THESE TRULY ARE THE BRAVE

UNIVERSITY PRESS OF FLORIDA

Florida A&M University, Tallahassee
Florida Atlantic University, Boca Raton
Florida Gulf Coast University, Ft. Myers
Florida International University, Miami
Florida State University, Tallahassee
New College of Florida, Sarasota
University of Central Florida, Orlando
University of Florida, Gainesville
University of North Florida, Jacksonville
University of South Florida, Tampa
University of West Florida, Pensacola

T0378161

THESE TRULY ARE THE BRAVE

An Anthology of African American
Writings on War and Citizenship

EDITED BY

A Yẹmisi Jimoh and Françoise N. Hamlin

University Press of Florida
Gainesville · Tallahassee · Tampa · Boca Raton
Pensacola · Orlando · Miami · Jacksonville · Ft. Myers · Sarasota

Publication of this book has been aided in part by grants from the University of Massachusetts Amherst and Brown University.

This book may be available in an electronic edition.

First cloth printing, 2015
First paperback printing, 2018

23 22 21 20 19 18   6 5 4 3 2 1

Library of Congress Cataloging-in-Publication Data
Jimoh, A Yẹmisi, 1957– author.
These truly are the brave : an anthology of African American writings on war and citizenship / A Yẹmisi Jimoh and Françoise N. Hamlin.
pages cm
Includes bibliographical references and index.
ISBN 978-0-8130-6022-4 (cloth)
ISBN 978-0-8130-6410-9 (pbk.)
1. American literature—African American authors. 2. African Americans—Literary collections. 3. African Americans—History. 4. War. 5. Citizenship. I. Hamlin, Françoise N., author. II. Title.
PS508.N3J55 2015
810.8'0896073—dc 3
2015003601

The University Press of Florida is the scholarly publishing agency for the State University System of Florida, comprising Florida A&M University, Florida Atlantic University, Florida Gulf Coast University, Florida International University, Florida State University, New College of Florida, University of Central Florida, University of Florida, University of North Florida, University of South Florida, and University of West Florida.

University Press of Florida
15 Northwest 15th Street
Gainesville, FL 32611-2079
http://upress.ufl.edu

We dedicate this book to the men and women of African descent, named and unknown, who fought for their freedom and that of their nation throughout the history of the United States of America.

Contents

Figures

Preface

This project began in 2001 with a paper presented by A Yẹmisi Jimoh at a meeting of The Space Between: Literature and Culture, 1914–1945. The research for that paper revealed a wide range of writings on issues of war, liberation, and citizenship by African Americans and an abundance of rich materials in disparate publications. Considering the importance of these materials for African American literary, historical, and political studies (especially in the burgeoning realm of African American Studies), Yẹmisi began teaching courses and collecting published versions of African American writings, speeches, and letters on citizenship and war. These documents span the nation's history from the eighteenth century to the twenty-first century. Many thanks to all of the students whose curiosity, probing questions, and challenging perspectives in those courses contributed to some of her early thoughts on the material in this volume.

The cross-disciplinary aspect, in particular the contextual grounding in history, of this volume developed in 2006 from a collaborative pedagogical endeavor between the editors, Françoise Hamlin and Yẹmisi Jimoh. We received support from a Mutual Mentoring Initiative through the Office of Faculty Development and a Small Grant in Support of Diversity, both from the University of Massachusetts Amherst. This grant support enabled us to design a cross-disciplinary undergraduate course on war, freedom, citizenship, and patriotism and a series of pedagogy seminars on cross-disciplinary teaching for graduate students. We appreciate the inquisitiveness of the undergraduates in the course and the dedication and perspicuity of the graduate students in the pedagogy seminars.

Additionally, we would like to thank all of our colleagues, family, friends, and others near and far (named and unnamed, remembered and misremembered) who passed along threads of information that deepened this volume immensely, especially Amritjit Singh (Ohio University), C. Lok Chua (San Francisco State University, Fresno), Seth Rockman (Brown University), Adriane Lentz-Smith (Duke University), Harley Erdman (University of Massachusetts Amherst), Kathy Perkins (University of Illinois), Maureen Honey (University of Nebraska), members of the Five Colleges Atlantic Seminar, colleagues in the W.E.B. Du Bois Department of Afro-American Studies at the University of Massachusetts Amherst, and colleagues in the Departments of Africana Studies and History at Brown University. Special thanks to Corey Walker, Paget Henry, Tricia Rose, Robert Self, Naoko Shibusawa, John Higginson, and Joye Bowman for their intellectual engagement with this project, and to Françoise's family for supporting her through this journey. Much appreciation also goes to Zahra Caldwell, Yẹmisi's graduate assistant, for her work to help make possible the completion of this manuscript. Added thanks to librarians whose support is essential to a project such as this, with special thanks to the Five Colleges librarians, most particularly at the W.E.B. Du Bois library at the University of Massachusetts Amherst.

For research support and permissions funding that aided in the production of this anthology, we also wish to thank the W.E.B. Du Bois Department of Afro-American Studies, University of Massachusetts Amherst; the College of Humanities and Fine Arts, University of Massachusetts Amherst; Center for Teaching and Faculty Development, University of Massachusetts Amherst; and the Humanities Fund in the Department of Africana Studies and the Department of History at Brown University.

For believing in and championing this project, we owe a deep debt of gratitude to Sian Hunter, our acquisitions editor at the University Press of Florida. Our thanks also go to the staff at the press for their patience, hard work, and grace.

These Truly Are the Brave indeed was a thoroughly collaborative project, drawing on the collective strengths of its editors and the support and wisdom of numerous others. We hope you find this volume and the wealth of information in it an illuminating journey and an intellectual pleasure.

A Note to Readers

War is central to the way the United States has imagined its identity as a nation. War also is a factor in citizens' expressions of national loyalty. *These Truly Are the Brave* collects poetry, fiction, plays, essays, newspaper articles, letters, interviews, and speeches that present African Americans speaking on issues related to questions of citizenship and the United States' engagement in wars. The varied perspectives (both literary and historical) in this collection oftentimes counter dominant narratives and complicate the meanings of national loyalty and citizenship in the country. No two groups or individuals have experienced what it means to be citizens of this country in the same way. Voluntary immigrants have their own narratives based on their points of origin and the status of their particular group in the new homeland. Yet, black people have lived in this land at least as long as their white counterparts, both having encountered the Indigenous peoples already here. Enslaved or free, black people in the United States well into the twentieth century lacked citizenship regardless of whether they were born in or dragged into the nation. The history of slavery, Jim Crow segregation, and internecine resistance by black people questions the consistency of the ideals at the center of the nation's identity. Therefore, the focus here on African Americans' citizenship claims and military participation challenges the very foundation on which popular narratives on democracy in the United States rest. In short, *These Truly Are the Brave* emphasizes how necessary it is to understand the historical context of African American commentaries on citizenship and war from the colonial era to the present in order to truly understand the United States and to provide nuance to dominant narratives on American military, political, and social histories.

A few black people served in military battles before the nation's founding, but during the Revolutionary War for Independence (1775–1783) a large number of black volunteers, about five thousand Patriots, made a difference in the racial makeup of the Continental Army. The Revolutionary forces indeed would be the most integrated army for almost two centuries, notwithstanding the severe color-based conflicts and inequities. During the Civil War (1861–1865), less than ninety years later, the U.S. military formally admitted black volunteers into the soldiering ranks of the Union forces only after the numbers of white enlistees declined. In the last months of the war, Confederate officials formally took similar action. With the formal organization of the U.S. Colored Troops (USCT) through enactment of General Order 143 in May 1863, black men gained the right to become official Union soldiers and veterans of that war, albeit in a segregated military.

The USCT continued active service after the Civil War. Posted on the western frontier to confront Indigenous peoples and later sent overseas in the Spanish-Cuban-U.S. War, their presence persistently caused tension at all levels of the military and in the communities surrounding their bases. This trend continued well into the twentieth century. African American intellectuals and the general public commented rigorously in black press outlets on the activities of black soldiers serving in a military for a segregated and unequal nation invested in empire-building ventures overseas, usually at the expense of other peoples of color. Editorials, letters, and articles emphasized the complicated and fraught situation that found black people, who lacked full citizenship rights, caught between national loyalty and Jim Crow conditions.

During World War I, African Americans' political and social struggles against Jim Crow doggedly challenged the military and heightened tension on bases overseas and at home. Attacks on black people, many of them uniformed veterans, marked multiple moments when these conflicts turned violent, particularly during the Red Summer of 1919. Tensions continued for the rest of the first half of that century, and only after considerable conflict and protest did conditions improve for African Americans in the military. In 1941, for instance, A. Philip Randolph challenged the U.S. government to lift the policy of segregation, and the black press galvanized civil rights organizations and allies to build momentum for what later would become a mass movement for civil rights. In 1950, the Korean War marked the first legally desegregated military operation since the Revolutionary War, yet not without continued racial discrimination and strife. The War in Vietnam forced the military to fully desegregate, fueled by the mass Civil Rights Movement coursing through the United States and punctuated by the assassination of Rev. Martin Luther King Jr. and the subsequent uprisings that in turn accelerated the Black Liberation/Black Power Movement during the 1960s and 1970s. By the turn of the twenty-first century, the U.S. military had transformed significantly, but only after African Americans since the colonial era had unfailingly and unflinchingly commented on citizenship and participated in wars.

These Truly Are the Brave includes Phillis Wheatley's poems from the eighteenth century; Susie Baker King Taylor's account of her work as a nurse and teacher for the USCT during the Civil War; W.E.B. Du Bois's 1918 "Close Ranks" announcement in *Crisis*; Claude McKay's seminal poem, "If We Must Die," published in 1919; Rev. Martin Luther King Jr.'s 1967 speech on Vietnam at Riverside Church; and many other selections that illustrate the long history of contradictions in war and the variety of ways that African Americans have challenged injustices and enacted national loyalty in the search for full citizenship in the United States. Thoroughly researched essays in this volume contextualize the political, cultural, and social landscape and situate the wide range of reactions that played out through a national dialogue during times of military conflict. These perspectives on war juxtapose military participation and displays of national loyalty with the long history of organized resistance against political and social injustice in the United States.

Black liberation struggles in North America, although occurring consistently, have varied in form. These struggles include insurrections on slaving ships, uprisings such as the one near the Stono River in the colony of South Carolina in 1739, urban uprisings in the Los Angeles neighborhood of Watts in 1965 and 1992, and organized movements such as the nineteenth-century abolitionists' movement and the mid-twentieth-century Civil Rights and Black Liberation/Black Power Movements. Thus, the historical contexts for this volume establish black people as actively resistant to bondage, inequality, and discrimination, and as using multiple ways to express discontent and claim citizenship. African Americans have corralled resources and made use of opportunities such as military service to try to change these inequities. A desire for liberty, fueled by the founding principles of the nation that inspired the Revolutionary War, has informed African American national loyalties.

Military service gave black men (and some women) new opportunities for life in the United States and a chance to reclaim citizenship that the nation had denied. For many African Americans, military service certainly did not embody national pride in or acceptance of the inequality that existed. Rather, such service challenged inequity and demonstrated the injustice of the nation's denial of full citizenship to African Americans. Military men and women exemplified sacrifice for a nation whose *promise* of equality had yet to be realized. Various voices in this volume have contested dominant definitions of patriotism, particularly when the color line has limited the rights of citizenship in the United States. Some African

Americans have rejected any performance of patriotism as folly, pointing to the contradictions between calls for national loyalty in the context of the nation's historical lack of commitment to equal rights. This anthology highlights the long history of African Americans wrestling with and contesting how the nation has placed black people in the democratic systems of the United States, even while African Americans have continued to wear the nation's military uniforms and have served as the nation's commander in chief. In short, *These Truly Are the Brave* encourages readers to challenge conventionally held definitions of patriotism, loyalty, citizenship, and freedom, using the voices of black people who themselves confronted these conventional meanings in their lifetimes.

These Truly Are the Brave opens with an introductory essay that advances innovative ways to approach the trajectory of citizenship among black people in the United States. The volume also has four chronological sections, each one beginning with a crucial turning point in African American military history.

Part 1, "Freedom, Democracy, and Equality? From Colonies to a Nation Divided," covers the colonial years to and including the Civil War, the period of legal enslavement for most black people and a period when the U.S. Constitution did not guarantee black citizenship rights. The essay in this part anchors the historical foundation upon which the major themes and questions of black citizenship and military participation rest.

Part 2, "The United States Enters the Global Stage: Empire, Worldwide War, and Democracy," negotiates America's involvement in conflicts abroad from the Spanish-Cuban-U.S. War and throughout World War I. It juxtaposes the mainstream rhetoric of democracy and empire against the dismantling of Reconstruction efforts and the establishment of Jim Crow as accepted legal racial policy on domestic soil.

Part 3, "The Double-V Campaign Challenges Jim Crow: World War II," examines World War II and the struggles around African Americans' increased military involvement overseas alongside the birth of the mass movement against inequality and the supremacist notions embedded in Jim Crow segregation in the United States.

Part 4, "Battles at Home and Abroad from Montgomery to Afghanistan," considers African Americans' shifting social and political terrain during the mass protest years following World War II and how that impacted military involvement in the wars in Korea, Vietnam, and the Persian Gulf and the most recent War on Terrorism.

EDITORIAL NOTES

By their very nature, anthologies are selective, and we as editors have made hard decisions regarding what to include in both the essays and the selections. At the center of *These Truly Are the Brave* readers will find a focus on African Americans' continual push for liberation, citizenship rights, and equality in military participation. This volume collects selections by eighty-nine writers and commentators who provide a wealth of responses to war, freedom, citizenship, and national loyalty. We have selected the texts of unfamiliar writers and have recovered little-known pieces by recognized names in African American literature, intellectual culture, and activism. Readers will find a number of familiar pieces as well.

The volume opens with a historical timeline that integrates dates found throughout the anthology with other relevant events in U.S. history. An introduction to the literature provides the scope, range, and organizing themes within and among the selections in *These Truly Are the Brave* while conceptualizing the way citizenship operates throughout the volume and within African American culture. Also, this introductory essay advances new ways to read citizenship in oft-quoted pieces as well as provocative ways to approach this issue in newly found sources. We have divided the historical periods into four parts and historical essays begin each part, providing context for the reproduced material. We have organized each part alphabetically by author, beginning each entry with brief pertinent biographical information and noting the relevant war for the selection where it is not evident in the title or text. There are three bibliographical resources: additional relevant readings by that author on the topic of war and citizenship that follow the individual selections; the "Selected Additional Literature on Citizenship and War" at the end of each part; and the comprehensive bibliography for the introduction and the part essays at the end of the volume, which also suggests further historical readings and secondary sources beyond those cited. At the back of the book we provided an appendix listing texts by theme and wars and two indexes (organized by title and author) to help readers with further interests and to facilitate locating selections from different points of entry.

Additionally, many authors published under more than one name, particularly women who married. In this volume, we generally have used the full names, particularly when those names will assist readers in locating other writings by the author or additional information on the writer. For example, we list Charlotte Forten Grimké rather than Charlotte Forten yet have decided to list Phillis Wheatley rather than Phillis Wheatley Peters. We have used brackets only to indicate publication under a pseudonym. We also could not find full bibliographic information for some of the authors, given the uneven record keeping for black peoples' birth and death dates throughout U.S. history. Similarly, due to the nature of publishing and the circulation of many sources in the eighteenth and nineteenth centuries (with self-publishing of speeches, pamphlets, and broadsides, for example), primary publication information in some cases is scarce. We have employed the contemporary usage for the names of wars, especially when these more recent terms work to address issues of empire-building, to appropriately recognize that the term American is hemispheric, or when the current terms accurately refer to the objectives of the wars. We thus refer to the French and Indian Wars/Seven Years' War, the Revolutionary War for Independence, the U.S.-Mexico War, the Spanish-Cuban-U.S. War, the U.S.-Philippines War, the War in Vietnam, and the War against Terrorism (also War against Terrorists).

Finally, we have taken great care to remain faithful to the voice and style of the original texts reproduced here to suggest the time of composition and the linguistic style and aesthetic choices of the writers or speakers. To that end, we follow the conventions of each writer on the use of particular group name identifiers (Negro, colored, Black, and so forth) for African Americans. Additionally, black speakers and writers in the United States have given the English language apt and eloquent turns of phrases or nuance and subtlety of tone (barely approximated on the page) that reflect the richness of African American culture. These qualities in the language we value highly and have retained. We also provide explanations in endnotes where necessary. On a few occasions, however, we have silently inserted paragraph breaks and/or shortened titles in eighteenth- and nineteenth-century prose (those writers tended to use long titles and to write in long paragraphs) and have corrected punctuation, capitalization, or obvious typographical errors simply for the purpose of clarity and ease of reading. All selections in *These Truly Are the Brave* end with the earliest dates that we could locate for their presentation or performance (speeches, readings, plays) and their publication.

HISTORICAL TIMELINE

1700   Escaped Africans establish earliest known Maroon communities in
        the Great Dismal Swamp of Virginia and North Carolina.
1712   New York City Slave Revolt.
1738   Fort Mose/Gracia Real de Santa Maria de Mose (later St. Augustine,
        Florida) becomes the first settlement for free black persons and
        runaways until 1763, when the British take over Florida.
1739   Stono Uprising (Stono, South Carolina).
1754   Beginning of the North American phase of the French and Indian
        Wars that ends in 1763 with the British controlling Canada and
        the land east of the Mississippi Valley.
1770   Crispus Attucks killed on 5 March during the Boston Massacre.
1772   Abolition of slavery in Britain, but not in the colonies.
1775   Philadelphia Quakers organize the Society for the Relief of Free
        Negroes Unlawfully Held in Bondage (later, in 1784, the Penn-
        sylvania Society for Promoting the Abolition of Slavery and the
        Relief of Free Negroes Unlawfully Held in Bondage), America's
        first antislavery society (14 April).
        19 April marks the official beginning of the American Revolution-
        ary War.
        Battle of Bunker Hill (May).
        Royal Ethiopian Regiment commandeered by the Earl of Dun-
        more stationed on the waters off the Norfolk, Virginia, coast
        (November).
1776   Continental Congress adopts Declaration of Independence (4 July).
1777   Prince Hall and other Bostonians petition for slavery's abolition in
        January.
        Vermont becomes first American state to abolish slavery (July).
        Battle of Brandywine in Pennsylvania (September).
1778   1st Rhode Island Regiment, the first black regiment, is raised (14
        February).
1781   Elizabeth Freeman files a freedom lawsuit in Massachusetts (wins
        her case in 1783).
1783   Treaty of Paris officially ends the Revolutionary War (signed on 3
        September).

1787   Constitutional Convention settles the matter of slavery—three-
        fifths of a state's enslaved population counts for the apportion-
        ment of representatives, electoral votes, and direct taxes.

        Northwest Ordinance/Freedom Ordinance, passed in July by the
        Congress of the Confederation of the United States, creates the
        Northwest Territory.

1789   The constitutional government of the United States of America
        begins on 4 March.

1790   First U.S. Naturalization Act is passed, permitting naturalization to
        free white persons who have lived in the country for two years
        and to their children under 21 years of age (March).

1791   Bill of Rights ratified.

        Beginning of the Haitian Revolution, a successful revolt against
        slavery and French colonization led by Toussaint L'Ouverture
        (ends in 1804).

1792   U.S. Congress expels all black people from the U.S. military.

1793   Fugitive Slave Act is passed, allowing capture and reenslaving of
        escaped captives (February).

1795   Naturalization Act extends residency to five years and requires re-
        nunciation of titles from and allegiance to foreign countries and
        affirmation that the applicant has no convictions resulting from
        joining the British Loyalist forces (January).

1798   U.S. Navy established.

        An Act to Establish Uniform Rule of Naturalization passes Con-
        gress as part of the Alien and Sedition Acts. It extends the
        residency requirement to fourteen years, disallows citizenship
        to persons from nations at war with the United States, allows
        imprisonment or deportation of "dangerous" immigrants, and
        criminalizes speech deemed unfavorable to the U.S. government.
        The naturalization act is repealed in 1802 (June).

1800   Gabriel Prosser attempts an uprising of enslaved persons near Rich-
        mond, Virginia, in the summer.

1803   United States negotiates the Louisiana Purchase (from France).

1804   Middlebury College, Vermont, gives an honorary MA degree to Le-
        muel Haynes, who had fought in the Continental Army during
        the Revolutionary War (February).

        New Jersey is the last northern state to pass gradual abolition.

1807   British abolition of the Atlantic trade in humans as property
        (March).

1808   United States abolishes international trade/importation of humans
        as property beginning on New Year's Day.

1812   War of 1812 begins (ends 1815).

        Louisiana Battalion of Free Men of Color, a militia unit of proper-
        tied black men, is organized.

1813   Black sailors serve in the Battle of Lake Erie (September).

1814   Andrew Jackson invites free black people to join the U.S. forces to
        win New Orleans from British troops (December).

        Francis Scott Key writes "The Star Spangled Banner (The Defense of
        Fort McHenry)," set to the tune of a British drinking song.

1815   Black soldiers fight alongside Major General Andrew Jackson to
        win New Orleans from British control (January).

1817   American Colonization Society founded.

        Seminole Wars are fought over Indigenous land in Florida; black
        Seminoles who have escaped enslavement participate (end in
        1850).

1820   The Missouri Compromise bans slavery in the new territories north
        of Missouri's southern border, the 36° 30" parallel.

        Army order prohibits black men from enlisting in the U.S. Army.

1822   Denmark Vesey's plans for a revolt in South Carolina are betrayed.

1823   Alexander Lucius Twilight is the first African American to graduate
        from an American institution of higher education (Middlebury
        College, Vermont).

1831   Samuel Francis Smith writes "America (My Country, 'Tis of Thee),"
        set to the tune of the British national anthem.

        Nat Turner's revolt, originally planned for July 4th, occurs in South-
        ampton County, Virginia, (21–23 August).

1833   American Anti-Slavery Society organizes in Philadelphia, com-
        posed of a group of male abolitionists from across the United
        States, including William Lloyd Garrison, Robert Purvis, James
        G. Barbadoes, and James McCrummill. Women form a separate
        antislavery society, including the daughters of black Revolution-
        ary War veteran James Forten. Both groups disband in 1870.

1834   The Slavery Abolition Act abolishes slavery in British colonies in
        the Americas and West Indies (1 August).

1838   Trail of Tears begins: forced removal of Native Americans from
        their homelands to designated territories in Oklahoma (ends
        1850).

1839   In January, Joseph Cinque and fifty-two others commandeer the
        illegal slaving ship *Amistad*, landing in the United States, where
        they secure their freedom after a famed court battle.

1841   Madison Washington and eighteen other captives orchestrate a mutiny aboard the *Creole* in November. They redirect the ship to the British West Indies, where they secure their freedom and that of the other captives aboard.

1846   U.S.-Mexico War begins.

1848   Treaty of Guadalupe Hidalgo ends the U.S.-Mexico War.

1849   John Horse, a black Seminole, establishes the Oklahoma settlement Wewoka after the United States reneges on a promise of freedom and tries to disarm black Seminoles.

1850   Compromise of 1850 (September).

The Fugitive Slave Law criminalizes the harboring of persons flee-ing captivity and authorizes the U.S. Marshals Service to capture and reenslave escapees (September).

The Underground Railroad is strengthened after the Fugitive Slave Law is enacted.

U.S. soldiers occupy the Panama Canal region (until 1856).

1854   The Kansas-Nebraska Act repeals the Missouri Compromise and advocates popular sovereignty.

William Walker and his mercenary army control Nicaragua and attempt to annex the rest of Central America (Costa Rica, Panama, Guatemala, El Salvador, and Honduras) to the United States as pro-slavery states.

1857   In *Dred Scott v. Sandford*, the Supreme Court rules that people of African descent have no legal rights and thus lack citizenship (March).

1858   Black abolitionists establish Crispus Attucks Day (5 March) in the Boston area.

1859   John Brown's raid on Harpers Ferry, Virginia (October).

1860   Abraham Lincoln is elected president of the United States.

1861   The Confederate States of America are formed. Confederates fire on Fort Sumter in Charleston Harbor, South Carolina, declaring war on the United States. Beginning of Civil War (12 April).

Congress passes a Confiscation Act, declaring enslaved persons will be "contraband of war" (6 August).

1862   General David Hunter forms 1st South Carolina Volunteers (spring).

President Lincoln signs the Militia Act, allowing "persons of African descent" enslaved in Confederate states to serve in the military and obtain freedom for themselves and their families through service (July).

Congress passes a second Confiscation Act, allowing persons

enslaved by rebels to bear arms in war and declaring those enslaved persons "forever free" (17 July).

Major General Benjamin Butler issues Order No. 63, organizing the Native Guards in Louisiana (Corps d'Afrique) (22 August).

Louisiana Native Guards becomes the first black regiment to receive official military recognition (September).

Earliest record of service for a black seaman, Moses Dallas, in the Confederate States Navy.

1863   President Abraham Lincoln's Emancipation Proclamation goes into effect on 1 January, emancipating enslaved persons in the rebelling states.

First U.S. military draft enacted (March).

Archer Alexander, whose likeness is sculpted on the Freedmen's Memorial Monument in Washington, D.C., may be among the last persons seized under the Fugitive Slave Law. Prior to his escape, he had betrayed his enslaver's plan to thwart the Union forces in Missouri (March).

First black military officer, Alexander T. Augusta, a surgeon for the 7th U.S. Colored Troops, earns the rank of major (April).

The U.S. War Department issues General Order No. 143, establishing a Bureau of Colored Troops (May).

Harriet Tubman leads the Combahee River Raid in South Carolina (June).

Battle of Milliken's Bend, Louisiana (7 June).

Siege of Port Hudson, Louisiana (May to July).

New York City Draft Riots (11–14 July).

Fifty-fourth and 55th Massachusetts charge Fort Wagner (18 July); William Harvey Carney carries U.S. flag. Carney belatedly receives the Medal of Honor in 1900.

1864   Battle of Olustee, Baker County, Florida (February).

Massacre at Fort Pillow, Tennessee (12 April).

Battle of Poison Springs, Arkansas (18 April).

Battle of the Crater, Petersburg, Virginia (30 July).

General Benjamin F. Butler commissions the Army of the James Medal to honor black Union soldiers' heroic acts of bravery (October).

1865   The Confederate Navy officially enlists black seamen (February).

The War Department establishes the Freedman's Bureau (3 March).

The Confederate Congress passes General Order 14 authorizing the Confederate States Colored Troops (13 March).

Jefferson Davis, president of the Confederate States, issues General
Order No. 14 allowing black men to join the Confederate Army
with the consent of their owners (23 March).

Confederate Army surrenders at Appomattox, ending the Civil War
(9 April).

John Wilkes Booth assassinates President Lincoln (14 April). Lincoln dies on 15 April.

Major General Gordon Granger arrives in Galveston, Texas, with
the announcement that slavery is officially ended. In many parts
of the United States, this date is an official holiday, Juneteenth,
recognizing the official release of the last enslaved black people
(19 June).

Thirteenth Amendment ratified (6 December).

Confederate veterans organize the Ku Klux Klan in Pulaski, Tennessee (24 December).

1866   Congress passes the Civil Rights Act over President Andrew Johnson's veto in April.

White mobs riot in Memphis in May following the disbanding of a
local black military unit.

The Army Reorganization Act authorizes six black regiments as
part of a regular standing army in July; includes the 9th and 10th
Cavalries and the 24th and 25th Infantries (otherwise known as
the Buffalo Soldiers).

Beginning of the Indian Wars (end in 1896).

1867   Reconstruction Acts passed.

1868   Fourteenth Amendment ratified (9 July).

1870   Fifteenth Amendment ratified (3 February).

First black student, James W. Smith, enrolled at West Point (but he
does not graduate).

Congress passes the first of three Enforcement Acts to reinforce
voting rights and freedom from vigilante attacks that hinder the
citizenship rights established in the Fourteenth and Fifteenth
Amendments. Includes federally enforced penalties for violations (May).

1871   Congress passes the second Enforcement Act, strengthening the
first Enforcement Act (February).

Congress passes the last of three Enforcement Acts, also known
as the Ku Klux Klan Act, which prohibits two or more persons
from conspiring to impede federally secured rights such as voting, an elected official's assumption of office, the functions of
government or law enforcement, or attempts to overthrow the

U.S. government. Includes federally enforced penalties for violations (April).

1872 The Freedman's Bureau closes.

First African Americans admitted to U.S. Naval Academy, including John Henry Conyers.

Frederick Douglass is nominated in absentia for vice-president on the Equal Rights Party ticket.

1873 The Supreme Court rules in the Slaughter-House Cases that the protections of the Fourteenth Amendment, particularly the Privileges or Immunities Clause, do not apply to state citizenship (April).

1875 The last biracial U.S. Congress in the nineteenth century passes the Civil Rights Act (also known as the Enforcement Act or Force Act), reinforcing basic civil rights of all persons, including equal access to public accommodations and protected rights to serve on juries. The act includes penalties that were missing from the act of 1866 (1 March).

1876 Freedwomen and men fully fund the Freedmen's Memorial Monument (also referred to as the Emancipation Memorial) that stands in Lincoln Park. Charlotte Scott, a formerly enslaved woman from Virginia, reportedly uses her first $5 earned as a free woman to begin the campaign for a monument in honor of Abraham Lincoln (14 April).

1877 Henry O. Flipper becomes first African American to graduate from West Point.

1883 The Supreme Court declares the 1875 Civil Rights Act unconstitutional.

1888 Monument to Crispus Attucks unveiled on Boston Commons.

1891 Citizens' Committee forms in New Orleans, Louisiana, to challenge the state's 1890 Separate Car Act. The committee recruits Homer Plessy for the 1892 test case against the East Louisiana Railroad.

1892 Francis Bellamy publishes an initial version of "The Pledge of Allegiance" in *The Youth's Companion*.

1893 Katherine Lee Bates writes "America the Beautiful," set to a tune by Samuel A. Ward.

1896 In *Plessy v. Ferguson*, the Supreme Court upholds segregation through the "separate but equal" ruling (18 May).

1898 Spanish-Cuban-U.S. War in Cuba (April to August).

Battle of San Juan Hill (1 July).

United States annexes Hawai'i by a joint resolution of Congress (7 July).

	Treaty of Paris gives the United States control of Guantanamo Bay in Cuba, Wake Island, Puerto Rico, the Philippines, and Guam (10 December).
1899	U.S.-Philippines War begins (ends in 1902).
1900	First Anti-Lynching Bill introduced in Congress by the lone black congressman George Henry White (January). The bill dies in the Judiciary Committee.
1903	Platt Amendment gives the United States intervention powers in Cuba and provides guidelines for how and when the United States can intervene in Cuban affairs (May).
1906	Brownsville Affair: townspeople accuse members of the 25th Infantry Regiment stationed in Brownsville, Texas, of killing a white citizen. Despite evidence to the contrary, 167 black soldiers receive dishonorable discharges from the military (13 August).
	Occupation of Cuba by U.S. forces under Platt Amendment extends into 1909.
1909	An interracial group establishes the National Association for the Advancement of Colored People (February).
1912	U.S. Marines occupy Nicaragua (ends in 1933).
1914	Archduke Franz Ferdinand of Austria assassinated, sparking World War I (28 June).
1915	More than 1.5 million African Americans begin migrating from the rural South for war industry employment as part of the Great Migration.
	U.S. Marines begin occupation of Haiti in July (ends August 1934).
1916	U.S. Marines begin occupation of the Dominican Republic (ends in 1924).
1917	United States annexes the Virgin Islands (31 March).
	United States enters World War I (6 April).
	Congress passes the Selective Service Act (May).
	Houston Riot in August after racial violence against members of the 24th Infantry Regiment causes a mutiny. A military court sentences nineteen black soldiers to death by hanging and discharges 108 from the army.
	Colonel Charles Young, a Buffalo Soldier, begins officers' training for black enlisted men at Fort Huachuca in Arizona, where he briefly serves as the commander.
	Over 1,000 men in the 17th Provisional Training Regiment at Fort Des Moines, Iowa, start officers' training; most of the successful candidates join the 92nd Division in France.

1918   Armistice ends World War I on 11 November.

Leonidas C. Dyer introduces the Dyer Anti-Lynching Bill in the U.S. House of Representatives. White Southern Democrats filibuster to prevent the Senate from voting.

Irving Berlin writes the first version of "God Bless America" (revised in 1938).

U.S. Marines occupy Panama (ends in 1920).

General John J. Pershing sends a memorandum advising the French to avoid crossing the color line by socializing with black troops (April).

1919   Treaty of Versailles signed (28 June).

Red Summer: tensions related to racism, immigration of Europeans, and unemployment spark riots in thirty-eight locales across the nation, including Chicago, Illinois; Longview, Texas; Charleston, South Carolina; Washington, D.C.; Knoxville, Tennessee; Elaine, Arkansas; Philadelphia, Pennsylvania; and Syracuse, New York.

1920   Nineteenth Amendment granting suffrage to women is ratified (18 August).

Marcus Garvey's Universal Negro Improvement Association and African Communities League (UNIA) creates the Pan-African/ Black Liberation flag.

1921   Race riot in Tulsa, Oklahoma, destroys black neighborhood.

1927   W.E.B. Du Bois and white supremacist Theodore Lothrop Stoddard focus on racial equality in New York radio debate (23 September).

Alain Locke and white supremacist Theodore Lothrop Stoddard debate the topic "Should the Negro be Encouraged to Cultural Equality?" in *Forum* (October).

1929   W.E.B. Du Bois and white supremacist Theodore Lothrop Stoddard meet at the Coliseum in Chicago for a debate organized by the Chicago Forum; their debate topic is "Shall the Negro Be Encouraged to Seek Cultural Equality?" (17 March).

1931   All-white jury convicts eight black youths in Scottsboro, Alabama, for the alleged rape of two white women.

Francis Scott Key's "Star Spangled Banner" becomes the official national anthem.

1934   Costigan-Wagner Anti-Lynching Bill is introduced in Congress.

1936   Commander Oliver Law, an African American, leads the integrated Abraham Lincoln Brigade, which formed surreptitiously, to fight in the Spanish Civil War (until 1939).

1939   World War II breaks out in Europe (1 September).

1940   The Selective Service Act allows all men from 18 to 34 years old to
        volunteer for military service, removing barriers against black
        volunteers.

1941   Benjamin O. Davis Sr. becomes the first black brigadier general in
        the U.S. Army (January).
        President Franklin D. Roosevelt issues Executive Order 8802,
        outlawing discrimination in federal employment and defense
        industries (25 June).

1941   Japan bombs Pearl Harbor and the United States enters World War
        II (7 December).

1942   The Double-V Campaign, which pushes for victory over racial op-
        pression at home and against the enemy abroad, begins in the
        Pittsburgh Courier (February).
        Black and white students in Chicago found the Committee of Racial
        Equity, later the Congress of Racial Equality (CORE). Their
        primary focus is inequality in the North and Mid-West. The co-
        chairs are George Houser and James Farmer.

1943   The War Department bans segregation in all recreational facilities
        and government transportation vehicles.
        Race riots erupt in Los Angeles (June), Detroit (June), Harlem (Au-
        gust), and forty-four other cities.

1944   Congress passes the Servicemen's Readjustment Act (also known
        as the GI Bill), which provides funds for education, loans for
        homes and businesses, and other aid to returning veterans.

1945   VE (Victory in Europe) Day ends World War II in Europe (8 May).
        VJ (Victory over Japan) Day (14 August) ends the war in the Pacific
        (celebrated on 15 August, the day the Japanese announced their
        surrender, or 2 September, the day of the ceremony of the formal
        surrender).

1947   President's Committee on Civil Rights, appointed by President Tru-
        man, publishes its report, *To Secure These Rights* (October).
        CORE tests the Supreme Court's ruling that segregation on inter-
        state transportation is unconstitutional. Four people, including
        Bayard Rustin, are arrested in Chapel Hill, North Carolina and
        put to labor on a chain gang.

1948   Truman desegregates the armed forces with Executive Order 9981
        (26 July).

1949   Wesley A. Brown becomes the first African American to graduate
        from the Annapolis Naval Academy.

1950   Korean War begins (25 June; ends with Korean War ceasefire armistice, 27 July 1953).

1951   All-black 24th Infantry (the Buffalo Soldiers) is officially disbanded (22 September).

1954   Dien Bien Phu, Vietnam, falls to the Viet Minh (7 May).

Supreme Court rules against the segregation of schools in *Brown v. Board of Education of Topeka, Kansas* (17 May).

1955   President Harry Truman provides aid to the French for war in Vietnam.

The Montgomery Bus Boycott begins in December (ends December 1956) and launches the leadership of Rev. Dr. Martin Luther King Jr.

1957   Congress passes a Civil Rights Act that focuses primarily on voting rights and establishes the U.S. Commission on Civil Rights and a civil rights division of the Justice Department; South Carolina Senator Strom Thurmond unsuccessfully filibusters the act for more than twenty-four hours.

1960   Four students (Joseph McNeil, Franklin McCain, Ezell Blair Jr., and David Richmond) begin a sit-in at the Woolworth's lunch counter in Greensboro, North Carolina, sparking a nationwide sit-in campaign (1 February).

Students and civil rights organizer Ella Baker found the Student Nonviolent Coordinating Committee (SNCC) at Shaw University in Raleigh, North Carolina; a student at Fisk University, Marion Berry, becomes the first chair (April).

1961   U.S. and Belgian support of rebel forces in the Congo leads to the murder of the democratically elected president Patrice Lumumba (January).

Freedom Riders organized by the Congress of Racial Equality (CORE) begin to test the 1960 Supreme Court ruling prohibiting segregation on interstate travel (May).

1962   Air Force veteran James Meredith desegregates the University of Mississippi (September).

1963   Rev. Dr. Martin Luther King Jr. pens the "Letter from the Birmingham Jail," one of the Civil Rights Movement's most notable documents, following coordinated mass protests against segregation in Birmingham, Alabama, since early April (16 April).

President John F. Kennedy delivers televised speech on civil rights (11 June).

Medgar Evers, Mississippi field secretary for the NAACP, is murdered in the driveway of his home in Jackson, Mississippi (12 June).

Historic March on Washington for Jobs and Freedom; Rev. Martin Luther King Jr. delivers his "I Have A Dream" speech (28 August).

Bombing of the 16th Street Baptist Church in Birmingham, Alabama, kills four young girls (15 September).

President John F. Kennedy assassinated (22 November).

1964   Fannie Lou Hamer, Robert Moses, Ella Baker, and others organize the Mississippi Freedom Democratic Party (MFDP), which takes a delegation to the Democratic National Convention in Atlantic City, New Jersey, to unseat Mississippi's all-white delegation (April and August).

The Council of Federated Organizations coordinates the Mississippi Freedom Summer Project, which recruits and trains over 800 black and white college students to provide voter education, organize black people to vote, and teach literacy and Black history, philosophy, and leadership courses in Freedom Schools in Mississippi (June–August).

Ku Klux Klan members murder Freedom Summer volunteer Andrew Goodman and Congress of Racial Equality (CORE) staff members James Chaney and Michael Schwerner in Neshoba County, Mississippi (June).

President Johnson signs Civil Rights Act (2 July).

Congress passes Gulf of Tonkin Resolution, authorizing President Johnson to initiate armed action against Vietnam (7 August).

1965   Jimmy Lee Jackson is shot by Alabama State Trooper. This incident becomes the pivotal moment for the Selma to Montgomery March (18 February).

James Reeb, a Unitarian minister from Boston, is attacked by white supremacists and subsequently dies in Selma, Alabama (9 March).

Civil rights worker Viola Liuzzo, a housewife from Detroit, is murdered along Highway 80 in Alabama by a Ku Klux Klan mob (25 March).

Malcolm X is assassinated in New York (21 February).

"Bloody Sunday," Selma, Alabama: police beat scores of civil rights protestors as they attempt to cross the Edmund Pettus Bridge from Selma to Montgomery (7 March). The third attempt to march from Selma to Montgomery succeeds, and marchers arrive on 25 March.

James Baldwin and William F. Buckley at the Cambridge Union Society debate the topic "Has the American Dream Been Achieved at the Expense of the American Negro?" Baldwin wins the debate 544–164 (18 February).

Uprisings across the nation's cities, including the Watts neighborhood in Los Angeles

President Johnson signs the Voting Rights Act (6 August).

1967   Martin Luther King Jr. delivers speech against the war in Vietnam at the Riverside Church in New York City (4 April).

1968   Martin Luther King Jr. is assassinated in Memphis, Tennessee (4 April).

President Johnson signs the Fair Housing Act on 11 April.

1972   New York congresswoman Shirley Chisholm campaigns for president on the Democratic Party's ticket as the first major-party black candidate and the first woman to run for the Democratic nomination. She receives 152 delegates.

1973   The Vietnam War officially ends with a peace agreement in Paris, France (27 January).

Military draft ends in the United States.

1975   Last American officials are airlifted out of Saigon, Vietnam (29 April).

1980   The United States begins supporting Contras in Nicaragua (continues until mid- to late 1980s).

1983   United States and Jamaica invade Grenada (October).

1984   Jesse Jackson seeks nomination for president on the Democratic Party's ticket (runs again in 1988).

1988   Lenora Fulani runs for president as an Independent and appears on the ballot in all fifty states.

1989   President George H. W. Bush appoints General Colin Powell as chair of the Joint Chiefs of Staff (August).

1991   Persian Gulf War, code-named Operation Desert Storm (January–February).

1996   Alan Keyes seeks nomination for president on the Republican Party's ticket (runs again in 2000 and 2008).

2001   President George W. Bush appoints General Colin Powell as U.S. Secretary of State (January).

Foreign terrorist attack on American soil (11 September).

U.S. and British forces launch airstrikes in Afghanistan (7 October).

2003   U.S. and allies invade Iraq (20 March).

2004   Carol Mosely Braun and Al Sharpton both seek nomination for president on the Democratic Party's ticket.

2007   U.S. begins President Bush's New Way Forward policy of "troop surge" in Iraq (February).

2008   Barack Hussein Obama, an African American, is elected 44th U.S. president (4 November).

2009   President Obama accepts the Nobel Prize for Peace (December).

President and Commander in Chief Barack Obama commits approximately 30,000 additional troops to Afghanistan (December).

2011   The United States completes its withdrawal of military personnel from Iraq.

Major General Marcia Anderson is promoted to two-star general, becoming the first African American woman to achieve that rank.

2013   The United States begins handing over control of military operations to Afghan armed forces.

2014   Michelle Janine Howard becomes the first woman four-star admiral in the U.S. Navy (1 July).

President Barack Obama authorizes air campaigns against terrorists in the group that refers to itself as the Islamic State (September).

Introduction

These Truly Are the Brave

The well-known narrative in the United States focusing on the pivotal events that precipitated the Revolutionary War for Independence (1775–1783) places a probable runaway from slavery, Crispus Attucks, at its center. From the founding of the United States in the eighteenth century, the nation's colonial inheritance of slavery and color circulated in the national narrative as race and operated at the center of economic, social, and political systems in the new nation.[1] Indeed, the subordination and enslavement of African peoples in British colonial North America and the displacement of Indigenous peoples made possible the United States as we currently know it. At the founding of the nation, the writers of its governing documents assigned most persons of African descent a subservient position outside the center of the nation's governing structures. Later, in 1832 President Andrew Jackson decided to uphold the idea of Georgia's states' rights and ignore the Supreme Court's decision in *Worcester v. Georgia*, which recognized the sovereignty of Native peoples to govern on their traditional lands, and thus the U.S. president similarly confirmed the nation's policy of subjection of Indigenous peoples. The founders of the United States, however, had written resistance to inequality and subordination into the founding documents of the new nation, making subsequent struggles for justice, liberty, and citizenship consistent with the nation's ideals.

From the colonial era forward, Africans in North America and their descendants have waged a protracted liberation struggle to secure due rights. The liberatory tactics toward this end have included underground resistance such as insurrections, revolts, and uprisings among enslaved black people, abolitionism, pamphleteering, escape, emigration, marronage, freedom suits (which were especially important for women, who used these suits to free their children as well),[2] literary art, vindicationist history, and public protests (speeches and peaceful resistance) designed to challenge the crafters of the nation's founding documents and those who had perpetuated policies and practices that excluded black people. Therefore, as 1783 brought the end of the Patriots' revolution, black people persisted in waging battles for freedom and justice, no longer as marginalized and enslaved colonial subjects but rather now as enslaved Americans in a democratic and ostensibly free society.[3] African Americans' participation in battles for liberation from slavery, the end of segregation, and equality of rights for all people in the United States combine with military participation to position black people as central to the shaping and reshaping of the nation's political and social structures. As part of these liberatory actions, black writers in the United States have commented in literature on what it has meant to be black and a soldier and on what it has meant to live in a nation that has unjustly denied citizenship rights to black people.

African American writers have produced an abundance of imaginative literature on citizenship, on wars from the writers' contemporary moment, and on past conflicts. These writers also have creatively reimagined wars known only through family or social and political history. Often black writers in the United States also have addressed concerns with war, citizenship, and inclusion while reclaiming images of black people from the false representations that frequently had circulated in the United States. Through literature, these writers have positioned African-descended people at the scene of wars and battles or have shown black people experiencing the impact of warfare, thereby claiming a place for African Americans in the country's heritage. These writers have recovered misplaced history, questioned African Americans' exclusions from citizenship, and challenged the United States to adhere to its principles of freedom, justice, and equality under the law.

African Americans' oral and written literature on war, liberation, and citizenship began during the British colonial era with poetry and auto-biographical writings of Africans enslaved by colonialists. The earliest known literary response by New World Africans to war in the colonies that later would become the United States is the folk poem "Bars Fight" by African-born Lucy Terry (see part 1). This poem responds to the battle at Deerfield, Massachusetts, in 1746, during one of the early Indian conflicts. These battles took place intermittently into the first decade of the twentieth century as the United States expanded westward, dislocating Indigenous peoples. Terry's poem was part of colonial folk legend, and was published in the *History of Western Massachusetts* in 1855. In her poem, Terry, whose husband, Abijah Prince, fought in the French and Indian War/Seven Years'

War and whose sons fought in the Revolutionary War for Independence, situates herself at the battle and presents a poetic eyewitness account of the events.[4] The speaker in Terry's poem shows no particular loyalty to British colonial New England as she graphically portrays the battle. Another young eyewitness to war, Olaudah Equiano, also African born, gives readers an autobiographical description of events during the French and Indian War/Seven Years' War in his *Interesting Narrative of the Life of Olaudah Equiano, or Gustavus Vassa, the African, Written by Himself*, published in 1789 (see part 1). Equiano's wish to enter the battle, an illustration of bravery, and his desire for liberty are crucial motifs found throughout more than 250 years of African American literature on war and literary responses to calls for patriotism. Equiano and Terry provide rare black voices speaking as eyewitnesses to colonial battles in North America.

Thirty years after Lucy Terry responded in poetry to war on colonial North American soil, Phillis Wheatley wrote that all humanity loves freedom and is "impatient of Oppression." Wheatley, whose poetry recalls her African childhood, also wrote several letters and poems that reject the unjust position of Africans in the colonial and revolutionary New World. Through their writings, Terry and Wheatley initiated an African American literary heritage of poetic, narrative, and expository responses to war, citizenship, and liberty. Indeed, Wheatley's representation of these issues is unlike that of other colonial-era black writers such as Olaudah Equiano (who was enslaved primarily at sea and ultimately became a British citizen), who remained silent about the American Revolution; Richard Allen who provided only two sentences on the Revolutionary War in the *Life, Experience, and Gospel Labours of the Rt. Rev. Richard Allen*, published in Philadelphia in 1833; and Jupiter Hammon, the colonial and revolutionary era Christian poet (enslaved in the prominent Lloyd family of New York—Loyalists), whose references to the war occur in 1783 in his essay "An Evening's Improvement" and in "A Dialogue Entitled the Kind Master and Dutiful Servant: A Line on the Present War," published together as a pamphlet. Hammon's writings on the war question whether the "Cruel and unnatural" Revolutionary War for Independence was punishment from God, and they allude to the Bible (Isaiah 2:4) in support of the idea of ending war, calling for nations to "seek for peace." Some of his other writings challenged people in his society who falsely presented themselves as Christians.[5] Ever since Phillis Wheatley actively (although at times subtly) engaged these issues in her letters and poetry, African American writers, orators, essayists, and dramatists have made their work a critical site in the struggle for democracy, justice, citizenship, liberty, and equity for all persons in the United States.

These writers provide a variety of perspectives on black people in the wars of the United States and on the protracted battles for liberation from slavery, Jim Crow segregation, and exclusion from citizenship rights. In doing so, African American writers also have rejected attempts to perpetuate the unspoken, albeit impossible, idea that European-descended peoples built and solely owned the new nation. This idea, of course, reflects a nation that never existed, as the presence of Indigenous peoples and the forced emigration of Africans clearly demonstrate. Throughout this literature, African American writers have represented war, patriots, and citizens in ways that have mirrored the history and varied experiences of black people in the United States. To this end, these writers frequently have deployed the power of biting irony through their uses of satire and parody. They have reimagined wars and have creatively reclaimed black images from false representations of cowardice and servility that had circulated at the center of the national narrative, and they have asserted entitlement to citizenship in the United States while adding to the nation's tradition of literary protest. African American literature on war and citizenship complicates and contests the dominant narratives of democracy in the United States and emphasizes two broad thematic issues: liberation and true citizenship.

Sarah Louisa Forten Purvis is among the numerous black writers whose ironic revisions of patriotic songs, symbols, and pledges have challenged the circulation of false and derogatory images of black people and have questioned the United States on the disjunction between its ideals and its practices of slavery, Jim Crow segregation in the South, and inequity and segregation in the North. In her poem "My Country," published in 1834 (see part 1), Forten refers to Samuel Francis Smith's patriotic song "America (My Country 'Tis of Thee)" (1831) and portrays enslaved black people as exiles living without rights and as strangers in their own land.[6] In this poem, Forten's speaker shows embarrassment because "falsehood" is associated with the flag of the United States. Other such writers who parody Smith's patriotic song and poetically convey African Americans' relationship to the nation include Frank Marshall Davis ("To Those Who Sing America"; 1948); W.E.B. Du Bois ("My Country 'Tis of Thee"; 1907; see part 2); and Joshua McCarter Simpson ("Song of the 'Aliened American'"; 1852; see part 1). Simpson and Du Bois parody Smith's patriotic song and poetically convey African Americans' relationship to the nation. In Simpson's poem, the

United States is a "Dark land of Slavery," while Du Bois's poem presents the nation as the "Late land of liberty." Davis's poem questions whether the nation has "forgotten / Something?" when people are asked to sing "On patriotic occasions" in a country where poverty, injustice, and inequity persist.[7]

Roscoe Conkling Jamison's poem "The Negro Soldiers" (see part 2), published in 1917 as a response to the U.S. entry into World War I, also contributes to the ongoing African American literary heritage of poetic, narrative, dramatic, and expository responses to patriotic iconography and songs. Jamison's poem echoes "The Star Spangled Banner" (1814), a response to the War of 1812 by Francis Scott Key. Yet Jamison's "truly brave" and the "truly free" soldiers are those who "cast aside / Old memories" and go to war for "Peace through Brotherhood, lifting glad songs, / Aforetime." Jamison's poem exposes once again the inconsistencies in the land of the free and the brave, where black soldiers have fought wars for the United States without the benefit of freedom and full citizenship for themselves. This poem also adds to the literary works that honor the deeds of black soldiers as well as the claims of those soldiers to the nation's soil through sacrifice overseas and liberatory actions at home. Among later writers, John O. Killens ironically uses the title of Irving Berlin's patriotic song in the short story "God Bless America" (1952; see part 4) and depicts the continued racialization of African Americans in the newly desegregated military during the Korean War. Similarly, Allia Matta, writing in the twenty-first century, has contributed to the tradition of African American parody with "Mymerica" (2005; see part 4). Matta has imagined white Americans laying exclusive claim to the United States, yet through the force of her poem she has ironically reinscribed in the twenty-first century both W.E.B. Du Bois's cutting questions from *The Souls of Black Folk*: "Your Country? How came it yours? . . . Would America have been America without her Negro People?" and Ralph Ellison's probing essay, "What America Would Be Like without Blacks," published in *Time* magazine in 1970.[8] Killens in his story and Matta in her poem are among a myriad of black writers, intellectuals, activists, and military personnel who have articulated the complex situation of African American citizenship and military participation.

Along with literary challenges to the values of patriotic songs and symbols that valorize U.S. ideals that have excluded black people, African Americans also have recast the assembly of patriots and drawn upon governing documents of the United States to reflect black life. When writers such as David Walker in the nineteenth century or the founders of the

Niagara Movement early in the twentieth century addressed issues of war, citizenship, and patriotism, they produced writings that were clearly stimulated by black people's relationship to national documents such as the Declaration of Independence, the Constitution, the national anthem, and the Emancipation Proclamation. In David Walker's *Appeal to the Coloured Citizens of the World* (1829; see part 1), for instance, with its preamble and four articles, and in the Niagara Movement's "Address to the Country" (1906; see part 2), which is structured by a preamble and five demands or resolutions, both treatises simulate the nation's founding documents, most notably the Constitution (which is composed of a preamble and seven articles). Additionally, in the Niagara Movement's "Address," there are clear echoes of the Declaration of Independence along with a demand for black people's "final emancipation," a reference to the Emancipation Proclamation.[9]

Likewise, when lending praise to the nation, African American writers have claimed their own celebratory and commemorative days (January 1st Emancipation Day; Pinkster Festivals; July 5th, protesting the hypocrisy of July 4th; various local Emancipation Days; and Juneteenth [19 June 1865], an emancipation celebration commemorating the official end of slavery in the United States once General Order No. 3, announcing the abolition of slavery, finally reached the last group of enslaved people in Texas), patriots, martyrs, and heroes of liberty (Toussaint L'Ouverture, Denmark Vesey, Nat Turner, Madison Washington, John Brown, Harriet Tubman, Malcolm X, Ella Baker, Martin Luther King Jr., Fannie Lou Hamer, Rosa Parks, and others), as well as symbols such as the Pan-African Liberation flag designed by followers of Marcus Garvey. These acts demonstrate the complicated, entwined tensions associated with definitions of patriotism and national heroes.[10] Black writers have focused on the Emancipation Proclamation and Abraham Lincoln for praiseworthy attention rather than on the Constitution or Thomas Jefferson or George Washington. Writers such as James Weldon Johnson, in his poem "Fifty Years" (1913),[11] and James Baldwin, in his "Letter to My Nephew" (1963; see part 4), place the Emancipation Proclamation, even with its limitations (which Frederick Douglass had challenged), in an esteemed cultural space of honor as a document that brought the United States closer to its ideals. When the Constitution receives acknowledgement in African American literature, writers focus their praise on the brilliance of its principles, as Ralph Ellison does in *Invisible Man*, while highlighting the nation's uneven implementation of them.

When African American writers focus on heroes and martyrs, they reclaim black images from inaccuracy by their persistent representations of and references to historical figures such as Crispus Attucks, Black Samson, Valaida Snow, and black soldiers presented in poetry, plays, essays, narratives, and oratory. For instance, by focusing on or making reference to Attucks, a probable runaway from slavery who played a central role in revolutionary events in colonial North America, and aligning him with prominent Africans in war such as Hannibal and with less-well-known black people on the battlefield, writers such as James Monroe Trotter, Olivia Bush-Banks, John A. Williams, and Chandler Owen have broadened a previously narrow view of African Americans who have engaged in battle and struggled for liberty. In this way, black writers have challenged the received narratives on slavery and exclusion.

Black writers also have taken due note of the fact that resistance against injustice and subordination appears in the founding documents of the United States and through literary reimaginings of legendary figures have portrayed black people's numerous acts of resistance. In his poem "Black Samson of Brandywine" (1903; see part 1), Paul Laurence Dunbar has recovered a legendary black war figure and has reimagined the nation's war for independence and liberty. Black Samson was reportedly at the Battle of Brandywine Creek in 1777, which ended in the British occupation of Philadelphia, the revolutionary capital. For Dunbar, heroic Samson refuted the dominant society's false narrative of black cowardice and subservience. Similarly, John Edgar Wideman's short story "Valaida" (see part 3) reimagines the experiences of the African American jazz trumpeter Valaida Snow, whom the Nazis reportedly held in their custody and later released.[12] Wideman's narrative has reconceptualized World War II by complicating the dominant war narrative and reviving the story of Valaida Snow. Many African American writers on war and citizenship have recovered extricated history through their literary art and have claimed a place for black people in the national heritage while resisting the country's silence on the lived reality of race in the United States. This literature has challenged the nation and contributed to its literary protest tradition, most particularly with the African American protest sonnets of Claude McKay, Helene Johnson, James Weldon Johnson, and others.[13]

While the ideals of the Revolutionary War for Independence have shaped the thinking of many African American writers who address issues of war and citizenship, their literary responses to the Civil War and World War II have inspired a considerable corpus of writings. The Civil War ended chattel slavery, and as Donald Yacovone has documented in *Freedom's Journey: African American Voices of the Civil War* (2004), in the decades following the war, a number of African American writers responded to the Civil War and its consequences.[14] James Baldwin has pointed out that World War II was a "turning point in the Negroes' relation to America." For Baldwin, World War II "was being fought . . . to bring freedom to everyone with the exception of Hagar's children" and the Japanese.[15] Both of these wars are central to the nation's history and have continued to inform the literary imaginary of African Americans.

Many African American writers have reimagined the Civil War. Yet in Shirley Graham Du Bois's play *It's Morning* (1940; see part 1) and in Pulitzer Prize–winner and former United States' poet laureate Natasha Trethewey's poetry collection *Native Guard* (2006; see part 1), readers will find perspectives on the subjects of battles, conquests, and power quite different from those emphasized by many other writers in literature on war.[16] Some black women writers, such as Graham Du Bois and Trethewey, have added domestic concerns to African American literary art on war. Shirley Graham Du Bois's play *It's Morning* illustrates this point.[17] Through the character of the enslaved mother Cissie, Graham Du Bois challenges masculinist heroism and illustrates a woman's defeat as she shows how a Civil War battle for freedom and liberty—as African Americans regularly portray it—also operates at the intimate level of an ongoing civil war focused on women's bodies within the supposed safety of the home, both national and private. War literature, nevertheless, often operates within a masculinist imaginary that centers on conquest and power. Thus, many black men and some black women writing on war have focused on the loss of male power and on efforts to establish that power in a society structured by patriarchy.[18] This concern with patriarchy was not the case, however, for Langston Hughes, a high school student in Cleveland, Ohio living by his own wits when the United States entered World War I. He wrote "The Red Cross Nurses" for his high school magazine, the Central High School *Monthly*.[19] Hughes's mature body of work on war and citizenship also provides an exception to this gendered view of war writing.[20]

African American literary production during World War I was substantial, as this war overlapped with the New Negro Movement in literature (1915–1930),[21] in which Hughes played a significant role. During the New Negro era, African American writers appeared in publications such as *Crisis, Opportunity, Negro World, Crusader, Messenger, Masses, Liberator,* and *New Masses* and in newspapers, magazines, and publishing houses at the center of the dominant society. Playwrights also presented their dramatic work on stage in community theatres, schools, and churches. Writers such as Angelina Weld Grimké and Mary Burrill found audiences for their plays through these outlets. Grimké's *Rachel* (first performed in 1916),[22] Alice Dunbar-Nelson's *Mine Eyes Have Seen* (1918; see part 2), and Burrill's *Aftermath* (1919; see part 2) draw upon war themes and contribute to African American lynching literature.[23] Literary responses to lynching, such as those found in the aforementioned plays, were published regularly and performed occasionally from the first decade of the twentieth century until the 1940s by groups such as the Krigwa Players, founded by W.E.B. Du Bois; the Howard Players, founded by Howard University's Thomas Montgomery Gregory; the Lafayette Players, spearheaded by Anita Bush; and Langston Hughes's Harlem Suitcase Theatre.

In African American lynching literature, writers' concerns with racial violence, including such violence against black veterans or military personnel, was a typical subject when this literature focused on World War I. The men and their families in Dunbar-Nelson's and Burrill's plays, for instance, contemplate how to respond to the call to war while accounting for the terror of racial violence and lynching at home. This violence along with the persistence of pseudo-scientific race theories throughout the early part of the twentieth century complicated African Americans' feelings of national pride, resulting in complex motives for fighting in wars. One well-known and quite typical poem from the era is Claude McKay's "If We Must Die," published in 1919 (see part 2). This poem is a critique of postwar violence against black people and a poetic declaration of the New Negro's explicit stance against the tyranny that permeated black life in the United States.[24] In terms of overt themes of war, poems such as Roscoe Conkling Jamison's "The Negro Soldiers" is atypical. Many World War I–era black writers centered on challenging racist stereotypes, appreciating the folk, and valuing the general cultural milieu of the New Negro. Despite the political and social justice emphasis of many New Negro era writers, they regularly encountered news reports on the war and black people's (including Africa and the African Diaspora) relationship to it, which were prevalent in *Crisis* and other black publications. Several months before the war's end and again nearly one year later, W.E.B. Du Bois, founder and editor of *Crisis*, published two volumes focused on World War I, the "Soldiers' Number" (June 1918) and a volume titled "First War History Number" (May 1919). Additionally, several issues of *Crisis* from 1917 through 1919 also featured war-related covers.

Many New Negro era writers often placed patriotism and the war on the margins of their texts, as their literary production focused primarily on racial uplift and local battles for citizenship, political and social justice, and equal rights.[25] This emphasis reflected the growing importance and political strength of the New Negro, a concept that was formulated in the 1890s and that prevailed throughout the 1950s. In *A New Negro for a New Century: An Accurate and Up-to-Date Record of the Upward Struggles of the Negro Race*, published in 1900 during the Philippines-U.S. War, Booker T. Washington, Fannie Barrier Williams, and N. B. Wood emphasized military service as central to the New Negroes' right to justice and equality.[26] Substantial numbers of New Negro writers took up the work of revising the dominating narratives on black life, contesting the derogatory images from that narrative in the United States, and of connecting local struggles to the struggles of suffering peoples around the world. During the early decades of the twentieth century and into the World War II years, for instance, New Negroes in their writings and speeches expressed concern about U.S. imperialism in the Philippines. The words of an anonymous black soldier in the Philippines who wrote in 1900 to the *New York Age* convey this concern (see part 2). Frequently articles in *Crisis* also reported on Africans in the wars. And black people in general responded to the atrocities of World War I, including the high death rates of Senegalese troops fighting with the French and African American men fighting in the U.S. armed services while it remained segregated. This Pan-African interest and a transnational viewpoint on injustice forms a persistent thread in African American literature.

World War II, which occurred during the Black Chicago Writers movement (1936–1949), has generated nearly as much response from African American writers as the Civil War. With the Double-V campaign, African Americans fought for victory on two fronts.[27] Through this campaign, black people again vigorously protested against inequality in the nation (a nation that also had confined over 100,000 Japanese American citizens in relocation prisons and confiscated their property) and in the military, while simultaneously engaging in the war overseas. During World War II, actual African American military resisters found a variety of ways to reject injustice and inequality in the armed services. Some of these resisters include Malcolm X, who feigned insanity during World War II and registered as a conscientious objector during the Korean War; William Henry Hastie, who resigned his position as civilian aide to the secretary of war in 1943 in protest against inequality in the military;[28] and Ralph Ellison, who served in the Merchant Marine to avoid a segregated military. African Americans' active resistance to injustice and inequity at home extended to political and social inequities everywhere, including concern for all colonial peoples and for the condition of peoples of color and the dispossessed around the globe.

In World War II veteran John O. Killens's novel *And Then We Heard the Thunder* (1963), he presents issues such as inequity and injustice in the military, in the United States, and internationally, through his central character Solly Saunders. This character nearly becomes convinced by a fellow soldier's praise for the Japanese as people of color competing equally as an imperial power with Western nations.[29] Solly also entertains thoughts of becoming a conscientious objector. Such literary representations were not solely the imaginative makings of creative writers, as demonstrated in historical studies of African Americans and Japanese during World War II.[30] Other writers including Ann Petry (*The Street*, 1946) and John A. Williams ("'Nam,'"1972; see part 4) have depicted various forms of resistance to military service, such as the dangerous practice of puncturing the eardrum to avoid service or to expedite discharge from the segregated military. As a testament to the impact of World War II on the imaginary of African Americans decades after the end of the war (as also is the case for the Civil War), a number of black writers, including Rosa Guy (*Bird at My Window*, 1966), World War II veteran John A. Williams (*Clifford's Blues*, 1998), and James McBride (*Miracle at St. Anna*, 2002) have continued to write compelling literature focused on this war.

The 1960s and 1970s mark another politically charged historical moment that produced an African American literary movement while the nation was at war, the Black Arts Aesthetics Movement (1965–1975).[31] Writers who were part of this literary and cultural movement, as was the case for New Negro Movement writers during World War I, did not produce a substantial body of literature that focused on the War in Vietnam. Rather, they presented the war as a backdrop in literature that emphasizes African Americans' political battles in the United States. Poems such as War in Vietnam veteran Haki Madhubuti's (Don L. Lee) "The Long Reality" (1967)[32] and short stories such as Toni Cade Bambara's "The Sea Birds Are Still Alive" (1977; see part 4) call attention to the structural analogies between the Vietnamese people's struggle against colonialism and African Americans' battles for liberation from inequity. This theme in Black Arts Aesthetics Movement (BAAM) literature revived transnational issues from African American writing of the World War II era. This Vietnam era literature also recalls World War I in its focus on inequality at home. Instead of emphasizing the War in Vietnam, BAAM writers addressed the discontent on the streets of the

United States, expressing frustration and anger over ongoing injustice. These writers were concerned primarily with their local battles, but they connected those fights, as did earlier writers, to struggles of peoples of color and subordinated peoples around the world. This time, the focus was on the Vietnamese, the Mozambique liberation movements, and other movements that also were battling oppression and moving against colonial and imperial powers.[33] A number of African American writers of the 1960s and 1970s were not part of BAAM, which had emerged alongside the Black Liberation/Black Power Movement. Yusef Komunyakaa, a veteran of the War in Vietnam, was one such writer. He collected a series of his poems on Vietnam in *Dien Cai Dau* (1988). In his innovative poetic narrative "The One-legged Stool" (see part 4), Komunyakaa points to the persistence of racial narratives in the United States and the ways those narratives had the potential to undermine the United States in the war. For other writers, such as Alice Walker in stories such as "Petunias,"[34] the problem of race during the Vietnam era is clear. The mother of a devastated war veteran has suffered at the hands of segregationists in Tranquil, Mississippi. In retaliation for the mother's civil rights work, the segregationists disinterred the ashes and bones of the woman's formerly enslaved great-grandmother (and the veteran's great-great-grandmother) and dumped them in the civil rights worker's flowerbed. In response, the veteran wanted to make a bomb with the knowledge he had acquired during the war.

The War in Vietnam ended in 1975, and by then the uprisings and revolts for equal rights and justice also had subsided, as had substantial numbers of literary responses to war by African American writers. While black writers' concerns with citizenship and equality under the law have persisted, African American and other writers have not yet had enough time to produce a substantial body of literature on the Gulf wars that began in the 1990s and continued into the twenty-first century or on the war in Afghanistan. A number of writers, however, have responded to the attacks of 11 September 2001 and to the war to protect the United States against terrorists' attacks. Lucille Clifton's poem "september song: a poem in 7 days" (2002; see part 4) exemplifies how African American writers have responded. She connects the United States to the long international history of "otherwheres" that have experienced violence and dispossession, naming Israel, Ireland, and Palestine. Clifton's poem also presents readers with yet another perspective on Irving Berlin's patriotic song "God Bless America" (1918) and on citizenship; the speaker reminds readers that "this is not the time / . . . to ask who is allowed to be / american."

Much of the literature by black writers focusing on war and African

American liberation struggles from the Revolutionary War for Independence to the present has included concerns about true citizenship. The nation's founders wrote the majority of black people into the Constitution as property, each human chattel valued at three-fifths of a whole person for purposes of representation. Later, the Naturalization Act of 1790 legally established a route to citizenship that was only for "free white persons." In 1857, in *Dred Scott v. Sandford*, the Supreme Court denied full citizenship to black people in the United States, ruling that the federal government did not have the power to regulate slavery in the U.S. western territories. This decision essentially reinforced the 1850 Compromise that included the Fugitive Slave Act, also imperiling the freedom of free black people, and the Kansas-Nebraska Act (1854), which had repealed the 1820 Missouri Compromise as well as nullified its slavery provisions. From that time to 1866, the whims of local officials determined the citizenship rights of black persons living in U.S. territories. Similarly, local laws in the states varied regarding the citizenship of black people. In this way, local and national laws and prevailing supremacist ideas preserved inequity and frequently violated African Americans' citizenship rights.

Free or enslaved, black people were merely inhabitants of the United States, not true citizens under the nation's laws. Before an audience in Boston in 1832, black abolitionist Maria Stewart presented a speech titled "Why Sit Ye Here and Die?" In that speech, Stewart asserted that she was a "true born American," who, along with other black people and black women in particular, deserved "equal rights and privileges."[35] Five years later, in 1837, Robert Purvis wrote in his *Appeal of Forty Thousand Citizens, Threatened with Disfranchisement, to the People of Pennsylvania* that black men were "citizens" who had fought "in the revolutionary struggle which achieved independence of our country. . . . Instead of being disfranchised, such men should be denominated fathers, and respected and honored as patriots of the country."[36] Ten years later, in 1847, before his break with the radical anti-Constitutional ideas of William Lloyd Garrison, Frederick Douglass addressed an audience in New York and asked, "What country have I? The Institutions of this Country do not know me—do not recognize me as a man. . . . I am not thought of or spoken of except as a piece of property. . . . Now, in such a country as this I cannot have patriotism. The only thing that links me to this land is my family, and the painful consciousness that here there are 3,000,000 of my fellow creatures groaning beneath the iron rod of the worst despotism that could be devised even in Pandemonium" (see part 1).[37]

So when the Supreme Court affirmed in law the unwritten national perspective that persons of African descent, whether free or enslaved, held indefinite status as citizens of the United States because their standing was subject to the caprice of local attitudes and laws, John S. Rock commented that black people, in the spirit of the Revolutionary War for Independence, should become a power that this nation would be "bound to respect."[38] His words joined the numerous contemporary responses to the notorious ruling by the Supreme Court in 1857 on Harriet and Dred Scott's freedom lawsuit for full citizenship, which has received ongoing comment in literature and oratory.

After the Civil War, Congress passed the Civil Rights Act of 1866, which conferred citizenship on black people in the United States. It passed a second Civil Rights Act in 1871 to protect the suffrage rights of African Americans, which were under attack by the Ku Klux Klan, and the Civil Rights Act of 1875 prohibited discrimination in public accommodations. Fearing equivocation on the provisions of these acts, Congress amended the Constitution as well. Indeed, in 1883, the Supreme Court overturned the Civil Rights Act of 1875. Then, despite ratification of the Fourteenth Amendment in 1868, which provides legal citizenship status not only to African Americans but also to all persons born in the nation, the Supreme Court, in 1896, reaffirmed the nation's subordination of black people and curtailed the citizenship of African Americans with its "separate but equal" decision in *Plessy v. Ferguson*.

The high court's decisions in 1857 and 1896 affirmed and upheld the segregation and exclusion of African Americans from the rights and privileges of the nation that black labor had helped establish and black military service had contributed to preserving for all except themselves. Until 1965 and the passage of the Voting Rights Act, African Americans unwillingly remained outside full legal citizenship in the United States. The Voting Rights Act became the final significant public policy designed to enforce the citizenship rights of African Americans that had been granted nearly 100 years earlier. Additional laws, judicial decisions, and legislation such as the Fair Housing Act of 1968 have continued the ongoing project of creating equality in the United States. Even though after 1965 black people were born in the United States with the presumption of full citizenship, African Americans engaged in an additional ten years of uprisings during the Black Liberation/Black Power Movement to ensure the enforcement of the civil rights laws. African Americans have persistently responded in writing and oratory to these contradictions in the citizenship status of black people in the United States.

During the first decade of the twentieth century, W.E.B. Du Bois, in his seminal book *The Souls of Black Folk* (1903), described black youths (Du Bois's "sons of night," including himself) questioning their exclusion from citizenship in the following way: "Why did God make me an outcast and a stranger in mine own house?" Throughout his writings, Du Bois asserted, nonetheless, that black people in the United States are Americans. For him, being American is not a homogenous (melting pot/assimilationist) experience for black people and indeed need not be. He argues that one should be able to be "both Negro and an American . . . without having the doors of opportunity closed roughly."[39] Du Bois's persistent calls for political and cultural equality and citizenship find similar expression in the several writings on this subject by James Baldwin, who presents his own version of Du Bois's multifaceted black person in the United States.

James Baldwin, in his essay "Stranger in the Village" (originally published in 1953 in *Harper's Magazine*), also stakes a claim to the United States for black people. African Americans, Baldwin notes, clearly have not been "visitor[s] to the West, but . . . citizen[s] there, an American." During the waning years of the Civil Rights Movement and the beginning of the Black Liberation/Black Power years, Baldwin remarked, in an essay titled "The American Dream and the American Negro," that "the American soil is full of the corpses of my ancestors, through four hundred years and at least three wars. Why is my freedom, my citizenship in question now? What one begs the American people to do, for all our sakes, is simply to accept our history." Two decades later, in *The Price of the Ticket* (1985), Baldwin observed that for black people living in the United States in the middle of the twentieth century, national calls to war and reciting the Pledge of Allegiance revealed the contradictions African Americans have had to take into account when thinking about citizenship. Patriotic symbols such as the flag "risked becoming . . . [a] shroud if you didn't know how to keep your distance and stay in your 'place.'" Importantly, though, Baldwin observed that the "romance of treason never occurred to . . . [African Americans] for the brutally simple reason that you can't betray a country you don't have. . . . And . . . [African Americans] did not wish to be traitors. We wished to be citizens."[40] Indeed, black writers, including Maria Stewart, Frederick Douglass, W.E.B. Du Bois, James Baldwin, and numerous others have eloquently and cogently presented a persistent line of thought asserting African American rights to an inheritance of citizenship.

Well into the twentieth century, the national contradictions that many early African American writers have addressed through time also have shaped the lived experiences of later writers such as William Melvin Kelley, who in his epigraph to *dəm* (1967) refers to black people as "in (not of) America."[41] Toni Morrison has echoed Baldwin, Du Bois, and Douglass on their attitudes toward the United States as the location of African Americans' national and family home where justice and equal rights have not yet been attained and are still due. In an interview with Robert Stepto during the U.S. bicentennial year, Morrison said, "I never felt like an American . . . I never felt like a citizen." Accordingly, in her fiction, Morrison has made place central, yet "not in terms of the country or the state."[42] For Morrison and many other African American writers, place and land have provided a sense of rootedness, an intimacy with a location that has become a home. In Morrison's novels *Beloved* (1987), *A Mercy* (2008), and *Home* (2012), she inscribes the United States using the metaphor of house and home by recalling the 1863 Emancipation Proclamation at 124 Bluestone in *Beloved* and by depicting Jacob Vaark's house in *A Mercy* as a site where black people had participated in building the house and are ineradicably part of the stories in it. In Morrison's *Home*, the life of a veteran from the war in Korea complicates the history of this country.[43] And, Morrison's blues-toned house in *Beloved*, as metaphor of the United States, is haunted by slavery. Her character Baby Suggs says, "Not a house in the country ain't packed to its rafters with some dead Negro's grief."[44] There is no back door at 124, no escape from the past of a partial emancipation enacted 124 years before the novel's publication, as that past inhabits the present. Ultimately, then, African Americans must enter the nation through the front door as the nation must acknowledge the ghosts in the rafters without succumbing to the power of the ghosts to possess the present. Similarly, in *A Mercy*, Morrison presents Jacob Vaark's unfinished house, with its missing windows, as another metaphor of this country. She further illustrates how the various forms of exploitation of persons in servitude in colonial North America became racialized before the Revolutionary War for Independence and the founding of the United States. So in a nation that is unformed and incomplete, Morrison's central character Florens writes her story on the walls and floor of Vaark's house. The story of Jacob Vaark's "grandiose" house, the story of this country, cannot be told without the stories of enslaved "Africs" such as Florens or the story of the novel's free blacksmith. Both of these tales are inscribed indelibly within Vaark's house. Morrison's title for her Korean War–era novel *Home* positions the United States as the home of African Americans and provides a useful way to explain the persistence in African American literature and social history of nineteenth-century ideas such as Frederick Douglass's and Martin Delany's references to black people as "a nation within a nation."[45] These black men recognize the difference between a country and a nation and assert that a people with a shared history, a shared language, a shared culture, and shared political solidarity, and who operate within defined geographical boundaries are a nation, even if they do not have the self-governance, social systems, structured economy, and sovereignty of a country.[46]

Also, Morrison is among the numerous black writers such as Ann Petry writer of *The Street* and the short story "In Darkness and Confusion" (1947; see part 3), John Edgar Wideman writer of the Homewood narratives, and many other writers who have depicted places in fiction illustrating African American life developing on its own terms, despite exclusion from true citizenship. Indeed, in his satirical novel *Middle Passage* (1990), Charles Johnson depicts Rutherford Calhoun (an escapee from slavery in New Orleans, found hiding on a ship bound for Africa to traffic in illegal human cargo) as a "marginalized American colored man," affirming his patriotism. Rutherford says that he is "of" this country; he longs for the United States, the only "*home*" he really knows.[47]

African American writers also have addressed United States' citizenship—denied, reclaimed, and affirmed—along with loyalty to the ideals of the nation in "America poems." In these poems, black writers have expressed their disappointment about the nation's inequality and posed a challenge to injustice. These poems include Langston Hughes's "I, Too, Sing America" (1925)[48] and Albery Allson Whitman's "Hymn to the Nation" (1877; see part 1), both of which inscribe the United States in the complex terms of African Americans' history. In their America poems, black writers have often used irony and parody to present their critique of the United States. This is the case for James Monroe Whitfield ("America," 1853; see part 1) and James Weldon Johnson ("To America," 1917; see part 2). In his poem, Johnson probes the country with questions such as "How would you have us, as we are? . . . / Strong, willing sinews in your wings? / Or tightening chains about your feet?" America poems by Johnson and other African American writers frequently have expressed disappointment in and a repudiation of the nation's inequality along with a desire for justice and inclusion. In African American literature from at least the eighteenth century, America poems, beginning with Phillis Wheatley's "America," which she tried unsuccessfully to publish in the United States in 1772, engage in a multifaceted dialogue with the similarly long history, of African heritage literature, particularly Africa poems, such as Wheatley's "On Being

Brought from Africa to America, published in 1773."[49] Both America poems and Africa poems convey versions of loss and reclamation, while together they inscribe the legacy of black people in the New World.

Black writers also have depicted pride in military service along with hope that the nation would fulfill and complete its gestures toward equality and freedom. Figures and topics such as Abraham Lincoln, Robert Gould Shaw,[50] black regiments, and significant battles such as Port Hudson, Fort Wagner, Fort Pillow, San Juan Hill, and the Battle of the Bulge are among the persistent themes of these writers. Paul Laurence Dunbar's poetry provides an example of the importance of these events on the imaginary of African American writers. In Dunbar's poem "Robert Gould Shaw," (see part 1) published in 1900, the speaker asks how the young officer became the man "To lead th' unlettered and despised droves / To Manhood's home and thunder at the gate," yet he still wonders whether Shaw's sacrifice was "but in vain!" This poem reveals the complicated operations of national loyalty in this country, as does much of the related literature by black writers in the United States.

Before 1965 and before the nation's laws upheld equal rights, African Americans claimed an inheritance of ownership rights to the land of their births through the sacrifice of generations of blood, sweat, and bones. African American literature, oratory, and essays demonstrate that some black people in the United States have located a sense of citizenship and feelings of national loyalty in that history and in the principles and ideals of the United States rather than in patriotic symbols, songs, and language. After 11 September 2001, a small window of opportunity for a new national narrative opened and quickly shut as deeply held racial attitudes and bigotry reformulated in new ways. Following the events of that day, African American writers such as Lucille Clifton urged the nation to interrogate unexamined notions of patriotic ideals and citizenship in the United States and to move outside the limitations of a black-white racial narrative that has inadequately and inaccurately explained the United States and its citizens. These writers convey how the history of the United States attests to the futility of rooting one's pride in nation in prefabricated pledges, songs, gestures, or symbols. They also remind readers that too frequently unexamined national loyalty has become a mechanism for silencing or forgetting both history and current lived experiences. Uncritical loyalty creates the pretense that all is well and always has been.

National pride that is blind to history and insensible to critique offers the false comfort of oblivion. In the poem "Reflections after the June 12th

March for Disarmament" (1984; see part 4), Sonia Sanchez, a participant in the Black Arts Aesthetics Movement era, tells the people of the United States, "Because we love the country, we challenge the country." This statement explains much of the literature on citizenship, national loyalty, and war by African Americans. The literature by these writers clearly demonstrates the hoped-for possibility that the United States will attain its highest and best aspirations. The long struggle to secure African American liberation and citizenship necessarily challenges the prevailing U.S. narratives on democracy. African Americans' writings and speeches on these issues provide further evidence that freedom from enslavement is insufficient without liberty, justice, and equity of all persons.

As nebulous assertions of a supposedly "post-racial" and, the disturbing erasure, a "post-black" United States abound in the nation's current popular narratives, the writers here provide valuable perspectives that displace Euro-American normative scripts, contribute to the disruption of black-white binaries, and clear a space for a post-supremacist United States. In such a nation, a plurality of narratives could proliferate and tell the varied interconnecting and often simultaneously diverging stories of its citizens.[51] Perhaps, then, Zora Neale Hurston's sentiments, in "Crazy for This Democracy" (1945),[52] that the nation suffers from a pox, could become a distant, historical memory, and her wish for the nation to be free of the disease so that she can know how democracy feels could become a reality, if not for her, at least for others. Hence, while the election and reelection of Barack Hussein Obama as the 44th president of the United States of America were not a cure for centuries of injustice, perhaps the United States has in some way made an important, even if irresolute, step toward a nation that may become substantially different from the one depicted in a significant portion of African American literature to date, some which we reprint here in *These Truly Are the Brave*.

NOTES

1. Williams, *Capitalism and Slavery*, 108–25.

2. Wong, *Neither Fugitive nor Free*, 130–49.

3. Nash, *The Forgotten Fifth*, 67. In *Reconstruction*, Eric Foner takes the view that the Civil War and Reconstruction are part of an unfinished revolution in the United States. For the view that black liberation activities worked to complete the American Revolution, see Outlaw, "Philosophy, African-Americans, and the Unfinished American Revolution," 46–47.

4. See Gerzina, *Mr. and Mrs. Prince.*

5. Hammon, "An Evening's Improvement" and Hammon, "A Dialogue Entitled the Kind Master and Dutiful Servant."

6. Smith's song was first performed at Park Street Church in Boston and was printed as a broadside 4 July 1831. He added another verse in 1832 to commemorate George Washington's centennial. See Branham, "'Of Thee I Sing': Contesting 'America,'" which also reports that alterations of patriotic songs to express the contradictions of the United States have a long history among black and white abolitionists and later advocates of social and political justice in the United States.

7. Davis, "To Those Who Sing America."

8. Du Bois, *The Souls of Black Folk*, 189; Ellison, "What America Would Be Like without Blacks."

9. Niagara Movement, "Negroes Want Equal Rights: The Niagara Movement Issues an Address to the Country," 4.

10. See Clark, *Defining Moments*; Kachun, *Festivals of Freedom*; Waldstreicher, *In the Midst of Perpetual Fetes.*

11. Johnson, "Fifty Years," 16.

12. Lusane, *Hitler's Black Victims*, 151–60.

13. Smith, "The Black Protest Sonnet"; Emanuel and Gross, *Dark Symphony*; Lederer, "The Didactic and the Literary in Four Harlem Renaissance Sonnets."

14. Yacovone, *Freedom's Journey.*

15. "Hagar's children" is an African American vernacular term describing the status of black people in the family of the United States. The term references the Old Testament story of Hagar in Genesis 16:1 and 21:8–21. See Baldwin, *The Price of the Ticket*, xiv–xv.

16. Trethewey, *Native Guard.*

17. Shirley Graham married W.E.B. Du Bois in 1951.

18. Ross, *Reforming Black Men in the Jim Crow Era*, 1–13, 94–104.

19. Hughes, "The Red Cross Nurses," 13.

20. Rampersad, *The Life of Langston Hughes*, 26–27. Among Hughes's war poetry are poems responding to the Spanish Civil War. In 1937, Hughes worked as a war correspondent in Spain.

21. Patton and Honey, "Contested Periodization," xxv–xxvii.

22. *Rachel: A Play in Three Acts*; see also Hill and Hatch, *A History of African American Theater.*

23. Mitchell, *Living with Lynching*, 1–18, 23–42. Literature written to protest lynching was part of a broad initiative among writers in the United States, not just black writers, especially in groups such as the Writers' League Against Lynching. African American writers played a central role in this important literary project.

24. See Tuttle, *Race Riot*; Ogletree and Sarat, *From Lynch Mobs to the Killing State*; McWhirter, *Red Summer*; and Whitaker, *On the Laps of Gods.*

25. Gaines, *Uplifting the Race*, 67–70, 76–80, 209–33; Gates and Jarrett, *The New Negro*, 10–14.

26. Gates and Jarrett, *The New Negro*, 1–20, 36–53.

27. This nationwide media campaign began in the *Pittsburgh Courier* in 1942, yet seg-

regation and injustice in the military and throughout the country had been crucial issues that the black press had addressed from the turn of the century.

28. See Ware, *William Hastie.*

29. During World War II, Japan engaged in its own project of empire-building. Due to the status of race in the United States, some African Americans felt that military success by peoples of color over Western colonizing nations simultaneously helped vindicate black people falsely maligned by charges of cowardice and unsuitability for battle while diminishing the power of supremacists. African Americans who held this view rarely recognized the supremacist ideas of other peoples of color.

30. Allen, "When Japan Was 'Champion of the Darker Races'" and "Waiting for Tojo."

31. The centrality of cultural and literary aesthetics during the 1960s and 70s is clear among writers who theorized the movement at the time. Larry Neal's term "Black Arts Movement/Black Art Aesthetic" accurately accounts for the full spectrum of literary activities during this cultural movement. This wide scope is represented in the usage here. See Neal, "Some Reflections on the Black Aesthetic"; also Hill et al., "African American History and Culture, 1960 to the Present," 1347, 1365.

32. Madhubuti initially published *Think Black* in 1966 independently in Chicago before Dudley Randall published Madhubuti's poems at Broadside Press. Randall founded this small independent press in 1965 in Detroit. Publication information for the self-published version (mimeographed) is unavailable. See Lee, *Think Black,* 22–23.

33. The Front for the Liberation of Mozambique (FRELIMO) was a coalition of groups that organized in 1962 against Portuguese colonialism in Mozambique. Portuguese colonial rule in Mozambique began in 1505.

34. Alice Walker, "Petunias," in *You Can't Keep a Good Woman Down: Stories.*

35. Stewart, "Why Sit Ye Here and Die?" 128.

36. Purvis, *An Appeal to Forty Thousand Citizens,* 133, 135.

37. Douglass, "Country, Conscience, and the Anti-Slavery Cause," 57.

38. Rock, "I Will Sink or Swim with My Race," 316.

39. Du Bois, *The Souls of Black Folk,* 8–9. Du Bois's views on retaining cultural distinctiveness in the United States among Negro or black people varied over time.

40. Baldwin, *The Price of the Ticket,* 88, 405, xv. Baldwin's essay "The American Dream and the American Negro" is a transcript of his debate with William F. Buckley at the Cambridge Union Society, Cambridge University, February 18, 1965. The *New York Times Magazine* published this "slightly condensed" transcript on March 7, 1965. Their debate topic is "Has the American Dream Been Achieved at the Expense of the American Negro?"

41. Kelley, *dɘm.*

42. Quoted in Stepto, "'Intimate Things in Place,'" 473.

43. In her fiction, Morrison frequently refers to wars, battles, and struggles. *The Bluest Eye* refers to World War I and World War II; *Sula* refers to the Trojan War, World War I, World War II, and the Civil Rights Movement; *Song of Solomon* and *Beloved* refer to the Civil War; *Tar Baby* refers to Vietnam; *Jazz* refers to World War I; *Paradise* refers to the Peloponnesian War, World War I, World War II, Korea, Vietnam, and Black Liberation; *Love* refers to World War I, Vietnam, and Black Liberation; and *Home* refers to World War I, World War II, and Korea.

44. Morrison, *Beloved*, 5.

45. Douglass, "The Present Condition and Future Prospects of the Negro People"; Delany, *The Condition, Elevation, Emigration and Destiny of the Colored People of the United States*.

46. This definition does not include Benedict Anderson's important yet complicated definition of these terms, as he does not account for the possibility of nations articulated or formed through lived experience. Here his concepts of "horizontal comradeship" (political solidarity) and "imagined political communities" obtain, but not, however, his view of sovereignty. See Anderson, *Imagined Communities*.

47. Johnson, *Middle Passage*, 169, 179.

48. Hughes, "I, Too," 46.

49. Phillis Wheatley's Poem "America," published posthumously in 1970 is among the earliest America Poems by a black writer, and her "On Being Brought From Africa to America," published in 1773 in *Poems on Various Subjects, Religious and Moral*, would be counted among Africa poems written by black writers. Although scholars know that Frances Ellen Watkins Harper's "Ethiopia" was published in 1854 in *Poems on Miscellaneous Subjects*, Kletzing and Crogman report a conversation with Harper stating that "Ethiopia" had been published earlier. Wheatley, *Poems on Various Subjects, Religious and Moral*; Kuncio, "Some Unpublished Poems of Phillis Wheatley"; Watkins [Harper], *Poems on Miscellaneous Subjects*; Kletzing and Crogman, *Progress of a Race*, 498–500.

50. Colonel Shaw's influence on the cultural imaginary of African Americans extends beyond literature. The nineteenth-century sculptor Edmonia Lewis, of African and North American Indigenous descent, made a bust of Shaw in 1864.

51. African immigrants could not become naturalized citizens of the United States until 1870. The continuing racialized nature of citizenship in the United States also is apparent in the Chinese Exclusion Act of 1882. See also *United States v. Wong Kim Ark* (1898), affirming the Fourteenth Amendment right to jus soli (citizenship by birth) and *United States v. Bhagat Singh Thind* (1923), a Supreme Court case that revoked Thind's citizenship as a "white person" or Aryan/Caucasian and reclassified immigrants from India as Asians.

52. Hurston, "Crazy for this Democracy."

1

FREEDOM, DEMOCRACY, AND EQUALITY?

From Colonies to a Nation Divided

In every human Breast, God has implanted a Principle, which we call Love of Freedom; it is impatient of Oppression, and pants for Deliverance; and by the Leave of our Modern Egyptians I will assert, that the same Principle lives in us. I desire not for their Hurt, but to convince them of the strange Absurdity of their Conduct whose words and actions are so diametrically opposite. . . . I humbly think it does not require the Penetration of a Philosopher to determine.

PHILLIS WHEATLEY, 1776

Robert Smalls and other Civil War sailors involved in capturing the *Planter*, a Confederate war vessel, and transporting it to the Union Army. Image from Joseph T. Wilson's *The Black Phalanx* (1890).

F OR AFRICAN AND AFRICAN-DESCENDED PEOPLE, alienation and discrimination were constant from the colonial period through the post–Civil War Reconstruction Era (1865–1877). This was the case regardless of whether a person had survived the Middle Passage or had been born in British North America and regardless of whether a person lived in legal slavery or had obtained legal freedom. Black people were denied basic rights, and persistent racial prejudice and brutal treatment exacerbated these losses, reinforced by the legality of slavery and justified by widespread belief in the dominant society that black people were racially inferior. Their lives curtailed by laws and customs, black people endured generations of injustice, hostility, and the absence of citizenship rights. Many fought for liberty from bondage or/and from the confines of the society that refused equality to black people. Military service offered one avenue for exercising agency in that pursuit.

Most of the wars in the colonies and the early United States involved struggles on North American soil: the Revolutionary War for Independence (1775–1783); continuing conflicts with Britain (War of 1812); war against the native peoples (during the Seven Years' War of 1756–1763 and throughout the nineteenth century); war against a neighboring nation (U.S.-Mexico War, 1846–1848); and war within the nation (Civil War, 1861–1865). Military service in this domestic arena provided a space where black men in particular could dispel commonly held, albeit false, beliefs about their inherent inferiority and situate themselves more solidly in the polity through their sacrifice, or so they had hoped. Despite black men's persistent military service, displays of courage, patriotism, and apparent loyalty, their efforts did not translate into the desired rewards of citizenship. More important, their military service throughout the history of the United States illuminates the varied and knotty definitions of patriotism that were inextricably linked to their pursuit of liberty.

Revolutionary anti-colonial battles in British North America informed and complicated subsequent attitudes toward citizenship and military service for New World Africans in the new nation. Black people participated in military service well before the War for Independence. During the colonists' struggles with the French and the Native American Indians that began in the late 1750s and continued through to the mid-1760s, a small number of black men, both enslaved and free, served on the British side (for example, Olaudah Equiano, whose writing is included here). During these wars, however, North American colonial militias made use of the black population only when enlisted white militiamen became scarce, relegating black men primarily to supportive roles as servants. Enslavers worried more about black insurrection than about conflict with the French or with native peoples on the frontier. This pattern of prejudicial selection for service would continue for two centuries.[1]

When they write about black participation and bravery in the Revolutionary War for Independence, historians often focus on the death of Crispus Attucks, and indeed, in 1888, Boston officials memorialized him with a statue (albeit after years of resistance to the idea). Attucks, likely a fugitive from slavery in Massachusetts, was one of five men killed after skirmishes with a British sentry on 5 March 1770. This selective commemoration of black participation in this war distorts the numbers who served, about 5,000 from a black population of half a million. By 1779, black soldiers represented one in seven men of the Continental Army, making it the most integrated U.S. Army until the Vietnam War almost 200 years later.[2]

Black peoples' allegiances were complicated, and during the Revolutionary War for Independence, the prize of liberation for enslaved people or improved social status for free women and men dictated loyalties. The colonials' complaint that precipitated the revolution against the British— the imposition of taxes without representation—was not necessarily black people's battle. For the most part, black people rooted their military service in the revolutionary potential for their freedom. As historian Benjamin Quarles states, "The Negro's role in the Revolution can best be understood by realizing that his major loyalty was not to a place nor to a people but to a principle."[3] Lemuel Haynes, born in 1753, served as a soldier in the Continental Army. He then became a minister and later received an honorary MA from Middlebury College in Vermont. In "Liberty Further Extended" (1776) Haynes unequivocally promoted the claim that the American Revolution should also free enslaved people.[4] While thousands of black men fought against the British, their identification with the new nation was not self-evident, particularly when the numbers who chose *not* to fight for colonialists' independence vastly outnumbered those who served in the Continental Army. Rough estimates of the number of black people who fled to British-controlled territory stands at around 100,000, although the number of those runaways who actually fought for King George III is unknown.[5]

On the first official day of hostilities, 19 April 1775, the militia that exchanged fire with the British in Lexington, Massachusetts, included black armed men, some free and some enslaved locally. After the Battle of Bunker Hill in May 1775, the Continental Congress raised an army to replace states' militias. This Continental Army was not yet institutionalized; it operated on loose military rules, populated by self-armed volunteers. After George Washington, a Virginia slaveholder, took command in July 1775, he forbade black men from serving. Southern delegates to the Continental Congress, who were heavily invested in slave labor for their economic well-being, pushed Washington toward an all-white army. They did not want to arm enslaved black men and stubbornly refused to include them, even when some owners were offered compensation.[6]

Nevertheless, free black men served in the colonial militia and in the Continental Army for a chance to acquire equal citizenship rights, perhaps even citizenship with suffrage rights attached to property requirements. One example of service was the black Boston-based militia company called the Bucks of America, who protected local property during the war. Governor John Hancock presented them with their own flag for their diligent service.[7] The Bucks of America and many other black soldiers saw the conflict as an opportunity to make a political impression on the winning side. Their quest for freedom also coalesced around the elimination of slavery, an institution that negatively marked all black people, free and enslaved.

The British, stretched to breaking point along the eastern coastline, actively recruited black soldiers and offered freedom to enslaved black men who would fight for the Crown. In November 1775, the Royal Ethiopian Regiment, commanded by John Murray, Earl of Dunmore, was stationed in the waters off the coast of Norfolk, Virginia. Those men sought their freedom by opposing the Continental Army. By August 1776, however, a devastating smallpox epidemic had ravaged their numbers. The British also raised the Black Company of Pioneers, composed of unarmed runaways, as part of a British provincial military unit. Other short-lived units formed in various places during the war, some armed, many not.[8]

After recognizing the tactical problem with runaways fighting alongside the British, George Washington reluctantly allowed freed black men to serve if they already had battle experience. As the battles advanced, generally only free black men and enslaved men acting as surrogates for their owners served until the end of the war. One notable exception was the segregated 1st Rhode Island Regiment, which included a company of black men whose enslavers sold them in 1778 to the Continental Army. Rhode

Island also allowed any volunteer his freedom and wages.[9] Black women, as with white women, could have no official military role but often worked as nurses and cooks in the war zones. This was the case with Elizabeth Barjona, a cook for the Continental Congress. Similarly, a black woman named Deborah Gannett served in uniform under the name Robert Shurtleff. According to the records of the Massachusetts Legislature, she enlisted in the 4th Massachusetts Regiment from May 1782 to sometime in 1783. The legislature paid her $170 in wages and awarded her an honorable discharge for her service.[10]

Black people assisted the war effort in other ways. Some worked as Continental Army spies, taking advantage of a dubious social status that allowed them to cross enemy lines without suspicion. In one instance, James, enslaved in Virginia, served as a spy by hovering around British camps and passing on information he overheard. His reward was his personal freedom (his owner was also compensated), and his actions clearly demonstrate how black people understood their options for how best to attain freedom. Many black people recognized that a more likely route to freedom came through individual manumission than through state-sanctioned emancipation. To accomplish their goals, some captives played on stereotypes, displaying a clear consciousness that countered prevailing racial attitudes that claimed black people were ignorant and childlike.[11]

Many black men working on merchant ships and whaling vessels joined local navies or the Continental Navy at the beginning of the war. Black sailors were not an anomaly; during the colonial era they commonly served on commercial or Royal Navy vessels. With a chronic shortage of volunteers, black sailors took a variety of jobs, from pilots to laborers, although the numbers and the freedom they had varied by colony. Sea vessels were popular choices for runaways because they provided a modicum of safety off shore. Privateer vessels offered better wages and more mobility than the navy and were easily able to attract recruits. James Forten (whose writing is included below), a founding father of abolitionism, served as a privateer during the war.[12]

In short, many black people knew their value to the war effort and negotiated for better conditions when they could. In January 1777, for instance, several free and enslaved black men in Boston, including Prince Hall, who had encouraged black military participation, petitioned for the abolition of slavery in Massachusetts (reprinted below). The Massachusetts Legislature rejected their petition. Many black people petitioned for freedom before and during the war, some as individuals, some as groups, but the majority of these petitions were unsuccessful because of the prevailing climate of injustice.[13]

Change came gradually as some northeastern states (Vermont in 1777, and Massachusetts, New Hampshire, Pennsylvania, Rhode Island, Connecticut, New York, and New Jersey in the following decades) ended slavery, at least on paper. Yet even as the cause of independence eventually unleashed the "first emancipation" in the North, the treatment of most black men who participated in the Revolutionary War for Independence set an unfortunate precedent. While many black Patriots earned accolades for their heroism (and many enslaved men in northern states who had fought won freedom), the nation forgot or ignored them later. The British, similarly, did not recognize most black Loyalists after the Revolutionary War for Independence, although some runaways did have opportunities to migrate to Nova Scotia and later to Sierra Leone, West Africa. Proven loyalty to a chosen side, for the most part, did not facilitate any marked progress for black people. This was underscored when both the Continental Army and British commanders sometimes offered enslaved black people as bounty to encourage white enlisters from areas where slave labor was highly valued. In these cases, both sides used black people as weapons of war, and military leaders reinforced the customary practice of black bodies as property that they bought, sold, stole, or gave away.[14]

After the last battle in October 1781, the national investment in slavery and supremacist beliefs won out, and maintaining slavery became economically and politically crucial to the new nation. Although emancipation came soon in many northeastern states, individuals and many businesses such as insurance and clothing manufacturers continued to benefit from the raw materials and industries (including cotton and textiles) of the slaveholding South. The Constitutional Convention of 1787 reflected the overwhelmingly strong sectionalist interest in retaining the institution of slavery, stunting the nation's revolutionary potential. After Congress passed the federal Fugitive Slave Law in 1793, even the North was no longer a legally safe haven for runaways.

U.S. citizenship consolidated along racial lines also. During the early years of nationhood, some black people again initiated individual freedom lawsuits. Most were unsuccessful, but some prevailed. For instance, in 1781, Elizabeth Freeman, the widow of a Revolutionary War soldier and an ancestor of W.E.B. Du Bois, was the first New World African woman to win her freedom through the courts based on the fact that Article 1 of the Massachusetts Constitution said that "all men are born free and equal."

Unlike plaintiffs in other freedom lawsuits, who downplayed or denied their African ancestry, asserting English heritage, or those who argued for their freedom based on their conversion to Christianity, Freeman pursued freedom as her legal and constitutional right. Some New World Africans sent collective group petitions to colonial and new state legislatures, like the one generated by the Sons of Africa, a group of black men from several towns in Massachusetts who sent their petition to the colonial legislature in 1773.[15] Despite these suits and petitions, when the new nation clarified citizenship in the 1790s with the Naturalization Act, it legally established citizenship for only "free white persons." Subsequent naturalization acts in 1795 and 1798 reinforced this law and focused on immigrants not on Africans. Accordingly, in spite of the Revolutionary War for Independence, true freedom and citizenship remained elusive for black people in the new United States.

The War of 1812 (1812–1815), carried out primarily at sea, continued the struggles with the British and precipitated a call for volunteers to boost the number of conscripted soldiers. After the Revolutionary War for Independence, Congress had disbanded the navy, resulting in a minimal defense system for the nation's vast coastline and shipping interests. In 1798, the U.S. government created its Navy against a backdrop of hostilities on the high seas in an undeclared war with France (1798–1800). Naval recruitment proved difficult at best, as sailors could earn higher wages working on merchant ships. While the law banned black men from service, the nation's needs eventually won out and they boarded naval vessels.

By 1812, nearly 85 percent of the black population in the United States was enslaved.[16] The navy initially used black sailors only in the poorest conditions, unacceptable to even the lowliest white sailor. Yet as the shortages continued, black men also operated the guns. These black sailors distinguished themselves in service. After a key event in 1813, the Battle of Lake Erie, which gave the United States control of much of the land that is now Michigan, Commander Oliver Hazard Perry wrote that "they [black sailors] seem to be absolutely insensible to danger."[17] While perhaps well meaning, his comment provoked much debate and consternation. Despite the reluctance of the armed forces to include black seamen, it was black men who answered the recruitment call, and by the end of the mostly naval war they comprised about one-sixth of the naval personnel. Many black men also contributed to the war effort on privateer vessels.

Repeating their practices of the Revolutionary War era, the British habitually impressed, or forced, men into service. At the center of the War of 1812 was the dispute over Britain's impressments of John Strachan, William Ware, and Daniel Martin, all of whom the United States claimed as residents (see John Williams's entry below).[18] At times, the British continued to appeal to enslaved men for their service with the promise of freedom. In 1814, almost 5,000 Chesapeake runaways fled to the British side, drawn by the promises of freedom in Canada or the West Indies or the opportunity to fight their captors. Under Admiral Alexander Cochrane, a unit nicknamed the "Black Marines" was noted for its participation in burning the Capitol Building and the president's house in Washington, D.C., in August 1814.[19] They were exceptions, however. Most captives did not trust Britain's intentions and were vividly aware of the ramifications if they failed in their missions or if the U.S. military caught them.

When the British attempted to take New Orleans in 1815, the Louisiana Battalion of Free Men of Color proved invaluable alongside General Andrew Jackson in the Battle of New Orleans. This battalion existed because in 1812 the Louisiana governor had permitted free propertied black men (and those who had paid taxes for two years) to form a militia unit. Louisiana had just entered the union (the United States bought the territory in 1803 from France and admitted it as a state in 1812), and the people there had lived under different racial norms. This rendered the black population in Louisiana somewhat different from the rest of the nation. For instance, the state had a number of refugees from the Saint Domingue (Haitian) army who had supported Napoleon. These men, led by white officers, sought to protect their own interests as they demonstrated national loyalty. The battalion had three black second lieutenants: Isidore Honoré, Vincent Populous (who became the first black officer of field-grade rank recognized by the United States), and Joseph Savary (whom Andrew Jackson promoted to major).[20] Andrew Jackson, anticipating an attack and recognizing the paucity of volunteers for an unpopular war, took the unusual action of issuing a proclamation urging freemen to take up arms against the British, offering them the same pay as white soldiers. However, they would remain under the command of white officers in segregated units. The U.S. victory in the war secured the nation's geographical boundaries and gave it geopolitical power. For the Louisiana Battalion, praises and promises echoed nationally in the wake of their service. Nevertheless, applause did not convert into equality and citizenship for the majority of black people.[21] The War of 1812 formally concluded with the Treaty of Ghent, signed in December 1814 and ratified in February 1815. During the entire war, the armed forces as a whole refused to enroll runaways and only accepted freemen, although some owners sent black enslaved men into service and collected their wages.[22]

The U.S. Army continued to resist arming black men. In 1820 the federal government again announced that black men could not enlist in the army, but they fought nonetheless.[23] The expansionist U.S. policy of Manifest Destiny, which declared that it was the nation's inevitable duty to expand coast to coast, precipitated another border conflict, this time over the annexation of Texas. Black men once again volunteered their services, hoping for better opportunities as payment for their service and loyalties. Although the all-white army excluded their participation during the U.S.-Mexico War (1846–1848), black people were present, either enslaved or as servants. Although this was a land war, the U.S. Navy blockaded Mexican commerce in the Gulf of Mexico, a maneuver that did not involve combat. About 1,000 black sailors participated in the blockade, as the number of white recruits had waned.[24] Critics of the war, however, such as abolitionist Frederick Douglass, saw the conflict as a means to expand slaveholding territory westward, illustrating the complicated and tangled arguments about the locus of loyalty and patriotism in African Americans' participation in U.S. military conquests.

Black military participation in the first half of the nineteenth century never translated into the desired rewards in civilian life. There were exceptions in localized areas, but they were few. Indeed, early nineteenth-century debates about slavery and the expansion of the nation created unprecedented tension. As a result, during the early decades of the nineteenth century black people witnessed an overall trend toward harsher treatment and a tightening of laws related to any form of freedom they might have had (whether free or enslaved). For some black people, the response to slavery became insurrection, as had occurred in Haiti (Saint Domingue) at the turn of the century. Some of the potential mass uprisings on U.S. soil include Gabriel Prosser's plans for armed revolt (using black Revolutionary War veterans) near Richmond, Virginia, in 1800; Denmark Vesey's endeavor in 1822 in South Carolina; Nat Turner's revolt in Southampton County, Virginia, in 1831; and John Brown's raid on Harpers Ferry in 1859 (funded by northern abolitionists, both black and white). Historians of slavery have documented that there were many more local and less-publicized attempts to take freedom by force, including smaller flashes of violence on plantations, on roadways, in homes, or on vessels.[25]

During the last decade before the Civil War, the nation split decisively along sectional lines as legislation passed through Congress and the Supreme Court weighed in on the slavery question. In 1850, Congress revised the Fugitive Slave Law, extending its reach and making it a crime to harbor runaways. In 1854, the Kansas-Nebraska Act allowed voters, at that time white and male, in the new territories to determine by popular vote whether slavery would be allowed; and in 1857, the Supreme Court confirmed the invalidity of full black citizenship in *Dred Scott v. Sandford*. The court concluded not only that the enslaved plaintiff Scott had no basis to sue for freedom but that *no* black person had "rights which the white man was bound to respect."[26]

The Civil War (1861–1865) shook the nation's foundations. In the midst of the political and warfront battles, heated discussions swirled about whether or not black people should serve in the war for the union. These discussions did not stop thousands of black men from once again volunteering their services. Black men again made choices about loyalty based on the prospect of emancipation or better social status. Once it became clear that President Abraham Lincoln would enforce emancipation, more black people sought freedom and full citizenship through military service. Either emancipation would occur, bringing (they hoped) citizenship and equality as freed men and women, or the Confederacy would win, bringing a worse fate for black people. They had everything to fight for.

With the Militia Act of July 1862, President Lincoln authorized the use of black labor in the army for building trenches and other work that supported armed troops. As with all the previous wars of the nation, black people were present, whether officially or not. The major issue remained whether or not the armed services would allow black men in combat units. Some field commanders simply ignored War Department directives not to arm black men. For example, in the spring of 1862, abolitionist general David Hunter, then commander of the U.S. Army's Department of the South, organized the 1st South Carolina Volunteers, a regiment of escapees from slavery. Similarly, in the fall of 1862, General John Phelps and Captain James Williams recruited for the 1st Regiment Kansas Volunteer Infantry (Colored), encouraging runaways from neighboring slave states to enlist. They mustered in January 1863 and became the first regiment of black troops in a northern state.[27]

On 22 August 1862, Major General Benjamin Butler issued General Order no. 63, which organized regiments from the Native Guards in Louisiana

(Corps d'Afrique). Many of these free black men were descendants of those who served with Andrew Jackson decades earlier.[28] The War Department allowed Butler to take this action at his own discretion but held back on a general policy to arm black men. Butler also had detained runaways as "contraband," or property seized from the enemy at war, when they crossed Union lines at Fort Monroe, Virginia during the summer of 1861. Lincoln took the view that runaways were contraband when he signed the First Confiscation Act on 6 August 1861, authorizing the seizure of rebel property, including human chattel. The president also actively thwarted actions by field officers who wanted to enlist black men. His paramount interest was to reunite the nation as quickly as possible; it was a "white man's war," a phrase commonly used at the time, often to minimize the issue of slavery and race as the cause of the conflict. In 1862, realizing that victory would not occur quickly, Lincoln gradually reversed his opinions on the prickly issue of slavery. He abolished slavery in the nation's capital in March and reluctantly signed the Second Confiscation Act in July, which allowed the government to seize property from rebels, although the law was rarely implemented. Soon word spread that Union forces were not returning runaways to rebel forces, and thousands of black people fled the South. Refugees traveled north aboard vessels, on foot, and by whatever other means they could secure to find some semblance of safety; some simply followed the army in "contraband" camps. Many people who escaped from slavery probably reasoned that the war was about their freedom; concerns about the preservation of the Union likely took second place to concerns about their own personal liberty.[29]

In these camps, Union troops oftentimes forced women to carry out vital tasks. Black women, mostly refugees following the Union army camps, served as laundresses, cooks, and nurses. Some women went beyond these gendered roles and participated more directly, disguised as men in combat or serving as spies and carriers of information over enemy lines. While records show that over 200,000 black men risked their lives during this war, the number of women is undocumented, in part because they may have passed as men. Documents do show that Maria Lewis passed as a white woman and served in the 8th New York Cavalry and that Lizzie Hoffman enlisted in the 45th Regiment Infantry U.S. Colored Troops. These are two of only a few black women who have been identified as soldiers. The most famous black female spy was Harriet Tubman, but lesser-known women such as Mary Elizabeth Bowser also served their nation by carrying information. Bowser, who had been freed and educated by her owner, Elizabeth Van Lew, positioned herself as an illiterate maid at Confederate president Jefferson Davis's dinner table and successfully gathered vital news from Davis and his generals that she relayed verbally to contacts. As many had done before her, she exploited stereotypes of docile black slave women.[30]

Black sailors served from the start of the Civil War. The Union Navy, again faced with a shortage of white recruits, also encountered a profusion of runaways, prompting it to enlist heavily from these numbers of able bodies and ensuring that black sailors served in every major naval battle in the war. The U.S. Navy had a better record of race relations than the U.S. Army; it integrated its crews and offered equal pay and better conditions to black sailors and rations for runaways and their families. In addition, by the end of 1862, as the navy competed with the army for black recruits, enlisters could enter at any rank commensurate with their prewar experiences. Therefore, despite ongoing and deep-seated prejudice and discrimination, the navy offered skilled black seamen and laborers more freedom and rights for their loyalty and service than their soldier counterparts received.[31]

On 22 September 1862, President Lincoln declared that he would order the emancipation of enslaved persons in the rebel states, and his Emancipation Proclamation went into effect on New Year's Day in 1863. The proclamation also stated that the U.S. military would begin receiving "persons of suitable condition" into "the armed service of the United States." Prominent black abolitionists, including Martin Delany and Frederick Douglass, both of whom had sons who served in the war, recruited across the nation for volunteers. The War Department's General Order 143, issued on 22 May 1863, outlined the process by which the army would form the U.S. Colored Troops (USCT). Thousands of black men, more than half from Confederate states, enlisted directly into the U.S. Army. One of the state units raised in 1863 was the 54th Massachusetts Volunteer Infantry Regiment, under the command of Colonel Robert Gould Shaw. The regiment enjoyed a huge send-off on the streets of Boston on 28 May 1863.[32]

Despite the willing service of black men, the U.S. Army restricted the number of black commissioned officers. The only two black officers in the 54th Massachusetts, for example, were chaplains. Of the 2.1 million soldiers in the Union army, about 186,000 were black men, yet only a handful of black officers existed, and they usually served as chaplains.[33] However, the first black major in 1863 also was the first black army surgeon, Alexander T. Augusta, who initially worked with the 7th USCT and later with a general army hospital in Georgia (see Alexander Augusta below). In 1890, Augusta became the first black officer laid to rest in Arlington national cemetery. Also, in 1865, Major Martin Delaney received a commission as the first black field officer.[34]

Black soldiers did not receive the same medical treatment as white soldiers. An inordinate percentage of black soldiers perished from a lack of sufficient medical care. Everyone suffered from the dire medical situation on the battlefield. This war killed thousands of men on both sides, but racism compounded black soldiers' agony, as white soldiers were given priority for treatment.[35] Corporal Henry Harmon wrote in October 1863, from Morris Island, South Carolina, about the treatment of the black soldiers who had survived an assault on Fort Wagner. Instead of comfort, "they receive nothing but the rough sympathies from rougher hands of their comrades in arms." He continued, "We too have suffered and died in defense of that starry banner which floats only over free men."[36]

Black soldiers also protested inequities in pay. Sometimes their objections took the form of direct action, such as the refusal of black troops from the 3rd South Carolina Infantry to fight.[37] Soldiers also protested in writing. An example is a letter from the 55th Massachusetts Volunteer Infantry Regiment signed by seventy-four soldiers. These protests created a moral crisis that forced the government to respond.[38] In September 1864, the federal government passed a statute that equalized pay for those who were free before the war and provided retroactive pay from April 1861. The law was amended in March 1865, after more protests, to include all men.[39] From then on the army maintained equal pay based on rank.

Black soldiers persisted in proving their mettle and honor despite the prejudice they encountered. Two examples stand out. Port Hudson, Louisiana, on 27 May 1863 was the first major engagement for black troops. It was a victory. The Union forces included the 1st Louisiana Native Guard. Even after he was wounded, Captain André Cailloux, a free man from New Orleans, carried out repeated attacks on the fort that controlled the Mississippi River before he was finally felled on the field.[40] The unit received high praises for bravery, suspending, if only for a moment, some of the unfounded doubt that persisted about black men's ability, skills, and willingness to fight. The second example was William H. Carney of the 54th Massachusetts, who had held fast to the Union flag during the storming of Fort Wagner in June 1863, despite severe injuries. Carney was the first black soldier to receive the newly created Medal of Honor. In all, around seventeen black soldiers were awarded the Medal of Honor. Some black soldiers received the Butler Medal, named after Major General Benjamin Butler, who commissioned the award in October 1864 to honor the valor of black soldiers under his command. Inscribed on the medal are the words *Ferro iis libertas perveniet* (Freedom will be theirs by the sword). It is the only medal the U.S. military ever struck specifically for black soldiers.[41]

Despite the huge human loss that the war exacted in the South, Confederates refused to formally enlist the armed services of free black men who volunteered, insisting that black men were "natural cowards" and unfit for combat. For the most part, black people who served in the Confederate military were confined to the roles of servants, laborers, scouts, and sailors. Some black people (enslaved and free) were forced to contribute by growing food for the military, transporting goods to the frontlines, or serving as pilots or deckhands for the Confederate navy. However, there is evidence that many were compelled to fight unofficially. In March 1865, with defeat looming, the Congress of the Confederate States finally allowed the owners of enslaved men to enlist them in the army. It was too little too late. Enlistment also opened up for free men. That free black people would enlist as Confederates baffles many today, yet some were property owners protecting their own interests and others likely sought favor with their neighbors in the hope that their loyalty would bring fairer treatment and benefits. Black Confederates used the war emergency to seek benefits for their families, like their unionist counterparts.[42]

In December 1862, Confederate president Jefferson Davis reinforced the southern economy of slavery and supremacist ideas during the war by extending the region's slave laws against insurrection to include black Union soldiers and their white officers. If captured, white officers faced execution, and the black soldiers confronted enslavement. The Confederates enforced this law at Fort Pillow. On 12 April 1864, Confederate general Nathan Bedford Forrest (who would later become the first Imperial Wizard of the Ku Klux Klan) and his troops surrounded and stormed Fort Pillow, just north of Memphis, Tennessee, which was under Union control. Union troops at the fortress were composed of about 600 black and white soldiers from the 11th United States Colored Infantry (which included the 2nd U.S. Colored Light Artillery and the 6th U.S. Colored Heavy Artillery) and the 13th Tennessee Volunteer Cavalry Regiment. The Confederates outnumbered the Union troops more than three to one. Controversy surrounds the details of the assault; some accounts claim that the Confederate troops massacred soldiers who had surrendered. Nevertheless, most of the black people, including runaways, perished, as did a significant number of the white soldiers serving with them.

Reports also included details of live burials and mutilations. At a congressional committee established to investigate the incident at Fort Pillow, a black civilian cook, Jacob Thompson, testified that the enemy "just called them out like dogs and shot them down. . . . They nailed some black sergeants to logs, and set the logs on fire." Ransome Anderson from Company B, 6th U.S. Colored Heavy Artillery, testified that Confederates placed wounded Union soldiers in houses that they bolted and burned to the ground. The National Park Service records that only sixty-two of the nearly 300 black soldiers survived. The incident produced a rallying cry for the Union: "Remember Fort Pillow!" This battle cry was particularly salient for black soldiers, who saw that failure meant enslavement or certain death.[43] Many other battles violated military rules of engagement, especially against black people.

Even black civilians in the North suffered. A mob of Irish immigrant men unable to pay $300 per man to avoid the first national draft sparked the Draft Riots in New York City in July 1863. Loath to free enslaved people whom they perceived to be competitors for their jobs, they beat and murdered local black men, women, and children on a four-day rampage, underscoring the ambivalence of some white people toward the northern black population.

During Reconstruction, black soldiers continued to serve, hoping for full citizenship rights as the dust settled from the war. Their expectations, however, were never realized. Although some black militias attempted to police Reconstruction in the southern states, they collapsed because unchecked violence and intimidation against them undermined their authority. For example, in the first days of May 1866, white mobs in Memphis attacked black soldiers who had just been mustered out of the U.S. Army and were awaiting transfer out of the city. Gangs destroyed black property and institutions in a freedmen's settlement in south Memphis, killing at least forty-six African American civilians. The mere presence of black soldiers in Memphis since 1863 enraged white residents to the point of murder, rape, pillage, and arson. White rioters quickly asserted their dominance and effectively limited black claims to freedom and citizenship in Memphis as soldiers or as civilians.[44] As the size of the standing army decreased to 25,000 in 1869, U.S. military leaders formed four black units, the 24th and the 25th Infantry Regiments and the 9th and 10th Cavalry Regiments. Black soldiers could wear the uniform, but these segregated units stayed under white command.

After the Civil War, most black regular military served in the West. While their families often traveled with these soldiers for the long western assignments, women did not serve as soldiers. However, there is one documented case, in 1866, of a cross-dressing woman who enlisted as a soldier into the 38th Infantry in St. Louis. Cathy Williams (William Cathay) served for three years in uniform. Only when she applied for a soldier's pension was her identity revealed. Her request was summarily denied.[45]

Struggles with native peoples over territory on the continent had continued in the midst of the nineteenth-century national crisis over slavery. This chapter of U.S. history involved conquest and annihilation, from the French-Indian Wars and local conflicts between settlers and Indians in the eighteenth century (see Lucy Terry's poem below) to the Seminole Wars (see Albery Allson Whitman's poem below) in the first half of the nineteenth century to the post–Civil War conflicts in the West. Black soldiers participated in these struggles.[46] As the nation expanded west to fulfill its vision of Manifest Destiny, the U.S. Army, including black soldiers, claimed the land inhabited by Indigenous peoples.

Black units comprised approximately 14 percent of the forces in the West. Scant evidence has survived that reveals the feelings of black soldiers about displacing and fighting against Indigenous peoples while the nation still treated the soldiers themselves so poorly. Some soldiers may have experienced discomfort over this situation; others apparently shared the values of the dominant culture and viewed themselves as soldiers and Americans on the opposite side of the Indigenous populations.[47] Sometime around 1870, Indigenous peoples on the frontier bestowed the nickname "Buffalo Soldiers" on black men. Although the meaning of the name varies, some Native American communities believed that African hair texture resembled that of a buffalo, an honored animal. Regardless of the symbolism, the units incorporated a buffalo on their crest.[48] Between sixteen and eighteen African Americans received the Medal of Honor during this period. These black soldiers at times faced violence from those people they were protecting, mostly white settlers who often escaped penalty for their crimes against black men in uniform.[49]

The U.S. armed forces moved very slowly to provide equal opportunities for black soldiers, and the unhurried pace reflected the prevailing attitudes in civilian society. West Point Military Academy admitted only a few black cadets. These men suffered regular beatings and humiliation disguised as hazing. Henry Ossian Flipper, born into slavery in Georgia in 1856, was the fifth black candidate to enter the academy but the first to graduate (1877). After his graduation, the army assigned him to the 10th Cavalry as a second lieutenant. Flipper became the first African American to command regular troops. It was ten years before another African American, John Hanks Alexander, graduated from West Point.

In April 1865, Frederick Douglass delivered a speech at the annual meeting of the Massachusetts Anti-Slavery Society in Boston, reflecting on possible new agendas for abolitionists. He stated, "There is something too mean in looking upon the Negro, when you are in trouble, as a citizen, and when you are free from trouble, as an alien." Recapping the Revolutionary War for Independence, the War of 1812, and then the Civil War, he noted that black man had "been a citizen just three times in the history of this government, and it has always been in time of trouble. In time of trouble, we are citizens. Shall we be citizens in war, and aliens in peace? Would that be just?"[50] Yet the United States quickly reconstructed systems of dominance in the decades after the war, creating a legal system aligned with segregation and controlled by violence, and one that ensured continued discrimination against African Americans. After Reconstruction, the promise of citizenship for African Americans quickly dissolved into a national betrayal of that promise and a return to the white supremacist status quo. The 1896 Supreme Court decision *Plessy v. Ferguson* put the final nail in the coffin of Reconstruction and gave support from the highest court in the land to the system of legal racial segregation known as Jim Crow.

NOTES

1. O'Shaughnessy, "Arming Slaves in the American Revolution," 186.

2. Buckley, *American Patriots*, 5.

3. Quarles, *The Negro in the American Revolution*, xxvii.

4. Lemuel Haynes, "Liberty Further Extended," Wendell Family Papers, MS Am1907, no. 608, Houghton Library, Harvard University, Cambridge, Massachusetts.

5. Bogin, "'Liberty Further Extended'"; Quarles, *The Negro in the American Revolution*, xxiii.

6. Astor, *The Right to Fight*, 11–12.

7. National Park Service, "George Middleton House," Boston African American, http://www.nps.gov/boaf/historyculture/george-middleton-house.htm, accessed 9 June 2014; Massachusetts Historical Society, African Americans and the End of Slavery in Massachusetts, http://www.masshist.org/endofslavery/?queryID=56, accessed 9 June 2014; Nell, *Colored Patriots of the American Revolution*, 24; Kaplan and Kaplan, *The Black Presence in the Era of the American Revolution*, 66–68.

8. Quarles, *The Negro in the American Revolution*, xix, 134–57; Nash, "Thomas Peters:

Millwright and Deliverer"; Pybus, *Epic Journeys of Freedom*; Whitman, *Challenging Slavery in the Chesapeake*.

9. Wilson, *The Black Phalanx*, 46–49, 59–61; Kaplan and Kaplan, *The Black Presence in the Era of the American Revolution*, 64–65.

10. Quarles, *Black Mosaic*, 104; Bond, "The Negro in the Armed Forces of the United States Prior to World War I," 268.

11. Quarles, *The Negro in the American Revolution*, 94–95; Wilson, *The Black Phalanx*, 69.

12. Quarles, *The Negro in the American Revolution*, 83–93; Kaplan and Kaplan, *The Black Presence in the Era of the American Revolution*, 44–64; Ramold, *Slaves, Sailors, Citizens*, 6–10; Bolster, *Black Jacks*, 1–6.

13. See Nell, *Colored Patriots of the American Revolution*; Nash, *Race and Revolution*; VanderVelde, *Redemption Songs*.

14. See Pybus, *Epic Journeys of Freedom*; Quarles, *The Negro in the American Revolution*, 106–9, 156–57; Wilson, *The Black Phalanx*, 122–26.

15. Lewis, *W.E.B. Du Bois*, 14; Du Bois, *The Suppression of the Slave Trade*, 62; Du Bois, *Dusk of Dawn*, 635–38; Sinha, "To 'Cast Just Obloquy' on Oppressors," 151–52.

16. Astor, *The Right to Fight*, 15.

17. Quoted in ibid., 16; Wilson, *The Black Phalanx*, 78–80; Ramold, *Slaves, Sailors, Citizens*, 11–15, 20.

18. Wilson, *The Black Phalanx*, 73–74.

19. Buckley, *American Patriots*, 48.

20. Ibid., 49.

21. Wilson, *The Black Phalanx*, 81–88.

22. Lemmon, *Frustrated Patriots*, 196; Ramold, *Slaves, Sailors, Citizens*, 23; Bond, "The Negro in the Armed Forces of the United States Prior to World War I," 277.

23. Buckley, *American Patriots*, 54.

24. Edgerton, *Hidden Heroism*, 21; Astor, *The Right to Fight*, 19; Ramold, *Slaves, Sailors, Citizens*, 19–20.

25. For examples, see Carroll, *Slave Insurrections in the United States, 1800–1865* and Franklin, *Runaway Slaves*.

26. *Dred Scott v. John F. A. Sandford*, 60 U.S. 393 (1856).

27. Smith, *Black Soldiers in Blue*, 21–23; *Report of the Adjutant General of the State of Kansas, 1861–'65*, esp. 11; The Museum of the Kansas National Guard, http://www.kansas-guardmuseum.org/dispunit.php?id=8, accessed 25 September 2014.

28. Bond, "The Negro in the Armed Forces of the United States Prior to World War I," 281.

29. Astor, *The Right to Fight*, 22, 25; Buckley, *American Patriots*, 82–85; Wilson, *The Black Phalanx*, 103–9; Quarles, *The Negro in the Civil War*, 76, 116–20.

30. See Lowry, *Harriet Tubman*; Larson, *Bound for the Promised Land*; Forbes, *African American Women during the Civil War*; Hine, Brown, and Terborg-Penn, *Black Women in America*; Eggleston, *Women in the Civil War*, 119–20; Varon, *Southern Lady, Yankee Spy*, 165–70; Hall, *Women on the Civil War Battlefront*, 203–20.

31. Ramold, *Slaves, Sailors, Citizens*, 4–5, 42–50; Bond, "The Negro in the Armed Forces of the United States Prior to World War I," 284.

32. Astor, *The Right To Fight*, 28.

33. Astor, *The Right to Fight*, 32; Reidy, "Armed Slaves and the Struggles for Republican Liberty in the U.S. Civil War," 285.

34. "Alexander Thomas Augusta," Arlington National Cemetery Website, http://www.arlingtoncemetery.net/ataugust.htm, accessed 9 June 2014; Quarles, *The Negro in the Civil War*, 203–4, 328. The army placed Augusta on detached service after white officers at the army hospital in Savannah, Georgia, complained about serving under his authority.

35. Smith, *Black Soldiers in Blue*, 41–42.

36. Quoted in Redkey, *A Grand Army of Black Men*, 35–36.

37. Smith, *Black Soldiers in Blue*, 51.

38. "Soldiers of the 55th Massachusetts," in Yacovone, *Freedom's Journey*, 163; Redkey, *A Grand Army of Black Men*, 205.

39. Astor, *The Right to Fight*, 28; and Redkey, *A Grand Army of Black Men*, 231.

40. Redkey, *A Grand Army of Black Men*, 138.

41. "Butler Medal," Civil War@Smithsonian, http://www.civilwar.si.edu/soldiering_butler_medal.html, accessed 9 June 2014.

42. Edgerton, *Hidden Heroism*, 33–35; Bond, "The Negro in the Armed Forces of the United States Prior to World War I," 278–80; Reidy, "Armed Slaves and the Struggles for Republican Liberty in the U.S. Civil War," 276–78, 280. See also Barrow, Segars, and Rosenburg, *Black Confederates* and Segars and Barrow, *Black Southerners in Confederate Armies*.

43. American Battlefield Protection Program, "Fort Pillow," CWSAC Battle Summaries, Heritage Protection Services, http://www.nps.gov/history/hps/abpp/battles/tn030.htm, accessed 9 June 2014.

44. See Hardwick, "'Your Old Father Abe Lincoln Is Dead and Damned.'"

45. See Tucker, *Cathy Williams*.

46. Halbert and Hall, *The Creek War of 1813 and 1814*, 32, 258–59.

47. Schubert, *Voices of the Buffalo Soldier*, 1–3.

48. Astor, *The Right to Fight*, 47, 54; Schubert, *Voices of the Buffalo Soldier*, 48; and Taylor, "African American Men in the American West," 108.

49. Schubert, *Voices of the Buffalo Soldier*, 115.

50. Douglass, "What the Black Man Wants."

ALEXANDER T. AUGUSTA

Freeborn in Virginia in 1825 and later trained as a physician at the University of Toronto Medical College, Alexander T. Augusta became the first of eight African Americans to receive commissions as U.S. Army surgeons during the Civil War. He mustered into the 7th Regiment United States Colored Troops as a major in 1863 and left military service in 1866 as the first African American lieutenant colonel. During Augusta's leadership of the medical corps for the United States Colored Troops, white physicians complained to President Lincoln because they did not want to report to a black man. Alexander T. Augusta died in Washington, D.C., in 1890.

From "Colored men have their rights that white men are bound to respect"

Washington, [D.C.]
May 15, 1863

Sir:

Inasmuch as many misstatements relative to the assault upon me in Baltimore have been made, I deem it necessary, in justice to myself, as well as to all parties concerned, to give to the public a true statement of the facts as they occurred.

I started from my lodgings in Mulberry Street, near Pine, about a quarter past nine o'clock, on the morning of 1st inst.,[1] in order to take the 10 a.m. train for Philadelphia. [. . .] I obtained my ticket from the agent, without the usual bond required of colored persons wishing to proceed North, and took my seat in the car—little expecting anyone would make an attack upon me then.

After remaining in my seat about five minutes, I heard someone conversing behind me, but paid no attention to what they were talking about, when of a sudden a boy about fifteen years of age, who appeared to be employed about the depot, came up behind me, and, swearing at me, caught hold of my right shoulder-strap, and pulled it off. I jumped up, and, turning towards him, found a man standing by his side who had directed me which car to get in, and while I was remonstrating with the boy for what he had done, he pulled the other one off; while at the same time the boy threatened to strike me with a club he held in his hand. I then turned towards the door of the car where I was standing, and found I was surrounded by about eight or ten roughs; and knowing that should I touch one of them all the rest would pounce upon me, I thought it best to take my seat and await what further issue might take place.

Shortly after I had taken my seat, the parties who had assaulted me left the car, and a policeman came in and stood near me. A person standing by asked him if he intended to interfere. He answered by saying it depended upon circumstances. I then turned towards him, and said to him, "If you are a policeman, I claim your protection as a United States officer, who has been assaulted without a cause." Just about that time, I was informed that the provost guards were in the car, and that I had better apply to them for protection. I called to the guards and told them I was a United States officer; that I had been assaulted and my shoulder-straps torn off by employees of the road, and that I claimed their protection. Having satisfied them of my connection with the service, they assured me of their protection. I might have gone on in that train, but I was determined to stop back, so as to have the parties punished, knowing full well that the same thing might occur again, unless a stop was put to it at once. I therefore went up to the provost marshal's office with one of the guard, and reported the facts to Lieut. Col. Fish, the provost marshal.

He examined my commission, and finding it was all right, said he did not care who it was, so he was a United States officer, and claimed his protection, he should have it to the fullest extent. He then deputed Lieut. Morris to accompany me to the depot and arrest the parties. The Lieutenant told me I was as much authorized as an officer to arrest them as he was; and that I had better go ahead of him and the guard, fearing that if the parties saw them they would get out of the way. He directed me, at the same time, that when I saw any one of the parties to go up to him and place my hand upon his shoulder and claim him as my prisoner, and he would be on hand to take him in charge. I knew this was an extraordinary step for me to take in Baltimore, but I told him I would do it. I accordingly went down to the depot, and when near it I recognized one of the parties crossing the street; I went up to him, and, while accusing him of taking off my straps, put my hand upon his shoulder and claimed him as my prisoner. I then ordered the guard to take him into custody, which he did. I then hunted around the depot for the boy, but could not find him. [. . .]

[Soon] a man, whom I learned afterwards to be named Hancock, emerged from the market and assaulted me. I called the guard across and had him taken into custody. We then proceeded to the office unmolested. [. . .] [Later] Lieut. Morris told me it was time to start for the depot, to take the one o'clock train. I got ready and we proceeded together, and every step we took after leaving the office, the crowd which was standing around the door increased. No one, however, interfered with me until we arrived at the corner of Pratt and President streets, when a man, whose name I since learned to be Dunn, was standing in our way, and as soon as I reached him, he dealt me a severe blow on the face, which stunned me for a moment and caused the blood to flow from my nose very freely. In an instant, Lieut. Morris seized him by the collar and held him fast; and I not knowing that there was anyone else in the crowd to protect me, made for the first door I saw open. When I reached it, a woman was standing there and pushed me back to prevent me from entering. In the meantime I looked back and saw a person with my cap and a revolver in his hand. He told me to stand still, that I was protected. I came down the steps, and proceeded between two guards with revolvers drawn until we reached the depot.

Upon our arrival, Lieut. Morris put the prisoner upon a settee,[2] and placed a guard over him, with orders to shoot him if he dared to stir from the spot. A short time after we arrived, two other persons were identified as having been engaged in the last assault upon me, and were arrested. I washed the blood from my face and prepared to take my seat in the cars, when an officer, whom I subsequently learned to be Major Robertson, of Maj. Gen. [Joseph] Hooker's staff, having learned the facts of the case from Lieut. Morris, came up to me and told me he was going to Philadelphia, and offered to protect me at the risk of his own life. The guard surrounded me with drawn revolvers, conducted me to the cars, and remained with me until the train started. During the same time we were waiting for the train to start, I learned from the guard that when I was struck by Dunn, they were in the crowd dressed in citizens' clothes, and were just about to shoot him when Lieut. Morris ordered them not to shoot, as he had the prisoner safe. [...]

Since my return to Washington, I have learned that some of the parties have been tried, and sent to Fort McHenry.

These, Mr. Editor, are the facts of the case, and I deny, in toto, the profane language attributed to me by the Baltimore *Clipper.*

Now it seems that, in this transaction, I have been blamed by two classes of persons. The first say that I should not have passed through Baltimore in uniform, because, say they, the people of Baltimore are opposed to it, and even Union men do not wish to see colored men wearing the United States uniform.

Well, in answer to this class, I will say that the people of Baltimore were opposed to the Massachusetts troops passing through there two years ago, and mobbed them, but the Government of the United States was strong enough to put down that spirit then, and I apprehend it is strong enough now to protect colored troops under similar circumstances. And furthermore, while I have always known Baltimore as a place where it is considered a virtue to mob colored people, still, I had a right to expect a safe transit through there after the resolution passed only two weeks before at the National Union League,[3] on the anniversary of the attack upon the Massachusetts troops, calling on the President of the United States to place not only spades but muskets in the hands of black men to put down the rebellion. And more especially, as I had only volunteered to bind up the wounds of those colored men who should volunteer, as well as those rebels and Copperheads whom the fortune of war might throw into my hands. But, sir, I may take still higher grounds than these to justify my course. For I hold that my position as an officer of the United States entitles me to wear the insignia of my office, and if I am either afraid or ashamed to wear them anywhere, I am not fit to hold my commission, and should resign it at once.

The other class that blame me are those who say I acted wrongly in not shooting down anyone who dared to interfere with me. Well, in answer to this class, I can only say that while I am aware that I had the authority as an officer of the United States to defend myself to that extremity, I do not think, had I have done so, I would have accomplished so much for liberty as I did by allowing those whose special duty it was to protect me.

The question has no doubt been frequently asked, "What has been gained by this transaction?" I will answer. It has proved that even in *rowdy Baltimore* colored men have their rights that white men are bound to respect. [. . .]

In conclusion, Mr. Editor, I desired to return my sincere thanks to Lieut. Col. Fish for his prompt protection, to Lieut. Morris for the alacrity with which he carried out Col. Fish's orders, to Major Robertson for his kindness in volunteering his services, and the brave men of the guard for risking their lives in my defence. I remain, sir, Yours, very respectfully,

A. T. Augusta
Bachelor of Medicine,
Surgeon U.S.V.

Excerpted from letter to the editor, *National Republican*, 16 May 1863, 1.

James Madison Bell

Abolitionist poet and orator James Madison Bell was born free in 1826 in Ohio. He presented his poetry to audiences throughout the country and was known as the Bard of the Maumee River in Ohio. Bell wrote "A Poem Entitled, the Day and the War" to recognize the first anniversary of the Emancipation Proclamation. He published the poem as a pamphlet and dedicated it to John Brown. In 1902, Bell died in Toledo.

From A Poem Entitled, The Day and the War[4]

[. . .] Though Tennyson, the poet king,
Has sung of Balaklava's charge,[5]
Until his thund'ring cannons ring
From England's center to her marge,[6]
The pleasing duty still remains
To sing a people from their chains—
To sing what none have yet assay'd,[7]
The wonders of the Black Brigade.[8]
The war had raged some twenty moons,
Ere they in columns or platoons,
To win them censure or applause,
Were marshal'd in the Union cause—
Prejudged of slavish cowardice,
While many a taunt and foul device
Came weekly forth with Harper's[9] sheet,
To feed that base, infernal cheat.

But how they would themselves demean,
Has since most gloriously been seen.
'Twas seen at Milliken's[10] dread bend!
Where e'en the Furies seemed to lend
To dark Secession all their aid,
To crush the Union Black Brigade.
The war waxed hot, and bullets flew
Like San Francisco's summer sand,
But they were there to dare and do,
E'en to the last, to save the land.
And when the leaders of their corps

Grew wild with fear, and quit the field,
The dark remembrance of their scars
Before them rose, they could not yield:
And, sounding o'er the battle din,
They heard their standard-bearer cry—
"Rally! and prove that ye are men!
Rally! and let us do or die!
For war, nor death, shall boast a shade
To daunt the Union Black Brigade!"

And thus he played the hero's part,
Till on the ramparts of the foe
A score of bullets pierced his heart,
He sank within the trench below.
His comrades saw, and fired with rage,
Each sought his man, him to engage
In single combat. Ah! 'twas then
The Black Brigade proved they were men!
For ne'er did Swiss! or Russ! or knight!
Against such fearful odds arrayed,
With more persistent valor fight,
Than did the Union Black Brigade!

As five to one, so stood their foes,
When that defiant shout arose,
And 'long their closing columns ran,
Commanding each to choose his man!
And ere the sound had died away,
Full many a ranting rebel lay
Gasping piteously for breath—
Struggling with the pangs of death,
From bayonet thrust or shining blade,
Plunged to the hilt by the Black Brigade.
And thus they fought, and won a name—
None brighter on the scroll of Fame;
For out of one full corps of men,
But one remained unwounded, when
The dreadful fray had fully past—
All killed or wounded but the last!

And though they fell, as has been seen,
Each slept his lifeless foes between,
And marked the course and paved the way
To ushering in a better day.
Let Balaklava's cannons roar,
And Tennyson his hosts parade,
But ne'er was seen and never more
The equals of the Black Brigade!

Then nerve thy heart, gird on thy sword,
For dark Oppression's ruthless horde
And thy tried friends are in the field—
Say which shall triumph, which shall yield?
Shall they that heed not man nor God—
Vile monsters of the *gory rod*—
Dark forgers of the *rack* and *chain*:
Shall *they* prevail—and Thraldom's[11] reign,
With all his dark unnumber'd ills,
Become eternal as the hills?
No! by the blood of freemen slain,
On hot-contested field and main,
And by the mingled sweat and tears,
Extorted through these many years
From Afric's patient sons of toil—
Weak victims of a braggart's spoil—
This bastard plant, the Upas tree,[12]
Shall not supplant our liberty! [. . .]

"A Poem Entitled, the Day and the War," Celebration of the First Anniversary of the President's Emancipation Proclamation, Platt's Hall, San Francisco, California, 1 January 1864.[13] Excerpted from *A Poem Entitled, the Day and the War, Delivered January 1, 1864, at Platt's Hall* (San Francisco: Agnew and Deffebach, Publishers, 1864).

Related writings by James Madison Bell: "What Shall We Do with the Contrabands" (1862); "An Anniversary Poem Entitled the Progress of Liberty" (1866).

BENJAMIN GRIFFITH BRAWLEY

Benjamin Griffith Brawley was born in 1882 in Columbia, South Carolina, the descendant of free black grandparents. He wrote poetry and was an influential educator and essayist who published widely on topics in literary history. He also taught at and served as dean of Morehouse College in Atlanta, Georgia, where he had earned a bachelor's degree. Brawley spent most of his professional life teaching and leading the department of English at Howard University. While employed at Howard, he died in 1939 after suffering a stroke.

My Hero (To Robert Gould Shaw)[14]

Flushed with the hope of high desire,
  He buckled on his sword,
To dare the rampart ranged with fire,
  Or where the thunder roared;
Into the smoke and flame he went,
  For God's great cause to die—
A youth of heaven's element,
The flower of chivalry.
This was the gallant faith, I trow,[15]
  Of which the sages tell;
On such devotion long ago
The benediction fell;
And never nobler martyr burned,
  Or braver hero died,
Than he who worldly honor spurned
To serve the Crucified.

And Lancelot and Sir Bedivere[16]
  May pass beyond the pale,
And wander over moor and mere[17]
  To find the Holy Grail;[18]
But ever yet the prize forsooth[19]
  My hero holds in fee;[20]
And he is Blameless Knight in truth,
And Galahad[21] to me.

"My Hero (To Robert Gould Shaw)" *Crisis* 10, no. 1 (May 1915): 37.

Related writings by Benjamin Griffith Brawley: "The Flag" (1905); "The Freedom of the Free: Emancipation Exposition Poem" (1913).

WILLIAM WELLS BROWN

William Wells Brown was born into slavery in Kentucky around 1814 and liberated himself through escape in 1834. After achieving his freedom, Brown worked as an abolitionist and published the *Narrative of William W. Brown, an American Slave: Written by Himself,* a liberation narrative detailing the events in his life and his escape. In 1853, Brown published, in London, *Clotel; or, the President's Daughter. A Narrative of Slave Life in the United States,* the first novel by a black writer born in the United States. Between 1860 and 1867, he retitled and revised this fictional narrative, producing three additional versions in his continuing effort to use fiction to support the abolition of slavery. In 1867, Brown added a section on the Civil War and Reconstruction (excerpted below) and changed the title to *Clotelle; or, the Colored Heroine, a Tale of the Southern States.* Brown died in 1884 in Massachusetts.

From Clotelle; or, the Colored Heroine, a Tale of the Southern States

[Clotelle is the daughter of Henry Linwood, a congressman from Virginia, and Isabella, whom Linwood purchased for $1,800 and hid in a small cottage to be his sexual slave. Henry's interest in Isabella wanes, so he marries Gertrude Miller, the daughter of a prominent Virginian. To appease Gertrude, Henry allows his cruel mother-in-law to sell Isabella and enslave his daughter Clotelle in the Millers' home. By passing as white and dressing as a man, Isabella escapes from her owner in Vicksburg, Mississippi. She returns to Richmond to retrieve Clotelle and is found out because of heightened security in the area following the recent uprising led by Nat Turner. The desperate mother commits suicide to avoid reenslavement.]

CHAPTER XVII: CLOTELLE

The curtain rises seven years after the death of Isabella. During that interval, Henry, finding that nothing could induce his mother-in-law to relinquish her hold on poor little Clotelle, and not liking to contend with one on whom a future fortune depended, gradually lost all interest in the child, and left her to her fate.

Although Mrs. Miller treated Clotelle with a degree of harshness scarcely equalled, when applied to one so tender in years, still the child grew every day more beautiful, and her hair, though kept closely cut, seemed to have improved in its soft, silk-like appearance. Now twelve years of age, and more than usually well-developed, her harsh old mistress began to view her with a jealous eye.

Henry and Gertrude had just returned from Washington, where the husband had been on his duties as a member of Congress, and where he had remained during the preceding three years without returning home. It was on a beautiful evening, just at twilight, while seated at his parlor window, that Henry saw a young woman pass by and go into the kitchen. Not aware of ever having seen the person before, he made an errand into the cook's department to see who the girl was. He, however, met her in the hall, as she was about going out.

"Whom did you wish to see?" he inquired.

"Miss Gertrude," was the reply.

"What did you want to see her for?" he again asked.

"My mistress told me to give her and Master Henry her compliments, and ask them to come over and spend the evening."

"Who is your mistress?" he eagerly inquired.

"Mrs. Miller, sir," responded the girl.

"And what's your name?" asked Henry, with a trembling voice.

"Clotelle, sir," was the reply.

The astonished father stood completely amazed, looking at the now womanly form of her who, in his happier days, he had taken on his knee with so much fondness and alacrity. It was then that he saw his own and Isabella's features combined in the beautiful face that he was then beholding. It was then that he was carried back to the days when with a woman's devotion, poor Isabella hung about his neck and told him how lonely were the hours in his absence. He could stand it no longer. Tears rushed to his eyes, and turning upon his heel, he went back to his own room. It was then that Isabella was revenged; and she no doubt looked smilingly down from her home in the spirit-land on the scene below.

On Gertrude's return from her shopping tour, she found Henry in a melancholy mood, and soon learned its cause. As Gertrude had borne him no children, it was but natural, that he should now feel his love centering in Clotelle, and he now intimated to his wife his determination to remove his daughter from the hands of his mother-in-law.

When this news reached Mrs. Miller, through her daughter, she became furious with rage, and calling Clotelle into her room, stripped her shoulders bare and flogged her in the presence of Gertrude.

It was nearly a week after the poor girl had been so severely whipped and for no cause whatever, that her father learned of the circumstance through one of the servants. With a degree of boldness unusual for him, he immediately went to his mother-in-law and demanded his child. But it was too late,—she was gone. To what place she had been sent no one could tell, and Mrs. Miller refused to give any information whatever relative to the girl.

It was then that Linwood felt deepest the evil of the institution under which he was living; for he knew that his daughter would be exposed to all the vices prevalent in that part of the country where marriage is not recognized in connection with that class. [. . .]

[A parson named Wilson in Natchez, Mississippi, purchases Clotelle as a gift for his own daughter, Georgiana. She surreptitiously teaches Clotelle to read. While enslaved by the Wilsons, Clotelle meets Jerome, an African, who worked as the Wilson's coachman. Jerome and Clotelle fall in love, and Clotelle teaches Jerome how to read. He decides not to marry Clotelle until after he can escape and take her as well. One day, Jerome refuses to be whipped by the parson and escapes before he had planned to do so. He is caught and jailed.]

CHAPTER XIX: THE TRUE HEROINE

In vain did Georgiana try to console Clotelle, when the latter heard, through one of the other slaves, that Mr. Wilson had started with the dogs in pursuit of Jerome. The poor girl well knew that he would be caught, and that severe punishment, if not death, would be the result of his capture. It was therefore with a heart filled with the deepest grief that the slave-girl heard the footsteps of her master on his return from the chase. The dogged and stern manner of the preacher forbade even his daughter inquiring as to the success of his pursuit. Georgiana secretly hoped that the fugitive had not been caught; she wished it for the sake of the slave, and more especially for her maid-servant, whom she regarded more as a companion than a menial. But the news of the capture of Jerome soon spread through the parson's household, and found its way to the ears of the weeping and heart-stricken Clotelle.

The reverend gentleman had not been home more than an hour ere some of his parishioners called to know if they should not take the negro from the prison and execute *Lynch law* upon him.

"No negro should be permitted to live after striking a white man; let us take him and hang him at once," remarked an elderly-looking man, whose gray hairs thinly covered the crown of his head.

"I think the deacon is right," said another of the company; "if our slaves are allowed to set the will of their masters at defiance, there will be no getting along with them,—an insurrection will be the next thing we hear of."

"No, no," said the preacher; "I am willing to let the law take its course, as it provides for the punishment of a slave with death if he strikes his master. We had better let the court decide the question. Moreover, as a Christian and God-fearing people, we ought to submit to the dictates of justice. Should we take this man's life by force, an Allwise Providence would hold us responsible for the act."

The company then quietly withdrew, showing that the preacher had some influence with his people.

"This," said Mr. Wilson, when left alone with his daughter,—"this, my dear Georgiana, is the result of your kindness to the negroes. You have spoiled every one about the house. I can't whip one of them, without being in danger of having my life taken."

"I am sure, papa," replied the young lady,—"I am sure I never did any thing intentionally to induce any of the servants to disobey your orders."

"No, my dear," said Mr. Wilson, "but you are too kind to them. Now, there is Clotelle,—that girl is completely spoiled. She walks about the house with as dignified an air as if she was mistress of the premises. By and by you will be sorry for this foolishness of yours."

"But," answered Georgiana, "Clotelle has a superior mind, and God intended her to hold a higher position in life than that of a servant."

"Yes, my dear, and it was your letting her know that she was intended for a better station in society that is spoiling her. Always keep a negro in ignorance of what you conceive to be his abilities," returned the parson.

It was late on the Saturday afternoon, following the capture of Jerome that, while Mr. Wilson was seated in his study preparing his sermon for the next day, Georgiana entered the room and asked in an excited tone if it were true that Jerome was to [be] hanged on the following Thursday.

The minister informed her that such was the decision of the court.

"Then," said she, "Clotelle will die of grief."

"What business has she to die of grief?" returned the father, his eyes at the moment flashing fire.

"She has neither eaten nor slept since he was captured," replied Georgiana; "and I am certain that she will not live through this."

"I cannot be disturbed now," said the parson; "I must get my sermon ready for to-morrow. I expect to have some strangers to preach to, and must, therefore, prepare a sermon that will do me credit."

While the man of God spoke, he seemed to say to himself,—

"With devotion's visage, and pious actions,
We do sugar over the devil himself."

Georgina did all in her power to soothe the feelings of Clotelle, and to induce her to put her trust in God. Unknown to her father, she allowed the poor girl to go every evening to the jail to see Jerome, and during these visits, despite her own grief, Clotelle would try to comfort her lover with the hope that justice would be meted out to him in the spirit-land.

Thus the time passed on, and the day was fast approaching when the slave was to die. Having heard that some secret meeting had been held by the negroes, previous to the attempt of Mr. Wilson to flog his slave, it occurred to a magistrate that Jerome might know something of the intended revolt. He accordingly visited the prison to see if he could learn anything from him, but all to no purpose. Having given up all hopes of escape, Jerome had resolved to die like a brave man. When questioned as to whether he know anything of a conspiracy among the slaves against their masters, he replied,—

"Do you suppose that I would tell you if I did?"

"But if you know anything," remarked the magistrate, "and will tell us, you may possibly have your life spared."

"Life," answered the doomed man, "is worth nought to a slave. What right has a slave to himself, his wife, or his children? We are kept in heathenish darkness, by laws especially enacted to make our instruction a criminal offence; and our bones, sinews, blood, and nerves are exposed in the market for sale."

"My liberty is of as much consequence to me as Mr. Wilson's is to him. I am as sensitive to feeling as he. If I mistake not, the day will come when the negro will learn that he can get his freedom by fighting for it; and should that time arrive, the whites will be sorry that they have hated us so shamefully. I am free to say that, could I live my life over again, I would use all the energies which God has given me to get up an insurrection."

Every one present seemed startled and amazed at the intelligence with which this descendant of Africa spoke.

"He's a very dangerous man," remarked one.

"Yes," said another, "he got some book-learning somewhere, and that has spoiled him."

An effort was then made to learn from Jerome where he had learned to read, but the black refused to give any information on the subject.

The sun was just going down behind the trees as Clotelle entered the prison to see Jerome for the last time. He was to die on the next day. Her face was bent upon her hands, and the gushing tears were forcing their way through her fingers. With beating heart and trembling hands, evincing the deepest emotion, she threw her arms around her lover's neck and embraced him. But, prompted by her heart's unchanging love, she had in her own mind a plan by which she hoped to effect the escape of him to whom she had pledged her heart and hand. While the overcharged clouds which had hung over the city during the day broke, and the rain fell in torrents, amid the most terrific thunder and lightning, Clotelle revealed to Jerome her plan for his escape.

"Dress yourself in my clothes," said she, "and you can easily pass the jailer."

This Jerome at first declined doing. He did not wish to place a confiding girl in a position where, in all probability, she would have to suffer; but being assured by the young girl that her life would not be in danger, he resolved to make the attempt. Clotelle being very tall, it was not probabl[e] that the jailer would discover any difference in them.

At this moment, she took from her pocket a bunch of keys and unfastened the padlock, and freed him from the floor.

"Come, girl, it is time for you to go," said the jailer, as Jerome was holding the almost fainting girl by the hand.

Being already attired in Clotelle's clothes, the disguised man embraced the weeping girl, put his handkerchief to his face, and passed out of the jail, without the keeper's knowing that his prisoner was escaping in a disguise and under cover of the night. [. . .]

[After changing into clothing that Clotelle has hidden for him, Jerome boards a steamer and pretends to be one of the workers. Unfortunately, he finds that the steamer is going to Kentucky rather than north. He escapes bounty hunters and then meets Quakers who help him escape to Canada, where he works for Mr. Streeter. Meanwhile, Clotelle remains in jail for three days after the jailer and the parson find out what she has done. She is sentenced to be flogged and is sold to Mr. Taylor from New Orleans. Clotelle escapes New Orleans for France with Captain Antoine Devenant, an officer in the French army who declares his love for her. Antoine and Clotelle marry in France.]

CHAPTER XXVII: TRUE FREEDOM

The history of the African race is God's illuminated clock, set in the dark steeple of time. The negro has been made the hewer of wood and the drawer of water for nearly all other nations. The people of the United States, however, will have an account to settle with God, owing to their treatment of the negro, which will far surpass the rest of mankind.

Jerome, on reaching Canada, felt for the first time that personal freedom which God intended that all who bore his image should enjoy. [. . .]

CHAPTER XXVIII: FAREWELL TO AMERICA

Three months had elapsed, from the time the fugitive commenced work for Mr. Streeter, when that gentleman returned from his Southern research, and informed Jerome that Parson Wilson had sold Clotelle, and that she had been sent to the New Orleans slave-market.

This intelligence fell with crushing weight upon the heart of Jerome, and he now felt that the last chain which bound him to his native land was severed. He therefore determined to leave America forever. His nearest and dearest friends had often been flogged in his very presence, and he had seen his mother sold to the negro-trader. An only sister had been torn from him by the soul-driver; he had himself been sold and resold, and been compelled to submit to the most degrading and humiliating insults; and now that the woman upon whom his heart doted, and without whom life was a burden, had been taken away forever, he felt it a duty to hate all mankind.

If there is one thing more than another calculated to make one hate and detest American slavery, it is to witness the meetings between fugitives and their friends in Canada. Jerome had beheld some of these scenes. The wife who, after years of separation, had escaped from her prison-house and followed her husband had told her story to him. He had seen the newly-arrived wife rush into the arms of the husband, whose dark face she had not looked upon for long, weary years. Some told of how a sister had been ill-used by the overseer; others of a husband's being whipped to death for having attempted to protect his wife. He had sat in the little log-hut, by the fireside, and heard tales that caused his heart to bleed; and his bosom swelled with just indignation when he thought that there was no remedy for such atrocious acts. It was with such feelings that he informed his employer that he should leave him at the expiration of a month.

In vain did Mr. Streeter try to persuade Jerome to remain with him; and late in the month of February, the latter found himself on board a small vessel loaded with pine-lumber, descending the St. Lawrence, bound for Liverpool. The bark, though an old one, was, nevertheless, considered sea-worthy, and the fugitive was working his way out. As the vessel left the river and gained the open sea, the black man appeared to rejoice at the prospect of leaving a country in which his right to manhood had been denied him, and his happiness destroyed.

The wind was proudly swelling the white sails, and the little craft plunging into the foaming waves, with the land fast receding in the distance, when Jerome mounted a pile of lumber to take a last farewell of his native land. With tears glistening in his eyes, and with quivering lips, he turned his gaze toward the shores that were fast fading in the dim distance, and said,—

"Though forced from my native land by the tyrants of the South, I hope I shall some day be able to return. With all her faults, I love my country still." [...]

CHAPTER XXXI: THE MYSTERIOUS MEETING

After more than a fortnight spent in the highlands of Scotland, Jerome passed hastily through London on his way to the continent.

It was toward sunset, on a warm day in October, shortly after his arrival in France, that, after strolling some distance from the Hotel de Leon, in the old and picturesque town of Dunkirk, he entered a burial-ground—such places being always favorite walks with him—and wandered around among the silent dead. All nature around was hushed in silence, and seemed to partake of the general melancholy that hung over the quiet resting-place of the departed. Even the birds seemed imbued with the spirit of the place, for they were silent, either flying noiselessly over the graves, or jumping about in the tall grass. [...] Jerome seated himself on a marble tombstone, and commenced reading from a book which he had carried under his arm. It was now twilight, and he had read but a few minutes when he observed a lady, attired in deep black, and leading a boy, apparently some five or six years old, coming up one of the beautiful, winding paths. As the lady's veil was drawn closely over her face, he felt somewhat at liberty to eye her more closely. While thus engaged, the lady gave a slight scream, and seemed suddenly to have fallen into a fainting condition. Jerome sprang from his seat, and caught her in time to save her from falling to the ground.

At this moment an elderly gentleman, also dressed in black, was seen approaching with a hurried step, which seemed to indicate that he was in some way connected with the lady. The old man came up, and in rather a confused manner inquired what had happened, and Jerome explained matters as well as he was able to do so. After taking up the vinaigrette,[22] which had fallen from her hand, and holding the bottle a short time to her face, the lady began to revive. During all this time, the veil had still partly covered the face of the fair one, so that Jerome had scarcely seen it. When she had so far recovered as to be able to look around her, she raised herself slightly, and again screamed and swooned. The old man now feeling satisfied that Jerome's dark complexion was the immediate cause of the catastrophe, said in a somewhat petulant tone,—

"I will be glad, sir, if you will leave us alone."

The little boy at this juncture set up a loud cry, and amid the general confusion, Jerome left the ground and returned to his hotel.

While seated at the window of his room looking out upon the crowded street, with every now and then the strange scene in the graveyard vividly before him, Jerome suddenly thought of the book he had been reading, and, remember[ed] that he had left it on the tombstone, where he dropped it when called to the lady's assistance. [. . .]

CHAPTER XXXII: THE HAPPY MEETING

After passing a sleepless night, and hearing the clock strike six, Jerome took from his table a [new] book, and thus endeavored to pass away the hours before breakfast-time. While thus engaged, a servant entered and handed him a note. Hastily tearing it open, Jerome read as follows:—

> "SIR,—I owe you an apology for the abrupt manner in which I addressed you last evening, and the inconvenience to which you were subjected by some of my household. If you will honor us with your presence to-day at four o'clock, I will be most happy to give you due satisfaction. My servant will be waiting with the carriage at half-past three.
> I am, sir, yours, &c.,
> J. DEVENANT JEROME FLETCHER, Esq.

Who this gentleman was, and how he had found out his name and the hotel at which he was stopping, were alike mysteries to Jerome. And this note seemed to his puzzled brain like a challenge. "Satisfaction?" He had not asked for satisfaction. However, he resolved to accept the invitation, and, if need be, meet the worst. At any rate, this most mysterious and complicated affair would be explained.

The clock on a neighboring church had scarcely finished striking three when a servant announced to Jerome that a carriage had called for him. In a few minutes, he was seated in a sumptuous barouche.[23]

Jerome alighted, and was shown into a superb room, with the walls finely decorated with splendid tapestry, and the ceilings exquisitely frescoed. The walls were hung with fine specimens from the hands of the great Italian masters, and one by a German artist. [. . .] A faint light, together with the quiet of the hour, gave beauty beyond description to the whole scene. A half-open door showed a fine marble floor to an adjoining room, with pictures, statues, and antiquated sofas, and flower-pots filled with rare plants of every kind and description.

Jerome had scarcely run his eyes over the beauties of the room when the elderly gentleman whom he had met on the previous evening made his appearance, followed by the little boy, and introduced himself as Mr. Devenant. A moment more and a lady, a beautiful brunette, dressed in black, with long black curls hanging over her shoulders, entered the room. Her dark, bright eyes flashed as she caught the first sight of Jerome. The gentleman immediately arose on the entrance of the lady, and Mr. Devenant was in the act of introducing the stranger when he observed that Jerome had sunk back upon the sofa, in a faint voice exclaiming,—

"It is she!"

After this, all was dark and dreary. How long he remained in this condition, it was for others to tell. The lady knelt by his side and wept; and when he came to, he found himself stretched upon the sofa with his boots off and his head resting upon a pillow. By his side sat the old man, with the smelling-bottle in one hand and a glass of water in the other, while the little boy stood at the foot of the sofa. As soon as Jerome had so far recovered as to be able to speak, he said,—

"Where am I, and what does all this mean?"

"Wait awhile," replied the old man, "and I will tell you all."

After the lapse of some ten minutes, Jerome arose from the sofa, adjusted his apparel, and said,—

"I am now ready to hear anything you have to say."

"You were born in America?" said the old man.

"I was," he replied.

"And you knew a girl named Clotelle," continued the old man.

"Yes, and I loved her as I can love none other."

"The lady whom you met so mysteriously last evening was she," said Mr. Devenant.

Jerome was silent, but the fountain of mingled grief and joy stole out from beneath his eyelashes, and glistened like pearls upon his ebony cheeks.

At this juncture, the lady again entered the room. With an enthusiasm that can be better imagined than described, Jerome sprang from the sofa, and they rushed into each other's arms, to the great surprise of the old gentleman and little Antoine, and to the amusement of the servants who had crept up, one by one and were hid behind the doors or loitering in the hall. When they had given vent to their feelings and sufficiently recovered their presence of mind, they resumed their seats.

"How did you find out my name and address?" inquired Jerome.

"After you had left the grave-yard," replied Clotelle, "our little boy said, 'Oh, mamma! if there ain't a book!' I opened the book, and saw your name written in it, and also found a card of the Hotel de Leon. Papa wished to leave the book, and said it was only a fancy of mine that I had ever seen you before; but I was perfectly convinced that you were my own dear Jerome."

As she uttered the last words, tears—the sweet bright tears that love alone can bring forth—bedewed her cheeks.

"Are you married?" now inquired Clotelle, with a palpitating heart and trembling voice.

"No, I am not, and never have been," was Jerome's reply.

"Then, thank God!" she exclaimed, in broken accents.

It was then that hope gleamed up amid the crushed and broken flowers of her heart, and a bright flash darted forth like a sunbeam.

"Are you single now?" asked Jerome.

"Yes, I am," was the answer.

"Then you will be mine after all?" said he with a smile. [. . .]

Although Clotelle had married young Devenant, she had not forgotten her first love, and her father-in-law now willingly gave his consent to her marriage with Jerome. Jerome felt that to possess the woman of his love, even at that late hour, was compensation enough for the years that he had been separated from her, and Clotelle wanted no better evidence of his love for her than the fact of his having remained so long unmarried. It was indeed a rare instance of devotion and constancy in a man, and the young widow gratefully appreciated it. [. . .]

This was the first evening that Jerome had been in her company since the night when, to effect his escape from prison, she disguised herself in male attire. How different the scene now. Free instead of slaves, wealthy instead of poor, and on the eve of an event that seemed likely to result in a life of happiness to both. . . .

[After ten years apart, Jerome and Clotelle marry in France. They return to the United States during the Civil War.]

CHAPTER XXXVI: THE RETURN HOME

The first gun fired at the American Flag, on the 12th of April, 1861, at Fort Sumter, reverberated all over Europe, and was hailed with joy by the crowned heads of the Old World, who hated republican institutions, and who thought they saw, in this act of treason, the downfall of the great American experiment. Most citizens, however, of the United States, who were then sojourning abroad, hastened home to take part in the struggle,— some to side with the rebels, others to take their stand with the friends of liberty. Among the latter, none came with swifter steps or more zeal than Jerome and Clotelle Fletcher. They arrived in New Orleans a week after the capture of that city by the expedition under the command of Major-Gen. B. F. Butler.[24] But how changed was society since Clotelle had last set feet in the Crescent City![25] Twenty-two years had passed; her own chequered life had been through many shifting scenes; her old acquaintances in New Orleans had all disappeared; and with the exception of the black faces which she beheld at every turn, and which in her younger days were her associates, she felt herself in the midst of strangers; and these were arrayed against each other in mortal combat. Possessed with ample means, Mr. and Mrs. Fletcher set about the work of assisting those whom the rebellion had placed in a state of starvation and sickness.

With a heart overflowing with the milk of human kindness, and a tear for every sufferer, no matter of what color or sect, Clotelle was soon known as the "Angel of Mercy."[26]

The "General Order No. 63,"[27] issued on the 22nd of August, 1862, by Gen. Butler, recognizing, and calling into the service of the Federal Government, the battalion of colored men known as the "Native Guard," at once gave full scope to Jerome's military enthusiasm; and he made haste to enlist in the organization.

The "Native Guard" did good service in New Orleans and vicinity, till ordered to take part in the siege of Port Hudson,[28] where they appeared under the name of the "First Louisiana,"[29]and under the immediate command of Lieut.-Col. Bassett.[30] The heroic attack of this regiment, made on the 27th of May, 1863, its unsurpassed "charge," its great loss, and its severe endurance on the field of battle, are incidents which have passed into history. The noble daring of the First Louisiana gained for the black soldiers in our army the praise of all Americans who value Republican institutions.

There was, however, one scene, the closing one in the first day's attack on Port Hudson, which, while it reflects undying credit upon the bravery of the negro, pays but a sorry tribute to the humanity of the white general who brought the scene into existence. The field was strewn with the dead, the dying, and the wounded; and as the jaded regiments were leaving the ground, after their unsuccessful attack, it was found that Capt. Payne,[31] of the Third Louisiana, had been killed; and his body, which was easily distinguished by the uniform, was still on the battle-field. The colonel of the regiment, pointing to where the body lay, asked, "Are there four men here who will fetch the body of Capt. Payne from the field?" Four men stepped out, and at once started. But, as the body lay directly under the range of the rebel batteries, they were all swept down by the grape, canister, and shell[32] which were let loose by the enemy. The question was again repeated, "Are there four men who will go for the body?" The required number came forth, and started upon a run; but, ere they could reach the spot, they were cut down. "Are there four more who will try?" The third call was answered in the affirmative, and the men started upon the double-quick. They, however, fell before getting as far as the preceding four. Twelve men had been killed in the effort to obtain the body of the brave Payne, but to no purpose. Humanity forbade another trial, and yet it was made. "Are there four more men in the regiment who will volunteer to go for Capt. Payne's body?" shouted the officer. Four men sprang forward, as if fearful that they would miss the opportunity of these last: one was Jerome Fletcher, the hero of our story. They started upon the run; and, strange to tell, all of them reached the body, and had nearly borne it from the field, when two of the number were cut down. Of these, one was Jerome. His head was entirely torn off by a shell. The body of the deceased officer having been rescued, an end was put to the human sacrifice.

CHAPTER XXXVII: THE ANGEL OF MERCY

The sad intelligence of Jerome's death was brought to Clotelle while she was giving her personal attention to the sick and wounded that filled the hospitals of New Orleans. For a time she withdrew from the gaze of mankind, and gave herself up to grief. Few unions had been productive of more harmonious feelings than hers. And this blow, so unexpected and at a time when she was experiencing such a degree of excitement caused by the rebellion, made her, indeed, feel the affliction severely.

But the newspaper accounts of the intense suffering of the Union prisoners in the rebel States aroused her, and caused her to leave her retirement. In the month of October, 1863, Clotelle resolved to visit Andersonville, Ga.,[33] for the purpose of alleviating the hardships of our sick and imprisoned soldiers, and at once put her resolution into effect by going immediately to that place. After crossing the lines, she passed as a rebel lady, to enable her the more successfully to carry out her object. On her arrival at Andersonville, Clotelle took up her abode with a private family, of Union proclivities, and commenced her work of mercy. [. . .]

Excerpted from *Clotelle; or, The Colored Heroine. A Tale of the Southern States* (Boston: Lee and Shepard, 1867).

Related writings by William Wells Brown: "Under the Stars and Stripes (A Lecture delivered before the Female Anti-Slavery Society of Salem, at Lyceum Hall)" (1847); "I Have No Constitution, and No Country" (1849); "Fling Out the Anti-Slavery Flag" (1849); "Madison Washington" (1863); *The Negro in the American Rebellion: His Heroism and His Fidelity* (1867); "Slave Revolt at Sea" (1867).

OLIVIA WARD BUSH-BANKS

Olivia Ward's parents were Montauk Indian and African American. Her career included work as the Montauk historian and as a writer of both journalism and literature. Although born in Sag Harbor, New York in 1869, she spent her childhood and young adulthood in New England following the death of her mother. Bush-Banks married Frank Bush in 1889 (they divorced after six years) and married Anthony Banks in 1916. During the New Negro era, Bush-Banks lived in Chicago, where she taught drama before returning to live in New York in the 1930s. A regular contributor to the *Colored American* magazine, she also wrote and worked as an editor for the *New Rochelle Westchester Record-Courier* and published two collections of poetry: *Original Poems* (1899) and *Driftwood* (1914). In 1944, Olivia Ward Bush-Banks died in New York.

Crispus Attucks[34]

The Nation's heart beat wildly,
  And keenly felt the coming strife;
The Country's call was sounding
  Brave men must offer life for life.

So long Great Britain's power
  Had sternly held unyielding sway,
The people yearned for freedom
  And cried, "Our blood must pave the way."

So, on the streets of Boston,
  Where madly rushed the British foe;
Men questioned with each other,
  "Who shall be first to strike the blow?"

Not that they shrank from duty,
  Ah, no! their lives they gladly gave;
But War, with all its terrors,
  Brings fear to hearts both true and brave.

But one, with fearless courage,
  Inspired them to activity,
And boldly led them forward
  With cheering shout, "For Liberty?"

In face of death and danger,
  He met the foe, this soldier true,
Till, charging full upon them,
  Their bayonets had pierced him through.

He fell, and o'er the pavement
  A Negro's blood was flowing free.
His sable hand was foremost
  To strike the blow for liberty.

It was a deed most valiant,
  And mighty was the work begun,
For War then waging fiercely,
  Ceased not till victory was won.

Naught but a slave was Attucks,
  And yet how grand a hero, too.
He gave a life for freedom,
  What more could royal sovereign do?

Well may we eulogize him!
  And rear a monument of fame.
We hold his memory sacred;
  We honor and revere his name.

A century has vanished,
  Yet, through the years still rolling on
We emulate his bravery
  And praise the deed he nobly done.

Then write in glowing letters
  These thrilling words in history,—
That Attucks was a hero,
  That Attucks died for Liberty.

Original Poems (Providence, R.I.: Louis A. Basinet Press, 1899).

Related writings by Olivia Ward Bush-Banks: "Crispus Attucks" (1899); "Abraham Lincoln" (1914); "Carney, The Brave Standard Bearer" (1914); "Unchained: 1863" (1914); "Wendell Phillips" (1914); *Collected Works of Olivia Ward Bush-Banks* (1991); "The Keepers of the House" (1991); "Black Communism" (1991); "What about Our Loyal Colored Americans?" (1991); "Doing Our Bit: Nov. 4, 1942" (1991).

SAMUEL CABBLE

Samuel Cabble worked as a waiter in Iowa before June 1863 when he enlisted as a private in the 55th Massachusetts Regiment. He remained in the army for the duration of the war. In the letter below, now housed in the National Archives, he writes to his wife, Leah Ward Cabble.

"I look forward to a brighter day"[35]

Dear Wife I have enlisted in the army[.] I am now in the state of Massachussetts but before this letter reaches you I will be in north Carolina and though great is the present national difficulties yet I look forward to a brighter day[, w]hen I shall have the opertunity of seeing you in the full enjoyment of fredom[.] I would like to no if you are still in slavery! if you are it will not be long before we shall have crushed the system that now opreses you[,] for in the Course of three months you shall have your liberty[.] great is the outpouring of the colered people that is now rallying with the hearts of lions against that very curse that has seperated you an me[.] yet we shall meet again and oh what a happy time that will be when this ungodly rebellion shall be put down and the curses of our land is trampled under our feet[.] I am a soldier now[,] and I shall use my utmost endeavers to strike at the rebellion and the heart of this system that so long has kept us in chains. Write to me just as soon as you git this letter[.] tell me if you are still living in the cabin where you use to live, tell eliza I send her my best respects and love[;] ike and sully likwise[.] I would send you some money but i now it is impossible for you to git it[.] I would like to see little jenkins now but I no it is impossibl at present[.] se[36] no more but remain your own afectionate husband until death[.]

Samuel Cabble to Leah Ward Cabble, after June 1863, Compiled Military Service Records of Volunteer Soldiers Who Served with the United States Colored Troops: 55th Massachusetts Infantry (Colored), Records of the Adjutant General's Office, 1780s–1917, Record Group 94.12.2, National Archives and Records Administration, Washington, D.C.

Frederick Douglass

Frederick Douglass was born around 1818 on the eastern shore of Maryland. In 1838, he escaped slavery and later traveled widely as an abolitionist orator. Douglass founded and published newspapers and wrote three autobiographical accounts of his life, including *Narrative of the Life of Frederick Douglass, An American Slave* (1845), a popular liberation narrative in which he outlined the terrors of slavery and his escape to freedom. Douglass died in 1895 at his home in Washington, D.C.

"What country have I?"[37]

[. . .] I do not doubt but that a large portion of this audience will be disappointed, both by the *manner* and the *matter* of what I shall this day set forth. The extraordinary and unmerited eulogies which have been showered upon me, here and elsewhere, have done much to create expectations which, I am well aware, I can never hope to gratify. I am here, a simple man, knowing what I have experienced in Slavery, knowing it to be a bad system, and desiring, by all Christian means, to seek its overthrow. I am not here to please you with an eloquent speech, with a refined and logical address, but to speak to you the sober truths of a heart overborne with gratitude to God that we have in this land, cursed as it is with Slavery, so noble a band to second my efforts and the efforts of others in the noble work of undoing the Yoke of Bondage, with which the majority of the States of this Union are now unfortunately cursed.

You are aware, doubtless, that my object in going from this country was to get beyond the reach of the clutch of the man who claimed to own me as his property. I had written a book giving a history of that portion of my life spent in the gall and bitterness and degradation of Slavery, and in which I also identified my oppressors as the perpetrators of some of the most atrocious crimes. This had deeply incensed them against me and stirred up within them the purpose of revenge, and, my whereabouts being known, I believed it necessary for me, if I would preserve my liberty, to leave the shores of America and take up my abode in some other land, at least until the excitement occasioned by the publication of my *Narrative* had subsided. I went to England, Monarchical England, to get rid of Democratic Slavery, and I must confess that, at the very threshold, I was satisfied that I had gone to the right place. Say what you will of England—of the degradation—of the poverty—and there is much of it there—say what you will of the oppression and suffering going on in England at this time, there is Liberty there, there is Freedom there, not only for the white man, but for the black man also. [. . .]

I cannot agree with my friend Mr. Garrison in relation to my love and attachment to this land. I have no love for America, as such; I have no patriotism. I have no country. What country have I? The Institutions of this Country do not know me—do not recognize me as a man. I am not thought of, spoken of, in any direction, out of the Anti-Slavery ranks, as a man. I am not thought of or spoken of, except as a piece of property belonging to some *Christian* Slaveholder, and all the Religious and Political Institutions of this Country alike pronounce me a Slave and a chattel. Now, in such a country as this I cannot have patriotism. The only thing that links me to this land is my family, and the painful consciousness that here there are 3,000,000 of my fellow creatures groaning beneath the iron rod of the worst despotism that could be devised even in Pandemonium,—that here are men and brethren who are identified with me by their complexion, identified with me by their hatred of Slavery, identified with me by their love and aspirations for Liberty, identified with me by the stripes upon their backs, their inhuman wrongs and cruel sufferings. This, and this only, attaches me to this land, and brings me here to plead with you, and with this country at large, for the disenthrallment of my oppressed countrymen, and to overthrow this system of Slavery which is crushing them to the earth.

How can I love a country that dooms 3,000,000 of my brethren, some of them my own kindred, my own brothers, my own sisters, who are now clanking the chains of Slavery upon the plains of the South, whose warm blood is now making fat the soil of Maryland and of Alabama, and over whose crushed spirits rolls the dark shadow of Oppression, shutting out and extinguishing forever the cheering rays of that bright Sun of Liberty, lighted in the souls of all God's children by the omnipotent hand of Deity itself? How can I, I say, love a country thus cursed, thus bedewed with the blood of my brethren? A Country, the Church of which, and the Government of which, and the Constitution of which are in favor of supporting and perpetuating this monstrous system of injustice and blood? I have not, I cannot have, any love for this country, as such, or for its Constitution. I desire to see it overthrown as speedily as possible and its Constitution shivered in a thousand fragments, rather than that this foul curse should continue to remain as now.

In all this, my friends, let me make myself understood. I do not hate America as against England, or against any other country or land. I love

Humanity all over the globe. I am anxious to see Righteousness prevail in all directions. I am anxious to see Slavery overthrown here; but, I never appealed to Englishmen in a manner calculated to awaken feelings of hatred or disgust, or to inflame their prejudices toward America as a nation, or in a manner provocative of national jealousy or ill-will; but I always appealed to their conscience—to the higher and nobler feelings of the people of that country, to enlist them in this cause. I always appealed to their manhood, that which preceded their being Englishmen, (to quote an expression of my friend Phillips), I appealed to them as men, and I had a right to do so. They are men, and the Slave is a man, and we have a right to call upon all men to assist in breaking his bonds, let them be born when and live where they may.

But it is asked, "What good will this do?" or "What good has it done?" "Have you not irritated, have you not annoyed your American friends and the American people rather than done them good?" I admit that we have irritated them. They deserve to be irritated. I am anxious to irritate the American people on this question. As it is in physics, so in morals, there are cases which demand irritation and counter-irritation. The conscience of the American public needs this irritation, and I would *blister it all over from center to circumference*, until it gives signs of a purer and a better life than it is now manifesting to the world. [...]

Excerpted from "Country, Conscience, and the Anti-Slavery Cause: An Address Delivered in New York, New York, May 11, 1847," *New York Daily Tribune*, 13 May 1847.

* * *

The War with Mexico[38]

From aught that appears in the present position and movements of the executive and cabinet—the proceedings of either branch of the national Congress—the several State Legislatures, North and South—the spirit of the public press—the conduct of leading men, and the general views and feelings of the people of the United States at large, slight hope can rationally be predicated of a very speedy termination of the present disgraceful, cruel, and iniquitous war with our sister republic. Mexico seems a doomed victim to Anglo Saxon cupidity and love of dominion. The determination of our slaveholding President[39] to prosecute the war, and the probability of his success in wringing from the people men and money to carry it on, is made evident, rather than doubtful, by the puny opposition arrayed against him. No politician of any considerable distinction or eminence, seems willing to hazard his popularity with his party, or stem the fierce current of executive influence, by an open and unqualified disapprobation of the war. None seem willing to take their stand for peace at all risks; and all seem willing that the war should be carried on, in some form or other. [. . .]

The people appear to be completely in the hands of office seekers, demagogues, and political gamblers. Within the bewildering meshes of their political nets, they are worried, confused, and confounded, so that a general outcry is heard—"Vigorous prosecution of the war!"—"Mexico must be humbled!"—"Conquer a peace!"—"Indemnity!"—"War forced upon us!"—"National honor!"—"The whole of Mexico!"—"Our destiny!"—"This continent!"—"Anglo Saxon blood!"—"More territory!"—"Free institutions!"—"Our country!" till it seems indeed "that justice has fled to brutish beasts, and men have lost their reason." The taste of human blood and the smell of powder seem to have extinguished the senses, seared the conscience, and subverted the reason of the people to a degree that may well induce the gloomy apprehension that our nation has fully entered on her downward career, and yielded herself up to the revolting idea of battle and blood. "Fire and sword," are now the choice of our young republic. The loss of thousands of her own men, and the slaughter of tens of thousands of the sons and daughters of Mexico, have rather given edge than dullness to our appetite for fiery conflict and plunder. [. . .]

We have no preference for parties, regarding this slaveholding crusade. The one is as bad as the other. The friends of peace have nothing to hope from either. [. . .] We know where to find the so called Democrats. They are the accustomed panderers to slaveholders: nothing is either too mean, too dirty, or infamous for them, when commanded by the merciless man stealers of our country. No one expects any thing honorable or decent from that party, touching human rights. They annexed Texas under the plea of extending the area of freedom. They elected James K. Polk, the slaveholder, as the friend of freedom; and they have backed him up in his Presidential falsehoods. They have used their utmost endeavors to crush the right of speech, abridge the right of petition, and to perpetuate the enslavement of the colored people of this country. But we do not intend to go into any examination of parties just now. That we shall have frequent opportunities of doing hereafter. We wish merely to give our readers a general portrait of the present aspect of our country in regard to the Mexican war, its designs, and its results, as they have thus far transpired. [. . .]

But, humble as we are, and unavailing as our voice may be, we wish to warn our fellow countrymen, that they may follow the course which they have marked out for themselves; no barrier may be sufficient to obstruct them; they may accomplish all they desire; Mexico may fall before them; she may be conquered and subdued; her government may be annihilated— her name among the great sisterhood of nations blotted out; her separate existence annihilated; her rights and powers usurped; her people put under the iron arm of a military despotism, and reduced to a condition little better than that endured by the Saxons when vanquished by their Norman invaders; but, so sure as there is a God of justice, we shall not go unpunished; the penalty is certain; we cannot escape; a terrible retribution awaits us. We beseech our countrymen to leave off this horrid conflict, abandon their murderous plans, and forsake the way of blood. Peradventure our country may yet be saved. Let the press, the pulpit, the church, the people at large, unite at once; and let petitions flood the halls of Congress by the million, asking for the instant recall of our forces from Mexico. This may not save us, but it is our only hope.

Excerpted from "The War with Mexico," *The North Star*, 21 January 1848.

* * *

Peace! Peace! Peace![40]

The shout is on every lip, and emblazoned on every paper. The joyful news is told in every quarter with enthusiastic delight. We are such an exception to the great mass of our fellow-countrymen, in respect to everything else, and have been so accustomed to hear them rejoice over the most barbarous outrages committed upon an unoffending people, that we find it difficult to unite with them in their general exultation at this time; and for this reason, we believe that by *peace* they mean *plunder*. In our judgment, those who have all along been loudly in favor of a vigorous prosecution of the war, and heralding its bloody triumph with apparent rapture, and glorifying the atrocious deeds of barbarous heroism on the part of wicked men engaged in it, have no sincere love of peace, and are not now rejoicing over *peace,* but *plunder.* They have succeeded in robbing Mexico of her territory, and are rejoicing over their success under the hypocritical pretence of a regard for peace. Had they not succeeded in robbing Mexico of the most important and most valuable part of her territory, many of those now loudest in their professions of favor for peace, would be loudest and wildest for war—war to the knife. Our soul is sick of such hypocrisy. We presume the churches of Rochester[41] will return thanks to God for peace they did nothing to bring about, and boast of it as a triumph of Christianity! That an end is put to the wholesale murder in Mexico, is truly just cause for rejoicing; but we are not the people to rejoice, we ought rather blush and hang our heads for shame, and in the spirit of profound humility, crave pardon for our crimes at the hands of a God whose mercy endureth forever.

"Peace! Peace! Peace!" *The North Star*, 17 March 1848.

*   *   *

Fellow Citizens: On Slavery and the Fourth of July[42]

[. . .] Friends and Fellow Citizens: [. . .] This [. . .] is the 4th of July. It is the birthday of your National Independence, and of your political freedom. This, to you, is what the Passover was to the emancipated people of God. It carries your minds back to the day, and to the act of your great deliverance; and to the signs, and to the wonders, associated with that act, and that day. This celebration also marks the beginning of another year of your national life; and reminds you that the Republic of America is now 76 years old. I am glad, fellow-citizens, that your nation is so young. Seventy-six years, though a good old age for a man, is but a mere speck in the life of a nation. Three score years and ten is the allotted time for individual men; but nations number their years by thousands. According to this fact, you are, even now, only in the beginning of your national career, still lingering in the period of childhood. [. . .] There is hope in the thought, and hope is much needed, under the dark clouds which lower above the horizon. [. . .] There is consolation in the thought that America is young. [. . .]

Fellow-citizens, I shall not presume to dwell at length on the associations that cluster about this day. [. . .] I am not wanting in respect for great men too—great enough to give fame to a great age. It does not often happen to a nation to raise, at one time, such a number of truly great men. The point from which I am compelled to view them is not, certainly, the most favorable; and yet I cannot contemplate their great deeds with less than admiration. They were statesmen, patriots and heroes, and for the good they did, and the principles they contended for, I will unite with you to honor their memory.

Fully appreciating the hardship to be encountered, firmly believing in the right of their cause, honorably inviting the scrutiny of an on-looking world, reverently appealing to heaven to attest their sincerity, soundly comprehending the solemn responsibility they were about to assume, wisely measuring the terrible odds against them, your fathers, the fathers of this republic, did, most deliberately, under the inspiration of a glorious patriotism, and with a sublime faith in the great principles of justice and freedom, lay deep the corner-stone of the national superstructure, which has risen and still rises in grandeur around you. [. . .] Of this fundamental work, this day is the anniversary. [. . .] I leave, therefore, the great deeds of your fathers to other gentlemen whose claim to have been regularly descended will be less likely to be disputed than mine!

My business, if I have any here to-day, is with the present. The accepted time with God and his cause is the ever-living now.

"Trust no future, however pleasant,
Let the dead past bury its dead;
Act, act in the living present,
Heart within, and God overhead."[43]

[. . .] Fellow-citizens, pardon me, allow me to ask, why am I called upon to speak here to-day? What have I, or those I represent, to do with your national independence? Are the great principles of political freedom and of natural justice, embodied in that Declaration of Independence, extended to us? and am I, therefore, called upon to bring our humble offering to the national altar, and to confess the benefits and express devout gratitude for the blessings resulting from your independence to us? [. . .]

But, such is not the state of the case. I say it with a sad sense of the disparity between us. I am not included within the pale of this glorious anniversary! Your high independence only reveals the immeasurable distance between us. The blessings in which you, this day, rejoice, are not enjoyed in common. The rich inheritance of justice, liberty, prosperity and independence, bequeathed by your fathers, is shared by you, not by me. The sunlight that brought life and healing to you, has brought stripes and death to me. This Fourth July is yours, not mine. You may rejoice, I must mourn. To drag a man in fetters into the grand illuminated temple of liberty, and call upon him to join you in joyous anthems, were inhuman mockery and sacrilegious irony. Do you mean, citizens, to mock me, by asking me to speak to-day? If so, there is a parallel to your conduct. And let me warn you that it is dangerous to copy the example of a nation whose crimes, lowering up to heaven, were thrown down by the breath of the Almighty, burying that nation in irrecoverable ruin! I can to-day take up the plaintive lament of a peeled and woe-smitten people!

"By the rivers of Babylon, there we sat down. Yea! we wept when we remembered Zion. We hanged our harps upon the willows in the midst thereof. For there, they that carried us away captive, required of us a song; and they who wasted us required of us mirth, saying, Sing us one of the songs of Zion. How can we sing the Lord's song in a strange land? If I forget thee, O Jerusalem, let my right hand forget her cunning. If I do not remember thee, let my tongue cleave to the roof of my mouth."[44]

My subject, then fellow-citizens, is AMERICAN SLAVERY. I shall see, this day, and its popular characteristics, from the slave's point of view. Standing, there, identified with the American bondman, making his wrongs mine, I do not hesitate to declare, with all my soul, that the character and conduct of this nation never looked blacker to me than on this 4th of July! Whether we turn to the declarations of the past, or to the professions of the present, the conduct of the nation seems equally hideous and revolting. America is false to the past, false to the present, and solemnly binds herself to be false to the future. Standing with God and the crushed and bleeding slave on this occasion, I will, in the name of humanity which is outraged, in the name of liberty which is fettered, in the name of the constitution and the Bible, which are disregarded and trampled upon, dare to call in question and to denounce, with all the emphasis I can command, everything that serves to perpetuate slavery—the great sin and shame of America! "I will not equivocate; I will not excuse";[45] I will use the severest language I can command. [. . .]

Must I undertake to prove that the slave is a man? That point is conceded already. Nobody doubts it. The slaveholders themselves acknowledge it in the enactment of laws for their government. [. . .] The manhood of the slave is conceded. It is admitted in the fact that Southern statute books are covered with enactments forbidding, under severe fines and penalties, the teaching of the slave to read or to write. When you can point to any such laws, in reference to the beasts of the field, then I may consent to argue the manhood of the slave. [. . .] The time for such argument is past. [. . .] For it is not light that is needed, but fire; it is not the gentle shower, but thunder. We need the storm, the whirlwind, and the earthquake. The feeling of the nation must be quickened; the conscience of the nation must be roused; the propriety of the nation must be startled; the hypocrisy of the nation must be exposed; and its crimes against God and man must be proclaimed and denounced.

What, to the American slave, is your 4th of July? I answer: a day that reveals to him, more than all other days in the year, the gross injustice and cruelty to which he is the constant victim. To him, your celebration is a sham; your boasted liberty, an unholy license; your national greatness, swelling vanity; your sounds of rejoicing are empty and heartless; your denunciations of tyrants, brass fronted impudence; your shouts of liberty and equality, hollow mockery; your prayers and hymns, your sermons and thanksgivings, with all your religious parade, and solemnity, are, to him, mere bombast, fraud, deception, impiety, and hypocrisy—a thin veil to cover up crimes which would disgrace a nation of savages. There is not a nation on the earth guilty of practices, more shocking and bloody, than are the people of these United States, at this very hour. [. . .]

To me the American slave-trade is a terrible reality. When a child, my soul was often pierced with a sense of its horrors. I lived on Philpot Street, Fell's Point, Baltimore, and have watched from the wharves, the slave ships in the Basin, anchored from the shore, with their cargoes of human flesh, waiting for favorable winds to waft them down the Chesapeake. [. . .]

By an act of the American Congress,[46] not yet two years old, slavery has been nationalized in its most horrible and revolting form. By that act, Mason & Dixon's line has been obliterated; New York has become as Virginia; and the power to hold, hunt, and sell men, women, and children as slaves remains no longer a mere state institution, but is now an institution of the whole United States. The power is co-extensive with the star-spangled banner and American Christianity. Where these go, may also go the merciless slave-hunter. Where these are, man is not sacred. [. . .] Your lawmakers have commanded all good citizens to engage in this hellish sport. Your President, your Secretary of State, your lords, nobles, and ecclesiastics, enforce, as a duty you owe to your free and glorious country, and to your God, that you do this accursed thing. Not fewer than forty Americans have, within the past two years, been hunted down and, without a moment's warning, hurried away in chains, and consigned to slavery and excruciating torture. [. . .]

The church of this country is not only indifferent to the wrongs of the slave, it actually takes sides with the oppressors. It has made itself the bulwark of American slavery, and the shield of American slave-hunters. Many of its most eloquent Divines, who stand as the very lights of the church, have shamelessly given the sanction of religion and the Bible to the whole slave system. They have taught that man may, properly, be a slave; that the relation of master and slave is ordained of God; that to send back an escaped bondman to his master is clearly the duty of all the followers of the Lord Jesus Christ; and this horrible blasphemy is palmed off upon the world for Christianity. For my part, I would say, welcome infidelity! welcome atheism! welcome anything! in preference to the gospel, as preached by those Divines! They convert the very name of religion into an engine of tyranny, and barbarous cruelty, and serve to confirm more infidels, in this age, than all the infidel writings of Thomas Paine, Voltaire, and Bolingbroke, put together, have done! [. . .]

Allow me to say, in conclusion, notwithstanding the dark picture I have this day presented of the state of the nation, I do not despair of this country. Oceans no longer divide, but link nations together. [. . .] Thoughts expressed on one side of the Atlantic are distinctly heard on the other.

The fiat of the Almighty, "Let there be Light,"[47] has not yet spent its force. No abuse, no outrage whether in taste, sport or avarice, can now hide itself from the all-pervading light. . . . Africa must rise and put on her yet unwoven garment. "Ethiopia shall stretch out her hand unto God."[48]

Excerpted from *Oration Delivered in Corinthian Hall, Rochester, by Frederick Douglass* (Rochester, N.Y.: Lee, Mann & Co., 1852).

*   *   *

From How to End the War[49]

To our mind, there is but one easy, short and effectual way to suppress and put down the desolating war which the slaveholders and their rebel minions are now waging against the American Government and its loyal citizens. Fire must be met with water, darkness with light, and war for the destruction of liberty must be met with war for the destruction of slavery. *The simple way, then, to put an end to the savage and desolating war now waged by the slaveholders, is to strike down slavery itself,* the primal cause of that war.

Freedom to the slave should now be proclaimed from the Capitol, and should be seen above the smoke and fire of every battle field, waving from every loyal flag! The time for mild measures is past. They are pearls cast before swine, and only increase and aggravate the crime which they would conciliate and repress. The weak point must be found, and when found should be struck with the utmost vigor. Any war is a calamity; but a peace that can only breed war is a far greater calamity. [. . .] The sooner this rebellion is put out of its misery, the better for all concerned. A lenient war is a lengthy war, and therefore the worst kind of war. Let us stop it, and stop it effectually—stop it before its evils are diffused throughout the Northern States—stop it on the soil upon which it originated, and among the traitors and rebels who originated the war. This can be done at once, by "carrying the war into Africa." Let the slaves and free colored people be called into service, and formed into a liberating army, to march into the South and raise the banner of Emancipation among the slaves. The South having brought revolution and war upon the country, and having elected and consented to play at that fearful game, she has no right to complain if some good as well as calamity shall result from her own act and deed.

The slaveholders have not hesitated to employ the sable arms of the Negroes at the South in erecting the fortifications which silenced the guns of Fort Sumter, and brought the star spangled banner to the dust. They often boast, and not without cause, that their Negroes will fight for them against the North. They have no scruples against employing the Negroes to exterminate freedom, and in overturning the Government. They work with spade and barrow with them, and they will stand with them on the field of battle, shoulder to shoulder, with guns in their hands, to shoot down the troops of the U. S. Government.—They have neither pride, prejudice nor pity to restrain them from employing Negroes *against white men, where slavery is to be protected and made secure*. Oh! that this Government would only now be as true to liberty as the rebels, who are attempting to batter it down, are true to slavery. [. . .] Every consideration of justice, humanity and sound policy confirms the wisdom of calling upon black men to take up arms in behalf of their country.

We are often asked by persons in the street as well as by letter, what our people will do in the present solemn crisis in the affairs of the country. Our answer is, would to God you would let us do something! We lack nothing but your consent. We are ready and would go, counting ourselves happy in being permitted to serve and suffer for the cause of freedom and free institutions. But you won't let us go. Read the heart-rending account we publish elsewhere of the treatment received by the brave fellows, who broke away from their chains and went through marvelous suffering to defend Fort Pickens[50] against the rebels.—They were instantly seized and put in irons and returned to their guilty masters to be whipped to death! Witness Gen.

Butler's[51] offer to put down the slave insurrection in the State of Maryland. The colored citizens of Boston have offered their services to the Government, and were refused. There is, even now, while the slaveholders are marshaling armed Negroes against the Government, [. . .] there is still, we say, weak and contemptible tenderness towards the blood thirsty, slaveholding traitors, by the Government and people of the country. Until the nation shall repent of this weakness and folly, [. . .] until they shall strike down slavery, the source and center of this gigantic rebellion, they don't deserve the support of a single sable arm. [. . .]

Excerpted from "How to End the War," *Douglass' Monthly*, May 1861, 451.

Related writings by Frederick Douglass: "The Heroic Slave" (1853); "The Claims of the Negro Ethnologically Considered" (1854); "The Unconstitutionality of Slavery" (1860); "Fighting the Rebels with Only One Hand" (1861); "Appeal to Congress for Impartial Suffrage" (1867); "I Denounce the So-Called Emancipation as a Stupendous Fraud" (1888).

LEWIS HENRY DOUGLASS

Lewis Henry Douglass, a son of Frederick Douglass, was born in 1840 in New Bedford, Massachusetts. He volunteered for military service during the Civil War and served as a sergeant major in the 54th Massachusetts Volunteer Infantry Regiment, commanded by Colonel Robert Gould Shaw. He suffered illness after the first battle at Fort Wagner that resulted in his discharge from service. Following the war, Douglass worked in government and as a newspaperman. He died in 1908.

"If I die tonight I will not die a coward"[52]

Morris Island,
S[outh] C[arolina]
July 20th, 1863

My Dear Father and Mother:

Wednesday July 8th, our regiment left St. Helena Island for Folly Island, arriving there the next day, and were then ordered to land on James Island, which we did. On the upper end of James Island is a large rebel battery with 18 guns. After landing we threw out pickets to within two miles of the rebel fortification. We were permitted to do this in peace until last Thursday, 16th inst.,[53] when at four o'clock in the morning the rebels made an attack on our pickets, who were about 200 strong. We were attacked by a force of about 900. Our men fought like tigers; one sergeant killed five men by shooting and bayoneting. The rebels were held in check by our few men long enough to allow the Conn[ecticut] [Infantry Regiment] to escape being surrounded and captured, for which we received the highest praise from all parties who knew of it. This performance on our part earned for us the reputation of a fighting regiment.

Our loss in killed, wounded and missing was forty-five. That night we took, according to our officers, one of the hardest marches on record through woods and marsh. The rebels we defeated and drove back in the morning. They, however, were reinforced by 14,000 men, we having only half a dozen regiments. So it was necessary for us to escape.

I cannot write in full, expecting every moment to be called into another fight. Suffice it to say we are now on Morris Island. Saturday night we made the most desperate charge of the war on Fort Wagner, losing in killed, wounded and missing in the assault, three hundred of our men. The splendid 54th is cut to pieces. All our officers, with the exception of eight, were either killed or wounded. Col. [Robert Gould] Shaw is prisoner and wounded. Major [Edward N.] Hallowell is wounded in three places, Adj't [Garth W.] James in two places. Serg't [Robert Simmons is killed, Nat[haniel] Hurley (from Rochester) is missing and a host of others.

I had my sword sheath blown away while on the parapet of the Fort. The grape and cannister, shell and minnies[54] swept us down like chaff, still our men went on and on, and if we had been properly supported, we would have held the Fort, but the white troops could not be made to come up. The consequence was we had to fall back, dodging shells and other missiles.

If I have another opportunity, I will write more fully. Goodbye to all; If I die tonight I will not die a coward. Goodbye.

Lewis

"From Charleston, The 55th Massachusetts at Fort Wagner—Letter from Sergeant Douglass," *Douglass' Monthly*, August 1863, 852–53.

Paul Laurence Dunbar

Joshua Dunbar, father of the well-known writer Paul Laurence Dunbar, escaped from slavery and served in the 55th Massachusetts Volunteer Infantry Regiment during the Civil War. The younger Dunbar used his father's experiences in slavery and war to inform several literary works. Paul Laurence Dunbar, a prolific writer, was born in 1872 in Dayton, Ohio. His collection of stories, *Folks from Dixie* (1898), was the first book of short stories by a black writer published in the United States. He became the best-known black poet among both white and black readers before his death in 1906 in Ohio.

Black Samson of Brandywine[55]

"In the fight at Brandywine, Black Samson, a giant negro armed with a scythe, sweeps his way through the red ranks . . ."

C. M. SKINNER'S *MYTHS AND LEGENDS OF OUR OWN LAND*

Gray are the pages of record,
    Dim are the volumes of eld;[56]
Else had old Delaware[57] told us
    More that her history held.
Told us with pride in the story,
    Honest and noble and fine,
More of the tale of my hero,
    Black Samson of Brandywine.
Sing of your chiefs and your nobles,
    Saxon and Celt and Gaul[58]
Breath of mine ever shall join you,
    Highly I honor them all.
Give to them all of their glory,
    But for this noble of mine,
Lend him a tithe of your tribute,
    Black Samson of Brandywine.
There in the heat of the battle,
    There in the stir of the fight,
Loomed he, an ebony giant,
    Black as the pinions of night.
Swinging his scythe like a mower

Over a field of grain,
Needless the care of the gleaners,
  Where he had passed amain.
Straight through the human harvest,
  Cutting a bloody swath,
Woe to you, soldier of Briton!
  Death is abroad in his path.
Flee from the scythe of the reaper,
  Flee while the moment is thine,
None may with safety withstand him,
  Black Samson of Brandywine.
Was he a freeman or bondman?
  Was he a man or a thing?
What does it matter? His brav'ry
  Renders him royal—a king.
If he was only a chattel,
  Honor the ransom may pay
Of the royal, the loyal black giant
  Who fought for his country that day.
Noble and bright is the story,
  Worthy the touch of the lyre,
Sculptor or poet should find it
  Full of the stuff to inspire.
Beat it in brass and in copper,
  Tell it in storied line,
So that the world may remember
  Black Samson of Brandywine.

"Black Samson of Brandywine," in *Lyrics of Love and Laughter* (New York: Dodd, Mead, 1903), 120–23.

* * *

The Colored Soldiers[59]

If the muse were mine to tempt it
  And my feeble voice were strong,
If my tongue were trained to measures,
  I would sing a stirring song.

I would sing a song heroic
    Of those noble sons of Ham,[60]
Of the gallant colored soldiers
    Who fought for Uncle Sam!

In the early days you scorned them,
    And with many a flip and flout
Said "These battles are the white man's,
    And the whites will fight them out."
Up the hills you fought and faltered,
    In the vales you strove and bled,
While your ears still heard the thunder
    Of the foes' advancing tread.

Then distress fell on the nation,
    And the flag was drooping low;
Should the dust pollute your banner?
    No! the nation shouted, No!
So when War, in savage triumph,
    Spread abroad his funeral pall—
Then you called the colored soldiers,
    And they answered to your call.

And like hounds unleashed and eager
    For the life blood of the prey,
Sprung they forth and bore them bravely
    In the thickest of the fray.
And where'er the fight was hottest,
    Where the bullets fastest fell,
There they pressed unblanched and fearless
    At the very mouth of hell.

Ah, they rallied to the standard
    To uphold it by their might;
None were stronger in the labors,
    None were braver in the fight.
From the blazing breach of Wagner[61]
    To the plains of Olustee,[62]
They were foremost in the fight
    Of the battles of the free.

And at Pillow![63] God have mercy
    On the deeds committed there,
And the souls of those poor victims
    Sent to Thee without a prayer.
Let the fulness of Thy pity
    O'er the hot wrought spirits sway
Of the gallant colored soldiers
    Who fell fighting on that day!

Yes, the Blacks enjoy their freedom,
    And they won it dearly, too;
For the life blood of their thousands
    Did the southern fields bedew.
In the darkness of their bondage,
    In the depths of slavery's night,
Their muskets flashed the dawning,
    And they fought their way to light.

They were comrades then and brothers,
    Are they more or less to-day?
They were good to stop a bullet
    And to front the fearful fray.
They were citizens and soldiers,
    When rebellion raised its head;
And the traits that made them worthy,
    Ah! those virtues are not dead.

They have shared your nightly vigils,
    They have shared your daily toil;
And their blood with yours commingling
    Has enriched the Southern soil.

They have slept and marched and suffered
    Neath the same dark skies as you,
They have met as fierce a foe-man,
    And have been as brave and true.

And their deeds shall find a record
    In the registry of Fame;
For their blood has cleansed completely

Every blot of Slavery's shame.
So all honor and all glory
    To those noble sons of Ham—
The gallant colored soldiers
    Who fought for Uncle Sam!

"The Colored Soldiers," in *Majors and Minors* (Toledo, Ohio: Hadley & Hadley, 1895),
50–52.

*   *   *

Robert Gould Shaw[64]

Why was it that the thunder voice of Fate
Should call thee, studious, from the classic groves,
Where calm-eyed Pallas[65] with still footstep roves,
And charge thee seek the turmoil of the state?
What bade thee hear the voice and rise elate,
Leave home and kindred and thy spicy loaves,
To lead th' unlettered and despised droves
To manhood's home and thunder at the gate?

Far better the slow blaze of Learning's light,
The cool and quiet of her dearer fane,[66]
Than this hot terror of a hopeless fight,
This cold endurance of the final pain,
Since thou and those who with thee died for right
Have died, the Present teaches, but in vain!

"Robert Gould Shaw," *Atlantic Monthly*, October 1900, 488.

*   *   *

Lincoln

Hurt was the nation with a mighty wound,
And all her ways were filled with clam'rous sound.
Wailed loud the South with unremitting grief,
And wept the North that could not find relief.
Then madness joined its harshest tone to strife:

A minor note swelled in the song of life.
Till, stirring with the love that filled his breast,
But still, unflinching at the right's behest,
Grave Lincoln came, strong handed, from afar,
The mighty Homer of the lyre[67] of war.
'T was he who bade the raging tempest cease,
Wrenched from his harp the harmony of peace,
Muted the strings, that made the discord,—Wrong,
And gave his spirit up in thund'rous song.
Oh mighty Master of the mighty lyre,
Earth heard and trembled at thy strains of fire:
Earth learned of thee what Heav'n already knew,
And wrote thee down among her treasured few.

"Lincoln," in *Lyrics of Love and Laughter* (New York: Dodd, Mead, 1903), 60.

Related writings by Paul Laurence Dunbar: "Our Martyred Soldiers" (1888); "Emancipation" (1890); "Memorial Day" (1893); *The Fanatics*, 1901; "Unsung Heroes" (1903); "When Dey Listed Colored Soldiers" (1903); "Dirge for a Soldier" (1903); "The Fourth of July and Race Outrages" (1903); "The Strength of Gideon" (1903).

OLAUDAH EQUIANO [GUSTAVUS VASSA]

After surviving capture by human traffickers in Essaka, West Africa around 1745 as well as captivity at sea in England and in the British North American colony of Virginia, Olaudah Equiano purchased his freedom in 1766 while enslaved in Montserrat. In his book *The Interesting Narrative of the Life of Olaudah Equiano*, the autobiographical abolitionist narrative excerpted below, Equiano reports on his activities during the Seven Years' War/French and Indian Wars while enslaved by British Royal Navy officer Michael Pascal. His narrative is silent on the Revolutionary War for Independence in the New World. In 1777, Equiano settled in England and became a founding member of the Sons of Africa, a black abolitionist group. He died in 1831 as a British citizen.

Life at Sea during the French and Indian War (Seven Years' War)[68]

[. . .] When I went on board this large ship, I was amazed indeed to see the quantity of men and the guns. However my surprise began to diminish as my knowledge increased; and I ceased to feel those apprehensions and alarms which had taken such strong possession of me when I first came among the Europeans, and for some time after. I began now to pass to an opposite extreme; I was so far from being afraid of any thing new which I saw, that, after I had been some time in this ship, I even began to long for a battle. [. . .]

My master [. . .] got an appointment to be sixth lieutenant of the *Namur*, which was then at Spithead,[69] sitting up for Vice-admiral Boscawen,[70] who was going with a large fleet on an expedition against Louisbourgh. [. . .] There was a very great fleet of men of war of every description assembled together for this expedition, and I was in hopes soon to have an opportunity of being gratified with a sea-fight. All things being now in readiness, this mighty fleet (for there was also Admiral Cornish's[71] fleet in company, destined for the East Indies) at last weighed anchor, and sailed. The two fleets continued in company for several days, and then parted; Admiral Cornish, in the *Lenox*, having first saluted our admiral in the *Namur*, which he returned. We then steered for America; but, by contrary winds, we were driven to Teneriffe,[72] where I was struck with its noted peak. Its prodigious height, and its form, resembling a sugar-loaf, filled me with wonder. We remained in sight of this island some days, and then proceeded for

America, which we soon made, and got into a very commodious harbour called St. George, in Halifax,[73] where we had fish in great plenty, and all other fresh provisions. We were here joined by different men of war and transport ships with soldiers; after which, our fleet being increased to a prodigious number of ships of all kinds, we sailed for Cape Breton in Nova Scotia. [. . .]

We arrived at Cape Breton in the summer of 1758: and here the soldiers were to be landed, in order to make an attack upon Louisbourgh. My master had some part in superintending the landing; and here I was in a small measure gratified in seeing an encounter between our men and the enemy. The French were posted on the shore to receive us, and disputed our landing for a long time; but at last they were driven from their trenches, and a complete landing was effected.

Our troops pursued them as far as the town of Louisbourgh. In this action many were killed on both sides. One thing remarkable I saw this day:—A lieutenant of the *Princess Amelia*, who, as well as my master, superintended the landing, was giving the word of command, and while his mouth was open a musquet ball went through it, and passed out at his cheek. I had that day in my hand the scalp of an indian king, who was killed in the engagement: the scalp had been taken off by an Highlander.[74]

Our land forces laid siege to the town of Louisbourgh, while the French men of war were blocked up in the harbour by the fleet, the batteries at the same time playing upon them from the land. This they did with such effect, that one day I saw some of the ships set on fire by the shells from the batteries, and I believe two or three of them were quite burnt. At another time, about fifty boats belonging to the English men of war, commanded by Captain George Balfour of the *Ætna fire-ship*, and another junior captain, Laforey, attacked and boarded the only two remaining French men of war in the harbour. They also set fire to a seventy-gun ship. [. . .] At last Louisbourgh was taken, and the English men of war came into the harbour before it, to my very great joy; for I had now more liberty of indulging myself, and I went often on shore. When the ships were in the harbour we had the most beautiful procession on the water I ever saw. All the admirals and captains of the men of war, full dressed, and in their barges, well ornamented with pendants, came alongside of the *Namur*. The vice-admiral then went on shore in his barge, followed by the other officers in order of seniority, to take possession, as I suppose, of the town and fort. Some time after this the French governor and his lady, and other persons of note, came on board our ship to dine. On this occasion our ships were dressed with colours of all kinds, from the topgallant-mast head to the deck; and this, with the firing of guns, formed a most grand and magnificent spectacle.

It was now winter; and one evening, during our passage home, about dusk, when we were in the channel, or near foundings, and were beginning to look for land, we descried seven sail of large men of war, which stood off shore. Several people on board of our ship said, as the two fleets were (in forty minutes from the first sight) within hail of each other, that they were English men of war; and some of our people even began to name some of the ships. By this time both fleets began to mingle, and our admiral ordered his flag to be hoisted. At that instant the other fleet, which were French, hoisted their ensigns, and gave us a broadside as they passed by. Nothing could create greater surprise and confusion among us than this: the wind was high, the sea rough, and we had our lower and middle deck guns housed in, so that not a single gun on board was ready to be fired at any of the French ships. I afterwards heard this was a French squadron, commanded by Mons. Conflans;[75] and certainly had the Frenchmen known our condition, and had a mind to fight us, they might have done us great mischief. But we were not long before we were prepared for an engagement. Immediately many things were tossed overboard; the ships were made ready for fighting as soon as possible; and about ten at night we had bent a new main sail, the old one being split. Being now in readiness for fighting, we wore ship,[76] and stood after the French fleet, who were one or two ships in number more than we. However we gave them chase, and continued pursuing them all night; and at day-light we saw six of them, all large ships of the line, and an English East Indiaman, a prize they had taken. We chased them all day till between three and four o'clock in the evening, when we came up with, and passed within a musquet shot of, one seventy-four gun ship, and the Indiaman also, who now hoisted her colours, but immediately hauled them down again. On this we made a signal for the other ships to take possession of her; and, supposing the man of war would likewise strike, we cheered, but she did not; though if we had fired into her, from being so near, we must have taken her. [. . .]

We chased all night; but the next day they were out of sight, so that we saw no more of them; and we only had the old Indiaman (called Carnarvon I think) for our trouble. After this we stood in for the channel, and soon made the land; and, about the close of the year [1758–1759], we got safe to St. Helen's. [. . .][77]

Excerpted from *Interesting Narrative of the Life of Olaudah Equiano, or Gustavus Vassa, the African, Written by Himself* (London: Printed for the author by T. Wilkins, 1789).

JAMES FORTEN

James Forten was born in 1766 to free parents in Philadelphia. He served in the Continental Navy on a privateer vessel. After returning to Philadelphia as a Revolutionary War veteran, he became an ardent abolitionist leader and built his fortune in the sailmaking business. Forten and his wife reared eight children. The excerpt below is from his pamphlet, published anonymously, in response to a bill proposed in the Philadelphia legislature that would have impeded the migration of black people into that state; the bill was unsuccessful. He later befriended William Lloyd Garrison and often published in the *Liberator* under the name "A Colored Philadelphian." Forten died in Philadelphia in 1842.

From Letters from a Man of Colour on a Late Bill before the Senate of Pennsylvania

Letter IV

[. . .] I proceed again to the consideration of the bill of unalienable rights[78] belonging to black men, the passage of which will only tend to show, that the advocates of emancipation can enact laws more degrading to the free man, and more injurious to his feelings, than all the tyranny of slavery, or the shackles of infatuated despotism. And let me here remark, that this unfortunate race of humanity, although protected by our laws, are already subject to the fury and caprice of a certain set of men, who regard neither humanity, law nor privilege. They are already considered as a different species, and little above the brute creation. They are thought to be objects fit for nothing else than lordly men to vent the effervescence of their spleen upon, and to tyrannize over, like the bearded Musselman[79] over his horde of slaves. Nay, the Musselman, thinks more of his horse, than the generality of people do of the despised black!—Are not men of colour sufficiently degraded? Why then increase their degradation? It is a well known fact, that black people, upon certain days of public jubilee, dare not to be seen after twelve o'clock in the day, upon the field to enjoy the times; for no sooner do the fumes of that potent devil, Liquor, mount into the brain, than the poor black is assailed like the destroying Hyena or the avaricious Wolf! I allude particularly to the Fourth of July—Is it not wonderful, that the day set apart for the festival of Liberty, should be bused[80] by the advocates of Freedom, in endeavoring to sully what they profess to adore. If men, though they know that the law protects all, will dare, in defiance of law, to execute their hatred upon the defenceless black, will they not by the passage of this bill, believe him still more a mark for their venom and spleen—Will they not believe him completely deserted by authority, and subject to every outrage brutality can inflict—too surely they will, and the poor wretch will turn his eyes around to look in vain for protection. Pause, ye rulers of a free people, before you give us over to despair and violation—we implore you, for the sake of humanity, to snatch us from the pinnacle of ruin, from that gulf, which will swallow our rights, as fellow creatures; our privileges, as citizens; and our liberties, as men!

There are [black] men among us of reputation and property, as good citizens as any men can be, and who, for their property, pay as heavy taxes as any citizens are compelled to pay. All taxes, except personal, fall upon them, and still even they are not exempted from this degrading bill. The villainous part of the community, of all colours, we wish to see punished and retrieved as much as any people can. Enact laws to punish them severely, but do not let them operate against the innocent as well as the guilty. Can there be any generosity in this? Can there be any semblance of justice, or of that enlightened conduct which is ever the boasted pole star of freedom? By no means. This bill is nothing but the ignus fatuus[81] of mistaken policy. [. . .]

I have done. My feelings are acute, and I have ventured to express them without intending either accusation or insult to any one. An appeal to the heart is my intention, and if I have failed, it is my great misfortune, not to have laid a power of eloquence sufficient to convince. [. . .]

Excerpted from "Letter IV," in *Letters from a Man of Colour on a Late Bill before the Senate of Pennsylvania* ([Philadelphia]: Pa.: 1813), 7–9.

CHARLOTTE FORTEN GRIMKÉ

Charlotte Forten, a free woman of color, poet, educator, and abolitionist, was the granddaughter of James Forten, niece of Sarah Louisa Forten, and a member of the Salem Female Anti-Slavery Society. Her poetry and essays appeared in prominent antislavery periodicals. Charlotte Forten was born in 1837 in Philadelphia. She traveled to the Sea Islands in 1862 to teach freedwomen and men; she also worked as a nurse to soldiers wounded at Fort Wagner. While in South Carolina, she wrote about her observations of events related to the Civil War. The *Atlantic Monthly* serialized her memoir, excerpted here, under the title "Life on the Sea Islands." Well after the war, Forten married Francis Grimké, the nephew of the Grimké sisters who were prominent abolitionists from South Carolina. Charlotte Forten Grimké died in 1914 in Washington, D.C.

"True manhood has no limitations of color"[82]

[. . .] New-Year's-Day—Emancipation-Day [1863][83]—was a glorious one to us. The morning was quite cold, the coldest we had experienced; but we were determined to go to the celebration at Camp Saxton,—the camp of the First Regiment South Carolina Volunteers,—whither the General [Rufus Saxton] and Colonel [Thomas Wentworth] Higginson had bidden us, on this, "the greatest day in the nation's history." We enjoyed perfectly the exciting scene on board the *Flora*. There was an eager, wondering crowd of the freed people in their holiday-attire, with the gayest of head-handkerchiefs, the whitest of aprons, and the happiest of faces. The band was playing, the flags streaming, everybody talking merrily and feeling strangely happy. The sun shone brightly, the very waves seemed to partake of the universal gayety, and danced and sparkled more joyously than ever before. Long before we reached Camp Saxton we could see the beautiful grove, and the ruins of the old Huguenot[84] fort near it. Some companies of the First Regiment [33rd USCT] were drawn up in line under the trees, near the landing, to receive us. A fine, soldierly-looking set of men. [. . .]

The celebration took place in the beautiful grove of live-oaks adjoining the camp. It was the largest grove we had seen. I wish it were possible to describe fitly the scene which met our eyes as we sat upon the stand, and looked down on the crowd before us. There were black soldiers in their blue coats and scarlet pantaloons, the officers of this and other regiments in their handsome uniforms, and crowds of lookers-on,—men, women, and the children, of every complexion, grouped in various attitudes under the moss-hung trees. The faces of all wore a happy, interested look. The exercises commenced with a prayer by the chaplain of the regiment. An ode, written for the occasion by Professor [John] Zachos, was read by him, and then sung. Colonel Higginson then introduced Dr. [William H.] Brisbane, who read the President's Proclamation, which was enthusiastically cheered. Rev. Mr. [Mansfield] French presented to the Colonel two very elegant flags, a gift to the regiment from the Church of the Puritans, accompanying them by an appropriate and enthusiastic speech. At its conclusion, before Colonel Higginson could reply, and while he still stood holding the flags in his hand, some of the colored people, of their own accord, commenced singing, "My Country, 'tis of thee." It was a touching and beautiful incident, and sent a thrill through our hearts. The Colonel was deeply moved by it. He said that that reply was far more effective than any speech he could make. [. . .]

After the meeting we saw the dress-parade, a brilliant and beautiful sight. An officer told us that the men went through the drill remarkably well,—that the ease and rapidity with which they learned the movements were wonderful. To us it seemed strange as a miracle,—this black regiment, the first mustered into the service of the United States, doing itself honor in the sight of the officers of other regiments, many of whom, doubtless, "came to scoff." The men afterwards had a great feast, ten oxen having been roasted whole for their especial benefit.

We went to the landing, intending to take the next boat for Beaufort;[85] but finding it very much crowded, waited for another. It was the softest, loveliest moonlight; we seated ourselves on the ruined wall of the old fort; and when the boat had got a short distance from the shore the band in it commenced playing "Sweet Home."[86] The moonlight on the water, the perfect stillness around, the wildness and solitude of the ruins, all seemed to give new pathos to that ever dear and beautiful old song. [. . .] We promenaded the deck of the steamer, sang patriotic songs, and agreed that moonlight and water had never looked so beautiful as on that night. At Beaufort we took the row-boat for St. Helena; and the boatmen, as they rowed, sang some of the sweetest, wildest hymns. It was a fitting close to such a day. Our hearts were filled with an exceeding great gladness; for, although the Government had left much undone, we knew that Freedom was surely born in our land that day. It seemed too glorious a good to realize,—this beginning of the great work we had so longed and prayed for. [. . .]

Notwithstanding the heat, we determined to celebrate the Fourth of July [1863] as worthily as we could. The freed people and the children of the different schools assembled in the grove near the Baptist Church. The flag was hung across the road, between two magnificent live-oaks, and the children, being grouped under it, sang "The Star-Spangled Banner" with much spirit. Our good General could not come, but addresses were made by Mr. [Edward] P[hilbrick],—the noble-hearted founder of the movement for the benefit of the people here, and from first to last their stanch and much-loved friend,—by Mr. [James] L[ynch], a young colored minister, and others. Then the people sang some of their own hymns; and the woods resounded with the grand notes of "Roll, Jordan, [R]oll."[87] They all afterward partook of refreshments, consisting of molasses and water,—a very great luxury to them,—and hard-tack.[88]

Among the visitors present was the noble young Colonel [Robert Gould] Shaw, whose regiment was then stationed on the island. We had met him a few nights before, when he came to our house to witness one of the people's shouts.[89] We looked upon him with the deepest interest. There was something in his face finer, more exquisite, than one often sees in a man's face, yet it was full of courage and decision. The rare and singular charm of his manner drew all hearts to him. He was deeply interested in the singing and appearance of the people. A few days afterwards we saw his regiment on dress-parade, and admired its remarkably fine and manly appearance. After taking supper with the Colonel we sat outside the tent, while some of his men entertained us with excellent singing. Every moment we became more and more charmed with him. How full of life and hope and lofty aspirations he was that night! How eagerly he expressed his wish that they might soon be ordered to Charleston! "I do hope they will give *us* a chance," he said. It was the desire of his soul that his men should do themselves honor,—that they should prove themselves to an unbelieving world as brave soldiers as though their skins were white. And for himself, he was like the Chevalier of old, "without reproach or fear."

After we had mounted our horses and rode away, we seemed still to feel the kind of clasp of his hand,—to hear the pleasant, genial tones of his voice, as he bade us good-bye, and hoped that we might meet again. We never saw him afterward. In two short weeks came the terrible massacre at Fort Wagner, and the beautiful head of the young hero and martyr was laid low in the dust. Never shall we forget the heart-sickness with which we heard of his death. We could not realize it at first,—we, who had seen him so lately in all the strength and glory of his young manhood. For days we clung to a vain hope; then it fell away from us, and we knew that he was gone. We knew that he died gloriously, but still it seemed very hard. Our hearts bled for the mother whom he so loved,—for the young wife, left desolate. And then we said, as we say now,—"God comfort them! He only can."

During a few of the sad days which followed the attack on Fort Wagner, I was in one of the hospitals of Beaufort, occupied with the wounded soldiers of the Fifty-fourth Massachusetts. The first morning was spent in mending the bullet-holes and rents in their clothing. What a story they told! Some of the jackets of the poor fellows were literally cut in pieces. It was pleasant to see the brave, cheerful spirit among them. Some of them were severely wounded, but they uttered no complaint; and in their letters which they dictated to their absent friends there was no word of regret, but the same cheerful tone throughout. They expressed an eager desire to get well, that they might "go at it again." Their attachment to their young colonel was beautiful to see. They felt his death deeply. One and all united in the warmest and most enthusiastic praise of him. He was, indeed, exactly the person to inspire the most loyal devotion in the hearts of his men. And with everything to live for, he had given up his life for them. Heaven's best gifts had been showered upon him, but for them he had laid them all down. I think they truly appreciated the greatness of the sacrifice. May they ever prove worthy of such a leader! Already, they, and the regiments of freedmen here, as well, have shown that true manhood has no limitations of color. [. . .]

Excerpted from "Life on the Sea Islands, Part II," *Atlantic Monthly*, June 1864, 668–70, 676–76.

Related writing by Charlotte Forten Grimké: "The Gathering of the Grand Army" (1890).

Sarah Louisa Forten Purvis

Sarah Louisa Forten was born free in 1814 to a prominent black abolitionist family of Philadelphia. In 1831, at the age of seventeen, she began publishing in the *Liberator* newspaper under pen names, including the name Ada, which she used for the poem below. She became a charter member of the Philadelphia Female Anti-Slavery Society and later became a policy-making leader in that organization. She married Joseph Purvis, whose brother also was a renowned abolitionist. Sarah Forten Purvis was the aunt of Charlotte Forten and daughter of Revolutionary War veteran and wealthy Philadelphia sailmaker James Forten. She died in 1857 at her family's home in Philadelphia.

My Country

Oh! speak not of heathenish darkness again,
Nor tell me of lands held in error's dread chain!
Where—where is the nation so erring as we,
Who claim the proud name of the "HOME OF THE FREE"?
What a throb do the lov'd ties of country awake
In the heart of the exile!—for time cannot break
The sweet vision of home, and all he loved well,
Which has thrown o'er his pathway a magical spell.
Can the name of "MY COUNTRY"—the deeds which we sing—
Be honored—revered—'midst pollution and sin?
Can the names of our fathers who perished in fight,
Be hallowed in story, midst slavery's blight?
When America's standard is floating so fair,
I blush that the impress of falsehood is there;
That oppression and mockery dim the high fame,
That seeks from all nations a patriot's name.
Speak not of "my country," unless she shall be,
In truth, the bright home of the "brave and the free!"
Till the dark stain of slavery is washed from her hand,
A tribute of homage she cannot command.

"My Country," *Liberator*, 4 January 1834, 4.

Related writing by Sarah Louisa Forten Purvis: "The Abuse of Liberty" (1831).

VIEVEE FRANCIS

Vievee Francis has published two collections of poetry. She was the recipient of the Cave Canem Fellowship in 2005 and 2007. In 2009, she received the Rona Jaffe Foundation Writers' Award. Her book of poems titled *Horses in the Dark* appeared in print in 2012. Francis teaches creative writing at Warren Wilson College in Asheville, North Carolina.

Frederick Douglass Speaks before the Anti–Mexican War Abolitionists[90]

Rise up with thunder
dissenting voice, and take your
place within the pantheon
of righteous forces.

We are accosted by the masses
of assumed patriots
who wave their flags and leaflets
overhead—but we will gather
their names, we will record
the atrocities, we will
face the prison cell
before we will support
an unjust war
thrust upon us
by executive insistence.

"Frederick Douglass Speaks before the Anti–Mexican War Abolitionists," in *Blue-Tail Fly* (Detroit: Wayne State University Press, 2006), 15.

*   *   *

South of Houston

My father said prayers that meant soon there would be none
of us left who were not servants to them. Houston[91] wanted us out.
The Texicans[92] bred like prairie dogs—towns springing up
out of nowhere, like dust funnels out of Chihuahua[93] sands, pushing us

further and further south. New laws[94] sweeping us out by day like
    lizards.
They grew to hate us, as if *we* were the masters
and the leash theirs to bite.

"South of Houston," in *Blue-Tail Fly* (Detroit: Wayne State University Press, 2006), 32.

FREEDOM PETITION TO THE MASSACHUSETTS COUNCIL AND HOUSE OF REPRESENTATIVES

This petition is among a number of similar pleas by African Americans to end slavery in Massachusetts. Individuals as well as groups filed freedom petitions such as the one below. The petitioners here have made the Declaration of Independence and the Revolutionary War for Independence the basis of their argument for liberation.

Black Abolitionists Declare Rights to Revolutionary Freedom[95]

To the Honorable Counsel and House of Representatives for the State of Massachusetts Bay, Jan. 13, 1777.

The petition of a great number of blacks detained in a state of slavery in the bowels of a free & Christian country humbly sheweth that your petitioners apprehend we have in common with all other men a natural and Unalienable Right to that freedom which the Great Parent of the Universe hath bestowed equally on all mankind, and which they have never forfeited by any compact or agreement whatever. But they were unjustly dragged by the hand of cruel Power from their dearest friends and some of them even torn from the embraces of their tender parents—from a populous, pleasant, and plentiful country and in violation of Laws of Nature and of Nations—and in defiance of all the tender feelings of humanity, brought here to be sold like beasts of burden and like them condemned to slavery for life among a people professing the mild Religion of Jesus—a people not insensible of the secrets of rational beings nor without spirit to resent the unjust endeavours of others to reduce them to a state of bondage and subjection.

Your honours need not to be informed that a life of slavery like that of your petitioners, deprived of every social privilege, of everything requisite to render life tolerable, is far worse than nonexistence.

In imitation of their laudable example of the good people of these States, your petitioners have long and patiently waited the event of petition after petition by them presented to the legislative body of this state and cannot but with grief reflect that their success hath been but too similar. They cannot but express their astonishment that it has never been considered that every principle from which Americans have acted in the course of their unhappy difficulties with Great Britain pleads stronger than a thousand arguments in favour of your petitioners that they therefore humbly beseech your honours to give this petition its due weight and consideration and cause an act of the legislature to be passed whereby they may be restored to the enjoyments of that which is the natural right of all men—and their children who were born in this land of liberty—may not be held as slaves after they arrive at the age of twenty one years. So may the inhabitants of this state, no longer chargeable with the inconsistency of acting themselves the part which they condemn and oppose in others, be prospered in their present glorious struggle for liberty and have those blessings to them, &c.

Lancaster Hill

Peter Bess

Brister Slenser

Prince Hall

Jack Pierpont

Nero Funelo

Newport Sumner

Job Look

Jeremy Belknap Papers, Massachusetts Historical Society, Boston, Massachusetts.

HENRY HIGHLAND GARNET

Henry Highland Garnet was born into slavery in 1815 in Maryland. His family escaped captivity when he was a young boy. He became an ordained Presbyterian minister and worked as an abolitionist. Garnet advocated that black people engage in armed rebellion and establish independent settlements either inside or outside the United States. He first presented the speech below in 1843 at the National Negro Convention (NNC) in Buffalo, New York. In 1882, Garnet died in Liberia while there on an appointment from the U.S. government.

From An Address to the Slaves of the United States of America[96]

Brethren and Fellow Citizens:—Your Brethren of the North, East, and West have been accustomed to meet together in National Conventions,[97] to sympathize with each other, and to weep over your unhappy condition. In these meetings we have addressed all classes of the free, but we have never, until this time, sent a word of consolation and advice to you. We have been contented in sitting still and mourning over your sorrows, earnestly hoping that before this day your sacred liberty would have been restored. But, we have hoped in vain. Years have rolled on, and tens of thousands have been borne on streams of blood and tears, to the shores of eternity. While you have been oppressed, we have also been partakers with you; nor can we be free while you are enslaved. We, therefore, write to you as being bound with you.

Many of you are bound to us, not only by the ties of a common humanity, but we are connected by the more tender relations of parents, wives, husbands, children, brothers, and sisters, and friends. As such we most affectionately address you. Slavery has fixed a deep gulf between you and us, and while it shuts out from you the relief and consolation which your friends would willingly render, it affects and persecutes you with a fierceness which we might not expect to see in the fiends of hell. [. . .]

Two hundred and twenty-seven years ago, the first of our injured race were brought to the shores of America. They came not with glad spirits to select their homes in the New World. They came not with their own consent, to find an unmolested enjoyment of the blessings of this fruitful soil. The first dealings they had with men calling themselves Christians, exhibited to them the worst features of corrupt and sordid hearts; and convinced them that no cruelty is too great, no villainy and no robbery too abhorrent for even enlightened men to perform, when influenced by avarice and lust. Neither did they come flying upon the wings of Liberty, to a land of freedom. But they came with broken hearts, from their beloved native land, and were doomed to unrequited toil and deep degradation. Nor did the evil of their bondage end at their emancipation by death. Succeeding generations inherited their chains, and millions have come from eternity into time, and have returned again to the world of spirits, cursed and ruined by American slavery.

The propagators of the system, or their immediate ancestors, very soon discovered its growing evil and its tremendous wickedness, and secret promises were made to destroy it. The gross inconsistency of a people holding slaves, who had themselves "ferried o'er the wave" for freedom's sake, was too apparent to be entirely overlooked. The voice of Freedom cried, "Emancipate yourselves." Humanity supplicated with tears for the deliverance of the children of Africa. Wisdom urged her solemn plea. The bleeding captive plead [*sic*] his innocence, and pointed to Christianity who stood weeping at the cross. [. . .] But all was in vain. Slavery had stretched its dark wings of death over the land, the Church stood silently by—the priests prophesied falsely, and the people loved to have it so. Its throne is established, and now it reigns triumphant.

Nearly three millions of your fellow-citizens are prohibited by law and public opinion, (which in this country is stronger than law) from reading the Book of Life. Your intellect has been destroyed as much as possible, and every ray of light they have attempted to shut out from your minds. The oppressors themselves have become involved in the ruin. They have become weak, sensual, and rapacious—they have cursed you—they have cursed themselves—they have cursed the earth which they have trod. [. . .]

The colonists threw the blame upon England. They said that the mother country entailed the evil upon them, and that they would rid themselves of it if they could. The world thought they were sincere, and the philanthropic pitied them. But time soon tested their sincerity. In a few years the colonists grew strong, and severed themselves from the British Government. Their independence was declared, and they took their station among the sovereign powers of the earth. The declaration[98] was a glorious document. Sages admired it, and the patriotic of every nation reverenced the God-like sentiments which it contained. When the power of Government returned to their hands, did they emancipate the slaves? No; they rather added new links to our chains. Were they ignorant of the principles of Liberty? Certainly they were not. The sentiments of their revolutionary orators fell in burning eloquence upon their hearts, and with one voice they cried, Liberty or Death. Oh what a sentence was that! It ran from soul to soul like electric fire, and nerved the arm of thousands to fight in the holy cause of Freedom. Among the diversity of opinions that are entertained in regard to physical resistance, there are but a few found to gainsay that stern declaration. We are among those who do not.

Slavery! How much misery is comprehended in that single word. What mind is there that does not shrink from its direful effects? Unless the image of God be obliterated from the soul, all men cherish the love of Liberty. The nice discerning political economist does not regard the sacred right more than the untutored African who roams in the wilds of Congo. Nor has the one more right to the full enjoyment of his freedom than the other. In every man's mind the good seeds of liberty are planted, and he who brings his fellow down so low, as to make him contented with a condition of slavery, commits the highest crime against God and man. Brethren, your oppressors aim to do this. They endeavor to make you as much like brutes as possible. When they have blinded the eyes of your mind—when they have embittered the sweet waters of life—then, and not till then, has American slavery done its perfect work.

TO SUCH DEGRADATION IT IS SINFUL IN THE EXTREME FOR YOU TO MAKE VOLUNTARY SUBMISSION. The divine commandments you are in duty bound to reverence and obey. If you do not obey them, you will surely meet with the displeasure of the Almighty. [. . .] The forlorn condition in which you are placed, does not destroy your moral obligation to God. You are not certain of heaven, because you suffer yourselves to remain in a state of slavery, where you cannot obey the commandments of the Sovereign of the universe. If the ignorance of slavery is a passport to heaven, then it is a blessing, and no curse, and you should rather desire its perpetuity than its abolition. God will not receive slavery, nor ignorance, nor any other state of mind, for love and obedience to him. Your condition does not absolve you from your moral obligation. The diabolical injustice by which your liberties are cloven down, NEITHER GOD, NOR ANGELS, OR JUST MEN, COMMAND YOU TO SUFFER FOR A SINGLE MOMENT. THEREFORE IT IS YOUR SOLEMN AND IMPERATIVE DUTY TO USE EVERY MEANS, BOTH MORAL, INTELLECTUAL, AND PHYSICAL THAT PROMISES SUCCESS. [. . .]

Brethren, it is as wrong for your lordly oppressors to keep you in slavery, as it was for the man thief to steal our ancestors from the coast of Africa.

You should therefore now use the same manner of resistance, as would have been just in our ancestors when the bloody foot-prints of the first remorseless soul-thief was placed upon the shores of our fatherland. The humblest peasant is as free in the sight of God as the proudest monarch that ever swayed a sceptre. Liberty is a spirit sent out from God, and like its great Author, is no respecter of persons.

Brethren, the time has come when you must act for yourselves. It is an old and true saying that, "if hereditary bondmen would be free, they must themselves strike the blow."[99] You can plead your own cause, and do the work of emancipation better than any others. The nations of the world are moving in the great cause of universal freedom, and some of them at least will, ere long, do you justice. The combined powers of Europe have placed their broad seal of disapprobation upon the African slave-trade. But in the slaveholding parts of the United States, the trade is as brisk as ever. They buy and sell you as though you were brute beasts. [. . .] Think of the undying glory that hangs around the ancient name of Africa—and forget not that you are native born American citizens, and as such, you are justly entitled to all the rights that are granted to the freest. Think how many tears you have poured out upon the soil which you have cultivated with unrequited toil and enriched with your blood; and then go to your lordly enslavers and tell them plainly, that you *are determined to be free.* [. . .] Point them to the increase of happiness and prosperity in the British West Indies since the Act of Emancipation.[100]

Tell them in language which they cannot misunderstand, of the exceeding sinfulness of slavery, and of a future judgment, and of the righteous retributions of an indignant God. Inform them that all you desire is FREEDOM, and that nothing else will suffice. Do this, and for ever after cease to toil for the heartless tyrants, who give you no other reward but stripes and abuse. If they then commence the work of death, they, and not you, will be responsible for the consequences. You had better all *die—die immediately*, than live slaves and entail your wretchedness upon your posterity. If you would be free in this generation, here is your only hope. However much you and all of us may desire it, there is not much hope of redemption without the shedding of blood. If you must bleed, let it all come at once—rather *die freemen, than live to be slaves.* It is impossible like the children of Israel, to make a grand exodus from the land of bondage. The Pharaohs are on both sides of the blood-red waters! You cannot move *en masse*, to the dominions of the British Queen—nor can you pass through Florida and overrun Texas, and at last find peace in Mexico. The propagators of American slavery are spending their blood and treasure, that they may plant the black flag in the heart of Mexico and riot in the halls of the Montezumas.[101] [...]

Fellow men! Patient sufferers! behold your dearest rights crushed to the earth! See your sons murdered, and your wives, mothers and sisters doomed to prostitution. In the name of the merciful God, and by all that life is worth, let it no longer be a debatable question whether it is better to choose LIBERTY or DEATH.

In 1822, Denmark Veazie [Vesey], of [Charleston], South Carolina, formed a plan for the liberation of his fellow men. In the whole history of human efforts to overthrow slavery, a more complicated and tremendous plan was never formed. He was betrayed by the treachery of his own people, and died a martyr to freedom. Many a brave hero fell, but history, faithful to her high trust, will transcribe his name on the same monument with Moses, Hampden, Tell, Bruce and Wallace, Toussaint L'Ouverture, Lafayette and Washington.[102] That tremendous movement shook the whole empire of slavery. The guilty soul-thieves were overwhelmed with fear. It is a matter of fact, that at that time, and in consequence of the threatened revolution, the slave States talked strongly of emancipation. But they blew but one blast of the trumpet of freedom and then laid it aside. [...]

The patriotic Nathaniel Turner[103] followed Denmark Veazie [Vesey]. He was goaded to desperation by wrong and injustice. By despotism, his name has been recorded on the list of infamy, [...] [yet] future generations will remember him among the noble and brave.

Next arose the immortal Joseph Cinque, the hero of the *Amistad*.[104] He was a native African, and by the help of God he emancipated a whole shipload of his fellow men on the high seas. And he now sings of liberty on the sunny hills of Africa and beneath his native palm-trees, where he hears the lion roar and feels himself as free as that king of the forest. Next arose Madison Washington,[105] that bright star of freedom, and took his station in the constellation of true heroism. He was a slave on board the brig *Creole*, of Richmond, bound to New Orleans, that great slave mart, with [...] [one] hundred and four others. Nineteen struck for liberty or death. But one life was taken, and the whole were emancipated, and the vessel was carried into Nassau, New Providence.

Noble men! Those who have fallen in freedom's conflict, their memories will be cherished by the true-hearted and the God-fearing in all future generations; those who are living, their names are surrounded by a halo of glory. Brethren, arise, arise! Strike for your lives and liberties. Now is the day and the hour. Let every slave throughout the land do this, and the days of slavery are numbered. [. . .]

It is in your power so to torment the God-cursed slaveholders that they will be glad to let you go free. [. . .] But you are a patient people. You act as though, you were made for the special use of these devils. [. . .] In the name of God, we ask, are you men? Where is the blood of your fathers? Has it all run out of your veins? Awake, awake; millions of voices are calling you! Your dead fathers speak to you from their graves. Heaven, as with a voice of thunder, calls on you to arise from the dust.

Let your motto be resistance! *resistance*! RESISTANCE! No oppressed people have ever secured their liberty without resistance. What kind of resistance you had better make, you must decide by the circumstances that surround you, and according to the suggestion of expediency. Brethren, adieu! Trust in the living God. Labor for the peace of the human race, and remember that you are FOUR MILLIONS!

"An Address to the Slaves of the United States of America," National Negro Convention, Buffalo, New York, 16 August 1843. Excerpted from *Walker's Appeal, with a Brief Sketch of His Life by Henry Highland Garnet and Also Garnet's Address to the Slaves of the United States of America* (New York: J. H. Tobitt, 1848), 89–97.

SHIRLEY GRAHAM DU BOIS

An activist and accomplished writer before her marriage to W.E.B. Du Bois in 1951, Shirley Graham was born in Indianapolis, Indiana, in 1896. She spent her childhood and youth in the various cities where her father, an African Methodist Episcopal minister, was assigned. She wrote plays, short stories, librettos, and musical scores and directed the Chicago Negro Unit of the Federal Theater Project of the Works Progress Administration in the 1930s. Shirley Graham also was a member of the Sojourners for Truth and Justice, a group that advocated for women's liberation. In 1961, she emigrated to Ghana with her husband, and they both became citizens of that West African country. She died in 1977 in China.

It's Morning[106]

A One-Act Play in Two Scenes

Note: The dialect in "It's Morning" is not uniform. It is not intended to be. Many African languages express different meanings by changes in pitch and volume. The most primitive of American Negroes indicate slight changes in meaning by changing vowel sounds. Also, the old type of Negro preachers used a biblical mode of expression which cannot be expressed in dialect. The song used in Scene II "Ah want Jesus to walk wid me," is one of the oldest of the Spirituals. As are most of these older songs, it is in the minor mode. Music for the other lyrics is original and harmonizes with the theme of the play.—S.G.

Characters

CISSIE, a Slave Woman

MILLIE, her fourteen-year-old daughter

PETE, her ten-year-old son

GRANNIE LOU, the oldest slave on the plantation, considered a little crazy

ROSE, a slave woman

PHOEBE, a slave woman

AUNT SUE, a slave woman

CRIPPLE JAKE, the banjo player

UNCLE DAVE, slave preacher from Green's plantation

SOLDIER, a white Union soldier

Other slaves, men and women, singers, small military band

Place: A Remote Plantation in the Deep South

Time: The last day in December, 1862
Early in the morning January 1, 1863

SCENE I

Place: Interior of Cissie's cabin.

Time: Nearly noon on the last day in December, 1862.

SCENE: *Bright morning sunshine streams through the open door and frameless window in the back of a rather large, sparsely furnished room. The walls are crudely plastered with old newspapers, but through the knotholes and cracks come bits of light, pointing up the strings of bright red peppers hanging near the fire, and reflecting in the piece of broken mirror above the hearth. The left wall is almost taken up by the wide, open fireplace in which burn heaps of pine cones. Pots and pans are on the hearth and over the flames an iron kettle hangs. On the shelf above sit an oil-lamp, and odds and ends of heavy dishes, while dried herbs hang from a nail. Fishing poles are in a corner of the room; a fishnet is draped along the wall. There are split-bottom chairs, a bench before the fire, a bare table down front left.*

When the curtain rises, a slave is discovered just outside the open door, chopping wood and singing as he works. He swings his ax in long, even strokes, beating out the rhythm of his song. Beyond him and through the window may be seen a field of dead, dried cottonstalks, standing naked in the sunshine. A few women are at work, digging up stalks or turning the earth. Within the room GRANNIE LOU *is bending over the fire and stirring the kettle with a long-handled spoon. She is shrunken and frail as a withered leaf. Her face is very black and wrinkled, her hands are bony and twisted. The bandana fastened about her head fits tight and smooth as a skull-cap, but it is a pleasing bit of color as she moves about. Between her toothless gums is stuck a lighted corn-cob pipe. She is humming to herself—a soft accompaniment to the woodchopper's song.*

 MAN. (*Singing*)
Don' min' wo'kin' from sun tuh sun
 Dis mawnin',
Don' min' wo'kin' from sun tuh sun
 Dis mawnin',
Don' min' wo'kin' from sun tuh sun Jus so Ah gets mah wo'k all
 done,
 Dis mawnin'.

Wen' tuh da ribbah tuh wade across, Dis mawnin',

Wen' tuh da ribbah tuh wade across, Dis mawnin',

Wen' tuh da ribbah tuh wade across, Ribbah so deep Ah had tuh
grab me a hoss,

Dis mawnin'.

Grabbed a donkey didn't hab no hair,

Dis mawnin',

Grabbed a donkey didn't hab no hair,

Dis mawnin',

Grabbed a donkey didn't hab no hair,

When Ah come to Ah wasn't dere,

Dis mawnin'.

(*There is the sound of laughter. The slave tosses his ax to one side and waves his hand to someone in the field. As he does so he sees something that catches and holds his attention. With his eyes still riveted, he stoops and absent-mindedly begins piling the wood in his arms. Now, he pauses and, sticking his head in the cabin, gives a quick look around. The old woman does not notice him and he says nothing. Then, as if anxious to get away, he piles the wood high in his arms and goes right. He gives a troubled look over his shoulder as he passes the window. Hardly has he disappeared when through the window may be seen* ROSE *and* PHOEBE, *whispering excitedly and watching someone approach. Upon the head of the taller woman is balanced a water pail. Both fall silent as* CISSIE *appears in the doorway, clinging there a moment, as if for support. They watch her grope her way across the floor to the table where she drops into a chair and leans forward, one hand hiding her face, the other hanging listlessly at her side. Her motionless figure casts a long shadow across the floor and somehow this shadow seems to spread and widen, blotting out the sunshine in the room. The old woman stops her humming, takes her pipe from her mouth, and gives Cissie a long, piercing look. Then without a word, she turns back to the fire.*

The two women hesitate in the doorway. Rose swings the pail of water from her head, sets it just inside the door and asks anxiously.)

ROSE. Has yo'all heared da word, Cissie?

CISSIE. (*dully*) Yes. . . . Dey's gwine in da mawnin'.

PHOEBE. (*choking back a cry*) Jesus! Jesus! In da mawnin'!

ROSE. (*comes downstage and clasps her hands*)

Oh, Lawd,

Look down an' see dis po' woman,

Bowed in huh grief an' woe,

He'p huh bear dis hebby cross,

An' make huh meek an' 'umble

Tuh dye will.

(*During* ROSE's *prayer,* AUNT SUE *appears at the threshold. She is older than the three women. Her ample frame in the clean cotton dress fills the doorway, her great bosom trembles with suppressed emotion and her kindly face is filled with sympathy as she stands listening. She waits until Rose is silent.*)

AUNT SUE. (*entering*)

Hit kain't be true, an' yet Ah knows it am,

Ole missie wouldn't touch a bite o' food,

She cry all day an' wish fuh massa Charles.

Dat man give huh no peace,

He say he will hab Millie gal,

Else tu'n us out tuh starve—an' missie, too.

PHOEBE. He'd do it kase he's cruel an' hard,

He's lak a beast dat's scented fresh, young meat,

He's old—He'll suck huh blood lak damp

swamp ting. (*She shudders*)

AUNT SUE. His jowls hang down lak empty 'tatah sacks,

An' 'bacca juice falls drippin' f'om his mouth,

Leavin' a trail o' slime whar he has passed.

(CISSIE *has sat motionless while the others talked. Now, she drops her hand from her face. Her eyes stare straight ahead. She speaks as if from a distance, with difficulty, still looking with horror upon a picture etched on her brain.*)

CISSIE. Ah seed him lick his lips an' smile an' grin,

Ole missie beg him wait till cotton bust,

An' promise him da best bales in da lot.

He say he wait no mo'. . . . He want da gal.

Ah seed his hands . . . dey touch huh golden breast,

She war so scared, she couldn't run . . .

An' den she scream . . . an' missie tell huh go.

Ah heared him laf . . . an' spit upon da floah!

(CISSIE *pulls herself to her feet and, as if weights are fastened to her limbs, drags across the floor toward the inner room. Outside is heard a girl's voice singing.*)

GIRL. Oh, see dat sun,

See how he run,

Don' yo' ebber let 'em catch yo',

Wid yo' wo'k undone.

Oh, see dat sun,

See how he run,

Don' yo' ebber let 'em catch yo'

Wid yo' wo'k undone,

(*Cissie disappears in the gloom of the other room.*)

ADDED VOICES. (*outside*) Oh! Ah'm a gonna shine,

Lawd, Ah'm a gonna shine.

AUNT SUE. (*shaking her head and looking after* CISSIE)

Cissie uster sing lak dat

Jes' lak huh gal.

PHOEBE and ROSE.(*astonished*) Cissie! Sing?

AUNT SUE. Yes, Cissie! she war beautiful!

Black as a berry an' lovely as da night,

Slender an' swift as a young colt

She nevah walk, jes' prance an' run about da place.

Ah seen da buckra[107] eyin' huh—an' she jes' laf.

Den come a day when she war very still,

Ah donno why, till one night seen huh slippin'

trough da shadows lak a hounded coon

crawls tuh his hole to lick his bleedin' wounds.

ROSE. Dey say dat she war proud, an' dat da

ovahseer swear he'd break huh will.

AUNT SUE. (*bitterly*) He did . . . An' when he'd come along da

row

She tremble lak a leaf, an' once she fall down cryin' at his feet.

He laf, an' kick huh wid his foot, not hard, but lak you'd kick a

bitch dat's large wid puppy, out of yo' path.

(*A deep sigh from the three women.*)

ROSE. Huh Millie's lak a flower,

She watch huh day an' night,

An' now . . .

PHOEBE. She know dat Millie's singin' days am gone

AUNT SUE. Yes, an' huh dancin', too. . . .

Po' lil gal—She'll mos' wish she war dead.

ROSE. An' Peter—Spite of he small an' weak,

He take to round da bargain out complete.

PHOEBE. Mussy Jesus! He'p us, Lawd!

(*The prayer is interrupted by Grannie dropping her spoon on the hearth with a loud clatter. The women give a start. They had forgotten her presence. Grannie breaks into high-pitched, crazy laughter.*)

GRANNIE. He! He! He! Ha! Ha!

PHOEBE. Mek huh stop! Somebody'll hyear.

ROSE. What's da mattah, grannie,

Why yo' all laf?

GRANNIE. (*mocking*) Mussy Jesus! Mussy Jesus!

(*She snickers while the women gasp.*)

Day don' hab tuh go, Ah tells yo',

Day don' hab tuh go!

AUNT SUE. Let huh talk.

We allus calls huh crazy, but who knows?

Maybe da Voodoo[108] wo'k dat way, maybe she bile up sompin'
    dat kin help.

(*Gently to the old woman*)

What is it, grannie, what dey kin do?

Might dey bof run away?

GRANNIE. (*in a cracked, singsong voice*)

Da ribbah's high, da rains dat fall las' week,

Make all da ma'shes tick wid mud an' deep.

AUNT SUE. Den what? . . . Why yo' all laf?

Hit's Cissie's chillun dat's been sole down ribbah.

Millie, huh gal, an' Pete, huh lil boy.

PHOEBE. Aw, Antie, why yo' askin' po' ole Lou?

GRANNIE. (*Sharply to Phoebe*) Shut yo' mouf!

Ah ain't so ole dat Ah don' member.

(*Turning to the others*)

Ain't Ah nebbah tole yo' bout dat 'oman

long time gone? Dey say she straight from jungles in

da far off Africa. . . . She nevah say.

Dat war a 'oman—straight lak tree, an' tall,

Swift as a lion an' strong as any ox.

Da sugah cane went down fo' huh big knife,

Lak cottonstalks under da fierces' hail—

No man could walk wid huh . . . An' sing!

She uster sing out in da fields . . .

Da niggahs wo'k dem days . . . When Ah war young.

(*Her voice dies away in a mumble of reminiscence. She turns back to her pots, forgetting her audience, forgetting the present, lost in the happy memories of her youth.* CISSIE *may be seen standing just within the doorway of the inner room. The women do not see her. Now they turn away from* GRANNIE *in disgust.*)

PHOEBE. Humph!

Ah tought yo' gonna tell us sompin' we

kin do to he'p po' Cissie an' huh gal,

An' all yo'all comes talkin' 'bout is some

cane-choppin' heathen dat kin sing.

Gwan! Anybody kin sing!

GRANNIE. (*facing about angrily*)

Ain't Ah tol' yo' shut yo' fat mouf, yo'?

Dat 'oman dar do mo' den sing! Lissen—

(*She gesticulates with her pipe. Cissie presses forward listening intently.*)

She hab tree sons, dey black an' tall lak she,

An' one day news comes dat dey sole huh sons down

ribbah. . . . Dey brings good price.

She say dey nebbah go. Da white folks laf,

but niggahs dassent laf—dey see huh face.

She don' say no'tin' mo', but go away,

An' early in da mawnin' call huh boys,

An' when dey come, she tell 'em to stan' close,

An' watch da sun come up out ob da hills.

Dey sort ob smile at huh an' look,

An' den dat 'oman lift huh big cane knife,

She cry out sompin' in a wild, strange voice,

An' wid one sweep she cut off all dey heads,

Dey roll down at huh feet—All tree ob dem.

(*The women give a gasp! It is* GRANNIE's *moment of triumph. She holds it. Then, with a shrug of her shoulders and a toothless grin, she turns back to her pots. Outside the girl's voice comes nearer. The women's heads bow, but in the background* CISSIE *remains standing as if spellbound.*)

GIRL. Oh! see dat sun,

See how he run,

Don' yo' ebbah let 'em catch yo',

Wid yo' wo'k undone,

Oh! Ah'm a-gonna shine,

Lawd, Ah'm a-gonna shine.

(*The song stops as the girl reaches the door. It is* MILLIE. *Her thin dress reveals the beautifully molded lines of young womanhood as she hesitates just outside in the sunshine. She is the color of burnished gold, and in her soft, wavy hair, framing the round face, are glints of copper. Her mouth is full and curves sweetly like a little child's. Her eyes are wide and know no shadows. Now, she puckers her brow anxiously as she sees the three women, silent and bowed. But the silence is broken by* CISSIE, *speaking from where she stands. Her voice is thick and harsh. The women look at each other in consternation. They are wondering how long she has been in the room.*)

CISSIE. Com' hyear, chile.

(MILLIE's *eyes fill with alarm at her mother's voice.*)

MILLIE. Mammy, mammy, Ah ain't done nottin'.

Ole missie tell me Ah kin go—

She say tuh hurry hyear an' look fuh yo'.

(*The girl advances timidly, looking from one woman to the other, noting the strained expressions.* CISSIE *stares at her with awful concentration.* MILLIE *stops uncertain.*)

MILLIE. What's de mattah, mammy?

What's da mattah wid ever'body today?

Ole missie, too. She lookin' powerful sad.

Hav' sompin' awful come to Massa Frank

Way at da war? . . . Why, hyear come Pete!

(PETE, *prancing on his spindly legs, has just entered the cabin. He is grinning widely and brings with him an air of exuberance which relieves the tension and seems to lift some of the shadows in the room. As if to avoid further questions,* CISSIE *walks rapidly to the fireplace and begins to busy herself at the hearth.* MILLIE *addresses the boy severely.*)

MILLIE. Hey, what yo'all doin' pussyfootin' off f'om wo'k dis
    time a day?

PETE. (*cheerfully*) Pussyfootin' yo'self!

(*He whirls on his bare feet*)

No mo' wo'k fuh me today,

Nottin' tuh do but go an' play!

    Hoopla! Hoopla!

(MILLIE *grins in spite of herself.* PETE *continues.*)

Is dar gwine be a pahty o' sompin'?

Us ain't had no pahty fuh Christmas.

(*Eagerly*) Maybe Massa Frank come back f'om da war!

He sho' giv' us pahties!

(CISSIE's *face is hidden as she bends over the hearth. Now, she speaks in a light, high, but slightly muffled voice.*)

CISSIE. No, Massa Frank ain't come back yet,

But us gwine tuh hab a pahty!

(*Pete bounds up with joy. The women show amazement. Cissie turns with a laugh. Her eyes are shining, her voice animated. She is galvanized into action. Each of the next lines is punctuated by some definite, playful motion.*)

CISSIE. Scour out da kettles,

Fill up da pails,

Run tell Cripple Jake to get his banjo down.

Fotch me a chicken,

Heap up da cones,

Ah'm cookin' up a mess o' victuals wid cawnpone.

Go quick! (*She grabs a pail and gives it to Pete, who rushes out.*)

Call Paul! (*She calls after him*)

We'll dance!

Tell all!

(*She gives* MILLIE *a playful push out the door. The merry voices of the two may be heard outside.*)

PHOEBE. A pahty!

Cissie, is yo' crazy?

(CISSIE *has remained standing near the door looking out after the children. As their happy voices fade, her shoulders sag. She seems to wither and shrink as she stands there, her back to the room. She speaks without turning, all the life gone from her voice.*)

    CISSIE. Dey gonna sing an' dance till dey kain't dance

    no mo'. Till sleep pulls hebby at dar lids,

    An' dey sinks down wid belly full o' joy.

    (*Almost in a whisper*)

    Happy will be der dreams—der long, long dreams.

    ROSE. (*Sudden fear clutching at her throat and thickening her
        voice.*)

    What yo' sayin', Cissie?

    What yo'all sayin'?

(CISSIE *whirls in the doorway like a wounded animal at bay. Her eyes are blazing. She speaks wildly.*)

    CISSIE. Dey ain't gwine, yo' hyear me?

    DEY. . . . ain't gwine . . . NEIDDAH!

(*She rushes out the door.*)

    GRANNIE. He! He! He! Ha! Ha! Ha!

CURTAIN

SCENE II

Place: Same interior as SCENE I.

Time: The hour just before the dawn of the following day.

SCENE: *The night of revelry has passed. The room, still bedecked for the party—with its half-emptied pots upon the hearth, table and bench pushed against the wall and piles of dirty dishes scattered about—is like an actress, when the comedy is finished, ghastly beneath her grease paint. A bright, gay cloth is draped at the window, the wooden shutter is closed. Spanish moss, gathered in the swamp, is festooned from the rafters of the unceiled room. When the room is lighter the little red berries of holly may be seen nestling in the thick bed of green bunches. Over the door sprays of mistletoe now droop— tiny, white pearls hanging heavy upon the wilted stems.*

When the curtain lifts the room is in deep shadow, lighted only by the fire which has burned down to a few glowing cones. The young folks have gone home, but there remain the older slaves who watch with CISSIE for the dawn.

For the most part they are huddled together near the fire, but several sit tense, staring into the shadows. CRIPPLE JAKE, alone in a corner, his rude crutch at his side, holds a banjo in his lap. At intervals he strums it softly. Slightly separated from the group, down front, crouches CISSIE. She sits like a graven image, except that from time to time her hand reaches out and touches the blade of the huge cane knife that lies beside her. The women are talking in whispers, glancing at CISSIE. Darkness and chill lie like a pall upon the room. A moment passes.

CISSIE. (*without turning her head*) Look out, Phoebe, see if hit ain't mos' sun-up.

(*The slaves hold their breath and every eye, except CISSIE's, follows PHOEBE as she goes to the door and opens it. Outside there is only darkness. A sigh of relaxation comes from the group.*)

PHOEBE. No, hit's still dark.

AUNT SUE. (*devoutly*) Tank yo', Jesus!

PHOEBE. (*still looking out, speaks again*) Why, hyear comes somebody!

(*Pause*) Hit's Uncle Dave . . . Uncle Dave from way ovah Green's plantation.

(*Several join PHOEBE at the door. In a moment an old man enters, walking feebly. His hair is a white halo about a gentle, wrinkled face. He is greeted warmly.*)

VOICES. Howdy, Uncle Dave.

Good mawnin', Uncle Dave.

Come right in.

ROSE. Praise da Lawd! Maybe she'll

listen to yo', Uncle Dave.

PHOEBE. Lawsy mussy! Yo'all ain't come all trough dat black swamp by yo'self, is yo'?

UNCLE DAVE. (*His voice is rich, and in it sounds the music of deep rivers.*)

Yes, chile,

Ah heared da han' ob God lay hebby on yo',

Ah prayed da master'd get me hyear on time. (*He looks around*) Whar be da chilluns?

ROSE. (*Pointing towards the other room*) In dar . . . Sleepin'.

ROSE. (*continuing*)

Dey eat dere full an' all us dance an' sing,

An' Cissie, dere, lafs loudes' of us all . . .

Po' lam's, deys plum tuck out, an' so dey sleepin' sound.

UNCLE DAVE. Thank God! An' Cissie . . . ?

(*The group opens up allowing him to see* CISSIE *who sits unheeding and motionless.*)

PHOEBE. (*loudly*) Hit's all dat black Lou's fault.

(*She is interrupted by several who motion warningly towards the other room.*)

VOICES. Sh-sh-sh-sh-sh!

She'll hyear!

(PHOEBE *continues angrily, but in a lower voice.*)

PHOEBE. She put a spell on Cissie,

Shuttin' huh eyes an' stoppin'

up huh ears tuh evahting

dat we kin do an' say.

She gotta evil eye,

Dat's what she got!

UNCLE DAVE. Dar now, daughtah,

De Lawd takes care ob his own,

Us ain't got no cause tuh fret.

(*A wavering wail comes softly from the banjo. It hangs suspended in the air a moment and Cripple Jake speaks.*)

CRIPPLE JAKE. Ah'm tinkin' bout dis ting—

Hebbin is a high an' a holy place,

Da chilluns done no wrong,

Dyin' will bring 'em joy,

Da good book say, "Lam's

In His bosom—safe."

While Cissie know dat

Livin's jes a slow decay

Wid worms gnawin' lak nits

Into dey heart an' soul.

ROSE. But Cissie kain't . . .

1st WOMAN. Dey'll beat huh mos' tuh death!

2nd WOMAN. She'll be a mu'deress!

3nd WOMAN. She'll bu'n in hell!

CRIPPLE JAKE. Yes, Cissie, will be lonely—now,

An' maybe fuh a t'ousand yeahs tuh come.

(*They turn at the unexpected sound of* CISSIE's *voice. It is low and vibrant.*)

CISSIE. But, when da saints ob God go marchin' home

Mah gal will sing! Wid all da pure, bright stars,

Tuhgedder wid da mawnin' stars—She'll sing!

(CISSIE's *head is lifted and for one moment a strange beauty illumines her black, gaunt face. A soft chord sounds from the banjo, gentle as wings brushing across the strings.*)

UNCLE DAVE. (*sternly*) We be forgettin' God!

Didn't He bring Daniel out ob da lion's den,

An' da Hebrew chillun out da fiery furnace,

Didn't He open up da Red Sea,

An' save Jonah from da belly ob da whale?

WOMEN. (*fervently*)Yes, ma Lawd!

Save us, Jesus.

(*The women begin to rock back and forth, humming softly.* UNCLE DAVE *moves down stage to* CISSIE. *He places his hand on her shoulder. She starts violently, but when she sees who it is she sinks back. The light has faded from her face.*)

WOMAN. (*Singing, with humming accompaniment.*)

Ah want Jesus tuh walk wid me,

Ah want Jesus tuh walk wid me,

All along mah hebbenly journey,

Ah want Jesus tuh walk wid me.

In mah sorrow, walk wid me,

In mah sorrow, walk wid me,

When mah hea't wid' in is breakin',

Ah want Jesus tuh walk wid me.

(*The singing sinks to a hum*)

UNCLE DAVE. Kain't yo' trus' de Lawd, daughtah? Hit's al wid Him. Yo' kain' stain yo' han's wid da blood ob yo' own chilluns.

CISSIE. (*wearily*) Ah tought da time is come. Dat man comin' fuh 'em at sun-sup.

UNCLE DAVE. (*fallen on his knees*)
Oh, Lawd! Our Lawd!
Sittin' on yo' great white throne,
Wid da stars a crown o' beauty fur
    yo' haid,
An' de earth a mighty footstool fur
    yo' feet,
Lean down ovah da ramparts of
    Hebbin dis mawnin'
An' see us 'umble sinners kneelin'
    hyear.
We been prayin' so long,
We been singin' so . . .

(*From the outside is heard the sound of a galloping horse. It draws rapidly nearer. There is the sound of pawing feet just outside the door. The horse neighs and in a moment comes loud knocking on the door.*)

VOICE. Open the door! Open the door!

CISSIE. Da man! He's come!

(CISSIE *clutches the knife, but does not yet rise. The slaves watch her terrified. Two men spring forward to hold the door. A woman cautiously cracks the shutter and peeps out. She jerks back and speaks with surprise.*)

WOMAN. Hit's a soldier!

VOICES. Soldiers?

(*The slaves spring up, perplexed, crowd to the window trying to see. The men are uncertain whether or not to hold the door. The pounding becomes more purposeful. The door is giving way.* CISSIE *rises swiftly. This new excitement means nothing to her. The time has come. Knife in hand, she slips unnoticed into the inner room. Just as she disappears, the outer door gives way admitting a white soldier. He is hardly more than a boy. His face is pale with emotion and, though he wears a torn and dusty blue uniform, he stands there poised like some radiant messenger of glad tidings. Behind him the sky is turning rosy with the dawn. He points upward, his voice exalting.*)

SOLDIER. Look! Look, the day has come!
The day for which we fought.
Stilled for a moment are the guns
And from the fallow earth do rise
The souls of those who fell
That they might see you go forth
Free to greet this Dawn!

(*The eager black folks gather round him at the door, questioning, their faces lifted.*)

VOICES. Free? Free?

SOLDIER. Free! Do you understand?

You're free! No longer slaves.

Loud sound the bugles and the drums,

The mighty armies march—

For this day sets you free!

(*While the soldier has been speaking from the distance, borne upon the fresh, morning breeze, comes spirited, marching music.*)

UNCLE DAVE. (*He falls upon his knees and lifts his hands towards the rising sun.*)

Thank God! Oh! Thank—

(*His words are cut short by a scream of terror coming from the inner room. Like puppets fastened on a single string, the black folks give a startled jerk and then freeze motionless. Outside the music draws nearer while from the room backs little PETE, his mouth still distended with his scream, his eyes dilated. There is a moment of tense waiting and CISSIE comes through the door, walking slowly and deliberately. In her arms is the lifeless body of MILLIE, her head fallen back. Cissie advances into the room towards the soldier, her face a deeply chiseled mask in ebony, with set, unseeing eyes.*)

CISSIE. Yo' come too late.

Mah gal is dead! Da boy yo' didn't wan' no how,

He's wo'thless in da fields—he is too weak.

But huh. . . . (*She extends the soft body*)

See how huh red blood falls hyear in da sun,

Hit's warm an' pure. . . . Come, dip yo' han's in it

She will not shrink away—Huh teahs will nevah

Choke huh song nor will huh limbs grow hebby

wid dispair. Mah gal is dead!

(*Everyone has crouched back except the young soldier, who stands as if paralyzed, his face turning white. Now, he finds his voice.*)

SOLDIER. My God! My God! What? What . . .

UNCLE DAVE. (*speaking from his knees*)

Cissie! Cissie, dis—dis ain't da man.

Dis am a Yankee soldier, come tuh tell us

Dat we's. . . .

(*The old man cannot finish. The word chokes in his throat. He buries his face in his hands. Outside a chorus of happy, singing voices is swelling, forming a joyous obligato to the music of the band.*)

VOICES. (*singing*)

Free, Free, Free

    Ah'm free, lil chillun,

Free! Free!

Free! Free! Free!

    Oh! Da sun ob God

Does sot us free dis mawnin'!

(*Through the door behind* CISSIE *has come* GRANNIE LOU. *She stumbles, rubbing her sleep-heavy eyes and shaking her shriveled frame. She sees Cissie facing the white man and her clouded brain can take in only one meaning for the scene.*)

SOLDIER. (*speaking gently to* CISSIE)

Do you hear them?

You're no longer a slave! You—

(*He is stopped by a burst of wild, loud laughter from* GRANNIE, *who points her skinny finger at the limp body.*)

GRANNIE. He! He! He! Ha! Ha! Ha!

Ah tole yo' . . . She don' hab tuh go!

He! He! He!

(*Several women rush to* GRANNIE, *soothing her as they would a child. Only bewilderment shows in* CISSIE's *face, but the boy soldier's poise is completely shattered. Flinging up his hand to shut out the sight, vainly trying to stop his ears, he rushes out into the morning sunshine. Two or three men follow him. Gradually Grannie is quieted. They lead her back into the sleeping room. Little* PETE *has buried his face in* AUNT SUE's *deep bosom. He is still shaking, but makes no sound. The women have dropped to their knees. They rock their bodies and give an occasional moan.*)

(CISSIE *walks to the door, her inert burden clasped to her breast. For a moment she stands in the bright sunshine, gazing out. The music has gradually diminished into the distance and now may be heard only faintly. The dew-drenched earth is sweet, bathed in the pure sunshine of the newborn day. Somewhere in the yard a cock crows. Cissie looks down into her child's face and speaks quietly.*)

CISSIE. Hit's mawnin'!

(*And from her throat there comes a cry of anguish as she falls to her knees. Above her, on the door, a single spray of mistletoe sways in the morning breeze and then falls gently on the upturned face of the child.*)

CURTAIN

It's Morning was performed at the Yale University Theatre, New Haven, Connecticut, on 5–7 February 1940, directed by Frederick Coe. It is published in *Black Female Playwrights: An Anthology of Plays before 1950*, edited by Kathy Perkins (Bloomington, Indiana: Indiana University Press, 1990), 211–24.

Frances Ellen Watkins Harper

Frances Ellen Watkins was born in 1825 as a free woman in Baltimore, Maryland. She attended the Academy for Negro Youth, which her uncle, William Watkins, ran. Her first book of poetry, *Autumn Leaves*, appeared in print in 1845. She was a prolific writer of poetry, journalism, and fiction. In the 1850s, after Congress strengthened the Fugitive Slave Act, Harper moved to Philadelphia and worked on the Underground Railroad. She was a highly regarded feminist and abolitionist lecturer, and in 1859, she became the first black writer in the United States to publish a short story. In 1860, Frances Watkins married Fenton Harper but would become a widow in 1864. She later became one of the founders of the National Association of Colored Women, serving as president for over fifteen years. Frances Harper died in 1911 in Philadelphia.

An Appeal to My Countrywomen

You can sigh o'er the sad-eyed Armenian
Who weeps in her desolate home.
You can mourn o'er the exile of Russia
From kindred and friends doomed to roam.

You can pity the men who have woven
From passion and appetite chains
To coil with a terrible tension
Around their heartstrings and brains.

You can sorrow o'er little children
Disinherited from their birth,
The wee waifs and toddlers neglected,
Robbed of sunshine, music and mirth.

For beasts you have gentle compassion;
Your mercy and pity they share.
For the wretched, outcast and fallen
You have tenderness, love and care.

But hark! from our Southland are floating
Sobs of anguish, murmurs of pain,
And women heart-stricken are weeping
Over their tortured and their slain.

On their brows the sun has left traces;
Shrink not from their sorrow in scorn.
When they entered the threshold of being
The children of a King were born.

Each comes as a guest to the table
The hand of our God has outspread,
To fountains that ever leap upward,
To share in the soil we all tread.

When ye plead for the wrecked and fallen,
The exile from far-distant shores,
Remember that men are still wasting
Life's crimson around your own doors.

Have ye not, oh, my favored sisters,
Just a plea, a prayer or a tear,
For mothers who dwell 'neath the shadows
Of agony, hatred and fear?

Men may tread down the poor and lowly,
May crush them in anger and hate,
But surely the mills of God's justice
Will grind out the grist of their fate.

Oh, people sin-laden and guilty,
So lusty and proud in your prime,
The sharp sickles of God's retribution
Will gather your harvest of crime.

Weep not, oh my well-sheltered sisters,
Weep not for the Negro alone,
But weep for your sons who must gather
The crops which their fathers have sown.

Go read on the tombstones of nations
Of chieftains who masterful trod,
The sentence which time has engraven,
That they had forgotten their God.

'Tis the judgment of God that men reap
The tares which in madness they sow,
Sorrow follows the footsteps of crime,
And Sin is the consort of Woe.

"An Appeal to My Countrywomen," in *Poems on Miscellaneous Subjects* (Boston: J. B. Yerrinton & Son, 1871).

Related writings by Frances Ellen Watkins Harper: "Bury Me in a Free Land" (1858); "To the Cleveland Union-Savers" (1861); "The Massachusetts Fifty-Fourth" (1863); "Lines to Miles O'Reiley" (also titled "The Other Side"; 1867); *Minnie's Sacrifice* (1869); "Words for the Hour" (1871); "The Deliverance" (1872); *Iola Leroy, or, Shadows Uplifted* (1892).

George Moses Horton

George Moses Horton was born around 1797 in North Carolina. He and his maternal family were owned as property by William Horton. George Moses Horton wrote his first collection of poems, *The Hope of Liberty*, to raise funds so he could buy his freedom and emigrate to Liberia. In 1845, he contributed a narrative of his life to a collection of his poems edited by Dennis Heartt. Horton probably died sometime in the 1880s in Philadelphia.

Jefferson in a Tight Place[109]

The Fox Is Caught
> The blood hounds, long upon the trail,
> Have rambled faithful, hill and dale;
> But mind, such creatures never fail,
>> To run the rebel down.
> His fears forbid him long to stop,
> Altho' he gains the mountain top,
> He soon is made his tail to drop,
>> And fleets to leave the hounds.

> Alas! He speeds from place to place,
> Such is the fox upon the chase;
> To him the mud is no disgrace,
>> No lair his cause defends.
> He leaves a law and seeks a dell,
> And where to fly 'tis hard to tell;
> He fears before to meet with hell;
>> Behind he has no friends.

> But who can pity such a fox,
> Though buried among the rocks?
> He's a nuisance among the flocks.
>> And sucks the blood of geese.
> He takes advantage of the sheep,
> His nature is at night to creep,
> And rob the flocks while the herdsmen sleep,
>> When dogs can have no peace.

But he is now brought to a bay,
However fast he run away,
He knows he has not long to stay,
    And assumes a raccoon's dress.
Found in a hole, he veils his face,
And fain would take a lady's place,[110]
But fails, for he has run his race,
    And falls into distress.

The fox is captured in his den,
The martial troops of Michigan
May hence be known the fleetest men,
    For Davis is their prey.
Great Babylon has fallen down,
A King is left without a crown,
Stripped of honors and renown,
    The evening ends the day.

"Jefferson in a Tight Place," in *Naked Genius* (Raleigh, North Carolina: W. B. Smith & Co., Publisher, 1865).

Related writings by George Moses Horton: "Liberty and Slavery" (1829); "Like Brothers We Met" (1865); "Lincoln Is Dead" (1865); "General Grant—The Hero of the War" (1865); "The Spectator of the Battle of Belmont" (1865); "The Dying Soldier's Message" (1865); "The Soldier on His Way Home" (1865); "Weep" (1865).

FENTON JOHNSON

A native of Chicago, Fenton Johnson was born into a well-to-do black family in 1888. He was a poet, playwright, fiction writer, and journalist. He co-founded two monthly magazines *The Champion* (1916) and *The Favorite* (1918). At the time of his death in 1958, Johnson had published three collections of poetry, a book of essays, and a short story collection.

De Ol' Sojer[111]

You say dat Ah ain't got no kintry nor no flag?
Dat Ah's a man dat's lowah dan de wustes' beast?
Look hyeah, you heish yo' mouf! You's dumb as any brute!
You see de stahs? You see de stripes dat mak' dis rag?
Ah cai'ed dem clean thoo all de thickes' ob de fight[112]
At Gettysbu'g an' Chattanooga[113] w'en ol' Def
Was rakin' in de men lak leaves dat drap an' drap
An' lay erpon de groun' ontwell dey tu'n to ash an' dust.
Ah fought to mak' dis lan a lan dat's free f'om wrong,
Dat dipped in blood will rise again, befo No'th an' Souf,
Ontwell it reach de blessed Th'one ob Gawd Hisse'f.

W'en Marstuh Lincum called de colo'ed man to fight
Huh! huh! Ah left de ol' plantashun quick as sin,
An' ran to whaih de Yankee ahmy held daih camp.
De Cunnle[114] wrapped de flag erroun' mah achin' bones,—
"Dis man is free!" he sayed, an' held up high his swo'd.
De sojers bowed, an' trumpets blowed—an' Ah was free.
Ah loved de Cunnle, an' Ah loved dat shiny flag,—
De stahs jes' lak de eyes ob Gawd on Freedom's night,
De stripes jes' lak what anguls waih on battlefiel's;
An' deep down' neaf de coat o' blue[115] dey put on me
Mah hea't was beatin' fu' to see dat flag triumph.
Thoo wintah snow, thoo summah heat Ah wu'ked an' bled,
An' faced de bullets dat de ribels shot at us,
Ontwell one day w'en Johnny' ribs[116] was lickin' us
De Cunnle say, "What man is brave enough to go
An' place his kintry's flag erpon de 'Federate fo't?"[117]
Not one would speak, de braves' 'mongst dem white wid feah,

An' Ah mahse'f all trimblin' to mah ve'y boot tops.
De Cunnle add: "Unless we git dat fo't we fail."
'Twas den Ah spoke, an' spoke mah wo'ds so brave an' true,
"Gib me de flag! To-night, good sah, dat fo't is yo'n!"
W'en night come on Ah ma'ched ahaid ob all de troops,
De Stahs an' Stripes awavin' in de summah breeze,
De gray coat[118] bayonets a-p'intin' at mah breas',
All ready fu' to jab dis body thoo an' thoo;
But w'en de moonlight pou'ed upon dis face o' mine
White tu'ned de ribel Gin'ul, an' he cried, "A slave!
A da'ky slave! O Gawd, hab muss on us all!"
De graycoats fiahed, de bullets rainin' thick as hail,
Dey got me in de hip, dey got me in de leg,
But Gawd dat led ol' Isr'ul was erpon mah side
An' Ah was strong enough to keep f'om earf dat flag.
De bluecoats an' de graycoats fought lak brothahs fight
While Ah went on an' on ontwell Ah retched de fo't
An' nailed ol' Marstuh Lincum's flag erpon de post.
Dey tote me back erpon de stretchah, so' wid' pain,
But on mah face de smile dat only fightahs smile,
A hero in de cause ob kintry, home an' Gawd.

An' w'en de kintry say dat Cuby[119] must be free
Mah boy, mah Lizy's Sam went fo'th to wah,
Ah gib him to de cause, an' tol' him fight lak sin
To keep de Stahs an' Stripes f'om drappin' to the groun'.
He lies somewhaih—mah Lizy's boy!—he lies somewhaih,
A bullet in his hea't, de flag erpon his breas'.
O Gawd ob Jacob, smile erpon dis Glohry rag
An' tell de folks dat he who fought to save daih lan'
Am jes' as much a sojer ob de Stahs an' Stripes
As any livin' No'th o' South, East o' West.

"De Ol' Sojer," in *Songs of the Soil* (New York: Trachtenberg Co, 1916), 13–15.

Related writings by Fenton Johnson: "The Soldiers of the Dusk" (1915); "Jubal's Free" (1915); "Mary on August the First" (1915).

BOSTON KING

Boston King was born into slavery in South Carolina around 1760 in what is now Charleston. His owner moved to the countryside after hearing rumors that British troops were coming to the city. During the British occupation of Charleston in 1780, King sought refuge with the British and fought as a Loyalist during the war. After the war, he settled in the Canadian province of Nova Scotia. The editors of *Methodist Magazine* serialized his "Memoirs of the Life of Boston King, a Black Preacher." King later settled in Sierra Leone, West Africa, where he taught (after receiving teacher training) and served as a missionary. He died in Sierra Leone in 1802.

From "Freedom and fear fighting for the Loyalists"[120]

[...] To escape [...] cruelty, I determined to go to Charles-Town, and I began to feel the happiness of liberty, of which I knew nothing before, although I was much grieved at first, to be obliged to leave my friends, and reside among strangers. [...]

I marched with the army to Chamblen[121]. [...] I tarried [...] about a year, and then left [...] and came to Nelson's-ferry.[122] Here I entered into the service of the commanding officer of that place. But our situation was very precarious, and we expected to be made prisoners every day; for the Americans had 1600 men, not far off; whereas our whole number amounted only to 250. But there were 1200 English about 30 miles off; only we knew not how to inform them of our danger, as the Americans were in possession of the country. Our commander at length determined to send me with a letter, promising me great rewards, if I was successful in the business. I refused going on horse-back, and set off on foot about 3 o'clock in the afternoon; I expected every moment to fall in with the enemy, whom I well knew would shew me no mercy. I went on without interruption, till I got within six miles of my journey's end, and then was alarmed with a great noise a little before me. But I stepped out of the road, and fell flat upon my face till they were gone by. I then arose, and praised the Name of the Lord for his great mercy and again pursued my journey, till I came to Mums-corner tavern. I knocked at the door, but they blew out the candle. I knocked again, and entreated the master to open the door. At last he came with a frightful countenance, and said, "I thought it was the Americans; for they were here about an hour ago, and I thought they were returned again." I asked, How many were there? He answered, "about one hundred."

I desired him to saddle his horse for me, which he did, and he went with me himself. When we had gone about two miles, we were stopped by the picket-guard, till the Captain came out with 30 men. As soon as he knew that I had brought an express from Nelson's-ferry, he received me with great kindness, and expressed his approbation of my courage and conduct in this dangerous business. Next morning, [the commanding officer] gave me three shillings, and many fine promises, which were all that I ever received for this service from him. However, he sent 600 men to relieve the troops at Nelson's ferry.

Soon after I went to Charles-Town, and entered on board a man of war. We stayed in the bay two days, and then sailed for New York, where I went on shore. [...]

In 1783, the horrors and devastation of the war happily terminated, and peace was restored between America and Great Britain, which diffused universal joy among all parties, except us, who had escaped from slavery, and taken refuge in the English army; for a report prevailed at New York, that all the slaves, in number 2000, were to be delivered up to their masters, although some of them had been three or four years among the English. This dreadful rumour filled us all with inexpressible anguish and terror, especially when we saw our old masters coming from Virginia, North Carolina, and other parts, and seizing up their slaves in the streets of New York, or even dragging them out of their beds. Many of the slaves had very cruel masters, so that the thoughts of returning home with them embittered life to us. For some days we lost our appetite for food, and sleep departed from our eyes. The English had compassion on us in the day of distress, and issued out a Proclamation, importing, that all slaves should be free who had taken refuge in the British lines, and claimed the sanction and privileges of the Proclamations respecting the security and protection of negroes. In consequence of this, each of us received a certificate from the commanding officer at New-York, which dispelled all our fears, and filled us with joy and gratitude. Soon after, ships were fitted out, and furnished with every necessary for conveying us to Nova Scotia. We arrived at Burch Town in the month of August, where we all safely landed. Every family had a lot of land, and we exerted all our strength in order to build comfortable huts before the cold weather set in. [...]

"Memoirs of the Life of Boston King, a Black Preacher. Written by Himself, during his Residence at Kingswood School," *The Methodist Magazine*, March–June 1798.

DUDLEY RANDALL

A veteran of World War II, writer, publisher, librarian, and the founder of Broadside Press in 1965, Dudley Randall was born in 1914 in Washington, D.C. into a middle-class family. His family moved to Detroit when he was a child. He published six volumes of poetry from 1966 to 1981. Randall also edited the important collection, *The Black Poets*, in 1971. He was the first poet laureate of Detroit and spent much of his life in that city. Randall died in Detroit in 2000.

Memorial Wreath[123]

(*It is a little known fact that 200,000 Negroes fought for freedom in the Union Army during the Civil War.*)

In this green month when resurrected flowers,
Like laughing children ignorant of death,
Brighten the couch of those who wake no more,
Love and remembrance blossom in our hearts
For you who bore the extreme sharp pang for us,
And bought our freedom with your lives.

                                    And now,
Honoring your memory, with love we bring
These fiery roses, white-hot cotton flowers
And violets bluer than cool northern skies
You dreamed of stooped in burning prison fields
When liberty was only a faint north star,
Not a bright flower planted by your hands
Reaching up hardy nourished with your blood.

Fit grave fellows you are for Douglass, Brown,
Turner and Truth and Tubman[124] . . . whose rapt eyes
Fashioned a new world in this wilderness.

American earth is richer for your bones;
Our hearts beat prouder for the blood we inherit.

Negro History Bulletin 26, no. 1 (1962): 76.

Related writings by Dudley Randall: "Roses and Revolution" (1948); "The Southern Road" (1966); "Shoe Shine Boy" (1966); "Pacific Epitaphs" (1970); "Straight Talk from a Patriot" (1970); "Courage: A Revolutionary Poem" (1973); "Blood Precious Blood" (1981).

HENRIETTA CORDELIA RAY

Henrietta Cordelia Ray was born into an abolitionist family around 1852 in New York City, where she would live until her death in 1916. She earned a degree from the University of the City of New York and then worked as a teacher and writer. Her writing received national recognition in 1876 when her poem "Lincoln" was featured at the dedication of the Freedmen's Memorial Monument in Washington, D.C. Her first book of poetry, *Sonnets*, was published in 1893, and her second book, *Poems*, appeared in print in 1910, collecting new poetry along with poems from her earlier book.

Robert G. Shaw[125]

When War's red banners trailed along the sky,
And many a manly heart grew all aflame
With patriotic love and purest aim,
There rose a noble soul who dared to die,
If only Right could win. He heard the cry
Of struggling bondmen and he quickly came,
Leaving haunts where learning tenders fame
Unto her honored sons; for it was ay
A loftier cause that lured him on to death.
Brave men who saw their brothers held in chains
Beneath his standard battled ardently.
O friend! O hero! Thou who yielded breath
That others might share Freedom's priceless gains,
In rev'rent love we guard thy memory.

"Robert F. Shaw,"[126] in *Poems* (New York: Grafton Press, 1910), 88.

Related writing by Henrietta Cordelia Ray: "Lincoln" (1876 at the Freedmen's Memorial; 1910).

GEORGE CLINTON ROWE

George Clinton Rowe was born in Litchfield, Connecticut in 1853. He left Litchfield in 1876 and lived in Virginia, Georgia, and South Carolina. Rowe was a minister of the Plymouth Congregational Church in Charleston, an editor and publisher of the weekly *Charleston Enquirer*, and a poet. He published pamphlets on important (primarily religious) figures and of his lectures. He also collected his poetry in two books. Rowe died in 1903.

The Reason Why[127]

It is the eve of battle;
    The soldiers are in line;
The roll of drum and bugle's blast
    Marshal that army fine.

The hour is fraught with mystery—
    A hush pervades that throng,
And each one thinks of home and friends,
And says at heart, "How long?"
The colonel rides before his men,
    His thoughtful brow is bare;
He calls the color-sergeant,[128]
    And tenders to his care

The nation's pride, the dear old flag—
    The loved *red*, *white* and *blue*,
And says, with earnest tones and grave:
    "I intrust *this* now to you.

"Yes, color-bearer, take in charge
    Your country's flag to-day,
And to the conflict bear it—
    The thickest of the fray.

"Bear it with lofty courage,
    And to it faithful be;
This flag has inspired thousands,
    And led to victory.

"Take it and never leave it,

'Tis a solemn charge to thee;
Bring back to *me* this banner,
This ensign of the free!"

"Colonel," the color-sergeant said,
Holding the flag on high;
"I'll bring it back or else report
To *God* the reason why!"

Away to the front he bears it,
Cheered on by comrades brave,
Anxious to liberate his race,
Bring freedom to the slave.

They charge upon Port Hudson,[129]
Where, sheltered by a wall,
The foemen cut them down like grass.
They bravely charge—but fall.

Yes, on that field, where thousands
Unheeding the tumult lie,
He left the flag, reporting
To *God* the reason why.

Another bears that flag along,
Holding it proud and high;
But the sergeant has reported
To *God* the reason why.

Oh, Christian soldier, going forth
To battle for the Lord,
Be filled with manly courage,
And proudly bear God's word.

It is the standard of your King,
Who rules the earth and sky;
You must win, through it, the vict'ry
Or tell *Christ* the reason why.

The war will soon be ended:

In the dust you soon will lie;
Go forth and conquer, or report
To God the reason why.

"The Reason Why," in *Thoughts in Verse and a Volume of Poems* (Charleston, S.C.: Kahrs, Stolze, & Welch, 1887).

Related writing by George Clinton Rowe: *Our Heroes: Patriotic Poems on Men, Women and Sayings of the Negro Race* (1890).

SARAH E. SHUFTEN

Sarah Shuften was the wife of John T. Shuften, editor of the *Colored American*, published in Augusta, Georgia, from 1865 to 1866.

Ethiopia's Dead[130]

A tribute to the memory of her sons who have fallen in the great struggle for liberty and independence.

Brave hearts! brave Ethiopia's dead
    On hills, in valleys lie,
On every field of strife, made red
    With gory victory.

Each valley, where the battle poured
    Its purple swelling tide,
Beheld brave Ethiopia's sword
    With slaughter deeply dyed.

Their bones bleach on the Southr'n hill,
    And on the Southern plain,
By [brook], and river, lake and rill,[131]
    And by the roaring main.[132]

The land is holy where they fought,
    And holy where they fell;
For by their blood, that land was bought
    That land they loved so well—
Then glory to that valiant band,
    The honored saviors of the land.

Oh! few and weak their numbers were,
    A handful of brave men,
But up to God they sent their prayer,
    And rushed to battle, then
The God of battle heard their cry,
    And crowned their deeds with victory.

From east to west, from hill to vale,
    Then be their names adored—

Europe, with all thy millions, hail!
    The Peace bought by their sword.

Asia, and Africa shall ring
    From shore to shore, their fame;
And fair Columbia[133] shall sing,
    Their glory, and their name.

Peace, with her olive branch, shall spread
    Her wings, o'er sea and shore,
And hearts no more with terror dread
    The battle's clashing roar.

Fair Afric's *free* and valiant sons,
    Shall join with Europe's band,
To celebrate in varied tongues,
    Our *free* and happy land

Till freedom's golden fingers trace,
    A line that knows no end,
And man shall meet in every face,
    A brother and a friend.

"Ethiopia's Dead," *Colored American* 1, no. 3 (30 December 1865): 4.

JOSHUA MCCARTER SIMPSON

Joshua McCarter Simpson spent his life in Ohio, where he was born free around 1820. He worked as an indentured laborer until the age of 21, and he was a practitioner of herbal medicine who educated himself before attending Oberlin College. Simpson collected his early poetry in his first book *Original Anti-Slavery Songs*. Before his death in 1876, Simpson published a second book of poetry, *The Emancipation Car, Being an Original Composition of Anti-Slavery Ballads, Composed Exclusively for the Under Ground Railroad* (1874), in which he appended a narrative on his life titled "How I Got My Education."

Song of the "Aliened American"

My country, 'tis of thee,
Dark land of Slavery,
    In thee we groan.
Long have our chains been worn—
Long has our grief been borne—
Our flesh has long been torn,
    E'en from our bones.

The white man rules the day—
He bears despotic sway,
    O'er all the land.
He wields the Tyrant's rod,
Fearless of man or God,
And at his impious nod,
    We "fall or stand."

O! shall we longer bleed?
Is there no one to plead
    The black man's cause?
Does justice thus demand
That we shall wear the brand,
And raise not voice nor hand
    Against such laws?

No! no! the time has come,
    When we must not be dumb,

We must awake.
We now "Eight Millions Strong,"
Must strike sweet freedom's song
And plead ourselves, our wrong—
 Our chains must break.

"Song of the 'Aliened American,'" in *Original Anti-Slavery Songs* (Zanesville, Ohio: Printed for the author, 1852).

Related writings by Joshua McCarter Simpson: "Fourth of July in Alabama" (1852); "Freedom's Call" (1852); "The Emancipation Car" (1852); "Onward and Upward" (1852); "The Fifteenth Amendment" (1852); and "Let the Banner Proudly Wave" (1874).

ROBERT SMALLS

Robert Smalls was born enslaved in 1839 in South Carolina. The Confederate Navy pressed him into service as a pilot. During the absence of the white crew on 13 May 1862, he commandeered the fully armed *CSS Planter* in Charleston, delivering it to the Union Navy. This action secured his freedom and that of the other black captives on board, which included his wife and children. He then served in the Union Navy, becoming the first black captain of a U.S. vessel. After the war, he learned how to read and write and became a respected Republican state senator and a U.S. Representative for South Carolina. In 1864, Smalls told the story of his capture of the *Planter* to an A.M.E. Church audience in Philadelphia. At his death in 1915, he had resided in South Carolina.

Commandeering Freedom:
Robert Smalls Pilots the Confederate Ship *Planter*[134]

While at the wheel of the *Planter*,[135] it occurred to me that I could not only secure my own freedom but that of numbers of my comrades. Moreover, I thought that the *Planter* might be of some use to "Uncle Abe."[136] I was not long in making my thoughts known to my wife. She desired to know the consequences in case I should be caught. I replied, "I shall be shot." "It is a risk, but you and I and our little ones must be free. I will go," said she, "for where you die I will die."

I reported my plans to the crew (all colored) and secured their secrecy and co-operation. On May 13, 1862, we took on board several large guns at the Atlantic Dock. At evening of that day, the Captain went home, leaving the boat in my care. At half past 3 o'clock in the morning of the 14th, I left the Atlantic Dock with the *Planter*, took on board my family and several other families, then proceeded down Charleston River slowly. On reaching Fort Sumter I gave the signal which was answered from the fort, thereby giving permission to pass. I then made speed for the blockading fleet. When out of range of Sumter's guns, I hoisted a white flag and at 5 a.m. reached a U.S. blockading vessel, commandeered by Captain Nichols, to whom I turned over the *Planter*.

"Captain Robert Smalls Addresses the General Conference of 1864, Daniel A. Payne Presiding," reprinted in *A.M.E. Church Review*, January–March 1955, 22–23, 31.[137]

GEORGE E. STEPHENS

George E. Stephens, born in 1832, was reared in Philadelphia by free parents who had left Virginia fearing violence in the aftermath of the Nat Turner uprising. A well-educated man, he had moved in abolitionist circles before the Civil War. During the war, he first volunteered as a cook and then enlisted in the 54th Massachusetts Volunteer Infantry in April 1863 as a first sergeant. After Stephens was wounded at Fort Wagner, he was mustered out of the army in July 1865 at the rank of first lieutenant. During the war, he regularly sent letters from the field to the *New York Weekly*. Stephens died in New York in 1888.

"How dare I be offered half the pay of any man, be he white or red?"[138]

Morris Island, S.C.
Aug. 1, 1864

Mr. Editor:

Two or three months ago, it was announced that Congress had passed a law equalizing the pay of colored troops. This was at the closing period of the session. The colored troops, which had been enlisted under the law of 1862, were unpaid. This was known, of course, at Washington. The noble Major [George] Stearns[139] was compelled to resign, because the pledges he had been authorized by Sec. [Edwin] Stanton[140] to make to the colored man were broken by the War Department, who refused to pay soldiers who had black skins more than seven dollars per month.

Thus free men were reduced to servitude. No matter what services he might render—no matter how nobly he might acquit himself—he must carry with him the degradation of not being considered a man, but a thing. The foreigner, the alien, of whatever color, or race, or country, are enrolled and paid like native Americans; but the latest refinement of cruelty has been brought to bear on us.

In the Revolutionary War, and in the War of 1812, colored men fought, and were enrolled, and paid, the same as the whites; and not only this, were drilled and enlisted indiscriminately in the same companies and regiments. Little did our forefathers think that they were forging chains for the limbs of their own race. Look how nobly [James] Forten, [John C.] Bowers, and [Joseph] Cassey,[141] and those colored patriots of the last war, rallied to the defence of Philadelphia; yet how were the colored people repaid? By stripping them in '36[142] of their right of franchise. Now the plan is to inveigle the black man into the service by false pretences, and then make him take half pay. If he doesn't take half pay and behave himself, as a vender[143] of religious tracts down here said, "Shoot 'em." Why, sir, the rebels have not reached the daring extreme of reducing free men to slaves. Does the Lincoln despotism think it can succeed? There are those who say, you should not talk so—"you hurt yourself." Let me say to those men, we cannot be injured more. There is no insult—there is no cruelty—there is no wrong, which we have not suffered. Torture, massacre, mobs and slavery. Do you think that we will tamely submit like spaniels to every indignity?

I shall speak hereafter my wrongs, and nothing shall prevent me but double irons or a pistol-ball that shall take me out of the hell I am now suffering: nearly eighteen months of service—of labor—of humiliation—of danger, and not one dollar. An estimable wife reduced to beggary, and dependent upon another man—what can wipe out the wrong and insult this Lincoln despotism has put upon us? Loyal men everywhere hurl it from power—dismember it—grind it to atoms! Who would have believed that all the newspaper talk of the pay of colored soldiers having been settled by Congress was a base falsehood? There is not the least sign of pay, and there are hints from those in authority that we will not get paid, and will be held to service by the terrors of our own bullets. Seventeen months and upwards! Suppose we had been white? Massachusetts would have inaugurated a rebellion in the East, and we would have been paid. But—Oh, how insulting!—because I am black, they tamper with my rights. How dare I be offered half the pay of any man, be he white or red.

This matter of pay seems to some of those having slaveholding tendencies a small thing, but it belongs to that system which has stripped the country of the flower of its youth. It has rendered every hamlet and fire-side in this wide country desolate and brought the country itself to bankruptcy and shame. It is a concomitant of the system. Like as the foaming waves point the mariner to the hidden rocks on which his storm-driven ship will soon be lost, this gross injustice reveals to us the hidden insidious principles on which the best hopes of the true patriot will be dashed.

G.E.S.

The Weekly Anglo-African (New York), 27 August 1864.[144]

SUSIE BAKER KING TAYLOR

Susie Baker was born into slavery in 1848 in Georgia. She traced her lineage to the first of her known enslaved relatives brought to the Georgia colony in the 1730s and found that her ancestry included persons who had served in the American Revolution. She used her knowledge of this lineage to assert her patriotic claim to the nation. During the Civil War, King traveled with her first husband, Edward King, a noncommissioned black officer in the Union Army. In 1863, she served as a cook, laundress, and nurse for the 1st South Carolina Volunteers (United States Colored Troops); in 1864, she was a laundress and nurse for the regiment. After the war, she taught freedmen in Georgia, then moved to New England, where she married again and became a founding member and later president of the Women's Relief Corps of the Grand Army of the Republic #67 in Boston. King self-published *Reminiscences of My Life in Camp with the 33rd United States Colored Troops* in 1902. She died in Boston in 1912.

A Nurse for the 33rd USCT[145]

[1863]

Some mornings I would go along the picket line, and I could see the rebels on the opposite side of the river. Sometimes as they were charging pickets they would call over to our men and ask for something to eat, or for tobacco, and our men would tell them to come over. Sometimes one or two would desert to us, saying, they "had no negroes to fight for." [. . .]

* * *

[1864]

Fort Wagner being only a mile from our camp, I went there two or three times a week, and would go up on the ramparts to watch the gunners send their shells into Charleston (which they did every fifteen minutes), and had a full view of the city from that point. Outside the fort there were many skulls lying about; I have often moved them [to] one side out of the path. The comrades and I would have quite a debate as to which side the men fought on. Some thought they were the skulls of our boys; others thought they were the enemy's; but as there was no definite way to know, it was never decided which could lay claim to them. They were a gruesome sight, those fleshless heads and grinning jaws, but by this time I had become accustomed to worse things and did not feel as I might have earlier in my camp life.

It seems strange how our aversion to seeing suffering is overcome in war,—how we are able to see the most sickening sights such as men with their limbs blown off and mangled by the deadly shells, without a shudder; and instead of turning away, how we hurry to assist in alleviating their pain, bind up their wounds, and press the cool water to their parched lips, with feelings only of sympathy and pity. [...]

Excerpted from *Reminiscences of My Life in Camp with the 33rd United States Colored Troops Late 1st S. C. Volunteers* (Boston: Published by the author, 1902).

LUCY TERRY PRINCE

Lucy Terry was born around 1724 in Africa, where she was kidnapped as a child and sold into slavery in colonial British North America. During the French and Indian Wars, she lived in Deerfield, Massachusetts, where she witnessed a surprise battle initiated by Indigenous men during the war. Terry's folk poem "Bars Fight," presented locally in 1746, records the incident. The poem was passed down orally for over a century before it was published in 1855. Terry later married Abijah Prince, a veteran of the wars who had obtained his freedom and purchased his wife's liberty. To save the family's property from terroristic attacks in southern Vermont, Lucy Terry Prince reportedly presented her case, with the help of a local official, before the Supreme Court in Vermont, even though she had no legal training. At the time of her death in 1821, Lucy Terry Prince lived in Vermont.

Bars Fight[146]

August 'twas the twenty-fifth,
Seventeen hundred forty-six,
The Indians did in ambush lay,
Some very valiant men to slay,
The names of whom I'll not leave out:
Samuel Allen like a hero fout,
And though he was so brave and bold,
His face no more shall we behold.

Eleazer Hawks was killed outright,
Before he had time to fight,—
Before he did the Indians see,
Was shot and killed immediately.

Oliver Amsden he was slain,
Which caused his friends much grief and pain.
Simeon Amsden they found dead
Not many rods distant from his head.

Adonijah Gillett, we do hear,
Did lose his life which was so dear,
John Sadler fled across the water,
And thus escaped the dreadful slaughter.

Eunice Allen see the Indians coming,
And hopes to save herself by running;
And had not her petticoats stopped her,
The awful creatures had not catched her,
Nor tommy hawked her on the head,
And left her on the ground for dead.
Young Samuel Allen, Oh, lack-a-day!
Was taken and carried to Canada.

"Bars Fight," in Josiah G. Holland, *History of Western Massachusetts*, vol. 2, part 3 (Springfield, Mass.: S. Bowles and Co., 1855), 360.

Natasha Trethewey

Born in Mississippi in 1966, Trethewey won the Pulitzer Prize for Poetry in 2007 for *Native Guard*. From 2012–2014, she served as the U. S. Poet Laureate Consultant in Poetry, appointed by the Library of Congress. She is the poet laureate of Mississippi and the director of creative writing at Emory University.

Elegy for the Native Guards[147]

Now that the salt of their blood Stiffens the saltier oblivion of the sea . . .

ALLEN TATE

We leave Gulfport at noon; gulls overhead
trailing the boat—streamers, noisy fanfare—
all the way to Ship Island.[148] What we see
first is the fort, its roof of grass, a lee[149]—
half reminder of the men who served there—
a weathered monument to some of the dead.

Inside we follow the ranger, hurried though
we are to get to the beach. He tells of graves
lost in the Gulf, the island split in half when
Hurricane Camille[150] hit,
shows us casemates,[151] cannons, the store that sells
souvenirs, tokens of history long buried.

The Daughters of the Confederacy[152]
has placed a plaque here, at the fort's entrance—
each Confederate soldier's name raised hard
in bronze; no names carved for the Native Guards—
2nd Regiment, Union men, black phalanx.[153]
What is monument to their legacy?
All the grave markers, all the crude headstones—
water-lost. Now fish dart among their bones,
and we listen for what the waves intone.
Only the fort remains, near forty feet high,
round, unfinished, half open to the sky,
the elements—wind, rain—God's deliberate eye.

"Elegy for the Native Guards," in *Native Guard: Poems* (New York: Houghton Mifflin, 2006), 44.

James Monroe Trotter

James Monroe Trotter was among the spokesmen when the soldiers of the 55th Massachusetts Infantry fought for equal pay for their service. Born into slavery sometime around 1842 in Mississippi, the child of a white father and an enslaved mother, Trotter and his mother later moved to Ohio; his father had relocated them so that they could live free after the father's marriage to a white woman. In 1878, Trotter published a book on African American music, *Music and Some Highly Musical People*. He married Virginia Isaacs, a descendant of Sally Hemmings, with whom President Jefferson had children. He was the father of William Monroe Trotter, the prominent newspaperman and advocate for equality. On 26 February 1892, James Monroe Trotter died in Boston.

The Fifty-Fourth at Wagner[154]

With Time's sure march came the day at last
  when slavery's strength
Defiance spoke, seemed all-potential, through
  the country's length;
In God's own time came the day at last, long
  much desired,
When black men, armed, themselves and friends
  with longing fired
To strike the monster wrong avenging deadliest
  blow;
To give the proof that, in contest with the country's
  common foe,
The spirit of liberty fills all men's souls, and in
  them burns alike,
While with it all may win when for it all in
  heart and hand unite.
"To arms! to arms!" with unpent souls, their
  valorous leaders cried;
"Now call they for help who erst[155] so long, so
  bitterly denied;
Strike, strike ye for freedom! rush quickly to
  the fore!
Thy great wrongs now forgot, but be slaves
  nevermore!"

And so, with gladdened eagerness, in hosts they
   bravely came
From North, from East, from West, and many,
   too, from Southern cane,
These dusky warriors, with life in hand, with
   purpose great,
To swell our ranks, to charge the foe, and
   honor give a race and state.
Night had her mantle thrown o'er Charleston's
   warlike isle;[156]
Silent, grim was Wagner; Sumter,[157] erst thunder-
   tongued, rested, while
All seemed peace, yet two armies, prepared for
   devastating fray.
Still, eager vigil kept far more than if 'twere
   open day.
"To front of column, Massachusetts fifty-
   fourth!" Thus the order came.
"'Tis what we wish!" their gallant Shaw[158] exultingly
   did quick exclaim;
"With most at stake, my men undaunted now
   do claim this hour
To glorious victory gain, at least to show no
   fear of slavery's power."
Momentous hour! A race on trial, which oft in
   this and other lands
Had filled the deadly breach, had helped to
   burst foul slavery's bands!
O shades of Attucks, Salem, Hannibal, O grand
   Toussaint,[159]
Thy valor's lost, thy fame is nough, if these
   now prove faint!
And so most valiant men, and so heroic leaders
   went
To meet the enemy's vantage fire behind strong
   entrenchment;
On, on they charge, who do not fall, [none] falter
   as they reach the walls,

'Midst deadly rain of cannister, 'midst piercing
    rifle-balls!
Not till many scaled the parapet,[160] or waited
    soldiers' graves,
Though thinned their ranks, their colonel
    sleeping with his braves,
Paused these black heroes whose standard-bearer's
    crown
Came in glory, as he cried, "The old flag never
    touched the ground!"[161]
Alas! that valor, unmindful of wounds or even
    death's sad blight,
Brought not victory to our worthy arms that
    fateful night!
Brought not victory? O dull the sight that cannot
    see
Triumph on a field of glory long held 'gainst
    odds for liberty!
Ay, noble men, dead and living, O "famous 54,"
In charge through deadly field, o'er firey ramparts
    then you bore
A race's honor, its friends' deep hopes, a state's
    free banner—
These, in thy keeping, were not lost, but saved
    in glorious manner!

"The Fifty-Fourth at Wagner," *Boston Commonwealth*, 8 December 1883.

SOJOURNER TRUTH

Born enslaved in 1797 in Ulster County, New York, Sojourner Truth (originally Isabella Baumfree) had no formal education. After escaping slavery in 1826, she became a famous abolitionist and women's rights advocate. Her well-known speech "Aren't I a Woman?" illustrates the contrasting experiences of enslaved and free women. She also participated in war relief for Union soldiers. Authorship of "The Valiant Soldiers," likely a folk composition, is unknown, although long attributed to Sojourner Truth. She died in Battle Creek, Michigan, in 1883.

The Valiant Soldiers[162]

(Tune—"John Brown")

The following song, written for the first Michigan Regiment of colored soldiers, was composed by Sojourner Truth during the war, and was sung by her in Michigan and Washington.

We are the valiant soldiers who've 'listed for the war;
We are fighting for the Union, we are fighting for the law;
We can shoot a rebel farther than a white man ever saw,
   As we go marching on.
Chorus—
   Glory, glory, hallelujah! Glory, glory, hallelujah!
   Glory, glory, hallelujah, as we go marching on.
Look there above the center, where the flag is waving bright;
We are going out of slavery, we are bound for freedom's light;
We mean to show Jeff Davis[163] how the Africans can fight,
   As we go marching on.[164]—
We are done with hoeing cotton, we are done with hoeing corn;
We are colored Yankee soldiers as sure as you are born.
When massa hears us shouting, he will think 'tis Gabriel's[165] horn,
   As we go marching on.—
They will have to pay us wages, the wages of their sin;
They will have to bow their foreheads to their colored, kith and kin;
They will have to give us house-room, or the roof will tumble in,
   As we go marching on.—
We hear the proclamation, massa, hush it as you will;
The birds will sing it to us, hopping on the cotton hill;

The possum up the gum tree couldn't keep it still,
    As he went climbing on.—
Father Abraham has spoken, and the message has been sent;
The prison doors have opened, and out the prisoners went
To join the sable army of African descent,
    As we go marching on.—

"The Valiant Soldiers," in *Narrative of Sojourner Truth; a Bondswoman of Olden Time* (Battle Creek, Mich.: Published for the author, 1878), 126.

DAVID WALKER

An outspoken abolitionist, David Walker initially presented some of the ideas in the *Appeal* in 1828 as a speech before the Massachusetts General Colored Association. The next year, he published the speech as a pamphlet. He was born in 1796 in North Carolina to a free woman and an enslaved father, which made Walker legally free because the status of a child followed that of the mother. Seeking greater opportunities, he moved to Boston and opened a business selling used clothing. Walker died in Boston in 1830 shortly after publication of his third edition of the *Appeal*.

From Walker's Appeal, in Four Articles: Together with a Preamble to the Coloured Citizens of the World, but in Particular, and Very Expressly, to Those of the United States of America

PREAMBLE

My dearly beloved Brethren and Fellow Citizens.

Having travelled over a considerable portion of these United States, and having, in the course of my travels, taken the most accurate observations of things as they exist—the result of my observations has warranted the full and unshaken conviction, that we, (coloured people of these United States), are the most degraded, wretched, and abject set of beings that ever lived since the world began; and I pray God that none like us ever may live again until time shall be no more. They tell us of the Israelites in Egypt, the Helots in Sparta, and of the Roman Slaves, which last were made up from almost every nation under heaven, whose sufferings under those ancient and heathen nations, were, in comparison with ours, under this enlightened and Christian nation, no more than a cipher—or, in other words, those heathen nations of antiquity, had but little more among them than the name and form of slavery; while wretchedness and endless miseries were reserved, apparently in a phial,[166] to be poured out upon our fathers, ourselves and our children, by *Christian Americans!*

These positions I shall endeavour, by the help of the Lord, to demonstrate in the course of this *Appeal*, to the satisfaction of the most incredulous mind—and may God Almighty, who is the Father of our Lord Jesus Christ, open your hearts to understand and believe the truth.

The *causes*, my brethren, which produce our wretchedness and miseries, are so very numerous and aggravating, that I believe the pen only of a Josephus or a Plutarch,[167] can well enumerate and explain them. Upon subjects, then, of such incomprehensible magnitude, so impenetrable, and so notorious, I shall be obliged to omit a large class of, and content myself with giving you an exposition of a few of those, which do indeed rage to such an alarming pitch, that they cannot but be a perpetual source of terror and dismay to every reflecting mind.

I am fully aware, in making this appeal to my much afflicted and suffering brethren, that I shall not only be assailed by those whose greatest earthly desires are, to keep us in abject ignorance and wretchedness, and who are of the firm conviction that Heaven has designed us and our children to be slaves and *beasts of burden* to them and their children. I say, I do not only expect to be held up to the public as an ignorant, impudent and restless disturber of the public peace, by such avaricious creatures, as well as a mover of insubordination—and perhaps put in prison or to death, for giving a superficial exposition of our miseries, and exposing tyrants. [. . .]

ARTICLE IV

I ask the candid and unprejudiced of the whole world, to search the pages of historians diligently, and see if the Antedeluvians[168]—the Sodomites[169]—the Egyptians—the Babylonians—the Ninevites[170]—the Carthagenians[171]—the Persians—the Macedonians—the Greeks—the Romans—the Mahometans[172]—the Jews—or devils, ever treated a set of human beings, as the white Christians of America do us, the blacks, or Africans. I also ask the attention of the world of mankind to the declaration of these very American people, of the United States.

A declaration made July 4, 1776.

It says, "When in the course of human events, it becomes necessary for one people to dissolve the political bands which have connected them with another, and to assume among the Powers of the earth, the separate and equal station to which the laws of nature and of nature's God entitle them. A decent respect for the opinions of mankind requires, that they should declare the causes which impel them to the separation.—We hold these truths to be self evident—that all men are created equal, that they are endowed by their Creator with certain unalienable rights: that among these, are life, liberty, and the pursuit of happiness that, to secure these rights, governments are instituted among men, deriving their just powers from the consent of the governed; that when ever any form of government becomes destructive of these ends, it is the right of the people to alter or to abolish it, and to institute a new government laying its foundation on such principles, and organizing its powers in such form, as to them shall seem most likely to effect their safety and happiness. Prudence, indeed, will dictate, that governments long established should not be changed for light and transient causes; and accordingly all experience hath shewn, that mankind are more disposed to suffer, while evils are sufferable, than to right themselves by abolishing the forms to which they are accustomed. But when a long train of abuses and usurpations, pursuing invariably the same object, evinces a design to reduce them under absolute despotism, it is their right it is their duty to throw off such government, and to provide new guards for their future security."

See your Declaration Americans! ! ! Do you understand your own language? Hear your language, proclaimed to the world, July 4th, 1776: "We hold these truths to be self evident—that ALL MEN ARE CREATED EQUAL! ! That they *are endowed by their Creator with certain unalienable rights*; that among these are life, *liberty*, and the pursuit of happiness! !" Compare your own language above, extracted from your Declaration of Independence, with your cruelties and murders inflicted by your cruel and unmerciful fathers and yourselves on our fathers and on us—men who have never given your fathers or you the least provocation.

Hear your language further! "But when a long train of abuses and usurpation, pursuing invariably the same object, evinces a design to reduce them under absolute despotism, it is their *right*, it is their *duty*, to throw off such government, and to provide new guards for their future security."

Now, Americans! I ask you candidly, was your sufferings under Great Britain, one hundredth part as cruel and tyrannical as you have rendered ours under you? Some of you, no doubt, believe that we will never throw off your murderous government and "provide new guards for our future security." If Satan has made you believe it, will he not deceive you? Do the whites say, I being a black man, ought to be humble, which I readily admit? I ask them, ought they not to be as humble as I? or do they think that they can measure arms with Jehovah? Will not the Lord yet humble them? or will not these very coloured people whom they now treat worse than brutes, yet under God, humble them low down enough? Some of the whites are ignorant enough to tell us, that we ought to be submissive to them, that they may keep their feet on our throats. And if we do not submit to be beaten to death by them, we are bad creatures and of course must be damned, &c. If any man wishes to hear this doctrine openly preached to us by the American preachers, let him go into the Southern and Western sections of this country—I do not speak from hear say—what I have written, is what I have seen and heard myself. No man may think that my book is made up of conjecture—I have travelled and observed nearly the whole of those things myself, and what little I did not get by my own observation, I received from those among the whites and blacks, in whom the greatest confidence may be placed.[. . .]

Excerpted from *Walker's Appeal, in Four Articles: Together with a Preamble to the Coloured Citizens of the World, but in Particular, and Very Expressly, to Those of the United States of America* (Boston: Published by David Walker, 1829).

Related writing by David Walker: "The Necessity of a General Union among Us" (1828).

PHILLIS WHEATLEY

Phillis Wheatley was born in Africa around 1753 and arrived in the New World on the slaving vessel *Phillis*. The Wheatley family, who had purchased her as human property, bestowed the name of the ship on the young girl. While she was not the first black writer to publish poetry in the United States, she was the first to publish a book of poetry: *Poems on Various Subjects, Religious and Moral* (1773). Even though Phillis Wheatley's domestic work in the Wheatley home ceased following the death of Susannah Wheatley in 1774, the poet remained the legal property of the Wheatley family until the death of John Wheatley in 1778, when her enslavers made legal provisions to release her from bondage. In 1778, she also married John Peters, a free black man. Her poem *Liberty and Peace, a Poem*, was published as a pamphlet under the name Phillis Peters. Her last poem published in the United States appeared in 1784, also under her married name. Phillis Wheatley Peters died in poverty later that year.

Letter Accompanying a Poem to General George Washington[173]

Sir, I Have taken the freedom to address your Excellency in the enclosed poem, and entreat your acceptance, though I am not insensible of its inaccuracies. Your being appointed by the Grand Continental Congress to be Generalissimo of the armies of North America, together with the fame of your virtues, excite sensation not easy to suppress. Your generosity, therefore, I presume, will pardon the attempt. Wishing your Excellency all possible success in the great cause you are so generously engaged in. I am,

Your Excellency's most obedient humble servant, Phillis Wheatley.
Providence, Oct. 26, 1775.

His Excellency Gen. Washington

Celestial choir! enthron'd in realms of light
Columbia's scenes of glorious toils I write.[174]
While freedom's cause her anxious breast alarms,
She flashes dreadful in refulgent arms.
See mother earth her offspring's fate bemoan,
And nations gaze at scenes before unknown!
See the bright beams of heaven's revolving light
Involved in sorrows and the veil of night!

The goddess[175] comes, she moves divinely fair,
Olive and laurel binds her golden hair:
Wherever shines this native of the skies,
Unnumber'd charms and recent graces rise.

Muse! bow propitious while my pen relates
How pour her armies through a thousand gates:
As when Eolus[176] heaven's fair face deforms,
Enwrapp'd in tempest and a night of storms;
Astonish'd ocean feels the wild uproar,
The refluent surges beat the sounding shore;
Or thick as leaves in Autumn's golden reign,
Such, and so many, moves the warrior's train.
In bright array they seek the work of war,
Where high unfurl'd the ensign[177] waves in air.
Shall I to Washington their praise recite?
Enough thou know'st them in the fields of fight.
Thee, first in place and honours,—we demand
The grace and glory of thy martial band.
Fam'd for thy valour, for thy virtues more,
Hear every tongue thy guardian aid implore!

One century scarce perform'd its destin'd round,
When Gallic[178] powers Columbia's fury found;
And so may you, whoever dares disgrace
The land of freedom's heaven-defended race!
Fix'd are the eyes of nations on the scales,
For in their hopes Columbia's arm prevails.
Anon Britannia droops the pensive head,
While round increase the rising hills of dead.
Ah! cruel blindness to Columbia's state!
Lament thy thirst of boundless power too late.

Proceed, great chief, with virtue on thy side,
Thy ev'ry action let the goddess guide.
A crown, a mansion, and a throne that shine,
With gold unfading, WASHINGTON! be thine.

"Mess. Dixon and Hunter: Pray Insert the Enclosed Letter and Verses, Written by the Famous Phillis Wheatley, the African Poetess, in Your Next *Gazette*," *Virginia Gazette*, 30 March 1776.

* * *

On the Death of General Wooster[179]

From this the muse rich consolation draws
He nobly perish'd in his Country's cause
His Country's Cause that ever fir'd his mind
Where martial flames, and Christian virtues join'd.
How shall my pen his warlike deeds proclaim
Or paint them fairer on the list of Fame—
Enough great Cheif[180]—now wrapt in shades around
Thy grateful Country shall thy praise resound
Tho' not with mortals' empty praise elate
That vainest vapour to th' immortal State
Inly[181] serene the expiring hero lies
And thus (while heav'nward roll his swimming eyes)[:]
["]Permit, great power while yet my fleeting breath
And Spirits wander to the verge of Death—
Permit me yet to paint fair freedom's charms
For her the Continent shines bright in arms
By thy high will, celestial prize she came—
For her we combat on the field of fame
Without her presence vice maintains full sway
And social love and virtue wing their way
O still propitious be thy guardian care
And lead *Columbia* thro' the toils of war.
With thine own hand conduct them and defend
And bring the dreadful contest to an end—
For ever grateful let them live to thee
And keep them ever virtuous, brave, and free—
But how, presumptuous shall we hope to find
Divine acceptance with th' Almighty mind—
While yet (O deed ungenerous!) they disgrace
And hold in bondage Afric's blameless race?
Let virtue reign—And thou accord our prayers
Be victory our's, and generous freedom theirs."
The hero pray'd—the wond'ring Spirit fled
And Sought the unknown regions of the dead—
Tis thine fair partner of his life, to find
His virtuous path and follow close behind—

A little moment steals him from thy Sight
He waits thy coming to the realms of light
Freed from his labours in the ethereal Skies
Where in Succession endless pleasures rise!

Mukhtar Ali Isani, "'On the Death of General Wooster': An Unpublished Poem by Phillis Wheatley," *Modern Philology* 77, no. 3 (1980): 306–9.

*   *   *

Liberty and Peace, a Poem[182]

LO! Freedom comes. Th' prescient Muse foretold,
  All Eyes th' accomplish'd Prophecy behold:
Her Port describ'd, "*She moves divinely fair,*
Olive and Laurel bind her golden Hair."
She, the bright Progeny of Heaven, descends,
And every Grace her sovereign Step attends;
For now kind Heaven, indulgent to our Prayer,
In smiling *Peace* resolves the Din of *War.*
Fix'd in *Columbia* her illustrious Line,
And bids in thee her future Councils shine.
To every Realm her Portals open'd wide,
Receives from each the full commercial Tide.
Each Art and Science now with rising Charms
Th' expanding Heart with Emulation warms.
E'en great *Britannia* sees with dread Surprize,
And from the dazzl'ing Splendors turns her Eyes!
Britain, whose Navies swept th'*Atlantic* o'er,
And Thunder sent to every distant Shore:
E'en thou, in Manners cruel as thou art,
The Sword resign'd, resume the friendly Part!
For *Galia's*[183] Power espous'd *Columbia's* Cause,
And new-born *Rome* shall give *Britannia* Law,
Nor unremember'd in the grateful Strain,
Shall princely *Louis'* friendly Deeds remain;
The generous Prince th' impending Vengeance eye's,
Sees the fierce Wrong, and to the rescue flies.
Perish that Thirst of boundless Power, that drew
On *Albion's*[184] Head the Curse to Tyrants due.

But thou appeas'd submit to Heaven's decree,
That bids this Realm of Freedom rival thee!
Now sheathe the Sword that bade the Brave attone
With guiltless Blood for Madness not their own.
Sent from th' Enjoyment of their native Shore
Ill-fated—never to behold her more!
From every Kingdom on *Europa*'s Coast
Throng'd various Troops, their Glory, Strength and Boast.
With heart-felt pity fair *Hibernia*[185] saw
Columbia menac'd by the Tyrant's Law:
On hostile Fields fraternal Arms engage,
And mutual Deaths, all dealt with mutual Rage;
The Muse's Ear hears mother Earth deplore
Her ample Surface smoak[186] with kindred Gore:
The hostile Field destroys the social Ties,
And ever-lasting Slumber seals their Eyes.
Columbia mourns, the haughty Foes deride,
Her Treasures plunder'd, and her Towns destroy'd:
Witness how *Charlestown*'s curling Smoaks arise,
In sable Columns to the clouded Skies!
The ample Dome, high-wrought with curious Toil,
In one sad Hour the savage Troops despoil.
Descending *Peace* the Power of War confounds;
From every Tongue celestial *Peace* resounds:
As from the East th' illustrious King of Day,
With rising Radiance drives the Shades away,
So Freedom comes array'd with Charms divine,
And in her Train Commerce and Plenty shine.
Britannia owns her Independent Reign,
Hibernia, *Scotia*,[187] and the Realms of *Spain*;
And great *Germania*'s ample Coast admires
The generous Spirit that *Columbia* fires.
Auspicious Heaven shall fill with fav'ring Gales,
Where e'er *Columbia* spreads her swelling Sails:
To every Realm shall *Peace* her Charms display,
And Heavenly *Freedom* spread her golden Ray.

Liberty and Peace (Boston: Warden and Russell, 1784).

Related writings by Phillis Wheatley: "On the Capture of General Lee" (1863); "America" (1970); *Complete Writings: Phillis Wheatley* (2001).

JAMES MONROE WHITFIELD

James Whitfield was born free in 1822 in New Hampshire. He was an abolitionist poet who at one point supported the emigration and resettlement of black people outside the United States. His book *America and Other Poems* appeared in print in 1853 and was dedicated to emigration advocate Martin Delany. Despite Whitfield's disagreement with Frederick Douglass on abolitionists' tactics, Douglass published a series of essays on abolition by Whitfield in the *North Star* in 1853. James Monroe Whitfield relocated to San Francisco, where he died in 1871.

America

AMERICA, it is to thee,
Thou boasted land of liberty,—
It is to thee I raise my song,
Thou land of blood, and crime, and wrong.
It is to thee, my native land,
From whence has issued many a band
To tear the black man from his soil,
And force him here to delve and toil;
Chained on your blood-bemoistened sod,
Cringing beneath a tyrant's rod,
Stripped of those rights which Nature's God
     Bequeathed to all the human race,
Bound to a petty tyrant's nod,
     Because he wears a paler face.
Was it for this, that freedom's fires
Were kindled by your patriot sires?
Was it for this, they shed their blood,
On hill and plain, on field and flood?
Was it for this, that wealth and life
Were staked upon that desperate strife,
Which drenched this land for seven long years
With blood of men, and women's tears?
When black and white fought side by side,
     Upon the well-contested field,—
Turned back the fierce opposing tide,
     And made the proud invader yield—

When, wounded, side by side they lay,
  And heard with joy the proud hurrah
From their victorious comrades say
  That they had waged successful war,
The thought ne'er entered in their brains
That they endured those toils and pains,
To forge fresh fetters, heavier chains
For their own children, in whose veins
Should flow that patriotic blood,
So freely shed on field and flood.
Oh no; they fought, as they believed,
  For the inherent rights of man;
But mark, how they have been deceived
  By slavery's accursed plan.
They never thought, when thus they shed
  Their heart's best blood, in freedom's cause
That their own sons would live in dread,
  Under unjust, oppressive laws:
That those who quietly enjoyed
  The rights for which they fought and fell,
Could be the framers of a code,
  That would disgrace the fiends of hell!
Could they have looked, with prophet's ken,
  Down to the present evil time,
  Seen free-born men, uncharged with crime,
Consigned unto a slaver's pen,—
Or thrust into a prison cell,
With thieves and murderers to dwell—
While that same flag whose stripes and stars
Had been their guide through freedom's wars
As proudly waved above the pen
Of dealers in the souls of men!
Or could the shades of all the dead,
  Who fell beneath that starry flag,
Visit the scenes where they once bled,
  On hill and plain, on vale and crag,
By peaceful brook, or ocean's strand,
  By inland lake, or dark green wood,
Where'er the soil of this wide land

Was moistened by their patriot blood,—
And then survey the country o'er,
    From north to south, from east to west,
And hear the agonizing cry
Ascending up to God on high,
From western wilds to ocean's shore,
    The fervent prayer of the oppressed;
The cry of helpless infancy
    Torn from the parent's fond caress
By some base tool of tyranny,
    And doomed to woe and wretchedness;
The indignant wail of fiery youth,
    Its noble aspirations crushed,
Its generous zeal, its love of truth,
    Trampled by tyrants in the dust;
The aerial piles which fancy reared,
    And hopes too bright to be enjoyed,
Have passed and left his young heart seared,
    And all its dreams of bliss destroyed.
The shriek of virgin purity,
    Doomed to some libertine's embrace,
Should rouse the strongest sympathy
    Of each one of the human race;
And weak old age, oppressed with care,
    As he reviews the scene of strife,
Puts up to God a fervent prayer,
    To close his dark and troubled life.
The cry of fathers, mothers, wives,
    Severed from all their hearts hold dear,
And doomed to spend their wretched lives
    In gloom, and doubt, and hate, and fear;
And manhood, too, with soul of fire,
And arm of strength, and smothered ire,
Stands pondering with brow of gloom,
Upon his dark unhappy doom,
Whether to plunge in battle's strife,
And buy his freedom with his life,
And with stout heart and weapon strong,
Pay back the tyrant wrong for wrong,

Or wait the promised time of God,
    When his Almighty ire shall wake,
And smite the oppressor in his wrath,
And hurl red ruin in his path,
And with the terrors of his rod,
    Cause adamantine[188] hearts to quake.
Here Christian writhes in bondage still,
    Beneath his brother Christian's rod,
And pastors trample down at will,
    The image of the living God.
While prayers go up in lofty strains,
    And pealing hymns ascend to heaven,
The captive, toiling in his chains,
    With tortured limbs and bosom riven,
Raises his fettered hand on high,
    And in the accents of despair,
To him who rules both earth and sky,
    Puts up a sad, a fervent prayer,
To free him from the awful blast
    Of slavery's bitter galling shame—
Although his portion should be cast
    With demons in eternal flame!
Almighty God! 'tis this they call
    The land of liberty and law;
Part of its sons in baser thrall
    Than Babylon or Egypt saw—
Worse scenes of rapine, lust and shame,
    Than Babylonian ever knew,
Are perpetrated in the name
    Of God, the holy, just, and true;
And darker doom than Egypt felt,
May yet repay this nation's guilt.
Almighty God! thy aid impart,
And fire anew each faltering heart,
And strengthen every patriot's hand,
Who aims to save our native land.
We do not come before thy throne,
    With carnal weapons drenched in gore,

Although our blood has freely flown,
    In adding to the tyrant's store.
Father! before thy throne we come,
    Not in the panoply of war,
With pealing trump, and rolling drum,
    And cannon booming loud and far;
Striving in blood to wash out blood,
    Through wrong to seek redress for wrong;
For while thou'rt holy, just and good,
    The battle is not to the strong;
But in the sacred name of peace,
    Of justice, virtue, love and truth,
We pray, and never mean to cease,
    Till weak old age and fiery youth
In freedom's cause their voices raise,
And burst the bonds of every slave;
Till, north and south, and east and west,
The wrongs we bear shall be redressed.

"America," in *America and Other Poems* (Buffalo, N.Y.: James S. Leavitt Company, 1853).

Related writings by James Monroe Whitfield: "Ode for the Fourth of July" (1853); "Yes! Strike Again That Sounding String" (1853); "How Long?" (1853); "A Poem" (1867).

ALBERY ALLSON WHITMAN

Albery Allson Whitman was born in Kentucky in 1851 to enslaved parents. He was orphaned at age twelve, yet later attended Wilberforce University and became a protégé of African Methodist Episcopal (A.M.E.) bishop Daniel A. Payne, president of the university. In 1870, Whitman became an A.M.E. minister. He published several books, including a volume of poetry titled *Poems on Miscelaneous Subjects* (1877), several book-length narrative poems such as *Not a Man, and Yet a Man* (1877) as well as *Twasinta's Seminoles* (1885), and the epic poem, *An Idyl of the South* (1901). Whitman was a prolific and highly regarded writer, affectionately referred to as poet laureate of the Negro race. He died in 1901.

From Hymn to the Nation[189]

[. . .] Fair Freedom travailed[190] 'neath an unknown sky,
And tho' the tyrant[191] shook his envious chain,
And tho' the bigot reared a gloomy fane,[192]
She bore our darling of the azure eye;[193]
Baptized its childhood in brave blood and tears,
But trumpted her independence in Great Britian's ears.

Astonished kingdoms heard of the new birth,
And royal vengeance drew her warring blade,
And bloody strokes upon Columbia[194] laid,
To smite the young offender to the earth;
Colonial hardships shivered where she went,
And border horrors thro' the years a thrill of sadness sent.

But patriotism bold, sustained the blow,
Returning deeper wounds with daring might—
For Freedom ever steels the stroke of right—
And cool determined Valor's proud arm so
Dismayed the imperial hosts, that baffled George[195]
Saw he could ne'er enslave the men who withstood Valley Forge.

A century has spun around the wheel
Of ages, and the years in noiseless flight
Have heaped their golden tributes to the right;
Till now religion in her heavenly zeal,

To mend life's ills walks hand in hand with lore,[196]
Where clank the chains of slaves in Law's offended ears no more. [...]
Tho' at the name Republic tyrants mocked,
Columbia has lived a hundred years
Thro' trials, triumphs, hopes, and doubts and fears,
And still she lives, tho' often tempest-rocked,
Republic yet, united, one and free,
And may she live; her name the synonyme of Liberty! [...]

"Hymn to the Nation," in *Poems on Miscellaneous Subjects* (Springfield, Ohio: Republic Printing Company, 1877).

*   *   *

From The End of the Whole Matter[197]

[Rodney, the hero, has escaped from slavery to Canada and has rescued Dora, Sir Maxey's daughter, from Indigenous people who had captured her in a raid. Sir Maxey had previously promised his daughter in marriage to the man who rescued her. When Sir Maxey realizes the jealousy of the white men who did not win Dora in marriage, he sells the hero to bounty hunters, who return Rodney to the Aylor plantation in Tennessee.

Leeona, the heroine, is from New Orleans, where her father also was her owner. She was her father's favorite, but she was sold to Aylor illegally and without her father's consent while she was visiting Tennessee. Rodney and Leeona become lovers, which infuriates their owner, who has designs on Leeona. With the help of Leeona and an elderly enslaved woman named Aunt Ameriky, Rodney escapes slavery again. He lives as a maroon in a cave and Leeona visits him regularly. Finally, they escape together to Florida before finally reaching freedom in Canada. During the Civil War, Rodney, now sixty, returns to the United States with his two sons to fight with the Union forces. He sees Aylor dying on the battlefield and gives his former enslaver a drink of water. Aylor recognizes Rodney and asks forgiveness. Following the war Rodney seeks reconciliation, peace, and equality.]

PROLOGUE

[...] The black man has a cause, deny who dares,
And him to vindicate my muse prepares.
A part of this great nation's hist'ry, he

Has made in valor and fidelity.
His sweat has poured to swell our ample stores,
His blood run freely to defend our shores. [...]

[...] Rodney had left his home in foreign lands,
And laid his life into our country's hands,
His struggling kindred's conquests proud to share,
For he beheld acknowledged manhood there.
And this the grandest day that ever rose
Upon his life, at its eventful close
Was bringing with it recollections sweet,
That made his old heroic heart with youth's emotions beat

His country's banner, soiled and battle-torn,
In sable hands before the columns borne,
Streamed in the setting sun's deep golden light,
And rivaled Heaven in her blazon bright.
The drums of victory clamored on his ear;
The bugle's wail of rest was ringing clear,
Thunder of wheels was in the distance roaring,
And into camp the weary victors pouring.
He saw that Slav'ry's days were numbered now,
Far death's cold damp hung on her pallid brow.

And looking now upon his left and right,
Two proud sons who had ridden thro' the fight
With him, rode there with martial mien and brave,
The off'rings which Leeona's bosom gave
The country that had chased her as a slave.
He saw his sons, and prouder felt than he
Who took Rebellion's sword from famous Lee.

This was the day when Southern chivalry
Beheld black manhood clothed in liberty,
Step from the shadow of his centuries
Of bondage, shake dejection from his eyes,
And to the awful verge of valor rise.
The day that heard the negro, scarred and maimed,
On sovereign battle's lips a man proclaimed.

The hosts of Sherman[198] marching to the sea,
Beneath Rebellion's trembling canopy
Swept like a thunder storm, whose lightnings catch
The shaking hills with hands of flame, and snatch
Their mighty forests down. [. . .]

Wrenching fair victory from brave hands and true
As e'er on foe the steel of battle drew [. . .]

The Union struck at proud Rebellion's heart;
Rebellion aimed at her same vital part,
And doubtless had a wound most painful made,
Had not the Union's negro arm displayed
Such valiant strength in warding off the blow,
And striking down the strong and gallant foe. [. . .]

Now let the vanquished his repentant face,
Lean in the victor's merciful embrace,
And let the victor, with his strong arm heal
The bleeding wounds that gape beneath his steel.
And may no partial hand attempt to lay

Of praise, as due along to blue or grey.
The warrior's wreath may well by both be worn [. . .]

And while America's escutcheon bright,
Is bathed in war-won Freedom's glorious light,
Forget it not, the colored man will fight.
More patriotism Sparta never knew,
A lance more knightly Norman never threw,
More courage never armed the Roman coasts,
With blinder zeal ne'er rode the Moslem hosts,
And ne'er more stubborn stood the Muscovite,[199]
Than stood the hated negro in the fight. [. . .]

Hail dawning Peace! Speed on thy glorious rise!
And with thy beams unseal the nation's eyes.
Let Islam in the blaze of scimitar[200]
Proclaim his rites, and gorge the fangs of war,
But peace be unto thee, land of our sires,

Whose sacred altar flames with holier fires!
Let lawlessness no longer stagger forth
With his destructive torch, nor South nor North;
And let the humblest tenant of the fields,
Secured of what his honest labor yields,
Pursue his calling, ply his daily care,
His home adorn and helpless children rear,
Assured that while our flag above him flies,
No lawless hand can dare molest his joys. [...]

Oh comrade freemen strike your hands to stand
Like walls of rock and guard our father-land!
Oh guard our homes and institutions free,
The price of blood and valor's legacy.
Awake to watch, ye sovereign sons of toil!
If despot feet e'er touch our country's soil,
Fly to the standard that by freemen born,
The glory of a hundred years has worn,
Blood-stained, yet bright, streaming, but battle-torn,
And *rally* till the last drop from the veins
Of free America flows on our plains.
Eternal vigilance must light the tower,
Whose granite strength can bide the evil hour,
Whose wave-dashed base defies the tempest's shock,
Builded upon the everlasting rock.
At last, proud land, let potent wisdom write
Her name above thy brow in glorious light,
And suffer ne'er thy hands to idle rest
Till learning lights thy humblest subject's breast.
In cities tall, and in the hamlet rude,
Suffer no partial hand to e'er exclude
A single poor from fair instruction's halls,
But write EQUALITY on all her walls.
An equal chance in life, an even start,
Give every one and let him play his part.
But who could, with complacence on his face,
First bind one's feet, then *challenge* for a race?
I would not own I was a thing so small,
I'd rather own I was no man at all,

Than show that I must some advantage take,
The race of life respectably to make.
Say my facilities must all be *best*,
Then write excelsior upon my crest?[201]
Nay, rather let me weed the hardest row,
And rise above by *toiling* from below. [...]

And soon, whoever to our bourne[202] shall come,
Jew, Greek or Goth, he here shall be at home.
Then Ign'rance shall forsake her crooked ways,
And poor old Caste there end her feeble days.

"The End of the Whole Matter," in *Not a Man, and Yet a Man* (Springfield, Ohio: Republic Printing Company, 1877).

*   *   *

From Twasinta's Seminoles; or, Rape of Florida[203]

[The name Twasinta in this poem is a fictional reference to both the native land of the people in this narrative and the people themselves. They are the Indigenous neighbors of the Seminoles. The hero, Atlassa, and others, were primarily loyal to Florida and secondarily to Spain. The three nineteenth-century Seminole Indian Wars (ca. 1816–1858) were the second major series of battles in the long-standing struggle—since colonial times—between the Indigenous peoples of North America and European settlers. Florida, the site of colonial battles primarily between Britain and Spain throughout the eighteenth century, was controlled by Spain after the U.S. Revolutionary War for Independence. By agreement between Spain and the United States, Florida became a U.S. territory in 1821. The multiethnic peoples of Spanish Florida are represented here by Twasinta; Palmecho, a Spaniard; Ewald, Palmecho's daughter with a Maroon woman; Atlassa, a Seminole; and Mickasuki, the Muskogee. The Seminoles[204] lived on land in present-day Florida. While Spain occupied Florida, Seminole land became a refuge for escaped captives from slavery (Maroons) and for free black people. The fictional Twasinta bands of Indians were strongly influenced by the Spanish. They also intermarried with Maroons. In this narrative, the Seminoles, Muskogee, and other native peoples eventually lost their land and conceded to allowing slavery among their peoples after Spain relinquished Florida to the United States in 1819, which took effect two years later. They were forced from their land in 1830 after Andrew Jackson's betrayal of the Muskogean people. Soldiers from the U.S. military capture Atlassa, the leader of Florida's people, but he escapes and reunites with them, becoming the leader of the exiled people on the Trail of Tears (1831–1838). Some will settle in so-called Indian Territory; others travel as far as Mexico and establish their own settlements.]

INVOCATION

IV

[. . .] Say, then, of that too soon forgotten race
That flourished once, but long has been obscure
In Florida, and where the seas embrace
The Spanish isles; say if e'er lives more pure
Warmed veins, or patriots could more endure
Around the altars of their native bourne!²⁰⁵
Say, when their flow'ry landscapes could allure,
What peaceful seasons did to them return,
And how requited labor filled his golden urn! [. . .]

CANTO I

XIX

Oh! sing it in the light of freedom's morn,
Tho' tyrant wars have made the earth a grave;
The good, the great, and true, are, if so, born,
And so with slaves, *chains do not make the slave!*
If high-souled birth be what the mother gave,—
If manly birth, and manly to the core,—
Whate'er the test, the man will he behave!
Crush him to earth and crush him o'er and o'er,
A man he'll rise at last and meet you as before. [. . .]

XLI

Was not thy standard on these shores unfurled? [206]—
Dominions named for thy "most Christian Queen"[207]
The smile-provoking jest of a New World,
Whose sons in battle had victorious been,
O'er English vet'rans, who had service seen?

Yea, when the luchre-loving Saxon grew
And fattened on the blood of slaves, I ween[208]
Not much remained for errant hands to do,
Except to seize and hold the weak in bondage too! [. . .]

XLVIII

Thus have we, Mickasukie, seen thy brave;
And, too, Twasinta, seen thy homes decline!
Thus have we found how yearns the poorest slave
For freedom—how at patriotism's shrine,
The ardor of the exile is divine:
And now, that in the tide of years o'erflown,
There's scarcely left a trace of thee and thine,
We pause and sigh, mid wrecks that time hath strewn;
Of all the world has been, how little now is known! [. . .]

CANTO II

VII

Tis hard to judge if hatred of one's race,
By those who deem themselves superior-born,
Be worse than that quiesence in disgrace,
Which only merits—and *should* only—scorn!
Oh! let me see the negro, night and morn,
Pressing and fighting in, for place and power!
If he a proud escutcheon[209] would adorn,
All earth is place—all time th' auspicious hour,
While heaven leans forth to see, oh! can he quail or cower? [. . .]

XXX

The very air uneasily did creep
Among the maples darkling over-head;
And as she reached her gateway on the steep,
She found Palmecho, prying out, who said:
"There's wrong abroad, my Ewald,[210] something dread
Is sure to happen," and while yet he spake,
A hasty footman from the forests sped—
It was an exile who his way did make
Straight to Palmecho, some alarming news to break.

XXXI

As Ewald passed, she heard Atlassa's name.
Wide thro' Twasinta spread the hasty news,
Like stubbles crackling in a wind-swept flame.
Ah! now was trouble's sombre currents loose!
With muttered threats and presages profuse,
The young men's speeches stirred the eager crowd;
Whilst old men thought up their ancestral views,
And triumphs, that well made the warrior proud—
But all for action were unanimous and loud. [. . .]

XXXV

"What troop is this that comes to mine abode!
What seek ye here! Intruders! will ye dare
To hoof my grounds? why shun yon open road?
Age quencheth not resentment! and beware,
Whoe'er ye be, or whence soe'er ye are,
Ye Come no further!" Rapid gestures told
How he was moved; but without heed or care,
On rode the soldiers till he had seized hold
One's reins, and felt a sabre's blow that laid him cold. [. . .]

XXXVIII

Atlassa's feerless plume was now in sight,
His Seminoles towards Twasinta cheered.
Twasinta answered with her valiant might,
And deaf'ning shouts did greet them as they neared!
Till on Palmecho's threshold they appeared
The tempest of rejoicings held its sway;
Then on the roof the flag of Spain was reared,
And Mickasukie's braves the live, long day,
Were thro' Twasinta led in many a festive way. [. . .]

CANTO III

XLIII

Upon assailants: Thus doth valor teach,
When roused to desperation's potent tests,
That "Liberty or Death," is one of God's behests! [. . .]

XLIV

Fierce Spirit of the Seminole! what fate
Can tame thy warring sons upon the field!
I see them for a Nation's strength *too* great
Outnumbered and outarmed they *will not* yield!
Till by the darkness they are well concealed,
They hold an army back and guard their dead;
Thus shall their immortality be sealed,
The bravest of the brave, to victory led,
By one whose plume would honor e'en a Bruce's head![211]

XLV

Down to the end of time be it proclaimed!
Up to the skies of fame let it be rung!
Wherever valor's sacrifice is named,
Whenever plaudits fire the human tongue;
Or by sweet strings expressed, or mortals sung
Let it go forth, and let mankind attest,
That, Seminoles and exiles, old and young,
Upon the bosom of their country prest;
By valiant deeds are shrined in ev'ry patriot breast! [. . .]

XLVIII

Or some Atlassa, who could call his braves
To turfy beds of glory in the dell,
Or vict'ry o'er those who would make them slaves!—
But for such men the wide earth were a hell,
Where vampire priests and kingly vultures fell,
Plucking the fleshless bones of human woe
Would perch thro' time! [. . .]

LIII

Of warriors round their chief, whose valiant brow
Is heavy with the horrors of the day!
Upon the turf the wounded in a row,
Painful but silent, for attention lay,—
The dead to Apalachi's shores[212] are borne away. [. . .]

CANTO IV

IV

"My native Florida! Adieu! Adieu!
I'm looking at the last pine on thy shore!
Soon other climes must come upon my view,
And thy sweet landscapes meet my eyes no more!
Oh! Florida! Hear now thy son implore!
In thy fair bosom still remember me;
And while the billows shall between us roar,
Or thy smooth sands shall hear a lisping sea,
Let these my latest vows revive and dwell in thee!" [. . .]

Excerpted from *The Rape of Florida* (St Louis, Missouri: Nixon-Jones Printing Co., 1884).[213]

Related writings by Albery Allson Whitman: *Leelah Misled* (1873); "Peace" (1877); "Custar's Last Ride" (1877); "Old Abe, the War Eagle of Wisconsin" (1877); "The Veteran" (1890); "Stonewall Jackson" (1890); "Grant" (1890); "The Fortunes of War" (1890); "The Freedman's Triumphant Song" (1893).

JOHN A. WILLIAMS

World War II Navy veteran, journalist, professor, and author of over twenty books, John A. Williams was born in 1925 in Jackson, Mississippi, and died 3 July 2015 in Paramus, New Jersey. He won several literary awards, including the Richard Wright-Jacques Roumain Award, the American Book Award, and the Phillis Wheatley Award. The selections below are excerpted from Williams's novel *Captain Blackman*.

1812[214]

[Abraham Blackman is a hero of the War in Vietnam who, while recuperating from war injuries, dreams that he has traveled through time and has relived events from a black military history course that he teaches. While time traveling, he takes part in almost all of the wars the United States has participated in, from the Revolutionary War for Independence to the War in Vietnam. After the Revolutionary War, Abraham Blackman, (moving in the opposite direction of the migratory flow of black people out of the South) travels to New Orleans and participates in the Battle of New Orleans, which occurred in 1815 and was the last battle of the War of 1812.]

[. . .] South he went, hearing from blacks along the way stories of Lafayette,[215] who told Washington to free the slaves, and Blackman knew as he walked that Washington, like a lot of people wanting to get right with God, would free his own slaves as he was dying, and ask his heirs, of which by blood he had none, to look out for the darkies until they were twenty-five. His body servant, William Lee, would be provided for, with freedom or not, no one would know. Blackman marched south.

South, to sit in the shadows of the Cathedral of St. Louis and the Cabildo,[216] in an inn for blacks, drinking and listening to the French, Spanish, English, and Creole being spoken here in the port of New Orleans.

Over his hot rum Blackman reflected that the talk was almost always the same until another ship sailed into the harbor with lowered sails and dropped anchor. The black sailors from those vessels then brought in all the world's gossip, enough of it to last until the arrival of the next ship. New Orleans was a sailors' town and while other inns in other parts of the city were also places of gossip, that gossip was about whites. In La Baleine Noire,[217] the black underside of the world was the topic of gossip, discussion, and speculation. For here they spoke of the black kingdom of Haiti, of York's journey with Lewis and Clark,[218] of distant African ports and hot tropical islands far to the south.

These days, however, most of the talk in this place of dim sea lanterns and smoky walls, was of the war and where black men, sailors and soldiers would fit in. The militias had been white for twenty years; not so the Navy.

Blackman was just taking down another hot rum when he was slapped heartily on the back. He knew without looking that it was old Griot, clown, raconteur, black patriot, ancient mariner. Always good for a laugh on these chilly days.

"Mornin sar!" Griot boomed, glancing around to see if his arrival had been properly noticed. "How's de big mon tis day, bien, bon?"

"Griot!" came a shout from across the room. "What's news? What the white folks gonna do with them Englishers sittin out inna harbor?"

"Yeah, Griot, you look like you know sumthin new."

His audience assured, Griot moved away from Blackman to the center of the room, tugging at his striped stocking cap. "Well, mens, we's gonna git us some war, now, don you worry none bout dat. But you know, I made de talk, dina make talk bout Strachan, Ware, n Martin,[219] bout dey bein black, n how dey come in here on leave from dey ship, de *Chesapeake*? Come in here feelin low."

Griot walked back and forth, spinning about to make sure every eye was upon him.

"Sar! Come in feelin low n talkin about how dey no walk de streets enywhere safe cause dey bein black n people spittin on dem n callin 'em names, wuthless black bastids n alla dat, and dey sailors inna Yewnity States Navy. A crime, sars, a crime!

"Cose dey sails away, sails out onna high seas and goddamn gumbo! Here come de Raidcoats." Griot got into a crouch, his arms out before him, one a little ahead of the other, and he moved his hands up and down, and Blackman saw two ships on heaving blue waters.

"De Raidcoats comin in de *Leopard*, puttin on evera patcha sail dey could find, an dey ketch up wid de *Chesapeake*,[220] gonna impress some me Yewnity States sailors. S'now dey snatches off dat boat dem t'ree boys, Strachan, Ware, n Martin, n puts dem in de Raidcoat navy! N den, genemuns, we goes t war."

Griot took a deep breath and circled in his space once again.

"De same niggers dat warent safe in eny Merican city now's de cause o dis whole war. Dat's what dey says. Man, dese white folks is a messa *gumbo!*"

Griot led the laughter. His bright red gums flashed in the dim light and Blackman, laughing himself, ordered Griot a hot rum. Griot had told the story before; it was an ironic tale, Blackman knew, and they laughed because it would've been too painful to cry. The laughter was dying now, as it always did when the irony of the war was realized. The drinks were going around now. Blackman basked in the fish-soup-smell of the kitchen, the bland odor of melting wax candles, liquor, and sailor sweat. Black, brown, tan, and white, the faces of the Negroes glistened in the hot inn; eyes shot here and there, trying not to miss any speaker who'd know anything about tomorrow. Their eyes also sought the British ships riding at anchor in the harbor, which could be seen through the small foc'sle-like windows of the inn.[221]

Tomorrow, Blackman thought, they will ask us to fight, and he looked around the room again. A lot of strangers, probably farmers who'd come in to find out what was going on. They'd not heard Griot before. This night in La Baleine Noire they were welcomed; war sat hard in the harbor, and all black men had the most to lose. Blackman looked up. Griot was at his side again.

"Well, Griot," Blackman said. "They'll ask us to fight, no?"

Griot nodded. "It's down t de skinnin o de shrimp, big man, an dey gonna be askin us to fight; dey gonna say 'now lissen y'all black fellers'—dey won't be callin us niggers t'morrow—'dem Raidcoats is in de harbuh, dey comin in here t take over Merica n youse black fellers is Mericans jes like de rest of us, so you got t he'p us fight.' Dey done said it befo n dey goan say it agin, big Abe."

"What you going to do, Griot?"

"Ah'll fight," he said simply.

Black Antoine from upriver joined them. "If they ask, us farmers'll fight, too." He clicked his clay pipe against his teeth. "Can't hardly say no, because before this white man'd let us stray loose at his back while he's fightin another man in his front, he'd see us dead."

Blackman shrugged. The truth.

Griot flapped his arms and laughed. "Fur a fack, now dey might even join togedder t git rid o niggers so dey kin fight in peace."

The inn stayed open all night, and the men in it drank, ate, and dozed, waiting for daybreak. Faintly, they heard the ships' bells ringing out in the harbor.

*   *   *

Blackman gazed at the man named Andrew Jackson. He might inspire confidence among whites, Blackman thought, but not in blacks. An exterminator. The Creeks would never recover from what this man with the scar on his face had done to them at Horseshoe Bend.[222] Had he done it before? Yes. Would he do it again? Yes, Blackman thought, for a man who'd kill Indians and a few blacks the way he'd done it at Horseshoe surely wouldn't hesitate to kill others. Eyeing the strong, lean face even more closely, Blackman felt that Jackson could take just as murderously as he gave. A tough competitor. One of those backwoodsmen who sometimes saw little difference between life and death; one of those who rose in the morning uncaring about making it back to his bed at night to sleep in peace. A chilling kind of man.

Jackson was speaking:[223]

"Through a mistaken policy, you have heretofore been deprived of participation in the glorious struggle for national rights in which our country is engaged. This shall no longer exist."

Blackman looked around him. Old Griot stood with the farmers Pierre, Odum, and Jones. Black Antoine on the other side. There were so many, Blackman thought, but why not? New Orleans was as rich with blacks, slave and free, as the soil from the Mississippi whose delta was only one hundred miles away. And with Creoles, the *passé blancs*.[224] They all knew that Jackson, with his fine and noble talk, was begging, had to be begging this cold morning in a frost-girded field, surrounded by blacks. Blackman thought of the streams of fine carriages, filled with ladies and gentlemen and bags and boxes, moving northward out of New Orleans. Poor Jackson, begging blacks to help defend the city because there were too few others.

But they let him continue:

"As sons of freedom, you are now called upon to defend our most inestimable blessings. As Americans, your country looks with confidence to her adopted children for valorous support as a faithful return for the advantages enjoyed under her mild and equitable government."

Griot threw back his head and roared, then slammed himself to the ground, still laughing. Jackson swung his eyes to another part of the crowd and continued, a flush spreading across his face.

"As fathers, husbands, and brothers," he went on, "you are summoned to rally around the standard of the Eagle, to defend all which is dear in existence. Your country, although calling for your exertions, does not wish you to engage in her cause without amply remunerating you for the services rendered. Your intelligent minds are not to be led away by false representations. Your love of honor would cause you to despise the men who would attempt to deceive you. In the sincerity of a soldier and the language of the truth, I address you."

Blackman could not believe what he was hearing, yet he was hearing it, this bold whitewash of history, this random throwing of compliments, all unmeant, all of which must have fought their way out of Jackson's bitter throat. Listen to him! Blackman thought. He knows what we think and he plays upon it. Honor, intelligence, truth.

"To every noble-hearted, generous freeman of color volunteering—"

A pulsing went through the crowd. So, that was the catch. Only freemen. They'd only have to give something, not the freedom from slavery whites thought they had now. They'd have to give slaves that freedom, and they wouldn't. They'd see New Orleans burned to the ground first, Blackman thought, before they loosed the slaves.

"—to serve during the present contest with Great Britain, and no longer, there will be paid the same bounty, in money and lands, now received by the white soldiers of the United States, viz.,[225] one hundred and twenty-four dollars in money, and one hundred and sixty acres of land. The noncommissioned officers and privates will also be entitled to the same monthly pay and daily rations, and clothes, furnished to any American soldier."

But the slaves, silently, like shadows, were already slipping away. Some with relief, Blackman imagined, for death in battle instead of freedom might've easily been their reward. Some were sad, for they'd have run the risk, fought and hoped to live, to become free men.

And you, Blackman, he said to himself, why are you here, why don't you go? No slave, but black, and there's a choice. Why stay?

He thought then of a quarter section. Land. Land bristling with tall pines, black with weather and heavy with turpentine; thought of magnolias in thick groves and streams and ponds and areas where the earth had been turned over to the warming sun and pulverized by plow and horse, and furrowed. He saw the first green shoots emerge from the black-brown soil and then bushes and then the corn, beans, cabbages, and the cotton. There would be cotton, off to a patch by itself, which would bring in the hard money. There would be so much land, 160 acres, that he wouldn't be able to see it all. And it would be his forever.

And his family's, for he thought, too, of a woman—wife, mother—and of children who would people the land. The woman would be strong, broad-shouldered, and under her flawless black skin the bones would be big. She'd walk about with that fine feminine grace large women possess, that grace they were forever conscious of wanting to have—and had because they weren't small—

"Sure could use a quarter section," Black Antoine said, and Blackman came out of his reveries to see him chewing nervously on his pipe.

"That's a lotta land, specially when all you've got now is ten acres."

"Griot, what about you?" Blackman said. "Still going?"

"Oh, Ah'll go," he said. "Git me dat quahtah section n sell it. Dat be wuth mo den de money." Griot looked at them with eyes that in the right light could've been called dead. He'd spent a lifetime dulling the flashes he knew could leap in them. Now, they always appeared lifeless, flat. But old acquaintances, long dead, some washed overboard in rough seas, others murdered in knife fights in ports halfway around the world, these had perceived the cunning that lay behind the flatness of his yellowed eyes.

Looking at Black Antoine, Griot saw a conniving hustler, a land-greedy farmer whose fields one day would burst with the white fluff of cotton bolls. Black Antoine would buy slaves and treat them worse than the white man. Black Antoine had plans and wasn't a good man to fight beside, Griot decided.

He would fight beside the Big Man, Blackman. Didn't know what he would be fighting for except the money and the land, and most of the land he'd put under cultivation for food. Looked like a family man. Hard-workin' big nigger. Could hitch a plow to himself and do just as good as a horse. Dreamer. Doer. Believer.

So Griot was prepared when Blackman said, "Sell it?"

And Black Antoine said, "I'll buy it."

*   *   *

To many a man, it would have been demeaning to beg for help from the blacks. To some degree Jackson felt this, but more, he was determined to win the battle he saw taking shape for New Orleans and the rest of the South. If you already had pirates, Choctaws, Creoles, and buckskinned Tennesseeans, it didn't make any difference about the niggers.

Now sitting in his quarters, Jackson almost smiled. That old fool who was rolling around on the ground this morning. All alone, too. Whatever the others felt about the high-flown speech, they didn't let it show. Land and money in exchange for services. That was fair enough, because if the British succeeded, there'd be nothing at all. You could promise the sky—and pay off, if you won. And he'd see to it that the niggers got exactly what he'd promised, no more and no less. As long as he had the power to do so, and if he won this battle, he thought, a vision of George Washington passing through his mind, he could come into almost unlimited power.

Two nights before Christmas, Jackson welcomed the news that the British had landed a squadron of troops and were making for New Orleans by way of the Villiers plantation. The men'd been missing life in the city and were getting restless. You couldn't treat them the way you did regulars; they'd pick up their rifles and start walking back home or wherever they came from.

Which group to send to head them off? The dragoons in their bright uniforms? No, they were the best of the few regulars he had. They were needed to set the example in bright daylight, in open field. His native Tennesseeans? The Indians? The pirates? The militia? The blacks with some equally unblooded young officers? [. . .] The black farmers would know every trail, nook, and cranny, Jackson thought again. He'd made a wise choice. [. . .]

*   *   *

For years, whenever they met they called each other the name the whites'd given them—Freejacks[226]—and they grew into a tough, isolated, proud clan, asking white men for nothing and giving nothing in return. Griot, whose land was adjacent to Blackman's, did not sell it after all, but leased it to Blackman. Black Antoine bought as much as he could and prospered.

Five years after the battle, Griot, hobbling now, his hair fringed with silver, came into La Baleine Noire, unrolled a parchment, and asked to have it hung so everyone could see. It read:

> February 18, 1820
> Office of the Adjutant General
> Office of the Inspector General
> No Negro or Mulatto will be received as a recruit of the Army.[227]

A group of men sitting around a table'd decided that, Blackman thought when he read it. Groups of white men were always sitting around tables deciding things about black people.

Excerpted from *Captain Blackman: A Novel* (Garden City, N.Y.: Doubleday, 1972).

Related writings by John A. Williams: *This Is My Country Too* (1964); *The Man Who Cried I Am* (1967); *Sons of Darkness, Sons of Light: A Novel of Some Probability* (1969); *Clifford's Blues* (1998).

SELECTED ADDITIONAL LITERATURE ON CITIZENSHIP AND WAR

Albert, Octavia V. Rogers. *The House of Bondage, or Charlotte Brooks and Other Slaves.* 1890. Reprint, New York: Oxford University Press, 1988.

Carter, Stephen L. *The Impeachment of Abraham Lincoln.* New York: Knopf, 2012.

Delany, Martin. "A Series of Four Tracts on National Polity." In *Martin R. Delany: A Documentary Reader,* edited by Robert S. Levine, 415–24. Chapel Hill: University of North Carolina Press, 2003.

———. "True Patriotism." In *Martin R. Delany: A Documentary Reader,* edited by Robert S. Levine, 137–40. Chapel Hill: University of North Carolina Press, 2003.

Hammon, Jupiter. "A Line on the Present War." [1783.] In Sondra A. O'Neale, *Jupiter Hammon and the Biblical Beginnings of African-American Literature,* 208–10. Metuchen, N.J.: Scarecrow Press, 1993.

Hopkins, Pauline. "A Dash for Liberty." [1901.] In *The Unforgetting Heart: An Anthology of Short Stories by African American Women (1859–1993),* edited by Asha Kanwar, 23–29. San Francisco: Aunt Lute, 1993.

Jacobs, Harriet. "Life among the Contrabands." [1862.] In *Incidents in the Life of a Slave Girl: A Norton Critical Edition,* edited by Nellie Y. McKay and Frances Smith Foster, 174–80. New York: W. W. Norton, 2001.

Jennings, Paul. *A Colored Man's Reminiscences of James Madison.* Brooklyn: George C. Beadle, 1865.

Johnson, Charles. *Middle Passage.* New York: Scribner, 1990.

Johnson, James Weldon. "Fifty Years," *New York Times,* 1 January 1913, 16.

Killens, John O. *And Then We Heard the Thunder.* New York: Knopf, 1963.

Moore, William. "The Spring of '65." [1925.] In *The Messenger Reader: Stories, Poetry, and Essays from* The Messenger Magazine, edited by Sondra Kathryn Wilson, 169–77. New York: Modern Library, 2000.

Morrison, Toni. *Beloved.* New York: Knopf, 1987.

———. *A Mercy.* New York: Knopf, 2008.

Nelson, Marilyn. "Juneteenth." In Marilyn Nelson, *The Fields of Praise: New and Selected Poems,* 93. Baton Rouge: Louisiana State University Press, 1997.

Packer, ZZ. "Dayward." *New Yorker,* 14 June 2010, 106–10.

Purvis, Robert. *An Appeal to Forty Thousand Citizens, Threatened with Disfranchisement, to the People of Pennsylvania. Pamphlets of Protest: An Anthology of Early African American Protest Literature, 1790–1860,* edited by Richard Newman, Patrick Rael, and Phillip Lapsansky, 133–42. New York: Routledge, 2001.

Pitts, Leonard, Jr. *Freeman.* Evanston, Ill.: Agate Bolden, 2012.

Rock, John S. "I Will Sink or Swim with My Race." 1858. In *Lift Every Voice: African American Oratory, 1787–1900,* edited by Philip S. Foner and Robert James Branham, 313–18. Tuscaloosa: University of Alabama Press, 1998.

Reed, Ishmael. *Flight to Canada: A Novel.* 1976. Reprint, New York: Atheneum, 1989.

Walker, Margaret. *Jubilee.* 1966. Reprint, New York: Bantam, 1967.

Yerby, Frank. "XXXVI." In Frank Yerby, *The Foxes of Harrow*, 395–408. New York: Dial Press, 1946.

ENDNOTES

1. *Instante mense*, a Latin term meaning in the current month.

2. Sofa.

3. The National Union League was a private, exclusive, patriotic organization composed primarily of economically successful men initially in Philadelphia (as the Union Club) and then nationally throughout the North. It was founded in 1862 during the Civil War and operated in support of Abraham Lincoln and the Union Army. After the war, newly freed black people throughout the South were encouraged to demonstrate loyalty to the Republican Party and the federal government by becoming members and establishing local clubs. Facing threats from the Ku Klux Klan, members in the South typically met in secret. The National Union League also was known as the Union League.

4. Civil War.

5. A failed charge, in 1854, on the Russian port of Balaclava by the British Light Brigade during the Crimean War. A poem by Alfred Tennyson memorializes the charge.

6. Margins.

7. Attempted to explain or present.

8. The African Brigade was comprised of the 1st Mississippi Infantry (African Descent) and the 9th and 11th Louisiana Regiment Infantry (African Corp/Corps d'Afrique).

9. *Harper's Magazine*, an influential political and literary publication founded in the 1850s. Drawings re-creating black soldiers in battle appeared in *Harper's*.

10. A battle on 7 June 1863 between black soldiers of the African Brigade, the 23rd Iowa Volunteer Infantry Regiment, and the 10th Illinois Volunteer Cavalry Regiment and the Confederate Army occurred at Milliken's Bend in Madison Parish, Louisiana. This battle was part of the successful siege of Vicksburg, Mississippi.

11. Slavery.

12. A poisonous tree; the term is often used to designate a negative or poisonous influence.

13. A black newspaper, *Pacific Appeal*, reported on James Madison Bell's presentation of this poem and excerpted a version. See "The Black Brigade," *Pacific Appeal*, 2 January 1864, 2.

14. Civil War.

15. Believe confidently.

16. Two knights from the legend of King Arthur and the Knights of the Round Table; Lancelot is associated with bravery and gallantry; Bedivere is considered a warrior. The French medieval poet, Chrétien de Troyes, wrote two of the earliest print versions of this legend: *Lancelot, Knight of the Cart* (ca. 1175–1181) and *Perceval, the Story of the Grail* (ca. 1135–1190).

17. Marshland and lakes or seas.

18. The quest of the Knights of the Round Table for the Holy Grail. In one version of

the Arthurian legend, the Holy Grail is the cup/chalice Jesus used at the last supper; in this version, it also is believed that Joseph of Arimathea used the same cup to collect the blood of Jesus on the cross. In another version, it is both a sacred plate/platter and the most honored spiritual understanding that a knight could acquire in his quest.

19. In truth.

20. To gain ownership by paying the established price; also to receive by inheritance.

21. Lancelot's son and a knight at the Round Table. Galahad finds the Holy Grail.

22. Miniature pendant used for perfume or smelling salts to revive consciousness.

23. A four-wheeled horse-drawn carriage.

24. Major General Benjamin Franklin Butler was the commander of the occupation of New Orleans in 1862 and organized the Union forces of the Louisiana Native Guard (73rd Regiment of the United States Colored Troops). The Butler Medal was named for him. He commissioned the medal in 1864 to honor black Civil War soldiers.

25. New Orleans.

26. During the Civil War this term referred to women who served as nurses and other medical workers.

27. This order formally authorized the Louisiana Native Guard (Corps d'Afrique/African Corps), a local militia composed of free men, to organize as Union troops. Their status as federal troops, however, was provisional, as there was not yet an official federal policy allowing black troops.

28. On 23 May 1863, Union troops seized Port Hudson in Louisiana and forced the Confederates to surrender on 3 July. This was the longest battle of the war and the first to involve black soldiers officially in the Union forces.

29. The 1st Louisiana Native Guard (African Corps) was sworn into service on 27 September 1862. They were one of several unofficial black regiments before the Emancipation Proclamation in January 1863 that allowed escaped black men to join the Union forces before the War Department issued its formal policy establishing black troops the following April. The 1st Louisiana Native Guard later was designated the 73rd Regiment, United States Colored Infantry under General Benjamin Butler.

30. Chauncy J. Bassett, the white commanding officer of the 1st Louisiana Native Guard (African Corps), was made commander over the existing black officers in the unit and led the unit before it received federal approval. Two officers, Captain André Cailloux and Second Lieutenant John Crowder, died at Port Hudson.

31. This reference is uncertain. It likely refers to Colonel Charles Jackson Paine, commander of the 2nd Louisiana Infantry Regiment (white), who was killed at Port Hudson. Union Brigadier General Halbert E. Paine was wounded but did not die at Port Hudson. Captain F. A. Payne was a Confederate officer who died at Port Hudson. The 3rd Louisiana Infantry Regiment (Corps d'Afrique) also participated in this battle. The events described here also correspond with reports of the death of a black Native Guard (Corps d'Afrique) soldier, Captain André Cailloux.

32. Grapes and canisters are two types of cannon projectiles designed to scatter and inflict massive injuries on people instead of targeting buildings or ships. Shells are fired from guns.

33. Site of the notorious Confederate prison that was hastily built to hold Union prison-

ers; also referred to as Camp Sumter. Thousands of Union prisoners of war died there of dehydration, malnutrition, and disease.

34. Revolutionary War for Independence.

35. Title supplied by volume editors; Civil War.

36. Say.

37. Title supplied by volume editors. Speech delivered on 11 May 1847 in New York.

38. The U.S.-Mexico War began in 1846 after the United States annexed Texas in 1845. Mexico never relinquished its claim to Texas while it was the independent Republic of Texas under Sam Houston. The war ended in 1848 with the signing of the Treaty of Guadalupe Hidalgo. The term Manifest Destiny reportedly appeared first in an essay by John O. Sullivan titled "Annexation," published in the July–August 1845 issue of *United States Magazine and Democratic Review*. The term conveys the notion of North American Europeans Christianizing and "civilizing" the entirety of the New World.

39. President James K. Polk of Tennessee.

40. U.S.-Mexican War.

41. Rochester, New York.

42. Title supplied by volume editors. Speech before the Rochester (New York) Anti-Slavery and Sewing Society on 5 July celebrating the 4 July 1776 adoption of the Declaration of Independence. Douglass later printed the speech as a pamphlet.

43. Reference to Henry Wadsworth Longfellow, "A Psalm of Life (What the Heart of the Young Man Said to the Psalmist)," *Knickerbocker, or New-York Monthly Magazine*, October 1838, 189.

44. Psalm 137:1–6.

45. This is a quotation from the first issue of William Lloyd Garrison's newspaper *The Liberator*. See "To the Public," *The Liberator* 1, no. 1 (1831): 1.

46. The Fugitive Slave Law of 1850 extended the 1793 law, making it a crime to harbor persons escaping from slavery. The 1850 law effectively criminalized the Underground Railroad and many other activities of abolitionists.

47. Genesis 1:3.

48. Psalm 68:31, sometimes referred to as the Ethiopian Prophecy.

49. Civil War.

50. Fort Pickens, located off the coast of Florida on Santa Rosa Island, had been unoccupied for at least a decade. It was a Union stronghold throughout the war, even though Florida joined the confederacy in 1861. Union forces that were transported by sea reinforced the fort. Both free and enslaved black people had lived in Florida ever since its occupation by Spain.

51. In the early days of the war, Major General Benjamin Franklin Butler offered Union troops to quash an uprising of enslaved people in Maryland. In 1861, he also advocated the policy of classifying persons who had escaped from slavery as war contraband, or property, and did not use them in battle. He later advocated that black troops should fight in the war and planned the successful battle (with both black and white troops) at New Market Heights near Richmond, Virginia. The Butler Medal, which he commissioned in 1864 to honor black Civil War soldiers, was named for him.

52. Civil War. Title supplied by volume editors.

53. *Instante mense*, a Latin term meaning the current month.

54. Grapes and canisters are two types of cannon projectiles designed to scatter and inflict massive injuries to people rather than to buildings or ships. Shells and minnies (also referred to as balls) are rifle ammunition.

55. Revolutionary War for Independence. A battle at Brandywine Creek near Philadelphia resulted in the British taking the revolutionary capital, then located at Philadelphia. Samson is a biblical figure endowed with great strength.

56. Old.

57. First state to sign the Constitution.

58. Saxon refers to Germany. The Celtic nations include Ireland, Scotland, Wales, Brittany, and other countries where Celtic languages are spoken. Gaul refers to France.

59. Civil War.

60. In the Old Testament, Ham was the son of Noah. Some interpretations of the story of Ham present him as cursed with black skin. The biblical account actually does not indicate this.

61. On 18 July 1863, the 54th Regiment Massachusetts Volunteer Infantry (United States Colored Troops) breached the Confederate lines at Fort Wagner on Morris Island, South Carolina. This second battle at Fort Wagner resulted in numerous Union casualties.

62. On 20 February 1864, Union and Confederate forces engaged in battle near Jacksonville, Florida. Numerous soldiers from the 54th Regiment Massachusetts Volunteer Infantry, the 8th infantry of the United States Colored Troops, and 35th North Carolina were reportedly murdered as prisoners.

63. On 12 April 1864, Confederates, led by General Nathan Bedford Forrest (a subsequent founder of the Ku Klux Klan), massacred Union soldiers and civilians at Fort Pillow in Tennessee; many had surrendered.

64. Civil War.

65. Pallas-Athena, goddess of war.

66. Fane: a temple, used here as a metaphor referring to the university.

67. Ancient stringed instrument often associated with the singing of poets.

68. Title supplied by volume editors.

69. A town in England.

70. Edward Boscawen ("Old Dreadnought"), an admiral in the Royal Navy. In 1758, he captured the French-controlled Louisbourg fortress in Canada, near Cape Breton Island, Nova Scotia.

71. Samuel Cornish invaded and captured Manila (under Spanish control) in response to Spain's entry into the war.

72. One of the Canary Islands colonized by Spain; located off the coast of Africa.

73. Nova Scotia, a province in Canada.

74. A person from the Scottish Highlands.

75. Henri de Brienne, a commander in the French navy.

76. Wore ship: The ship intentionally used the wind to veer in another direction in pursuit of the French vessels.

77. England.

78. The Bill of Rights (1791) comprises the first ten amendments to the Constitution of the United States. It includes individual rights that were not part of the Constitution, which primarily protected property rights and established a governmental structure.

79. Muslim.

80. Abused.

81. The term—actually *ignis fatuus*—refers to the illusion of light that occurs over swamps. Often the term is used to refer to someone being misled. Forten is suggesting that while the new bill limiting the movement of free black persons in Philadelphia was proposed as helpful, it really was quite the opposite. For more information on the bill and Forten's response see Winch, "The Making and Meaning of James Forten's *Letters from a Man of Colour.*"

82. Civil War.

83. The Emancipation Proclamation became effective on 1 January 1863. This document called for the freedom of enslaved people in the rebel states; persons enslaved in states loyal to the Union were not included in the provisions of this document.

84. French Protestants. Although the earliest Huguenot settlement in South Carolina, which was established in the sixteenth century, failed, later settlements in South Carolina in the seventeenth century thrived.

85. In May 1862, General David Hunter in Beaufort, South Carolina, advocated for black men to participate in the war. He organized the first regiment of black soldiers to fight for the Union. The regiment was unauthorized. Secretary of War Edwin Stanton ordered them to disband.

86. "Home, Sweet Home," a song from an opera by John Howard Payne that is famously known by the second line: "Be it ever so humble, there's no place like home."

87. A spiritual in the African American musical tradition.

88. A type of biscuit made with simple ingredients.

89. A ritual spiritual practice among black people in the New World.

90. U.S.-Mexico War.

91. Samuel Houston was the first president of the independent Republic of Texas after the battle of San Jacinto in 1836. He became a senator from Texas after it was annexed by the United States in 1845. Houston also fought in the Creek Wars with Andrew Jackson and later lived among the Cherokees on Indian Territory created by the United States.

92. Former residents of the Republic of Texas (never recognized by Mexico), which became part of the United States in 1845.

93. Name of the capital city of the state of Chihuahua in northern Mexico. U.S. forces occupied the city in 1847 during the U.S.-Mexico War. Colonel Alexander Doniphan led the U.S. forces.

94. Laws of the United States, including the imposition of slavery.

95. Title supplied by volume editors.

96. Frederick Douglass denounced Garnet's speech. The National Negro Convention delegation rejected by one vote Garnet's call for ending slavery by uprisings and insurrections. Douglass later paraphrased Garnet in his own Civil War recruiting broadside, "Men of Color To Arms! To Arms! Now or Never": "Let us rather die freemen than live to be slaves." Garnet published his address together with David Walker's *Appeal* in 1848.

97. The National Negro Convention movement began on 15 September 1830 in Philadelphia, Pennsylvania, at the Bethel A.M.E. Church and continued until 1864. Primary concerns of the members of the convention were resettlement of free persons of color in

Canada, the liberation of black people from slavery, and equality for black people in the United States. They did not advocate resettlement in Africa.

98. Declaration of Independence.

99. Quote from Lord Byron's long poem (published from 1812–1818) "Childe Harold's Pilgrimage," Canto II, Stanza 76.

100. In 1833, Britain began a protracted process of abolishing slavery in the United Kingdom. Britain abolished slavery in the Caribbean effective 1 August 1838. Many black people in the United States saw this and the end of the Haitian Revolution (1791–1804) as signal events in the liberation of bondspersons and the abolition of slavery.

101. After the fall of the viceroyalty of New Spain in 1821 and the establishment of Mexico under its own constitution in 1824, settlers from the relatively new United States of America lived in Mexico. Garnet is referring to the creation of the Republic of Texas during the Texas Revolution (1835–1836), following President Antonio López de Santa Anna's attempt to reorganize Mexico's governmental structure.

Montezumas: Garnet is referring to the ancient Sinagua people of present-day Arizona and the Montezuma Castle, or cliff dwellings, they constructed in the Arizona hills.

102. Garnet names heroic figures his audience would know: Moses, the biblical figure; Hampden, perhaps the religious radical Bishop Renn Dickson Hampden; [William] Tell of Switzerland, a legendary figure believed to be responsible for the Swiss rebellion against Austria's House of Habsburg; [Robert the] Bruce and [Sir William] Wallace, leaders of battles against the kingdom of England during the Wars of Scottish Independence in the thirteenth and fourteenth centuries; Toussaint L'Ouverture, the leader of the Haitian Revolution (1791–1804) that ended slavery in Haiti and established the country as an independent black nation; Lafayette, a French military officer who fought at the Battle of Brandywine (a British success) and secured French troops to fight in the Continental Army during the American Revolution; and [George] Washington, commander of the Continental Army.

103. Nat Turner led an insurrection in Southhampton County, Virginia in 1831.

104. In 1839, after the end of the international slave trade in 1808, Joseph Cinque and fifty-two other men commandeered the illegal slave ship that was transporting them and others to Cuba. They redirected the ship to the United States, where their trial for mutiny ended with their freedom.

105. In 1841, Madison Washington commandeered the slave ship transporting him and others in the internal slave trade from Virginia to New Orleans. Washington initially wanted to sail the ship to Liberia but then redirected it to Nassau, Bahamas, a British Caribbean Island colony where slavery had been abolished. Writers such as Frederick Douglass ("The Heroic Slave," 1853), William Wells Brown ("Madison Washington," 1863; and "Slave Revolt at Sea," 1867), Lydia Maria Child ("Madison Washington," 1865), and Pauline Hopkins ("A Dash for Liberty," 1901) retell this event in literature.

106. Civil War.

107. A white man, typically from the poor or laboring classes, especially a boss, trader, or overseer.

108. Folk healing practices and spiritual beliefs.

109. Jefferson Davis, president of the Confederacy.

110. Here Horton alludes to the apocryphal tale that Jefferson Davis fled wearing a dress.

111. Civil War and Spanish-Cuban-U.S. War.

112. The best-known of the Union flag bearers was William Harvey Carney, who took up the flag at the battle of Fort Wagner after the initial flag bearer was killed.

113. Civil War battles near Gettysburg, Pennsylvania, and Chattanooga, Tennessee. President Abraham Lincoln delivered the Gettysburg Address on 19 November 1863 and dedicated the cemetery at Gettysburg, which was the site of the most numerous casualties during the war.

114. Very likely Colonel Thomas Wentworth Higginson of the 1st South Carolina Volunteers (3rd USCT), which was composed of escaped captives from slavery.

115. The blue uniform of the Union Army.

116. The term Johnny Reb referred to Confederate soldiers.

117. Fort Wagner at Morris Island, South Carolina.

118. The gray uniform of the Confederate Army.

119. Spanish-Cuban-U.S. War (1898).

120. Revolutionary War for Independence. Title supplied by volume editors.

121. Headquarters of British general Charles Cornwallis, located near Camden, South Carolina. Cornwallis also served in the Battle of Brandywine Creek in Pennsylvania.

122. In 1780, Colonel Francis Marion, ignoring Cornwallis's defeat of General Horatio Gates's Continental forces at Camden, South Carolina, and later Colonel Thomas Sumter's defeat, destroyed British boats at Murray's Ferry and Nelson's Ferry before defeating British forces that occupied the home of Colonel Sumter, located near Nelson's Ferry. A ferry, similar to a dock, is a location where water vessels are loaded.

123. Civil War. Randall published a somewhat different version of "Memorial Wreath" in the *Afro-American* (Baltimore), 25 May 1946, 18.

124. Frederick Douglass, John Brown, Nat Turner, Sojourner Truth, and Harriet Tubman were either active abolitionists or leaders of antislavery actions.

125. Civil War.

126. "Robert F. Shaw" is the printed title for Ray's poem in her book. We have corrected the title for this volume because it is difficult to determine if the error is the poet's or the printer's.

127. Civil War.

128. Flag or standard bearer; this is an allusion to Anselmas Planciancois, a color sergeant in the 1st Louisiana Native Guards (Corps d'Afrique).

129. On 23 May 1863, Union troops seized Port Hudson in Louisiana, and on 3 July, they forced the Confederates to surrender. This was the longest battle of the war and the first to involve black soldiers officially in the Union forces.

130. Civil War. Throughout the eighteenth and nineteenth centuries black people frequently referred to themselves as Ethiopian or African, the former being a metonym for people of African descent.

131. Brook.

132. High seas.

133. A poetic or metaphorical name for the United States. Sometimes personified in literature and art as the goddess of liberty or democracy.

134. Civil War. Title supplied by volume editors.

135. A Confederate vessel.

136. Abraham Lincoln.

137. Bishop Benjamin Tucker Tanner founded the *A.M.E. Church Review* in July 1884. This report was initially published in the nineteenth century.

138. Title supplied by volume editors.

139. Stearns advocated for enlisting black men in the Union forces. He recruited escaped captives from Canada and free men from the western states for the 54th Regiment Massachusetts Volunteer Infantry and led the general recruitment effort for black soldiers. He also requested that the men receive equal pay. Stearns resigned after the War Department reneged on the promise of equal pay.

140. Secretary of War.

141. Prominent nineteenth-century black abolitionists.

142. In 1838, Pennsylvania became one state in a long line of northern states that rescinded or restricted voting rights for black men.

143. Vendor.

144. Founded in 1859 by Thomas Hamilton in New York.

145. Civil War. Title supplied by volume editors.

146. Meadow. This fight between the Native Indians and the colonial settlers on a meadow/bars in Deerfield, Massachusetts, was one among many battles during the various Indian Wars that took place throughout the colonies.

147. During the Civil War, the 1st Regiment Corps d'Afrique were free men who had volunteered for the Confederate Army in 1861 but were rejected. The Union forces later mustered some of the men into service. The 2nd Regiment Corps d'Afrique, primarily escaped captives from slavery, mustered into service on October 1862.

148. An island off Mississippi where the 2nd Regiment Corps d'Afrique was headquartered. Ship Island was a base for captured Confederates during the Civil War. Fort Massachusetts, located on the island, was incomplete when the war began.

149. A shelter from cold and wind.

150. A disastrous Gulf Coast hurricane that made landfall in Mississippi in 1969 and caused thousands of deaths in Mississippi, Louisiana, and Alabama. The Hurricane split Ship Island into two parts, now referred to as West Ship Island and East Ship Island.

151. A housing for holding a gun while firing.

152. A women's organization for descendants of persons who served in the military of the Confederate States of America.

153. Phalanx is a term from ancient military warfare referring to an imposing group of soldiers organized in a mass. Joseph T. Wilson uses the term Black Phalanx to refer to black military personnel in wars for the United States from the Revolutionary War for Independence through to the Civil War.

154. The second Civil War battle at Fort Wagner, located on Morris Island, South Carolina, is well known for the fighting of the 54th Regiment Massachusetts Volunteer Infantry.

155. Formerly.

156. Morris Island is near Charleston, South Carolina.

157. Forts in South Carolina. Fort Wagner is where the 54th Massachusetts Volunteer Infantry Regiment fought, and Fort Sumter is the site where the Civil War began, on 12 April 1861.

158. Colonel Robert Gould Shaw.

159. Shades: ghosts. The poem refers to black Revolutionary War heroes Crispus Attucks and Peter Salem; Hannibal, the Carthaginian general and military strategist who invaded Italy in the first century BCE; and Toussaint L'Ouverture, leader of the Haitian Revolution.

160. A low protective wall of earth or stone, designed to protect soldiers.

161. Reported as the words of William Harvey Carney of the 54th Regiment Massachusetts Volunteer Infantry, the flag-bearer for the second Battle of Fort Wagner.

162. Civil War. This song, often attributed to Sojourner Truth, very likely is a folk composition. Lindley Miller, a white officer in the First Arkansas regiment, collected a version from black troops. His title is "Song of the First of Arkansas."

163. Jefferson Davis, president of the Confederacy.

164. The chorus follows each set of dashes.

165. Gabriel is a high angel in the Koran, the Bible, and the Hebrew scriptures. He is a messenger or intermediary between God and humanity. Christian interpretations of Gabriel indicate that he will blow his horn to signal the last days and God's judgment of humanity.

166. Vial: a small container.

167. Josephus was a first-century historian of Jewish culture. He was Jewish (Yosef ben Matityahu) but became a Roman citizen. Plutarch was a Greek historian who became a Roman citizen.

168. Antediluvians lived before the Old Testament flood and did not survive.

169. Sodomites live in the Old Testament city of Sodom that God destroyed (along with Gomorrah, Admah, and Zeboim).

170. Ninevites resided in the ancient and great town of Nineveh.

171. Carthage was an ancient city-state in northern Africa and an empire possessing lands along the coast of the Mediterranean Sea.

172. Followers of the Muslim prophet Mohammad.

173. Title supplied by volume editors; Revolutionary War for Independence.

174. A name applied to the New World colonies of Europe in the eighteenth century. Wheatley uses the term as a poetic or metaphorical name for the hoped-for new nation. During the eighteenth and nineteenth centuries, poets and artists personified Columbia as the goddess of liberty or democracy; this use in literature by a writer in the New World may have begun with Wheatley. See Moore, "The Name 'Columbia,'" which refers to Phillis Wheatley in similar terms.

175. Columbia.

176. Aeolus, the Greek god who holds back fierce winds, some of which were thought to have separated Europe from Africa, creating the opening for the Mediterranean Sea.

177. National flag.

178. French.

179. Revolutionary War for Independence. Wheatley's letter to Mary Wooster, the wife

of General David Wooster, indicates that Mrs. Wooster commissioned this poem. General Wooster died on 27 April 1777 after receiving a wound during the Battle of Ridgefield.

180. Chief.

181. Inwardly.

182. Wheatley published this poem as a pamphlet under the name Phillis Peters.

183. France.

184. Britain.

185. Ireland.

186. "Smoak" is an eighteenth-century variant of smoke, here suggesting the earth's displeasure with dead bodies spread across her surface smoldering and bloodied from the fires of war; the sense of horror is associated with this word.

187. Scotland.

188. Unbreakable or stonelike.

189. Revolutionary War for Independence.

190. Gave birth with difficult labor pains.

191. Britain.

192. Flag.

193. Perhaps blue skies.

194. A poetic or metaphorical name for the United States, sometimes personified in poetry and art as the goddess of liberty or democracy.

195. King George III of England.

196. Stories from daily life; also earthly concepts.

197. Civil War.

198. Union general William Tecumseh Sherman.

199. Sparta was an ancient Greek city-state praised for its military prowess. Normans are people of northern France (Normandy) who are recognized for their military ideas. A Muscovite is a Russian, derived from the name of the capital city, Moscow.

200. A curved sword.

201. Excelsior is a Latin term meaning excellence or always higher. A crest is the uppermost section of a coat of arms, located just below the motto. The term crest sometimes is used as a metonym for coat of arms.

202. Bourne: boundaries, here meaning land or country.

203. Indian Wars (Seminole Wars).

204. Seminole is a variant of the Muskogean word *simanóli*, meaning wild, and the Spanish term *cimarrones*, which refers to runaways in Latin America. Maroon also is a variant of *cimarrones*.

205. Bourne: boundaries, here meaning land or country.

206. Spain.

207. Very likely Queen Isabella II of Spain.

208. Suppose.

209. The shield on a coat of arms.

210. The Spaniard Palmecho's daughter.

211. Robert the Bruce was a fourteenth-century Scottish warrior king who fought for and won Scotland's independence from England.

212. Apalachi: A reference to the North American Indigenous Apalachian people,

known as the Appalachian Cherokee Nation, and their native mountainous land in present-day West Virginia, Kentucky, Tennessee, and Virginia.

213. While Whitman's first version of this narrative poem appeared in print in 1884 under the title *The Rape of Florida*, the author revised and corrected this poem in 1885 and 1890. Excerpts from the 1885 version are presented here.

214. War of 1812. Title supplied by volume editors.

215. Marie-Joseph Lafayette, a French military officer who was one of George Washington's generals and fought at the Battle of Brandywine (a British success) in the Continental Army during the American Revolution. Lafayette later brought French troops to fight alongside Washington's army.

216. St. Louis Cathedral in New Orleans was established in 1720 and remains in use. Spanish colonialists built the Cabildo (meeting place of the government/city council, or *cabildo*) in 1795 to replace the capitol building that was destroyed by fire in 1788; the Cabildo is next to the St. Louis Cathedral.

217. The Black Whale, an inn for black sailors.

218. York was enslaved by William Clark and traveled with him and Meriwether Lewis on their expedition from Pittsburgh, Pennsylvania, to the Pacific Coast, which took place in 1803–1806. They reached the Pacific Coast at the mouth of the Columbia River in present-day Oregon.

219. John Strachan, William Ware, and Daniel Martin escaped from the Royal Navy ship *Melampus* in 1807 after the British impressed (forced) them into service. The practice of impressment permitted the Royal Navy to force able-bodied British men into service (often by boarding ships at sea) when they needed additional manpower. Sometimes the Royal Navy overlooked the rule regarding citizenship. The Royal Navy often pressed American men into service. If a man could not prove his citizenship, he often could not avoid being pressed. Daniel Martin, a black man, was unable to show protections from impressment. John Strachan and William Ware (a free man of color) were impressed even though they had protections papers. This event and a series of others following it precipitated an escalation into war between Britain and the United States.

220. The *Leopard*, a British ship, attacked the *Chesapeake* in an attempt to recover Strachan, Ware, and Martin from the United States.

221. Forecastle: the sailors' living quarters at the bow of a ship.

222. In 1814, a band of the Muskogee (Creek) Indians were simultaneously allies of the British and at war with other bands of the Muskogee nation. The ongoing battles between the United States and the British-allied band of Indians ended in the decisive battle of the Creek War at Horseshoe Bend in Alabama, when General Andrew Jackson took Creek lands from the bands that had supported the United States.

223. John A. Williams quotes directly from Andrew Jackson's proclamation on 21 September 1814, "To the Free Colored Inhabitants of Louisiana."

224. Passing for white is the practice among persons with a portion of African ancestry to deny their African lineage and claim solely their European American ancestry. The Creoles in New Orleans—some with and some without African ancestry—complicate the practice of passing for white in the United States. The previously Spanish and French colonial heritage of Louisiana had established different laws and social policies regarding who

was classified as black, white, or Creole. Louisiana Creoles typically have French ancestry along with any combination of Native American Indian, African, or Spanish ancestry. Creoles constitute an entirely separate group in New Orleans, a category that does not exist in the United States outside of Louisiana, which is sometimes considered the northernmost point of the Caribbean.

225. Abbreviation for the Latin term *videlicet*, which means to wit, that is, or namely.

226. Freejacks lived near present-day New Orleans in a community composed of persons who very likely had African, Haitian, Spanish, and French ancestry or heritage comprising any combination of the aforementioned groups. When Louisiana became a state in 1812, prior to the war, the residents of this community fought vigorously then and later to avoid being classified as black people by the United States because under the French, as well as the Spanish, law and social policy, they were not considered black.

227. Williams quotes an actual War Department general order. Congress strengthened and clarified this act with a second act in 1821 that restricted military service to free white males.

2

THE UNITED STATES ENTERS THE GLOBAL STAGE

Empire, Worldwide War, and Democracy

Up, up, ye men of bronze!
Breathe now a freeman's breath!
And claim your liberty in life
Or freedom in your death!

WILLIAM PICKENS, SEPTEMBER 1924

Buffalo Soldiers photographed in 1898 at Camp Wikoff, Montauk Point, New York. Image courtesy of the National Archives and Records Administration.

THROUGHOUT THE NINETEENTH CENTURY, the western borders of the United States expanded across the continent and military struggles consolidated the geographical growth. Soon those wars left the shores of the continent. After the Civil War, the United States began its quest to become an imperialist power with significant political, economic, and military influence. These years also mark a time of intense social disturbance domestically: the population expanded as new immigrants arrived, the North industrialized rapidly, and the country worked to recover from the brutal civil war that had disrupted (but had not destroyed) the racial status quo. In the midst of all of these events, African Americans continued to seek and claim their rightful places in the nation. By the turn of the twentieth century, the United States had a new vision of itself in relation to the rest of the world. This new perspective included a foreign policy based on an imperialist relationship with people of color. Three significant military engagements showcase this new international presence: the Spanish-Cuban-U.S. War (1898), the resulting struggles in the U.S.-Philippines War (1899–1902), and World War I. Each of these wars revealed the persistent realities of domestic and international race relations.[1]

The post–Civil War and the Reconstruction Amendments (Thirteenth, Fourteenth, and Fifteenth) abolished slavery, conferred citizenship on all persons born in the United States, and extended the vote to black men. These changes seemed to suggest a turning point that presaged expanded opportunities for most black people. But the promise of liberty was betrayed as northern and southern politicians battled for power in Congress, using the freedoms of African Americans as the pawn. The debacle of the 1876 presidential election and the back-room compromise that put Rutherford B. Hayes in the White House facilitated and hastened the betrayal of black citizens. As Republican reformers backed off from the commitments of Reconstruction laws, a period of violent political and social retrenchment unfolded. The political and civic participation of black people diminished in the face of extralegal violence intended to halt their demonstrations of citizenship. Nathan Bedford Forrest, a Confederate military leader during the Civil War, helped found the Ku Klux Klan in Tennessee in 1867, one of many secret vigilante groups established at this time to "police" and subjugate black people by creating and propagating fear. Engaging in campaigns of intimidation, bribery, arson, and murder, these domestic terror groups helped enforce the Black Codes, or state laws designed to limit the rights and movement of African Americans in the late 1880s and 1890s. The U.S. Supreme Court validated these disfranchising and discriminatory codes with the *Plessy v. Ferguson* (1896) decision, which upheld the constitutionality of the notion of "separate but equal" and set the cornerstone for race relations in the United States for almost seventy years.[2]

Black soldiers entered the Spanish-Cuban-U.S. War in 1898 in the context of this stultifying and debilitating racial repression at home. After the Civil War, they had served mainly in the West (particularly as the Buffalo Soldiers of the 9th and 10th Cavalries and the 24th and 25th Infantry Regiments), where they helped patrol the frontier and in many ways conducted imperialist missions against the Indigenous peoples of the North American continent. As the U.S. conflict with Spain intensified and war seemed likely, the military moved black soldiers to camps in the southeast and on the East Coast of the United States, where they encountered violence and rampant discrimination. Many white southerners, still smarting from the loss of the Civil War, resented the presence of black uniformed soldiers in their midst. For their part, black soldiers resented Jim Crow treatment.

In response to pressure from black communities, eight states accepted black volunteers in their militias, and the militias of three states had black officers. Nevertheless, the War Department continued to segregate federal military camps.[3] With hard feelings on both sides, black and white Americans (local citizens and military personnel) engaged in a number of violent clashes that typically ended in one-sided reports claiming that black soldiers were unmanageable and unfit for service. These reports, often promoted in the mainstream press, were highly inaccurate. Black regiments had a lot of experience. They were battle tested from their experiences in the West, more so than white regiments, which had higher rates of turnover and desertion. Black soldiers were high performing and ready to demonstrate their abilities, and except for a few times when extreme provocation necessitated self-defense or protection, they endured the abuse from locals and the press.[4]

The catalyst for the Spanish-Cuban-U.S. War revealed the intentions of the United States overseas. When the U.S.S. *Maine* sank in Havana Bay in February 1898, the United States blamed Spain. The definitive cause of this event was never determined despite multiple investigations later, including the most probable report that indicated a sailor's error in the boiler room.

Nevertheless, tensions had escalated between isolationists and imperialists in the United States. Imperialists used sensationalist news reports of the deaths of the 260 sailors aboard the *Maine* as a convenient justification for war, masking their eagerness to dominate the Spanish colony. The United States declared war against Spain in April 1898 and a patriotic zeal swept the nation that briefly united U.S. citizens across color and regional lines.[5] The war was billed as a "war to save humanity" and to save Cubans from the tyranny of Spanish imperialists. For many African Americans, military participation was an obligation of citizenship and a test of loyalty. In fact, black troops, mostly Buffalo Soldiers, made up about 13 percent of the U.S. forces in Cuba.[6]

The Spanish seemed a formidable foe after years of honing their skills against insurgent Cuban forces, but disease, particularly an outbreak of yellow fever, wreaked havoc on the island and affected fighting soldiers. President William McKinley's administration believed that supposedly racially determined biological differences endowed African Americans with natural immunity to tropical diseases. This is one reason for the military's deployment of significant numbers of black soldiers for this war, rather than, as some people had believed and hoped, as a reward for the years of service on the western frontiers. However, racialized biological determinism proved erroneous. The army ordered many black soldiers to nurse yellow fever patients in hospitals after the disease had decimated the military staff. In spite of the false science that claimed that black soldiers were immune to this disease, a huge number of black soldiers became sick. The 24th Infantry Regiment assigned to work in the hospitals reported losing six of their fifteen officers and 258 of their 456 enlisted men to the disease.[7]

The U.S. victory in Cuba can be directly attributed to the performance of black troops, yet Theodore Roosevelt and his "Rough Riders" (1st U.S. Volunteer Cavalry Regiment) have dominated the memory of this brief, 100-day war. Indeed, Roosevelt's role in orchestrating the war by recognizing Cuba as a geographically strategic acquisition clearly highlighted his ambition and political power. He managed to get a volunteer regiment mustered into service with himself as leader, even though he only had National Guard training. He also managed to get his regiment into a war in which few other volunteer units saw combat. However, it was black troops that facilitated important and strategic victories.[8]

At Las Guásimas, for instance, because of the disorganized leadership of U.S. troops, Spanish troops managed to ambush the Rough Riders under Colonel Roosevelt's command. The swift actions and bravery of the 10th

Cavalry saved the beleaguered volunteer unit from complete destruction. Sergeant Louis Bowman, a black 10th Cavalry trooper who later published his story in the *Tampa Morning Tribune*, stated in no uncertain terms that "if it had not been for the timely aid of the Tenth Cavalry, the Rough Riders would have been exterminated."[9] At the time, Roosevelt had only praise for the black soldiers with whom he fought side by side. Indeed, the performance of the 24th Infantry proved crucial in the capture of San Juan Hill, a significant win that signaled Spain's defeat and elicited glowing reports from the battlefield. Black units suffered huge losses in Cuba, not just to yellow fever. The 10th Cavalry, who kept pushing forward from their positions, lost about 20 percent, including twelve officers, early in the campaign. A total of 50 percent of its officers were killed or wounded.[10]

African American responses to this war varied. Most civilian African Americans viewed the war in Cuba through the lens of deteriorating race relations in the United States, and many exposed the irony of helping those abroad given the racism implicit in the endeavor. As one writer put it, it was "a war launched in the name of humanity by a nation enamored of Anglo-Saxon supremacy."[11] Why fight, many argued, for the deliverance of others or the further oppression of peoples of color by empire-building Americans when the real fight for salvation was at home? This language, formed at a point when the United States became an occupying power, would be honed in the "Double V" campaign during the opening years of World War II, nearly fifty years later. Opinions on the war in Cuba, among black public figures and punctuated by African Americans' reports from the field itself, appeared in the growing black press. Papers such as the *New York Age* and the New Orleans *Crusader*, mostly distributed locally and circulated by black porters and passengers on the railroads, recorded the heated debates among black people and the torn commitments they felt about the imperialist project. For the most part, despite the hostile environment at home, African Americans (particularly soldiers) saw the war as the first opportunity since Emancipation to win official recognition from the military and the nation.[12]

After the war, black troops returned to bases in the South and faced violence again, this time from local residents and white volunteers who had not seen battle. If anything, by proving their loyalty and skill in the international field, black soldiers raised the ire of large segments of the white population that was determined to force them back into their "place." Press reports typically overemphasized and distorted episodes where black soldiers defended themselves against provocation from white citizens or military personnel. In addition, Theodore Roosevelt, early in 1899 in a *Scribner's Magazine* article, went out of his way to embellish his account of the events in Cuba by accusing black troops of cowardice and by omitting their rescue mission.[13] In response, Sergeant Presley Holliday wrote a letter to the *New York Age* (below) that was published soon after Roosevelt's article. Holliday addressed Roosevelt's inaccuracies, stating that his remarks were "uncalled for and uncharitable and . . . altogether ungrateful." Roosevelt, however, continued to devalue the contributions, ability, and patriotism of the black soldiers who had rescued his unit. Roosevelt's re-creation of his role in events catapulted him to celebrity status and ultimately into the presidency.[14]

Heightened rage about the progress of black people played out not only in the military but also in many towns across the country. In November 1898, for example, a few months before Roosevelt's article, white supremacists in Wilmington, North Carolina, used fraud and intimidation to unseat legitimately elected black officials in the city. Impatient to seize power, a white mob rampaged through black sections of Wilmington, destroying black-owned businesses and homes and terrorizing or killing black people they encountered. Approximately 1,500 African Americans left the city, forfeiting their property. This riot set the tone for race relations in the state for decades afterward. President William McKinley did nothing, thereby emboldening white supremacists throughout the South. Atrocities where whites enforced their perceived supremacy through violence and intimidation occurred often, well into the mid-twentieth century.[15]

Although the treatment of the black soldiers who participated in the Spanish-Cuban-U.S. War tested the national loyalty of all African Americans, at least two ideological camps developed. Some supported imperialism as a show of patriotism that might open up more opportunities. Many also remained loyal to the Republican Party, which was still viewed as the party of Lincoln. However, others were decidedly anti-imperialist and pointed to the increasing terrorism against black people and the deliberate rewriting of black participation in Cuba to support their position. Among this latter group were African Americans who refused to be silent about exporting white supremacist behavior to other peoples of color.[16] Notably, Bishop Henry McNeal Turner of the African Methodist Episcopal Church published a commentary (below) that sought to dissuade black men from enlisting in the army, citing accounts of mistreatment of black troops on home soil and openly questioning what African Americans had achieved through military service.

Victory in Cuba set a course for American expansion and imperialism. Spain also surrendered territories in the Philippines, Guam, and Puerto Rico in the Treaty of Paris, signed in December 1898. That year, the United States also annexed the Kingdom of Hawai'i after overthrowing Queen Lili'uokalani in 1893, and in January 1899, the United States appropriated uninhabited Wake Island. The United States was now an empire with strategic geographical posts in the Pacific that provided direct access to Asia. Manifest Destiny had spilled far beyond the shores of the continent by the turn of the twentieth century.

The U.S. imperialist project quickly encountered local drives for independence. The Treaty of Paris precipitated the Philippines-U.S. War. In February 1899, Emilio Aguinaldo, a prominent Filipino nationalist, led thousands in guerrilla warfare against U.S. occupation. In response, the U.S. military shipped about 70,000 soldiers to the islands. By this point, many African American civic groups had adopted a clear anti-imperialist tone, including the National Afro-American Council; the National Negro Anti-Imperial, Anti-Expansion, and Anti-Trust League; and the Black Man's Burden Association. Reports from the Philippines suggested that the racism, violence, and brutality of white Americans surpassed that of the Spanish colonialists who had preceded them. One anonymous letter to the *New York Age* in 1900 (below) condemned the occupation as "highway robbery" of persons of color and questioned the involvement of black troops in helping imperialists plunder another nonwhite population. Prominent Howard University professor Kelly Miller wrote a biting social commentary on the Filipino struggle, excoriating the official rhetoric of humanitarianism and stating that the U.S. imperial conquest had no consent from the people. He also questioned the position of black troops, stating that they would be unworthy of the rights they claimed at home—even going so far as to write that they would forfeit those rights—if they supported the imperialist endeavor: "How, with consistency, could the despoilers of the brown man's rights in Manila, upbraid the nullifiers of the black man's rights in Mississippi?" Miller asked. "The pill of imperialism may be sugar-coated to the taste, but the negro swallows it to his own political damnation."[17]

While members of the four black segregated army units, the Buffalo Soldiers, fought on the islands, the army was reluctant to send black volunteers, doubting their loyalty in light of black protests against the war at home. In a calculated political move, President McKinley, looking toward the upcoming elections, authorized two black volunteer regiments (the 48th and 49th Infantries).[18] As some had feared, however, when black soldiers became part of the occupational forces, the United States transported Jim Crow to the Pacific along with troops. Public spaces on the islands were segregated. White troops insulted both Filipino civilians and black soldiers.[19]

There were a few small gains for black military men in this era. A small number of black soldiers were commissioned as officers for the Philippine Scouts (Filipino recruits into the U.S. Army), and black seaman Robert Penn won a Medal of Honor for his bravery during the Spanish-Cuban-U.S. War. But overall, attitudes about black men in uniform continued to reflect the nation's ambivalence toward African American citizens.

The navy, which had had a relatively open policy toward black seamen, began to change in the beginning of the twentieth century, particularly after Theodore Roosevelt became president in 1901. In this period, the navy upgraded its fleet to steel and steam. The new ships required machine operators, not navigators or sail handlers, and naval recruiting altered to focus on trained engineers. This shift in skills resulted in a downsizing of black sailors (who were mostly put on shore duty), and the navy relegated those who remained on board to the boiler room or to servant work.[20] The navy became the "Great White Fleet," reflecting the preferred color for the paint on the new ships and for the men who operated them. The proportion of African Americans serving as mess men in the navy increased from 29 to 49 percent from 1870 to 1890, and by 1906, African Americans represented only 5 percent of the navy. This figure dropped to 2 percent during World War I. As a result of the military's access to cheaper labor sources leading to an increase in foreign enlistments, more Filipinos served in the navy by 1914 than African Americans. For black men, the Naval Academy at Annapolis at the turn of the century proved more hostile than West Point, and the few black sailors suffered so severely that none finished. Because of all this, black seamen never advanced to higher positions.[21]

In short, the two wars that decimated Spain's empire increased the ongoing debates about why black people would want to serve in the U.S. military, particularly given the racial tensions within the United States. The Spanish-Cuban-U.S. War had "multiplied the black man's grievances," and Roosevelt's fictitious accounts about Cuba had insulted African American soldiers.[22] Complex loyalties informed African American responses to both wars. Black soldiers, trained and committed to serving their country, demonstrated their patriotism by carrying out military orders. Yet for some African Americans, both at home and at war, a growing sense of a political alliance with other peoples of color prompted a disavowal of the imperialist endeavors of the United States.

In peacetime, black soldiers continued to experience intense racial prejudice and hostility from white civilians living around their garrisons. Some white politicians petitioned the War Department to remove black troops from their districts. A particularly egregious incident in August 1906 highlighted the complicit racism in all corners of society, from the local saloon owner to the U.S. president. The 1st Battalion of the 25th Infantry Regiment was based for less than three weeks at Fort Brown, Texas, which bordered Brownsville. After numerous incidents of provocation from civilians who rigidly maintained the color line in the town, the army ordered black soldiers to stay in the garrison to avoid confrontations. During the night of 13 August someone fired shots in town, damaging property, killing one person and wounding a few others. The locals blamed supposedly rogue black soldiers who, they claimed, had scaled the walls and fired indiscriminately.

Unable to identify any individuals and basing their decisions on flimsy evidence at best, Secretary of War William Taft and President Roosevelt enforced an excessive punishment: they dismissed without honor every black soldier present that night at Fort Brown, 167 in total. Senate investigations in the following months questioned the validity of the evidence and concluded that no proof existed to warrant such a harsh punishment. Only in 1972, and under political pressure, did President Richard Nixon push the military to award honorable discharges to the soldiers. The sole survivor, Dorsie Willis, was given a token compensation of $25,000 in consideration of the earnings, pension, and honor he had lost.[23]

Just over a decade after the Fort Brown incident, on 6 April 1917, the United States entered World War I after closely monitoring the bloodshed in Europe for nearly three years. President Woodrow Wilson proclaimed that the nation declared war to protect democracy. This noble reason for aiding the Allies in Europe did little to ameliorate the situation for African Americans at home, where white supremacy and Jim Crow segregation continued. And the military marched in lockstep with these values. At the onset of the war, the approximately 10,000 black soldiers in the standing army remained in the segregated units of the Buffalo Soldiers, the small number of African Americans in the Navy were below the decks in service positions, and other branches of the U.S. military remained essentially white.[24]

Among a new generation of black intellectuals, debates raged about the nation's entry into the war. In the pages of the *Crisis* (below), the official publication of the National Association for the Advancement of Colored People (NAACP), editor W.E.B. Du Bois urged African Americans to "close ranks," to put aside the struggles of African Americans and take up the national war effort, hoping for social and political advancement afterward. In contrast, some of his contemporaries doubted that the practice of failing to reward military service with equality would change. Among the dissenters were two labor activists who were also editors of *The Messenger* magazine, A. Philip Randolph and Chandler Owen (below). These men published articles on the hypocrisy of sending African Americans to fight for democracy in Europe while black people endured unequal treatment at home. Some African Americans "closed ranks" as Du Bois had suggested, and others protested as Randolph and Owen suggested. These patterns of the debate reflected the conversations that had unfolded nearly two decades earlier during the U.S. imperial wars.

On 18 May 1917, in the early weeks of the U.S. engagement, as the need for additional troops became apparent Congress passed the Selective Service Act, which required all eligible men to register. About 350,000 African Americans signed up. Many were eager to be part of the nation's push onto the world stage and anticipated better opportunities in the military than they would have as civilians enduring the injustices of prejudice and Jim Crow. Military quotas limiting the number of African Americans thwarted the aspirations of many for service. This occurred because the U.S. military initially emphasized frontline combat, and the armed services refused to deploy black men in Europe. More black men may have registered to wear military uniform, but in parts of the South exploited black labor drove the huge plantation economy, keeping many black men in the fields (see John Matheus's play below).[25]

When African Americans finally received conscription notices, they lived in segregated quarters on military bases, often in the South, and received insufficient training in inferior environments. While most white draftees occupied decent barracks and received intense training, most black soldiers did not. The armed services also prohibited black men from firing weapons. In some camps black soldiers lived in overcrowded and unsanitary tents without floors or warm blankets, some wore discarded Civil War uniforms (if they received any at all), and lacked sufficient clothing and supplies for the changeable climates. Once again, the bases, located near firmly segregated civilian communities, became sites of conflict and violence. On 23 August 1917, conflict occurred in Houston, Texas, after a series of smaller incidents between disgruntled local white civilians and police and black civilians and soldiers posted at Camp Logan. When reports of a white mob shooting on the base began to circulate among the black troops, members of the 24th Infantry stationed there marched, in protest, on Houston, shooting anyone who got in their way. For them, self-protection was about honor and pride. They valued the uniform they wore and demanded respect. Shots fired on both sides killed several people, both soldiers and civilians. In response, the army tried the rioting soldiers in courts-martial, meting out the harshest punishments of execution or life sentences, but never addressing Houston's white population's blatant provocation and unlawful violence.[26]

The NAACP, established in 1909, protested acts of violence directed toward black people, calling national attention to racially motivated atrocities and seeking the right for black men to fight for the nation. In May 1917, in response to intense lobbying, the War Department established a training camp for black officers at Fort Des Moines, Iowa. Just under 650 junior officers received commissions that October: 106 captains, 329 first lieutenants, 204 second lieutenants, and 2 majors.[27] The orders these new officers received sent them to service units and they had few, if any, opportunities to lead. By the end of the war, a reported 1,353 black officers had served, but their rankings were low and relatively few became company commanders. White troops regularly requested and received transfers to avoid serving under black leadership, and white officers received priority for positions leading black troops. When these white officers evaluated black servicemen, they relied on prejudicial reports and the pseudoscience of eugenics instead of reviewing records of loyalty and bravery. Their reports claimed that black men were not suited for war and tended to categorize all black soldiers as "combat risks." These evaluations also failed to take into account inequalities in training and opportunities. The U.S. military used such reports to strengthen their policy to keep black men in low ranks and deny them the right to fight in combat even after the implementation of a federal "work or fight" order to the Selective Service Act in 1918.[28]

The work-or-fight rule became another way to control black labor. It allowed local draft boards to force unemployed men to work in war industries or join the military. It also permitted local authorities to order men to leave their jobs unrelated to defense for work in war industries in the local area or to enter the military. Local officials in states such as Georgia, Florida, Louisiana, Virginia, and Alabama enacted similar laws that forced black women to do domestic work, pay fines, or go to jail instead of living on their husbands' military allotments. Black men across the South protested these attempts to mandate forced work for black women. Draft board authorities also furloughed black soldiers against their will and forced them to work on farms picking cotton or other crops in the area. They also forced civilian black men to work locally at wages far below what they would receive in the military. Local authorities used the work-or-fight policy and farm furloughs to perpetuate existing coercive labor practices that exploited southern African Americans. Some influential planters in the Mississippi Delta lobbied for deferments for their strong and able-bodied tenants or sharecroppers so they could keep them in the fields. Ironically, many southern states sent more white men to the war in order to keep local agricultural economies functioning with cheap black labor.[29]

By the spring of 1918, a significant number of African Americans had finally received induction notices. The increased number of black soldiers expanded the ranks of the 92nd Infantry Division (which was organized in November 1917 with early draftees) and the 93rd Infantry Division (established in December of that year from army regulars and former black National Guardsmen). Even though warehousing black units on American bases caused local instability, top military commanders balked at the notion of sending black troops to Europe under the U.S. flag. Most of the Buffalo Soldiers remained outside the European theatre, along the Mexican border or in the Philippines or Hawai'i. Only about 11 percent of black men in the armed services saw combat during the war and most of these fought with the French military, not U.S. troops. The 92nd, poorly trained and commanded by disinterested white leaders, performed dismally during the Meuse-Argonne campaign and suffered further under accusations of cowardice and ineptitude, a stigma that was hard to remove from the public record.[30]

Regiments from the 93rd Division fought under the French flag. The 369th U.S. Infantry (a regiment of the 93rd Division) from New York, the "Men of Bronze," or Les Enfants Perdus (the lost children), as the French called them, underscoring the black unit's abandonment by the United States, had to rely on French material support for their campaigns. The U.S. military had suspended all leaves, so the 369th spent more time in combat than any other American infantry unit, and still it beat the Germans. In a secret memorandum dated 7 August 1918 with the subject line "Concerning Black American Troops," General John J. Pershing advised the French to refrain from "spoiling" or socializing with African Americans in an effort to maintain the U.S. colorline. French officials, for the most part, ignored the directive and in December 1918 awarded the Croix de Guerre to the 369th for bravery. The Germans had nicknamed them the "Hell Fighters" due to their mettle and efficiency on the battlefield. They were the most decorated unit of the war, albeit by France. More than 3,000 casualties from the 93rd Division belied claims that African Americans were cowardly and unwilling to fight. The men returned to a ticker-tape parade down Fifth Avenue in New York in February 1919, the first such reception for black veterans, but the U.S. military refused to let them march in uniform in the French parade on 14 July 1919 in Paris (Bastille Day).[31]

Women also served abroad during World War I. They contributed in significantly smaller numbers than the men and worked as civilians instead of military personnel. White women supported the Allies through the American Red Cross or the Army Nurse Corps or as telephone operators. These organizations refused to accept black women eager to serve. The YMCA sponsored a few African American women who went to Europe. Addie Hunton and Kathryn Johnson spent fifteen months in France and documented their experiences and those of black soldiers in *Two Colored Women with the American Expeditionary Forces*. Similarly, a small number of black women volunteers such as the "colored yeowomen" performed clerical duties for the navy in Washington, D.C. Overall, however, black women's efforts to be included in official war efforts as equals failed.[32]

African American men who returned from the war were changed, but the nation they returned to remained unchanged in terms of race relations. Immense hostility awaited the uniformed black veterans who came home. Membership in the Ku Klux Klan boomed and its members employed terrorism and violence—with the tacit approval of local and state law enforcement—to enforce Jim Crow laws and customs. Lynchings continued unpunished across the country. During the notorious Red Summer of 1919, violence against African American veterans intensified. Du Bois, disappointed and angered by the continued maltreatment of black soldiers and civilians despite their patriotic efforts, resumed his push for full citizenship for all. Between the wars, African Americans issued vigorous challenges to persistent violations of their civil rights, including lynching, and against the widely proliferating and false ideas about human character and intelligence.

NOTES

1. Here, the term imperialism refers to the dominant military, political, social, and economic influence of the United States abroad.

2. See Du Bois, *Black Reconstruction*; Du Bois, *The Souls of Black Folk*; Foner, *Reconstruction*; Dailey, Gilmore, and Simon, *Jumpin' Jim Crow*; Litwack, *Trouble in Mind*.

3. Gatewood, "Black Americans and the Quest for Empire," 551–52; Scott, *The Unwept*, 73–75.

4. Gatewood, "Negro Troops in Florida, 1898," 2–15; Astor, *The Right to Fight*, 59–63; Edgerton, *Hidden Heroism*, 49.

5. Edgerton, *Hidden Heroism*, 48; Astor, *The Right to Fight*, 57.

6. Scott, *The Unwept*, 13.

7. Ibid., 151, 181–91; Bonsal, "The Negro Soldier in War and Peace," 325; Bond, "The Negro in the Armed Forces of the United States Prior to World War I," 286.

8. See Gatewood, "Black Americans and the Quest for Empire."

9. Quoted in Scott, *The Unwept*, 122.

10. Edgerton, *Hidden Heroism*, 53.

11. Gatewood, "Black Americans and the Quest for Empire," 546.

12. Thompson, "The Black Press," 333–40.

13. Edgerton, *Hidden Heroism*, 55; Roosevelt, "The Rough Riders."

14. Bond, "The Negro in the Armed Forces of the United States Prior to World War I," 285; Lentz-Smith, *Freedom Struggles: African Americans and World War I*, 19–20.

15. Litwack, *Trouble in Mind*, 312–15; North Carolina Office of Archives & History, "1898 Wilmington Race Riot Commission," www.history.ncdcr.gov/1898-wrrc/, accessed 9 June 2014; Lentz-Smith, *Freedom Struggles: African Americans and World War I*, 17–18.

16. Gatewood, "Black Americans and the Quest for Empire," 566; Gatewood, "Negro Troops in Florida, 1898," 1.

17. Kelley Miller, "Anti-Imperialist Broadside No. 11: The Effect of Imperialism on the Negro Race" (1900), N. E. Negro Anti-Imperialist League, Boston, Mass., http://memory.loc.gov/ammem/rbpehtml/rbpebibAuthors27.html (click on Miller, Kelley), accessed 9 June 1914.

18. Gatewood, "Black Americans and the Quest for Empire," 559–60.

19. Lentz-Smith, *Freedom Struggles: African Americans and World War I*, 57–58.

20. Buckley, *American Patriots*, 159.

21. Ramold, *Slaves, Sailors, Citizens*, 182–84; Edgerton, *Hidden Heroism*, 59–60.

22. Gatewood, "Black Americans and the Quest for Empire," 555.

23. Astor, *The Right to Fight*, 79–89; Lentz-Smith, *Freedom Struggles: African Americans and World War I*, 59–60.

24. Farrar, "The Black Soldier in Two World Wars," 350; Lentz-Smith, *Freedom Struggles: African Americans and World War I*, 37.

25. Mennell, "African-Americans and the Selective Service Act of 1917," 275–87; Farrar, "The Black Soldier in Two World Wars," 350.

26. See Barbeau and Henri, *The Unknown Soldiers*; Farrar, "The Black Soldier in Two World Wars," 351; Spencer, Spencer, and Wright, "World War I as I Saw It," 143–44; Lentz-Smith, *Freedom Struggles: African Americans and World War I*, 59–69, 121, 171; Edgerton, *Hidden Heroism*, 73.

27. Scott, "The Participation of Negroes in World War I," 290.

28. Hastie, "Negro Officers in Two World Wars," 316–18; Scott, "The Participation of Negroes in World War I," 289–90; Farrar, "The Black Soldier in Two World Wars," 351.

29. Shenk, "*Work or Fight*," 5–9, 34–47; Woodruff, *American Congo*, 49.

30. See Barbeau and Henri, *The Unknown Soldiers*; Keene, "Americans as Warriors," 16–17; Spencer, Spencer, and Wright, "World War I as I Saw It," 148–49; Du Bois, "The Negro Soldier in Service Abroad during the First World War," 324.

31. See Harris, *Harlem's Hell Fighters*; Little, *From Harlem to the Rhine*; Roberts, *The American Foreign Legion*; Slotkin, *Lost Battalions*; Farrar, "The Black Soldier in Two World Wars," 351–52; Lentz-Smith, *Freedom Struggles: African Americans and World War I*, 109–10.

32. See Hunton and Johnson, *Two Colored Women with the American Expeditionary Forces*; Miller, *The History of the World War for Human Rights*, 597–98.

A.M.E. CHURCH: *Voice of Missions*

The missionary societies of the A.M.E. Church have their origins in the nineteenth century. Sarah Allen, wife of A.M.E. Church founder Richard Allen, formed the short-lived Daughters of Conference (which Richard Allen referred to as the Dorcas Society) in 1824. In 1840, Reverend William Paul Quinn was appointed as the first General Missionary of the A.M.E Church, and in 1844 the Parent Home and Foreign Missionary Society became the official national missionary organization of the A.M.E. Church. Several of the bishops' wives established the first women's missionary society of the A.M.E. Church in 1874, the Women's Parent Mite Missionary Society, which became a national organization at the next meeting of the General Conference of the church. There were no chapters in the South. Bishop Henry McNeal Turner spearheaded the second women's missionary society in 1893, the Women's Home and Foreign Missionary Society; most of its chapters were in the South. The A.M.E Church women's missionary societies raise funds in support of missionary work. Local missionary work in the A.M.E. Church was primarily, although not exclusively, performed by women; international missionary work was primarily assigned to husband and wife teams. From 1893 to 1900, Bishop Turner (one of the most vociferous opponents of the war in Cuba) edited the *Voice of Missions* newspaper (headquartered in Atlanta, Georgia), which published the article reprinted below.

The Negro Should Not Enter the Army[1]

It is about time for the ministers of the A.M.E. Church[2] who, in the aggregate, are the most progressive, enlightened and racial of the Africanite ministry of the world, with the highest regard for all other denominations, to begin to tell the young men of our race to stay out of the United States army. If it is a white man's government, and we grant it is, let him take care of it. The Negro has no flag to defend. There is not a star in the flag of this nation, out of the forty odd, that the colored race can claim, nor is there any symbol signalized in the colors of the flag that he can presume to call his, unless it would be the stripes, and the stripes are now too good for him. He is only regarded as entitled to powder and lead and the burning fagots.[3] He has no civil, social, political, judicial or existing rights any longer. He may exist, be or live till the lynchers say he must die, and when they get ready to demand his life, the nation, from President McKinley down, down and down to the most contemptible white riff-raff, says well done! If not in words, they say it by their silence, and those who did enlist some months ago, were abused, misrepresented and vilified when they even passed through the country, worse than brutes would have been.

If they came out of the cars and walked about the depot, they were charged with trying to kill men, women and children, and fire the cities and villages. If they sat in the cars and failed to get out, the newspapers branded them with cowardice, and said they were afraid, they knew what would follow, while one town would telegraph to the next that Negro soldiers would pass through. "Have your armed police at the railroad station, armed to the teeth and ready to shoot them down upon the slightest provocation." Yet the same towns and villages were ready to supply them with all the rot-gut whiskey they were able to purchase, to transform them into maniacs and human devils, if these soldiers were low enough to drink the infernal drug. We now ask, in the face of these facts, and they are not half told, what does the Negro want to enlist, lay his life upon the alter [sic] of the nation, and die for? What is to be gained? Where is the credit? Who will accord it to him? In what particular will the race be benefited?

Suppose the Negro should enlist in great numbers and go to the Spanish islands and help to subjugate the territory now in dispute, and subordinate it to the dictatorial whim of the United States. What right, what privilege, what immunity, what enjoyment, what possession will he be the recipient of? A Cuban from Havana who was compelled to ride with us in a jim-crow⁴ car a week ago, and who was as mad as vengeance at this restriction of his manhood, told us that the diabolical prejudice of the United States was being exhibited there, and his curse-words were sulphuretic vengeance itself. He said "This valuing a man by his color was unknown in Cuba until the scoundrels and villains of this country went there." He showed us papers which represented him as a great business man, dealing in the finest tobacco and cigars, yet he was compelled to ride in the jim-crow car or be mobbed at every station, and this Cuban was not a black man.

We ask the young men of the Negro race if you have got any life to throw away for such a country as this? If you have a spare life on hand, that you wish to dispose of by sacrifice, for mercy's sake, for honor's sake, for manhood's sake, and for common sense sake throw it away for a better purpose, in a nobler act, in doing something that will perpetuate your memory, to say the least.

While we are the first Africanite Chaplain in the history of the nation, and have once been proud of the flag of this nation as it waved and flaunted in the air, as a Negro we regard it a worthless rag. It is the symbol of liberty, of manhood sovereignty and of national independence to the white man, we grant, and he should justly be proud of it, but to the colored man, that has any sense, any honor, and is not a scullionized fool, it is a miserable dirty rag.

We repeat that the A.M.E. ministry, yes, and the Negro ministry of the country should fight the enlistment of colored men in the United States army, as they would liquor brothels, thievery, breaking the Sabbath, or any crime even in the catalogue of villainy. The Negro minister of the gospel who would encourage enlistment in the United States army in the conditions things are now, encourages murder and the shedding of innocent blood for nothing, as the foolish young men do not know what steps they are taking. Moreover, the bulk of the white people do not want colored soldiers. Our own governor[5] disapproves of it. The majority of the white press is against it. They regard the black soldiers as monstrosities, and we regard them monstrosities also. Again we say to the colored men, stay out of the United States army. Take no oath to protect any flag that offers no protection to its sable defenders. If we had the voice of seven thunders, we would sound a protest against Negro enlistment till the very ground shook below our feet.

"The Negro Should Not Enter the Army," *The Voice of Mission* (1 May 1899).

A Black Soldier in the Philippine Islands

This anonymous letter by an African American soldier serving in the Philippines in the 25th Infantry reveals both the racism in the U.S. Army and black soldiers' awareness of their precarious positions as participants in empire-building at the expense of peoples of color.

"We don't want these islands"[6]

Editor, *New York Age*[7]

I have mingled freely with the natives and have had talks with American colored men here in business and who have lived here for years, in order to learn of them the cause of their [Filipinos'] dissatisfaction and the reason for this insurrection, and I must confess they have a just grievance. All this never would have occurred if the army of occupation would have treated them as people. The Spaniards, even if their laws were hard, were polite and treated them with some consideration; but the Americans, as soon as they saw that the native troops were desirous of sharing in the glories as well as the hardships of the hard-won battles with the Americans, began to apply home treatment for colored peoples: cursed them as damned niggers, steal [from] and ravish them, rob them on the street of their small change, take from the fruit vendors whatever suited their fancy, and kick the poor unfortunate if he complained, desecrate their church property, and after fighting began, looted everything in sight, burning, robbing the graves.

This may seem a little tall—but I have seen with my own eyes carcasses lying bare in the boiling sun, the results of raids on receptacles for the dead in search of diamonds. The [white] troops, thinking we would be proud to emulate their conduct, have made bold of telling their exploits to us. One fellow, member of the 13th Minnesota, told me how some fellows he knew had cut off a native woman's arm in order to get a fine inlaid bracelet. On upbraiding some fellows one morning, whom I met while out for a walk (I think they belong to a Nebraska or Minnesota regiment, and they were stationed on the Malabon[8] road) for the conduct of the American troops toward the natives and especially as to raiding, etc., the reply was: "Do you think we could stay over here and fight these damn niggers without making it pay all it's worth? The government only pays us $13 per month: that's starvation wages. White men can't stand it." Meaning they could not live on such small pay. In saying this they never dreamed that Negro soldiers would never countenance such conduct. They talked with impunity of "niggers" to our soldiers, never once thinking that they were talking to home "niggers" and should they be brought to remember that at home this is the same vile epithet they hurl at us, they beg pardon and make some effeminate excuse about what the Filipino is called.

I want to say right here that if it were not for the sake of the 10,000,000 black people in the United States, God alone knows on which side of the subject I would be. And for the sake of the black men who carry arms and pioneer for them as their representatives, ask them to not forget the present administration[9] at the next election. Party be damned! We don't want these islands, not in the way we are to get them, and for Heaven's sake, put the party in power that pledged itself against this highway robbery [the Democratic Party]. Expansion is too clean a name for it.

[Unsigned]

Reprinted in *Wisconsin Weekly Advocate*, 17 May 1900.[10]

Samuel Alfred Beadle

Little is known about Samuel Alfred Beadle, who was born in Georgia in 1857. He was a trained lawyer and worked in a law office in Mississippi. Beadle wrote three books, *Sketches from Life in Dixie* (1899), *Adam Shuffler* (1901), and *Lyrics of "The Under World"* (1912). He died in 1932 in Chicago.

Lines

Suggested by the Assaults made on the Negro Soldiers as they passed through the south on their way to and from our war with Spain.[11]

How I love my country you have heard,
    And I would you were noble and free
In spirit and deed, as in word,
    And your boasted humanity.
I love you, my country, I do,—
    Here's a heart, a soul that is thine,
Pregnant with devotion for you,
    And blind to your faults as to mine.

The standard of morals is high;
    When fixed by my brother for me,
It goes towering up to the sky
    With a dazzling purity.
For a bench he sits on a skull,
    And is a judge austere and stern,
With whom my demurrers are null,
    And my pleadings, though just, are spurned.

I've carried your flag to the front[12]
    Through pestilence, battles and storms;
Of the carnage of war took the blunt,
    Obeyed your command, "Carry arms!"
And gone with you down to the death,
    With the thorns of caste on my head;
Defended your home and your hearth,
    And wept o'er the bier[13] of your dead.

As the smoke of the fight goes by,
    And the bugle calls to repose,
By my countryman's hands I die,
    As well as by the hands of its foes;
Yet I love you, my country, I do,
    Here's a heart, a soul that is thine,
Pregnant with devotion for you,
    And blind to your faults as to mine.

"Lines," in *Sketches from Life in Dixie* (Chicago: Scroll Publishing, 1899).

Related writings by Samuel Alfred Beadle: "Strike for Equal Rights" (1899); "My Country" (1912).

Mary Burrill

Born in Washington, D.C., in 1881, Mary Burrill was an educator and play-wright who pressed against tense boundaries of race and gender. In 1919, she wrote on the controversial topic of birth control and about the impact of lynching on black soldiers at war. At the time of her death in 1946, she lived in New York.

Aftermath: A One-Act Play of Negro Life

Time: The present

Place: The Thornton cabin in South Carolina.

It is late afternoon of a cool day in early spring. A soft afterglow pours in at the little window of the Thornton cabin. The light falls on MILLIE, *a slender brown girl of sixteen, who stands near the window ironing. She wears a black dress and a big gingham apron. A clothes-horse weighted down with freshly ironed garments is nearby. In the rear there is a door leading out to the road. To the left, another door leading into the other room of the cabin. To the right there is a great stone hearth blackened by age. A Bible rests on the mantel over the hearth. An old armchair and a small table on which is a kerosene lamp are near the hearth. In the center of the room sits a well-scrubbed kitchen table and a substantial wooden chair. In front of the hearth, in a low rocking chair drawn close to the smouldering wood fire, sits* MAM SUE *busily sewing. The many colors in the old patchwork quilt that she is mending, together with the faded red of the bandanna on her head, contrast strangely with her black dress. Mam Sue is very old. Her ebony face is seamed with wrinkles; and in her bleared, watery eyes there is a world-old sorrow. A service flag containing one star hangs in the little window of the cabin.*

MAM SUE: (*crooning the old melody*).

O, yes, yonder comes mah Lawd,

He is comin' dis way

Wid his sword in his han'

O, yes, yonder comes—(*A burning log falls apart, and Mam Sue suddenly stops singing and gazes intently at the fire. She speaks in deep mysterious tones to Millie, who has finished her task and has come to the hearth to put up her irons.*) See dat log dah, Millie? De one fallin' tuh de side dah wid de big flame lappin' 'round hit? Dat means big doin's 'round heah tonight!

MILLIE: (*with a start*) Oh, Mam Sue, don' you go proph'sying no mo'! You seen big doin's in dat fire de night befo' them w'ite devuls come in heah an' tuk'n po' dad out and bu'nt him!

MAM SUE: (*calmly*) No, Millie, Ah didn' see no big doin's dat night—Ah see'd *evul* doin's an' Ah tole yo' po' daddy to keep erway f'om town de nex' day wid his cotton. Ah jes knowed dat he wuz gwine to git in a row wid dem w'ite debbils—but he wou'd'n lis'n tuh his ole mammy—De good Lawd sen' me dese warnin's in dis fiah, jes lak He sen' His messiges in de fiah to Moses.[14] Yo' chillun bettah lis'n to—

MILLIE: (*nervously*) Oh, Mam Sue, you skeers me when you talks erbout seein' all them things in de fire—

MAM SUE: Yuh gits skeered cause yuh don' put yo' trus' in de good Lawd! He kin tek keer o' yuh no mattuh whut com'!

MILLIE: (*bitterly*). Sometimes I thinks that Gawd's done fu'got us po' cullud[15] people. Gawd didn' tek no keer o' po' dad and *he* put *his* trus' in Him! He uster set evah night by dis fire at dis here table and read his Bible an' pray—but jes look whut happen' to dad! That don' look like Gawd wuz tekin' keer—

MAM SUE: (*sharply*). Heish yo' mouf, Millie! Ah ain't a-gwine to 'ave dat sinner-talk 'roun' hyeah! (*Derisively.*) Gawd don't tek no keer o' yuh? Ain't yuh bin prayin' night an' mawnin' fo' Gawd to sen' yo' brudder back f'om de war 'live an' whole? An' ain't yuh git dat lettah no longer'n yistiddy sayin' dat de fightin's all done stopp't an' dat de blessid Lawd's done brung yo' brudder thoo all dem battuls live an' whole? Don' dat look lak de Lawd's done 'membered yuh?

MILLIE: (*thoughtfully*). I reckon youse right, Mam Sue. But ef anything had a-happen' to John I wuz'n evah goin' to pray no mo'!

(*Millie goes to the clothes-horse and folds the garments and lays them carefully into a large basket. Mam Sue falls again to her crooning.*)

MAM SUE:

O, yes, yonder comes mah Lawd,

He's comin' dis way-a.

MILLIE: Lonnie's so late gittin' home tonight; I guess I'd bettah tek Mis' Hart's wash home tonight myse'f.

MAM SUE: Yas, Lonnie's mighty late. Ah reckons you'd bettah slip erlon' wid hit. (MILIE *gets her hat from the adjoining room and is about to leave with the basket when Mam Sue calls significantly.*) Millie?

MILLIE: Yas, Mam Sue.

MAM SUE: (*firmly*) Don' you fu'git to drap dat lettah fu' John in the Pos' Awfus ez yuh goes by. Whah's de lettah?

MILLIE: (*reluctantly*). But, Mam Sue, please don' lets—

(*A knock is heard. Millie opens the door and REVEREND LUKE MOSEBY enters. Moseby is a wiry little old man with a black, kindly face, and bright, searching eyes; his woolly hair and beard are snow-white. He is dressed in a rusty black suit with a coat of clerical cut that comes to his knees. In one hand he carries a large Bible, and in the other, a stout walking stick.*)

MILLIE: Good evenin', Brother Moseby, come right in.

REV. MOSEBY: Good eben', Millie. Good eben', Mam Sue. I jes drap't in to see ef you-all is still trus'in'[16] de good Lawd an'—

MAM SUE: Lor', Brudder Moseby, ain't Ah bin trus'n' de good Lawd nigh onter dese eighty yeah! Whut fu' yuh think Ah's gwine to quit w'en Ah'm in sight o' de Promis' Lan'?[17] Millie, fetch Brudder Moseby dat cheer.

MOSEBY: (*drawing his chair to the fire*). Dat's right, Mam Sue, you jes a-keep on trus'n' an' prayin' an evah thing's gwine to come aw-right. (*Observing that Millie is about to leave.*) Don' lemme 'tain[18] yuh, Millie, but whut's all dis good news wese bin heahin' 'bout yo' brudder John? Dey say he's done won some kind o' medal ober dah in France?

MILLIE: (*brightening up*). Oh, yes, we got a lettah day befo' yestiddy fom John tellin' us all erbout it. He's won de War Cross![19] He fought off twenty Germuns all erlone an' saved his whole comp'ny an' the gret French Gen'rul come an' pinned de medal on him, *hisse'f*!

MOSEBY: De Lawd bles' his soul! Ah know'd dat boy wud mek good!

MILLIE: (*excited by the glory of it all*). An' he's been to Paris, an' the fines' people stopp't him when they seen his medal, an' shook his han' an' smiled at him—an' he kin go evahwhere, an' dey ain't nobody all the time a-lookin' down on him, an' a-sneerin' at him 'cause he's black; but evahwhere they's jes gran' to him! An' he sez it's the firs' time evah in his life he's felt lak a real, sho-nuf man!

MOSEBY: Well, honey, don't de Holy Book say, "De fust shill be las' and de las' shill be fust"?

MAM SUE: (*fervently*). Dat hit do! An' de Holy Book ain't nebber tole no lie!

MOSEBY: Folks ober in Char'ston is sayin' dat some sojers is gwine to lan' dah today or tomorrer. Ah reckons day'll all be comin' 'long soon now dat de war's done stopp't.

MILLIE: I jes hates the thought of John comin' home an' hearin' 'bout dad!

MOSEBY. (*in astonishment*). Whut! Yuh mean to say yuh ain't 'rite him 'bout yo' daddy, yit?

MAM SUE. Dat she ain't! Millie mus' 'ave huh way! She 'lowed huh brudder ough'n be tole, an' dat huh could keep on writin' to him jes lak huh dad wuz livin'—Millie allus done de writin'—An' Ah lets huh 'ave huh way—

MOSEBY: (*shaking his head in disapproval*). Yuh mean tuh say—

MILLIE: (*pleadingly*). But, Brother Moseby, I couldn't write John no bad news w'ilst he wuz way over there by hisse'f. He had 'nuf to worry him with death a-starin' him in the face evah day!

MAM SUE: Yas, Brudder Moseby, Millie's bin carryin' on dem lies in huh lettahs fu' de las' six months; but today Ah jes sez to huh—Dis war done stopp't now, an' John he gwine to be comin' home soon, an' he ain't agwine to come hyeah an' fin' me wid no lie on mah soul! An' Ah med huh set down an' tell him de whole truf. She's gwine out to pos' dat lettah dis minute.

MOSEBY: (*still disapproving*). No good nebber come—

(*The door is pushed violently open, and* LONNIE, *a sturdy black boy of eighteen rushes in breathlessly.*)

LONNIE: Mam Sue! Millie! Whut'da yuh think? John's come home!

MILLIE: (*speechless with astonishment*). John? Home? Where's he at?

MAM SUE: (*incredulously*). Whut yuh sayin'? John done come home? Bles' de Lawd! Bles' de Lawd! Millie, didn' Ah tell yuh sumpin wuz gwine tuh happen?

LONNIE: (*excitedly*). I wuz sweepin' up de sto' jes befo' leavin' an' de phone rung—it wuz John—he wuz at Char'ston—jes landid! His comp'ny's waitin' to git de ten o'clock train fu' Camp Reed[20] whah dey's goin' to be mustered out.

MOSEBY: But how's he gwine to get erway?

LONNIE: Oh, good evenin', Brother Moseby, Ise jes so 'cited I didn't see yuh—Why his Cap'n done give him leave to run over heah 'tell de train's ready. He ought tuh be heah now 'cause it's mos' two hours sence he wuz tallkin'—

MAM SUE: Whuffo yuh so long comin' home an' tellin' us?

LONNIE: (*hesitatingly*). I did start right out but when I git to Sherley's corner I seen a whole lot of them w'ite hoodlums[21] hangin' 'round de feed sto'—I jes felt like dey wuz jes waitin' dah to start sumpin, so I dodged 'em by tekin' de long way home.

MILLIE: Po' Lonnie! He's allus dodgin' po' w'ite trash!

LONNIE: (*sullenly*). Well, yuh see whut dad got by not dodgin' 'em.

MOSEBY: (*rising to go*) Ah mus' be steppin' 'long now. Ah got to stop in to see ole man Hawkins; he's mighty sick. Ah'll drap in on mah way back fu' a word o' prayer wid John.

MAM SUE: Lonnie, yu'd bettah run erlon' as Brudder Moseby go an' tote dat wash tuh Mis' Ha't.[22] An' drap in Mis' Hawkins' sto' an' git some soap an' starch; an' Ah reckons yu'd bettah bring me a bottle o' linimint[23]—dis ole pain done come back in mah knee. (*To Moseby.*) Good eben, Brudder Moseby.

MOSEBY: Good eben, Mam Sue; Good eben, Millie, an' Gawd bles' yuh.

LONNIE: (*as he is leaving*). Tell John I'll git back fo' he leaves.

(*Lonnie and Moseby leave. Millie closes the door behind them and then goes to the window and looks out anxiously.*)

MILLIE: (*musingly*). Po' John! Po' John! (*Turning to Mam Sue.*) Mam Sue?

MAM SUE: Yas, Millie.

MILLIE: (*hesitatingly*). Who's goin' to tell John 'bout dad?

MAM SUE: (*realizing for the first time that the task must fall to someone*). Dunno. Ah reckons yu'd bettah.

MILLIE: (*going to Mam Sue and kneeling softly at her side*). Mam Sue, don' let's tell him now! He's got only a li'l hour to spen' with us—an' it's the firs' time fu' so long! John loved daddy so! Let 'im be happy jes a li'l longer—we kin tell 'im the truth when he comes back fu' good. Please, Mam Sue!

MAM SUE: (*softened by Millie's pleading*). Honey chile, John gwine to be askin' for his daddy fust thing—dey ain't no way—

MILLIE: (*gaining courage*). Oh, yes, 'tis! We kin tell 'im dad's gone to town—anything, jes so's he kin spen' these few li'l minutes in peace! I'll fix the Bible jes like dad's been in an' been a-readin' in it! He won't know no bettah!

(*Millie takes the Bible from the mantel and opening it at random lays it on the table; she draws the old armchair close to the table as her father had been wont to do every evening when he read his Bible.*)

MAM SUE: (*shaking her head doubtfully*). Ah ain't much on actin' dis lie, Millie.

(*The soft afterglow fades and the little cabin is filled with shadows. Millie goes again to the window and peers out. Mam Sue falls again to her crooning.*)

MAM SUE: (*crooning*).

O, yes, yonder comes mah Lawd,
  He's comin' dis way
Wid his sword in his han'—
(*To Millie.*) Millie, bettah light de lamp; it's gittin' dark—
He's gwine ter hew dem sinners down
  Right lebbal to de groun'
Oh, yes, yonder comes mah Lawd—

(*As Millie is lighting the lamp, whistling is heard in the distance. Millie listens intently, then rushes to the window. The whistling comes nearer; it rings out clear and familiar—"Though the boys are far away, they dream of home".[24]*)

MILLIE: (*excitedly*). That's him! That's John, Mam Sue!

(*Millie rushes out of doors. The voices of JOHN and Millie are heard from without in greetings. Presently, John and Millie enter the cabin. John is tall and straight—a good soldier and a strong man. He wears the uniform of a private in the American Army. One hand is clasped in both of Millie's. In the other, he carries an old fashioned valise.*[25] *The War Cross is pinned on his breast. On his sleeve three chevrons*[26] *tell mutely of wounds suffered in the cause of freedom. His brown face is aglow with life and the joy of homecoming.*)

JOHN: (*eagerly*). Where's Dad? Where's Mam Sue?

MAM SUE: (*hobbling painfully to meet him*). Heah's ole Mam Sue! (*John takes her tenderly in his arms.*) Bles' yo' heart, chile, bles' yo' heart! Tuh think dat de good Lawd's done lemme live to see dis day!

JOHN: Dear old Mam Sue! Gee, but I'm glad to see you an' Millie again!

MAM SUE: Didn' Ah say dat yuh wuz comin' back hyeah?

JOHN: (*smiling*). Same old Mam Sue with huh faith an' huh prayers! But where's dad? (*He glances toward the open Bible.*) He's been in from de field, ain't he?

MILLIE. (*without lifting her eyes*). Yes, he's come in but he had to go out ag'in—to Sherley's feed sto'.

JOHN: (*reaching for his cap that he has tossed upon the table*). That ain't far. I've jes a few minutes so I'd bettah run down there an' hunt him up. Won't he be surprised!

MILLIE: (*confused*). No—no, John—I fu'got; he ain't gone to Sherley's, he's gon' to town.

JOHN: (*disappointed*). To town? I hope he'll git in befo' I'm leavin'. There's no tellin' how long they'll keep me at Camp Reed. Where's Lonnie?

MAM SUE: Lonnie's done gone to Mis' Ha't's wid de wash. He'll be back to-reckly.[27]

MILLIE: (*admiring the medal on his breast*). An' this is the medal? Tell us all erbout it, John.

JOHN: Oh, Sis, it's an awful story—wait 'til I git back fu' good. Let's see whut I've got in dis bag fu' you. (*He places the worn valise on the table and opens it. He takes out a bright-colored dress pattern.*) That's fu' you, Millie, and quit wearin' them black clothes.

(*Millie takes the silk and hugs it eagerly to her breast, suddenly there sweeps into her mind the realization that she cannot wear it, and the silk falls to the floor.*)

MILLIE: (*trying to be brave*). Oh, John, it's jes lovely! (*As she shows it to Mam Sue.*) Look, Mam Sue!

JOHN: (*flourishing a bright shawl*). An' this is fu' Mam Sue. Mam Sue'll be so gay!

MAM SUE: (*admiring the gift*). Who'd evah b'lieved dat yo' ole Mam Sue would live to be wearin' clo'es whut huh gran'chile done brung huh fom Eu'ope!

JOHN: Never you mind, Mam Sue, one of these days I'm goin' to tek you an' Millie over there, so's you kin breathe free jes once befo' yuh die.

MAM SUE: It's got tuh be soon, 'cause dis ole body's mos' wo'e out; an' de good Lawd's gwine to be callin' me to pay mah debt 'fo' long.

JOHN: (*showing some handkerchiefs, with gay borders*). These are fu' Lonnie. (*He next takes out a tiny box that might contain a bit of jewelry.*) An' this is fu' Dad. Sum'pin he's been wantin' fu' years. I ain't goin' to open it 'till he comes.

(*Millie walks into the shadows and furtively wipes a tear from her eyes.*)

JOHN: (*taking two army pistols from his bag and placing them on the table*). An' these las' are fu' *youahs truly*.

MILLIE: (*looking at them, fearfully*). Oh, John, are them youahs?

JOHN: One of 'em's mine; the other's my Lieutenant's. I've been cleanin' it fu' him. Don' tech 'em—'cause mine's loaded.

MILLIE: (*still looking at them in fearful wonder*). Did they learn yuh how to shoot 'em?

JOHN: Yep, an' I kin evah mo' pick 'em off!

MILLIE: (*reproachfully*). Oh, John!

JOHN: Nevah you worry, li'l Sis, John's nevah goin' to use 'em 'less it's right fu' him to. (*He places the pistols on the mantel—on the very spot where the Bible has lain.*) My! but it's good to be home! I've been erway only two years but it seems like two cent'ries. All that life ovah there seems like some awful dream!

MAM SUE: (*fervently*). Ah know it do! Many's de day yo' ole Mam Sue set in dis cheer an' prayed fu' yuh.

JOHN: Lots of times, too, in the trenches when I wuz dog-tired, an' sick, an' achin' wid the cold I uster say: well, if we're sufferin' all this for the oppressed, like they tell us, then Mam Sue, an' Dad, an' Millie come in on that—they'll git some good ou'n it if I don't! An' I'd shet my eyes an' fu'git the cold, an' the pain, an' them old guns spittin' death all 'round us; an' see you folks settin' here by this fire—Mam Sue, noddin, an' singin'; Dad a spellin' out his Bible—(*He glances toward the open book.*) Let's see whut he's been readin'—(*John takes up the Bible and reads the first passage upon which his eye falls.*) "But I say unto you, love your enemies, bless them that curse you, an' do good to them that hate you"[28]—(*He lets the Bible fall to the table.*) That ain't the dope they been feedin' us soljers on! 'Love your enemies!' It's been—git a good aim at 'em, an' let huh go!

MAM SUE: (*surprised*). Honey, Ah hates to hyeah yuh talkin' lak dat! It sound lak yuh done fu'git yuh Gawd!

JOHN: No, Mam Sue, I ain't fu'got God, but I've quit thinkin' that prayers kin do ever'thing. I've seen a whole lot sence I've been erway from here. I've seen some men go into battle with a curse on their lips, and I've seen them same men come back with never a scratch; an' I've seen men whut read their Bibles befo' battle, an' prayed to live, left dead on the field. Yes, Mam Sue, I've seen a heap an' I've done a tall lot o' thinkin' sence I've been erway from here. An' I b'lieve it's jes like this—be-yon' a certain point prayers ain't no good! The Lawd does jes so much for you, then it's up to you to do the res' fu' yourse'f. The Lawd's done His part when He's done give me strength an' courage; I got tuh do the res' fu' myse'f!

MAM SUE: (*shaking her head*). Ah don' lak dat kin' o' talk—it don' 'bode no good!

(*The door opens and Lonnie enters with packages. He slips the bolt across the door.*)

JOHN: (*rushing to Lonnie and seizing his hand*). Hello, Lonnie, ole man!

LONNIE: Hello, John. Gee, but Ah'm glad tuh see yuh!

JOHN: Boy, you should 'ave been with me! It would 'ave taken some of the skeeriness out o' yuh, an' done yuh a worl' o' good.

LONNIE: (*ignoring John's remark*). Here's the soap an' starch, Millie.

MAM SUE: Has yuh brung mah linimint?

LONNIE: Yassum, it's in de packige.

MILLIE: (*unwrapping the package*). No, it ain't, Lonnie.

LONNIE: Mis' Hawkins give it tuh me. Ah mus' a lef it on de counter. Ah'll git it w'en Ah goes to de train wid John.

MILLIE: (*showing him the handkerchief*). See whut John done brought you! An' look on de mantel! (*Pointing to the pistols.*)

LONNIE: (*drawing back in fear as he glances at the pistols*). You'd bettah hide them things! No cullud man bettah be seen wid dem things down heah!

JOHN: That's all right, Lonnie, nevah you fear. I'm goin' to keep 'em an' I ain't a-goin' to hide 'em either. See them (*pointing to the wound chevrons on his arm*), well, when I got them wounds, I let out all the rabbit-blood[29] 'at wuz in me! (*Defiantly.*) Ef I kin be trusted with a gun in France, I kin be trusted with one in South Car'lina.

MAM SUE: (*sensing trouble*). Millie, you'd bettah fix some suppah fu' John.

JOHN: (*looking at his watch*). I don' want a thing. I've got to be leavin' in a little while. I'm 'fraid I'm goin' to miss dad after all.

(*The knob of the door is turned as though someone is trying to enter. Then there is a loud knock on the door.*)

JOHN: (*excitedly*). That's Dad! Don't tell him I'm here!

(*John tips hurriedly into the adjoining room. Lonnie unbolts the door and MRS. ELEN HAWKINS enters.*)

MRS. HAWKINS: Lonnie fu'got de liniment so I thought I bettah run ovah wid hit, 'cause when Mam Sue sen' fu' dis stuff she sho' needs hit. Brudder Moseby's been tellin' me dat John's done come home.

JOHN: (*coming from his hiding place and trying to conceal his disappointment*). Yes, I'm here. Good evenin', Mis' Hawkins. Glad to see you.

MRS. HAWKINS: (*shaking hands with John*). Well, lan' sakes alive! Ef it ain't John sho'nuf! An' ain't he lookin' gran'! Jes

look at dat medal a-shining' on his coat! Put on yuh cap, boy,
an' lemme see how yuh look!

JOHN: Sure! (*John puts on his overseas cap and, smiling, stands
at attention a few paces off, while Mam Sue, Lonnie, and Millie
form an admiring circle around him.*)

MRS. HAWKINS: Now don' he sholy look gran'! I knows yo'
sistah, an' gran'-mammy's proud o' yuh! (*A note of sadness
creeps into her voice.*) Ef only yuh po' daddy had a-lived to see
dis day!

(*John looks at her in amazement. Millie and Mam Sue stand transfixed with
terror over the sudden betrayal.*)

JOHN: (*looking from one to the other and repeating her words
as though he can scarcely realize their meaning*). 'Ef your po'
daddy had lived—' (*To Millie.*) Whut does this mean?

(*Millie sinks sobbing into the chair at the table and buries her face in her
hands.*)

MRS. HAWKINS: Lor', Millie, I thought you'd tole him!

(*Bewildered by the catastrophe that she has precipitated, Selena Hawkins slips
out of the cabin.*)

JOHN: (*shaking Millie almost roughly*). Come, Millie, have you
been lyin' to me? Is Dad gone?

MILLIE: (*through her sobs*). I jes hated to tell you—you wuz so
far erway—

JOHN: (*nervously*). Come, Millie, for God's sake don' keep me in
this su'pense! I'm a brave soldier—I kin stan' it—did he suffer
much? Wuz he sick long?

MILLIE: He wuzn't sick no time—them w'ite devuls come in
heah an' dragged him—

JOHN: (*desperately*). My God! You mean they lynched dad?

MILLIE: (*sobbing piteously*). They burnt him down by the big
gum tree!

JOHN: (*desperately*). Whut fu', Millie? What fu'?

MILLIE: He got in a row[30] wid ole Mister Withrow 'bout the
price of cotton—an' he called dad a liar an' struck him—an'
dad he up an' struck him back.

JOHN: (*brokenly*). Didn' they try him? Didn' they give him a
chance? Whut'd the Sheriff do? An' the Gov-nur?

MILLIE: (*through her sobs*). They didn't do nothin'.

JOHN: Oh, God! Oh, God! (*Then recovering from the first bitter anguish and speaking.*) So they've come into ouah home, have they! (*He strides over to* LONNIE *and seizes him by the collar.*) An' whut wuz you doin' when them hounds come in here after dad?

LONNIE: (*hopelessly*). They wuz so many of 'em come an' git 'im—whut could Ah do?

JOHN: Do? You could 'ave fought 'em like a man!

MAM SUE: (*pleadingly*). Don't be too hard on 'im, John, wese ain't got no gun 'round heah!

JOHN: Then he should 'ave burnt their damn kennels ovah their heads! Who was it leadin' 'em?

MILLIE: Old man Withrow and the Sherley boys, they started it all.

(*Gradually assuming the look of a man who has determined to do some terrible work that must be done,* JOHN *walks deliberately toward the mantel where the revolvers are lying.*)

JOHN: (*bitterly*). I've been helpin' the w'ite man git his freedom, I reckon I'd bettah try now to get my own!

MAM SUE: (*terrified*). Whut yuh gwine ter do?

JOHN: (*with bitterness growing in his voice*). I'm sick o' these w'ite folks doin's—we're 'fine, trus'worthy feller citizuns' when they're handin' us out guns, an' Liberty Bonds,[31] an' chuckin' us off to die; but we ain't a damn thing when it comes to handin' us the rights we done fought an' bled fu'! I'm sick o' this sort o' life—an' I'm goin' to put an end to it!

MILLIE: (*rushing to the mantel, and covering the revolvers with her hands*).Oh, no, no, John! Mam Sue. John's gwine to kill hisse'f!

MAM SUE: (*piteously*). Oh, mah honey, don' yuh go do nothin' to bring sin on yo' soul! Pray to de good Lawd to tek all dis fiery feelin' out'n yo' heart! Wait 'tel Brudder Moseby come back—he's gwine to pray—

JOHN: (*his speech growing more impassioned and bitter*). This ain't no time fu' preachers or prayers! You mean to tell me I mus' let them w'ite devuls send me miles erway to suffer an'

> be shot up fu' the freedom of people I ain't nevah seen, while they're burnin' an' killin' my folks here at home! To Hell with 'em!

(*He pushes* MILLIE *aside, and seizing the revolvers, thrusts the loaded one into his pocket and begins deliberately to load the other.*)

> MILLIE: (*throwing her arms about his neck*). Oh, John, they'll kill yuh!
>
> JOHN: (*defiantly*). Whut ef they do! I ain't skeered o' none of 'em! I've faced worse guns than any sneakin' hounds kin show me! To Hell with 'em! (*He thrusts the revolver that he has just loaded into Lonnie's hands.*) Take this, an' come on here, boy, an' we'll see what Withrow an' his gang have got to say!

(*Followed by Lonnie, who is bewildered and speechless, John rushes out of the cabin and disappears in the gathering darkness.*)

Curtain.

Aftermath: A One-Act Play of Negro Life, The Liberator 2, no. 4 (April 1919): 10–14.

OLIVIA WARD BUSH-BANKS

See part 1, p. 65 for biographical note.

A Hero of San Juan[32]

Among the sick and wounded ones,
  This stricken soldier boy lay,
With glassy eye and shortened breath;
  His life seemed slipping fast away.

My heart grew faint to see him thus,
  His dark brown face so full of pain,
I wondered if the mother's eyes
  Were looking for her boy in vain.

I bent to catch his feeble's words:
  "I am so ill and far from home.
I feel so strange and lonely here;
  You seem a friend, I'm glad you've come.

"I want to tell you how our boys
  Went charging on the enemy.
'Twas when we climbed up Juan's hill;
  And there we got the victory.

"The Spaniards poured a heavy fire;
  We met it with a right good will.
We saw the Seventy-first[33] fall back,
  And then our boys went up the hill.

"Yes, up the hill, and gained it, too;
  Not one brave boy was seen to lag.
Old Glory o'er us floating free,
  We'd gladly died for that old flag."

His dim eye brightened as he spoke;
  He seemed unconscious of his pain;
In fancy on the battlefield
  He lived that victory o'er again.

And I; I seemed to grasp it, too,—
  The stalwart form, the dusky face
Of those black heroes, climbing up
  To win fair glory for their race.

The Spaniards said, that phalanx[34] seemed
  To move like one black, solid wall
They flung defiance back at Death,
  And, answering to that thrilling call,

They fought for Cuban liberty.
  On Juan's hill those bloody stains
Mark how these heroes won the day
  And added honor to their names.

March on, dark sons of Afric's race,
  Naught can be gained by standing still;
Retreat not, 'quit[35] yourselves like men
  And, like these heroes, climb the hill,

Till pride and prejudice shall cease;
  Till racial barriers are unknown.
Attain the heights where over all,
  Equality shall sit enthroned.

"A Hero of San Juan," in *Original Poems* (Providence, R.I.: Louis A. Basinet Press, 1899).

CHARLES WADDELL CHESNUTT

Charles Waddell Chesnutt was born in 1858 to free parents in Ohio. He spent his youth in South Carolina after the Civil War. Chesnutt published numerous books, a play, and a wealth of essays, articles, and stories that appeared in newspapers and magazines over two decades. In 1887, he was admitted to the Ohio Bar and maintained a legal office to keep his family afloat. Charles Chesnutt was living in Cleveland at the time of his death in 1932.

Acquit Yourselves Like Men: An Address to Colored Soldiers at Grays Armory, Cleveland, Ohio[36]

You young men have a great opportunity. You have really been selected for a superior sort of service. In the early ages of history the warrior, the fighting man, was the great man of the community to whom all others deferred. The field of battle was the pathway to glory. The great epic poems, of the world's literature, consist mainly of the recital of the warlike deeds of their heroes, and in modern times successful generals have been rewarded in aristocratic countries with titles and estates, in our country and the countries south of ours by election to the presidency; and the common soldiers by pensions and medals and the grateful acclaims of their fellow citizens. [. . .]

*   *   *

A careful study of the causes of this present war leaves no other conclusion but that Germany was guided by selfish motives from the first; that she was the aggressor, and wished to despoil France and Belgium of their colonies and their coal and coke fields so that she might extend her place in the sun. There have been many such wars. Our own Civil War was fought on the one side because the South wished to extend slavery politically over the whole country.

Then there are men and nations who fight for principle, from high and noble motives. No nation should go to war for any other reason. In this present war, France and Belgium are fighting for their altars and their fires, their hearths and their homes. Invaded by a ruthless enemy, it was either fight or perish. England's motives were high. She could not admit that a solemn treaty was a mere scrap of paper, or that her guarantee of the neutrality of Belgium was a hollow sham. And she foresaw that France once conquered, England would be invaded; and the great governmental system which she had built up during the centuries, embracing one fourth of the most fertile and best governed land on the earth's surface, would become a mere appanage[37] of Germany.

Other countries were drawn into the war by various motives, until came the time of the U.S. of America, as we call our country. We have gone into this war largely it would seem, for altruistic reasons. We believe in the principle of democracy. We have not, sad to say always lived up to it—far from it—but all our wars have been in support of it, and each one brings us nearer to its realization. The Revolutionary War resulted in the Constitution, which established the principle of free government for white men. They did not find it as free as it seemed on paper, and many old abuses, rooted in the customs and thoughts of the people, flourished for a long time after the Revolution, customs and laws which were not consistent with the doctrine of freedom and equality.

The cause of democracy was given a further impetus by the Civil War. It resulted in the war amendments, which involved the abolition of slavery and the enfranchisement of the former slaves. Yet we all know that many of the old abuses still linger. Our Spanish-American War was an unselfish war for the most part, and it resulted in the emancipation of Cuba from the tyranny of Spain.

But no one of our wars was ever based upon a higher motive than this one. We might have kept out of it, by some sacrifice of war profits during the first two years of it, and some loss of self-respect and the respect of other nations. But we were confronted by a situation in which the freer and more democratic nations of Europe were in a death grip with an arrogant autocracy which was threatening to conquer and reduce them to vassalage. The very fundamental principle of democracy was at stake. At first it might not have seemed important that the German people should be willing to live under such a government, it was up to them to change if they did not like it. But when they attempted to force it on the whole world, with threats directed even to America, then it became apparent that the real future of democracy depended upon the destruction of autocracy everywhere. The Russian people rose and cast it out, and made it easy for the U.S. to say that not only the rest of the world, but Germany herself must be made safe for democracy.[38]

Now, young men, soldiers, you have been selected to take part in this noble work. You have a glorious opportunity to participate in a great adventure. In Europe, in the Middle Ages, the soldiers of the Cross[39] crossed Europe to free the Holy Sepulcher from the hands of the infidel. It is your privilege to cross the seas to help tear down the German eagle of autocracy and replace it with the banner of democracy. You will see new countries, hear other tongues, meet and fraternize with some of the finest people in the world. You risk your lives, of course, but we all have to die sooner or later, and reduced to percentages the risks of war are not so much greater than those of working on a railroad or driving a motor car. Your preliminary military training will give you erect figures, firm muscles, quick reactions, it will cultivate all the manly virtues, and when you return to civil life, as most of you will, you will be all the better for your excursion to Europe at the expense of Uncle Sam.

And when you do reach the scene of hostilities and find yourselves at the front, you will give a good account of yourselves. Any man who suggests a doubt as to the fighting qualities of the Negro brands himself as ignorant of history.

The war records of the U.S. are filled with instances of the gallantry and devotion to duty of colored soldiers. The first man killed in the Revolutionary struggle was a mulatto, Crispus Attucks. He was buried from Faneuil Hall, his body was followed to the grave by a procession in columns six deep, with a long file of coaches belonging to the most distinguished citizens, and there is a monument to his memory on Boston Common.

The death of Major Pitcairn, of the English forces, at the hands of Peter Salem, a Negro soldier, ended the battle of Bunker Hill in favor of liberty. [. . .]

Negroes fought among the white soldiers in all the New England regiments, and some in separate battalions, and the military records of the day give them full credit for their gallantry.

The free colored men of Louisiana were organized into a regiment by General Andrew Jackson during the War of 1812, and three months later, after the battle of Mobile, General Jackson addressed the same troops as follows:

> Soldiers! The President of the U.S. shall be informed of your conduct on the present occasion, and the voice of the representatives of the American nation shall applaud your valor, as your general now praises your ardor.

Negro soldiers and sailors rendered valiant service in the war of 1812, and constituted about one-fourth of the American forces engaged in the battle of Lake Erie.

Before colored troops were enrolled under the flag of the Union in the Civil War, there had been several instances of their bravery and daring upon the high seas. You remember the case of the schooner *S. J. Waring*, from New York, bound to South America. She was captured on the passage by a rebel privateer, and a prize crew put on board, and the vessel set sail for the port of Charleston. Three of the original crew were retained on board, among them a black man named William Tillman, the steward and cook of the schooner. One night, when the prize crew were asleep, Tillman, with a heavy club, put the captain and the mate out of commission, released a Yankee who was a prisoner in irons, and between them they overcame the crew, and Tillman as master, took the vessel to the port of New York. The New York *Tribune* said of this event: "To this colored man was the nation indebted for the first vindication of its honor on the sea." [. . .] The federal government awarded to Tillman the sum of $6,000.00 as prize money for the capture of the schooner; all loyal journals joined in praise of this heroic act, and even when the news reached England the Negro's bravery was applauded.

An instance with which we are more familiar was that of Captain Robert Smalls, pilot on the rebel steamer *Planter* in Charleston harbor, who carried the steamer away from under the very guns of the enemy and delivered her to the blockading Union squadron. [. . .] Colored troops were first employed in the Civil War at New Orleans, then in possession of General Benjamin F. Butler. [. . .] For several years after [. . .] [the Civil War] war broke out, there was a great deal of discussion as to whether the Negroes would fight. Here you have an advantage over the colored men who fought in the Civil War. There was some suggestion from Southern sources a little while ago that Negro soldiers would not be wanted in this war [World War I]; but these suggestions received no attention from the government, and you are going into the war at the very beginning. [. . .]

*   *   *

The Colonels of your regiments, in this war, with some few exceptions, will, certainly at the beginning, be white men, largely because they have had the training and experience to qualify them for regimental command. Let us hope they will all be of the quality of Colonel Shaw, men under whose leadership it will be an honor to fight. All white officers who have led colored men praise their soldierly qualities, and seldom care to command any other kind of troops after having once had experience with them.[. . .]

The valor of the colored troops in the Spanish-American war at San Juan Hill, and in the recent Mexican unpleasantness at Carrizal, are too fresh in your minds to need recalling. Suffice it to say that their conduct added to the laurels already won by men of their race in our wars.

You are going into war again as colored troops. There are some of us who would like to see you fighting in the regiments with white men, side by side. It would be a better example of the democracy for which we are fighting. But, as I said before, manners and customs are slow to change, and the American army has been organized in accordance with the traditions of the past, by which the colored men are placed in different units. But there are some compensating advantages. Fighting as colored soldiers, any gallant deeds they may perform, will be credited to them as such. If they storm a difficult position, capture a redoubt, put a battalion of Huns to flight, the credit for it will be given to them and cannot be stolen by some white man. Any laurels that you may win in this war will thus be a gain, not only to yourselves and to your race, but to the cause of democracy, because it will prove, if proof were needed, the Negro's worth as a citizen and a patriot, and will bring that much nearer the day when the U.S. will be as safe for real democracy as it is trying to make the rest of the world. [. . .]

You will not be called upon to shoot down any man of color. It is a curious fact that black men, whose ancestors were brought across the ocean to this country in slave ships several generations ago to work for white men, are now being sent across the ocean in comfortable transports to kill white men. If any of you has any lurking grudge against the white race for its historic attitude toward the Negro, let him take it out on the Germans. They never did anything for you. The English in their colonies have treated black men fairly. They abolished slavery in their western possessions a generation before it ended in the United States, and have established in them a real democracy.[40] The French African colonies are administered in accordance with the French political doctrine of liberty, equality, fraternity, and their friendly attitude toward colored Frenchmen and travelers is traditional. The white men of the U.S. sacrificed half a million men for the freedom of the slave, which was only made possible by saving the Union. The Germans, on the other hand, are harsh in their Colonial administration, which is conducted with slight regard for the rights or feelings of the natives. Shortly after the war broke out, when the French and English were bringing black troops from Africa, the Germans criticized them for bringing black men to Europe to fight white men, as a reproach to civilization—this from men who torpedo peaceful merchant vessels and leave their crews to drown, men who have left Belgium like a sucked orange, who have bombed peaceful civilian populations, and slaughtered women and children, and who have preached and practiced the doctrine of ruthless frightfulness. We shall look to you to show the world that it is not because your faces are dark that they object to your fighting them, but because you are such good soldiers, such fearless fighters, that they are afraid to face you.

You are going from Cleveland to receive your military training in a section of the country where the climate is congenial, but where the social atmosphere, if not hostile, is at least not particularly friendly to colored soldiers. You will find some laws which you do not like, some customs which are not in accord with the more liberal customs of the North, and you will very naturally feel inclined to resent certain things. But you cannot change the laws or social customs of the South during your brief stay there, and it will be necessary for you to exercise a certain amount of patience. This will not be a subject for reproach, but rather for praise; for a man who must expect to face the cold and hunger of the trenches, the shrapnel and cold steel of the enemy, poisonous gasses, and all the rigors of the battlefield, it ought to be a small matter to endure with dignified patience an occasional sneer or even a contemptuous word, and to consider the source, and value it no more than the unworthy motive behind it is worth. You will be in camps with Northern white soldiers, who will have a friendly disposition toward you. Your officers will do all they can to promote harmony and good feeling, not only for your sake and for the sake of the army, but for their own sake; for an officer who cannot maintain order in his own regiment is not the ideal commander. Guard against any repetition of the unfortunate affair at Houston.[41]

Your friends at the North are on guard. They will see to it that your comfort and well being are looked after. The War Department under our fair-minded friend, Secretary Baker, is showing an increasing disposition to be fair to the colored soldiers. Already over six hundred colored officers have been commissioned,[42] and you will be led largely by men of your own race. Generals and Colonels may plan the actions and dispose the forces, but the captains and lieutenants lead the real fighting, and you will have the opportunity to prove that men of your race can lead as well as they can fight, and thus nail another lie which seems to die hard. [. . .]

Young men, Cleveland looks to you to win praise for yourselves and your city. As I have said, you are setting out upon a great adventure, with a great shining goal before you. You will be doing your bit for humanity and for freedom, and we at home will be doing ours to aid you, to sustain you, with our resources, with our prayers, with our best wishes, confident that victory will rest upon your banners. Acquit yourselves like men, and when you return, covered with glory and honor, your fellow citizens will welcome you with open arms and open hearts. Good-bye and Good Luck!

Excerpted from "Address to Colored Soldiers at Grays Armory," in *Charles W. Chesnutt: Essays and Speeches*, edited by Joseph R. McElrath Jr., Robert C. Leitz III, and Jesse S. Crisler (Stanford, Calif.: Stanford University Press, 1999), 449–58.

Related writings by Charles Waddell Chesnutt: "The Future of the Negro" (1882); "The Future American" (1900); "Cicely's Dream" (1899); *The Marrow of Tradition* (1901); *The Colonel's Dream* (1905); "Perry Centennial" (1913).

JOSEPH SEAMON COTTER JR.

The son of a highly respected formerly enslaved educator and writer, Joseph Seamon Cotter Jr. was born in 1895 in Kentucky. The younger Cotter spent his brief life as a journalist, playwright, and poet. He published *The Band of Gideon and Other Lyrics* in 1918. The sonnet form appealed to Cotter, and his sonnet series "Out of the Shadows" and selections of his poetry titled "Poems" were published in the *A.M.E. Zion Quarterly Review* after his death in 1919.

Moloch[43]

Old Moloch walks the way tonight
On Flanders'[44] poppied field,
Where foe meets foe in steel and might
And never one shall yield.

Old Moloch of the fiery shrine,
Deep in the throes of pain,
Cries for the bleeding anodyne
Of flesh of youths again.

Heart of my heart went out tonight,
Where Moloch holds the way,
To lads of brown and black and white
Who blazon Freedom's day.

Tear down the shrine of Moloch there,
    From crimson field and glen,
Tear down the shrine of Moloch where
    It shames the hearts of men.

"Moloch," *A.M.E. Zion Quarterly Review* (1921).

Related writings by Joseph Seamon Cotter Jr.: "Sonnet to Negro Soldiers" (1918); "The Band of Gideon" (1918); "O, Little David, Play on Your Harp" (1918); "Theodore Roosevelt" (1921); *On the Fields of France* (1920); "Ode to Democracy" (1990).

W. A. DOMINGO

Wilfred A. Domingo was born in Kingston, Jamaica, in 1889. After arriving in the United States, he worked as a journalist and contributed to many activist publications, including A. Philip Randolph's *Messenger*. He also served as the first editor of Marcus Garvey's *Negro World* and was a founding member of the African Blood Brotherhood (1919–1924). Domingo's political education and activism included involvement with the activities of Marcus Garvey until they parted ways over political differences. Domingo was aligned with socialism before he eventually moved to the Communist Party. He spent the last two decades of his life organizing for Jamaican independence. The essay below was published in 1919 and responds to the racial violence of that summer. W. A. Domingo died in 1968.

From If We Must Die

America won the war that was alleged to be fought for the purpose of making the world safe for democracy, but in the light of recent happenings in Washington, the Capital city, and Chicago,[45] it would seem as though the United States is not a part of the world. In order to win the war President Wilson employed "force, unstinted force," and those who expect to bring any similar desirable termination to a just cause can do no less than follow the splendid example set them by the reputed spokesman of humanity. That the lesson did not take long to penetrate the minds of Negroes is demonstrated by the change that has taken place in their demeanor and tactics. No longer are Negroes willing to be shot down or hunted from place to place like wild beasts; no longer will they flee from their homes and leave their property to the tender mercies of the howling and cowardly mob. They have changed, and now they intend to give men's account of themselves. If death is to be their portion, New Negroes[46] are determined to make their dying a costly investment for all concerned. If they must die they are determined that they shall not travel through the valley of the shadow of death alone, but that some of their oppressors shall be their companions.

This new spirit is but a reflex of the great war, and it is largely due to the insistent and vigorous agitation carried on by younger men of the race. The demand is uncompromisingly made for either liberty or death, and since death is likely to be a two-edged sword it will be to the advantage of those in a position to do so to give the race its long-denied liberty. [. . .]

Counter irritants are useful in curing diseases, and Negroes are being driven by their white fellow citizens to investigate the curative values inherent in mass action, revolvers and other lethal devices when applied to social diseases.

The New Negro has arrived with stiffened back bone, dauntless manhood, defiant eye, steady hand and a will of iron. His creed is admirably summed up in the poem ["If We Must Die" by] [. . .] Claude McKay, the black Jamaican poet. [. . .]

Excerpted from "If We Must Die," *The Messenger*, September 1919.[47]

W.E.B. Du Bois

Born in 1868, three years after the end of the Civil War, in Great Barrington, Massachusetts, W.E.B. Du Bois became a preeminent scholar, activist, educator, and writer. He was a founding member, with William Monroe Trotter and others, of the Niagara Movement in 1905. Some members of this group of activists for political and social justice and equality aligned with others in 1909 to found the National Association for the Advancement of Colored People (NAACP). After decades of writing and activism produced insufficient change in the United States, Du Bois relocated to Ghana and became a citizen of that newly independent African nation. He died in Ghana in 1963, one day before the March on Washington.

My Country 'Tis of Thee[48]

My country tis of thee,
Late land of liberty,
   Of thee I sing.
Land where my father's pride
Slept where my mother died,
From every mountain side
   Let freedom ring!

My native country thee,
Land of the slave set free,
   Thy fame I love.
I love thy rocks and hills
And o'er thy hate which chills,
My heart with purpose thrills,
   To *rise* above.

Let laments swell the breeze,
And wring from all the trees,
   Sweet freedom's song.
Let laggard tongues awake,
Let all who hear partake,
Let Southern silence quake
   The sound prolong.

Our fathers' God to thee
Author of Liberty
    To thee we sing
Soon may our land be bright,
With Freedom's happy light
Protect us by Thy might,
    Great God our King.

"My Country 'Tis of Thee," *Horizon* 2 (November 1907): 5–6.

*   *   *

Close Ranks[49]

This is the crisis of the world. For all the long years to come men will point to the year 1918 as the great Day of Decision, the day when the world decided whether it would submit to military despotism and an endless armed peace—if peace it could be called—or whether they would put down the menace of German militarism and inaugurate the United States of the World.

We of the colored race have no ordinary interest in the outcome. That which the German power represents today spells death to the aspirations of Negroes and all darker races for equality, freedom and democracy. Let us not hesitate. Let us, while this war lasts, forget our special grievances and close our ranks shoulder to shoulder with our white fellow citizens and the allied nations that are fighting for democracy. We make no ordinary sacrifice, but we make it gladly and willingly, with our eyes lifted to the hills.

"Close Ranks," *Crisis* 16 (July 1918): 111.

*   *   *

A Philosophy in Time of War

First. This is OUR country. We have worked for it, we have suffered for it, we have fought for it; we have made its music, we have tinged its ideals, its poetry, its religion, its dreams; we have reached in this land our highest modern development, and nothing, humanly speaking, can prevent us from eventually reaching here the full stature of our manhood. Our country is at war. The war is critical, dangerous and worldwide. If this is OUR country, then this is OUR war. We must fight it with every ounce of blood and treasure.

Second. Our country is not perfect. Few countries are. We have our memories and our present grievances. This nation has sinned against the light, but it has not sinned as Germany has. Its continued existence and development is the hope of mankind and of black mankind, and not its menace. We must fight, then, for the survival of the Best against the threats of the Worst.

Third. But what of our wrongs? cry a million voices with strained faces and bitter eyes. Our wrongs are still wrong. War does not excuse disfranchisement, "Jim-Crow"[50] cars or social injustices, but it does make our first duty clear. It does say deep to the heart of every Negro American: We shall not bargain with our loyalty. We shall not profiteer with our country's blood. We shall not hesitate the fraction of a second when the God of Battles summons his dusky warriors to stand before the armposts of His Throne. Let them who call for sacrifice in this awful hour of pain fight for the rights that should be ours; let them who make the laws writhe beneath each enactment that oppresses us,—but we? Our duty lies inexorable and splendid before us, and we shall not shirk.

Fourth. Calm and with soul serene, unflurried and unafraid, we send a hundred thousand black sons and husbands and fathers to the Western Front, and behind them, rank on rank, stand hundreds of thousands more.

We are the Ancient of Days,[51] the First of Races and the Oldest of Men. Before Time was, we are. We have seen Egypt and Ethiopia, Babylon and Persia, Rome and America,[52] and for that flaming Thing, Crucified Right, which survived all this staggering and struggling of men—for that we fight today in and for America; not for a price, not for ourselves alone, but for the World.

Fifth. Protest, my brother, and grumble. I have seen the Vision and it shall not fade. We want victory for ourselves—dear God, how terribly we want it—but it must not be cheap bargaining, it must be clean and glorious, won by our own manliness, and not by the threat of the footpad. In the day of our lowest travail we did not murder children and rape women to bring our freedom nearer. We played the game and freedom came. So, too, today our souls are ours, but our bodies belong to our country.

Patience, then, without compromise; silence without surrender; grim determination never to cease striving until we can vote, travel, learn, work and enjoy in peace—all this, and yet with it and above it all the tramp of our armies over the bloodstained lilies of France to show the world again what the loyalty and bravery of black men means.

"A Philosophy in Time of War," *Crisis* 16 (August 1918): 164–65.

* * *

Our Special Grievances

The leading editorial in the July *Crisis,* called "Close Ranks," has been the subject of much comment. To a few it has seemed to indicate some change of position on the part of the National Association for the Advancement of Colored People and *The Crisis.* It is needless to say that it indicates nothing of the sort. This Association and this magazine stand today exactly where they have stood during the eight years of their work; *viz.,*[53] for the full manhood rights of the American Negro.

The July editorial is not in the slightest degree inconsistent with these principles. It was submitted to prominent members and officers of the Board before printing and found no objection.

The editorial seeks to say that the *first* duty of an American is to win the war and that to this all else is subsidiary. It declares that whatever personal and group grievances interfere with this mighty duty must wait.

It does not say that these grievances are *not* grievances, or that the temporary setting aside of wrongs make them right. But it *does* say, and *The Crisis* repeats the word, that any man or race that seeks to turn his country's tragic predicament to his own personal gain is fatally cheating himself. [. . .]

Did Negroes refuse to serve in the draft until they got the right to vote? No, they stormed the gates of the Army for the right to fight. Did they refuse commissions because their army school was segregated? No, they were eager to enter and diligent to learn. Have we black men for one moment hesitated to do our full duty in this war because we thought the country was not doing its full duty to us? Is there a single Negro leader who advised by word, written or spoken, rebellion and disloyalty? Certainly not. Then somebody "forgot his special grievance" and fought for his country, and to him and for him *The Crisis* speaks. *The Crisis* says, *first* your Country, then your Rights!

"Our Special Grievances," *Crisis* 16 (September 1918): 216–17.

*   *   *

Returning Soldiers

We are returning from war! *The Crisis* and tens of thousands of black men were drafted into a great struggle. For bleeding France and what she means and has meant and will mean to us and humanity, and against the threat of German race arrogance, we fought gladly and to the last drop of blood; for America and her highest ideals, we fought in far-off hope; for the dominant Southern oligarchy entrenched in Washington, we fought in bitter resignation. For the America that represents and gloats in lynching, disfranchisement, caste, brutality and devilish insult—for this, in the hateful upturning and mixing of things, we were forced by vindictive fate to fight also.

But today we return! We return from the slavery of uniform which the world's madness demanded us to don to the freedom of civil garb. We stand again to look America squarely in the face and call a spade a spade. We sing: This country of ours, despite all its better souls have done and dreamed, is yet a shameful land.

It *lynches*.

And lynching is barbarism of a degree of contemptible nastiness unparalleled in human history. Yet for fifty years we have lynched two Negroes a week, and we have kept this up right through the war.

It *disfranchises* its own citizens.

Disfranchisement is the deliberate theft and robbery of the only protection of poor against rich and black against white. The land that disfranchises its citizens and calls itself a democracy lies and knows it lies.

It encourages *ignorance*.

It has never really tried to educate the Negro. A dominant minority does not want Negroes educated. It wants servants, dogs, whores and monkeys. And when this land allows a reactionary group by its stolen political power to force as many black folk into these categories as it possibly can, it cries in contemptible hypocrisy: "They threaten us with degeneracy; they cannot be educated."

It *steals* from us.

It organizes industry to cheat us. It cheats us out of our land; it cheats us out of our labor. It confiscates our savings. It reduces our wages. It raises our rent. It steals our profit. It taxes us without representation. It keeps us consistently and universally poor, and then feeds us on charity and derides our poverty.

It *insults* us.

It has organized a nationwide and latterly a worldwide propaganda of deliberate and continuous insult and defamation of black blood wherever found. It decrees that it shall not be possible in travel nor residence, work nor play, education nor instruction, for a black man to exist without tacit or open acknowledgement of his inferiority to the dirtiest white dog. And it looks upon any attempt to question or even discuss this dogma as arrogance, unwarranted assumption and treason.

This is the country to which we Soldiers of Democracy return. This is the fatherland for which we fought! But it is *our* fatherland. It was right for us to fight. The faults of *our* country are *our* faults. Under similar circumstances, we would fight again. But by the God of Heaven, we are cowards and jackasses if, now that that war is over, we do not marshal every ounce of our brain and brawn to fight a sterner, longer, more unbending battle against the forces of hell in our own land.

We *return*.

We *return from fighting*.

We *return fighting*.

Make way for Democracy! We saved it in France, and by the Great Jehovah, we will save it in the United States of America, or know the reason why.

"Returning Soldiers," *Crisis* 18 (May 1919): 13–14.

Related writings by W.E.B. Du Bois: *The Souls of Black Folk* (1903); "Africa for Africans" (1917); "The Massacre of East St. Louis" (1917); *Black Reconstruction: An Essay toward a History of the Part Which Black Folk Played in the Attempt to Rescue Democracy in America, 1860–1880* (1935); *In Battle for Peace: The Story of My Eighty-Third Birthday* (1952); "On Stalin" (1953).

PAUL LAURENCE DUNBAR

See part 1, p. 82 for biographical note.

The Conquerors: The Black Troops in Cuba[54]

Round the wide earth, from the red field your valour has won,
Blown with the breath of the far-speaking gun,
   Goes the word.
Bravely you spoke through the battle cloud heavy and dun.
Tossed though the speech toward the mist-hidden sun,
   The world heard.

Hell would have shrunk from you seeking it fresh from the fray,
Grim with the dust of the battle, and gray
   From the fight.
Heaven would have crowned you, with crowns not of gold but of bay,[55]
Owning you fit for the light of her day,
   Men of night.

Far through the cycle of years and of lives that shall come,
There shall speak voices long muffled and dumb,
   Out of fear.
And through the noises of trade and the turbulent hum,
Truth shall rise over the militant drum,
   Loud and clear.

Then on the cheek of the honester nation that grows,
All for their love of you, not for your woes,
   There shall lie
Tears that shall be to your souls as the dew to the rose;
Afterward, thanks that the present yet knows
   Not to ply!

"The Conquerors: The Black Troops in Cuba," *The Bookman* 8, no. 4 (December 1898): 373.

ALICE RUTH MOORE DUNBAR-NELSON

A native of New Orleans, Alice Dunbar-Nelson was born in 1875. She was an educator, a journalist, an editor, a women's rights activist, and a writer. Dunbar-Nelson published her first book, a collection of poetry, stories, and essays titled *Violets and Other Tales*, in 1895. This book and her collection of short stories, *The Goodness of St. Rocque* (1899), present complex narratives of ethnicity, race, and language, especially those of the Louisiana Creole. Although she retained her first husband Paul Laurence Dunbar's last name throughout her life, their marriage ended in 1902. She was the co-editor of the *A.M.E. Church Review* from 1913 to 1914 and of the Wilmington *Advocate*, a newspaper that she and her third husband, the journalist Robert J. Nelson, published from 1920 until her death. Alice Dunbar-Nelson died in 1935 in Philadelphia.

Mine Eyes Have Seen[56]

A PLAY IN ONE ACT.

CHARACTERS

DAN: *The Cripple.*

CHRIS: *The Younger Brother.*

LUCY: *The Sister.*

MRS. O'NEILL: *An Irish Neighbor.*

JAKE: *A Jewish Boy.*

JULIA: *Chris' Sweetheart.*

BILL HARVEY: *A Muleteer.*

CORNELIA LEWIS: *A Settlement Worker.*

Time: Now

Place: A manufacturing city in the northern part of the United States.

SCENE *Kitchen of a tenement. All details of furnishing emphasize sordidness—laundry tubs, range, table covered with oil cloth, chairs. Curtain discloses* DAN *in a rude imitation of a steamer chair, propped by faded pillows, his feet covered with a patch-work quilt. Practicable window at back.*

LUCY *is bustling about the range preparing a meal. During the conversation she moves from range to table, setting latter and making ready the noon-day meal.*

DAN *is about thirty years old; face thin, pinched, bearing traces of suffering. His hair is prematurely gray; nose finely chiselled; eyes wide, as if seeing BE-YOND. Complexion brown.*

LUCY *is slight, frail, brown-skinned, about twenty, with a pathetic face. She walks with a slight limp.*

DAN: Isn't it most time for him to come home, Lucy?

LUCY: It's hard to tell, Danny, dear; Chris doesn't come home on time any more. It's half-past twelve, and he ought to be here by the clock, but you can't tell any more—you can't tell.

DAN: Where does he go?

LUCY: I know where he doesn't go, Dan, but where he does, I can't say. He's not going to Julia's any more lately. I'm afraid, Dan, I'm afraid!

DAN: Of what, Little Sister?

LUCY: Of everything; oh, Dan, it's too big, too much for me—the world outside, the street—Chris going out and coming home nights moody-eyed; I don't understand.

DAN: And so you're afraid? That's been the trouble from the beginning of time—we're afraid because we don't understand.

LUCY: (*coming down front, with a dish cloth in her hand.*) Oh, Dan, wasn't it better in the old days when we were back home—in the little house with the garden, and you and father coming home nights and mother getting supper, and Chris and I studying lessons in the dining-room at the table—we didn't have to eat and live in the kitchen then, and—

DAN: (*grimly.*)—And the notices posted on the fence for us to leave town because niggers had no business having such a decent home.

LUCY: (*unheeding the interruption.*)—And Chris and I reading the wonderful books and laying our plans—

DAN:—To see them go up in the smoke of our burned home.

LUCY: (*continuing, her back to DAN, her eyes lifted, as if seeing a vision of retrospect.*)—And everyone petting me because I had hurt my foot when I was little, and father—

DAN:—Shot down like a dog for daring to defend his home—

LUCY:—Calling me "Little Brown Princess," and telling mother—

DAN:—Dead of pneumonia and heartbreak in this bleak
  climate.

LUCY:—That when you—

DAN: Maimed for life in a factory of hell! Useless—useless—
  broken on the wheel. (*his voice breaks in a dry sob.*)

LUCY: (*coming out of her trance, throws aside the dish-cloth, and
  running to DAN, lays her cheek against his and strokes his
  hair.*) Poor Danny, poor Danny, forgive me, I'm selfish.

DAN: Not selfish, Little Sister, merely natural.

(*Enter roughly and unceremoniously CHRIS. He glances at the two with their
arms about each other, shrugs his shoulders, hangs up his rough cap and
mackinaw[57] on a nail, then seats himself at the table, his shoulders hunched
up; his face dropping on his hand. LUCY approaches him timidly.*)

LUCY: Tired, Chris?

CHRIS: No.

LUCY: Ready for dinner?

CHRIS: If it is ready for me.

LUCY: (*busies herself bringing dishes to the table.*) You're late
  to-day.

CHRIS: I have bad news. My number[58] was posted today.

LUCY: Number? Posted? (*pauses with a plate in her hand.*)

CHRIS: I'm drafted.

LUCY: (*drops plate with a crash. DAN leans forward tensely, his
  hands gripping the arms of his chair.*) Oh, it can't be! They
  won't take you from us! And shoot you down, too? What will
  Dan do?

DAN: Never mind about me, Sister. And you're drafted, boy?

CHRIS: Yes—yes—but—(*he rises and strikes the table heavily
  with his hand.*) I'm not going.

DAN: Your duty—

CHRIS:—Is here with you. I owe none elsewhere, I'll pay none.

LUCY: Chris! Treason! I'm afraid!

CHRIS: Yes, of course, you're afraid, Little Sister, why shouldn't
  you be? Haven't you had your soul shrivelled with fear since
  we were driven like dogs from our home? And for what?
  Because we were living like Christians. Must I go and fight
  for the nation that let my father's murder go unpunished?

That killed my mother—that took away my chances for making a man out of myself? Look at us—you—Dan, a shell of a man—

DAN: Useless—useless—

LUCY: Hush, Chris!

CHRIS:—And me, with a fragment of an education, and no chance—only half a man. And you, poor Little Sister, there's no chance for you; what is there in life for you? No, if others want to fight, let them. I'll claim exemption.

DAN: On what grounds?

CHRIS: You—and Sister. I am all you have; I support you.

DAN: (half rising in his chair.) Hush! Have I come to this, that I should be the excuse, the woman's skirts for a slacker[59] to hide behind?

CHRIS: (clenching his fists.) You call me that? You, whom I'd lay down my life for? I'm no slacker when I hear the real call of duty. Shall I desert the cause that needs me—you—Sister—home? For a fancied glory? Am I to take up the cause of a lot of kings and politicians who play with men's souls, as if they are cards—dealing them out, a hand here, in the Somme—a hand there, in Palestine—a hand there, in the Alps—a hand there, in Russia[60]—and because the cards don't match well, call it a misdeal, gather them up, throw them in the discard, and call for a new deal of a million human, suffering souls? And must I be the Deuce of Spades?[61]

(During the speech, the door opens slowly and JAKE lounges in. He is a slight, pale youth, Hebraic, thin-lipped, eager-eyed. His hands are in his pockets, his narrow shoulders drawn forward. At the end of CHRIS's speech he applauds softly.)

JAKE: Bravo! You've learned the patter well. Talk like the fellows at the Socialist meetings.

DAN and LUCY: Socialist meetings!

CHRIS: (defiantly.) Well?

DAN: Oh, nothing; it explains. All right, go on—any more?

JAKE: Guess he's said all he's got breath for. I'll go; it's too muggy in here. What's the row?

CHRIS: I'm drafted.

JAKE: Get exempt. Easy—if you don't want to go. As for me—
(*door opens, and* MRS. O'NEILL *bustles in. She is in deep mourning, plump, Irish, shrewd-looking, bright-eyed.*)

MRS. O'NEILL: Lucy, they do be sayin' as how down by the chain stores they be a raid on the potatoes, an' ef ye're wantin' some, ye'd better be after gittin' into yer things an' comin' wid me. I kin kape the crowd off yer game foot—an' what's the matter wid youse all?

LUCY: Oh. Mrs. O'Neill, Chris has got to go to war.

MRS. O'NEILL: An' ef he has, what of it? Ye'll starve, that's all.

DAN: Starve? Never! He'll go, we'll live.

(LUCY *wrings her hands impotently.* MRS. O'NEILL *drops a protecting arm about the girl's shoulder.*)

MRS. O'NEILL: An' it's hard it seems to yer? But they took me man from me year before last, an' he wint afore I came over here, an' it's a widder I am wid me five kiddies, an' I've niver a word to say but—

CHRIS: He went to fight for his own. What do they do for my people? They don't want us, except in extremity. They treat us like—like—like—

JAKE: Like Jews in Russia, eh? (*he slouches forward, then his frame straightens itself electrically.*) Like Jews in Russia, eh? Denied the right of honor in men, eh? Or the right of virtue in women, eh? There isn't a wrong you can name that your race has endured that mine has not suffered, too. But there's a future, Chris—a big one. We younger ones must be in that future—ready for it, ready for it—(*his voice trails off, and he sinks despondently into a chair.*)

CHRIS: Future? Where? Not in this country? Where?

(*The door opens and* JULIA *rushes in impulsively. She is small, slightly built, eager-eyed, light-brown skin, wealth of black hair; full of sudden shyness.*)

JULIA: Oh, Chris, someone has just told me—I was passing by—one of the girls said your number was called. Oh, Chris, will you have to go? (*She puts her arms up to* CHRIS' *neck; he removes them gently, and makes a slight gesture towards* DAN'S *chair.*)

JULIA: Oh, I forgot. Dan, excuse me. Lucy, it's terrible, isn't it?

CHRIS: I'm not going, Julia.

MRS. O'NEILL: Not going!

DAN: Our men have always gone, Chris. They went in 1776.[62]

CHRIS: Yes, as slaves. Promised a freedom they never got.

DAN: No, gladly, and saved the day, too, many a time. Ours was the first blood shed on the altar of National liberty. We went in 1812, on land and sea. Our men were through the struggles of 1861.[63]

CHRIS: When the Nation was afraid not to call them. Didn't want 'em at first.

DAN: Never mind; they helped work out their own salvation. And they were there in 1898[64]—

CHRIS: Only to have their valor disputed.

DAN:—And they were at Carrizal,[65] my boy, and now—

MRS. O'NEILL: An' sure, wid a record like that—ah, 'tis me ould man who said at first 'twasn't his quarrel. His Oireland[66] bled an' the work of thim divils to try to make him a traitor nearly broke his heart—but he said he'd go to do his bit—an' here I am.

(*There is a sound of noise and bustle without, and with a loud laugh,* BILL HARVEY *enters. He is big, muscular, rough, his voice thunderous. He emits cries of joy at seeing the group, shakes hands and claps* CHRIS *and* DAN *on their backs.*)

DAN: And so you weren't torpedoed?

HARVEY: No, I'm here for a while—to get more mules and carry them to the front to kick their bit.

MRS. O'NEILL: You've been—over there?[67]

HARVEY: Yes, over the top, too. Mules, rough-necks, wires, mud, dead bodies, stench, terror!

JULIA (*horror-stricken*): Ah—Chris!

CHRIS: Never, mind, not for mine.

HARVEY: It's a great life—not. But I'm off again, first chance.

MRS. O'NEILL: They're brutes, eh?

HARVEY: Don't remind me.

MRS. O'NEILL (*whispering*): They maimed my man, before he died.

JULIA (*clinging to* CHRIS): Not you, oh, not you!

HARVEY: They crucified children.

DAN: Little children? They crucified little children.

CHRIS: Well, what's that to us? They're little white children. But here, our fellow-countrymen throw our little black babies in the flames—as did the worshippers of Moloch,[68] only they haven't the excuse of a religious rite.

JAKE: (*slouches out of his chair, in which he has been sitting brooding.*) Say, don't you get tired sitting around grieving because you're colored? I'd be ashamed to be—

DAN: Stop! Who's ashamed of his race? Ours the glorious inheritance; ours the price of achievement. Ashamed! I'm *proud*. And you, too, Chris, smouldering in youthful wrath, you, too, are proud to be numbered with the darker ones, soon to come into their inheritance.

MRS. O'NEILL: Aye, but you've got to fight to keep yer inheritance. Ye can't lay down when someone else has done the work, and expect it to go on. Ye've got to fight.

JAKE: If you're proud, show it. All of your people—well, look at us! Is there a greater race than ours? Have any people had more horrible persecutions—and yet—we're loyal always to the country where we live and serve.

MRS. O'NEILL: And us! Look at us!

DAN: (*half tears himself from the chair, the upper part of his body writhing, while the lower part is inert, dead.*) Oh, God! If I were but whole and strong! If I could only prove to a doubting world of what stuff my people are made!

JULIA: But why, Dan, it isn't our quarrel? What have we to do with their affairs? These white people, they hate us. Only today I was sneered at when I went to help with some of their relief work. Why should you, my Chris, go to help those who hate you?

(CHRIS *clasps her in his arms, and they stand, defying the others.*)

HARVEY: If you could have seen the babies and girls—and old women—if you could have (*covers his eyes with his hand*).

CHRIS: Well, it's good for things to be evened up somewhere.

DAN: Hush, Chris! It is not for us to visit retribution. Nor to wish hatred on others. Let us rather remember the good that has come to us. Love of humanity is above the small con-

siderations of time or place or race or sect. Can't you be big
enough to feel pity for the little crucified French children—
for the ravished Polish girls, even as their mothers must have
felt sorrow, if they had known, for *our* burned and maimed
little ones? Oh, Mothers of Europe, we be of one blood,[69] you
and I!

*(There is a tense silence. JULIA turns from CHRIS, and drops her hand.
He moves slowly to the window and looks out. The door opens quietly, and
CORNELIA LEWIS comes in. She stands still a moment, as if sensing a difficult situation.)*

CORNELIA: I've heard about it, Chris, your country calls you.
(CHRIS *turns from the window and waves hopeless hands at*
DAN *and* LUCY.) Yes, I understand; they do need you, don't
they?

DAN *(fiercely)*: No!

LUCY: Yes, we do, Chris, we do need you, but your country
needs you more. And, above that, your race is calling you to
carry on its good name, and with that, the voice of humanity
is calling to us all—we can manage without you, Chris.

CHRIS: You? Poor little crippled Sister. Poor Dan—

DAN: Don't pity me, pity your poor, weak self.

CHRIS: *(clenching his fist.)* Brother, you've called me two names
today that no man ought to have to take—a slacker and a
weakling!

DAN: True. Aren't you both? *(leans back and looks at* CHRIS
speculatively.)

CHRIS: *(makes an angry lunge towards the chair, then flings
his hands above his head in an impatient gesture.)* Oh, God!
(Turns back to window.)

JULIA: Chris, it's wicked for them to taunt you so—but Chris—
it *is* our country—our race—

*(Outside the strains of music from a passing band are heard. The music comes
faintly, gradually growing louder and louder until it reaches a crescendo. The
tune is "The Battle Hymn of the Republic,"[70] played in stirring march time.)*

DAN: *(singing softly.)* "Mine eyes have seen the glory of the
coming of the Lord!"

CHRIS: (*Turns from the window and straightens his shoulders.*)
And mine!

CORNELIA: "As He died to make men holy, let us die to make
them free!"

MRS. O'NEILL: An' ye'll make the sacrifice, me boy, an' ye'll be
the happier.

JAKE: Sacrifice! No sacrifice for him, it's those who stay behind.
Ah, if they would only call me, and call me soon!

LUCY: We'll get on, never fear. I'm proud! Proud! (*her voice
breaks a little but her head is thrown back.*)

(*As the music draws nearer, the group breaks up and the whole roomful rushes
to the window and looks out. CHRIS remains in the center of the floor, rigidly
at attention, a rapt look on his face. DAN strains at his chair, as if he would
rise, then sinks back, his hand feebly beating time to the music, which swells
to a martial crash.*)

Curtain

Mine Eyes Have Seen was performed at Dunbar High School, Washington, D.C., on 10
April 1918. It was published as *Mine Eyes Have Seen, Crisis* 15 (April 1918): 271–75.

*　　*　　*

I Sit and Sew[71]

I sit and sew—a useless task it seems,
My hands grown tired, my head weighed down with dreams—
The panoply of war, the martial tred of men,
Grim-faced, stern-eyed, gazing beyond the ken
Of lesser souls, whose eyes have not seen Death,
Nor learned to hold their lives but as a breath—
But—I must sit and sew.

I sit and sew—my heart aches with desire—
That pageant terrible, that fiercely pouring fire
On wasted fields, and writhing grotesque things
Once men. My soul in pity flings
Appealing cries, yearning only to go
There in that holocaust of hell, those fields of woe—
But—I must sit and sew.—

The little useless seam, the idle patch;
Why dream I here beneath my homely thatch,
When there they lie in sodden mud and rain,
Pitifully calling me, the quick ones and the slain?
You need me, Christ! It is no roseate dream
That beckons me—this pretty futile seam,
It stifles me—God, must I sit and sew?

"I Sit and Sew," in *The Dunbar Speaker and Entertainer*, edited by Alice Moore Dunbar-Nelson (Naperville, Ill.: J. L. Nichols & Co., 1920): 145.[72]

F. GRANT GILMORE

Little is known about Frederick Grant Gilmore, who probably was born in 1870. In 1908 he published a collection of poetry, *Masonic and Other Poems*. He was a writer and barber in Rochester, New York, and a member of the Frederick Douglass Club. Gilmore also is listed on the masthead of the *Rochester Sentinel*, a local black newspaper. Very likely he was a resident of Rochester, New York, at the time the Henry Conolly Company published *"The Problem": A Military Novel*, the source for the following excerpt.

A Battle in the Philippines[73]

[Sergeant William "Lanky" Henderson is a member of the 9th Cavalry Buffalo Soldiers and fought at San Juan Hill. He is now in the Philippines. Freda Waters, a Red Cross nurse who attended to William Henderson in Cuba, and her supposed adopted brother Henry Fairfax, a white army surgeon, are on board the naval ship *America* headed to the Philippines. Henry has previously attempted unsuccessfully to have Sergeant Henderson imprisoned because they are rivals for Freda's love. Freda is engaged to Henry Fairfax.

At this point, "the secret of (Freda's) heritage" remains intact. William is in love with Freda and she with him, yet their love is forbidden because Sergeant Henderson is a black man, and all, including Freda herself, believe that Freda is white.]

[. . .] [Aboard] the transport "America," speeding ten thousand miles away from home and loved ones, to take up the arduous labors of doctor and nurse for the glory of the Stars and Stripes, were Freda and Sergeant Fairfax. Anxious hearts wished them "Bon Voyage," and prayed that God would care for and return them to those who loved them. [. . .]

Like a huge swan rode the transport "America" over the raging sea. She was one of the products of American genius, and majestically buffeted the angry waves in mute defiance. On board were hearts thrilled with patriotism, soldiers, and seamen; each man eager to reach the scene of action, so that he may add one more star to his individual crown. In company with those rough and determined sons of liberty were a number of soft, soothing hearts, whose interest was to bring a God-like influence over their companions, and to render aid in times when only the physical power gives way. [. . .]

Among that number of living angels was Freda, clad in a delicate blue with an emblem of the Red Cross upon her arm. The "America," after a few days out from port, with her machinery working harmoniously and all well on board, seemed to be proud of her burden, and, coming proudly out from a few storms, rested quietly on the smooth sea. It seemed as if she was guided by an unseen hand and, although piloted by experienced and trained masters, the All-seeing Eye looked down and shaped the successful course.

To break the monotony of time, diverse sources of amusement were proposed, and among the many was a musicale to be given in the salon, and on the program was the name of Freda, who had volunteered to render two vocal selections. After the evening meal, the band played the opening number, a medley comprising patriotic airs; concluding with "My Country, Tis of Thee." All present arose, joining in the chorus. Near the last, Miss Freda Waters was introduced, and she chose for her selection that old inspiring song, "Just a Song at Twilight,"[74] and in the course of its rendition, her thoughts seemed to leave those who surrounded her, to join with those who were far away, and when she came to the part of the song which says:

"Though my heart beat weary,
Sad the day and long."

A tear escaped from her eye, and she pictured a tall, dark military form standing in the shrubbery, awaiting a fond good bye. The song ended, and amid deafening applause, she was asked to sing again. Awakening from her lethargy, and realizing that she was only an instrument of pleasure for those aboard, she responded, singing, "Coming Thro' the Rye."[75] The lightness of the character of this vocal effort seemed to lift her heart from a load of depression. She was soon one of the happy throng and the center of attraction. Surgeon Fairfax seemed a little piqued at the attention shown her and, instead of feeling proud of her accomplishments, he sulked in an envious mood that brought forth much criticism and words of derision and other taunting remarks were passed.

"Why, the Surgeon's jealous! See how cross he looks! I feel sorry for the poor fellow!"

Freda, noticing the attitude of the Surgeon towards his comrades, went to him and looked tenderly into his eyes, saying, "Come, Surgeon, you may take me on deck, where I can enjoy the night's cooling breeze, and we will talk of home."

These words had a comforting effect. He gallantly gave Freda his arm, and they were soon strolling the companion deck. [. . .]

"Land Ahoy!" was the welcome cry one pleasant morning, when, far out in the distant horizon, a dark, narrow strip was observed by the man on watch, as the bow of the "America" forged forward, seeming ever eager to decrease the longitude that would bring her nearer to port. The pleasure that had surmounted many faces gave way to one of serious thoughts of what the future would bring forth. Orders were given by the officers in charge to prepare for landing, and soon this craft, bearing the sons and daughters of liberty, was at anchor. The welcome demonstration to the "America" by the seacraft lying in harbor gave a new impetus to the ambition of those on board. The shrieks of the smaller craft, and the booming of cannon of the old sea-fighters, seemed to say to the "America," "We are glad that you have come." Soon tug boats and lighters ran alongside and the task of unloading was begun. A launch, bearing the crest U.S.N. was one of the first to reach the transport. Important cablegrams and cipher messages were given to the commanders and officers. They contained orders from Washington as to the plans laid out by the commander of the army and navy. The health officers, giving a clean bill, permitted soldiers to leave ship. The nurses were taken ashore and proceeded to the legation at Manila. All seemed pleased to be again on terra firma. But Oh, how different from home, and what work would be expected of this large family! [. . .]

In the harbor of Manila lay several transports which had preceded the "America." On board of one of these was Sergeant Henderson, in company with his famous Ninth and Tenth Cavalries. He had been ashore for some time and knew nothing of the coming of his soul's ideal [Freda] and his arch enemy, Surgeon Fairfax. Will he never escape him? Will it bring him happiness to learn that, although he will soon see her, yet he will be hounded like a criminal? The memory of that fateful day clings ever to him. The note, the shrubbery, the discovery, the accusation, the trial and his release, were like a specter, ever ready to haunt his dreams and to appear at all times when life seemed bright. It is thus the will of fate, that no matter where we are, or where we go, its ever-powerful influences are keenly felt by us. How to escape we know not; only the power of faith brings us peace.

*   *   *

"Henderson, the transport "America" is in the harbor and among the many passengers are Surgeon Fairfax and his foster-sister, Freda." This was the surprising news that greeted Henderson when he returned to headquarters, by his commander-in-chief. A rush of blood to the temples, followed by rapid palpitating heart beats, took immediate possession of the almost perfect physical man. Never before in his memory had this feeling of awe taken control of him. There was a presentment of grave forebodings. There are times in our lives, when apprised by an enemy, we are able to place ourselves on guard, as a panther crouches for an attack when suddenly confronted by an approaching foe. This intelligence, perceived by Henderson, had an opposite effect, and he knew not what to do, what to say, or how to act. The dictates of his heart craved for a meeting with Freda, but the knowledge in satisfying his heart's desire would only incite acts of hostile intent by the Surgeon. In open conflict he had no fear of him or any other man, but to harm him would wound her; so after the temporary feeling had worn off, he resolved, that from that moment he would cease to see her, thereby avoiding all unpleasantness. He looked his commander straight in the face, saying, "General [Funston], it is a pleasure to know that our friends will be near us again, but I trust our time will be short in these climes. While here you may assign me to foreign duty if you like; I would much prefer it."

The General honored Henderson, and the deep admiration he had for this black hero was of such that he would lay down his life to serve him. He thoroughly knew the situation and the innermost thought of the Sergeant. He pitied him, and firmly grasping his hand, he said, "Henderson, I am your friend, and I charge you to be on your guard at all times and to be guided solely by your conscience. I have no doubt as to your pure and good intentions, and I trust you will ever be able to do what is right in the sight of God and man. We have some unpleasant tasks to perform and I will need you." [. . .]

One pleasant afternoon a gala fete, in honor of General Funston's birthday, was celebrated. Among that number that had other duties to perform [than to attend General Funston's Birthday party] was Sergeant Henderson, who was in charge of a detachment to round up the marauding guerrillas. He had been gone for some time and no word had been received from him. A feeling of apprehension for his safety was felt by his commanders. After the day was well spent in pleasures befitting the occasion, a grand ball at the legation being the climax, and which was in the height of gaiety, Henderson returned. A hurried consultation between him and the General of the condition of affairs was held, and a new plan of action was inaugurated. At this time soldiers brought to the hospital a wounded comrade. While bending over him they heard him say, "Send help at once! A band of Filipino bandits have captured some of our men." Before further information could be gotten from this wounded soldier he lapsed into unconsciousness.

"Henderson," said the General, "I must have reliable and trustworthy men to go in pursuit of those devils. Will you accept this commission? It is beset with many dangers and requires a cool and level head. Select from your number only those whom you can rely upon in the face of danger. When will you start?"

"At once," replied Henderson.

Nearby, unnoticed and unobserved, stood Surgeon Fairfax. They little dreamed that this man who had sworn to be true to his flag and country would plot the destruction of a brave comrade. The feeling of hatred was so great that the desecration of the honor of his country was a small matter to him. [...]

When all was quiet and the city asleep, forms of five men were seen in the dim moonlight, skulking in and about the legation. Anyone familiar with those forms could readily see that they belonged to a band that meant no good to those sleeping citizens. There was one who did see them. Surgeon Fairfax saw them while on an unfriendly mission, and he soon recognized the leader whom he well knew. [...] After several detours, Fairfax came upon him. Pinto [a local Filipino], feeling secure that he was unrecognized, was about to pass when a rough hand was placed on his shoulder, and he found himself looking into the muzzle of a revolver held by Fairfax.

"Throw up your hands, Pinto! I know you. What are you here for? You are here for no good purpose. How did you manage to evade the outpost? Speak low; for if you make one cry I will send a bullet crashing through your brain."

Pinto, surprised, stood as commanded.

"Me mean no harm."

"You lie! Now listen! I know who you are. I know what you have come to do. You have come here to rob the legation and, perhaps, murder. Come with me; I have something to say to you." And keeping his captive under cover he marched him to a secluded spot. Far away from the sounds of any of the guards, he lowered his revolver and said:

"Pinto, I have a job on hand, and if you help me I will help you. There is a man whom I want to put out of the way. If you will do this I will let you go and give you one thousand dollars after you have done this work."

"Me do it, Surgeon," said Pinto.

"There are soldiers sent to bring you in, and they have gone down by the four forks. You will find them at the bridge. They are in charge of a man named Henderson. Now, if you will guide me to the place, one thousand dollars is yours. Will you do it? He has an hour's start of us, but as you know the road, we can overtake him."

"Me do it! Me do it!"

In the gleam of the moonlight these two arch conspirators bonded themselves for the death of an innocent hero, whose whole thought was to do his duty for the glory of his country. Pinto was allowed to go and give orders to his companions, and in a little while two figures were seen stealthily evading the guards, and were soon out on the highroads.

Henderson, with a small detachment of men, after reaching the four forks, gave orders to separate; each man taking a different course, while he, himself, stood near the bridge. In the stillness of the night this brave Othello stood there; his thoughts seemed to drift back to many incidents of his past life, and in that far-off wilds he saw a face that smiled, inspiring him with confidence to do his duty as his conscience directed. He pictured a hospital tent and a sleeping woman, resting in repose after a strenuous day, dreaming of nothing but her duty toward mankind. In the deep stillness of the night he prayed to God that no harm would befall her. While thus employed with his thoughts he heard a sound, and before he realized, he stood face to face with Surgeon Fairfax, disguised as a Filipino.

They sprang at each other, and were soon in a deathlike struggle. Taken unawares, Henderson was unable to draw his revolver. Fairfax attempted to pierce Henderson with his sword, but discovered that it was no easy task. He was soon joined by another, whom he recognized as Pinto. Henderson, being of an athletic build, was almost a match for both of them, and after wrenching the sword from Fairfax's hand, he was able to draw his revolver and fire. The shot was heard by some of the men, and fearing capture they escaped.

Before accompanying Pinto on his dangerous mission, Fairfax assumed a disguise, which in his mind would assist him in carrying out his nefarious project. After his escape from Henderson he was forced to leave his sword behind. He little thought Henderson recognized him, but the knowledge that Henderson had his sword with his name engraved upon the blade, gave him foreboding thoughts of impending danger. How to establish an alibi he did not know. After arriving at the legation, he returned to his apartments, and from all appearances was Surgeon Fairfax again.

Henderson, being joined by his comrades, who, hearing the report, gave orders for a courier to return to the legation. He fully recognized his assailant as Freda's foster brother; then, looking at the sword, his suspicions were confirmed.

"What shall I do? If I denounce this man as a traitor, it will break her heart. To remain silent is a gross neglect of duty. The General shall know!"

With this determined thought he, too, returned to the legation. Having been preceded by the courier, who, in a measure, exaggerated the facts as to the encounter, when Henderson arrived he was met by the General and other members of the staff.

Freda, hearing of the skirmish in which Henderson was personally engaged, was the first to greet him with, "Are you hurt?"

The General heard the report of Henderson, in which he told of his meeting with Pinto. Henderson, looking into the face of Freda, decided to remain silent as to his real assailant, and, turning, said, "General, there is a traitor among us. You shall know who it is later; but before he answers to Uncle Sam, I swear by the gods, he shall answer to me." [. . .]

Excerpted from *"The Problem": A Military Novel* (Rochester, N.Y.: Henry Conolly Co., 1915).

PRESLEY HOLLIDAY

Presley Holliday served in the all-black 10th Cavalry during the Spanish-Cuban-U.S. War. This letter to the editor of the *New York Age* meticulously lauds the performance and heroism of African American soldiers in the conflict in Cuba in 1899 and directly challenges and refutes the accounts of black cowardice Theodore Roosevelt published in *Scribner's Magazine*.

"The colored soldier . . . properly belongs among the bravest and most trustworthy in the land"[76]

April 22, 1899

To the Editor of the New York Age:

Having read in The Age of April 13 an editorial entitled "Our Troops in Cuba," which brings to my notice for the first time a statement made by Colonel [Theodore] Roosevelt, which, though in some parts true, if read by those who do not know the exact facts and circumstances surrounding the case, will certainly give rise to the wrong impression of colored men as soldiers, and hurt them for many a day to come, and as I was an eye-witness to the most important incidents mentioned in that statement, I deem it a duty I owe, not only to the fathers, mothers, sisters and brothers of those soldiers, and to the soldiers themselves, but to their posterity and the race in general, to be always ready to make an unprejudiced refutation of such charges, and to do all in my power to place the colored soldier where he properly belongs—among the bravest and most trustworthy of this land.

In the beginning, I wish to say that from what I saw of Colonel Roosevelt in Cuba, and the impression his frank countenance made upon me, I cannot believe that he made that statement maliciously. I believe the Colonel thought he spoke the exact truth. But did he know, that of the four officers connected with two certain troops of the Tenth Cavalry one was killed and three were so seriously wounded as to cause them to be carried from the field, and the command of these two troops fell to the first sergeants, who led them triumphantly to the front? Does he know that both at Las Guásima[s][77] and San Juan Hill the greater of troop B, of the Tenth Cavalry,[78] was separated from its commanding officer by accidents of battle and was led to the front by its first sergeant?[79]

When we reached the enemy's works on San Juan Hill[80] our organizations were very badly mixed, few company commanders having their whole companies or none of somebody else's company. As it was, Capt. [James W.]

Watson, my troop commander, reached the crest of the hill with about eight or ten men of his troop, all the rest having been accidentally separated from him by the thick underbrush during the advance, and being that time, as was subsequently shown to be the firing line under some one else, pushing to the front. We kept up the forward movement, and finally halted on the heights overlooking Santiago, where Colonel Roosevelt, with a very thin line had preceded us, and was holding the hill. Here Captain Watson told us to remain while he went to another part of the line to look for the rest of his troop. He did not come to that part of the field again.

The Colonel made a slight error when he said his mixed command contained some colored infantry. All the colored troops in that command were cavalrymen. His command consisted mostly of Rough Riders, with an aggregate of about one troop of the Tenth Cavalry, a few of the Ninth and a few of the First Regular Cavalry, with a half dozen officers. Every few minutes brought men from the rear, everybody seeming to be anxious to get to the firing line. For a while we kept up a desultory fire, but as we could not locate the enemy (he all the time keeping up a hot fire on our position), we became disgusted, and lay down and kept silent. Private [Lewis] Marshall was here seriously wounded while standing in plain view of the enemy, trying to point them out to his comrades.

There were frequent calls for men to carry the wounded to the rear, to go for ammunition, and as night came on, to go for rations and entrenching tools. A few colored soldiers volunteered, as did some from the Rough Riders. It then happened that two men of the Tenth were ordered to the rear by Lieutenant [R. J.] Fleming, Tenth Cavalry, who was then present with part of his troop, for the purpose of bringing either rations or entrenching tools, and Colonel Roosevelt seeing so many men going to the rear, shouted to them to come back, jumped up and drew his revolver, and told the men of the Tenth that he would shoot the first man who attempted to shirk duty by going to the rear, that he had orders to hold that line and he would do so if he had to shoot every man there to do it. His own men immediately informed him that "you won't have to shoot those men, Colonel. We know those boys." He was also assured by Lieutenant Fleming, of the Tenth, that he would have no trouble keeping them there, and some of our men shouted, in which I joined, that "we will stay with you, Colonel."

Everyone who saw the incident knew the Colonel was mistaken about our men trying to shirk duty, but well knew that he could not admit of any heavy detail from his command, so no one thought ill of the matter. In as much as the Colonel came to the line of the Tenth the next day and told the men of his threat to shoot some of their members and, as he expressed it, he had seen his mistake and found them to be far different men from what he supposed, I thought he was sufficiently conscious of his error not to make a so ungrateful statement about us at a time when the Nation is about to forget our past service.

Had the Colonel desired to note the fact, he would have seen that when orders came the next day to relieve the detachment of the Tenth from that part of the field, he commanded just as many colored men at that time as he commanded at any other time during the twenty-four hours we were under his command, although colored as well as white soldiers were going and coming all day, and they knew perfectly well where the Tenth Cavalry was posted, and that it was on a line about four hundred yards further from the enemy than Colonel Roosevelt's line. Still when they obtained permission to go to the rear, they almost invariably came back to the same position. Two men of my troop were wounded while at the rear for water and taken to the hospital and, of course, could not come back.

Our men always made it a rule to join the nearest command when separated from our own, and those who had been so unfortunate as to lose their way altogether were, both colored and white, straggling up from the time the line was established until far into the night, showing their determination to reach the front. In explaining the desire of our men in going back to look for their comrades, it should be stated that, from the contour of the ground, the Rough Riders were so much in advance of the Tenth Cavalry that, to reach the latter regiment from the former, one had really to go straight to the rear and then turn sharply to the right; and further, it is a well known fact, that in this country most persons of color feel out of place when they are by force compelled to mingle with white persons, especially strangers, and although we knew we were doing our duty, and would be treated well—as long as we stood to the front and fought, unfortunately some of our men (and these were all recruits with less than six months' service) felt so much out of place that when the firing lulled, often showed their desire to be with their commands. None of our older men did this. We knew perfectly well that we could give as much assistance there as anywhere else, and that it was our duty to remain until relieved. And we did. White soldiers do not, as a rule, share this feeling with colored soldiers. The fact that a white man knows how well he can make a place for himself among colored people need not be discussed here.

I remember an incident of a recruit of my troop, with less than two months' service, who had come up to our position during the evening of the 1st, having been separated from the troop during the attack on San Juan Hill. The next morning, before the firing began, having seen an officer of the Tenth, who had been sent to Colonel Roosevelt with a message, returning to the regiment, he signified his intention of going back with him, saying he could thus find the regiment. I remonstrated with him without avail and was only able to keep him from going by informing him of the Colonel's threat of the day before. There was no desire on the part of this soldier to shirk duty. He simply didn't know that he should not leave any part of the firing line without orders. Later, while lying in reserve behind the firing line, I had to use as much persuasion to keep him from firing over the heads of his enemies as I had to keep him with us. He remained with us until he was shot in the shoulder and had to be sent to the rear.

I could give many other incidents of our men's devotion to duty, of their determination to stay until the death, but what's the use? Colonel Roosevelt has said they shirked, and the reading public will take the Colonel at his word and go on thinking they shirked. His statement was uncalled for and uncharitable, and considering the moral and physical effect the advance of the Tenth Cavalry had in weakening the forces opposed to the Colonel's regiment, both at Las Guásima[s] and San Juan Hill, altogether ungrateful, and has done us an immeasurable lot of harm.

And further, as to lack of qualifications for command, I will say that when our soldiers, who can and will write history, sever their connections with the Regular Army, and thus release themselves from their voluntary status of military lockjaw, and tell what they saw, those who now preach that the Negro is not fit to exercise command over troops, and will go no further than he is led by white officers, will see in print held up for public gaze, much to their chagrin, tales of those Cuban battles that have never been told outside the tent and barrack room-tales that it will not be agreeable for some of them to hear. The public will then learn that not every troop or company of colored soldiers who took part in the assaults on San Juan Hill or El Caney[81] was led or urged forward by its white officer.

It is unfortunate that we had no colored officers in that campaign, and this thing of white officers for colored troops is exasperating, and I join with The Age in saying our motto for the future must be: "No officers. No soldiers."

Presley Holliday
Troop B, 10th Cavalry
Fort Ringgold, Tex.

New York Age,[82] 11 May 1899.

Roscoe Conkling Jamison

Roscoe Conkling Jamison, born 1886 in Tennessee, was a poet. He was the adopted son of Monroe Franklin Jamison (formerly enslaved) who edited the Colored Methodist Episcopal Church publications *Christian Index* and *Christian Advocate*. Roscoe Jamison's father also was a bishop in the church, which was founded in 1870. In 1922, James Weldon Johnson included one poem by Jamison in *The Book of American Negro Poetry*. Roscoe Conkling Jamison died 28 March 1918 in Phoenix, Arizona.

The Negro Soldiers[83]

These truly are the Brave,
These men who cast aside
Old memories, to walk the blood-stained pave
Of Sacrifice, joining the solemn tide
That moves away, to suffer and to die
For Freedom—when their own is yet denied!
O Pride! O Prejudice! When they pass by,
Hail them, the Brave, for you now crucified!

These truly are the Free,
These souls that grandly rise
Above base dreams of vengeance for their wrongs,
Who march to war with visions in their eyes
Of Peace through Brotherhood, lifting glad songs,
Aforetime, while they front the firing line.
Stand and behold! They take the field today,
Shedding their blood like Him now held divine,
That those who mock might find a better way!

"The Negro Soldiers," *Crisis* 14, no. 5 (September 1917): 249.

FENTON JOHNSON

See part 1, p. 130 for biographical note.

The New Day[84]

From a vision red with war I awoke and saw the Prince
of Peace hovering over No Man's Land.
Loud the whistles blew and the thunder of cannon was
drowned by the happy shouting of the people.
From the Sinai that faces Armageddon[85] I heard this chant
from the throats of white-robed angels:
  Blow your trumpets, little children!
  From the East and from the West,
  From the cities in the valley,
  From God's dwelling on the mountain,
  Blow your blast that Peace might know
  She is Queen of God's great army.
  With the crying blood of millions
  We have written deep her name
  In the Book of all the Ages;
  With the lilies in the valley,
  With the roses by the Mersey,[86]
  With the golden flower of Jersey
  We have crowned her smooth young temples.
  Where her footsteps cease to falter
  Golden grain will greet the morning,
  Where her chariot descends
  Shall be broken down the altars
  Of the gods of dark disturbance.
  Nevermore shall men know suffering,
  Nevermore shall women wailing
  Shake to grief the God of Heaven.
  From the East and from the West,
  From the cities in the valley,
  From God's dwelling on the mountain,
  Little children, blow your trumpets!
From Ethiopia,[87] groaning 'neath her heavy burdens, I
heard the music of the old slave songs.

I heard the wail of warriors, dusk brown, who grimly
fought the fight of others in the trenches of Mars.[88]
I heard the plea of blood-stained men of dusk and the
crimson[89] in my veins leapt furiously.
    Forget not, O my brothers, how we fought
    In No Man's Land that peace might come again!
    Forget not, O my brothers, how we gave
    Red blood to save the freedom of the world!
    We were not free, our tawny hands were tied;[90]
    But Belgium's plight and Serbia's[91] woes we shared
    Each rise of sun or setting of the moon.
    So when the bugle blast had called us forth
    We went not like the surly brute of yore
    But, as the Spartan,[92] proud to give the world
    The freedom that we never knew nor shared.
    These chains, O brothers mine, have weighed us down
    As Samson[93] in the temple of the gods;
    Unloosen them and let us breathe the air
    That makes the goldenrod the flower of Christ.
    For we have been with thee in No Man's Land,
    Through lake of fire and down to Hell itself;
    And now we ask of thee our liberty,
    Our freedom in the land of Stars and Stripes.
    I am glad that the Prince of Peace is hovering over No
    Man's Land.

"The New Day," in *Victory!: Celebrated by Thirty-Eight American Poets*, edited by William Stanley Braithwaite (Boston: Small, Maynard, and Co., 1919), 30–31.

JAMES WELDON JOHNSON

James Weldon Johnson was born into a black middle-class family in Florida in 1871. In 1920, he became the first African American to hold the office of national secretary of the National Association for the Advancement of Colored People (NAACP). Johnson was a renowned anthologist, writer, and educator. He was also an attorney who served as a U.S. diplomat in Venezuela and Nicaragua. Johnson wrote, edited, or co-edited now-classic books such as *God's Trombones* (1927), *The Book of American Negro Spirituals* (1925), and *The Book of American Negro Poetry* (1922). He also wrote the words to "Lift Every Voice and Sing," which many African Americans have adopted as a song of group pride and honor, often referred to as the "Negro (or Black) National Anthem." Johnson died in 1938 from injuries he suffered when a train hit the car he was driving in Maine.

To America

How would you have us, as we are—
Or sinking 'neath the load we bear?
Our Eyes fixed forward on a star—
Or gazing empty at despair?

Rising or falling? Men or things?
With dragging pace or footsteps fleet?
Strong, willing sinews in your wings?
Or tightening chains about your feet?

"To America," *Crisis* 15, no. 1 (November 1917): 13.

Related writings by James Weldon Johnson: "Life Every Voice and Sing" (1900); "Fifty Years" (1913); "The Color Sergeant" (1917); "Father, Father Abraham" (1917); "The Young Warrior" (1917); "And the Greatest of These Is War" (1917).

JOHN F. MATHEUS

John F. Matheus was born in 1887 in West Virginia. He wrote short stories, plays, and other literature during the New Negro era and won several *Opportunity* and *Crisis* magazine literary contests. As a scholar and professor, Matheus traveled to Cuba and Haiti to gather information for his opera *Ouanga!*, which focuses on the Haitian revolutionary leader Jean-Jacques Dessalines. He also was part of a delegation from the League of Nations in 1930 that investigated reports of slavery in Liberia, a country that black people from the United States had colonized in West Africa in 1820. Matheus died in Florida in 1983.

'Cruiter[94]

Characters

GRANNY, aged seventy-seven, a typical Negro "Mammy"

SONNY, her grandson, aged twenty-three

SISSY, his wife, aged twenty

A WHITE MAN, a recruiting agent for a Northern munitions factory

Scene: A farm cottage in lower Georgia.

Time: Just after the entry of the United States into the World War.

Early morning and Spring, 1918, in lower Georgia. The rising of the curtain reveals the large room of a Negro cabin. The walls are the reverse of the outside weatherboarding. A kerosene lamp is on a shelf. At the end of the room looking toward the audience is a door leading to a bedroom, where the starchy whiteness of a well-made bed is visible. In front of the spectators, at the rear of the room, is a window without glass, half-closed by a heavy wooden shutter. Four feet from the window is a door, wide open, leading to a garden. Rows of collards are seen, an old hoe, and in the background a path to the big road.

On the right is a wide, old-fashioned fireplace, where a big pine log makes a smoldering blaze. GRANNY, her head swathed in a blue bandana, is bending over the fire, stirring the contents of a huge iron kettle. In the center of the room is a rough table. A hunk of salt pork is on the table and a rusty knife. Under the window is another table supporting a fifteen quart galvanized iron bucket. A gourd dipper[95] is hanging on the wall between the window and the door. Under the gourd a tin washpan is suspended. Below the basin is a box in which oranges have been crated. A backless chair is under the center table. A mongrel dog is curled under it.

SCENE I

> GRANNY: (*with her profile to the audience, stirring the kettle and singing*)
> Nobody knows de trouble Ah've seen,
> Nobody knows but Jesus;
> Nobody knows de trouble Ah've seen[96]

(*stopping abruptly*)—Ah mus' put some mo' watah to dese plague-taked grits. (*walks to the water bucket, takes down the gourd dipper and fills it with water. Returning to the kettle she slowly pours in the water, stirring as she pours and singing*) "Nobody knows de trouble Ah've seen"—dah now! (*hobbles to the open door and looks across the big road toward the east*) 'Pears like Sonny and Sissy ought to be hyar. It is (*squinting at the sun*) it's mighty nigh onto six o'clock. (*A rooster crows lustily beyond the door. She claps her hands and stamps her feet*)—Skat! Skat, sir. Yo' honery rascal—bringin' me company so early in the mornin'. Ah ain't wantin' to see nobody wid all Ah got tuh do. (*A mocking bird sings.*) Jes' listen tuh dat bird. Hallelujah! Praise de Lam'.[97] (*sings*)
> Oh, when de world's on fiah,
> Ah wants God's bosom
> Fo' mah piller.[98]

(*goes to the table in the center of the room and begins to slice the bacon*) "Fo' mah piller." (*voice is heard outside*)

> SONNY: Whoa, mule, whoa, Ah say.

> GRANNY: (*putting the bacon in a large iron spider[99]*) Ah knowed dey'd be a-gwine fum de field. (*sound of two pairs of shoes is heard; the heavy tread of Sonny, the lighter tread of Sissy*)

> SONNY: (*wearing brogans and overalls*) Mo'in', Granny. Dat bacon sho' smells good.

> SISSY: (*enters, wearing a blue calico wrapper*) How yo' feelin', Granny?

> GRANNY: Ah ain't feelin' so peart dis mo'in'. Mus' be needin' some spring tonic.

> SONNY: (*taking down the washpan and dipping water from the bucket into the pan*) Well, us done planted a haf'n acre co'n. (*washing his face vigorously*) Ah don't know whut Ah'm goin' to do 'bout de cotton dis yeah, ef Ah don't go tuh wah.

SISSY: (*dropping down in the doorsill*) Phew! Mah back is sho' breakin'—stoopin' an' stoopin', drappin' dat co'n.

GRANNY: Well, yo' know yo' po' pappy allus use tuh put in de cotton tuh pay Mistah Bob fo' he's rations fum de Commissary.

SONNY: But dere warn't nary a pesky ole weevil then neither.
'Sides Mistah Bob done tol' me de guv'ment wanted somethin'
t'eat. Say dat de Germans ah goin' to sta've us out an' we mus'
plant co'n an' 'taters an' sich. He lows, too, Ah got tuh gi' 'em
all us maks dis yeah, 'scusin'[100] ouh keep, tuh he'p him fo' not
sendin' me to camp.[101]

GRANNY: How come? He ain't no sheriff.

SONNY: Don't kere, he somethin' t'other wif dis here Draftin' Bo'd.
Yo know dey done sent off Aunt Ca'line's crazy Jim?

GRANNY: Mah Jesus! Mah Jesus! Yo'se all Ah's lef', Sonny. Gi' it
tuh him. Yo' sho'll git kilt ef yo' has to go off fightin'; like yo'
gran'pappy bruder, Samuel, was kilt, when he jined de Yankee
Army.[102]

SONNY: But 'tain't his'n an' Ah jest as leef[103] die a fightin' dan stay
heah an' tek his sass an 'uptiness an' gi' him all Ah mak, lak Ah
was on de chain gang.[104]

SISSY: (*coming in from the doorsill and throwing out the dirty water
in the basin*) Sonny, Sonny, don't yo' know dese hyar whi' foks?

SONNY: (*wiping his hands on his overalls*) Don't Ah know 'em?
Co'se Ah knows 'em. When Ah was in town Sat'day didn't Ah
see Mistah Bob 'sputin' wif ol' Judge Wiley? Didn't Ah heah him
say dis wah was raisin' hell wid his business, takin' all de niggahs
fum de plantations?

GRANNY: Ah knowed dis here disturbance was comin', 'cause Ah
seed a light in de sky eb'ry night dis week.

SISSY: (*washing her hands and wiping them on her dress*) Where's
dey takin' 'em to, Sonny? Do yo' think dey goin' to take yo'?

SONNY: How does Ah know? Whatevah whi' fo'ks wants o' we-all,
we-all jes' nacherly got tuh do, Ah spose, but Ah ain't ter gwine
tuh give Mistah Bob all my wuk an' Sissy's fo' tuh keep me out a
wah. Ah ain't skeered.

GRANNY: Boy, yo' don't know whut yo' talkin' 'bout. Ah done seed
one wah. Men kilt, heads shot off—all de whi' fo'ks in dey big

houses, de wimmins, cryin' dey eyes out an' ol' Gen'ral Sherman[105] shootin' an' sottin' on fiah[106] evahthing waht 'ud bu'n.
(*mechanically takes the spider off the fire, then the kettle of grits,
dishing up both on a large, heavy crockery platter*)

SISSY: (*looking at GRANNY with tenderness. She and SONNY
exchange glances, showing appreciation of her*) Heah, Granny,
lemme he'p yo' fix breakfas'.

GRANNY: Go 'way chile. Yo' got a heap to do he'pin' Sonny all day
in de field.

SISSY: Oh, that ain't nothin'. (*pulling out the backless chair, then
bringing up the orange box and turning it lengthwise so that she
and SONNY can sit upon it*)

SONNY: (*patting Sissy's hand*) Po' chile, Ah ain't gwine to have yo'
wukin' dis er-way. 'Tain't right.

SISSY: Hush, chile, Granny's askin' de blessin'.

GRANNY: (*bowing her head*) Bress dis food we'se 'bout tuh receive
fo' Christ's sake. Amen. (*She serves their plates generously of the
bacon and grits and some gravy made with the bacon*)

SONNY: (*eating with his knife*) Er, ah, Granny—

GRANNY: Sonny, de co'n meal's 'bout gone. Dere's enough fo'
co'npone to-day.

SONNY: (*laying down his knife*) Sissy, don't lemme fergit to take
some co'n meal when Ah goes tuh town to-morrow, Sat'day, ef
us is heah.

SISSY: Ef us is heah? Whut yo' mean, Sonny?

GRANNY: He mean ef de Lawd's willin'. How come, chile, yo' don't
tek Him into yo' plannin'?

SONNY: (*absent-mindedly*) No, Granny, Ah means jes' whut Ah
say, ef all o' us is heah.

SISSY and GRANNY: (*looking at SONNY in amazement*) Wha' we
gwine tuh be?

SONNY: (*hangin' his head*) Ah don't know how to tell yo' 'bout it.
Ah been a-thinkin' an' a-plannin' an' skeered to let on.

SISSY: (*impatiently*) Whut's yo' talkin' 'bout?

SONNY: (*doggedly*) Ah'm talkin' 'bout leavin' heah.

GRANNY: How we goin' tuh leave? Wha' to? Hit teks heaps o'
money to git away.

SONNY: Yo' don't have tuh have no money, no nuthin'. Jes' git away.

SISSY: (*incredulous*) How?

GRANNY: What's ailin' yo' boy?

SONNY: When Ah was in town las' Sat'day a whi' man done tol' me he was lookin' fo' wukers.

GRANNY: Whut whi' man?

SONNY: He said he was a 'cruiter. Lots a fo'ks ah talkin' 'bout him. Yo' all out heah in de country, yo' don't know nothin' 'bout whut's goin' on. Ah'm tellin' yo'. He sez tuh me ez Ah was standin' in de Gen'ral Sto', kin' o' whisperin' lak: "Do yo' wan' tuh mek some money?"

GRANNY: Be keerful o' dese heady fo'ks. Dey ain't out fuh no good.

SONNY: But, Granny, he talked hones'.

GRANNY: Ah know dey ain't no mo' wuk roun' heah dan whut we all is doin'.

SONNY: But dis ain' 'round heah.

SISSY: Wha' is ut, Sonny?

SONNY: Up No'th.

SISSY: (*lighting up*) Up No'th!

GRANNY: (*with scorn*) UP NO'TH!

SONNY: (*bubbling with enthusiasm*) Yes. Up No'th—wha' we kin be treated lak fo'ks. He told me he would tek us all, tek us an' put us on de train at River Station below town, 'cause a deputy sheriff done 'rested a pa'cel[107] o' niggahs, whut was tryin' tuh follow some other 'cruiter.

SISSY: Wha' he now? When could he come?

SONNY: He say he wus comin' tuh see 'bout it Friday, today. (*with hesitation*) Dat's why Ah had to tell yo' all.

GRANNY: Up No'th? Sonny, dey tell me it's too col' up No'th.

SONNY: No, Granny, de 'cruiter say us kin live ez wa'm ez down heah—houses all het by steam. An' Sissy won't have to wuk in no fields neither, ner yo'.

GRANNY: But Ah done been down heah seventy-seven yeahs.

SONNY: (*triumphantly*) But, Granny, Ah won't have tuh leave yo' tuh fight de wa' 'gin dem Germans.

GRANNY: Who say so?

SONNY: De 'cruiter.

GRANNY: How he know?

SONNY: Oh—Ah jes' knows he knows. He sounds lak it when he
talks.

SISSY: Sonny, why wouldn't yo' have to go tuh wa'?

SONNY: He say somethin' Ah don't quite git de meanin' ob, but Ah
'membahs dis. He say Ah could wuk in some kin' o' a—a 'nition
factory,[108] wha' dey meks guns an' things, tuh fight de Germans.
Dat's why Ah wouldn't have to go.

GRANNY: (*looking off into space and tapping her foot slowly*) But
yo' can't believe dese whi' fo'ks. Dey're sich liars.

SONNY: But he's tellin' de troof.

SISSY: Ah hope he's tellin' de troof.

SONNY: (*emphatically*) He is. He's talkin' sense.

GRANNY: Eat yo' breakfus', chillun. Hit's gittin' col'. 'Spec yo'll nebbah heah any mo' fum dat 'cruiter. (*They begin to eat. GRANNY
gets up to get some hot grits, carrying the pot around and replen-
ishing each plate*)

SONNY: (*his mouth full*) We wuk—wuk—wuk. Whut does us git
fo' ut? Ouah victuals an' keep. De mules git dat. We ain't no bettern de mules down heah.

GRANNY: Yo' ain't seen no slavery days, Sonny.

SONNY: Why, slavery days ah right heah now.

GRANNY: Dey can't sell yo'.

SONNY: But dey kin buy us. Ole Mistah Bob thinks he's done
bought us. Dey put bloodhounds on some po' niggah who was
tryin' tuh leave ol' man Popperil's plantation. Whut's dat but
slavery?

SISSY: But, Sonny, Lincum[109] done sot us free. Didn't he, Granny?

GRANNY: 'Course he did. Sonny know dat.

SONNY: He ain't sot me free. (*an automobile horn is heard at a
distance*)

SONNY: (*jumping from the orange crate and speaking joyfully*) Dere
now. Whut did Ah say? Ah bet dat's him, de 'cruiter.

GRANNY: Comin' on Friday. No day to mek new business on
Friday. Bad luck's bound to follow yo'.

SISSY: 'Pears[110] lak tuh me bad luck's been follerin' us. (*the horn

sounds near. They all go to the door to look) There 'tis, comin'
down de road lickity-split.

SONNY: Sho' nuf! Sissy, da hit is, an' hit sho' looks lak de 'cruiter's
cah.

GRANNY: Looks say nuthin'.

SONNY: See. He's stoppin' right by ouah place.

SISSY: Sho' is. (*a brisk voice is heard*) Hey there!—(*steps sound.
THE WHITE MAN is seen coming down the path. He stops in
front of the open door, hat on and wearing gloves. He talks rapidly
and with finality*)

THE WHITE MAN: This woman your wife?

SONNY: Yas, this is her, Mr. 'Cruiter, an' hyah is mah Granny.
(GRANNY *nods her head coldly*)

THE WHITE MAN: Well, everything is ready. I came through the
country[111] early this morning to avoid other cars on the road.
If you say the word I will be back here after you about eleven
o'clock to-night. Don't miss this opportunity, folks.

GRANNY: Yo' don't know whut yo're axin', Mistah 'Cruiter.

THE WHITE MAN: Why, Missus, I am giving this boy a chance to
get out, to be a man, like anybody else, make plenty money and
have time to enjoy it. (*turning to* SISSY) What do you say? Don't
you want to live like a lady and wear fine clothes?

SISSY: (*grinning bashfully*) Yas, sir.

SONNY: 'Course, Mr. 'Cruiter, Ah sho' wants tuh go.

THE WHITE MAN: You know there are many jumping at the
chance.

GRANNY: Honey, yo' can't tell him now. Whut yo' gwine tuh do
wif yo' things?

SONNY: Us ain't got nothin' nohow, Granny.

THE WHITE MAN: (*looking at his watch*) Well, I must hurry. Tell
you what I'll do. I have to come down the road tonight anyway
as far as the adjoining plantation.

SISSY: (*turning to* GRANNY) Mistah Popperil's place.

THE WHITE MAN: I'll blow the horn three times. If you want to
come I'll take you. Don't miss this chance of your lifetime. Good
wages, transportation to Detroit straight, a good job waiting for
you and freedom. (*he leaves hastily*)

GRANNY: (*sinks down on the steps*) Huh! (SISSY *looks at* SONNY *expectantly.* SONNY *stands undecided, scratching his head. The automobile is heard leaving in the distance, down the big road*)

GRANNY: (*singing*)

Nobody knows de trouble Ah've seen,

Nobody knows but Jesus.

(SISSY *and* SONNY *stand looking on the ground.*) 'Twon't be right fo' tuh run dat er-way—widout tellin' nobody. 'Tain't Christian, Sonny.

SONNY: Ah ain't stud'in' 'bout Christian.[112]

GRANNY: Yo' talk lak a po' sinnah, boy.

SISSY: Well, Granny, let us try it. Come on.

GRANNY: Ef we leave dis place dis a-way, we dasn't come back, even of yo' didn't lak it.

SONNY: Ah wish Ah knowed what tuh do.

GRANNY: Yo' ain't got no faith, son. Yo' ought tuh trust God, lak us did way back dar in slavery days. An' He heard ouah prayahs.

SISSY: Sonny prays, Granny.

SONNY: But Ah neveh gits no answer.

SISSY: Mebbe dis is an answer.

SONNY: (*looking at the heavens*) De sun's risin'. Even of we go we got tuh keep on wukin' today, 'cause ol' Mistah Bob's liable to come heah any time.

GRANNY: Sonny, Sissy, Ah can't leave dis place. Why, bress me,[113] my mammy's died heah, ol' Missus is buried heah, yo' gran'daddy crossed ovah Jordan[114] in dis ve'y house, yo' own po' mammy, atter yo' worthless pappy was kilt in de cotton mill, died heah too. Ah'm too puny to leave heah now, too far gone mahself.

SONNY: Granny, ain't Ah allus wuked and he'p to tek kere o' yo' evah sence Ah been big enough to hoe a row?

GRANNY: Yo' has been a mighty dutiful chile, Sonny. Ah ain't sayin' nuttin' 'gin yo' honey. Ah ain't wantin' tuh stan' in yo' light. But Ah can't he'p ut. Ah can't beah tuh leave heah, wha all mah fo'ks ah a-layin'[115] an' go 'way 'mongst heathen people.

SISSY: But, Granny, you'd be happy wif us, won't yo'?

GRANNY: Yas, chile, Ah'd be happy all right, but Ah'm lak
  Ephraim[116] Ah reckon, wedded to mah idols. (*forcing the words*)
  Yo'-all go 'long an' lemme stay heah.

SONNY: (*fiercely*) But, Granny, yo' know how Mistah Bob's gwine
  tuh tek it, when he fin's us done gone. Ah nevah'd feel safe leavin'
  yo' behin'.

GRANNY: Dat's a'right. Ain't Ah wuked fo' he's pappy?

SONNY: He ain't keerin' fo' 'at.[117] He's liable to th'ow yo' out wif
  nuttin'.

GRANNY: Ain't dis mah cabin? (*looks around tenderly*) Ain't Ah
  lived heah fo' fifty yeahs?

SONNY: But it's on Mistah Bob's lan'.

GRANNY: Yo' kin sen' me some money an' excusin' de asthma an'
  de misery in mah head Ah kin keep a youngah 'oman dan me
  pantin', when it come tuh wuk.

SISSY: Granny, yo' mus' come wid us.

SONNY: Ah can't think o' leavin' yo' behin'.

GRANNY: (*getting up from the steps and walking wearily into the
  kitchen*) Don't pester me now. Mebbe—mebbe—Ah knowed
  trouble was comin', seein' dem lights in de elements.

SISSY: (*whispers to* SONNY) She say "Mebbe."

SONNY: (*whispering*) Ah wished Ah knowed what to do.

GRANNY: (*looking up and seeing them whispering*) Go long, chillun yo' needn't be keepin' secrets fum yo' ol' Granny. Mebbe
  yo're right; mebbe Ah'm right. Dis is a cu'ios worl' anyhow. But
  dat whi' man ain't come back yit. Dey ain't tekin' niggahs on
  steam cahs fo' nuttin'. Whi' fo'ks is whi' fo'ks.

SONNY: Well, Granny, we'll see.

GRANNY: Ah'll fix yo'-all's dinner an' bring it down yander to de
  bottom tree.

SONNY: (*to* SISSY) Come on, Sissy, us'll put in one day more anyhow. (*They leave. As the sound of their footsteps ceases the rooster
  is heard to crow again*)

GRANNY: (*going to the door*) Plague tek yo' honery self. (*picks up
  a spoon and throws in direction of the sound*) Cl'ar out a heah—
  crowin' up company. Ah don't need no 'cruiters. (*She becomes
  silent and then sings*)

Down in de Valley—couldn't heah mah Jesus,

Couldn't heah nobody pray, O Lord![118]—

SCENE II

Same Place: Ten forty-five that night. The faint glow of the kerosene lamp accentuates the desolate shadows. GRANNY is sitting on the backless chair, her hands folded. SISSY is packing clothes in an old dress suitcase. A big bag with a string tied around it rests beside GRANNY. SONNY, dressed in overalls and a gray coat, walks back and forth as he talks.

GRANNY: He ain't comin'.

SONNY: 'Tain't time yit. (*looking at his dollar watch*) It's only a quarter tuh 'leven.

GRANNY: He ain't comin', Ah say.

SONNY: Don't put a bad mouf on us, Granny.

SISSY: (*to* SONNY) Come heah, he'p me shet dis thing. (SONNY *helps her close the stuffed suitcase*)

GRANNY: Bad mouf, chile, Ah's been sittin' heah prayin' fo' yo'-all. We ain't nuttin', but wif de ol' Marster[119] we ah pow'ful strong.

SISSY: (*holding her head*) Mah head's turnin' 'round all in a whirl.

SONNY: Ah yo' ready, Granny?

GRANNY: Reckon so.

SISSY: Do yo' think he's comin'?

SONNY: Sho'.

GRANNY: (*shaking her head*) Can't keep fum thinkin' 'bout yo' mammy, how she wouldn't wan' yo' tuh leab heah dis a-way.

SONNY: Ah believe she'd wan' us tuh go.

SISSY: Whut yo' all talkin' 'bout sich fo'? Yo' mak me skeert.

GRANNY: 'Tain't no use bein' skeert. Yo' got tuh face de ol' Marster some o' dese times.

SISSY: Oh, Ah ain't skeert o'no ol' Marster, but yo' mek me think o'ghos'es.

SONNY: Ah'm skeert o' de clutches o' ol' Mistah Bob. He don't mean us no good. Ah jes' know ef mammy an' pappy could speak dey'd shoo us on.

GRANNY: How yo' know so much?

SONNY: Ain't Ah done seed de way he looked at niggahs—wicked lak he could swallow 'em whole?

GRANNY: (*sighs*)—Lordy! Lordy!

SISSY: Whut time is it, Sonny?

SONNY: (*looking at his watch*)—Ten tuh 'leven.

GRANNY: (*singing*)—O Lordy, Lordy, won't yo' ketch mah groan.

SONNY: Us ain't goin' tuh no funeral, Granny. Ah feels lak it's a picnic—a 'Mancipation Celebration picnic.[120]

SISSY: Ah'm rarin' tuh go, too, 'specially sence yo' tol' me 'bout de schools up yander. Ouah chillun kin go tuh whi' fo'ks school.

GRANNY: Whi' fo'ks ain't goin' treat niggahs wif book learnin' any bettern we-all.

SONNY: We kin treat each othah bettah den. Ah kin treat mahself bettah. An' so kin mah chillun.

GRANNY: Yo' young niggahs ah sho' uppity, but Ah hope yo' ain't got no wool ovah yo' eyes. We mought a sont ouah chickens tuh Sis Ca'line.

SISSY: She mought a tol' somebody, too, an' dere we'd be.

GRANNY: Yo' got dat box fixed for Berry?

SONNY: He's already in ut. He ain't used tuh bein' shut up lak dat, de lazy varmint.

GRANNY: (*walks to the door and looks out*) The stars ah shinin'. (*comes back and gets a drink from the bucket*)

SISSY: (*excitedly*) SAKES ALIVE! Ah see de lights a-comin', 'mobile lights.

SONNY: (*running to the door*) She is. We goin' 'fum heah.

GRANNY: (*moodily silent. The glare from the headlights of the automobile lights up the room, shining in through the open door. GRANNY looks in wonder at the light*) Ah, chillun, de Lawd is wif us. (*sings*) Shine on me. Let de light fum de lighthouse, shine on me.[121]

(*The chug of the engine is heard and the grinding of the brakes, as the car pulls up. The horn blows three times. THE WHITE MAN runs down the walk*)

THE WHITE MAN: Are you ready? We have no time to lose.

SONNY: We's waitin'. (*gathers up bag, suitcase and hat and starts towards the door*)

SISSY: Don't forget Berry.

THE WHITE MAN: Who's Berry?

SISSY: De dog.

THE WHITE MAN: What do you mean? We can't take dogs on this trip.

GRANNY: Whut's de mattah wif yo', man? Think we're goin' tuh leave Berry?

THE WHITE MAN: See here. It is impossible to take any dog. He'll make too much noise and besides I can't be bothered looking out for him.

SONNY: Well, Berry'll have tuh stay heah, dat's all.

GRANNY: Den Ah stays too.

SONNY: Whut yo' say?

GRANNY: (stubbornly) Ah ain't goin' tuh leave Berry.

THE WHITE MAN: Ah, come on—cut the argument. We got to make that train.

SISSY: (worried) He kin fend fo' hisself.

GRANNY: Go on yo' chillun, go on. Ah don't wan' tuh go nohow. Ah jes' been a-pretendin' tuh git yo' started. Ah kin git along. Ain't Ah got along wif whi' fo'ks fo' seventy yeahs an' mo'?

SONNY: (angrily) Whut yo' wan' tuh act dis a-way fo'?

THE WHITE MAN: Well, come on or stay, people. Time's passing.

SONNY: Ah'm goin', Granny. Don't yo' see Ah can't stay heah? Ef Ah stay Ah'm goin' tuh git kilt fo' sassin' dese whi' fo'ks; ef Ah go tuh wa', Ah hastuh leave yo' jes' de same an' mebbe git kilt. Ef Ah go No'th and die, Ah'll be a dead free man. (he puts down bundles and embraces GRANNY) Mah po' ol' Granny. Ah'm goin' tuh send yo' plenty a money an' Ah'll be back, come Christmas, mebbe to tek yo' atter we gits settled.

GRANNY: (frightened) Don't, don't come back, not heah. Promise me dat, chile. Yo' know Mistah Bob. He git yo'.

SONNY: No, he won't. Ah'll show him.

THE WHITE MAN: (impatiently) We must be going.

SISSY: Fo' God,[122] Granny, come on.

GRANNY: (firmly) Ah done said mah say.

SONNY: Den, good-bye, Granny. (gives her money) Ah send yo' plenty mo' fust pay day an' Ah'm goin' tuh have a pay day ebery week.

SISSY: (kissing GRANNY) Good-bye.

GRANNY: (her arms around them both) Mah po' chillun. Mah po' chillun. (*They tear themselves from her embrace.* THE WHITE MAN *leads the way to the car.* SONNY *takes up the suitcase, but leaves the bag. Sissy follows. The sound of the three pairs of footsteps dies away*)

SONNY and SISSY: (*calling from the car*) Granny?

GRANNY: (*standing in the doorway*) CHILLUN.

SISSY: Pray fo' us, Granny. (*the car is heard lurching ahead. The light disappears. The sounds die away.* GRANNY *stands for a minute in the deep silence, looking in the direction of the vanished car. A whining is heard. She looks out in the darkness*)

GRANNY: Bress mah soul! Berry! (*She pulls in a crated box, containing the cur. She gets a poker and pries the box open. The dog is wild with appreciation*) Come heah, Berry. (*pulls up the backless chair by the table and sits down, patting the dog*) Berry, you'se all Ah got lef' now. (*rests her elbow on the table, shuts her eyes*) Lordy, Ah'm so tiahed, so tiahed. (*She sits up suddenly, listening attentively*) Who dat knockin' at mah do'? (*She gets up slowly and looks out. Nothing. Shuts the door and bolts it. Sits down again and buries her face in her hands. Again she raises up and listens*) Who dat, knockin' agin? (*Once more she gets up more painfully, unbolts and opens the door. Nothing. Closing it, she totters feebly to the chair*) Berry, Ah'm tuckered out. (*croons*) "Somebody knock-in' at mah do'!"[123] (*stops. Listens*) Come in. (*falls back in chair, her head rests on the table, her arms limp. She mumbles*) Come in, 'Cruiter. Reckon Ah'm all ready.

Curtain

'*Cruiter*, in *Plays of Negro Life: A Source-Book of Native American Drama*, edited by Alain Locke and Montgomery Gregory (New York: Harper and Row, 1927), 187–204.

CLAUDE MCKAY

Claude McKay was born in 1889 in Jamaica and was given the birth name Festus Claudius McKay. He traveled to the United States in 1912 to pursue his education at Booker T. Washington's Tuskegee Institute. McKay later studied at Kansas State University, never completing a degree program at either institution. A prominent participant in the New Negro Movement in literature, he wrote numerous poems, stories, essays, and books. McKay lived in New York, London, Russia, North Africa, and Chicago. In the 1940s, he became a U.S. citizen and converted to Catholicism. He died in Chicago in 1948.

If We Must Die

If we must die—let it not be like hogs
Hunted and penned in an inglorious spot,
While round us bark the mad and hungry dogs,
Making their mock at our accursed lot.
If we must die—oh, let us nobly die,
So that our precious blood may not be shed
In vain; then even the monsters we defy
Shall be constrained to honor us though dead!

Oh, Kinsmen! We must meet the common foe;
Though far outnumbered, let us show us brave,
And for their thousand blows deal one death-blow!
What though before us lies the open grave?
Like men we'll face the murderous, cowardly pack,
Pressed to the wall, dying, but fighting back!

"If We Must Die," *Liberator* 2, no. 7 (July 1919): 21.

Related writings by Claude McKay: "The Little Peoples" (1919); "America" (1921); "The White House" (1922); "The Soldier's Return" (1923); "America in Retrospect" (1926); *Home to Harlem* (1928); "Tiger" (1946).

NIAGARA MOVEMENT

The Niagara Movement was founded in 1905 by a group of African American men determined to obtain political and social justice and equality.[124] William Monroe Trotter, later the founder in 1921 of the *Boston Guardian*, and W.E.B Du Bois, the prominent scholar and professor at Atlanta University, were two among the four primary leaders of this group. Du Bois started two short-lived magazines, *Moon* and *Horizon*, to promote the ideas of the group. The members of the Niagara Movement rejected the ideas of Booker T. Washington, whose influence over the National Afro-American Council frequently excluded them from policy-making decisions. The selection below was generated at the second annual meeting of the Niagara Movement at Harpers Ferry, West Virginia, in 1906, where Du Bois disseminated the demands to Niagara Movement members. By 1911, the Niagara Movement had ceased meeting and had disbanded.

Address to the Country

The men of the Niagara Movement coming from the toil of the year's hard work and pausing a moment from the earning of their daily bread turn toward the nation and again ask in the name of ten million the privilege of a hearing. In the past year the work of the Negro hater has flourished in the land. Step by step the defenders of the rights of American citizens have retreated. The work of stealing the black man's ballot has progressed and the fifty and more representatives of stolen votes still sit in the nation's capital. Discrimination in travel and public accommodation has so spread that some of our weaker brethren are actually afraid to thunder against color discrimination as such and are simply whispering for ordinary decencies.

Against this, the Niagara Movement eternally protests. We will not be satisfied to take one jot or tittle less than our full manhood rights. We claim for ourselves every single right that belongs to a freeborn American, political, civil and social; and until we get these rights we will never cease to protest and assail the ears of America. The battle we wage is not for ourselves alone but for all true Americans. It is a fight for ideals, lest this, our common fatherland, false to its founding, become in truth the land of the thief and the home of the Slave—a by-word and a hissing among the nations for its sounding pretensions and pitiful accomplishment.

Never before in the modern age has a great and civilized folk threatened to adopt so cowardly a creed in the treatment of its fellow-citizens born and bred on its soil. Stripped of verbiage and subterfuge and in its naked nastiness the new American creed says: Fear to let black men even try to rise lest they become the equals of the white. And this is the land that professes to follow Jesus Christ. The blasphemy of such a course is only matched by its cowardice.

In detail our demands are clear and unequivocal:

First, we would vote; with the right to vote goes everything: Freedom, manhood, the honor of your wives, the chastity of your daughters, the right to work, and the chance to rise, and let no man listen to those who deny this. We want full manhood suffrage, and we want it now, henceforth and forever.

Second. We want discrimination in public accommodation to cease. Separation, in railway and street cars, based simply on race and color, is un-American, un-democratic, and silly. We protest against all such discrimination.

Third. We claim the right of freemen to walk, talk, and be with them that wish to be with us. No man has a right to choose another man's friends, and to attempt to do so is an impudent interference with the most fundamental human privilege.

Fourth. We want the laws enforced against rich as well as poor; against Capitalist as well as Laborer; against white as well as black. We are not more lawless than the white race, we are more often arrested, convicted, and mobbed. We want justice even for criminals and outlaws. We want the Constitution of the country enforced. We want Congress to take charge of Congressional elections. We want the Fourteenth amendment[125] carried out to the letter and every State disfranchised in Congress which attempts to disfranchise its rightful voters. We want the Fifteenth amendment[126] enforced and no State allowed to base its franchise simply on color.

The failure of the Republican Party in Congress at the session just closed to redeem its pledge of 1904[127] with reference to suffrage conditions at the South seems a plain, deliberate, and premeditated breach of promise, and stamps that party as guilty of obtaining votes under false pretense.

Fifth. We want our children educated. The school system in the country districts of the South is a disgrace and in few towns and cities are the Negro schools what they ought to be. We want the national government to step in and wipe out illiteracy in the South. Either the United States will destroy ignorance or ignorance will destroy the United States.

And when we call for education we mean real education. We believe in work. We ourselves are workers, but work is not necessarily education.

Education is the development of power and ideal. We want our children trained as intelligent human beings should be, and we will fight for all time against any proposal to educate black boys and girls simply as servants and underlings, or simply for the use of other people. They have a right to know, to think, to aspire.

These are some of the chief things which we want. How shall we get them? By voting where we may vote, by persistent, unceasing agitation; by hammering at the truth, by sacrifice and work. We do not believe in violence, neither in the despised violence of the raid nor the lauded violence of the soldier, nor the barbarous violence of the mob, but we do believe in John Brown, in that incarnate spirit of justice, that hatred of a lie, that willingness to sacrifice money, reputation, and life itself on the altar of right. And here on the scene of John Brown's martyrdom we reconsecrate ourselves, our honor, our property to the final emancipation of the race which John Brown died to make free.

Our enemies, triumphant for the present, are fighting the stars in their courses. Justice and humanity must prevail. We live to tell these dark brothers of ours—scattered in counsel, wavering and weak—that no bribe of money or notoriety, no promise of wealth or fame, is worth the surrender of a people's manhood or the loss of a man's self-respect. We refuse to surrender the leadership of this race to cowards and trucklers.[128] We are men; we will be treated as men. On this rock we have planted our banners. We will never give up, though the trump of doom find us still fighting.

And we shall win. The past promised it, the present foretells it. Thank God for John Brown! Thank God for Garrison and Douglass! Sumner and Phillips, Nat Turner and Robert Gould Shaw,[129] and all the hallowed dead who died for freedom! Thank God for all those to-day, few though their voices be, who have not forgotten the divine brotherhood of all men white and black, rich and poor, fortunate and unfortunate.

We appeal to the young men and women of this nation, to those whose nostrils are not yet befouled by greed and snobbery and racial narrowness: Stand up for the right, prove yourselves worthy of your heritage and whether born north or south dare to treat men as men. Cannot the nation that has absorbed ten million foreigners into its political life without catastrophe absorb ten million Negro Americans into that same political life at less cost than their unjust and illegal exclusion will involve?

Courage brothers! The battle for humanity is not lost or losing. All across the skies sit signs of promise. The Slav[130] is raising in his might, the yellow millions are tasting liberty, the black Africans are writhing toward the light, and everywhere the laborer, with ballot in his hand, is voting open the gates of Opportunity and Peace. The morning breaks over blood-stained hills. We must not falter, we may not shrink. Above are the everlasting stars.

"Negroes Want Equal Rights: The Niagara Movement Issues an Address to the Country," *New York Times*, 20 August 1906, 4.

CHANDLER OWEN

Chandler Owen was born in North Carolina in 1889. He joined the socialist party while studying economics at Columbia University in 1916. There he formed a deep friendship with A. Philip Randolph and together, in 1917, they founded *The Messenger*. Fiery articles such as the one below prompted a Justice Department raid of the journal's office and charges of espionage. At the trial, the judge publicly mocked Owen and Randolph. Owen later moved to Chicago, where he spent the rest of his life and continued writing and editing for radical socialist journals. He also owned a successful public relations company. Owen died in 1967.

From The Failure of Negro Leadership

The Negro leaders have failed. It is hard to admit. Race-pride revolts against it. But the remedy lies in recognizing the condition and setting out to remedy it. Negro leaders like Dr. W.E.B. Du Bois, Kelly Miller, William Pickens, Archibald Grimke, James W. Johnson, Robert Russa Moton, Fred R. Moore, Wm. H. Lewis and Chas. W. Anderson[131] are a discredit to Negroes and the laughing stock among whites.

We have no ill-feeling toward these men. Many of them have held out the best light (or the least poor) for the race during the last ten or twenty years. We have admired them and we recognize their full merit and worth. We do not now impugn the motives of most of them. We impeach their methods. We do not hold that reality actuates them. But we bring against them the worst indictment of the modern world—ignorance—ignorance of the methods by which to achieve the ends aimed at.

Let us take Dr. Du Bois, for example. He has done some good work in stimulating the formation of the National Association for the Advancement of Colored People. He has persistently and consistently stood for the abolition of disfranchisement, discrimination and Jim Crowism.[132] He has fought to secure larger measure of support for institutions of higher education and to increase public and high school facilities for Negroes. As a general principle he has opposed segregation. Lynch law he has condemned directly. He fortunately supported woman suffrage though his reasons therefore were not sound and sufficient.

Still Dr. Du Bois has frequently urged the adoption of many measures which defeat his very purposes and aims. To illustrate: He opposes, we believe sincerely, segregation. Yet he was among the first to advocate a Jim

Crow training camp for Negroes. [. . .] The Jim Crow camp is indefensible—military duty not being a benefit, but a burden, shunned and rejected from early history by those who could escape from its hideous clutches and its grim tentacles.

Lynch law, Dr. Du Bois condemns directly, but he has seldom, if ever, shown a grasp of its true causes and the probable remedy. One has not seen where the Doctor ever recognized the necessity of the Negroes getting into labor unions in the South as a means of eliminating the Negro as a scab, allaying thereby the ill-feeling against him by the working white man, while at the same time, limiting and controling the supply of labor, which would increase the demand for labor both white and black. Moreover, this would be the strongest blow which peonage could be dealt.

Instead, however, we see Dr. Du Bois and all the other Negro editors and leaders herald in big headlines, "Negroes Break Strike!" As though that were something to exult in. [. . .] They should be explaining to Negroes the necessity of allying themselves with the workers' motive power and weapon—the Labor Union and the Strike.

Another evidence of the almost criminal incompetence and cringing compromise of the whole array of Negro leaders named in the beginning of this article is their recent endeavor to raise funds for the families of the colored men conscripted into the Army and Navy. A string of names of "so-called big Negroes" have given their endorsement and consent to the scheme. Now a very elementary examination will reveal the farce of attempting to give any wholesome and fundamental relief to those families by the petty charitable scheme which they have adopted. [. . .]

The impossibility of ever touching the surface of this problem by any hit and miss petty charity should have suggested itself to men like Du Bois, Pickens, Kelly Miller and James W. Johnson, who must have had some study of elementary economics.

Again, we hear Prof. Wm. Pickens, Du Bois and Kelly Miller talking in superlative sureness of how the Negroes' participation in this war will remove race prejudice. Since when has the subject race come out of a war with its rights and privileges accorded for such participation? Leaving out the question of color entirely where is the history to support this spurious promise? Did not the Negro fight in the Revolutionary War with Crispus Attucks dying first (which is not important nor material), and come out to be a miserable chattel slave in this country for nearly one hundred years after? Did not the Negro only *incidentally* secure freedom from physical slavery in the Civil War, only to have peonage fastened upon him almost immediately thereafter, becoming the victim of Ku Klux Klanism, oppression and unspeakable cruelty which were directly perpetrated by the South and condoned by the North. Did not the Negro take part in the Spanish-American War only to be discharged without honors and without a hearing by the president who rose into political prestige and power upon their valor in that war? And have not race prejudice and race hate grown in this country since 1898?[133] The same story must be told of Ireland. She has always helped England in her wars, but she has remained under the feet of the English oppressor for the last eight hundred years.

Professor Du Bois, Kelly Miller and William Pickens, this stuff you are giving out is sheer "clap-trap." It is repelled by the modern Negro student of economics and political science. It is offensive and repulsive. [. . .]

But when you are known to be the leading Negro professors, it makes us ashamed to consider what men like Professor Charles Beard, Scott Nearing, Overstreet, Albert Bushnell Hart and E.R.A. Seligman[134] must think when they read these pigmy opinions and this puerile, credulous interpretation of history from men who are supposed to have given their lives to the study of science, but who are little short of mental manikins and intellectual lilliputians.

Truly the Negro leaders have failed. Most of them are too old to be reformed, which means "re-educated." The hope of the race rests in new leaders with a more thorough grasp of scientific education, and a calm but uncompromising courage.

Excerpted from "The Failure of Negro Leadership," *The Messenger*, January 1918, 23–24.

ANNE BETHEL SPENCER

Anne Bethel Spencer was born on a plantation in Virginia in 1882 and lived most of her life in that state. She worked as a librarian and a New Negro era civil rights activist who also wrote poetry. She welcomed a number of luminaries of the period to her Queen Anne–style home in Lynchburg, Virginia. Spencer was also a poet. While her output was small, her poetry appeared in magazines and anthologies such as *Crisis, Opportunity, The Book of American Negro Poetry*, and *The New Negro*. Spencer died in Virginia in 1975.

The Wife-Woman

Maker-of-Sevens in the scheme of things
From earth to star;
Thy cycle holds whatever is fate, and
Over the border the bar.
Though rank and fierce the mariner
Sailing the seven seas,
He prays as he holds his glass[135] to his eyes,
Coaxing the Pleiades.[136]

I cannot love them; and I feel your glad
Chiding from the grave,
That my all was only worth at all, what
Joy to you it gave,
These seven links the *Law* compelled
For the human chain—
I cannot love *them*; and *you*, oh,
Seven-fold months in Flanders[137] slain!

A jungle there, a cave here, bred six
And a million years,
Sure and strong, mate for mate, such
Love as culture fears;
I gave you clear the oil and wine;
You saved me your hob and hearth[138]—
See how *even* life may be ere[139] the
Sickle[140] comes and leaves a swath.

But I can wait the seven of moons,
Or years I spare,
Hoarding the heart's plenty, nor spend
A drop, nor share—
So long but outlives a smile and
A silken gown;
Then gayly clad I reach up from my shroud,
And you, glory-clad, reach down.

"The Wife-Woman," in *The Book of American Negro Poetry*, edited by James Weldon Johnson (New York: Harcourt, Brace and Company, 1922), 171–72.

MELVIN BEAUNORUS TOLSON SR.

Poet, educator, and mayor of Langston, Oklahoma, Melvin Beaunorus Tolson was born in 1898 in Missouri. He was selected as the poet laureate
of Liberia in 1947 and wrote his poem *Libretto for the Republic of Liberia* to
commemorate the centennial of that nation's independence in 1847. Tolson
published this centennial poem in 1953. As a professor at Wiley College,
an historically black college in Marshall, Texas, Tolson coached the debate
team, the Wiley Forensic Society, which won a highly touted tournament
against the University of Southern California in 1935. *Harlem Gallery* (1965),
a long poem based in his extensive research on the New Negro era, was the
last work he published during his lifetime. Tolson died in Dallas, Texas, in
1966.

A Legend of Versailles[141]

Lloyd George and Woodrow Wilson and Clemenceau[142]—
The Big Three: England, America, and France—
Met at Versailles. The Tiger[143] ached to know
About the myth to end war's dominance.

"One moment, gentlemen," the Tiger said,
"Do you really want a lasting peace?" And then
Lloyd George assented with his shaggy head
And Woodrow Wilson, nodding, chafed his chin.

"The price of such a peace is great. We must give
Up secret cartels, spheres of power and trade;
Tear down our tariff walls; let lesser breeds live
As equals; scrap the empires we have made."

The gentlemen protested, "You go too far."
The Tiger shouted, "You don't mean peace, but war!"

"A Legend of Versailles," in Melvin B. Tolson, *Rendezvous with America* (New York: Dodd,
Mead, 1944), 65.

Related writings also by Melvin Beaunorus Tolson: "Dark Symphony" (1939); *Rendezvous
with America* (1944).

LUCIAN BOTTOW WATKINS

Born in Virginia in 1878 to formerly enslaved parents who could read but could not write, Lucian Bottow Watkins wrote prolifically. His published writings include *Voices of Solitude* (1903) and *Old Log Cabin* (1910). James Weldon Johnson included three of Watkins's poems in *The Book of American Negro Poetry*. Little is known about Watkins's life beyond the autobiographical statement in his book, which summarizes his military service: he was a veteran of the 10th Cavalry, a Buffalo Soldier, who served in the U.S.-Philippines War. After receiving an honorable discharge, he reenlisted for training as a medic. He was finally discharged in 1907. Watkins died around 1921.

The Negro Soldiers of America: What We Are Fighting For[144]

We fight—and for DEMOCRACY
    Lord, we are glad of this sweet chance
To brave whatever hells there be
    Beside the bleeding heart of France![145]

We fight—for all who suffer pain,
    We give our souls in sympathy;
We fight that Liberty may reign
    From Berlin unto Tennessee.

To Tennessee—where last we saw
    Infernal brands of death applied
To men—our men, within the law,
    But "lawless" as they moaned and died.

In Tennessee—where vain, it seems,
    Have been the gifts of passing years,
Where vain have been the eternal dreams
    And toil of Lincoln,[146] sad with tears;

In Tennessee—where Life's best part
    Rich "pearls are cast before the swine,"[147]
CHRIST'S GOLDEN RULE that rules the heart[148]
    And keeps man nearer The Divine.

In Tennessee—where Wrong is Might
    With Hate and Horror on the throne,

Where GOD'S DEMOCRACY of LIGHT
AND LOVE, it seems, has never shone.

In Tennessee—and all her kin[149]
Of sister criminals, year by year,
Who've lost the consciousness of sin,
The tenderness that is a tear.

We fight—and for DEMOCRACY
We'll dare Atlantic's[150] tragic foam,
Go "over the top"—Lord, let us see
PEACE AND HAPPINESS AT HOME!

"The Negro Soldiers of America: What We Are Fighting For," *Richmond Planet*, 2 March 1918, 1.

SELECTED ADDITIONAL LITERATURE ON CITIZENSHIP AND WAR

Bennett, Gwendolyn B. "Wedding Day." In *Double-Take: A Revisionist Harlem Renaissance Anthology*, edited by Venetria K. Patton and Maureen Honey, 511–16. New Brunswick, N.J.: Rutgers University Press, 2001.

Childress, Alice. *Wedding Band: A Love-Hate Story in Black and White*. 1966. Reprint, New York: Samuel French, 1973.

Daly, Victor. *Not Only War: A Story of Two Great Conflicts*. 1932. Reprint, New York: Mc-Grath, 1969.

Dove, Rita. "The Return of Lieutenant James Reese Europe." In Rita Dove, *American Smooth*, 66. New York: Norton, 2004.

Edmonds, Randolph. "Yellow Death." 1935. In Randolph Edmonds, *The Land of Cotton and Other Plays*, 180–204. Washington, D.C.: Associated Publishers, 1942.

Ellison, Ralph. *Invisible Man*. New York: Random House, 1952.

Fauset, Jesse. *There Is Confusion*. 1924. Reprint, Boston: Northeastern University Press, 1993.

Grimke, Archibald H. "Her Thirteen Soldiers." 1919. In *The Messenger Reader: Stories, Poetry, and Essays from* The Messenger Magazine, edited by Sondra Kathryn Wilson, 6–8. New York: Modern Library, 2000.

Miller, May. "Stragglers in the Dust." In *Black Female Playwrights: An Anthology of Plays before 1950*, edited by Kathy A. Perkins, 145–52. Bloomington: Indiana University Press, 1990.

Morrison, Toni. *Sula*. New York: Random House, 1973.

Pickens, William. "Up, Sons of Freedom!" 1924. In *The Messenger Reader: Stories, Poetry, and Essays from* The Messenger Magazine, edited by Sondra Kathryn Wilson, 39–40. New York: Modern Library, 2000.

"Soldiers Number." Special issue, *Crisis* 16, no. 2 (June 1918).

Wood, N. B. "Heroes and Martyrs." In *The New Negro: Readings on Race, Representation, and African American Culture, 1892–1938*, edited by Henry Louis Gates Jr. and Gene Andrew Jarrett, 36–53. Princeton, N.J.: Princeton University Press, 2007.

ENDNOTES

1. Spanish-Cuban-U.S. War and U.S.-Philippines War.

2. The African Methodist Episcopal Church had its beginnings in 1787, when Richard Allen, Absalom Jones, and other African-descended worshipers in the Methodist Church protested their unfair treatment and left the church. This group formed the Free African Society. Richard Allen later established the Bethel African Church (the forerunner of the African Methodist Episcopal Church) in 1794 in Philadelphia. In 1816, Bethel and several other churches combined to form the African Methodist Episcopal Church and begin a national presence.

3. A fagot refers to items in a bundle. In this instance, a bundle of wood for a fire, presumably to lynch black people.

4. Jim Crow: The term Jim Crow dates from at least the 1820s, when it was used by the white minstrel performer Thomas Rice in the song "Jump Jim Crow." Throughout the nineteenth century it was used as a pejorative term for African Americans. After the end of Reconstruction in 1877, the term referred to the laws and policies in the United States that enforced the separation of black and white people.

5. Allen Daniel Candler also was a supporter of the Democratic Party's white primaries.

6. U.S.-Philippines War.

7. The *New York Age* was a black newspaper founded by prominent journalist Timothy Thomas Fortune along with Walter Sampson and (very likely) George Parker in 1881. The initial names of the newspaper were the *Globe* and then the *Freeman*. This publication became the *New York Age* in 1888 after Fortune's brother Emanuel Fortune and another investor, Jerome Peterson, joined the paper.

8. A road leading to the coastal city of Malabon, a stronghold for the Philippines Islands' independence movement during the war against the occupation by the United States.

9. Of Republican president William McKinley.

10. Richard Montgomery founded this African American newspaper in 1898.

11. Spanish-Cuban-U.S. War.

12. Probably an allusion to both William Harvey Carney of the 54th Massachusetts Voluntary Infantry, who carried the U.S. flag during the Civil War, and George Berry of the 10th Cavalry Regiment of the United States Army (Buffalo Soldiers), who carried the flag for his own unit and for the 3rd Cavalry Regiment, a white unit, when they lost their standard bearer.

13. A coffin prepared for viewing the dead or any other platform or board on which the dead are viewed.

14. Moses is a prophet in a number of religious traditions. Old Testament accounts of Moses report that God came to Moses in the form of a burning bush.

15. Colored.

16. Trusting.

17. In the Christian Old Testament and the Jewish Tanakh, God promises the Israelites a home in Canaan, which is frequently referred to as the Promised Land. African American writers often use this term metaphorically to refer to a land where black people can live in freedom.

18. Detain.

19. The French Army awarded the Croix de Guerre (Cross of War) to black soldiers who fought with the French during World War I. The U.S. military did not allow black troops to fight with its white troops.

20. Camp Reed in Jackson, Tennessee.

21. In 1919, white mobs targeted African Americans, especially veterans, in racial attacks. James Weldon Johnson, a prominent African American, referred to the summer of 1919 as the Red Summer because of the large number of attacks on black people. Many African Americans responded to these attacks by fighting back.

22. Harriet.

23. Liniment: a lotion containing pain-relieving ingredients that are applied to the skin.

24. Lena Ford (lyrics) and Ivor Novello (music), both British, wrote "Keep the Home-Fires Burning ('Till the Boys Come Home)" in 1914. The song was popular during the war.

25. A small suitcase.

26. A chevron is a V-shaped military stripe sewn onto soldiers' uniforms to indicate rank, grade of service, and other distinctions.

27. Directly.

28. Matthew 5:44.

29. Fear.

30. Quarrel.

31. World War I war bonds sold in the United States to generate capital for the war. People were encouraged to buy Liberty Bonds to demonstrate patriotism.

32. A battle waged on 1 July 1898 at San Juan Hill in Cuba during the Spanish-Cuban-U.S. War.

33. 71st New York Volunteer Regiment.

34. A large number of infantry soldiers advancing with weapons. Bush-Banks made slight alterations to this poem when she published it in *Driftwood*. This line was enclosed in quotation marks in her 1914 version: "That phalanx seemed / To move like one black, solid wall."

35. Acquit.

36. World War I. Title supplied by volume editors. The precise date of this speech is unknown. It likely occurred in 1917.

37. That is, England would become a dependent land of Germany.

38. Paraphrase of Woodrow Wilson's well-known statement of 2 April 1917 that "the world must be made safe for democracy."

39. Allusion to the words "soldiers of the Cross," used by Pope Urban II in 1095 to admonish all Christians to join the army of Christ during the violent Christian Crusades against Islam and Judaism.

40. Britain abolished slavery in the New World colonies, but not in India, in 1833.

41. A dispute 23 August 1917 between black soldiers from the 24th Infantry Regiment stationed at Camp Logan, near Houston, Texas, and a white police officer resulted in a riot. Over 100 soldiers were court-martialed. Several soldiers received the death penalty and were hanged.

42. Des Moines was designated the training camp for African American officers in 1917.

43. An Old Testament figure (Leviticus 18:21 and 20:2; Jeremiah 32:35; and Isaiah 30:33 and 57:9) who requires extreme sacrifices—usually children—in order to be appeased. Certain idolatrous, apostate Israelites sacrificed children to a fiery statue referred to as Moloch. This figure often is represented as a ghoul in human form.

44. Flanders Field, located in Belgium, was the site of heavy casualties during World War I.

45. Race riots instigated by white vigilante attacks against black veterans began in Washington, D.C., on 19 July 1919 and continued sporadically until October. Black soldiers and citizens fought back when attacked. In addition to these cities, significant conflicts occurred in Omaha, Nebraska, and Elaine, Arkansas.

46. The term New Negro began circulating regularly in the United States around 1895. It refers to a concerted effort among black people to challenge color-based stereotypes, injustices, and inequality and to interact in society without subordination to anyone. There were cultural, social, and political dimensions to the New Negro era, which lasted throughout the 1950s.

47. In 1917, A. Philip Randolph and Chandler Owen established *The Messenger* in New York as a socialist magazine.

48. When this poem was published in Du Bois's *Horizon* magazine, he preceded it with the following words: "Of course you have faced the dilemma: it is announced, they all smirk and rise. If they are ultra, they remove their hats and look ecstatic; then they look at you. What shall you do? Noblesse oblige, you cannot be boorish, or ungracious, and too, after all, it is your country and you do love its ideals if not all of its realities. Now, then, I have thought of a way out. Arise, gracefully remove your hat, and tilt your head. Then sing as follows, powerfully and with deep unction. They'll hardly note the little changes, and their feelings and your conscious will thus be saved."

49. World War I.

50. Jim Crow: This term refers to the laws and policies in the United States that enforced the separation of black and white people.

51. The fulfillment of prophecy; also the eternal.

52. Locations of highly developed societies.

53. Abbreviation for the Latin term *videlicet*; namely.

54. Spanish-Cuban-U.S. War.

55. The Greeks and Romans wove the leaves of the bay laurel into crowns to honor their athletic and military heroes. The coins of the British Crown were initially minted in gold, but Dunbar could be simply referring to money.

56. World War I.

57. A short (usually plaid) coat made of heavy felt wool.

58. President Woodrow Wilson signed the Selective Service Act into law on 18 May 1917. Every male of draft age was required to register. Men were selected for service based on a lottery.

59. During World War I, "slackers" were men who did not comply with the law requiring them to register for military service. Registration was compulsory, and slacker raids rounded up unregistered men. In 1918, the E. G. Renesch company of Chicago created a promotional poster, "The Colored Man Is No Slacker," designed to encourage black men to register.

60. All are locations of bloody battles and high casualties during World War I. The Somme is a river in France near where a major battle occurred that resulted in over one million deaths; Palestine and Syria were the locations of several battles between the Allied forces and the Turkish Ottoman Empire (German allies); and the Italian Alps was the location of bloody battles between the Allied Italian forces and the Austrian-Hungarian forces. The Russians fought against the Austrians and then the Germans in World War I.

61. He is playing on words, as the term spade is slang for a black person. He also may be referring to the card game Spades in which the lowest card in the spades suit can beat or trump higher cards—including aces—that are not spades. Alternatively, the primary reference here could be to the card-shark hoax referred to as the "deuce of spades," in which the sucker card is the deuce or two of spades.

62. Revolutionary War for Independence.

63. The Civil War.

64. Spanish-Cuban-U.S. War. Colonel Theodore Roosevelt questioned the bravery of the black soldiers when he commented on the war in an article in *Scribner's* magazine in 1899.

65. The 10th Cavalry Buffalo Soldiers, under the command of General John Pershing, attempted to capture Francisco Pancho Villa at Carrizal, Mexico, in 1916. They battled the Mexican Army (Villa's foe) instead.

66. Ireland.

67. On the battlefield in Europe.

68. An Old Testament figure that requires extreme sacrifices—usually children—in order to be appeased. Certain idolatrous apostate Israelites sacrificed children to Moloch.

69. An allusion to Acts 17: 26 in the Bible. Black writers frequently refer to this passage to support the concept of one humanity.

70. A popular Civil War song written by Julia Ward Howe in 1861 that was published in the *Atlantic Monthly* in 1862. Dan sings the first line of the song and Cornelia speaks a line from the fifth verse.

71. World War I.

72. A note in the *Dunbar Speaker* indicates an earlier publication of Dunbar-Nelson's poem in the *A.M.E. Church Review*. We were unable to locate this prior publication.

73. U.S.-Philippines War; title supplied by volume editors.

74. "Love's Old Sweet Song" was written in 1886 by Graham Clifton Bingham; music by James Lyman Malloy.

75. "Comin' thro' the Rye" is a bawdy drinking song written by Scottish poet Robert Burns. He often wrote in Scots English.

76. Title supplied by volume editors.

77. The first battle in the Spanish-Cuban-U.S. war took place near Santiago, Cuba, on 24 June 1898. It sometimes is referred to as a skirmish.

78. The 10th Cavalry: a segregated unit of the U.S. Army, formed in 1866. These men and the men of the 9th Cavalry were later referred to as Buffalo Soldiers by the Native Americans. They were posted mainly in the West and participated in relocating Native peoples to the part of the country referred to as Indian Territory.

79. Sergeant John Buck.

80. A battle waged on 1 July 1898 that brought fame to Colonel Theodore Roosevelt and the 1st United States Volunteer Cavalry, referred to as the Rough Riders. This regiment initially was under the command of Colonel Leonard Wood, who retired and left the men in the hands of Roosevelt. The 9th and 10th Cavalry fought alongside the Rough Riders, but Roosevelt minimized their participation in an article published in 1899 in *Scribner's Magazine* under the title "The Rough Riders."

81. One of three important battles occurring on 1 July 1898. The other two battles are San Juan Hill and Kettle Hill.

82. The editors of the *New York Age*, a black-owned newspaper, received numerous letters in response to Theodore Roosevelt's comments in *Scribner's Magazine* in 1899.

83. World War I.

84. World War I.

85. Mount Sinai is the location where Moses received the Ten Commandments, or God's laws for humanity. Armageddon is the battle between good and evil that takes place at the end of the world in biblical prophecy.

86. A river in England; also a river in Nova Scotia where formerly enslaved captives escaped and where the British settled formerly enslaved Loyalists after the war.

87. Common nineteenth-century name used to refer to African and African descended peoples.

88. The Roman god of war.

89. Blood.

90. Perhaps an oblique reference to the reports—from as early as 1908—of the Belgians cutting off the hands of Africans in the Congo.

91. Belgium, a neutral nation, was invaded by the Germans during World War I. Flanders Field in Belgium was a site of heavy war losses. Austrian-Hungarian forces invaded Serbia after a Serbian assassinated Franz Ferdinand, the heir to the Austro-Hungarian throne.

92. The Spartans were citizens of Sparta, Greece, whose military training made their skill at war legendary.

93. Samson is an Old Testament figure with superhuman strength. He would lose his strength if he cut his hair.

94. World War I.

95. A receptacle for retrieving liquids or other substances. Dried and hollowed-out gourd plants have a wood-like appearance and make good ladles, cups, bottles, and bowls.

96. "Nobody Knows the Trouble I've Seen," a traditional spiritual.

97. Lamb; a reference to Jesus, who is called the Lamb of God in several places in the Bible.

98. "When the World's on Fire," a traditional gospel song.

99. An iron frying pan raised above the fire on three iron feet.

100. Excusing; with the exception of.

101. Boot camp.

102. The Union army in the Civil War.

103. Leef: a term of Middle English origin meaning willingly, here suggesting that Sonny finds that fighting and dying in the war would be better than turning his wages over to Bob.

104. A gang of prison workers restrained with heavy chains that connect them while they work.

105. William Tecumseh Sherman, a Union general during the Civil War, made a devastating march through Georgia, captured Atlanta, and ordered the destruction of the city by fire.

106. Setting on fire.

107. Arrested a passel, or many. As black laborers, who had worked in conditions resembling slavery, migrated out of the South after Reconstruction ended in 1877, many southern towns enacted laws that made it difficult for northern recruiters to do their work. The towns frequently authorized sheriff's officers and other law enforcement officials to arrest black people who attempted to leave.

108. Ammunition or munitions factory.

109. Lincoln.

110. Appears.

111. Country: rural area, back woods.

112. He does not care about or is not paying attention to Christianity.

113. Bless me.

114. Crossing over Jordan River is a frequent metaphor for death in African American literature. It simultaneously suggests freedom as well.

115. Buried.

116. Ephraim is the rebellious son of Rachel and Jacob in the Old Testament. His stubborn refusal to follow religious laws and his jealousy of the tribe of Judah resulted in Ephraim's exile. Granny suggests that she will not follow Sonny so will be exiled from the Promised Land in the North because she is stubborn and is too old to let go of her life in the South.

117. That.

118. "Couldn't Hear Nobody Pray," a traditional spiritual.

119. God.

120. Emancipation Celebrations were held on 1 January to commemorate the day the Emancipation Proclamation went into effect in 1863.

121. "Light from Your Lighthouse (Shine on Me)," a traditional spiritual.

122. For God's sake.

123. "Somebody's Knocking at My Door," a traditional spiritual. In some African American folk beliefs, such phantom knocking, especially if it occurs three times, signals an impending death. Sinners or those not ready to transition into death refuse to answer the door.

124. The Niagara Movement's Declaration of Principles resulted from this first meeting. Trotter opposed women's participation in the movement, but Du Bois's insistence that they should won out, and women attended the second meeting in 1906.

125. The Fourteenth Amendment conferred citizenship to all persons born in the United States.

126. The Fifteenth Amendment extended the vote to black men.

127. This is a reference to the 1904 election, which returned Theodore Roosevelt to the presidency pledging Republican support of voting reform.

128. Trucklers: servile or obsequious people.

129. This is a list of abolitionists and Civil War heroes. John Brown was an abolitionist whose raid in 1859 on the federal arsenal at Harpers Ferry was celebrated at this meeting of the Niagara Movement in 1906; [William Lloyd] Garrison was an abolitionist and the founder of the *Liberator*, which he published from 1831 to 1866; [Frederick] Douglass escaped slavery in 1838 and became a prominent abolitionist who worked with Garrison for many years; [Charles] Sumner was a Boston lawyer, politician, and antislavery advocate; and [Wendell] Phillips was a Boston attorney, abolitionist, and social justice advocate.

Nat Turner led an insurrection in Southhampton County, Virginia, in 1831; Robert Gould Shaw was a colonel in the Union Army and the commander of the 54th Regiment Massachusetts Volunteer Infantry.

130. Slavic peoples (Croats, Czechs, Poles, Serbs, Slovaks, and others) of the Austro-Hungarian Empire began to press for independence in the late nineteenth century.

131. Du Bois was a major intellectual leader who founded *Crisis* magazine in 1910 and co-founded the National Association for the Advancement of Colored People (NAACP) in 1909. Miller was a prominent professor at Howard University, which was established for black students. Pickens was a renowned educator who taught in historically black universities and colleges, including Morgan College, where he became vice-president. He also held a national position in the NAACP and is credited with expanding its membership into the South. Grimké, one of the founders of the NAACP, was a black lawyer and a descendant of the complicated white abolitionist Grimké family. Johnson was a lawyer, diplomat, and writer and a prominent figure in the NAACP. Moton became president of Tuskegee Institute upon the death of Booker T. Washington in 1915. Moore, a member of Booker T. Washington's National Negro Business League, edited the *Colored American* magazine after Washington helped him purchase it. Moore later edited T. Thomas Fortune's *New York Age*, also partially financed by Washington. Lewis was a lawyer who became an assistant attorney general of the United States. Anderson's friendship with Booker T. Washington elevated him to the highest federal position held by an African American, collector of internal revenue in New York.

132. Jim Crowism: This term refers to the practice of racial separation based on the laws and policies in the United States.

133. The year of the Spanish-Cuban-U.S. War.

134. Prominent white intellectuals: historian Charles Beard, economist Scott Nearing, philosopher H. A. Overstreet, historian Albert Bushnell Hart, and economist E.R.A. Seligman.

135. Telescope.

136. A constellation of stars frequently referred to as the Seven Sisters. It can be seen easily from earth.

137. Flanders field, a site of heavy losses during World War I, is located in Belgium.

138. Hob: a small ledge on a fireplace where items can be placed and kept warm. The hearth is the floor of the fireplace, especially the bricks in front of the opening.

139. Before.

140. Of death.

141. Two major meetings, the first in Paris in January 1919 and the second in Versailles, France, in June that same year, resulted in a treaty that established the conditions for peace following World War I. The treaty also established the League of Nations. The United States opposed the League of Nations and refused to sign the treaty.

142. Names of the leaders of the "Big Three": British prime minister David Lloyd George; U.S. president Woodrow Wilson; and French premier Georges Clemenceau.

143. Premier Georges Clemenceau became known as the Tiger because of his passionate desire for strong punitive measures against Germany in order to pay for the devastation in France.

144. World War I.

145. The 369th Infantry Regiment of black soldiers fought alongside the French allies because the U.S. military did not allow them to fight with white U.S. soldiers.

146. President Abraham Lincoln's dream of freedom promised during the Civil War and never realized.

147. This phrase is from Matthew 7:6.

148. The Golden Rule ("Do unto others as you would have them do unto you") is found in Luke 6:31.

149. Other southern states where Jim Crow law prevailed.

150. The Atlantic Ocean: where many African peoples died during the Middle Passage; also the ocean that symbolizes the pathway between the United States and war on the European continent.

3

THE DOUBLE-V CAMPAIGN CHALLENGES JIM CROW

World War II

In Far-off Rabaul
I died for democracy.
Better I fell
In Mississippi.

DUDLEY RANDALL, 1971

WACs photographed during the World War II era. Image courtesy of the National Archives and Records Administration.

A NUMBER OF positive developments in the participation of African Americans in the military occurred during and after World War II, but not without bitter struggles. The interwar years had enabled African Americans to develop a sharper Pan-African consciousness in part as a response to colonial and imperial conquests against black people around the world. For instance, the U.S. occupation of Haiti (1915–1934) elicited strong reactions from the black press and the National Association for the Advancement of Colored People (NAACP). Black citizens wrote to their newspapers and to the State Department. In the midst of increased racial violence at home, African Americans' empathy toward beleaguered Haitians grew. Similarly, African Americans' opposition to the occupation of Haiti remained constant into the 1930s, as documented on the pages of the *Crisis*, the NAACP's official publication. In addition, general resistance to Benito Mussolini's imperial invasion of Ethiopia (1935–1936) spilled onto the streets in the United States. Relationships between African Americans and Italian Americans deteriorated after heavyweight boxer Joe Louis beat Italian Primo Carnera in June 1935. Following that contentious boxing match, conflicts between the two groups flared for the next year, especially in New York and New Jersey. Western powers did little to halt Italy's blatant violations of international law, but the black press and black citizens criticized the U.S. government for its failure to speak out. Pan-African solidarity also prompted relief drives in black communities across the country.[1]

Despite African Americans' growing consciousness as international citizens, the U.S. military remained predominantly white. The War Department at this time used eugenics-inspired reports (particularly a 1925 pseudo-scientific report on brain size from the Army War College) to disqualify black people as soldiers, and the Executive Office did little to change such practices. By the 1940s, the NAACP had grown into a formidable organization that forcefully used its lobbying finesse and the U.S. justice system to push aggressively for equality in civil society and the military. For example, they supported legislators who tried, albeit unsuccessfully, to include a nondiscrimination clause in the Selective Training and Service Act of 1940 and worked alongside the black press to publicize injustice.[2] While President Franklin D. Roosevelt had a spotty record regarding national race relations, his wife, Eleanor Roosevelt, exercised her considerable influence to champion black rights. In March 1941, for example, she supported the inclusion of black pilots in the Air Corps by taking a flight piloted by a black airman from the Tuskegee Army Air Field in Alabama. Within two months of Mrs. Roosevelt's request, the first squadron of black airmen had enrolled at the airfield as part of a successful experiment to train black fighter pilots. The Tuskegee Airmen, as they became known, served the nation heroically during World War II, particularly in North Africa.[3]

Due to the absence of strong support from Roosevelt's White House, only small adjustments occurred related to desegregating the military. A few black men received promotions in the armed forces before the United States entered World War II. When the war began in 1939, just five of the 5,000 African Americans serving in the active regular army were officers, and three of them were chaplains. Approximately 500 black officers existed on paper in the Army Reserves and the National Guard—about half of 1 percent of the Officers' Reserve Corps.[4] In 1941, Benjamin O. Davis Sr., who had served in the Spanish-Cuban-U.S. War, became the first black brigadier general in the U.S. Army. In 1936 his son, Benjamin O. Davis Jr., had become the only African American during the interwar years to graduate from West Point. He served during World War II and became a U.S. Air Force general in 1998. But by March 1945, only 1 percent of the African Americans in the military were officers, in a pool where officers overall constituted 11 percent of the military.[5]

As with previous military engagements, many black men spoke out by venting their frustrations in the black press or writing letters to military and government officials. A. Philip Randolph, president of the Brotherhood of Sleeping Car Porters, and Bayard Rustin, a young social justice activist, threatened to gather thousands of African Americans to protest the double standard of American democracy in a massive march on Washington that they scheduled for 1 July 1941. In his call for a march, Randolph proclaimed that there was "a crisis of democracy." Responding to pressure from these activists and others, President Roosevelt signed Executive Order 8802 on 25 June 1941, banning discrimination in defense industries. The order established the President's Committee on Fair Employment Practice to investigate and report violations. In six months, half of the government's contractors had added black employees to their labor force.[6]

In 1942, the U.S. armed services remained segregated. Only 2 percent of the volunteer forces were African American. Officials rejected most black men because the segregated units and training facilities lacked space. On 31

January of that year, James G. Thompson, a cafeteria worker in the Cessna aircraft plant in Kansas, wrote a letter to the editor of the *Pittsburgh Courier*, published with the title "Should I Sacrifice to Live Half-American?" Thompson debuted the catch-phrase that called for a double victory for democracy at home and abroad. The editors of the *Courier* immediately introduced the Double-V campaign in their pages, which asked America to rally for victory against overseas fascists and victory against Jim Crow. This campaign publicized the continued hypocrisy of discriminatory policies in the military and gave new impetus to the long-standing fight for equality.

The Double-V campaign epitomized the raised expectations of black people about the possibilities for substantive change during this global conflict. African Americans actively invested in the war. Black groups and companies bought substantial numbers of war bonds, demonstrating their patriotism and their desire to see economic as well as sociopolitical returns for their loyalty after the war.[7] Black people also responded in large numbers to blood drives around the nation, despite rules in the Red Cross and the military that segregated blood supplies.

The NAACP actively monitored military discrimination. Its executive secretary, Walter White, visited troops abroad and reported his findings in letters and articles. The NAACP's *Crisis* and other black publications reported on most of the debates about African American military participation. Whether printing letters from soldiers on active duty, field reports from military camps, soldiers' complaints about poor treatment (see the letter from soldiers at Fort Logan below), or debates among intellectuals about the social and political meanings of the war for African Americans, the black press demonstrated the black community's patriotic support and continued discontent with unequal treatment.

Defenses against racist attacks went beyond letter writing or occasional fistfights. Aaron Henry, a GI stationed in Hawai'i during the war, later recalled moments of resistance against discrimination and insult. Black soldiers would boycott the segregated movie screenings that allotted one night to white men and the next to black servicemen. They also chose to attend church services off the base after one chaplain described the weather as "raining pitch forks and nigger babies." Army corporal Amzie Moore's duties included countering Japanese anti-U.S. propaganda, including Japanese broadcasts about the immorality of American segregation. Moore recollected, "We were promised [by the army] that after the war was over, things would be different. . . . Somehow or another, some of us didn't believe it, others did." He joined the NAACP while in the service, reasoning,

"Here I'm being shipped overseas, and I [have] been segregated from this man whom I might have to save or he save my life. I didn't fail to tell it."[8]

Despite pressure from civilian organizations, the military establishment was slow to change. Although the number of black soldiers had increased to about 100,000 by January 1942, less than thirty black soldiers had entered officer candidate schools. Only after further coercion did these numbers rise. As their predecessors had done during World War I, military leaders during World War II generally kept black soldiers out of combat zones by extending their training periods and by using other delaying tactics (see Aeron Bells below). Considerable public pressure nudged the army to deploy the 93rd Division to the Southwest Pacific in 1944, late in the war. In addition, African American servicemen and women continued to face problems on bases in the South. The iron fist of local Jim Crow laws and customs prevailed, even after March 1943 when the War Department banned segregation in all recreational facilities and in government transportation vehicles (see Georgia Douglas Johnson below).[9] Uniformed soldiers frequently became targets of civilian attacks. Riots occurred in Beaumont, Texas; Detroit, Michigan; and other cities during the summer of 1943 (see Langston Hughes and Ann Petry below).[10]

The war, which took place on multiple international fronts and required large numbers of troops and personnel, ultimately gave African Americans more access to the armed services than was available to them during World War I. However, in some cases, the military capitulated to foreign racism, maintaining segregation, for instance, in Australia to appease the "White Australia" policy of its ally.[11] In some European countries, though, a lot of African Americans experienced life without Jim Crow and the possibility of positive social interactions regardless of race. Many soldiers who later reflected on their service overseas noted the irony that although there were numerous instances of camaraderie with their fellow white soldiers in moments of engagement with the enemy, violence and resentment from them were rampant in social situations, particularly those involving interactions with local white women.[12]

In short, a pattern developed throughout Europe where black soldiers confronted animosity from their white colleagues in the U.S. military but mostly had good relations with local white populations. For instance, Britain welcomed U.S. troops, both black and white. Most black soldiers recall pleasant experiences fraternizing with members of local communities, who expressed gratitude for the men's service. On 14 October 1943, *The Times* of London quoted the statement of Brigadier-General Benjamin O. Davis that black troops "had been profuse in their praise of the way in which they had been received by British soldiers and the British public," although he said that "there had been resentment on the part of some white American troops against the way in which British people had entertained coloured troops." U.S. officials, uneasy about the interracial contact, particularly with roughly 100,000 black troops stationed in Britain, spread rumors about the supposed lecherousness of black men and circulated documents that attempted to skew the more tolerant race relations there.[13]

Despite the obstacles, from 1941 to 1945, the number of black enlisted personnel rose from 5,000 to over one million, and half of these served overseas. African Americans became pilots, officers, and marines (the Marine Corps enlisted black men as volunteers in June 1942 after a directive from Roosevelt). They entered all the branches of the military, although wherever they enlisted, they faced racism and segregation. For instance, black marines could not train with white marines in Parris Island, South Carolina, or San Diego, California. Instead, they trained at Montford Point, the segregated facility at Camp Lejeune, North Carolina. Approximately 20,000 trained there from 1942 to 1949. In general, black officers did not receive commissions and black military personnel were consistently underutilized. Indeed, three-fourths of the African Americans in uniform remained restricted to service and supply units, although many participated in combat because the military needed boots on the ground.

The army provided more opportunities for African Americans than any other branch of the military.[14] The navy remained the most segregated division. The low number of white recruits in 1942 forced Secretary of the Navy Frank Knox, who had been one of the "Rough Riders" in the Spanish-Cuban-U.S. War, to reluctantly agree to train limited numbers of black sailors, although not above the rank of petty officer. James Forrestal, who replaced Knox when he died, successfully experimented with desegregating the navy on a small scale in 1944. All sixteen black men who entered the segregated officer training program at Camp Robert Smalls (named after a black naval Civil War hero—see Part 1) in 1944 passed their tests, but only thirteen received commissions; they referred to themselves as the "Golden Thirteen." The Naval Academy in Annapolis did not desegregate until June 1945. The first African American to graduate was Wesley A. Brown in 1949.[15]

By the end of 1944, the military faced a massive shortage of fighting soldiers, and black service troops under General Dwight Eisenhower could volunteer for combat in Europe. Although they fought in segregated units and comprised only 4 percent of U.S. combat forces, black soldiers contributed greatly to the Allied victory. On 1 November 1944, a *New York Times* article documented the historic 92nd Infantry Division's sixty-eight days of progress on the Italian front line, praising the unit's endurance in comparison to that of "more experienced divisions." Noting their pride, the reporter stressed that the black soldiers saw themselves as Americans doing their duty: "Negro officers say they want above all to be regarded as American fighting men. Yet they admit their men want to do particularly well as a matter of race pride."[16]

Many black soldiers performed admirably. As had been the case in U.S. wars since the eighteenth century, the armed forces downplayed black heroism during World War II. However, in response to increased pressure from civic and national organizations (such as the NAACP), the black press, and veterans, the nation slowly and belatedly acknowledged some of those who served. One particular case is Dorie Miller, a black messman aboard the *U.S.S. West Virginia* in Pearl Harbor. As the first U.S. hero of World War II, he carried his wounded ship captain out of harm's way and gunned down four enemy planes. However, only after an intense campaign from African Americans did he finally receive the Navy Cross (see Gwendolyn Brooks below).[17] For most others, recognition took decades. A 1993 army-commissioned study revealed discrimination in the awarding of the Medal of Honor. Since then, Presidents Clinton, Bush, and Obama have recognized scores of black veterans among the hundreds they have acknowledged, most posthumously. The Tuskegee Airmen finally received recognition for their service, including a Congressional Gold Medal in 2007, and the Montford Point Marines received the same honor in 2012.

Before World War II, only a handful of black women served in the armed forces. In response to increased black activism and government oversight of the armed services during World War II, the Women's Army Auxiliary Corps, later the Women's Army Corps (WAC), accepted black women from its inception in 1942. The Women Accepted for Volunteer Emergency Service (WAVES), also established in 1942, permitted black women to enlist in the navy two years after its founding. The 6888th Central Postal Directory Battalion was the only group of African American WACs to serve overseas during the war, 855 women in all (see Gladys O. Thomas-Anderson below). They were able to serve partly because of pressure from the NAACP, the National Council of Negro Women, and the black press. Major Charity Adams became the first WAC black officer; she retired after the war as a lieutenant-colonel, the highest possible WAC rank. In addition, approximately 130 black army nurses and Red Cross women traveled to England.

These women knew they were trailblazers and expected equal treatment. As did their male counterparts, African American women believed that through their service they could demonstrate their rightful claim to their nation and help improve their own life chances. Similarly, just as black men in the military did, these women endured attacks, both physical and psychological. Civilian black women also found employment domestically in the industries that fueled the war effort. Thus, many more black women contributed to the nation's defense than ever before.[18]

Many black soldiers, buoyed by their experiences in Europe where they had seen the potential of life without Jim Crow, returned home to a segregated nation. Mississippian Haywood Stephney recalled, "When you're not exposed to much you don't get much. But after seeing what some of the other world was doing then I realized how far behind I was. As we began to move and stir around and learn other ways then we had a choice—a comparison." While at war in France, Medgar Evers realized that "the whole world wasn't like Mississippi." When Aaron Henry returned to his hometown in Mississippi, he saw veterans telling stories about their travels, "and the word had spread that conditions in Coahoma County had not been ordained by God."[19] Like Aaron Henry, Amzie Moore, and Medgar Evers, many veterans were transformed by their travels. Some benefited from the Servicemen's Readjustment Act (the GI Bill) of 1944. Some of these veterans became leaders and active participants in the mass civil rights movement of the following decades, taking up the challenge to fight vigorously for democracy at home just as they had done abroad.[20]

NOTES

1. Scott, "Black Nationalism in the Italo-Ethiopian Conflict, 1934–1936," 134–50; Plummer, *Rising Wind.*

2. See Sullivan, *Lift Every Voice*; Buckley, *American Patriots*, 262.

3. Moye, *Freedom Flyers*, 50–52; Buckley, *American Patriots*, 272–73, 282–83; Moore, *Fighting for America*, 24–26, 28–29. See also Moye, *Freedom Flyers.*

4. Hastie, "Negro Officers in Two World Wars," 319.

5. Stouffer et al., *The American Soldier*, 501–2.

6. Randolph, "Call to Negro America," 292; Buckley, *American Patriots*, 270–71; Moore, *Fighting for America*, 26–29.

7. Plummer, *Rising Wind*, 85.

8. Examples from Aaron Henry conversation with Jerry DeMuth at Henry's home, Clarksdale, Mississippi, 3 August, 1964, Jerry DeMuth Papers, 1962–1987, SC3065, Wisconsin Historical Society; Forman, *The Making of Black Revolutionaries*, 224, 279; Raines, *My Soul Is Rested*, 233.

9. Hastie, "Negro Officers in Two World Wars," 320; Stillman, "Negroes in the Armed Forces," 140; McGuire, *Taps for a Jim Crow Army*, 132–33.

10. Gerstle, *American Crucible*, 210–20.

11. Moore, *Fighting for America*, 48–49.

12. White, *A Man Called White*, 277–85, 292. See also Lee, *The Employment of Negro Troops*.

13. Davis quoted in Thorne, "Britain and the Black G.I.s," 342–51; Smith, *When Jim Crow Met John Bull*, 139–40; Moore, *To Serve My Country, To Serve My Race*, 120; McMillen, *Remaking Dixie*, 97. See also Hachey, "Walter White and the American Negro Soldier in World War II."

14. Scott, "The Participation of Negroes in World War I," 292; Buckley, *American Patriots*, 316–17; Stillman, "Negroes in the Armed Forces," 141.

15. Hastie, "Negro Officers in Two World Wars," 320–21; Ramold, *Slaves, Sailors, Citizens*, 184, 185; Buckley, *American Patriots*, 304–5; Astor, *The Right to Fight*, 268.

16. Bracker, "Negro Unit Proud of Gains in Italy."

17. Buckley, *American Patriots*, 275; Astor, *The Right to Fight*, 160–61.

18. See Moore, *To Serve My Country*; Hine, "Black Professionals and Race Consciousness"; Hastie, "Negro Officers in Two World Wars," 322.

19. McMillen, *Remaking Dixie*, 102; Vollers, *Ghosts of Mississippi*, 31; Henry, *Fire Ever Burning*, 70.

20. Stillman, "Negroes in the Armed Forces," 140. See also Hamlin, *Crossroads at Clarksdale*.

AERON D. BELLS

In 1942, Aeron D. Bells, a college-educated African American living in Texas, wrote to William H. Hastie, a civilian aide to Secretary of War Henry Stimson, to ask for clarification of the rules that prevented qualified black volunteers from entering the army as officers. Hastie's archive contains numerous complaints from qualified African Americans who were barred from service in the U.S. military beyond entry-level ranks.

"Local prejudice, or an official order from Washington"[1]

Houston, Texas
May 20, 1942
Mr. W. H. Hasty,[2]
Negro Adviser,
Sec'y of War,
Washington, D.C.

My Dear Sir:

I am a young Negro . . . age 33 years today. . . . I am a former student of Wiley College,[3] Marshall, Texas, and more recent of Iowa University, Iowa City, Iowa. . . . A Science Major studying for the degree of M.D. until I was forced to quit due to financial reverses. At present and for the past several years, I have been with the Post Office, this city. My salary $2100. At the outbreak of the war I heard a Nationwide broadcast for Volunteer Officer Candidates [V.O.C]. Realizing that my wife and family could not exist off my salary as a Non-Com[4] or as a private, and wishing to fulfill my obligation to my country, I inquired into the field of V.O.C. For some time I was given the old "run-a-round," but today I was told by my board (local board #15 Selective Service) that it had been advised by its headquarters at Austin, Texas, that NEGROES WERE NOT ACCEPTED IN THE ARMY AS VOLUNTEER OFFICER CANDIDATES. Will you kindly tell me whether this is local prejudice, or an official order from Washington. I am sure that you will agree with me when I say that the situation is "Confusing," for I fail to see why I WILL BE FORCED TO SHED MY BLOOD on Democracy's battlefields as a Private, and am refused to volunteer as an officer candidate to fulfill the same job.

I will appreciate any light that you may be able to shed on this confused soul.

May I remain,
Respectfully Yours,
Aeron D. Bells
#4702 Vernon Street
Houston, Texas.

"Not Accepted as Volunteer Officer Candidates," in *Taps for a Jim Crow Army: Letters from Black Soldiers in World War II*, edited by Phillip McGuire (Santa Barbara, California: ABC-Clio, 1982), 9.

GWENDOLYN BROOKS

A Pulitzer Prize–winning poet and the second poet laureate of Illinois, Gwendolyn Brooks was born in 1917 in the home of her maternal grandparents in Topeka, Kansas. The family soon moved to Chicago, where Brooks lived until her death in 2000. Early in her long career as a writer, she edited serial publications such as the *Champlain Weekly*, which she started as a teenager, contributed to the *Chicago Defender* newspaper, and participated in Richard Wright's South Side Writers' Group. Brooks lived in and wrote about Chicago and was among the Black Chicago Writers literary movement in the 1930s and 1940s. Her many books include *Annie Allen* (1949), which won a Pulitzer Prize, *The Bean Eaters* (1960), *In the Mecca* (1968), *Primer for Blacks* (1980), and her only novel *Maud Martha* (1953). Several poems in her collection *A Street in Bronzeville* (1945) focus on World War II.

Negro Hero

to suggest Dorie Miller[5]

I had to kick their law into their teeth in order to save them.
However I have heard that sometimes you have to deal
Devilishly with drowning men in order to swim them to shore.
Or they will haul themselves and you to the trash and the fish beneath.
(When I think of this, I do not worry about a few
Chipped teeth.)

It is good I gave glory, it is good I put gold on their name.
Or there would have been spikes[6] in the afterward hands.
But let us speak only of my success and the pictures in the Caucasian
    dailies[7]
As well as the Negro weeklies.[8] For I am a gem.
(They are not concerned that it was hardly The Enemy my fight was
    against
But them.)

It was a tall time. And of course my blood was
Boiling about in my head and straining and howling and singing me
    on.
Of course I was rolled on wheels of my boy itch to get at the gun.
Of course all the delicate rehearsal shots of my childhood massed in
    mirage before me.

Of course I was child
And my first swallow of the liquor of battle bleeding black air dying
  and demon noise
Made me wild.

It was kinder than that, though, and I showed like a banner my
  kindness.
I loved. And a man will guard when he loves.
Their white-gowned democracy[9] was my fair lady.
With her knife lying cold, straight, in the softness of her sweet-flowing
  sleeve.
But for the sake of the dear smiling mouth and the stuttered promise I
  toyed with my life.
I threw back!—I would not remember
Entirely the knife.

Still—am I good enough to die for them, is my blood bright enough to
  be spilled,
Was my constant back-question—are they clear
On this? Or do I intrude even now?
Am I clean enough to kill for them, do they wish me to kill
For them or is my place while death licks his lips and strides to them
In the galley[10] still?

(In a southern city a white man said
Indeed, I'd rather be dead;
Indeed, I'd rather be shot in the head
Or ridden to waste on the back of a flood
Than saved by the drop of a black man's blood.)[11]

Naturally, the important thing is, I helped to save them, them and a
  part of their democracy.
Even if I had to kick their law into their teeth in order to do that for
  them.
And I am feeling well and settled in myself because I believe it was a
  good job,
Despite this possible horror: that they might prefer the
Preservation of their law in all its sick dignity and their knives

To the continuation of their creed
And their lives.

"Negro Hero," in *Common Ground*, June 1945, 44–45.

*   *   *

the white troops had their orders
but the Negroes looked like men

They had supposed their formula was fixed.
They had obeyed instructions to devise
A type of cold, a type of hooded gaze.
But when the Negroes came they were perplexed.
These Negroes looked like men. Besides, it taxed
Time and the temper to remember those
Congenital iniquities that cause
Disfavor of the darkness. Such as boxed
Their feelings properly, complete to tags—
A box for dark men and a box for Other[12]—
Would often find the contents had been scrambled.
Or even switched. Who really gave two figs?
Neither the earth nor heaven ever trembled.
And there was nothing startling in the weather.

"the white troops had their orders but the Negroes looked like men," in *A Street in Bronzeville* (New York: Harper and Brothers, 1945).

Related writings by Gwendolyn Brooks: "Gay Chaps at the Bar" (1945); "The Progress" (1945); "The Anniad" (1949); "Third Sermon on the Warpland" (1981).

Ruby Berkley Goodwin

Ruby Berkley Goodwin was born in 1903 in Du Quoin, Illinois, a mining town. Her memoir, *It's Good to Be Black* (1953), recounts her experiences growing up in a small community of black people in southern Illinois. The family moved to California in the 1920s. Goodwin's poetry appeared in publications such as *Ebony Rhythm*, and she collected her poems in two books, *From My Kitchen Window* (1942) and *A Gold Star Mother Speaks* (1944). Goodwin worked as a syndicated columnist, as secretary/publicist for Hattie McDaniel and Ethel Waters, and as a movie and stage actor in productions that included *Member of the Wedding*. She died in 1961 in Los Angeles.

Guilty

(A Negro soldier was killed by a bus driver in a southern state because he did not know the jim crow[13] section of the car)

I did not know my place—
That is the crime for which I died.
I did not know where to sit,
Or how to bow low,
Or when to say "Yes, sir," to Mr. George.

I grew up with stardust in my eyes,
Stardust gathered from a million
Hopes and dreams of great men
Who died to make this a strong free nation.

True, all was not stardust.
I remembered Jamestown, Virginia,[14]
And Harper's Ferry.[15]
But a war was fought to end the shame
Of human slavery, or so I was told
By my teachers in New York.

I became a man and I heard
Of the Four Freedoms,[16]
How good they sounded to me:

Freedom from want,
No more breadlines,

No more Salvation Army clothes,
No more relief doles,[17]
No more hard-boiled case workers.

Freedom to worship,
I could sing "Steal Away" and "Ave Maria"[18]
On Beale Street or in Carnegie Hall.[19]
I could serve an invisible God
Or worship an image of gold or brass.
Freedom of speech,
I could laugh with Rochester[20] on the radio,
Disagree with the Dies committee,[21]
Yell for the Brooklyn Dodgers,
Or criticize the President.

And freedom from fear.
That was the greatest freedom
Of them all;
For the man who has no fear
Is the only free man in the world.

I wrapped the Four Freedoms around me
When I put on my uniform
And started south to become a soldier
To save the world from tyranny.

But I did not know my place—
That is the crime for which I died.
I did not know where to sit,
Or how to bow low,
Or when to say "Yes, sir," to Mr. George.

"Guilty," in *Ebony Rhythm: An Anthology of Contemporary Negro Verse*, edited by Beatrice M. Murphy (New York: Exposition Press, 1948), 68–69.

Related writings by Ruby Berkley Goodwin: *A Gold Star Mother Speaks* (1944); "Democracy Challenges America" (1949).

SHIRLEY GRAHAM DU BOIS

See part 1, p. 108 for biographical note.

Tar

It was the moan of the saxophones that did it—deep down, lingering and warm. Mary turned abruptly and began pushing her way towards the door. "Easy there, honey. What's the hurry?" "Lady, can I . . . ?" "Hands off, Alabama,[22] I seen her first!" "Some chick!" "Tall, slim mamma!"

No good. She had to get out. As usual, on Saturday night, the place was crowded, but nobody seemed to mind. Deep red leather, black lacquer, smooth floors, laughter, smoke and good music. No mistake about the music! The U.S.O.[23] down the street offered no competition to the Savoy.[24] Weekends there were always plenty of men in uniform. Plenty of men—not in uniform. Why should there be so many? Why weren't they in the army with—Tom?

Down the street Mary drew a deep breath that hurt. Lenox Avenue was rakish without being tawdry. The air was good, touched lightly with the pungent odor of barbecue, and there were sounds of loud and easy friendliness. But without a glance either way, Mary turned off the avenue into 140th Street, gradually leaving lights and haunting saxophones behind.

This was the way they usually went home—she and Tom—clinging to each other, shadowed by the trees. Then the throb of the saxophones was part of all the breathless night. No—it was pain.

Crazy idea—going to the Savoy without Tom. She had thought to run into some lonely soldier from down home. They were all over Harlem—gawky, slow speaking dark boys from Mississippi, Alabama and Georgia—anxious and defiant, crude and proud.

They turned to Mary like cornflowers to sunshine. Mary was one of them. She wasn't long come from Georgia herself.

That's why she could never get over the wonder of Tom. He was so sure of himself. He knew so well what he was going to do—had everything figured out. Nothing was going to stop him. And she had fitted into all his plans. "You're the missing link," Tom had grinned. "Right out of heaven into my arms! Oh, Baby!" Imagine calling Georgia heaven! Tom, who had made heaven for her. Smart Tom, who went downtown to school all day and worked nights. (All except that one night a week when he took her dancing at the Savoy.) Georgia and heaven, Tom and music and the bridges he told her he was learning to build, the shining clean home they were going to have—all mixed up like molasses—sweet!

Then the dirty Japs dropped bombs on Pearl Harbor![25]

Lord, Tom was mad! "Just like that. Right out of the sky on Sunday morning. Few more months and I'd be finished—set to build all the roads and canals and bridges in the world. But the army needs engineers *right now*!" Just before Christmas he had come in all excited. The entire class was going to be commissioned—wouldn't have to wait till June. All fellows were going into the army right away! He was going to be an officer! And Mary didn't say a mumbling word.

But there seemed to be some delay, and Tom fussed and fumed. Then for several evenings he was very quiet. Mary's heart ached. She recognized *the look*. She'd seen it on the face of a child who had been slapped hard. She even remembered it in the eyes of a kitten, which had been kicked. You see, Tom had been so sure! One night he was downright glum until unexpectedly he said, Aw hell, he was going to the army anyway. Wouldn't take long—he'd soon get to officers' training camp. They'd see, he had muttered darkly. He'd build bridges yet!

Now he was gone.

The odor of burnt hair assailed Mary's nostrils when she let herself into the walk-up apartment. Cleo was home—had converted the tiny kitchen into a beauty salon. Bits of hair still clung to the sink. With smoking iron she was transforming the thick, spongy mass of her head into a carefully designed and glistening coiffure.

Cleo was not, however, happy. Her Saturday evening had been a total loss. Washing and pressing her own hair was a chore to which she had been forced only through dire necessity. For Cleo sang in the Abyssinian Baptist Church choir. Attendance at morning service was obligatory. Nor dare she fall below the high standards set by Brother Powell. She sang second alto and intended "to shine for Jesus"—literally. Now, her voice was aggrieved.

"Two hours—two hours I wait at Maybelle's for this shampoo and curl. Then—what you think happens?"

"What?" asked Mary, knowing it must have been terrific.

"In walks that great big balook of a sailor of hers, and she goes wild! Not nary another head tonight—said I didn't have no appointment—walks right out leavin' two customers. Would you believe it? After two hours!"

"Well . . ." began Mary, doubtfully, "if he was here only one evening, I guess . . ."

"This damn war is ruinin' the country—just ruinin' it," Cleo's voice was bitter.

Mary paused long enough to cluck sympathetically, then sidled into the living room and threw up the window.

"Say," called Cleo, "Mrs. Van Dyke phoned. Wants you to come in Monday."

Mary didn't answer, and Cleo appeared in the doorway, hot iron poised.

"You hear what I said. Mrs. Van Dyke . . ."

"I heard you."

Mary had thrown herself down on the couch and was fumbling with the radio. She added without spirit. "Fat old thing!" Cleo eyed her suspiciously.

"Where you been?" A direct question.

"I stopped by the Savoy."

Mary didn't look up. She didn't need to. Tom might just as well be standing there on the rug. Through the pregnant silence the radio began to sputter.

Cleo hadn't liked Tom. She considered him "uppity."[26] And Cleo felt responsible for Mary. There was some sort of vague relation between the two families. It was Cleo who had suggested that Mary come north. Mary, she said, had a future.

For Mary sewed. Ever since she was a little girl she had been putting pieces together in striking and unusual patterns. And her tiny stitches were perfect. Now, what she could do with a length of cloth was something. She had a feeling for colors, too. The white folks in Maxwell were crazy about her. They all said Aunt Ross's gal was a well-mannered little thing.

"But," Cleo had urged, "why stay in such a dump workin' your fingers to the bone for fifty cents a day when you can come to New York and in a little while have your own shop on Seventh Avenue. Look at Madame Walker!"[27]

Mary couldn't very well look at Madame Walker—but she got the point. So did Aunt Ross, for that matter. There wasn't anybody else to consult. So that's how Mary came to be in Harlem sharing an apartment on West 136th Street with the veteran New Yorker, Cleo. And she was doing very well. Cleo had mentioned Mary's abilities to her boss. All her friends were delighted to find such an "unspoiled" seamstress.

Cleo cooked. She was a good cook, but she had no illusions about her future. She refused to live in[28]—got what she could out of her nights as she went along, and accepted fate. But Mary was different. Mary had talent!

And a girl with talent didn't have to get gaw-gaw over the first fast talker who came along. For all his big talk about bridges, the only work that "engineering student" did was odd job man around the Taft Hotel[29]—nights.

Mary had protested. "But Tom's putting in all his time studying. He's going to . . ."

"Bridges!" Cleo had snorted. "Don't make sense for a colored man—no future!"

No, she had not approved. And him going to the army hadn't helped matters. Mary had wanted Tom to marry her before he left. He had explained to a tight-lipped Cleo, "Engineers get in mighty tough spots. Wouldn't be fair to her. When I come back . . . if everything's okay . . . I mean—if I'm all here—you know . . . then we'll . . ." He had turned away from Mary's hungry eyes.

That was six months ago. And look at her now! Limp as a rag—no ambition—not interested in good customers—Mrs. Van Dyke, for instance . . . and her living on Central Park, South!

"This night," Cleo told herself, "I gotta speak my mind!"

But Mary didn't hear a word of it.

For Mary was listening to the radio. Thousands of other people heard that same announcement. They didn't know the man was talking straight to Aunt Ross's Mary—was telling her what she could do—how she could join up with Tom and help get this war over—quickly.

No, she didn't hear a word Cleo said. After she had written down an address she leaned far out the window and watched the blinking lights of a mail carrier high over head. The throbbing of its engines was music. She thought again of the saxophones, but now it was sweet. For she was feeling the beauty of a plane—all silver in the sunlight. How wonderful it would be to make even the tiniest part of a great plane!

It had never occurred to any of Mary's satisfied customers that she knew a war was going on. She said nothing the next afternoon until the job was finished. Then stooping over to pick up a long basting thread from the thick rug she announced in her husky, honey-thick drawl, "I won't be comin' next week."

The lady was annoyed. These girls, so utterly unreliable.

"I signed up for a defense course."

When the lady remonstrated, Mary was a bit apologetic. (Cleo had told her bluntly she was a fool.)

"I figured I ought do somethin' to help. I . . . I . . . don't think this," she lifted the silken folds, "is awful important. You reckon 'tis?"

Because Mary was skilled in cutting cloth on a bias and fitting uneven edges, she did exceptionally well in the sheet metal class. She took the advanced course. Then showed her certificate proudly.

"Now what?" Cleo asked.

"I'm going into the plane factory."

But Mary didn't get into that factory. Nothing daunted, she tried another and another and another. She stood in long lines day after day—clutching her certificate. At night she had crazy dreams—about flying and dropping through clouds—of her color fading out when she blew a saxophone. One night she dreamed she was green! After a while her face did get sort of ashy. She couldn't just keep on living on Cleo. She put her certificate away.

The customers welcomed her back gladly. "After all," they said. One lady mentioned the circumstances to her husband. "She's so *disappointed*. I thought there was a shortage of help." The husband thought so too and immediately gave Mary a letter to a friend of his. Mary took the letter gratefully. It asserted that she was "honest" and "a personable negress."

Mary got a job—filling vats with tar. She stood and poured tar all night—going on at twelve and returning in the morning spattered with tar.

"For heaven's sake," Cleo asked, "must you push in the tar with your nose?"

"Seems like I'm awful clumsy. It's so thick. I'll move up soon. Everybody has to start with tar."

The folks for whom Cleo cooked went south for the winter. Because Cleo's flesh yearned for the golden warmth of Texas sunshine, she went with them.

It was cold and damp the April morning Cleo returned. She shivered in the dark hallway as she fitted her key. Inside, water was running. From the bathroom door she surveyed Mary vigorously scrubbing tar from her forearms. Mary was thinner.

"Look," Cleo demanded, "you still pourin' tar? Ain't you been promoted?" Mary shook her head.

"The old so and so . . ." Cleo began, but Mary stopped her.

"Just had a long letter from Tom." Her eyes were shining.

Cleo was trying to stuff her coat into the tiny hall closet. Perhaps the state of that closet rendered her voice acid as she commented, "Naturally Tom's awful busy right now buildin' bridges over the Rhine."[30]

"Tom didn't say nothin' 'bout bridges this time." Then why was Mary's voice singing? "That morning they'd been unloading a ship when . . ."

"Unloading ships—Tom?" Cleo experienced a grim satisfaction. Engineers and their "tough places," indeed!

" . . . planes come. Tom said they was rushin' the stuff to cover when machine fire riddled the wharf."

"Was he . . . ?"

"Not Tom! The tank he was rollin' was shot to pieces and tar gushed all over him—knocking him down—burying him in tar. He said nothing could have hit him. And when they was gone and he managed to get up . . . Lord, he mustta been a sight!" And Mary laughed.

Cleo found herself moistening her lips as she finally managed to close the closet door. Then she turned back to Mary, who asked, "Can't you just see Tom in that tar?"

She shook the soap from her eyes, leaned over and carefully removed a bit of tar from behind her left ear.

Cleo grinned. "You don't do so bad yourself."

"I'll get it all off. I'm stopping by the Savoy tonight. Count Basie's[31] there."

Mary studied a spot just above her right elbow and frowned slightly.

"I reckon it'll take a heap of tar for all the new roads we gotta make. Yeh—a lotta tar!"

"Tar," *Negro Story*, March–April 1945, 9–13.

LANGSTON HUGHES

A writer in multiple genres, Langston Hughes produced a prolific body of work that addresses nearly every aspect of life in general and black life in particular. He was born in 1902 in Joplin, Missouri and lived in a number of cities throughout the United States, finally settling in Harlem. His literary career spanned three major African American literary movements that he participated in: the New Negro Movement in literature, the Black Chicago Writers movement, and the Black Arts Aesthetic Movement. He wrote a number of poems on war and citizenship throughout his long career. James Langston Hughes died in New York City in 1967.

Beaumont to Detroit: 1943[32]

Looky here, America
What you done done—
Let things drift
Until the riots come.

Now your policemen
Let your mobs run free.
I reckon you don't care
Nothing about me.

You tell me that hitler[33]
Is a mighty bad man.
I guess he took lessons
From the ku klux klan.

You tell me mussolini's[34]
Got an evil heart.
Well, it mus-a been in Beaumont
That he had his start—

Cause everything that hitler
And mussolini do,
Negroes get the same
Treatment from you.

You jim crowed[35] me
Before hitler rose to power—

And you're STILL jim crowing me
Right now, this very hour.

Yet you say we're fighting
For democracy.
Then why don't democracy
Include me?

I ask you this question
Cause I want to know
How long I got to fight
Both HITLER—AND JIM CROW.[36]

"Beaumont to Detroit: 1943," *Common Ground*, Autumn 1943, 104.

Related writings by Langston Hughes: "Our Land" (1923); "I, Too, Sing America" (1925); "Let America Be America Again" (1936); *The Em-Fuehrer Jones* (1938); "America," (1925); "The Colored Soldier" (1931); "America's Young Black Joe" (1940); "Brothers" (1941; radio play); "The Ballad of Margie Polite" (1943); "For This We Fight" (1943); "Will V-Day Be Me Day Too" (1944); "PVT Jim Crow" (1945; radio play); "In the Service of My Country" (1945; radio play); "American Heartbreak" (1951); *Simple's Uncle Sam* (1965); "War" (1967); "Un-American Investigators" (1967); *Jericho-Jim Crow* (1964).

Georgia Douglas Johnson

Poet, playwright, columnist, Georgia Douglas Johnson was born in Georgia in 1880. Her home, the renowned S Street Salon in Washington, D.C., was the gathering place for the leading artists and writers of the New Negro era. She also was a member of the Writers' League Against Lynching, founded in 1934. Johnson, who is credited with coining the term lynching plays, had written lynching dramas prior to her membership in this diverse group of writers, and she added more while she was a member. From 1910 until her death in 1966, Georgia Douglas Johnson lived in Washington, D.C.

Black Recruit

At home, I must be humble, meek,
Surrendering the other cheek;
Must be a coward over here,
And yet, a brave man—over there.

This sophistry[37] is passing strange,
Moves quite beyond my mental range—
Since I must be a hero there,
Shall I prepare by crawling here?

Am I a faucet that you turn
To right—I'm cold—to left—I burn!
Or but a golem[38] wound to spring
This way or that—a soulless thing!

He surely is a master-man
Who formulated such a plan.

"Black Recruit," in *Ebony Rhythm: An Anthology of Contemporary Negro Verse*, edited by Beatrice M. Murphy (New York: Exposition Press, 1948), 94.

Bob Kaufman

Robert Garnell Kaufman was born in 1925 in New Orleans. In the 1940s, he served in the U.S. Merchant Marine. One of the Beat poets in the 1950s, Kaufman reportedly coined the term "beatnik." Kaufman, William J. Margolis, and John Kelly founded the Beats literary magazine *Beatitude*, publishing the first issue on 9 May 1959. After President John F. Kennedy's assassination, Kaufman launched a protest by taking a vow of silence, which he refused to break until after the war in Vietnam had ended. He published three broadsides (*Second April* in 1959, *Abominist Manifesto* in 1959, *Does the Secret Mind Whisper?* in 1960) and three volumes of poetry, *Solitudes Crowded with Loneliness* (1965), *The Golden Sardine* (1967), and *The Ancient Rain: Poems 1956-1978* (1981). Kaufman's last book of poetry appeared in print before he abandoned writing and retreated again into silence. Kaufman was living in San Francisco in 1986 at the time of his death.

War Memoir: Jazz, Don't Listen to It at Your Own Risk

In the beginning, in the wet
Warm dark place,
Straining to break out, clawing at strange cables
Hearing her screams, laughing
"Later we forgave ourselves, we didn't know"
Some secret jazz
Shouted, wait, don't go.
Impatient, we came running, innocent
Laughing blobs of blood and faith.
To this mother, father world
Where laughter seems out of place
So we learned to cry, pleased
They pronounced human.
The secret jazz blew a sigh
Some familiar sound shouted wait
Some are evil, some will hate.
"Just Jazz, blowing its top again"
So we rushed and laughed.
As we pushed and grabbed
While Jazz blew in the night
Suddenly we were too busy to hear a sound
We were busy shoving mud in men's mouths,

Who were busy dying on the living ground
Busy earning medals, for killing children on deserted streetcorners
Occupying their fathers, raping their mothers, busy humans were
Busy burning Japanese in atomicolorcinescope
With stereophonic screams,
What one hundred percent red blooded savage would waste precious
    time
Listening to jazz, with so many important things going on
But even the fittest murderers must rest
So we sat down in our blood-soaked garments,
And listened to jazz
                    lost, steeped in all our dreams
We were shocked at the sound of life, long gone from our own
We were indignant at the whistling, thinking, singing, beating,
    swinging

Living sound, which mocked us, but let us feel sweet life again
We wept for it, hugged, kissed it, loved it, joined it, we drank it,
Smoked it, ate with it, slept with it
We made our girls wear it for lovemaking
Instead of silly lace gowns,
Now in those terrible moments, when the dark memories come
The secret moments to which we admit no one
When guiltily we crawl back in time, reaching away from ourselves
We hear a familiar sound,
Jazz, scratching, digging, bluing, swinging jazz,
And we listen
And we feel
And live.

"War Memoir: Jazz, Don't Listen at Your Own Risk," in *The Ancient Rain: Poems, 1956–1978*
(New York: New Directions Publishing, 1981), 32–33.

CORA BALL MOTEN

Cora Ball Moten appears to have been an active writer from 1928 to 1931, publishing serialized fiction and other pieces in black newspapers throughout the United States. Her work appeared in the *Afro-American* (Baltimore), the *Chicago Defender*, the *Pittsburgh Courier*, the *Advocate* (Portland, Oregon), the *Norfolk Journal and Guide* (Virginia), and others. Moten's writing appeared again in print in the 1940s, including this selection from *Opportunity* magazine.

Negro Mother to Her Soldier Son

Your tiny fingers kneaded my dark breast
like wind-stirred petals on the jungle bloom
of my fierce love for you, flesh of my flesh.
My knotted hands, work-calloused thru the years,
Once smoothed the fleecy softness of your hair.
That touch, remembered, thrills my fingers still.
My tortured heart bleeds yet for those deep hurts,
that strewed the bitter way your small feet trod
thru "their" white hate and scorn of your dark skin.

And now, with theirs, who crucified my hope,
your stunted life is staked to free a world;
your life, love's perfect gift, hate-shaped by "them"
to make a clown to hang their jokes upon,
a scapegoat, forfeit for the things "they" prize.

Was it for this I dreamed great dreams for you,
the dreams "they" killed, my son?
    But this—for these,
the born and unborn—every race and creed
on whom the shadow falls of men turned brutes
beneath the crooked cross and Hell-born sun;[39]
I pledge your twisted life to make—for these,
a wick to light a new world's candle flame.
I weave it on the loom of my own grief.

From you, my son, and your dark, outcast breed,
I take a solemn vow, that nevermore

shall manhood's measure be a shade of skin,
nor any race degrade its brother-men.

I charge you by the agony and pain
of mothers, dark and fair, whose sons today,
have sealed the bond of Freedom with their blood,
to lay my gift upon Her altar stone,
and bid the mockers match it *if they dare*—
my one, best, dearest gift, my son, *my—son.*

"Negro Mother to Her Soldier Son," *Opportunity*, April 1943, 76.

Related writing by Cora Ball Moten: "Hell: Beneath the Shadows of American Hypocrisy" (1929).

ANN LANE PETRY

Ann Lane was born in 1908 in Old Saybrook, Connecticut. She primarily wrote fiction, even though she was a trained pharmacist prepared to work in her family's business. She also published poetry, wrote books for young people, and worked as a journalist. During the war years, Petry lived in New York while her husband George Petry was away at war. While in New York, she wrote her first novel *The Street* (1946), which includes passages focusing on World War II. Petry also was the women's editor and a columnist for Adam Clayton Powell Jr.'s *People's Voice* newspaper. She returned to Old Saybrook, Connecticut, in 1947, where she died in 1997. In the story reprinted here, her fictional account of the Harlem riots of 1943 reimagines two central issues: a segregated military and racial injustice.

In Darkness and Confusion

William Jones took a sip of coffee and then put his cup down on the kitchen table. It didn't taste right and he was annoyed because he always looked forward to eating breakfast. He usually got out of bed as soon as he woke up and hurried into the kitchen. Then he would take a long time heating the corn bread left over from dinner the night before, letting the coffee brew until it was strong and clear, frying bacon, and scrambling eggs. He would eat very slowly—savoring the early-morning quiet and the just-rightness of the food he'd fixed.

There was no question about early morning being the best part of the day, he thought. But this Saturday morning in July it was too hot in the apartment. There were too many nagging worries that kept drifting through his mind. In the heat he couldn't think clearly—so that all of them pressed in against him, weighed him down.

He pushed his plate away from him. The eggs had cooked too long; much as he liked corn bread, it tasted like sand this morning—grainy and coarse inside his throat. He couldn't help wondering if it scratched the inside of his stomach in the same way.

Pink was moving around in the bedroom. He cocked his head on one side, listening to her. He could tell exactly what she was doing, as though he were in there with her. The soft heavy sound of her stockinged feet as she walked over to the dresser. The dresser drawer being pulled out. That meant she was getting a clean slip. Then the thud of her two hundred pounds landing in the rocker by the window. She was sitting down to comb her hair. Untwisting the small braids she'd made the night before. She would unwind them one by one, putting the hairpins in her mouth as she went along. Now she was brushing it, for he could hear the creak of the rocker; she was rocking back and forth, humming under her breath as she brushed.

He decided that as soon as she came into the kitchen he would go back to the bedroom, get dressed, and go to work. For his mind was already on the mailbox. He didn't feel like talking to Pink. There simply had to be a letter from Sam today. There had to be.

He was thinking about it so hard that he didn't hear Pink walk toward the kitchen.

When he looked up she was standing in the doorway. She was a short, enormously fat woman. The only garment she had on was a bright pink slip that magnified the size of her body. The skin on her arms and shoulders and chest was startlingly black against the pink material. In spite of the brisk brushing she had given her hair, it stood up stiffly all over her head in short wiry lengths, as though she wore a turban of some rough dark gray material.

He got up from the table quickly when he saw her. "Hot, ain't it?" he said, and patted her arm as he went past her toward the bedroom.

She looked at the food on his plate. "You didn't want no breakfast?" she asked.

"Too hot," he said over his shoulder.

He closed the bedroom door behind him gently. If she saw the door was shut, she'd know that he was kind of low in his mind this morning and that he didn't feel like talking. At first he moved about with energy—getting a clean work shirt, giving his shoes a hasty brushing, hunting for a pair of clean socks. Then he stood still in the middle of the room, holding his dark work pants in his hand while he listened to the rush and roar of water running in the bathtub.

Annie May was up and taking a bath. And he wondered if that meant she was going to work. Days when she went to work she used a hot comb on her hair before she ate her breakfast, so that before he left the house in the morning it was filled with the smell of hot irons sizzling against hair grease.

He frowned. Something had to be done about Annie May. Here she was only eighteen years old and staying out practically all night long. He hadn't said anything to Pink about it, but Annie May crept into the house at three and four and five in the morning. He would hear her key go in the latch and then the telltale click as the lock drew back. She would shut the door very softly and turn the bolt. She'd stand there awhile, waiting to see if they woke up. Then she'd take her shoes off and pad down the hall in her stockinged feet.

When she turned the light on in the bathroom, he could see the clock on the dresser. This morning it had been four-thirty when she came in. Pink, lying beside him, went on peacefully snoring. He was glad that she didn't wake up easy. It would only worry her to know that Annie May was carrying on like that.

Annie May put her hands on her hips and threw her head back and laughed whenever he tried to tell her she had to come home earlier. The smoky smell of the hot irons started seeping into the bedroom and he finished dressing quickly.

He stopped in the kitchen on his way out. "Got to get to the store early today," he explained. He was sure Pink knew he was hurrying downstairs to look in the mailbox. But she nodded and held her face up for his kiss. When he brushed his lips against her forehead he saw that her face was wet with perspiration. He thought, With all that weight she must feel the heat something awful.

Annie May nodded at him without speaking. She was hastily swallowing a cup of coffee. Her dark thin hands made a pattern against the thick white cup she was holding. She had pulled her hair out so straight with the hot combs that, he thought, it was like a shiny skullcap fitted tight to her head. He was surprised to see that her lips were heavily coated with lipstick. When she was going to work she didn't use any, and he wondered why she was up so early if she wasn't working. He could see the red outline of her mouth on the cup.

He hadn't intended to say anything. It was the sight of the lipstick on the cup that forced the words out. "You ain't workin' today?"

"No," she said lazily. "Think I'll go shopping." She winked at Pink and it infuriated him.

"How do you expect to keep a job when you don't show up half the time?" he asked.

"I can always get another one." She lifted the coffee cup to her mouth with both hands and her eyes laughed at him over the rim of the cup.

"What time did you come home last night?" he asked abruptly.

She stared out of the window at the blank brick wall that faced the kitchen. "I dunno," she said finally. "It wasn't late."

He didn't know what to say. Probably she was out dancing somewhere. Or maybe she wasn't. He was fairly certain that she wasn't. Yet he couldn't let

Pink know what he was thinking. He shifted his feet uneasily and watched Annie May swallow the coffee. She was drinking it fast.

"You know you ain't too big to get your butt whipped," he said finally.

She looked at him out of the corner of her eyes. And he saw a deep smoldering sullenness in her face that startled him. He was conscious that Pink was watching both of them with a growing apprehension.

Then Annie May giggled. "You and who else?" she said lightly. Pink roared with laughter. And Annie May laughed with her.

He banged the kitchen door hard as he went out. Striding down the outside hall, he could still hear them laughing. And even though he knew Pink's laughter was due to relief because nothing unpleasant had happened, he was angry. Lately every time Annie May looked at him there was open, jeering laughter in her eyes, as though she dared him to say anything to her. Almost as though she thought he was a fool for working so hard.

She had been a nice little girl when she first came to live with them six years ago. He groped in his mind for words to describe what he thought Annie May had become. A Jezebel, he decided grimly. That was it.

And he didn't want Pink to know what Annie May was really like. Because Annie May's mother, Lottie, had been Pink's sister. And when Lottie died, Pink took Annie May. Right away she started finding excuses for anything she did that was wrong. If he scolded Annie May he had to listen to a sharp lecture from Pink. It always started off the same way: "Don't care what she done, William. You ain't goin' to lay a finger on her. She ain't got no father and mother except us . . ."

The quick spurt of anger and irritation at Annie May had sent him hurrying down the first flight of stairs. But he slowed his pace on the next flight because the hallways were so dark that he knew if he wasn't careful he'd walk over a step. As he trudged down the long flights of stairs he began to think about Pink. And the hot irritation in him disappeared as it usually did when he thought about her. She was so fat she couldn't keep on climbing all these steep stairs. They would have to find another place to live—on a first floor where it would be easier for her. They'd lived on this top floor for years, and all the time Pink kept getting heavier and heavier. Every time she went to the clinic the doctor said the stairs were bad for her. So they'd start looking for another apartment and then because the top floors cost less, why, they stayed where they were. And—

Then he stopped thinking about Pink because he had reached the first floor. He walked over to the mailboxes and took a deep breath. Today there'd be a letter. He knew it. There had to be. It had been too long a time since they had had a letter from Sam. The last ones that came he'd said the same thing. Over and over. Like a refrain. "Ma, I can't stand this much longer." And then the letters just stopped.

As he stood there, looking at the mailbox, half-afraid to open it for fear there would be no letter, he thought back to the night Sam graduated from high school. It was a warm June night. He and Pink got all dressed up in their best clothes. And he kept thinking, Me and Pink have got as far as we can go. But Sam—he made up his mind Sam wasn't going to earn his living with a mop and a broom. He was going to earn it wearing a starched white collar and a shine on his shoes and a crease in his pants.

After he finished high school Sam got a job redcapping[40] at Grand Central.

He started saving his money because he was going to go to Lincoln—a college in Pennsylvania.[41] It seemed like it was no time at all before he was twenty-one. And in the army. Pink cried when he left. Her huge body shook with her sobbing. He remembered that he had only felt queer and lost. There was this war and all the young men were being drafted. But why Sam—why did he have to go?

It was always in the back of his mind. Next thing Sam was in a camp in Georgia. He and Pink never talked about his being in Georgia. The closest they ever came to it was one night when she said, "I hope he gets used to it quick down there. Bein' born right here in New York there's lots he won't understand."

Then Sam's letters stopped coming. He'd come home from work and say to Pink casually, "Sam write today?" She'd shake her head without saying anything.

The days crawled past. And finally she burst out. "What you keep askin' for? You think I wouldn't tell you?" And she started crying.

He put his arm around her and patted her shoulder. She leaned hard against him. "Oh, Lord," she said. "He's my baby. What they done to him?'

Her crying like that tore him in little pieces. His mind kept going around in circles. Around and around. He couldn't think what to do. Finally one night after work he sat down at the kitchen table and wrote Sam a letter. He had written very few letters in his life because Pink had always done it for him. And now standing in front of the mailbox he could even remember the feel of the pencil in his hand; how the paper looked—blank and challenging—lying there in front of him; that the kitchen clock was ticking and it kept getting louder and louder. It was hot that night, too, and he held the pencil so tight that the inside of his hand was covered with sweat.

He had sat and thought a long time. Then he wrote: "Is you all right? Your Pa." It was the best he could do. He licked the envelope and addressed it with the feeling that Sam would understand.

He fumbled for his key ring, found the mailbox key and opened the box quickly. It was empty. Even though he could see it was empty he felt around inside it. Then he closed the box and walked toward the street door.

The brilliant sunlight outside made him blink after the darkness of the hall. Even now, so early in the morning, it was hot in the street. And he thought it was going to be a hard day to get through, what with the heat and its being Saturday and all. Lately he couldn't seem to think about anything but Sam. Even at the drugstore where he worked as a porter, he would catch himself leaning on the broom or pausing in his mopping to wonder what had happened to him.

The man who owned the store would say to him sharply, "Boy, what the hell's the matter with you? Can't you keep your mind on what you're doing?" And he would go on washing windows, or mopping the floor or sweeping the sidewalk. But his thoughts, somehow, no matter what he was doing, drifted back to Sam.

As he walked toward the drugstore he looked at the houses on both sides of the street. He knew this street as he knew the creases in the old felt hat he wore the year round. No matter how you looked at it, it wasn't a good street to live on. It was a long cross-town street. Almost half of it on one side consisted of the backs of the three theaters on 125th Street[42]— a long blank wall of gray brick. There were few trees on the street. Even these were a source of danger, for at night shadowy, vague shapes emerged from the street's darkness, lurking near the trees, dodging behind them. He had never been accosted by any of those disembodied figures, but the very stealth of their movements revealed a dishonest intent that frightened him. So when he came home at night he walked an extra block or more in order to go through 125th Street and enter the street from Eighth Avenue.

Early in the morning like this, the street slept. Window shades were drawn down tight against the morning sun. The few people he passed were walking briskly on their way to work. But in those houses where the people still slept, the window shades would go up about noon, and radios would blast music all up and down the street. The bold-eyed women who lived in these houses would lounge in the open windows and call to each other back and forth across the street.

Sometimes when he was on his way home to lunch they would call out to him as he went past, "Come on in, Poppa!" And he would stare straight ahead and start walking faster.

When Sam turned sixteen it seemed to him the street was unbearable. After lunch he and Sam went through this block together—Sam to school and he on his way back to the drugstore. He'd seen Sam stare at the lounging women in the windows. His face was expressionless, but his eyes were curious.

"I catch you goin' near one of them women and I'll beat you up and down the block," he'd said grimly.

Sam didn't answer him. Instead he looked down at him with a strangely adult look, for even at sixteen Sam had been a good five inches taller than he. After that when they passed through the block, Sam looked straight ahead. And William got the uncomfortable feeling that he had already explored the possibilities that the block offered. Yet he couldn't be sure. And he couldn't bring himself to ask him. Instead he walked along beside him, thinking desperately, We gotta move. I'll talk to Pink. We gotta move this time for sure.

That Sunday after Pink came home from church they looked for a new place. They went in and out of apartment houses along Seventh Avenue and Eighth Avenue, 135th Street, 145th Street. Most of the apartments they didn't even look at. They just asked the super how much the rents were.

It was late when they headed for home. He had irritably agreed with Pink that they'd better stay where they were. Thirty-two dollars a month was all they could afford.

"It ain't a fit place to live, though," he said. They were walking down Seventh Avenue. The street looked wide to him, and he thought with distaste of their apartment. The rooms weren't big enough for a man to move around in without bumping into something. Sometimes he thought that was why Annie May spent so much time away from home. Even at thirteen she couldn't stand being cooped up like that in such a small amount of space.

And Pink said, "You want to live on Park Avenue? With a doorman bowin' you in and out? 'Good mornin' Mr. William Jones. Does the weather suit you this mornin'?'" Her voice was sharp, like the crack of a whip.

That was five years ago. And now again they ought to move on account of Pink not being able to stand the stairs anymore. He decided that Monday night after work he'd start looking for a place.

It was even hotter in the drugstore than it was in the street. He forced himself to go inside and put on a limp work coat. Then broom in hand he went to stand in the doorway. He waved to the superintendent of the building on the corner. And watched him as he lugged garbage cans out of the areaway and rolled them to the curb. Now, that's the kind of work he didn't want Sam to have to do. He tried to decide why that was. It wasn't just because Sam was his boy and it was hard work. He searched his mind for the reason. It didn't pay enough for a man to live on decently. That was it. He wanted Sam to have a job where he could make enough to have good clothes and a nice home.

Sam's being in the army wasn't so bad, he thought. It was his being in Georgia that was bad. They didn't treat black people right down there. Everybody knew that. If he could figure out some way to get him farther north, Pink wouldn't have to worry about him so much.

The very sound of the word Georgia did something to him inside. His mother had been born there. She had talked about it a lot and painted such vivid pictures of it that he felt he knew the place—the heat, the smell of the earth, how cotton looked. And something more. The way her mouth had folded together whenever she had said, "They hate niggers down there. Don't you never none of you children go down there."

That was years ago; yet even now, standing here on Fifth Avenue, remembering the way she said it turned his skin clammy cold in spite of the heat. And of all the places in the world, Sam had to go to Georgia. Sam, who was born right here in New York, who had finished high school here—they had to put him in the army and send him to Georgia.

He tightened his grip on the broom and started sweeping the sidewalk in long, even strokes. Gradually the rhythm of the motion stilled the agitation in him. The regular back-and-forth motion was so pleasant that he kept on sweeping long after the sidewalk was clean. When Mr. Yudkin, who owned the store, arrived at eight-thirty he was still outside with the broom. Even now he didn't feel much like talking, so he only nodded in response to the druggist's brisk "Good morning! Hot today!"

William followed him into the store and began polishing the big mirror in back of the soda fountain. He watched the man out of the corner of his eye as he washed his hands in the back room and exchanged his suit coat for a crisp white laboratory coat. And he thought maybe when the war was over Sam ought to study to be a druggist instead of a doctor or a lawyer.

As the morning wore along, customers came in in a steady stream. They got Bromo-Seltzers, cigarettes, aspirin, cough medicine, baby bottles. He delivered two prescriptions that cost five dollars. And the cash register rang so often it almost played a tune. Listening to it he said to himself, Yes, Sam ought to be a druggist. It's clean work and it pays good.

A little after eleven o'clock three young girls came in. "Cokes," they said, and climbed up on the stools in front of the fountain. William was placing new stock on the shelves and he studied them from the top of the step-ladder. As far as he could see, they looked exactly alike. All three of them. And like Annie May. Too thin. Too much lipstick. Their dresses were too short and too tight. Their hair was piled on top of their heads in slicked set curls.

"Aw, I quit that job," one of them said. "I wouldn't get up that early in the morning for nothing in the world."

That was like Annie May, too. She was always changing jobs. Because she could never get to work on time. If she was due at a place at nine, she got there at ten. If at ten, then she arrived about eleven. He knew, too, that she didn't earn enough money to pay for all the cheap, bright-colored dresses she was forever buying.

Her girl friends looked just like her and just like these girls. He'd seen her coming out of the movie houses on 125th Street with two or three of them. They were all chewing gum and they nudged each other and talked too loud and laughed too loud. They stared hard at every man who went past them.

Mr. Yudkin looked up at him sharply, and he shifted his glance away from the girls and began putting big bottles of Father John's medicine[43] neatly on the shelf in front of him. As he stacked the bottles up he wondered if Annie May would have been different if she'd stayed in high school. She had stopped going when she was sixteen. He had spoken to Pink about it. "She oughtn't to stop school. She's too young," he'd said.

But because Annie May was Pink's sister's child, all Pink had done had been to shake her head comfortably. "She's tired of going to school. Poor little thing. Leave her alone."

So he hadn't said anything more. Pink always took up for her. And he and Pink didn't fuss at each other like some folks do. He didn't say anything to Pink about it, but he took the afternoon off from work to go to see the principal of the school. He had to wait two hours to see her. And he studied the pictures on the walls in the outer office, and looked down at his shoes while he tried to put into words what he'd say—and how he wanted to say it.

The principal was a large-bosomed white woman. She listened to him long enough to learn that he was Annie May's uncle. "Ah, yes, Mr. Jones," she said. "Now in my opinion—"

And he was buried under a flow of words, a mountain of words, that went on and on. Her voice was high-pitched and loud, and she kept talking until he lost all sense of what she was saying. There was one phrase she kept using that sort of jumped at him out of the mass of words—"a slow learner."

He left her office feeling confused and embarrassed. If he could only have found the words he could have explained that Annie May was bright as a dollar. She wasn't any "slow learner." Before he knew it he was out in the street, conscious only that he'd lost a whole afternoon's pay and he never had got to say what he'd come for. And he was boiling mad with himself. All he'd wanted was to ask the principal to help him persuade Annie May to finish school. But he'd never got the words together.

When he hung up his soiled work coat in the broom closet at eight o'clock that night he felt as though he'd been sweeping floors, dusting fixtures, cleaning fountains and running errands since the beginning of time itself. He looked at himself in the cracked mirror that hung on the door of the closet. There was no question about it; he'd grown older-looking since Sam had gone into the army. His hair was turning a frizzled gray at the temples. His jawbones showed up sharper. There was a stoop in his shoulders.

"Guess I'll get a haircut," he said softly. He didn't really need one. But on a Saturday night the barbershop would be crowded. He'd have to wait a long time before Al got around to him. It would be good to listen to the talk that went on—the arguments that would get started and never really end. For a little while all the nagging worry about Sam would be pushed so far back in his mind, he wouldn't be aware of it.

The instant he entered the barbershop he could feel himself begin to relax inside. All the chairs were full. There were a lot of customers waiting. He waved a greeting to the barbers. "Hot, ain't it?" he said, and mopped his forehead.

He stood there a minute, listening to the hum of conversation, before he picked out a place to sit. Some of the talk, he knew, would be violent, and he always avoided those discussions because he didn't like violence—even when it was only talk. Scraps of talk drifted past him.

"White folks got us by the balls—"

"Well, I dunno. It ain't just white folks. There's poor white folks gettin' their guts squeezed out, too—"

"Sure. But they're white. They can stand it better."

"Sadie had two dollars on 546 yesterday and it came out and—"

"You're wrong, man. Ain't no two ways about it. This country's set up so that—"

"Only thing to do, if you ask me, is shoot all them crackers and start out new—"

He finally settled himself in one of the chairs in the corner—not too far from the window and right in the middle of a group of regular customers who were arguing hotly about the war. It was a good seat. By looking in the long mirror in front of the barbers he could see the length of the shop.

Almost immediately he joined in the conversation. "Them Japs ain't got a chance—" he started. And he was feeling good. He'd come in at just the right time. He took a deep breath before he went on. Most every time he started talking about the Japs the others listened with deep respect. Because he knew more about them than the other customers. Pink worked for some navy people and she told him what they said.

He looked along the line of waiting customers, watching their reaction to his words. Pretty soon they'd all be listening to him. And then he stopped talking abruptly. A soldier was sitting in the far corner of the shop, staring down at his shoes. Why, that's Scummy, he thought. He's at the same camp where Sam is. He forgot what he was about to say. He got up and walked over to Scummy. He swallowed all the questions about Sam that trembled on his lips.

"Hiya, son," he said. "Sure is good to see you."

As he shook hands with the boy he looked him over carefully. He's changed, he thought. He was older. There was something about his eyes that was different than before. He didn't seem to want to talk. After that first quick look at William he kept his eyes down, staring at his shoes.

Finally William couldn't hold the question back any longer. It came out fast. "How's Sam?"

Scummy picked up a newspaper from the chair beside him. "He's all right," he mumbled. There was a long silence. Then he raised his head and looked directly at William. "Was the las' time I seen him." He put a curious emphasis on the word "las.'"

William was conscious of a trembling that started in his stomach. It went all through his body. He was aware that conversation in the barbershop had stopped. It was like being inside a cone of silence in which he could hear the scraping noise of the razors—a harsh sound, loud in the silence. Al was putting thick oil on a customer's hair and he turned and looked with the hair-oil bottle still in his hand, tilted up over the customer's head. The men sitting in the tilted-back barber's chairs twisted their necks around—awkwardly, slowly—so they could look at Scummy.

"What you mean—the las' time?" William asked sharply. The words beat against his ears. He wished the men in the barbershop would start talking again, for he kept hearing his own words. "What you mean—the las' time?" Just as though he were saying them over and over again. Something had gone wrong with his breathing too. He couldn't seem to get enough air in through his nose.

Scummy got up. There was something about him that William couldn't give a name to. It made the trembling in his stomach worse.

"The las' time I seen him he was O.K." Scummy's voice made a snarling noise in the barbershop.

One part of William's mind said, Yes, that's it. It's hate that makes him look different. It's hate in his eyes. You can see it. It's in his voice, and you can hear it. He's filled with it.

"Since I seen him las'," he went on slowly, "he got shot by a white MP.[44] Because he wouldn't go to the nigger end of a bus. He had a bullet put through his guts. He took the MP's gun away from him and shot the bastard in the shoulder." He put the newspaper down and started toward the door; when he reached it he turned around. "They court-martialed him," he said softly. "He got twenty years at hard labor. The notice was posted in the camp the day I left." Then he walked out of the shop. He didn't look back.

There was no sound in the barbershop as William watched him go down the street. Even the razors had stopped. Al was still holding the hair-oil bottle over the head of his customer. The heavy oil was falling on the face of the man sitting in the chair. It was coming down slowly—one drop at a time.

The men in the shop looked at William and then looked away. He thought, I mustn't tell Pink. She mustn't ever get to know. I can go down to the mailbox early in the morning and I can get somebody else to look in it in the afternoon, so if a notice comes I can tear it up.

The barbers started cutting hair again. There was the murmur of conversation in the shop. Customers got up out of the tilted-back chairs. Someone said to him, "You can take my place."

He nodded and walked over to the empty chair. His legs were weak and shaky. He couldn't seem to think at all. His mind kept dodging away from the thought of Sam in prison. Instead the familiar detail of Sam's growing up kept creeping into his thoughts. All the time the boy was in grammar school he made good marks. Time went so fast it seemed like it was just overnight and he was in long pants. And then in high school.

He made the basketball team in high school. The whole school was proud of him, for his picture had been in one of the white papers. They got two papers that day. Pink cut the pictures out and stuck one in the mirror of the dresser in their bedroom. She gave him one to carry in his wallet.

While Al cut his hair he stared at himself in the mirror until he felt as though his eyes were crossed. First he thought, Maybe it isn't true. Maybe Scummy was joking. But a man who was joking didn't look like Scummy looked. He wondered if Scummy was AWOL.[45] That would be bad. He told himself sternly that he mustn't think about Sam here in the barbershop—wait until he got home.

He was suddenly angry with Annie May. She was just plain no good. Why couldn't something have happened to her? Why did it have to be Sam? Then he was ashamed. He tried to find an excuse for having wanted harm to come to her. It looked like all his life he'd wanted a little something for himself and Pink and then when Sam came along he forgot about those things. He wanted Sam to have all the things that he and Pink couldn't get. It got to be too late for them to have them. But Sam—again he told himself not to think about him. To wait until he got home and in bed.

Al took the cloth from around his neck and he got up out of the chair. Then he was out on the street heading toward home. The heat that came from the pavement seeped through the soles of his shoes. He had forgotten how hot it was. He forced himself to wonder what it would be like to live in the country. Sometimes on hot nights like this, after he got home from work, he went to sit in the park. It was always cooler there. It would probably be cool in the country. But then it might be cold in winter—even colder than the city.

The instant he got in the house he took off his shoes and his shirt. The heat in the apartment was like a blanket—it made his skin itch and crawl in a thousand places. He went into the living room, where he leaned out of the window, trying to cool off. Not yet, he told himself. He mustn't think about it yet.

He leaned farther out of the window, to get away from the innumerable odors that came from the boxlike rooms in back of him. They cut off his breath, and he focused his mind on them. There was the greasy smell of cabbage and collard greens, smell of old wood and soapsuds and disinfectant, a lingering smell of gas from the kitchen stove, and over it all Annie May's perfume.

Then he turned his attention to the street. Up and down as far as he could see, folks were sitting on the stoops. Not talking. Just sitting. Somewhere up the street a baby wailed. A woman's voice rose sharply as she told it to shut up.

Pink wouldn't be home until late. The white folks she worked for were having a dinner party tonight. And no matter how late she got home on Saturday night, she always stopped on Eighth Avenue to shop for her Sunday dinner. She never trusted him to do it. It's a good thing, he thought. If she ever took a look at me tonight she'd know there was something wrong.

A key clicked in the lock and he drew back from the window. He was sitting on the couch when Annie May came in the room.

"You're home early, ain't you?" he asked.

"Oh, I'm going out again," she said.

"You shouldn't stay out so late like you did last night," he said mildly. He hadn't really meant to say it. But what with Sam—

"What you think I'm going to do? Sit here every night and make small talk with you?" Her voice was defiant. Loud.

"No," he said, and then added, "but nice girls ain't runnin' around the streets at four o'clock in the mornin'." Now that he'd started he couldn't seem to stop. "Oh, I know what time you come home. And it ain't right. If you don't stop it, you can get some other place to stay"

"It's O.K. with me," she said lightly. She chewed the gum in her mouth so it made a cracking noise. "I don't know what Auntie Pink married a little runt like you for, anyhow. It wouldn't bother me a bit if I never saw you again." She walked toward the hall. "I'm going away for the weekend," she added over her shoulder, "and I'll move out on Monday."

"What you mean for the weekend?" he asked sharply. "Where you goin'?"

"None of your damn business," she said, and slammed the bathroom door hard.

The sharp sound of the door closing hurt his ears so that he winced, wondering why he had grown so sensitive to sounds in the last few hours. What'd she have to say that for, anyway, he asked himself. Five feet five wasn't so short for a man. He was taller than Pink, anyhow. Yet compared to Sam, he supposed he was a runt, for Sam had just kept on growing until he was six feet tall. At the thought he got up from the chair quickly, undressed, and got in bed. He lay there trying to still the trembling in his stomach; trying even now not to think about Sam, because it would be best to wait until Pink was in bed and sound asleep so that no expression on his face, no least little motion, would betray his agitation.

When he heard Pink come up the stairs just before midnight he closed his eyes. All of him was listening to her. He could hear her panting outside on the landing. There was a long pause before she put her key in the door.

It took her all that time to get her breath back. She's getting old, he thought. I mustn't ever let her know about Sam.

She came into the bedroom and he pretended to be asleep. He made himself breathe slowly. Evenly. Thinking I can get through tomorrow all right. I won't get up much before she goes to church. She'll be so busy getting dressed she won't notice me.

She went out of the room and he heard the soft murmur of her voice talking to Annie May. "Don't you pay no attention, honey. He don't mean a word of it. I know menfolks. They's always tired and out of sorts by the time Saturdays come around."

"But I'm not going to stay here anymore."

"Yes, you is. You think I'm goin' to let my sister's child be turned out? You goin' to be right here."

They lowered their voices. There was laughter. Pink's deep and rich and slow. Annie May's high-pitched and nervous. Pink said, "You looks lovely, honey. Now, have a good time."

The front door closed. This time Annie May didn't slam it. He turned over on his back, making the springs creak. Instantly Pink came into the bedroom to look at him. He lay still, with his eyes closed, holding his breath for fear she would want to talk to him about what he'd said to Annie May and would wake him up. After she moved away from the door he opened his eyes.

There must be some meaning in back of what had happened to Sam. Maybe it was some kind of judgment from the Lord, he thought. Perhaps he shouldn't have stopped going to church. His only concession to Sunday was to put on his best suit. He wore it just that one day and Pink pressed the pants late on Saturday night. But in the last few years it got so that every time he went to church he wanted to stand up and yell, "You goddamn fools! How much more you goin' to take?"

He'd get to thinking about the street they lived on, and the sight of the minister with his clean white collar turned hind side to and sound of his buttery voice were too much. One Sunday he'd actually gotten on his feet, for the minister was talking about the streets of gold up in heaven; the words were right on the tip of his tongue when Pink reached out and pinched his behind sharply. He yelped and sat down. Someone in back of him giggled. In spite of himself a slow smile had spread over his face. He stayed quiet through the rest of the service but after that, he didn't go to church at all.

This street where he and Pink lived was like the one where his mother had lived. It looked like he and Pink ought to have gotten further than his mother had. She had scrubbed floors, washed and ironed in the white folks' kitchens. They were doing practically the same thing. That was another reason he stopped going to church. He couldn't figure out why these things had to stay the same, and if the Lord didn't intend it like that, why didn't He change it?

He began thinking about Sam again, so he shifted his attention to the sounds Pink was making in the kitchen. She was getting the rolls ready for tomorrow. Scrubbing the sweet potatoes. Washing the greens. Cutting up the chicken. Then the thump of the iron. Hot as it was, she was pressing his pants. He resisted the impulse to get up and tell her not to do it.

A little later, when she turned the light on in the bathroom, he knew she was getting ready for bed. And he held his eyes tightly shut, made his body rigidly still. As long as he could make her think he was sound asleep she wouldn't take a real good look at him. One real good look and she'd know there was something wrong. The bed sagged under her weight as she knelt down to say her prayers. Then she was lying down beside him. She sighed under her breath as her head hit the pillow.

He must have slept part of the time, but in the morning it seemed to him that he had looked up at the ceiling most of the night. He couldn't remember actually going to sleep.

When he finally got up, Pink was dressed and ready for church. He sat down in a chair in the living room away from the window, so the light wouldn't shine on his face. As he looked at her he wished that he could find relief from the confusion of his thoughts by taking part in the singing and shouting that would go on in church. But he couldn't. And Pink never said anything about his not going to church. Only sometimes like today, when she was ready to go, she looked at him a little wistfully.

She had on her Sunday dress. It was made of a printed material—big red and black poppies splashed on a cream-colored background. He wouldn't let himself look right into her eyes, and in order that she wouldn't notice the evasiveness of his glance, he stared at the dress. It fit snugly over her best corset, and the corset in turn constricted her thighs and tightly encased the rolls of flesh around her waist. She didn't move away, and he couldn't keep on inspecting the dress, so he shifted his gaze up to the wide cream-colored straw hat she was wearing far back on her head. Next he noticed that she was easing her feet by standing on the outer edges of the high-heeled patent leather pumps she wore.

He reached out and patted her arm. "You look nice," he said, picking up the comic section of the paper.

She stood there looking at him while she pulled a pair of white cotton gloves over her roughened hands. "Is you all right, honey?" she asked.

"Course," he said, holding the paper up in front of his face.

"You shouldn't talk so mean to Annie May," she said gently.

"Yeah, I know," he said, and hoped she understood that he was apologizing. He didn't dare lower the paper while she was standing there looking at him so intently. Why doesn't she go, he thought.

"There's grits and eggs for breakfast."

"O.K." He tried to make his voice sound as though he were so absorbed in what he was reading that he couldn't give her all of his attention. She walked toward the door, and he lowered the paper to watch her, thinking that her legs looked too small for her body under the vastness of the printed dress, that women were sure funny—she's got that great big pocketbook swinging on her arm and hardly anything in it. Sam used to love to tease her about the size of the handbags she carried.

When she closed the outside door and started down the stairs, the heat in the little room struck him in the face. He almost called her back so that he wouldn't be there by himself—left alone to brood over Sam. He decided that when she came home from church he would make love to her. Even in the heat the softness of her body, the smoothness of her skin, would comfort him.

He pulled his chair up close to the open window. Now he could let himself go. He could begin to figure out something to do about Sam. There's gotta be something, he thought. But his mind wouldn't stay put. It kept going back to the time Sam graduated from high school. Nineteen seventy-five his dark blue suit had cost. He and Pink had figured and figured and finally they'd managed it. Sam had looked good in the suit; he was so tall and his shoulders were so broad it looked like a tailor-made suit on him. When he got his diploma everybody went wild—he'd played center on the basketball team, and a lot of folks recognized him.

The trembling in his stomach got worse as he thought about Sam. He was aware that it had never stopped since Scummy had said those words "the las' time." It had gone on all last night until now there was a tautness and a tension in him that left him feeling as though his eardrums were strained wide open, listening for sounds. They must be a foot wide open, he thought. Open and pulsing with the strain of being open. Even his nostrils were stretched open like that. He could feel them. And a weight behind his eyes.

He went to sleep sitting there in the chair. When he woke up his whole body was wet with sweat. It musta got hotter while I slept, he thought. He was conscious of an ache in his jawbones. It's from holding 'em shut so tight. Even his tongue—he'd been holding it so still in his mouth it felt like it was glued there.

Attracted by the sound of voices, he looked out of the window. Across the way a man and a woman were arguing. Their voices rose and fell on the hot, still air. He could look directly into the room where they were standing, and he saw that they were half-undressed.

The woman slapped the man across the face. The sound was like a pistol shot, and for an instant William felt his jaw relax. It seemed to him that the whole block grew quiet and waited. He waited with it. The man grabbed his belt and lashed out at the woman. He watched the belt rise and fall against her brown skin. The woman screamed with the regularity of clockwork. The street came alive again. There was the sound of voices, the rattle of dishes. A baby whined. The woman's voice became a murmur of pain in the background.

"I gotta get me some beer," he said aloud. It would cool him off. It would help him to think. He dressed quickly, telling himself that Pink wouldn't be home for hours yet and by that time the beer smell would be gone from his breath.

The street outside was full of kids playing tag. They were all dressed up in their Sunday clothes. Red socks, blue socks, danced in front of him all the way to the corner. The sight of them piled up the quivering in his stomach. Sam used to play in this block on Sunday afternoons. As he walked along, women thrust their heads out of the opened windows, calling to the children. It seemed to him that all the voices were Pink's voice saying, "You, Sammie, stop that runnin' in your good clo'es!"

He was so glad to get away from the sight of the children that he ignored the heat inside the barroom of the hotel on the corner and determinedly edged his way past girls in sheer summer dresses and men in loud plaid jackets and tight-legged cream-colored pants until he finally reached the long bar.

There was such a sense of hot excitement in the place that he turned to look around him. Men with slicked, straightened hair were staring through half-closed eyes at the girls lined up at the bar. One man sitting at a table close by kept running his hand up and down the bare arm of the girl leaning against him. Up and down. Down and up. William winced and looked away. The jukebox was going full blast, filling the room with high, raw music that beat about his ears in a queer mixture of violence and love and hate and terror. He stared at the brilliantly colored moving lights on the front of the jukebox as he listened to it, wishing that he had stayed at home, for the music made the room hotter.

"Make it a beer," he said to the bartender.

The beer glass was cold. He held it in his hand, savoring the chill of it, before he raised it to his lips. He drank it down fast. Immediately he felt the air grow cooler. The smell of beer and whiskey that hung in the room lifted.

"Fill it up again," he said. He still had that awful trembling in his stomach, but he felt as though he were really beginning to think. Really think. He found he was arguing with himself.

"Sam mighta been like this. Spendin' Sunday afternoons whorin'."

"But he was part of me and part of Pink. He had a chance—"

"Yeah. A chance to live in one of them hell-hole flats. A chance to get himself a woman to beat."

"He woulda finished college and got a good job. Mebbe been a druggist or a doctor or a lawyer—"

"Yeah. Or mebbe got himself a stable of women to rent out on the block—"

He licked the suds from his lips. The man at the table nearby had stopped stroking the girl's arm. He was kissing her—forcing her closer and closer to him.

"Yeah," William jeered at himself "That coulda been Sam on a hot Sunday afternoon—"

As he stood there arguing with himself he thought it was getting warmer in the bar. The lights were dimmer. I better go home, he thought. I gotta live with this thing some time. Drinking beer in this place ain't going to help any. He looked out toward the lobby of the hotel, attracted by the sound of voices. A white cop was arguing with a frowzy-looking girl who had obviously had too much to drink.

"I got a right in here. I'm mindin' my own business," she said with one eye on the bar.

"Aw, go chase yourself." The cop gave her a push toward the door. She stumbled against a chair.

William watched her in amusement. "Better than a movie," he told himself.

She straightened up and tugged at her girdle. "You white son of a bitch," she said.

The cop's face turned a furious red. He walked toward the woman, waving his nightstick. It was then that William saw the soldier. Tall. Straight. Creases in his khaki pants. An overseas cap cocked over one eye. Looks like Sam looked that one time he was home on furlough, he thought.

The soldier grabbed the cop's arm and twisted the nightstick out of his hand. He threw it half the length of the small lobby. It rattled along the floor and came to a dead stop under a chair.

"Now what'd he want to do that for?" William said softly.

He knew that night after night the cop had to come back to this hotel. He's the law, he thought, and he can't let—Then he stopped thinking about him, for the cop raised his arm. The soldier aimed a blow at the cop's chin. The cop ducked and reached for his gun. The soldier turned to run.

It's happening too fast, William thought. It's like one of those horse race reels they run over fast at the movies. Then he froze inside. The quivering in his stomach got worse. The soldier was heading toward the door. Running. His foot was on the threshold when the cop fired. The soldier dropped. He folded up as neatly as the brown-paper bags Pink brought home from the store, emptied, and then carefully put in the kitchen cupboard.

The noise of the shot stayed in his eardrums. He couldn't get it out. "Jesus Christ!" he said. Then again, "Jesus Christ!" The beer glass was warm. He put it down on the bar with such violence some of the beer slopped over on his shirt. He stared at the wet place, thinking Pink would be mad as hell. Him out drinking in a bar on Sunday. There was a stillness in which he was conscious of the stink of the beer, the heat in the room, and he could still hear the sound of the shot. Somebody dropped a glass, and the tinkle of it hurt his ears.

Then everybody was moving toward the lobby. The doors between the bar and the lobby slammed shut. High, excited talk broke out.

The tall thin black man standing next to him said, "That ties it. It ain't even safe here where we live. Not no more. I'm goin' to get me a white bastard of a cop and nail his hide to a street sign."

"Is the soldier dead?"[46] someone asked.

"He wasn't movin' none," came the answer.

They pushed hard against the doors leading to the lobby. The doors stayed shut.

He stood still, watching them. The anger that went through him was so great that he had to hold on to the bar to keep from falling. He felt as though he were going to burst wide open. It was like having seen Sam killed before his eyes. Then he heard the whine of an ambulance siren. His eardrums seemed to have been waiting to pick it up.

"Come on, what you waitin' for?" He snarled the words at the people milling around the lobby doors. "Come on!" he repeated, running toward the street.

The crowd followed him to the 126th Street entrance of the hotel. He got there in time to see a stretcher bearing a limp khaki-clad figure disappear inside the ambulance in front of the door. The ambulance pulled away fast, and he stared after it stupidly.

He hadn't known what he was going to do, but he felt cheated. Let down. He noticed that it was beginning to get dark. More and more people were coming into the street. He wondered where they'd come from and how they'd heard about the shooting so quickly. Every time he looked around there were more of them. Curious, eager voices kept asking, "What happened? What happened?" The answer was always the same. Hard, angry. "A white cop shot a soldier."

Someone said, "Come on to the hospital. Find out what happened to him."

In front of the hotel he had been in the front of the crowd. Now there were so many people in back of him and in front of him that when they started toward the hospital, he moved along with them. He hadn't decided to go, the forward movement picked him up and moved him along without any intention on his part. He got the feeling that he had lost his identity as a person with a free will of his own. It frightened him at first. Then he began to feel powerful. He was surrounded by hundreds of people like himself. They were all together. They could do anything.

As the crowd moved slowly down Eighth Avenue, he saw that there were cops lined up on both sides of the street. Mounted cops kept coming out of the side streets, shouting, "Break it up! Keep moving. Keep moving."

The cops were scared of them. He could tell. Their faces were dead white in the semidarkness. He started saying the words over separately to himself. Dead. White. He laughed again. Dead. White. The words were funny said separately like that. He stopped laughing suddenly because a part of his mind repeated, Twenty years, twenty years.

He licked his lips. It was hot as all hell tonight. He imagined what it would be like to be drinking swallow after swallow of ice-cold beer. His throat worked and he swallowed audibly.

The big black man walking beside him turned and looked down at him. "You all right, brother?" he asked curiously.

"Yeah," he nodded. "It's them sons of bitches of cops. They're scared of us." He shuddered. The heat was terrible. The tide of hate quivering in his stomach made him hotter. "Wish I had some beer," he said.

The man seemed to understand not only what he had said but all the things he had left unsaid. For he nodded and smiled. And William thought this was an extraordinary night. It was as though, standing so close together, so many of them like this—as though they knew each other's thoughts. It was a wonderful thing.

The crowd carried him along. Smoothly. Easily. He wasn't really walking. Just gliding. He was aware that the shuffling feet of the crowd made a muffled rhythm on the concrete sidewalk. It was slow, inevitable. An ominous sound, like a funeral march. With the regularity of a drumbeat. No. It's more like a pulse beat, he thought. It isn't a loud noise. It just keeps repeating over and over. But not that regular, because it builds up to something. It keeps building up.

The mounted cops rode their horses into the crowd. Trying to break it up into smaller groups. Then the rhythm was broken. Seconds later it started again. Each time the tempo was a little faster. He found he was breathing the same way. Faster and faster. As though he were running. There were more and more cops. All of them white. They had moved the colored cops out.

"They done that before," he muttered.

"What?" said the man next to him.

"They moved the black cops out," he said.

He heard the man repeat it to someone standing beside him. It became part of the slow shuffling rhythm on the sidewalk. "They moved the black cops." He heard it go back and back through the crowd until it was only a whisper of hate on the still hot air. "They moved the black cops."

As the crowd shuffled back and forth in front of the hospital, he caught snatches of conversation. "The soldier was dead when they put him in the ambulance." "Always tryin' to fool us." "Christ! Just let me get my hands on one of them cops."

He was thinking about the hospital and he didn't take part in any of the conversations. Even now across the long span of years he could remember the helpless, awful rage that had sent him hurrying home from this same hospital. Not saying anything. Getting home by some kind of instinct.

Pink had come to this hospital when she had had her last child. He could hear again the cold contempt in the voice of the nurse as she listened to Pink's loud grieving. "You people have too many children anyway," she said.

It left him speechless. He had his hat in his hand and he remembered how he wished afterward that he'd put it on in front of her to show her what he thought of her. As it was, all the bitter answers that finally surged into his throat seemed to choke him. No words would come out. So he stared at her lean, spare body. He let his eyes stay a long time on her flat breasts. White uniform. White shoes. White stockings. White skin.

Then he mumbled, "It's too bad your eyes ain't white, too." And turned on his heel and walked out.

It wasn't any kind of answer. She probably didn't even know what he was talking about. The baby dead, and all he could think of was to tell her eyes ought to be white. White shoes, white stockings, white uniform, white skin, and blue eyes.

Staring at the hospital, he saw with satisfaction that frightened faces were appearing at the windows. Some of the lights went out. He began to feel that this night was the first time he'd ever really been alive. Tonight everything was going to be changed. There was a growing, swelling sense of power in him. He felt the same thing in the people around him.

The cops were aware of it, too, he thought. They were out in full force. Mounties, patrolmen, emergency squads. Radio cars that looked like oversize bugs crawled through the side streets. Waited near the curbs. Their white tops stood out in the darkness. "White folks riding in white cars." He wasn't aware that he had said it aloud until he heard the words go through the crowd. "White folks in white cars." The laughter that followed the words had a rough, raw rhythm. It repeated the pattern of the shuffling feet.

Someone said, "They got him at the station house. He ain't here." And the crowd started moving toward 123rd Street.

Great God in the morning, William thought, everybody's out here. There were girls in thin summer dresses, boys in long coats and tight-legged pants, old women dragging kids along by the hand. A man on crutches jerked himself past to the rhythm of the shuffling feet. A blind man tapped his way through the center of the crowd, and it divided into two separate streams as it swept by him. At every street corner William noticed someone stopped to help the blind man up over the curb.

The street in front of the police station was so packed with people that he couldn't get near it. As far as he could see they weren't doing anything. They were simply standing there. Waiting for something to happen. He recognized a few of them: the woman with the loose, rolling eyes who sold shopping bags on 125th Street; the lucky-number peddler—the man with the white parrot on his shoulder; three sisters of the Heavenly Rest for All movement—barefooted women in loose white robes.

Then, for no reason that he could discover, everybody moved toward 125th Street. The motion of the crowd was slower now because it kept increasing in size as people coming from late church services were drawn into it. It was easy to identify them, he thought. The women wore white gloves. The kids were all slicked up. Despite the more gradual movement he was still being carried along effortlessly, easily. When someone in front of him barred his way, he pushed against the person irritably, frowning in annoyance because the smooth forward flow of his progress had been stopped.

It was Pink who stood in front of him: He stopped frowning when he recognized her. She had a brown-paper bag tucked under her arm and he knew she had stopped at the corner store to get the big bottle of cream soda she always brought home on Sundays. The sight of it made him envious, for it meant that this Sunday had been going along in an orderly, normal fashion for her while he—She was staring at him so hard he was suddenly horribly conscious of the smell of the beer that had spilled on his shirt. He knew she had smelled it, too, by the tighter grip she took on her pocketbook.

"What you doing out here in this mob? A Sunday evening and you drinking beer," she said grimly.

For a moment he couldn't answer her. All he could think of was Sam. He almost said, "I saw Sam shot this afternoon," and he swallowed hard.

"This afternoon I saw a white cop kill a black soldier," he said. "In the bar where I was drinking beer. I saw it. That's why I'm here. The glass of beer I was drinking went on my clothes. The cop shot him in the back. That's why I'm here."

He paused for a moment, took a deep breath. This was how it ought to be, he decided. She had to know sometime and this was the right place to tell her. In this semidarkness, in this confusion of noises, with the low, harsh rhythm of the footsteps sounding against the noise of the horses' hoofs.

His voice thickened. "I saw Scummy yesterday," he went on. "He told me Sam's doing time at hard labor. That's why we ain't heard from him. A white MP shot him when he wouldn't go to the nigger end of a bus. Sam shot the MP. They gave him twenty years at hard labor."

He knew he hadn't made it clear how to him the soldier in the bar was Sam; that it was like seeing his own son shot before his very eyes. I don't even know whether the soldier was dead, he thought. What made me tell her about Sam out here in the street like this, anyway? He realized with a sense of shock that he really didn't care that he had told her. He felt strong, powerful, aloof. All the time he'd been talking he wouldn't look right at her. Now, suddenly, he was looking at her as though she were a total stranger. He was coldly wondering what she'd do. He was prepared for anything.

But he wasn't prepared for the wail that came from her throat. The sound hung in the hot air. It made the awful quivering in his stomach worse. It echoed and reechoed the length of the street. Somewhere in the distance a horse whinnied. A woman standing way back in the crowd groaned as though the sorrow and the anguish in that cry were more than she could bear.

Pink stood there for a moment. Silent. Brooding. Then she lifted the big bottle of soda high in the air. She threw it with all her might. It made a wide arc and landed in the exact center of the plate-glass window of a furniture store. The glass crashed in with a sound like a gunshot.

A sigh went up from the crowd. They surged toward the broken window. Pink followed close behind. When she reached the window, all the glass had been broken in. Reaching far inside, she grabbed a small footstool and then turned to hurl it through the window of the dress shop next door. He kept close behind her, watching her as she seized a new missile from each store window that she broke.

Plate-glass windows were being smashed all up and down 125th Street— on both sides of the street. The violent, explosive sound fed the sense of power in him. Pink had started this. He was proud of her, for she had shown herself to be a fit mate for a man of his type. He stayed as close to her as he could. So in spite of the crashing, splintering sounds and the swarming, violent activity around him, he knew the exact moment when she lost her big straw hat; when she took off the high-heeled patent leather shoes and flung them away, striding swiftly along in her stockinged feet. That her dress was hanging crooked on her.

He was right in back of her when she stopped in front of a hat store. She carefully appraised all the hats inside the broken window. Finally she reached out, selected a small hat covered with purple violets, and fastened it securely on her head.

"Woman's got good sense," a man said.

"Man, oh, man! Let me get in there," said a raw-boned woman who thrust her way forward through the jam of people to seize two hats from the window.

A roar of approval went up from the crowd. From then on when a window was smashed it was bare of merchandise when the people streamed past it. White folks owned these stores. They'd lose and lose and lose, he thought with satisfaction. The words "twenty years" reechoed in his mind. I'll be an old man, he thought. Then: I may be dead before Sam gets out of prison.

The feeling of great power and strength left him. He was so confused by its loss that he decided this thing happening in the street wasn't real. It was so dark there were so many people shouting and running about, that he almost convinced himself he was having a nightmare. He was aware that his hearing had now grown so acute he could pick up the tiniest sounds: the quickened breathing and the soft, gloating laughter of the crowd; even the sound of his own heart beating. He could hear these things under the noise of the breaking glass, under the shouts that were coming from both sides of the street. They forced him to face the fact that this was no dream but a reality from which he couldn't escape. The quivering in his stomach kept increasing as he walked along.

Pink was striding through the crowd just ahead of him. He studied her to see if she, too, were feeling as he did. But the outrage that ran through her had made her younger. She was tireless. Most of the time she was leading the crowd. It was all he could do to keep up with her, and finally he gave up the attempt—it made him too tired.

He stopped to watch a girl who was standing in a store window, clutching a clothes model tightly around the waist. "What's she want that for?" he said aloud. For the model had been stripped of clothing by the passing crowd, and he thought its pinkish torso was faintly obscene in its resemblance to a female figure.

The girl was young and thin. Her back was turned toward him, and there was something so ferocious about the way her dark hands gripped the naked model that he resisted the onward movement of the crowd to stare in fascination. The girl turned around. Her nervous hands were tight around the dummy's waist. It was Annie May.

"Ah, no!" he said, and let his breath come out with a sigh.

Her hands crept around the throat of the model and she sent it hurtling through the air above the heads of the crowd. It landed short of a window across the street. The legs shattered. The head rolled toward the curb. The waist snapped neatly in two. Only the torso remained whole and in one piece.

Annie May stood in the empty window and laughed with the crowd when someone kicked the torso into the street. He stood there, staring at her. He felt that now for the first time he understood her. She had never had anything but badly paying jobs—working for young white women who probably despised her. She was like Sam on that bus in Georgia. She didn't want just the nigger end of things, and here in Harlem there wasn't anything else for her. All along she'd been trying the only way she knew how to squeeze out of life a little something for herself.

He tried to get closer to the window where she was standing. He had to tell her that he understood. And the crowd, tired of the obstruction that he had made by standing still, swept him up and carried him past. He stopped thinking and let himself be carried along on a vast wave of feeling. There was so much plate glass on the sidewalk that it made a grinding noise under the feet of the hurrying crowd. It was a dull, harsh sound that set his teeth on edge and quickened the trembling of his stomach.

Now all the store windows that he passed were broken. The people hurrying by him carried tables, lamps, shoeboxes, clothing. A woman next to him held a wedding cake in her hands—it went up in tiers of white frosting with a small bride and groom mounted at the top. Her hands were bleeding, and he began to look closely at the people nearest him. Most of them, too, had cuts on their hands and legs. Then he saw there was blood on the sidewalk in front of the windows, blood dripping down the jagged edges of the broken windows. And he wanted desperately to go home.

He was conscious that the rhythm of the crowd had changed. It was faster, and it had taken on an ugly note. The cops were using their nightsticks. Police wagons drew up to the curbs. When they pulled away, they were full of men and women who carried loot from the stores in their hands.

The police cars slipping through the streets were joined by other cars with loudspeakers on top. The voices coming through the loudspeakers were harsh. They added to the noise and confusion. He tried to listen to what the voices were saying. But the words had no meaning for him. He caught one phrase over and over: "Good people of Harlem." It made him feel sick. He repeated the words "of Harlem." We don't belong anywhere, he thought. There ain't no room for us anywhere. There wasn't no room for Sam in a bus in Georgia. There ain't no room for us here in New York. There ain't no place but top floors. The top-floor black people. And he laughed and the sound stuck in his throat.

After that he snatched a suit from the window of a men's clothing store. It was a summer suit. The material felt crisp and cool. He walked away with it under his arm. He'd never owned a suit like that. He simply sweated out the summer in the same dark pants he wore in winter. Even while he stroked the material, a part of his mind sneered—you got summer pants; Sam's got twenty years.

He was surprised to find that he was almost at Lenox Avenue, for he hadn't remembered crossing Seventh. At the corner the cops were shoving a group of young boys and girls into a police wagon. He paused to watch. Annie May was in the middle of the group. She had a yellow fox jacket dangling from one hand.

"Annie May!" he shouted. "Annie May!" The crowd pushed him along faster and faster. She hadn't seen him. He let himself be carried forward by the movement of the crowd. He had to find Pink and tell her that the cops had taken Annie May.

He peered into the dimness of the street ahead of him, looking for her; then he elbowed his way toward the curb so that the people could see the other side of the street. He forgot about finding Pink for directly opposite him was the music store that he passed every night coming home from work. Young boys and girls were always lounging on the sidewalk in front of it. They danced a few steps while they listened to the records being played inside the shop. All the records sounded the same—a terribly magnified woman's voice bleating out a blues song in a voice that sounded to him like that of an animal in heat—an old animal, tired and beaten, but with an insinuating know-how left in her. The white men who went past the store smiled as their eyes lingered on the young girls swaying to the music.

"White folks got us comin' and goin'. Backwards and forwards," he muttered. He fought his way out of the crowd and walked toward a no-parking sign that stood in front of the store. He rolled it up over the curb. It was heavy and the effort made him pant. It took all his strength to send it crashing through the glass on the door.

Almost immediately an old woman and a young man slipped inside the narrow shop. He followed them. He watched them smash the records that lined the shelves. He hadn't thought of actually breaking the records but once he started, he found the crisp, snapping noise pleasant. The feeling of power began to return. He didn't like these records, so they had to be destroyed.

When they left the music store there wasn't a whole record left. The old woman came out of the store last. As he hurried off up the street he could have sworn he smelled the sharp, acrid smell of smoke. He turned and looked back. He was right. A thin wisp of smoke was coming through the store door. The old woman had long since disappeared in the crowd.

Farther up the street he looked back again. The fire in the record shop was burning merrily. It was making a glow that lit up that part of the street. There was a new rhythm now. It was faster and faster. Even the voices coming from the loudspeakers had taken on the urgency of speed.

Fire trucks roared up the street. He threw his head back and laughed when he saw them. That's right, he thought. Burn the whole damn place down. It was wonderful. Then he frowned. "Twenty years at hard labor." The words came back to him. He was a fool. Fire wouldn't wipe that out. There wasn't anything that would wipe it out.

He remembered then that he had to find Pink. To tell her about Annie May. He overtook her in the next block. She's got more stuff, he thought. She had a table lamp in one hand, a large enamel kettle in the other. The lightweight summer coat draped across her shoulders was so small it barely covered her enormous arms. She was watching a group of boys assault the steel gates in front of a liquor store. She frowned at them so ferociously he wondered what she was going to do. Hating liquor the way she did, he half expected her to cuff the boys and send them on their way up the street.

She turned and looked at the crowd in back of her. When she saw him she beckoned to him. "Hold these," she said. He took the lamp, the kettle and the coat she held out to him, and he saw that her face was wet with perspiration. The print dress was darkly stained with it.

She fastened the hat with the purple flowers securely on her head. Then she walked over to the gate. "Git out the way," she said to the boys. Bracing herself in front of the gate, she started tugging at it. The gate resisted. She pulled at it with a sudden access of such furious strength that he was frightened. Watching her, he got the feeling that the resistance of the gate had transformed it in her mind. It was no longer a gate—it had become the world that had taken her son, and she was wreaking vengeance on it.

The gate began to bend and sway under her assault. Then it was down. She stood there for a moment, staring at her hands—big drops of blood oozed slowly over the palms. Then she turned to the crowd that had stopped to watch.

"Come on, you niggers," she said. Her eyes were little and evil and triumphant. "Come on and drink up the white man's liquor." As she strode off up the street, the beflowered hat dangled precariously from the back of her head.

When he caught up with her she was moaning, talking to herself in husky whispers. She stopped when she saw him and put her hand on his arm.

"It's hot, ain't it?" she said, panting.

In the midst of all this violence, the sheer commonplaceness of her question startled him. He looked at her closely. The rage that had been in her was gone, leaving her completely exhausted. She was breathing too fast in uneven gasps that shook her body. Rivulets of sweat streamed down her face. It was as though her triumph over the metal gate had finished her. The gate won anyway, he thought.

"Let's go home, Pink," he said. He had to shout to make his voice carry over the roar of the crowd, the sound of breaking glass.

He realized she didn't have the strength to speak, for she only nodded in reply to his suggestion. Once we get home she'll be all right, he thought. It was suddenly urgent that they get home, where it was quiet, where he could think, where he could take something to still the tremors in his stomach. He tried to get her to walk a little faster, but she kept slowing down until, when they entered their own street, it seemed to him they were barely moving.

In the middle of the block she stood still. "I can't make it," she said. "I'm too tired."

Even as he put his arm around her she started going down. He tried to hold her up, but her great weight was too much for him. She went down slowly, inevitably, like a great ship capsizing. Until all of her huge body was crumpled on the sidewalk. "Pink" he said. "Pink. You gotta get up," he said over and over again.

She didn't answer. He leaned over and touched her gently. Almost immediately afterward he straightened up. All his life, moments of despair and frustration had left him speechless—strangled by the words that rose in his throat. This time the words poured out.

He sent his voice raging into the darkness and the, awful confusion of noises. "The sons of bitches," he shouted. "The sons of bitches."

"In Darkness and Confusion," in *Cross Section 1947: A Collection of New American Writing*, edited by Edwin B. Seaver (New York: Simon and Schuster, 1947), 98–128.

SOLDIERS AT FT. LOGAN, COLORADO

Sent anonymously to the *Pittsburgh Courier* on behalf of soldiers stationed at Ft. Logan, this letter echoes the dire situation and poor treatment that black men serving in the military have suffered since the Civil War.

"We'd rather die on our knees as a man, than to live in this world as a slave"[47]

938th Quartermaster[48] Plt.
April 26, 1943
Transportation Air Base
Fort Logan, Colorado
The Pittsburgh Courier[49]

Dear Sirs:

We are soldiers who are stationed in Fort Logan, Colorado. We would appreciate it to the highest if our little article was printed in your paper against discrimination. We are colored soldiers who have been discriminated against terribly to the extent where we just can't possible stand any more. We're supposed to be representing part of the Army in which we're fighting for equality, justice and humanity so as all men, no matter of race, color, or creed, can be free to worship any way that they please.

Here on the Post we're treated like dogs. We work on different positions, sometimes for 9 or 10 hours daily. In the mornings we report to one particular job and at noon we are taken from the former one into a complete new one by orders of the white N.C.O.s (meaning Non-commissioned Officers)[50] and at these jobs we work at a very tiresome task, one that is unfit for even a dog. And yet the whites which are supposed to be a labor battalion just sit down and watch us do their work.

Even in eating time we were told to remain at attention outside the messhall until the whites have finished eating, then we go and eat what's left over—food which is cold, tasteless and even sometimes dirty from sitting on tables from left overs. [...]

We all here have come from the Easten States such as New York, Brooklyn[,] . . . and we're not accustomed to discrimination and their rules. We have now come to the conclusion that before we'd be a slave, We'd rather be carried to our graves and go home to the Lord and be saved. In fact[,] we'd rather die on our knees as a man, than to live in his world as a slave. [...]

Just give us a chance to show our color.

Excerpted from "No One's Fools," in *Taps for a Jim Crow Army*, edited by Phillip McGuire (Santa Barbara, California: ABC-Clio, 1982), 64–65.

GLADYS O. THOMAS-ANDERSON

A member of the 6888th Central Postal Battalion, U.S. Army Corps, Private Thomas-Anderson was among the first black women to serve in the Women's Army Corps (WAC). Under the command of Major Charity Adams (later Early), this unit was the first battalion of black women to serve overseas in the U.S. military during World War II.

"An honor to be in the Army and be black, too. We were the beginning."[51]

My brother and I always did things together. When the war was going on in Europe, he knew they were going to draft him eventually so he went in because he was unemployed and had no prospects. When he went, I wanted to go, too, but my mother said no. I was only eighteen. But at twenty-one I decided to go in. [. . .] I was sent to Des Moines. [. . .] We had to go to basic training every morning and had to fall in line. Then we'd work on how to salute and make our turns. I wanted to travel, and after training we were all sent to different places. I was sent to an Army Air Force installation. I was supposed to be in the military, yet they made me pay my own way to California. [. . .]

Then I heard that the Army had decided they wanted to send black WAC[s][52] overseas. Even though I wanted to go, they told me they weren't going to send me, that they weren't taking any girls from my base. But one day I went out to get my cleaning and my lieutenant said, "Where the hell were you? Get ready—you are going overseas." That's how I became a part of the 6888th Battalion.[53]

On February 3, 1945, we left for Scotland on the *Ile de France*. [. . .] We were treated better in Europe than in the States. They thought we were beautiful. A lot of them had never seen a black girl dressed in a uniform. They'd whistle at us all the time. You could go anywhere you wanted; there was nothing you couldn't do. We never saw signs that said Colored Only. [. . .]

Sorting the mail took a lot of concentration and it was dull. [. . .] We worked eight-hour shifts around the clock. We never had the same schedule. Just when you got used to one schedule, it would shift. But mail was important to the GIs, because it was something that came from home. It was a way they could find out what was going on. It was personal and raised their spirits. We did a bang-up job of it, too. The mail had been sitting in a warehouse for a long time before we sorted it all out.

In Birmingham, [England,] we slept in an old school. We took cold showers and our beds were on the floor. There were about ten of us to a room. Six months later we transferred to Rouen, France, near Paris, and my job didn't change at all. Paris was magical. It was the most exciting thing to be in this group and be in Paris. You could drink out of any water fountain you wanted to. We went to lots of parties, dance halls, and had a lot of fun. I knew I was there to do a job, which I tried my best to do. But I also wanted to have some fun. [...] I had never been out of Detroit.

I'm proud that I was able to serve. I'm proud that I was chosen. I was awarded the Victory Medal, Good Conduct Medal, and Army of Occupation Medal.[54] It was an honor to be in the Army and be black, too. We were the beginning. We were the ones who set the pattern. Now you have black pilots and so forth. It's a wonderful era. I've always been proud to be an American, and even more so after being in the service.

Excerpted from "Gladys O. Thomas-Anderson, Private, Women's Army Corps, 1944–1946," in *We Were There: Voices of African American Veterans from World War II to the War in Iraq*, edited by Yvonne Latty (New York: Amistad, 2004), 33–38.

JOHN EDGAR WIDEMAN

John Edgar Wideman was born in Washington, D.C., in 1941. He was a Rhodes Scholar and the first chairperson and founder of Black Studies at the University of Pennsylvania. Wideman has published numerous books, including ten novels, several collections of short stories, as well as essay collections and memoirs. His well-known Homewood Trilogy—*Damballah* (1981), *Hiding Place* (1981), *Sent for You Yesterday* (1983)—portrays the life and history of the Pittsburgh community of his youth. In 2014 John Edgar Wideman retired from teaching at Brown University. He lives in New York.

Valaida[55]

Whither shall I go from thy spirit?
Or whither shall I flee from thy presence?[56]

Bobby[57] tell the man what he wants to hear. Bobby lights a cigarette. Blows smoke and it rises and rises to where I sit on my cloud overhearing everything. Singing to no one. Golden trumpet from the Queen of Denmark across my knees. In my solitude.[58] Dead thirty years now and meeting people still. Primping loose ends of my hair. Worried how I look. How I sound. Silly. Because things don't change. Bobby with your lashes a woman would kill for, all cheekbones, bushy brows and bushy upper lip, ivory when you smile. As you pretend to contemplate his jive questions behind your screen of smoke and summon me by rolling your big, brown-eyed-handsome-man eyeballs to the ceiling where smoke pauses not one instant, but scoots through and warms me where I am, tell him, Bobby, about "fabled Valaida Snow who traveled in an orchid-colored Mercedes-Benz, dressed in an orchid suit, her pet monkey rigged out in an orchid jacket and cap, with the chauffeur in orchid as well." If you need to, lie like a rug, Bobby. But don't waste the truth, either. They can't take that away from me. Just be cool. As always. Recite those countries and cities we played. Continents we conquered. Roll those faraway places with strange-sounding names around in your sweet mouth. Tell him they loved me at home too, a down-home girl from Chattanooga, Tennessee, who turned out the Apollo,[59] not a mumbling word from wino heaven[60] till they were on their feet hollering and clapping for more with the rest of the audience. Reveries of days gone by, yes, yes, they haunt me, baby, I can taste it. Yesteryears, yesterhours. Bobby, do you also remember what you're not telling him? Blues lick in the middle of a blind flamenco[61] singer's moan. Mother Africa stretching her crusty, dusky hands forth,[62] calling back her far-flung children. Later that same night both of us bad on bad red wine wheeling round and round a dark gypsy cave. Olé. Olé.

Don't try too hard to get it right, he'll never understand. He's watching your cuff links twinkle. Wondering if they're real gold and the studs real diamonds. You called me Minnie Mouse. But you never saw me melted down to sixty-eight pounds soaking wet. They beat me, and fucked me in every hole I had. I was their whore. Their maid. A stool they stood on when they wanted to reach a little higher. But I never sang in the cage, Bobby. Not one note. Cost me a tooth once, but not a note. Tell him that one day, I decided I'd had enough and walked away from their hell. Walked across Europe, the Atlantic Ocean, the whole U.S. of A. till I found a quiet spot to put peace back in my soul, and then I began performing again. My tunes. In my solitude. And yes. There was a pitiful little stomped-down white boy in the camp I tried to keep the guards from killing, but if he lived or died I never knew. Then or now. Monkey and chauffeur and limo and champagne and cigars and outrageous dresses with rhinestones, fringe and peekaboo slits. That's the foolishness the reporter's after. Stuff him with your MC b.s., and if he's still curious when you're finished, if he seems a halfway decent sort in spite of himself, you might suggest listening to the trumpet solo in My Heart Belongs to Daddy, *hip him to* Hot Snow,[63] *the next to last cut, my voice and Lady Day's[64] figure and ground, ground and figure* Dear Lord above, send back my love.

He heard her in the bathroom, faucets on and off, on and off, spurting into the sink bowl, the tub. Quick burst of shower spray, rain sound spattering plastic curtain. Now in the quiet she'll be polishing. Every fixture will gleam. *Shine's what people see. See something shiny, don't look no further, most people don't.* If she's rushed she'll wipe and polish faucets, mirrors, metal collars around drains. Learned that trick, when she first came to the city and worked with gangs of girls in big downtown hotels. *Told me, said, Don't be fussing around behind in there or dusting under them things, child. Give that mirror a lick. Rub them faucets. Twenty more rooms like this one here still to do before noon.* He lowers the newspaper just enough so he'll see her when she passes through the living room, so she won't see him looking unless she stops and stares, something she never does. She knows he watches. Let him know just how much was enough once upon a time when she first started coming to clean the apartment. Back when he was still leaving for work some mornings. Before they understood each other, when suspicions were mutual and thick as the dust first time she bolted through his doorway, into his rooms, out of breath and wary eyed like someone was chasing her and it might be him.

She'd burst in his door and he'd felt crowded. Retreated, let her stake out the space she required. She didn't bully him but demanded in the language of her brisk efficient movements that he accustom himself to certain accommodations. They developed an etiquette that spelled out precisely how close, how distant the two of them could be once a week while she cleaned his apartment.

Odd that it took him years to realize how small she was. Shorter than him and no one in his family ever stood higher than five foot plus an inch or so of that thick straight, black hair. America a land of giants and early on he'd learned to ignore height. You couldn't spend your days like a country lout gawking at the skyscraper heads of your new countrymen. No one had asked him so he'd never needed to describe his cleaning woman. Took no notice of her height. Her name was Clara Jackson and when she arrived he was overwhelmed by the busyness of her presence. How much she seemed to be doing all at once. Noises she'd manufacture with the cleaning paraphernalia, her humming and singing, the gum she popped, heavy thump of her heels even though she changed into tennis sneakers as soon as she crossed the threshold of his apartment, her troubled breathing, asthmatic wheezes and snorts of wrecked sinuses getting worse and worse over the years, her creaking knees, layers of dresses, dusters, slips whispering, the sighs and moans and wincing ejaculations, addresses to invisible presences she smuggled with her into his domain. *Yes, Lord. Save me, Jesus. Thank you, Father.* He backed away from the onslaught, the clamorous weight of it, avoided her systematically. Seldom were they both in the same room at the same time more than a few minutes because clearly none was large enough to contain them and the distance they needed.

She was bent over, replacing a scrubbed rack in the oven when he'd discovered the creases in her skull. She wore a net over her hair like serving girls in Horn and Hardart's.[65] Under the webbing were clumps of hair, defined by furrows exposing her bare scalp.[66] A ribbed yarmulke of hair pressed down on top of her head. Hair he'd never imagined. Like balled yarn in his grandmother's lap. Like a nursery rhyme. *Black sheep. Black sheep, have you any wool?* So different from what grew on his head, the heads of his brothers and sisters and mother and father and cousins and everyone in the doomed village where he was born, so different that he could not truly consider it hair, but some ersatz substitute used the evening of creation when hair ran out. Easier to think of her as bald. Bald and wearing a funny cap fashioned from the fur of some swarthy beast. Springy wires of it jutted from the netting. One dark strand left behind, shocking him when he discovered it marooned in the tub's gleaming, white belly, curled like a question mark at the end of the sentence he was always asking himself. He'd pinched it up in a wad of toilet paper, flushed it away.

Her bag of fleece had grayed and emptied over the years. Less of it now. He'd been tempted countless times to touch it. Poke his finger through the netting into one of the mounds. He'd wondered if she freed it from the veil when she went to bed. If it relaxed and spread against her pillow or if she slept all night like a soldier in a helmet.

When he stood beside her or behind her he could spy on the design of creases, observe how the darkness was cultivated into symmetrical plots and that meant he was taller than Clara Jackson, that he was looking down at her. But those facts did not calm the storm of motion and noise, did not undermine her power any more than the accident of growth, the half inch he'd attained over his next tallest brother, the inch eclipsing the height of his father, would have diminished his father's authority over the family, if there had been a family, the summer after he'd shot up past everyone, at thirteen the tallest, the height he remained today.

Mrs. Clara. Did you know a colored woman once saved my life?

Why is she staring at him as if he's said, Did you know I slept with a colored woman once? He didn't say that. Her silence fusses at him as if he did, as if he'd blurted out something unseemly, ungentlemanly, some insult forcing her to tighten her jaw and push her tongue into her cheek, and taste the bitterness of the hard lump inside her mouth. Why is she ready to cry, or call him a liar, throw something at him or demand an apology or look right through him, past him, the way his mother stared at him on endless October afternoons, gray slants of rain falling so everybody's trapped indoors and she's cleaning, cooking, tending a skeletal fire in the hearth and he's misbehaving, teasing his little sister till he gets his mother's attention and then he shrivels in the weariness of those sad eyes catching him in the act, piercing him, ignoring him, the hurt, iron and distance in them accusing him. Telling him for this moment, and perhaps forever, for this cruel, selfish trespass, you do not exist.

No, Mistah Cohen. That's one thing I definitely did not know.

His fingers fumble with a button, unfastening the cuff of his white shirt. He's rolling up one sleeve. Preparing himself for the work of storytelling. She has laundered the shirt how many times. It's held together by cleanliness and starch. A shirt that ought to be thrown away but she scrubs and sprays and irons it; he knows the routine, the noises. She saves it how many times, patching, mending, snipping errant threads, the frayed edges of cuff and collar hardened again so he is decent, safe within them, the blazing white breast he puffs out like a penguin when it's spring and he descends from the twelfth floor and conquers the park again, shoes shined, the remnants of that glorious head of hair slicked back, freshly shaved cheeks raw as a baby's in the brisk sunshine of those first days welcoming life back and yes he's out there in it again, his splay-foot penguin walk and gentleman's attire, shirt like a pledge, a promise, a declaration framing muted stripes of his dark tie. Numbers stamped inside the collar. Mark of the dry cleaners from a decade ago, before Clara Jackson began coming to clean. Traces still visible inside the neck of some of his shirts she's maintained impossibly long past their prime, a row of faded numerals like those he's pushing up his sleeve to show her on his skin.

The humped hairs on the back of his forearm are pressed down like grass in the woods where a hunted animal has slept. Gray hairs the color of his flesh, except inside his forearm, just above his wrist, the skin is whiter, blue veined. All of it, what's gray, what's pale, what's mottled with dark spots is meat that turns to lard and stinks a sweet sick stink to high heaven if you cook it.

Would you wish to stop now? Sit down a few minutes, please. I will make a coffee for you and my tea. I tell you a story. It is Christmas soon, no?

She is stopped in her tracks. A tiny woman, no doubt about it. Lumpy now. Perhaps she steals and hides things under her dress. Lumpy, not fat. Her shoulders round and padded. Like the derelict women who live in the streets and wear their whole wardrobes winter spring summer fall. She has put on flesh for protection. To soften blows. To ease around corners. Something cushioned to lean against. Something to muffle the sound of bones breaking when she falls. A pillow for all the heads gone and gone to dust who still find ways at night to come to her and seek a resting place. He could find uses for it. Extra flesh on her bones was not excess, was a gift. The female abundance, her thickness, her bulk reassuring as his hams shrink, his fingers become claws, the chicken neck frets away inside those razor-edged collars she scrubs and irons.

Oh you scarecrow. Death's-head stuck on a stick. Another stick lashed crossways for arms. First time you see yourself dead you giggle. You are a survivor, a lucky one. You grin, stick out your tongue at the image in the shard of smoky glass because the others must be laughing, can't help themselves, the ring of them behind your back, peeking over your scrawny shoulders, watching as you discover in the mirror what they've been seeing since they stormed the gates and kicked open the sealed barracks door and rescued you from the piles of live kindling that were to be your funeral pyre. Your fellow men. Allies. Victors. Survivors. Who stare at you when they think you're not looking, whose eyes are full of shame, as if they've been on duty here, in this pit, this stewpot cooking the meat from your bones. They cannot help themselves. You laugh to help them forget what they see. What you see. When they herded your keepers past you, their grand uniforms shorn of buttons, braid, ribbons, medals, the twin bolts of frozen lightning, golden skulls, eagles' wings,[67] their jackboots gone, feet bare or in peasant clogs, heads bowed and hatless, iron faces unshaven, the butchers still outweighed you a hundred pounds a man. You could not conjure up the spit to mark them. You dropped your eyes in embarrassment, pretended to nod off because your body was too weak to manufacture a string of spittle, and if you could have, you'd have saved it, hoarded and tasted it a hundred times before you swallowed the precious bile.

A parade of shambling, ox-eyed animals. They are marched past you, marched past open trenches that are sewers brimming with naked, rotting flesh, past barbed-wire compounds where the living sift slow and insubstantial as fog among the heaps of dead. No one believes any of it. Ovens and gas chambers. Gallows and whipping posts. Shoes, shoes, shoes, a mountain of shoes in a warehouse. Shit. Teeth. Bones. Sacks of hair. The undead who huddle into themselves like bats and settle down on a patch of filthy earth mourning their own passing. No one believes the enemy. He is not these harmless farmers filing past in pillaged uniforms to do the work of cleaning up this mess someone's made. No one has ever seen a ghost trying to double itself in a mirror so they laugh behind its back, as if, as if the laughter is a game and the dead one could muster up the energy to join in and be made whole again. I giggle. I say, Who in God's name would steal a boy's face and leave this thing?

Nearly a half century of rich meals with seldom one missed but you cannot fill the emptiness, cannot quiet the clamor of those lost souls starving, the child you were weeping from hunger, those selves, those stomachs you watched swelling, bloating, unburied for days and you dreamed of opening them, of taking a spoon to whatever was growing inside because you were so empty inside and nothing could be worse than that gnawing emptiness. Why should the dead be ashamed to eat the dead? Who are their brothers, sisters, themselves? You hear the boy talking to himself, hallucinating milk, bread, honey. Sick when the spoiled meat is finally carted away.

Mistah Cohen, I'm feeling kinda poorly today. If you don mind I'ma work straight through and gwan home early. Got all my Christmas still to do and I'm tired.

She wags her head. Mumbles more he can't decipher. As if he'd offered many times before, as if there is nothing strange or special this morning at 10:47, him standing at the china cupboard prepared to open it and bring down sugar bowl, a silver cream pitcher, cups and saucers for the two of them, ready to fetch instant coffee, a tea bag, boil water and sit down across the table from her. As if it happens each time she comes, as if this once is not the first time, the only time he's invited this woman to sit with him and she can wag her old head, stare at him moon eyed as an owl and refuse what's never been offered before.

The tattoo is faint. From where she's standing, fussing with the vacuum cleaner, she won't see a thing. Her eyes, in spite of thick spectacles, watery and weak as his. They have grown old together, avoiding each other in these musty rooms where soon, soon, no way round it, he will wake up dead one morning and no one will know till she knocks Thursday, and knocks again, then rings, pounds, hollers, but no one answers and she thumps away to rouse the super with his burly ring of keys.

He requires less sleep as he ages. Time weighs more on him as time slips away, less and less time as each second passes but also more of it, the past accumulating in vast drifts like snow in the darkness outside his window. In the wolf hours before dawn this strange city sleeps as uneasily as he does, turning, twisting, groaning. He finds himself listening intently for a sign that the night knows he's listening, but what he hears is his absence. The night busy with itself, denying him. And if he is not out there, if he can hear plainly his absence in the night pulse of the city, where is he now, where was he before his eyes opened, where will he be when the flutter of breath and heart stop?

They killed everyone in the camps. The whole world was dying there. Not only Jews. People forget. All kinds locked in the camps. Yes. Even Germans who were not Jews. Even a black woman. Not gypsy. Not African. American like you, Mrs. Clara.

They said she was a dancer and could play any instrument. Said she could line up shoes from many countries and hop from one pair to the next, performing the dances of the world. They said the Queen of Denmark had honored her with a gold trumpet. But she was there, in hell with the rest of us.

A woman like you. Many years ago. A lifetime ago. Young then as you would have been. And beautiful. As I believe you must have been, Mrs. Clara. Yes. Before America entered the war. Already camps had begun devouring people. All kinds of people. Yet she was rare. Only woman like her I ever saw until I came here, to this country, this city. And she saved my life.

Poor thing.

I was just a boy. Thirteen years old. The guards were beating me. I did not know why. Why? They didn't need a why. They just beat. And sometimes the beating ended in death because there was no reason to stop, just as there was no reason to begin. A boy. But I'd seen it many times. In the camp long enough to forget why I was alive, why anyone would want to live for long. They were hurting me, beating the life out of me but I was not surprised, expected no explanation. I remember curling up as I had seen a dog once cowering from the blows of a rolled newspaper. In the old country lifetimes ago. A boy in my village staring at a dog curled and rolling on its back in the dust outside the baker's shop and our baker in his white apron and tall white hat striking this mutt again and again. I didn't know what mischief the dog had done. I didn't understand why the fat man with flour on his apron was whipping it unmercifully. I simply saw it and hated the man, felt sorry for the animal, but already the child in me understood it could be no other way so I rolled and curled myself against the blows as I'd remembered that spotted dog in the dusty village street because that's the way it had to be.

Then a woman's voice in a language I did not comprehend reached me. A woman angry, screeching. I heard her before I saw her. She must have been screaming at them to stop. She must have decided it was better to risk dying than watch the guards pound a boy to death. First I heard her voice, then she rushed in, fell on me, wrapped herself around me. The guards shouted at her. One tried to snatch her away. She wouldn't let go of me and they began to beat her too. I heard the thud of clubs on her back, felt her shudder each time a blow was struck.

She fought to her feet, dragging me with her. Shielding me as we stumbled and slammed into a wall.

My head was buried in her smock. In the smell of her, the smell of dust, of blood. I was surprised how tiny she was, barely my size, but strong, very strong. Her fingers dug into my shoulders, squeezing, gripping hard enough to hurt me if I hadn't been past the point of feeling pain. Her hands

Part 3. The Double-V Campaign Challenges Jim Crow: World War II · 387

were strong, her legs alive and warm, churning, churning as she pressed me against herself, into her. Somehow she'd pulled me up and back to the barracks wall, propping herself, supporting me, sheltering me. Then she screamed at them in this language I use now but did not know one word then, cursing them, I'm sure, in her mother tongue, a stream of spit and sputtering sounds as if she could build a wall of words they could not cross.

The kapos[68] hesitated, astounded by what she'd dared. Was this black one a madwoman, a witch? Then they tore me from her grasp, pushed me down and I crumpled there in the stinking mud of the compound. One more kick, a numbing, blinding smash that took my breath away. Blood flooded my eyes. I lost consciousness. Last I saw of her she was still fighting, slim, beautiful legs kicking at them as they dragged and punched her across the yard.

You say she was colored?

Yes. Yes. A dark angel who fell from the sky and saved me.

Always thought it was just you people over there doing those terrible things to each other.

He closes the china cupboard. Her back is turned. She mutters something at the metal vacuum tubes she's unclamping. He realizes he's finished his story anyway. Doesn't know how to say the rest. She's humming, folding rags, stacking them on the bottom pantry shelf. Lost in the cloud of her own noise. Much more to his story, but she's not waiting around to hear it. This is her last day before the holidays. He'd sealed her bonus in an envelope, placed the envelope where he always does on the kitchen counter. The kitchen cabinet doors have magnetic fasteners for a tight fit. After a volley of doors clicking, she'll be gone. When he's alone preparing his evening meal, he depends on those clicks for company. He pushes so they strike not too loud, not too soft. They punctuate the silence, reassure him like the solid slamming of doors in big sedans he used to ferry from customer to customer. How long since he'd been behind the wheel of a car? Years, and now another year almost gone. In every corner of the city they'd be welcoming their Christ, their New Year with extravagant displays of joy. He thinks of Clara Jackson in the midst of her family. She's little but the others are brown and large, with lips like spoons for serving the sugary babble of their speech. He tries to picture them, eating and drinking, huge people crammed in a tiny, shabby room. Unimaginable, really. The faces of her relatives become his. Everyone's hair is thick and straight and black.

"Valaida," in *Fever: Twelve Stories* (New York: Penguin, 1989), 27–40.

Related writing by John Edgar Wideman: "Rashad" (1981).

Gwendolyn Williams

Gwendolyn Williams published this short story in *Crisis* magazine. Additional biographical information is not available.

Heart against the Wind

No part of the day is more beautiful than the twilight with its faint tinge of gold left by the sun as it disappeared beyond the horizon. It brings a quietness that rests the very soul; it distills a gentleness upon the world that is the magic of dancing stars and another new moon.

Lys sat at her desk by the window and gazed raptly at the evening sky. It would be dark in another hour; then that lovely pale sky would become inky so that the stars would be as specks of glistening metal and the moon would be all silvery in her flight across the heavens. It would be dark, and she'd be alone again. Alone for how many more nights? Lys's expression changed, and her eyes fell on the letter she had just written Stephen. Stephen! How glad she would be when he came home again. How different she hoped the word "home" would be then. . . .

Dearest Stephen:

How's everything with you? Where are you? Don't tell me; I know. You're far off in a strange land where you will see many wonderful things probably both beautiful and horrid, and I won't be there to share them all with you. You're sorry, aren't you? I wish I were there beside you wading through the mud or whatever it is you wade through at any time.

I didn't write to say that though. I am writing to make an announcement: We are going to have a baby. I waited this long to tell you, because I had to be absolutely certain. And, Stephen, forgive me for being so cruel, but I don't want it. Doesn't that sound bad! You are shocked; I can see the sad shame for me creep into your eyes; then I see you catch your head with your hands as you number the reasons why I should be one of the happiest women in the world. Of course, I picture the whole thing.

So much has happened to change me! You long to know why I don't want our child. First of all he has no heritage. Stephen, a heritage is more than an innate quality—it's a birthright. He has no birthright; he's a little black boy. He can be anything. A doctor, lawyer, businessman, or even an actor or a preacher. He might be a teacher or pull people's teeth without giving them gas.[69] But there are other things: those possibilities must run parallel with hate, prejudice, and any outrage that might occur. If all the unkindness in existence could be erased—

Secondly, he has no country. No, don't take that literally. I suppose what I mean is does his country want him. His ancestors died with the scars of chains and whips upon them, but that was yesterday, and yesterday is dead. Today is important, Stephen. Through the years black men have proved themselves to the country, but the country . . . to be honest, the people of the country have never thanked them for their faithfulness.

The oration at Gettysburg[70] has lived through the ages as a masterpiece; yet those words delivered so hopefully have not had much meaning for the step-citizens of our country. Shall we listen to our son recite them some day? Of course, and he shall weep over their futility. He shall grow up observing the Fourth of July. Truly, we will never tell him that independence is a reality for some and a lie for others. No. We shall hang out the proud flag and pledge allegiance to it. Independence is freedom, so maybe by the time he is eighteen he will be free. A black boy's freedom is measured out by teaspoonsful.

He shall swear by his constitutional rights. He can lick any man who dares him to board a trolley or demands that he sit in the back of a train. He shall spit in the face of fear and want; he shall worship as he chooses whom he chooses, and he shall say what he pleases to say and to the right people.[71] I'm laughing, Stephen.

Gettysburg, July the Fourth, and constitutional rights are ashes. The people who read them have made them so. They have degraded the words associated with them so that they are destroyed surely as if lighted by a match. There was no speech, no declaration; the bill of rights is a hoax. Because it does not work both ways.

Stephen, why are you fighting? It boils down to the fact that you are on a foreign soil to free the enslaved peoples of a foreign land while at home they step on the faces of your brothers. A man can be murdered for no other reason than he is black. We are slaves of a modern age. Who will free us this time that there is no Lincoln and no states seceding from the Union? And we won't stoop to violence because we are a few. And we acknowledge the good privileges we have been permitted.

What difference does it make about the color of a man's skin? A man's a man in spite of that—with ambition, passion, and blood flowing in his veins. All men have a head with hair upon it until neglect or age eats away the roots; and eyes, a nose, a mouth; also every normal body is a trunk with the correct appendages attached. All men have that whether they are white, black, brown, red or foreign. Strip one at random and prove it for yourself.

And women. A woman is subject to the same dangers when she conceives a child and again when she is in labor in spite of her color. The babe in her womb is recipient of the same opportunities to be perfect or afflicted.

All men spring from the same source. Sure, and all men die. There is evidence that no man is superior to another; if he were, his progeny would inherit the earth, and he would be as God, with life everlasting.

Oh, Stephen! I would rather destroy this child and go to hell than to deliver it into a world like this where those who cry democracy and are so prolix in their love of freedom are reeking with hypocrisy. He will have friends, our son, but he will also have foes. And, Stephen, could he fight them!

I'd rather he never know the anguish of being black nor the pride—nor the injustice of being an unsung hero.

Tears stole down Lys's cheeks. She crushed the paper; it dropped short of the wastebasket and made a slight thud on the floor. There it lay until the wind, blowing in the open window, chased it into a corner.

Lys sighed. She lifted another mail form from the box, dipped her pen in the ink. She studied the blank paper for a while. She must write against the thoughts in her heart. Stephen had enough to go through without her writing a lot of foolishness over there to him.

But things were in such a muddle that they didn't even make horse sense. One way you looked at it, it was downright funny: here we are trying to help fight a war and promote a victory for freedom. How do you spell it! What does it mean! There are those who know; and still there are those who believe it is the state of being the boss of everything and everybody this side of tan. It's a lust for power, any kind of power, over the step-citizens of this country. It's the talking against nazis, fascists,[72] and all the other ists, isms, et cetera.

It will be, as it has been, a shame if a country whose people have sworn by Liberty fails to sponsor a fair play program after this great world struggle. How will they curb the laughter if they help to win a struggle for the freedoms of other peoples and changes its spots in the very places where they should not have been for bigger spots.

We all ought to begin now to count the differences that color established in some circles. If we did, Lys wondered, would we be honest enough to apologize for the instances where prejudices were silly?

She began to laugh. It was absurd to realize that a country of such distinguished folks should sponsor a promulgation so like the one it was striving to liquidate. Democracy is an example of a serpent which gorged itself on a supposed prey and didn't find out till too late that it was eating its own tail.[73]

Lives have been forfeited, liberty has been raped, and happiness has been pursued into the gutter.

Lys twisted a button and the room flooded with light. With the light came a fresh point of view, Stephen's point of view: We men will fight for what we have now, that's more than we have had before; it's worth something, but maybe we won't be wrong in expecting some more of that which we honestly deserve.

And there was Stephen, and all black people, in the room.

Her pen touched the paper.

Dearest Stephen,

We are going to be the proud parents, within this year, of a very special citizen. Don't worry about me, everything is going swell.

I've waited so long to tell you because I had to get me straightened out on a few points which you can well guess.

All the folks say howdy and send best wishes for your continued safety.

. . .

Love, love, love,

Lys

"Heart against the Wind," *Crisis* 51, no. 3 (January 1944): 18, 26.

SELECTED ADDITIONAL LITERATURE ON CITIZENSHIP AND WAR

Cullen, Countee, and Owen Dodson. "The Third Fourth of July: A One-Act Play. *Theatre Arts* 30 (1946): 488–93.

Davis, Frank Marshall. "Peace Is a Fragile Cup." 1948. In *Black Moods: Collected Poems*, edited by John Edgar Tidwell, 164–66. Urbana: University of Illinois Press, 2002.

———. "To Those Who Sing America." 1948. In *Black Moods: Collected Poems*, edited by John Edgar Tidwell, 129–30. Urbana: University of Illinois Press, 2002.

Ellison, Ralph. "Flying Home." *Cross Section 44*. Ed. Edwin Seaver. New York: L. B. Fischer, 1944. 469-85.

———. "The Negro and the Second World War." In *Cultural Contexts for Ralph Ellison's Invisible Man*, edited by Eric Sundquist, 233–40. Boston: Bedford/St. Martins, 1995.

French, Albert. *Patches of Fire: A Story of War and Redemption*. New York: Vintage, 1998.

Fuller, Charles. *A Soldier's Play*. New York: Hill and Wang, 1982.

Guy, Rosa. *Bird at My Window*. Philadelphia: Lippincott, 1966.

Himes, Chester. *If He Hollers, Let Him Go*. 1945. Reprint, Cambridge, Mass.: Da Capo, 2002.

———. "Let Me at the Enemy—An' George Brown." In *The Collected Stories of Chester Himes*, 36–47. New York: Thunder's Mouth, 1990.

———. *Lonely Crusade*. 1947. Reprinted Cambridge, Mass.: Da Capo, 1997.

———. "Two Soldiers." In *The Collected Stories of Chester Himes*, 61–64. New York: Thunder's Mouth, 1990.

Hurston, Zora Neale. "Crazy for This Democracy." *Negro Digest* 4 (December 1945): 45–48.

Killens, John O. *And Then We Heard the Thunder*. Washington, D.C.: Howard University Press, 1984.

Major, Clarence. *Dirty Bird Blues*. San Francisco: Mercury House, 1996.

McBride, James. *Miracle at St. Anna: A Novel of the Buffalo Soldiers of World War II*. New York: Riverhead, 2002.

Nelson, Marilyn. "Tuskegee Airfield." In *The Fields of Praise*, 41–44. Baton Rouge: Louisiana State University Press, 1997.

Petry, Ann. *The Street*. Boston: Houghton Mifflin, 1946.

Smith, William Gardner. *Last of the Conquerors*. 1948. Reprint, Madison, New Jersey: Chatham, 1973.

Tompkins, Grace W. "The Smell of Death." [1945.] In *Bitter Fruit: African American Women on World War II*, edited by Maureen Honey, 203–4. Columbia: University of Missouri Press, 1999.

Thompson, James G. "Should I Sacrifice to Live 'Half-American'?" *Pittsburgh Courier*, 31 January 1942, 3.

Williams, John A. *Clifford's Blues*. Minneapolis: Coffee House Press, 1998.

ENDNOTES

1. Title supplied by volume editors.

2. William Henry Hastie resigned from the Department of War in protest against continued segregation in the U.S. armed forces.

3. Wiley College, founded in 1873, is among the several Historically Black Colleges and Universities (HBCU) established to educate black students before predominately white colleges and universities in the United States were desegregated. Other HBCUs include Wilberforce University (1855); Atlanta University (1865); Howard University (1866); Augusta Institute (1867), later Morehouse College; Philander Smith (1877); Tuskegee (1881); and Atlanta Baptist Female Seminary (1881), later Spelman College.

4. Noncommissioned officers do not have their own command and are under the command of commissioned officers. Many commissioned officers enter military service as officers because they have education or experience and have received officers' training. Others spend numerous years working through the enlisted ranks to become an officer.

5. Doris "Dorie" Miller was a cook in the U.S. Navy aboard the USS *West Virginia* when the Japanese attacked Pearl Harbor on 7 December 1941. After the Japanese torpedoed the ship, Miller, a black man, came on deck and held off the Japanese using a machine gun. For his bravery, Dorie Miller received the Navy Cross from Admiral Chester W. Nimitz on 27 May 1942.

6. An allusion to lynching, possibly creating an analogy between Dorie Miller and the crucifixion of Jesus.

7. Daily newspapers.

8. Weekly newspapers such as the *Chicago Defender*, the *Pittsburgh Courier*, the *New York Amsterdam News*, and the *Baltimore Afro-American*.

9. The goddess of liberty or democracy often is depicted by artists and writers in a white gown. During the nineteenth century, writers frequently used this literary metaphor. In the eighteenth century, the poet Phillis Wheatley used this image effectively.

10. The galley, located at the bottom of the ship, is the food preparation area where mess men such as Dorie Miller worked.

11. Blood supplies were segregated during World War II.

12. The remains of black and white soldiers were not supposed to be buried in the same ground.

13. Jim Crow: The term Jim Crow dates from at least the 1820s, when it was used by the white minstrel performer Thomas Rice in the song "Jump Jim Crow." Throughout the nineteenth century it was used as a pejorative term for African Americans. After the end of Reconstruction in 1877, the term referred to the laws and practices in the United States that enforced the separation of black and white people.

14. The first Africans known to be sold as slaves in British North America arrived at Jamestown, Virginia, in 1619.

15. On 16 October 1859, white abolitionist John Brown along with his black (Osborne Anderson, Louis S. Leary, Dangerfield Newby, Shields Green, and John A. Copeland) and white abolitionist co-conspirators seized the federal arsenal located near the ships dock named Harpers Ferry in West Virginia.

16. On 6 January 1941, President Franklin Delano Roosevelt addressed Congress and set out the Four Freedoms: freedom of speech; freedom to worship as one chooses; freedom from want; and freedom from fear.

17. Public aid for the poor.

18. "Steal Away" is an African American spiritual. "Ave Maria" is a prayer in the Catholic tradition dating from the Middle Ages. The song "Ave Maria" ("Ellens Dritter Gesang") was composed in 1825 by Franz Schubert, taking lyrics from Walter Scott's poem "The Lady of the Lake," which was published in 1810.

19. Beale Street is a famous street in Memphis, Tennessee, where well-known jazz and blues musicians played and developed the Memphis blues style. The music district in Harlem, located around 133rd Street between 5th and 7th Avenues, became known as Beale Street or Jungle Alley in the 1920s because its musical environment was similar to that in Memphis. Carnegie Hall is the world-renowned musical performance venue on 7th Avenue in Midtown Manhattan.

20. Eddie Anderson, a black actor, became famous on *The Jack Benny Program*, a radio and television show from the 1930s through the 1950s. He played Rochester Van Jones, comedian Jack Benny's valet/sidekick.

21. The official name of the Dies Committee was the House Committee on Un-American Activities (HUAC). Congressman Martin Dies chaired HUAC at its inception in 1938 and influenced its activities throughout World War II.

22. Slang term for a black migrant from the South now living in the North.

23. United Service Organizations (private groups of U.S. citizens) support U.S. military personnel, often providing them with entertainment, food, and other items that bring feelings of home to the military environment.

24. The Savoy Ballroom was a popular dance spot where patrons tried out new dances such as the Lindy Hop (the signature Savoy dance) and the Rhumboogie. The Savoy, which had a special dance floor, opened in 1926 on Lenox Avenue in Harlem. It closed in 1958.

25. 7 December 1941. This incident marked the beginning of U.S. involvement in World War II.

26. Slang term for those whom others believe behave above their position in life.

27. Sarah Breedlove, as Madame C. J. Walker (using her husband Charles Joseph Walker's initials), became very wealthy after developing a line of black hair-care products distributed through the Madame C. J. Walker Manufacturing Company.

28. As a maid in her employer's home.

29. A hotel located in New York's Times Square. The hotel was named for President William Taft in 1931.

30. A river in Germany.

31. William "Count" Basie was a jazz bandleader, pianist, and composer. From the 1930s into the 1960s, he led the Count Basie Orchestra.

32. In 1943, several riots erupted across the United States as African Americans—in response to different incidents—insisted on the same equality and democracy that black soldiers had fought to ensure that others receive. The riots in Beaumont, Texas and Detroit, Michigan, occurred in June. In Beaumont, the clashes lasted two days. In response, the governor of Texas declared martial law and cancelled Juneteenth celebrations. The Detroit riot lasted three days and ended only after President Roosevelt sent in federal troops. Riots also occurred in New York; Los Angeles (known as the Zoot Suit riots); Washington, D.C.; Philadelphia; Mobile; St. Louis; and Baltimore.

33. Adolf Hitler, the autocratic, Austrian-born leader of the Nazi Party in Germany. He was responsible for ordering the genocidal killing of Jews and others in Germany.

34. Mussolini: Prime minister of Italy during World War II and an ally of Hitler. He was the leader of fascist Italy and head of the National Fascist Party. Italian partisans executed him at the end of the war.

35. The term "Jim Crow" refers to the laws and practices in the United States that enforced the separation of black and white people.

36. Allusion to the Double-V Campaign initiated in 1941 in the *Pittsburgh Courier* newspaper and promoted in black newspapers across the United States. The campaign challenged the United States to bring equality, democracy, and justice to African Americans while bringing those same benefits to Europeans.

37. False yet seemingly plausible arguments deliberately contrived to appear to have a basis in sound reasoning.

38. In Jewish folk tradition, a golem is a creature that has the appearance of a human but lacks human qualities in terms of character, morals, and so forth. Typically, golems are man-made and demonstrate humanity's attempt to replicate the work of God.

39. "Crooked cross" is a reference to the Nazi flag of Germany; the "Hell-born sun" refers to the sun disk on the Japanese flag.

40. A redcap is a baggage handler at a train station.

41. Lincoln University in Pennsylvania (known as Ashmun Institute until 1866) was founded in 1854 to educate black men. It is among the several Historically Black Colleges and Universities established to educate black students before higher education was available to them at predominately white institutions of higher education in the United States. Another historically black institution, Lincoln University in Missouri, was founded in 1866 through the initiative of the 62nd United States Colored Troops (USCT) and with the support of the 65th USCT.

42. 125th Street is the main business thoroughfare in New York City's Harlem neighborhood.

43. A health tonic or patent medicine developed in the nineteenth century, used primarily as a cold and cough medicine.

44. Military police.

45. Absent without leave (without official permission).

46. In 1943, several riots erupted across the United States. The two-day riot in Harlem began on Sunday, 1 August, in response to a rumor that a police officer had killed a black soldier who had intervened in the officer's arrest of a black woman. The soldier did not die. The scenes in this story are Petry's fictional representation of those events. Ralph Ellison also fictionalized the Harlem riot in his 1952 novel *Invisible Man*. James Baldwin wrote about the riot in "Harlem Hoodlums," *Newsweek*, 9 August 1943.

47. Title provided by volume authors.

48. Quartermaster units are responsible for provisions and supplies other than ammunition and medicine.

49. An African American newspaper founded in 1907 by Edwin Harleston. Robert Lee Vann was its publisher until 1940. During the war and in response to a letter from James G. Thompson to the newspaper, publisher Ira Lewis initiated the Double-V campaign, which ran from 7 February 1942 until 1943. This campaign challenged the United States to bring equality, democracy, and justice to African Americans while bringing those same benefits to Europeans. The *Pittsburgh Courier* had a national circulation throughout the 1940s. This African American newspaper and others such as the *Chicago Defender* and the *Baltimore Afro-American* frequently published reports of abuses against black soldiers.

50. NCOs do not have their own command and are under the command of commissioned officers.

51. Title provided by volume editors.

52. On 1 July 1943, President Roosevelt signed a bill making the Women's Army Auxiliary Corps (WAAC), a civilian support organization that was established in 1942, an official part of the U.S. Army. That year the WAAC became the WAC. WACs were assigned ranks commensurate with those of their male counterparts. The WAC ceased to exist after December 1978 as the regular army assimilated women.

53. The 6888th Central Postal Directory Battalion of the WAC was composed of black women; they were the only black women the U.S. military sent to serve in Europe.

54. The Victory Medal was awarded to all military personnel who served during World War II. The Good Conduct Medal was awarded for model performance of duties as an active member of the army. The Army of Occupation Medal was awarded for service of thirty days or more in occupied territories during World War II.

55. Valaida Snow was born into an African American musical family around 1902 in

Chattanooga, Tennessee. She became a renowned jazz trumpeter in the 1930s. While on tour in Europe and leading an all-women's band, she was arrested in Denmark and held for eighteen months (1940–1942) in the Nazi concentration camp Wester-Faengle. She died in New York in 1956.

56. Psalm 139:7.

57. Probably Bobby Smith, leader of the Bobby Smith Orchestra and a jazz saxophonist. He frequently played with Erskine Hawkins, who composed "Tuxedo Junction" with Bill Johnson, a member of the Original Creole Orchestra.

58. An allusion to the jazz song "In My Solitude," composed in 1934 by Duke Ellington, lyrics by Irving Mills and Eddie DeLange.

59. The Apollo is a popular entertainment venue in Harlem. This building opened in 1914 as Hurtig and Seamon's New Burlesque Theater; its owners did not admit black patrons. The theater received the name Apollo in 1934 and opened with an emphasis on African American entertainment.

60. Inexpensive seats in the balcony.

61. A lively form of string music and dance with origins in Andalusia in southern Spain. Frequently, the music is attributed, perhaps in error, to the people referred to as Gypsies.

62. An allusion to Psalm 68:31. Many African Americans have interpreted this passage as a metaphor affirming the connection among all African peoples and predicting their empowerment as well as their Christianity.

63. Valaida Snow recorded "My Heart Belongs to Daddy" as a single in 1939. She recorded the album *Hot Snow* in 1937.

64. Jazz singer Billie Holiday.

65. A restaurant in Philadelphia.

66. Her hair is probably plaited in braids or in cornrows, a type of braid that is close to the scalp and parted into several rows.

67. A list of Nazi symbols, including the swastika.

68. A prisoner who took on low-level jobs overseeing others in German concentration camps.

69. Nitrous oxide, or laughing gas, was widely used to relax patients during dental procedures before the development of Novocain.

70. Gettysburg is the site of the most casualties in a single battle during the Civil War and the location of a Union victory. President Abraham Lincoln delivered an address at Gettysburg on 19 November 1863, when he dedicated the military cemetery at the site.

71. An allusion to the Four Freedoms outlined by President Franklin D. Roosevelt: freedom from fear, freedom from want, freedom of speech, and freedom to worship as one chooses.

72. Nazi: a popular term for members of Adolf Hitler's National Socialist Party in Germany. Their ideology and the resulting atrocities caused World War II. Fascists: persons who subscribe to fascism, a system of rule by a sole leader (autocrat) who believes that the interest of the nation or race supersedes the interests of individuals and justifies political, economic, and social oppression. Hitler's Germany was fascist.

73. Reference to the ancient Ouroboros, a mythological symbol depicted by a snake eating its own tail.

4

Battles at Home and Abroad from Montgomery to Afghanistan

My conscience won't let me go shoot my brother, or some darker people, or some poor hungry people in the mud for big powerful America. [. . .] They [the Vietnamese] never called me Nigger. They never lynched me. They didn't put [. . .] dogs on me. They didn't rob me of my nationality. [. . .] How can I shoot them? [. . .] Just take me to jail.

MUHAMMAD ALI, 1967

Make them respect you [. . .]
Decision making isn't easy for a girl at war
I can get that suit just as well as a boy.

MISS FLAME (CORPORAL KISHA POLLARD),
9TH COMMUNICATION BATTALION, U.S. MARINE CORPS, IRAQ WAR

Faith Ringgold, *Flag for the Moon: Die Nigger*, Black Light Series #10, 36 × 50, oil on canvas. Copyright © Faith Ringgold, 1969, reproduced by permission of Faith Ringgold.

A FTER WORLD WAR II, the United States asserted itself as a superpower entrenched in a Cold War with the Soviet Union. Both sides competed globally for allies and influence. The isolationist tendencies that had shielded the nation from international scrutiny, particularly in terms of its treatment of African Americans and others, dissipated as the Cold War flashed hot in two major arenas: Korea (1950–1953) and Vietnam (1955–1975). During these decades, black freedom activists and political strategists again pointed out the contradiction of spreading democracy abroad while African Americans and others in the United States lacked basic human rights. Occupation forces in Europe remained segregated into the 1950s. At home, black citizens across the country organized into mass movements to finally kill Jim Crow laws.[1]

During his first term, which began in 1945, President Harry Truman committed the Democrats to a civil rights platform. His administration, which was in the midst of the escalating Cold War, encountered intense political pressure to establish equal rights and outlaw blatant voting restrictions. Much of this pressure came from groups such as the National Association for the Advancement of Colored People (NAACP) and from the report of his Presidential Committee on Civil Rights. The committee's report, *To Secure These Rights*, issued in 1947, condemned segregation and recommended sweeping civil rights legislation. With the signing of Executive Order 9981 in July 1948, Truman desegregated the military, bypassing a hostile Congress dominated by southern, senior-ranked senators. Desegregation began first at U.S. military bases; the executive order mandated that all who served be treated equally. Thus, notwithstanding considerable political maneuverings and resistance in the military to executive directions, the Korean War became the first integrated war in the twentieth century (see Hopkins and Killens below).[2]

Even with the pressure for military and national reform that had been building since the 1940s, change occurred slowly. Ironically, the deactivation of the last units of the famed Buffalo Soldiers precipitated integration on the battlefield. Segregation had always affected the performance of African Americans in the military, who bore the brunt of racism that often affected morale. Black soldiers had difficulty trusting white commanding officers who treated their African American subordinates with neglect and indifference. The constant battering of black soldiers' self-confidence coupled with poor training, insufficient supplies, and inadequate tactical communication created a mutual lack of respect between black and white military personnel. Consequently, black soldiers encountered resentment when they entered the battlefield in South Korea in 1950. Officers evaluated them as lazy and inept, assessments that pandered to long-existing stereotypes. Despite these obstacles, Private First Class William Thompson of the 24th Infantry became the first African American to win the Medal of Honor in Korea (the first since the Spanish-Cuban-U.S. War).[3]

Both negative assessments of black soldiers from white officers and GIs as well as newspaper reports reflected biased perspectives that ignored the conditions black combat soldiers faced. The black regiments did not receive time off to recuperate between campaigns and the military did not replenish their rations to the same levels as those of similarly situated white troops. White troops received brief retraining before their redeployment into combat; African American troops did not. The military leadership finally deactivated the Buffalo Soldier regiment in October 1951, reassigning men to the 9th Infantry Division, which thus became the first integrated regiment in Korea. Unfortunately, the U.S. armed services continued to send young, undertrained black soldiers to the frontlines to replace the injured, and this practice only augmented bitterness on both sides of the color line.[4]

The War in Vietnam was the first military engagement with an integrated U.S. Army from the beginning since black and white men fought side by side in the Continental Army almost 200 years earlier (see Part 1). As with the Korean conflict, the military bases in the United States experienced a relatively smoother transition than those overseas.[5] In Vietnam, African Americans continued to face discrimination that frequently led to scuffles with their prejudiced leaders and the white soldiers. In combat, however, black and white fought and died side by side.

As battles continued in Vietnam, foreign and domestic politics intertwined in the United States. The expanding War in Vietnam, the deployment of hundreds of thousands of U.S. troops, and the burgeoning black mass freedom struggle in the United States met at various flashpoints in the 1950s and 1960s (see Bond, Baldwin, Edwards, and Harper below). For many African Americans, the military still offered hope for fair treatment, and thousands enlisted, seeking change in their economic and political position within the nation. In the early 1960s, high morale dominated an army of volunteers and military careerists who believed the political rhetoric of success and U.S. invincibility in the faraway Asian country (see Rodgers below).

The Tonkin Resolution, which authorized military maneuvers prior to an official declaration of war by Congress, escalated the war to new heights. This resolution passed a month after President Johnson had signed the Civil Rights Act in the summer of 1964. The nation's latest civil rights legislation was the result of many years of mass civil disobedience and public demonstrations that placed the Civil Rights Movement in the context of the international struggle for black freedom. Many of the leaders of this mass movement were World War II veterans, including Aaron Henry (the Mississippi state NAACP president) and Medgar Evers (NAACP field secretary). These movements radicalized and politicized many young civilians who publicly questioned the structures of power and the character of the national leaders and demanded equal treatment with more vigor than ever before. As part of this quest, and in contrast to the mood of the early 1960s that had supported U.S. intervention, these young people questioned a military draft that disproportionately enlisted people of color and the poor into combat units.[6]

By the mid- to late sixties the tide had begun to turn against the war. The draft, the huge casualty rate, and the fact that there were few signs of success contributed to this shift in public opinion. The draft transported to Vietnam thousands of disfranchised black soldiers who felt disconnected from the United States. Many of these men came with the radical politics of Black Liberation and Black Power, the belief in black political and economic self-determination and the cultural pride sparked by the Black Arts Aesthetics Movement. These youthful and often angry soldiers had a global understanding of the war's racial politics. For them, the presence of the United States in Vietnam signified continuing imperial conquests over peoples of color (for examples, see Holcomb, Komunyakaa, Bambara, and Williams below). In this war, America's (and by extension, Europe's) enemies were not white, and habitually official rhetoric utilized derogatory and racialized language that belittled the North Vietnamese. This language, often spoken in the presence of African Americans, circulated easily and often in the White House, the government, the media, and on the frontlines, only exacerbating racial tensions in the military.[7]

With Black Power came a vocalized allegiance by many African Americans to people of color globally, one that more forcefully challenged U.S. involvement in Vietnam and viewed it in part as a racial battle. This perspective prompted the famous 1967 statement of outspoken heavyweight boxer and conscientious objector Muhammad Ali: "They [Vietnamese] never called me Nigger." Even prominent civil rights leader Rev. Martin Luther King Jr. broke ranks with the Johnson administration. On 4 April 1967, he gave an impassioned speech at the Riverside Church in New York against the war (see below), exactly one year before his assassination. Growing nationwide antiwar demonstrations helped mark the 1960s as a turbulent decade, one that ended with low morale, resentful veterans, and a military mired in cover-ups and manipulated reports.[8] In 1968, eleven presidential advisors on the Kerner Commission reported on the extensive urban riots of the previous year and identified two separate societies in the United States, one black and the other white, "separate and unequal."[9] That year, the army reflected the same racial problems in its ranks that existed in civilian society, as more African Americans, influenced by the new political climate of Black Power, began to speak out with increased vigor against racism in the ranks.[10]

After the war, the U.S. military restructured to improve its racial dynamics in an effort to avoid repeating the Vietnam experience. The social situation in the country had changed somewhat by the late 1960s. While opinions about the military ran the gamut in black communities, more radical groups (such as nationalists and conservatives on each end of the spectrum, both of which lamented the deterioration of race relations), more assimilated groups (those who benefited most from the social and political changes), and those higher up in rank became less critical of black military service.[11] The "New Army" returned to volunteerism in 1973. They recruited the self-motivated—those seeking training, a college education, and expanded opportunities. As a result, a record number of black volunteers entered the military, people very different from the disillusioned draftees of the 1960s. The U.S. armed services became the most meritocratic institution in the nation, albeit not free of problems. From 1971 to 1974, the proportion of black enlisted personnel in the army increased from 14.4 to 19.9 percent (in the navy, the proportion rose from 5.4 to 8.1 percent). By 1980, 27.2 percent of the army was black. Other military services witnessed similar growth in the proportion of black servicepeople over the same time span. Reserve Officers Training Corps (ROTC) programs at historically black colleges and universities and military academies recruited intensively. African Americans, including General Colin Powell, achieved high-ranking positions in the military. Powell climbed the leadership ranks to become chairman of the Joint Chiefs of Staff in 1989, and later he served as secretary of state under President George W. Bush.[12]

In January and February 1991, Operation Desert Storm removed Iraq from oil-rich Kuwait with a multilateral coalition supported by the United Nations. The air campaign took thirty-eight days, the ground war only four. The New Army, fully desegregated and with more women serving than ever before, also had better trained and educated troops. In 1991 29 percent of the army was African American, as were three-fifths of some combat units. African Americans accounted for 20 percent of the total U.S. troops in the Gulf. While many interpreted this as progress, the number of African Americans on the front lines was disproportionate to the number of African Americans in the general population. Clearly, social reforms in civilian life had not fully eradicated racism. Nor was the military entirely free of bias, as is evident in testimonies from black Persian Gulf veterans (see Pennick below). Many soldiers, both black and white, developed devastating illnesses after they returned home that military doctors refused to attribute to their exposure to chemicals during desert warfare. The military dismissed some veterans as liars, which meant that they suffered inadequate treatment, deteriorating health, and an array of unfortunate consequences ranging from permanent disabilities, cancers, and homelessness to death.[13]

Redress for historical wrongs against African American service men and women took time. Not until 1988 did the 24th Infantry Regiment of the Buffalo Soldiers receive vindication from accusations of cowardice; the regiment finally received its due honors for its triumphs from 1869 to 1951 as the military actively worked to rectify its errors and include the valiant contributions of African Americans. In the 1990s, the United States awarded commendations, many posthumously, to African Americans for military deeds dating from the late nineteenth century. Included in these reversals was an official White House apology in 1995 to Tuskegee Airmen, whom the army had reprimanded in 1945 for a nonviolent protest against Jim Crow treatment in Indiana.[14] More recently, in 2011, Major General Marcia Anderson became the first African American woman promoted to the rank of a two-star general; in 2014 Michelle Janine Howard became the first woman and first African American woman promoted to the rank of a four-star admiral in the U.S. Navy; and in 2017, West Point selected, an African American woman, Simone Askew as its First Captain, the highest ranking cadet.

Early in the twenty-first century, the terrorists' attacks on 11 September 2001 unified most of the nation against an enemy that did not have national borders. In response, President George W. Bush initiated the War on Terrorism, first entering Afghanistan in 2001 seeking to dismantle Al-Qaeda, the group claiming responsibility for the attacks (see Baraka and Clifton below). The Bush administration then launched Operation Iraqi Freedom in 2003. Although the engagement in Iraq yielded few positive results, it managed to unseat and execute Iraq's president Saddam Hussein. The war proceeded with an unclear agenda, and as casualties mounted, President Bush met fierce opposition and political backlash. In African American communities (as in the nation in general), most of the antiwar sentiment concerned the rising costs of the war, which necessitated reduced spending on domestic programs for the needy. Additional resistance to the war centered on concerns over adequate support services for returning veterans, many of whom suffered from debilitating psychological disabilities or were maimed and injured in the new twenty-first-century warfare that involved street-level bombings. In 2005, a Pew Research Center poll reported that twice as many African Americans as whites were against the war. Because the high risks associated with this war outweighed the opportunities for education and training in the military, black enlistment in the army dropped a dramatic 41 percent from 2000 to 2005, resulting in an overall recruiting deficit.[15] The new military messages stressing patriotism fell short and could not overcome the general misgivings about the rationale for the war, the military's overemphasis on recruiting the poor and people of color, the lack of representation from affluent families on the front lines, and the persistent racism at home (which was underscored by the federal government's missteps following Hurricane Katrina in New Orleans in 2005). These issues eroded the patriotic emotions that coalesced across the nation immediately following the attacks on 9/11.

In January 2009, Barack Hussein Obama became the forty-fourth president of the United States and the commander in chief of the armed forces. The first African American to hold this position, President Obama led a military engaged in active warfare on two fronts: Iraq and Afghanistan. Under his leadership, American military involvement in Iraq decreased. In 2009 he won the Nobel Peace Prize. He was the third sitting president to receive this award; his predecessors were Theodore Roosevelt and Woodrow Wilson. In his acceptance speech, President Obama echoed mantras from social movements and past U.S. presidents: "A just peace includes not only civil and political rights—it must encompass economic security and opportunity. For true peace is not just freedom from fear, but freedom from want."[16] However, since then, President Obama initiated a surge of troops in Afghanistan and in 2011 directed a U.S. Special Unit to kill Al-Qaeda leader Osama Bin Laden in Pakistan. In May 2014 the president announced the plan to gradually withdraw American troops from Afghanistan over 2.5 years to yield more resources to confront burgeoning terrorist threats elsewhere. In September 2014 he responded to threats by the Islamic State of Iraq and the Levant (ISIL) by authorizing offensive air strikes, reescalating U.S. military maneuvers in the region.[17] And so the long-term war against foreign terrorism continues, as the rhetoric of equality and justice prevails in American society, despite the reality.

NOTES

1. See Parker, "When Politics Becomes Protest."

2. Edgerton, *Hidden Heroism*, 162–65; Buckley, *American Patriots*, 338–43; Motley, *The Invisible Soldier*, 17. See also Sullivan, *Lift Every Voice*.

3. Buckley, *American Patriots*, xxiv, 350–57; Edgerton, *Hidden Heroism*, 166–68; U.S. Army Center of Military History, "Black Soldier, White Army: The 24th Infantry in Korea," http://www.army.mil/cmh-pg/books/korea/24th.htm, accessed 9 October 2014.

4. Astor, *The Right to Fight*, 350–58; Buckley, *American Patriots*, xxiv, 358; Edgerton, *Hidden Heroism*, 167–68.

5. Buckley, *American Patriots*, 361.

6. Ibid., 337–41; Astor, *The Right to Fight* 386–87.

7. Edgerton, *Hidden Heroism*, 184.

8. Remnick, *King of the World*, 287; Gorn, *Muhammad Ali*, 138; Lipsyte, "'I Don't Have to Be What You Want Me to Be,' Says Muhammad Ali," 93; Martin Luther King Jr., "Beyond Vietnam: A Time to Break Silence," American Rhetoric Online Speech Bank, http://www.americanrhetoric.com/speeches/mlkatimetobreaksilence.htm, accessed 10 June 2014.

9. "Report of the National Advisory Commission on Civil Disorders," The Eisenhower Foundation, http://www.eisenhowerfoundation.org/docs/kerner.pdf, accessed 10 June 2014.

10. Butler, "Affirmative Action in the Military," 202; Buckley, *American Patriots*, xxv; Astor, *The Right to Fight*, 409–22; Edgerton *Hidden Heroism*, 182, 184–85. See also Loeb, "MIA: African American Autobiography of the Vietnam War"; Hall, "The Response of the Moderate Wing of the Civil Rights Movement to the War in Vietnam"; Fendrich, "The Returning Black Vietnam-Era Veteran"; Terry, *Bloods: An Oral History of the Vietnam War by Black Veterans*; Black, *Soul Soldiers*; and Westheider, *Fighting on Two Fronts*.

11. See Weigert, "Stratification, Ideology, and Opportunity Beliefs among Black Soldiers."

12. Astor, *The Right to Fight* 493; Butler, "Affirmative Action in the Military," 203; Powell, *My American Journey*.

13. Butler, "Affirmative Action in the Military," 196, 203–5; Buckley, *American Patriots*, 433–35, 457, 465; Edgerton, *Hidden Heroism*, 188–90.

14. Buckley, *American Patriots*, 479–83.

15. Dave Moniz, "Opportunities, Opposition to Iraq War Cut into Recruiting," *USA Today*, 4 November 2005, http://www.usatoday.com/news/nation/2005-11-03-army-blacks-inside_x.htm, accessed 10 June 2014; Joseph Williams and Kevin Baron, "Military Sees Big Decline in Black Enlistees," *Boston Globe*, 7 October 2007, http://www.boston.com/news/nation/washington/articles/2007/10/07/military_sees_big_decline_in_black_enlistees/, accessed 10 June 2007.

16. "Remarks by the President at the Acceptance of the Nobel Peace Prize," White House press release, 10 December 2009, http://www.whitehouse.gov/the-press-office/remarks-president-acceptance-nobel-peace-prize, accessed 10 June 2014.

17. Mark Landler, "U.S. Troops to Leave Afghanistan by End of 2016," *New York Times*, 27 May 2014, http://www.nytimes.com/2014/05/28/world/asia/us-to-complete-afghan-pullout-by-end-of-2016-obama-to-say.html?_r=0, accessed 10 July 2014; Zeke J. Miller, "Obama Says U.S. Will Bomb ISIS in Syria, Train Rebels," *Time Magazine*, 10 September 2014, http://time.com/3319658/obama-isis-speech-iraq-syria/, accessed 9 October 2014.

ELLA BAKER

Born in Virginia in 1903, Ella Josephine Baker was a principal organizer and adviser to the founders of the Student Nonviolent Coordinating Committee (SNCC) in 1960. At that time, she had three decades' experience as a civil rights activist and grassroots organizer. She had previously worked as the director of the Young Negroes' Cooperative League, as director of branches for the National Association for the Advancement of Colored People (NAACP), and as president of the New York branch. She also had assisted in early organizing work for the Southern Christian Leadership Conference (SCLC) and had worked at newspapers such as the *American West Indian News* and the *Negro National News*. Baker lived a life committed to human rights and equality and died in New York City in 1986. She presented the speech below to the Institute of the Black World in Atlanta in 1969.

From The Black Woman in the Civil Rights Struggle

[...] I've always thought first and foremost of people as individuals. [...] Wherever there has been struggle, black women have been identified with that struggle. During slavery there was a tremendous amount of resistance in various forms. Some were rather subtle and some were rather shocking. One of the subtle forms was that of feigning illness. [...] One of the other forms of resistance which was perhaps much more tragic and has not been told to a great extent is the large number of black women who gave birth to children and killed them rather than have them grow up as slaves. There is a story of a woman in Kentucky who had borne thirteen children and strangled each of them with her own hands rather than have them grow up as slaves. Now this calls for a certain kind of deep *commitment* and *resentment. Commitment* to freedom and deep *resentment* against slavery. [...]

I think the period that is most important to most of us now is the period when we began to question whether we really wanted in. Even though the sit-in movement started off primarily as a method of getting in, it led to the concept of questioning whether it was worth trying to get in. The first effort was to be able to sit down at the lunch counters. When you look back and think of all the tragedy and suffering that the first sit-iners went through, you begin to wonder. Why pay a price like that for the privilege of eating at lunch counters? There were those who saw from the beginning that the struggle was much bigger than getting a hamburger at a lunch counter. There were those who saw from the beginning that it was part of the struggle for full dignity as a human being. So out of that came two things that to me are very significant. First, there was the concept of the trained finding their identity with the masses. Another thing that came out of it at a later period was that of leadership training. As the young people moved out into the community and finally were able to be accepted, they began to discover indigenous leaders. [...]

Around 1965 there began to develop a great deal of questioning about what is the role of women in the struggle. Out of it came a concept that black women had to bolster the ego of the male. This implied that the black male had been treated in such a manner as to have been emasculated both by the white society and black women because the female was the head of the household. We began to deal with the question of the need of black women to play the subordinate role. I personally have never thought of this as being valid because it raises the question as to whether the black man is going to try to be a man on the basis of his capacity to deal with issues and situations rather than be a man because he has some people around him who claim him to be a man by taking subordinate roles.

I don't think you could go through the Freedom Movement without finding that the backbone of the support of the Movement were women. When demonstrations took place and when the community acted, usually it was some woman who came to the fore. [...]

In order for us as poor and oppressed people to become a part of a society that is meaningful, the system under which we now exist has to be radically changed. This means that we are going to have to learn to think in *radical* terms. I use the term radical in its original meaning—getting down to and understanding the root cause. It means facing a system that does not lend itself to your needs and devising means by which you change that system. That is easier said than done. But one of the things that has to be faced is, in the process of wanting to change that system, how much have we got to do to find out who we are, where we have come from and where we are going. About twenty-eight years ago I used to go around making speeches, and I would open up my talk by saying that there was a man who had a health problem and he was finally told by the doctor that they could save his sight or save his memory, but they couldn't save both. They asked him which did he want and he said, "Save my sight because I would rather see where I am going than remember where I have been." I am saying as you must say, too, that in order to see where we are going, we not only must remember where we've been, but *we must understand where we have been.* This calls for a great deal of analytical thinking and evaluation of methods that have been used. We have to begin to think in terms of where do we really want to go and how can we get there.

Finally, I think it is also to be said that [civil rights organizing] is not a job that is going to be done by all the people simultaneously. Some will have to be in cadres, the advanced cadres, and some will have to come later. But one of the guiding principles has to be that we cannot lead a struggle that involves masses of people without getting the people to understand what their potentials are, what their strengths are.

"The Black Woman in the Civil Rights Struggle," speech given at the Institute of the Black World, Atlanta, Georgia, 1969. Excerpted from "The Black Woman in the Civil Rights Struggle," in Joanne Grant, *Ella Baker: Freedom Bound* (New York: John Wiley and Sons, 1998), 227–32.

JAMES BALDWIN

Renowned writer, intellectual, and activist James Baldwin was born in 1924 in New York City. His literary corpus includes novels, plays, poetry, and collections of essays. After the letter below initially appeared in the *Progressive*, Baldwin published it as part of his influential and important book-length essay *The Fire Next Time* (1963). During the 1960s, Baldwin frequently wrote and spoke on issues of civil rights and citizenship in the United States. He attended the 1963 March on Washington and participated in the march from Selma to Montgomery in 1965. Baldwin had expatriated to France in 1948, where he died in 1987.

My Dungeon Shook: Letter to My Nephew on the One Hundredth Anniversary of the Emancipation

Dear James:

I have begun this letter five times and torn it up five times. I keep seeing your face, which is also the face of your father and my brother. Like him, you are tough, dark, vulnerable, moody—with a very definite tendency to sound truculent because you want no one to think you are soft. You may be like your grandfather in this, I don't know, but certainly both you and your father resemble him very much physically. Well, he is dead, he never saw you, and he had a terrible life; he was defeated long before he died because, at the bottom of his heart, he really believed what white people said about him. This is one of the reasons that he became so holy. I am sure that your father has told you something about all that. Neither you nor your father exhibit any tendency towards holiness: you really *are* of another era, part of what happened when the Negro left the land and came into what the late E. Franklin Frazier[1] called "the cities of destruction." You can only be destroyed by believing that you really are what the white world calls a *nigger*. I tell you this because I love you, and please don't you ever forget it.

I have known both of you all your lives, have carried your Daddy in my arms and on my shoulders, kissed and spanked him and watched him learn to walk. I don't know if you've known anybody from that far back; if you've loved anybody that long, first as an infant, then as a child, then as a man, you gain a strange perspective on time and human pain and effort. Other people cannot see what I see whenever I look into your father's face, for behind your father's face as it is today are all those other faces which were his.

Let him laugh and I see a cellar your father does not remember and a house he does not remember and I hear in his present laughter his laughter as a child. Let him curse and I remember him falling down the cellar steps, and howling, and I remember, with pain, his tears, which my hand or your grandmother's so easily wiped away. But no one's hand can wipe away those tears he sheds invisibly today, which one hears in his laughter and in his speech and in his songs. I know what the world has done to my brother and how narrowly he has survived it. And I know, which is much worse, and this is the crime of which I accuse my country and my countrymen, and for which neither I nor time nor history will ever forgive them, that they have destroyed and are destroying hundreds of thousands of lives and do not know it and do not want to know it. One can be, indeed one must strive to become, tough and philosophical concerning destruction and death, for this is what most of mankind has been best at since we have heard of man. (But remember: *most* of mankind is not *all* of mankind.) But it is not permissible that the authors of devastation should also be innocent. It is the innocence which constitutes the crime.

Now, my dear namesake, these innocent and well-meaning people, your countrymen, have caused you to be born under conditions not very far removed from those described for us by Charles Dickens in the London of more than a hundred years ago. (I hear the chorus of the innocents screaming, "No! This is not true! How *bitter* you are!"—but I am writing this letter to *you*, to try to tell you something about how to handle *them*, for most of them do not yet really know that you exist. I *know* the conditions under which you were born, for I was there. Your countrymen were *not* there, and haven't made it yet. Your grandmother was also there, and no one has ever accused her of being bitter. I suggest that the innocents check with her. She isn't hard to find. Your countrymen don't know that *she* exists, either, though she has been working for them all their lives.)

Well, you were born, here you came, something like fifteen years ago; and though your father and mother and grandmother, looking about the streets through which they were carrying you, staring at the walls into which they brought you, had every reason to be heavy-hearted, yet they were not. For here you were, Big James, named for me—you were a big baby, I was not—here you were: to be loved. To be loved, baby, hard, at once, and forever, to strengthen you against the loveless world. Remember that: I know how black it looks today, for you. It looked bad that day, too, yes, we were trembling. We have not stopped trembling yet, but if we had not loved each other none of us would have survived. And now you must survive because we love you, and for the sake of your children and your children's children.

This innocent country set you down in a ghetto in which, in fact, it intended that you should perish. Let me spell out precisely what I mean by that, for the heart of the matter is here, and the root of my dispute with my country. You were born where you were born and faced the future that you faced because you were black and *for no other reason*. The limits of your ambition were, thus, expected to be set forever. You were born into a society which spelled out with brutal clarity, and in as many ways as possible, that you were a worthless human being. You were not expected to aspire to excellence: you were expected to make peace with mediocrity. Wherever you have turned, James, in your short time on this earth, you have been told where you could go and what you could do (and *how* you could do it) and where you could live and whom you could marry. I know your countrymen do not agree with me about this, and I hear them saying, "You exaggerate." They do not know Harlem, and I do. So do you. Take no one's word for anything, including mine—but trust your experience. Know whence you came. If you know whence you came, there is really no limit to where you can go. The details and symbols of your life have been deliberately constructed to make you believe what white people say about you. Please try to remember that what they believe, as well as what they do and cause you to endure, does not testify to your inferiority but to their inhumanity and fear. Please try to be clear, dear James, through the storm which rages about your youthful head today, about the reality which lies behind the words *acceptance* and *integration*. There is no reason for you to try to become like white people and there is no basis whatever for their impertinent assumption that *they* must accept *you*. The really terrible thing, old buddy, is that *you* must accept *them*. And I mean that very seriously. You must accept them and accept them with love. For these innocent people have no other hope. They are, in effect, still trapped in a history which they do not understand; and until they understand it, they cannot be released from it. They have had to believe for many years, and for innumerable reasons, that black men are inferior to white men. Many of them, indeed, know better, but, as you will discover, people find it very difficult to act on what they know. To act is to be committed, and to be committed is to be in danger. In this case, the danger, in the minds of most white Americans, is the loss of their identity. Try to imagine how you would feel if you woke up one morning to find the sun shining and all the stars aflame. You would be frightened because it is out of the order of nature.

Any upheaval in the universe is terrifying because it so profoundly attacks one's sense of one's own reality. Well, the black man has functioned in the white man's world as a fixed star, as an immovable pillar: and as he moves out of his place, heaven and earth are shaken to their foundations. You, don't be afraid. I said that it was intended that you should perish in the ghetto, perish by never being allowed to go behind the white man's definitions, by never being allowed to spell your proper name. You have, and many of us have, defeated this intention; and, by a terrible law, a terrible paradox, those innocents who believed that your imprisonment made them safe are losing their grasp of reality. But these men are your brothers—your lost, younger brothers. And if the word *integration* means anything, this is what it means: that we, with love, shall force our brothers to see themselves as they are, to cease fleeing from reality and begin to change it. For this is your home, my friend, do not be driven from it; great men have done great things here, and will again, and we can make America what America must become. It will be hard, James, but you come from sturdy, peasant stock, men who picked cotton and dammed rivers and built railroads, and, in the teeth of the most terrifying odds, achieved an unassailable and monumental dignity. You come from a long line of great poets, some of the greatest poets since Homer. One of them said, *The very time I thought I was lost, My dungeon shook and my chains fell off.*[2]

You know, and I know, that the country is celebrating one hundred years of freedom one hundred years too soon. We cannot be free until they are free. God bless you, James, and Godspeed.

Your uncle,
James

"Letter to My Nephew," *The Progressive*, December 1962. Reprinted as "My Dungeon Shook: Letter to My Nephew on the Hundredth Anniversary of the Emancipation," in James Baldwin, *The Fire Next Time* (New York: Dial Press, 1963), 17–24.[3]

Related writings by James Baldwin: "The Discovery of What It Means to Be an American" (1959); "Nobody Knows My Name" (1961); "The American Dream and the American Negro" (1965); "Why I Left America" (1970).

TONI CADE BAMBARA

Born in 1939 in New York City, Toni Cade Bambara was a novelist, filmmaker, anthologist, educator, and activist. She published five books and wrote or produced several screenplays. Bambara traveled to Cuba in 1973 and to Vietnam with the Anti-Imperialist Feminist Women's delegation in 1975. Bambara died in 1995 in Atlanta, Georgia. In 1997, the West African nation of Ghana honored Toni Cade Bambara with a stamp bearing her image.

The Sea Birds Are Still Alive[4]

Newspapers swirled around the deck. Sheets of print sucked up under the boat's tin roofing, shredded, then dropped into the water. A centerfold—ragged from its windswept journey across feet, between the bench legs, in and out among the closely woven baskets—smacked up flat against the side railings, buzzing loudly. Eyes swiveled away from the cabin of the pilot, whose whistle had just warned a freighter turning too widely. But the ensnared paper vibrating against the rusty rails held attention for only a moment. Some on board could read the script. Others couldn't read at all. For most, it didn't matter what the censored papers chose to say. The situation was confused enough without reports from the government press.

Rebel forces in the countryside have been subdued, it would say in the morning. By evening the wiped-out forces were reported in control of two villages. A particularly menacing commando unit were now prisoners of the Americans, one paper would say. Another would claim that victory for the Royal Army.[5] Turmoil in the city was attributed to roving bandits on page one, to foreign paid provocateurs on page two, then denied altogether on page three. Everything under control, the papers boasted.

But someone, perhaps students stirred up by the Chinese professors at the universities, had made attacks on the embassies, said the papers. And someone in national uniform—unemployed actors, perhaps—had been raiding the markets extorting fees and molesting women. Everything under control. As for the disruption of the prince's birthday celebration, clearly that was the work of juvenile delinquents, and parents needed to exert more control. A recent issue of the daily laid the city disturbances at the feet of irresponsible women whose husbands would be fined.

The country woman in a long, striped skirt kicked at the papers caught between her baskets and spat betel juice[6] in the prince's face. He flew over the side, disgraced. Some passengers laughed, others scowled. The old grandmother on her haunches plucked at the long, striped skirt for attention, then shared her toothless grin with any one else who cared to join them in their daring ridicule of royalty.

Eyes speckled and rimmed red, the grandmother studied the old gentleman on the side bench before her. He would neither smile nor scowl. He simply sat, his soft cloth shoes spread open in a V, a long clay pipe cold in his hand. The old woman looked again and saw that his other hand was missing. In a schoolteacher gesture that flooded where her memory of schooldays should have been, he ran a hand lazily over his jaw, worrying the hairs sprouting from his chin. She scanned his soft cloth suit for patriotic pins, wondering which war had martyred him, had pulled him from his classroom and left some district untutored. He sat straight and proud, one hand, chin whiskers, cold pipe. Her smile was different now. He had come to the end of his tobacco, but he had, she thought, much face left.

The vendors, mostly young children and the very old, checked the straps on their wooden trays, fussed over the paper cones of nuts and beans, the hanks of shoelaces, the tins of balms and nostrums, the rice-paper blobs of caramels. They sat cross-legged on the deck together, backs against the pilot's cabin. They chatted, ignoring the newspapers swirling around their wares.

The refugees kept watch over their belongings, slapping at the newspapers tangled round their feet, bunching up between the bundles of their household goods. Whatever explanation the papers offered, the situation meant for them upheaval and poor payment for the things too big to transport.

The country woman in the long, striped skirt squatted among her baskets and gave the sour curds a shake. She unwrapped her waistband, planning out her errands of the day, and wound the cloth around the old grandmother's head brushed bald by the wind lunging through the rails. Looking around at the foreigners, lip curling, the country woman spat in the direction of two new black shoes.

The foreigners glanced at the spit, at the soldier near the pilot's cabin who would not look, at the pairs and pairs of dark eyes, and sat. Newspapers tumbled unnoticed over their briefcases and shoes. Their situation was never recounted in those papers. Racing from country to country, exchanging currency from one that looked like stage money to another just as unreal, convinced they were being cheated, certain they were being mistreated, body alert for pickpockets, feet stinging from leather shoes, back stiff to insult or argument that their respective governments had committed unspeakable crimes, vile and filthy deeds.

Queuing up on endless lines for visas, permits, letters of transit. Trying to read an overseas newspaper for some trace of their own situation and finding none there either. The only attention, sardonic and scathing, in the rebel press, of all places. Slumped over for hours on hard benches at airports or railroad terminals or in offices where people spat and soldiers looked in the other direction. This soldier with blanked eyes and face staring off toward the horizon, a flurry of newspaper encircling his head. The foreigners sat, windblown, despised.

The pilot bent to stuff newspapers in his shoes to muffle the vibrations from the engine. For him the situation meant doubled-up hours transporting trucks and baggage and soldiers and an endless array of passengers ever anxious about the possibility of mines in the waters. The papers assured daily in increasingly strident tones that there was nothing to fear. But daily the people gathered on the jetties to watch the divers surface with one more mine the Americans were supposed to have removed.

The screech of sea birds made all heads turn toward the back of the boat. There a young girl, reckless near the edge where the wind swept in to balloon her clothes out and threatened to lift her from the deck, was flinging food to the birds who swooped and squabbled in scattered formation, flapping greedily after the rusting boat, snatching morsels out of the air one hair away from the foam churned high by the boat paddles. Or suspended in midair awaited the next pitch of bread, trying to fend off, without losing prime position in front of the girl, the rest of the flock, picking, clutching, nicking a wing, an eye.

One bird now in a downward spiral, beak overloaded, neck broken, wailing, then disappearing from view in a flurry of claws.

The passengers near the back of the boat where the tin roof ended and the full force of the wind began mumbled disapproval. Poor people starving in the countryside, starving in the cities, oxen too weak to pull a plow, chickens too scrawny to bother, and here right before their eyes good food wasted on worthless birds.

Two hill women on their straw mats, needles poised over the patches they snipped and stitched hurriedly, looked up, then sank their heads in sorrow over the waste of food. Quickly they picked up their pace. If they didn't hurry, they'd have nothing to sell. Nothing to sell, then nothing to eat and nothing to wear. They'd be run in their rags from the hotels where foreigners jingled loose change. Canadians, Americans, Australians, Europeans picking over their work and sneering, stalking away in dazzling shoes or staying to haggle ruthlessly in broken tongues. One of the women stabbed herself cruelly to fix her mind on the work at hand. To substitute for the pain she felt hopeless to deal with, with a pain she could understand.

A young man with a hard, brown face leaned over the rail to spit. Not at the girl and the wanton waste, but in answer to the Frenchwoman's question was he making his home in the city. Home. In '46 when the United States notified the families their island was needed for nuclear tests, he'd been a child peeping through the chinks in the bamboo awning, peeping at shells along the seashore. He couldn't even walk yet, much less protest. And the islanders, bowed down by centuries of servitude to the Spanish, the French, the Japanese, the Americans, complied.

The lovely atoll that was home devastated by two decades of atomic, then hydrogen, blasts. For years, with no compensation money, they waited for an unseen needle on an unknown gauge to record the radiation level and announce it safe to return home. They waited, complied, were rerouted, resettled at this camp or that island, the old songs gone, the dances forgotten, the elders and the ancient wisdoms put aside, the memory of home scattered in the wind.

Home for him had been a memory of yellow melons and the elders with their tea sitting right outside his window under the awning. Home after that, a wicker basket and his father's uncle's pallet in muddy tent cities, flooded wooden barracks, compounds with loudspeakers but no vegetation and no work to keep one's dignity upright. Meager rations in one country, hostility in the next.

Then finding home among islanders who remembered home, a color, a sound, the shells, the leaping fish, the cool grottoes. And home among other people foreign but not foreign, people certain that humanity was their kin, the world their home. Home with people like that who shared their next-to-nothing things and their more-than-hoped-for wealth of spirit. Home with people who watched other needles on other gauges that recorded the rising winds.

The young man with the hard, brown face leaned over the rail, the wind shoving his hair flat like that earlier wind had bowed the island grasses down outside his window. But one sturdy stem had remained upright; dark green, defiant, it had imprinted indelibly on his brain. The young man smiled, the wind drawing his lips back, baring his teeth. It was a good time in history to be on the earth, to be on the boat going home. He leaned way over, examining the holes below that bled rust with each grumble of the engine, each turn of the wooden paddles. Then he straightened, back stiff with the conviction that he, like many others going home now, was totally unavailable for servitude.

The notebook pages fluttered and threatened to fly off in the wind. The correspondent leafed through, the heels of her hands holding down the months and months of notes. Her mouth full of paper clips, she tried to make some order and find a section of blank papers that would get her through the stage she now anticipated: agricultural, commercial, industrial operations, foreign and domestic, taken over by a provisional revolutionary authority. She flipped through the filled pages.

. . . summit conferences . . . cloak and dagger . . . solidarity banners . . . May I see your papers? . . . ginger candy with too many hairs for eating . . . crepe-paper flowers for the dead . . . sabotage at the plants . . . mass arrests . . .

. . . Your papers, please . . . ox collars turned plant hangers priced for tourists and not farmers . . . Sorry, no journalists allowed . . . borders closed . . . defections in the army . . . the people's militia growing every day . . . the Indian widow in endless exile having disgraced her family rejecting suttee, knocking on her hotel door with another nightmare to relate, haunted by her husband still burning on the funeral pyre . . . bellboys peeking through the transom . . . hauled before the secret police and questioned about the other foreigners in the hotels . . . double agents . . .

. . . the Slavic woman at the Exchange in harlequin glasses from Hollywood and plastic wedgies from the Caribbean . . . babies wrapped in newspapers dying near their dying mothers on floors of prison cells . . . braziers in the street and families huddled round roasting rat, some people said . . . the Ugandan diplomat in alligator shoes holdin forth in the café bar . . . the landlord's daughter caught in a roundup, for the rally had been held right outside her dressmaker's shop, heard the revolution was coming and the rich would be slaughtered, blackened her teeth and sold the family treasures in the market, parceled out the lands to the tenants and waited for the revolution to come, bitter that none came in two weeks she returned to the estate looking for a dentist and a handout. . . .

. . . Your letters of introduction, please . . . parachutes overhead and the people fleeing, expecting bombs, missiles of some sort or another, the packages floating down could perhaps be medicines or leaflets; coming out of hiding they discover boxes of brandied peaches and tinned pheasant marked for the general in the district . . . Your identification card, please . . .

. . . USAID[7] officers in the company of known assassins . . . death squadrons . . . torture quotas . . . students rounded up on the steps of the university library . . . sentences but not trial notes posted under glass outside municipal buildings . . . schoolboys and merchants on the army payroll . . . the arrest of the schoolteacher who'd led her to the DMZ then mysteriously turned waxworks . . .

She had logged incessantly, sent numerous cables to the wire service, conducted interviews in caves, in hallways, in swamps in the dead of night under fire, translated graffiti on the walls of paramilitary organizations under the guise of manufacturing plants seized by the student-worker coalition, decoded purloined documents her paper grumbled about paying for, ignored the summons home. She could not go home now, not yet, not when the victory of the people was so close at hand.

She closed the looseleaf and zippered it tight. She had missed Paris in the spring of '68.[8] She would not miss this moment of history emerging right before her eyes. Cadres pouring into the cities from the liberated zones, organizing women, students, workers boldly in view of the demoralized national troops. She could write now as she never had before. Her earlier work so like the travel posters over her desk in Paris, interesting but didn't mean she'd been there.

She was there now. She felt she was already in the mobilized city. Could feel herself shoving through the revolving doors of the Imperial Palace Hotel, which some joked should be called the Anti-Imperialist Hotel. Heels clicking over the tile, tongue clumsy with the language, cautious with the questions, certain in the times. A room with no transom. The view of the streets and the cadres at outdoor rallies. "Why are our people poor?" they would begin. She felt she was already there, in the moment.

The little girl feeding the birds bumped the correspondent out of her reverie and excused herself in French, much to the woman's surprise. But of course. The correspondent examined the clothes, the black hair, the round face with the dark eyes and high cheekbones, and remembered where she was. She clutched the precious cargo in her lap, spitting out one twisted paper clip that skidded over the deck, then disappeared over the side. She ignored the wind, the squawling birds, the little girl. She was also unaware of the soldier who now watched her in convoluted hatred.

On the long bench by the pilot's cabin, the American sat amid a muddle of luggage, his own and the bags of poor folk crowding him. Eight years, he was thinking, eight damn years making a name for myself in the Department of the Interior, learning the languages almost of the Midwest Indians, and now transferred to some godforsaken outpost in the middle of east hell. An encampment where he'd oversee the refugees evacuated by the United States in its war against the Reds. He'd been told at orientation that the last typhoon of salt water had caved in the dikes and swept away the agricultural project, so he'd have to start from scratch. What did he know about constructing dikes or irrigating land and suchlike?

They'd run him through a crash course of languages and cultures, but hadn't explained much about the agricultural project, except that he was to see to it that the dike was built and the cyclone fence repaired at once. He ran a hand across his bristly face and smiled. It had been quite a course. But then he frowned, thinking of all the papers he'd had to sign, declarations of discretion, secrecy. No one at the Defense Department had answered to his satisfaction the charges about germ and chemical research being conducted at the camp. It wasn't just the troublemakers this time making those charges. Rumors were rife even in responsible Washington circles.

He looked around the boat. The people, the rusting hulk, the birds caterwauling in the rear. When he'd missed his plane and lost contact with the other new officers headed for the camp, he'd waited foolishly in the airport for word from them. But scientists were like that—brisk, brusque, cold. And so he'd had to make his own way to the post. And why so many scientists? Twenty years before when he'd joined the service, Red China and North Korea had accused the United States of germ warfare. He'd known that for a lie. Germ warfare was a violation of international law, after all. But this time . . . and responsible people . . . and those biochemists were scheduled to work only three-hour shifts in the infirmary . . . He hugged his briefcase.

His briefcase bulged with material he was to release in flyers, bark out over loudspeakers, feed to the press. Toxic fallout from defoliants does not endanger the health, the flyers argued. As for the charges of germ warfare, so much enemy propaganda, the material said. But do not eat shellfish, other flyers said, and avoid deep-root vegetables. And check in at the dispensary once a month, it warned in bold caps.

The American rearranged his body on the hard bench and wondered who was sitting in his leather chair back in Washington. He yearned to kick off his shoes, buzz for a drink, bury his stocking feet in the deep, gray carpet. Exasperated, chilled, unshaven, knees aching, he stretched, cocky in the knowledge that Pine Ridge Reservation[9] would never have been disrupted had he been at his desk. They'd see. He'd be recalled. Twenty-eight years of good service. Eight years at the Interior and now outside, put out to pasture. He'd be recalled. They'd see.

His eyes rested for a moment on the blob of brown spit near his shoes and then he studied the passengers again, testing himself. He'd been tutored with stacks of *National Geographic* to enable him to distinguish the various stocks of people indigenous to the Mekong,[10] the Indian Ocean, the Pacific. Hue, eye size and slant, bone structure, hairline. But looking round the deck, he was forced to frown again. For other than the Frenchwoman and other obvious Europeans, everyone looked like the Indians from Minnesota or the Hawaiians on TV or the Mexicans recently moved into his daughter's neighborhood. The children's eyes didn't even have a hint of slant. He thought of the two colored children who'd gone to his son's high school. Did their eyes suddenly slant after graduation?

The pilot pulled his cap down to watch undetected the fat man by the coil of ropes, leaning into the wind looking like an ancient Victory from the schoolbooks or the statue winging the grill of the Mercedes below deck. It was the landlord from his district, impatient to get back to civilization. The landlord who made the crossing once a year at election time, who would arrive in the district in traditional dress, the incongruous leather shoes mocking the ploy. The press at his elbow, his assistants assembling the people, he would promise an irrigation pump and the new road once more. The press out of earshot, he would threaten to evict the farmers from the land.

Prodded by the landlord's assistants, the people would line up to shake the fat hand, to deposit their votes on yellow slips of paper into his beefy paw. Then stepping back, he would turn and march with his entourage back to the jetty. He was now returning to the city in the Western suit worn under the costume, his Mercedes below deck with the tithes of rice and chickens he always collected, the sticky black boxes the tribesmen brought down from the hills, the sacks of grain for brew the landlord himself had outlawed in the district.

The pilot clenched his jaws and gripped the wheel rather than crash through the cabin window and throttle the fat man. No impulsive actions, the cadres had cautioned the people. Timing and patience, collective push, discipline. It would be a long war, had been a long war. The pilot could not remember a time of peace except in the words of the old songs. But soon the people would confront the rich grown fat off the blood and bones of the people. Would accuse them face to face in the people's tribunals. It was just a matter of time and the reign of terror would be over and life could start anew. The landlords, the war lords, the imperialists were no match for the force of the people, the force of justice, once the people moved together.

The pilot yanked his cap lower and straightened over the wheel. He could be patient. The leaders spoke wisdom to the people and shared their hardships. And he would do his part, no longer envious of their leadership. He watched the churning waters, proud of his part in history. For as the master pilot often said to him, it's not the water in front that pulls the river along. It's the rear guard that is the driving force.

The pilot thought of the rear guard. Thought of the widow woman who hid the cadres in her storage sheds and under her hut, who cooked for the young men of the district, proud in her hatred for the enemy, proud in her love for the country and the nation coming soon. She was doing her part filling up the quivers with new arrows, rosining the twine for the crossbow, stirring in the pot where the poison brewed.

And no one told her any more that that was no way to defend the district, not against B-52's and F 1104's, incendiary gels and M-16's. No one told her that any more, not after she had ambushed the soldiers who'd penetrated their line. No one told her, for the widow woman had and would again, had been taught she could and should by the fighters before her cutting arrows in the crawl space under the huts of old, sharpening arrowheads by the light of trapped-firefly lanterns, chanting the war songs and the old prayers and the new creeds of allegiance to a new day, urging the children to hurry with the branches, the branches and the mud hens, for an offering had to be burned on the temple steps. No one told the widow woman not to, even now when the temple steps were green-black with soil mold, slick with greasy votives. For the widow woman was the vessel of the old stratagems, a walking manual, having lost a grandfather, a father, six uncles, four sons, two husbands, and a daughter to the French, the Japanese, the Americans. No one told her not to, for the district was too busy listening as she related, stirring in the pots, how the people of old planted stakes in the waters to ensnare and wreck the enemy ships.

The pilot looked away from the water and back to the landlord. Watched him hard till his image faded and the vision of the women of old feeding arrows into the men's quivers blurred with the image of the young girls of his district feeding bullet belts into the guns.

What sounded like the twang of a bowstring made the pilot twist round toward the back of the boat. Strained heads lifted passengers from the benches, eager to see for themselves what the frenzied woman and the little girl were doing. With wire from her unbound hair, the mother of the girl whipped in slashing motions, slicing rust from the rails, ripping feathers from the birds, making siren sounds with the wire that recalled for most aboard the long nights of shelling. Two students leaned their packs against the side railings and rushed forward stamping, flapping their jackets, bellowing the birds away. In a scatter the birds flew off.

Birds will get vicious when they're fed and then rejected, thought the researcher, fishing out a pen to take notes. People as well, he mused, then nodded agreement with the notion. The chaotic situation in the country was just that: natives supported by foreign aid, sustained, educated, taught a superior way of life, strike out in adolescent pique when abandoned. "The Dependency Complex of the Colored Peoples," he wrote. It did occur to him that the natives had first banded together, struck out, and then drove the aid away. But who could trust poorly trained native journalists to keep events in order?

The researcher had done a study at home of the Afro-Brazilian personality that had won him a university chair and accolades from people that mattered. But jealous colleagues had written scathing critiques of the book, challenging him to evaluate his profile of the African, Indian, and Latin character in light of what had emerged in revolutionary Cuba.

"Could be, my friend, that you've confused the coping mechanisms of the oppressed with racial character," Professor Amado had said over sherry. The snide remark of other most esteemed colleagues still ringing in his ears now left him stinging in his clothes despite the cold wind chafing his neck.

"Dependency Complex," he underlined twice, slicing through the index cards he used for notes. Fatalistic, lazy, irresponsible, no sense of time. It was true throughout the colored world. It explained those people's condition of poverty.

Rows of dark, sleepy faces swam before his eyes: the dock workers he had interviewed, the fisherfolk, the beggars, the servants at his in-laws' estate, the vagabonds in the cities. He examined the faces, the postures, the mien of passengers on board, tucking his feet under the bench as the woman with the blowing hair ushered the little girl past. "Fed, then abandoned, birds and people will attack," he wrote, planning his next book and his counter-remarks for the most esteemed Professor Amado.

The mother led the girl back to their seats, the passengers along the way grabbing the small hand and leading the child to the next hand outstretched. The mother kept her head down, waiting for the brown leather shoes that marked their places next. She sat, her unbound hair hard to gather up with the wind sweeping under the tin roofing. The little girl raised up on her knees and caught up the billowing hair in bunches, and the mother secured it at last with the wire.

The gentleman in brown shoes kept his eyes all the while averted, tried not to notice when the hair blew all over his shoulder and chest, giving him a wayward beard. He stared up at the corrugated tin roofing so like the poorer houses in his district. Tin sheets held together with rusted bolts no longer holding against the wind. Nothing these days was holding against the winds, thinking of his family scattered. One son lost to Coca-Cola and bell-bottoms, hair so long the gentleman was ashamed to call him kin. Another son gone underground and no word sent in years and years. His unmarried sister leaving his household without his permission, dreams of Paris, London, and New York salons taking her off, defying his authority, rejecting the suitor so carefully selected, so carefully groomed by the two families in question. The outraged family invading his home, backing him up against the piles of fashion magazines abandoned by his sister. He with no bride to offer and no face left.

His mealtimes of late explosive scenes, the magazines flung across the room upsetting the bowls and his digestion. White-faced models in Asian fashions asprawl on the floor and his daughter screaming.

"What cannibals," kicking at the faces in the book. "Occidental cadavers draped in the clothing of the dead. The murdered dead. In the skin of the dead. Our dead they murdered, disemboweled, then they stepped into the skins. Look, look," his daughter would demand, bringing the magazines to the table. "Look what they've done to their eyes," jabbing her finger. He no longer said she was a fool to get so upset over Occidentals who chose to draw dark slants on their eyes. It only made her wild. There was no peace in his house any more, no calm. Each day, each meal, his daughter became a hurricane uncontained, blowing his composure apart.

Then his daughter, without his permission, joined the women's union and the women's detachment of the band who called themselves the People's Army.[11] Leaving home each morning to hop a truck with other brazen women to work at the salt flats, or shoot guns in the woods, or pitch manure for the forbidden co-op farms downriver. She would argue with him, shout into his face, call him feudal, fool, collaborator, corrupt. And he would go back into the house breathless. And never once these days did his wife say he was right. She was all but mute and seemingly paralyzed, for she made no move to censure the wild daughter.

The gentleman in brown shoes squinted up at the slits of sky, wondering if the roof would hold or fly off, the bolts no match for the irresistible winds. His authority no match for the hurricane that was his daughter. His sovereignty dissolved like the near-worthless currency he carried strapped around his belly, waterlogged in the money belt, having been stashed in the well, hidden from the soldiers and the people's militia. It had mildewed. And despite the drying by the fire, the money never seemed to recover. He was off to the city now uncomfortable to try to float a loan on damp collateral and rebuild his household. What was to become of him now that his seed was scattered in the winds? Who would manage the land, keep up the line, the traditions? Not the transistor-radio son who stayed in the movie houses now. His wife was far too old for further family. He wondered if indeed he should find a new wife and start again.

The little girl smoothed her mother's hair back from her temples and wondered if the gentleman was tipping away because of the boat's lurching or because of them. She felt a quivering in her mother's body and feared that any minute her mother might bolt from her grasp, thrash about on the deck, pitch herself over the side. At night sometimes, the girl would awaken to her mother's reliving of the torture. Memory surging through her body as she rolled around on the floor, banging down the chairs, doubling up tightly, then springing apart as though taunted by an electric prod, hands tight between her legs protecting what'd been violated.

"Nothing," she'd moan. "I'll tell you nothing," her head jerking as though some unseen hand had her by the hair. "You'll never break our spirits. We cannot be defeated."

"Nothing. I'll tell you nothing . . ." Over and over, louder and louder, thrashing about on the hard-swept dirt floor, flinging away into the walls the women who rushed in from the next hut but could never hold her down and only sometimes could shove a bit of wood between her teeth to keep her from swallowing her own tongue.

"Nothing. I'll tell you nothing." The girl might manage to get her mother's head up off the floor and into her lap. "You'll never break our spirits," soothing the temples. "We cannot be defeated," rocking, rocking.

The little girl continued her brushing and smoothing, wondering if the gentleman could be relied upon if her mother bolted. If she herself didn't panic, she would demand he jump to aid the minute the first words were blurted out. "Nothing. I'll tell you nothing." It would take nimble timing, for often the bourgeoisie would not touch the miserable shoeless. "You'll never break our spirit." But then the engine was switched off and her mother relaxed, looking over the side, her face full in the wind. "We cannot be defeated." It had been the vibrations of the boat, the girl concluded, that had made her mother shiver. It had been the lurching of rough waters that had tipped the gentleman away from them.

The mother grasped her daughter's hand and avoided looking just yet at the gathering on the landing. She watched instead the women pounding clothes on the rocks, shooing mud hens from the wash, chasing the pigs from the soap. Workers from the textile plant farther down were spreading strips of newly dyed cloth across the grass to dry. Around tents of mosquito netting humped over bamboo poles, women and young girls moved in a circle, stitching up the hems, moving round and round as in the country dances of old. Closer by, some workers round the braziers huddled, coaxing brochettes and threading wild onions and hunks of mud hens on twigs while an old woman at a separate fire watched the rice boil up.

Rising slowly, the mother wound a bit of cloth into a coil for her head. The gentleman helped her hoist the bundles onto the coil, stepping back fast when their hands touched in her hair. The deck shivered violently when the lower ramp clanked down, and she lost her balance against his body that was there then wasn't there. She held her daughter's shoulder as the oxen loped off from the deck below, cyclists weaving in and out among the porters unloading crates and sacks and the sticky black boxes that caused murmurs, the trucks sputtering in the wet sand then honking people out of the way. When the top ramp banged down, she steadied herself against her daughter, and they followed the soldier off; he then quickly joined a group of uniformed men by a cement bunker from a war before.

The taxi driver rushed forward to grab the American's luggage. He wrestled the handbags from the Frenchwoman, collared everybody in shoes. Gabbing loudly in snatches of this language and that, he loaded suitcases onto his humpback taxi, stuffing, jamming the bags into the rack. He ticked off the meter in his mind, not sure just yet how to stuff and jam the owners of the luggage into the car. Once more he brushed by the weighted-down woman and the stumbling girl to check the suspicious-looking young man with the hard brown face. There was something about him, a look he had seen before. A look that could mean money. He studied the young man's tracks in the sand, and his meter jumped. Rubber treads from downed American planes. Ho Chi Minh[12] sandals. Just in from the border. Tall, brown, thin, hard, thirty or so. Someone might pay plenty even in the dwindling market these days of revolution. The driver crowded five into his humpback taxi and sped off, already peddling the information in his mind.

A young boy with a wheelbarrow had been studying the passengers, on the watch for shoes with big heels that could mean smuggling and might mean a meal for him, on watch for baskets with false bottoms that might mean new clothes for him if the tip paid off. He wheeled among the workers gathered at the landing for news of the downriver districts, just as he daily wheeled among the civil servants gathered at the airport for news of the world. Other people on the landing were there to greet relatives, come to squeeze into already overcrowded rooms in the city.

No shoes or baskets worth noting, the barrow boy shifted his attention to the squat woman in the straw hat who seemed to be waiting for the crowd to disperse before approaching the woman with the bundle on her head and the little girl overloaded with smaller bundles. He recognized the squat woman in the conical hat. She worked at the Imperial Palace, which some joked would be called the People's Palace soon. She shined shoes in the arcade, boiled sheets out back, served coffee in the rooms, and seemed to be ever out walking—no doubt involved in something clandestine, something worth uncovering. Rebel or paid informer, he hadn't decided. He had been told to simply keep his eyes open.

He watched the two women meet and speak. The squat one using her straw hat to fan then shield the other from the sun. The boy wheeled his barrow in closer, for they would be needing him for the bundles. The wind blew their words the other way, so he moved in closer still and began loading up.

"a good girl   used to hard work . . ."

"in good hands   don't worry   will not be abused . . ."

"a permit for my husband's release   soon the family will be reunited   Can you find room for our things?"

"Soon the country will be free," the squat woman was saying, looking directly into his mouth. "Then we'll all be reunited."

"news of your son   alive though sickly   consumption damp cells and   and your baby?"

"Dead."

The barrow boy awaited instructions, looking from the mother to the girl to the squat woman from the Imperial Palace Hotel.

The mother bent and embraced her daughter, then quickly turned and trotted back up the boat ramp. For a moment the girl felt the breeze from her mother's leave-taking more strongly than the currents off the bay. But soon the wind picked up again as the boat eased out. The wind weighted with soap from the washerwomen was heavy on her, enclasping her, jamming up her nose.

At the precinct bunker, they'd stuffed hoses up her nose and pumped in soapy water, fish brine, water from the district's sewer till her belly swelled up, bloated to near bursting. Then they beat her with the poles, sticks, rods of bamboo, some iron till she vomited, nearly drowning. She told them nothing. Heard none of their questions, her own prayers too loud in her ears to hear anything but her own hopes that her brothers did not betray the cadres in the cellars, in the temples, in the woods.

Coming to on a ribbed floor, the door of the metal cage swung wide and the moon spilling in, she smelled the soap again on the uniform of the man in boots who told her her brothers had been freed. She smelled the soap on him and could not move, had to be shoved past the bamboo fence and iron barbs. He had stuffed a pack of food into her arms clutched round her belly. A pack of food wrapped in plantain leaves and elephant ears. A pack she clutched unnoticed all the way home and all the way to the temple, then all the way to the jetty.

Of course she had expected the sea birds to drop down poisoned into the waters. Had not thought they'd live through the food long enough to attack her. She had been caught off-guard so preoccupied, thinking about the soldier in his boots who'd set her free and given her perfectly good food, as it turned out. And pitying him. For what shame would overwhelm him when he reexperienced his natural self and knew once more right from wrong. But that, the elders had taught her in the spring, was the wonderful thing about revolution. It gave one a chance to amend past crimes, to change, to be human. And that is why, the elders had taught her in the rainy season, the youth were so important, for they would prove to the ancestors that it had not been foolish to fight for the right to be free, to be human. And that was why, the elders had taught her in the first crop season, that she herself mattered, that what she did or did not do would matter for the yet unborn.

So in winter when they took her from the schoolhouse and dragged her off for interrogation, she was already an elder in her mind.

The woman from the Imperial Palace walked just behind the barrow boy, looking sadly at his grimy, spare body, wondering who had recruited him and for what, but had not fed him. She took the little girl's hand as she'd been doing for so long, training the youth for the Front.[13] Wondering how she'd look in her vendor apron stationed at the embassies, in the market, at the Exchange, in the hotel lobbies hawking combs, acting as guide, securing information about troop movements. The woman from the hotel tried to keep her mind on the work at hand and the days ahead as the cadres prepared for the liberation of the city. Tried not to fret over the sickly barrow boy with the swollen hands. He may not have a mother, she was thinking, but he certainly has a future.

The barrow boy stole a glance at the girl and the squat woman walking hand in hand at his side now, just one or two paces behind him, so close he knew they could hear him groaning. It wasn't the weight of the barrow that hurt, but the grasping of the handles that shot pain up his arms, down his legs, scattered through his body, lodging hot up under his tongue. He shoved ahead, staring at his greenish puffy hands, wishing instead he walked between them, clasping theirs.

"The Sea Birds Are Still Alive," in *The Sea Birds Are Still Alive: Collected Stories* (New York: Random House, 1977), 71–93.

AMIRI BARAKA

Amiri Baraka (Everett Leroy Jones) was born in Newark, New Jersey in 1934. He has received the American Book Award and for a brief time was the poet laureate of New Jersey. Baraka coined the phrase Black Art as a positive term for the artistic production of black people. The phrase would later become associated with the Black Arts Aesthetics Movement of the 1960s, in which Baraka was a participant. He wrote the poem excerpted below immediately after the terrorists' attacks on the World Trade Center on 11 September 2001. Amiri Baraka died in Newark, New Jersey, on 9 January 2014.

From Somebody Blew Up America[14]

(All thinking people
oppose terrorism
both domestic
& international . . .
But one should not
be used
to cover the other)

They say it's some terrorist, some

   barbaric

    A Rab, in

  Afghanistan

It wasn't our American terrorists
It wasn't the Klan or the Skin heads
Or the them that blows up nigger
Churches, or reincarnates us on Death row

It wasn't Trent Lott[15]
Or David Duke or Giuliani
Or Schundler, Helms retiring

It wasn't
the gonorrhea in costume
the white sheet diseases

That have murdered black people
Terrorized reason and sanity
Most of humanity, as they pleases

They say (who say? Who do the saying)

Who is them paying
Who tell the lies
Who in disguise
Who had the slaves
Who got the bux out the Bucks

Who got fat from plantations
Who genocided Indians
Tried to waste the Black nation

Who live on Wall Street
The first plantation
Who cut your nuts off
Who rape your ma
Who lynched your pa

Who got the tar, who got the feathers
Who had the match, who set the fires
Who killed and hired
Who say they God & still be the Devil [. . .]

Who/ Who/ Who/

Who stole Puerto Rico
Who stole the Indies, the Philippines, Manhattan
Australia & the Hebrides
Who forced Opium on the Chinese [. . .]

Who made Bush president

Who believe the confederate flag need to be flying

Who talk about democracy and be lying

WHO/ WHO/ WHOWHO/ [. . .]

Who cut off peoples hands in the Congo
Who invented Aids Who put the germs
In the Indians' blankets

Who thought up "The Trail of Tears"[16]
Who blew up the Maine
& started the Spanish American War

Who got Sharon back in Power
Who backed Batista, Hitler, Bilbo,
Chiang Kai-shek[17]

who WHO WHO

Who decided Affirmative Action had to go
Reconstruction, The New Deal,
The New Frontier, The Great Society [. . .]

Who WHO Who WHO

Who make money from war

Who make dough from fear and lies
Who want the world like it is
Who want the world to be ruled by imperialism and
National oppression and
terror
violence, and hunger and poverty.

Who is the ruler of Hell?
Who is the most powerful

Who you know ever
                    Seen God
But everybody seen
                    The Devil [. . .]

Excerpted from *Somebody Blew Up America* ([Oakland, Calif.],[18] blackdotpress, 2001).

Related writings by Amiri Baraka: "Letter to Jules Feiffer" (1961); "The Last Days of American Empire (Including Some Instructions for Black People)" (1964); The System of Dante's Hell (1965); *Why Is We Americans?* (2002)

JULIUS W. BECTON JR.

Julius Wesley Becton Jr. was born in 1926 in Pennsylvania. He served in the U.S. army for nearly four decades (1944–1983), retiring as a highly decorated lieutenant general after commanding the VII Corps in Europe during the Cold War. After retiring from the military, Becton continued his career in public service. He was president of his alma mater, Prairie View A&M University (1989–1994), and served as the superintendent of the Washington, D.C., public school district (1996–1998). He has now retired from public life.

"We were pioneers"[19]

When President Truman signed Executive Order 9981[20] in 1948, which ended segregation in the military, I was in the Reserves and in training at Aberdeen Proving Ground in Maryland. I remember the post commander assembled all the officers and he read the order to the assembled group. He then said, "As long as I am commander here, there will be no change."

I wasn't surprised or upset. It was typical Army leadership—Jim Crow and segregation were here to stay. That was the sentiment of the Army at the time. Blacks could not lead. There was not much of anything they would let us do. At that time I was in college studying to be a doctor, but I really didn't want to be one. That was my father's dream. He only had a third-grade education and my mother dropped out in the tenth grade. I was married and expecting a youngster, and my stipend at school was not enough to meet my family obligations or a mortgage. So in 1949 I went back on active duty and was assigned to Fort Bliss, Texas. I was the mess officer.

One time our unit drove from Texas to Fort Bragg in North Carolina. The first night out in Van Horn, Texas, I had to write up a list of supplies. The men had wanted certain things we didn't have. So some of the other officers and I went into a drugstore and started buying what we needed. We spent hundreds of dollars, and the store manager was happy. So I sat down at the counter to eat an ice cream cone and the sheriff, who was in the store, turned pale and said, "Boy, get away from that counter." I was like, Who said that? I turned and saw a great big badge and a .45 on a scrawny little fellow. He then said to my major, "You need to teach that boy something." I paid for the ice cream and left. My major told him that I wasn't from around there and didn't know. But I just wanted to get back to my unit as soon as possible. There was a certain comfort in numbers.

I went to Korea in 1950 with the 2nd Division. It was all white except for two battalions. The black units were pulled out and not deployed with the regiment. We were sent somewhere else. They weren't sure how we would do. They sent us to Pohang-Dong on the east coast and we saw some minor action. Eventually, they sent us back to the regiment because they needed personnel. [...]

I got hit with shrapnel from mortar rounds in the right thigh. There were about eighteen to twenty of us and many of us got hit. I was sent to a hospital in Japan and stayed as little time as I could because there was a rumor we would be home for Christmas. So I rushed and rejoined the regiment at the 38th parallel in Korea, just south of Runari, about thirty miles south of the Yalu River. I was leading an element up a hill and got shot in the Achilles' heel between the tendon and bone. I was very lucky. That wound saved my life, because thirty-six hours later my battalion lost all of its officers except a handful. They were either killed or captured. I was sent back to the hospital in Japan and the nurses said, "Not you again." This time I didn't rush back. It was clear we were not going home for Christmas. The Chinese had entered the war.

I returned in February of 1951. At that time the unit was integrated. No longer was there an effort to keep blacks together. I was the only officer left from the original group and became the company commander. I held that position until I rotated home to Camp Edwards, Massachusetts. Camp Edwards was integrated, but I joined an all-black service unit. Our job was cleaning the post and running the major mess hall. We had about five hundred soldiers and we ran the kitchen, ordered supplies, and followed the master Army menus. None of the other people at the base had been in Korea, and here I was with two Purple Hearts and a Silver Star doing cleaning work. I didn't feel good about that. I had just spent the better part of a year in Korea, in which I was fighting for my county and fighting to prove I was qualified. The president had signed an order basically saying the military was desegregated, and I had come to an all-black mess unit. I knew there was a better way some place, and I was going to find it. I put in for a transfer and got out. I got reassigned to Indiantown Gap Military Reservation[21] and was involved in basic training.

My career kept going along. I was promoted and took every opportunity to learn. During the Vietnam War, I was the commander of the Airborne Cavalry Squadron.

In Vietnam there were not a lot of senior black officers, and that created the wrong impression. About 20 percent of the enlisted men were black, yet less than 10 percent of them were officers. It created the impression that the Army didn't care. [. . .]

When I left Vietnam I was selected to be colonel and sent to the National War College.[22] When I graduated in 1971, there were no black generals. In 1972, I was one of five blacks selected to be brigadier general. I was the first in that group to be promoted and the sixth general in Army history.

I retired in 1983. [. . .] I'm very proud of what I accomplished. We were pioneers. We saw the good and the bad, we saw the Army go from its segregated past to where it is today. Now I can't think of a finer place for black Americans to be.

Excerpted from "Julius W. Becton Jr., Army Lieutenant General, 1944–1983; Army Reserves, 1943, 1946–1948, World War II, Korea, and Vietnam," in *We Were There: Voices of African American Veterans from World War II to the War in Iraq*, edited by Yvonne Latty (New York: Amistad, 2004), 77–81.

JULIAN BOND

Born in 1940 in Nashville, Tennessee, Horace Julian Bond would become one of the founders of the Student Nonviolent Coordinating Committee (SNCC) in 1960, when he was a Morehouse College student in Atlanta. He served as the group's communications director from 1961 to 1966. He also helped found the Southern Poverty Law Center, serving as its president from 1971 to 1979. He would later chair the NAACP (1998–2010). Bond wrote this poem, inspired by Langston Hughes, while still at Morehouse. It was published in 1960 in the first edition of SNCC's newsletter, *The Student Voice*.[23] Julian Bond died 15 August 2015 in Fort Walton Beach, Florida.

I Too, Hear America Singing

I too, hear America singing
  But from where I stand
I can only hear Little Richard
  And Fats Domino.
But sometimes,
I hear Ray Charles
  Drowning in his own tears
  or Bird
Relaxing at Camarillo
  Or Horace Silver doodling,
Then I don't mind standing
  a little longer.

"I Too, Hear America Singing," *The Student Voice*, June 1960, 4.

Lucille Clifton

Thelma Lucille Sayles was born in 1936 in Depew, New York. She studied at Howard University where she met Fred Clifton, the man she would later marry. Among her numerous poetry collections, she has claimed the National Book Award, Pulitzer Prize nominations, and many other literary honors. Her first poetry collection *Good Times* (1969) received notice in the *New York Times*, and her book *Generations: A Memoir* recounts the history of her father's family, tracing their ancestry to Dahomey (present-day Benin). In 1999, Clifton became the chancellor of the Academy of American Poets; she was also the poet laureate of Maryland. Clifton has received other accolades, including an Emmy Award. At the time of her death in 2010, Lucille Clifton lived in Maryland. The excerpt below is from a poem she wrote in response to the terrorists' attacks on 11 September 2001.

From september song: a poem in 7 days[24]

1   tuesday 9/11/01

thunder and lightning and our world
is another place   no day
will ever be the same   no blood
untouched

they know this storm in otherwheres
israel ireland palestine
but God has blessed America
we sing

and God has blessed America
to learn that no one is exempt
the world is one   all fear

is one   all life   all death
all one

2   wednesday 9/12/01

this is not the time
i think
to note the terrorist

inside
who threw the brick
into the mosque
this is not the time
to note
the ones who cursed
Gods other name
the ones who threatened
they would fill the streets
with arab children's blood
and this is not the time
i think
to ask who is allowed to be
american   America
all of us gathered under one flag
praying together safely
warmed by the single love
of the many tongued God [. . .]

4   friday 9/14/01

some of us know
we have never felt safe

all of us   americans
weeping

as some of us have wept
before

is it treason to remember

what have we done
to deserve such villainy

nothing we reassure ourselves
nothing

5 saturday 9/15/01

i know a man who perished for his faith.
others called him infidel, chased him down
and beat him like a dog.   after he died
the world was filled with miracles.
people forgot he was a jew and loved him.
who can know what is intended?   who can understand
the gods? [. . .]

7 monday sundown 9/17/01

Rosh Hashanah

i bear witness to no thing
more human than hate

i bear witness to no thing
more human than love

apples and honey
apples and honey

what is not lost
is paradise

"September Suite" was presented on *Morning Edition*, NPR, 27 August 2002. Excerpted from "september song: a poem in 7 days," *Mercy* (Rochester, N.Y.: BOA Editions, 2004), 43–49.[25]

Related writings by Lucille Clifton: "At Gettysburg" (1989); "At Nagasaki" (1989); "crazy horse instructs his men but in their grief they forget" (1989); "the message of crazy horse" (1989).

Junius Edwards

Junius Edwards was born in 1929 in Alexandria, Louisiana. He served in the Korean War and later attended the University of Oslo in Norway. His writing career took off in 1958 following his receipt of first prize in the *Writer's Digest* short story contest. In 1959, Edwards received the Eugene F. Saxton Fellowship for Creative Writing, which resulted in several short stories and a novel on the Korean War. Edwards's novel, *If We Must Die* (1963), expands the story reprinted here. When he died in 2008, Junius Edwards was living in New York City, where he had owned an advertising agency.

Liars Don't Qualify[26]

Will Harris sat on the bench in the waiting room for another hour. His pride was not the only thing that hurt. He wanted them to call him in and get him registered so he could get out of there. Twice, he started to go into the inner office and tell them, but he thought better of it. He had counted ninety-six cigarette butts on the floor when a fat man came out of the office and spoke to him.

"What you want, boy?"

Will Harris got to his feet.

"I came to register."

"Oh, you did, did you?"

"Yes sir."

The fat man stared at Will for a second, then turned his back to him.

As he turned his back, he said, "Come on in here."

Will went in.

It was a little office and dirty, but not so dirty as the waiting room. There were no cigarette butts on the floor here. Instead, there was paper. They looked like candy wrappers to Will. There were two desks jammed in there, and a bony little man sat at one of them, his head down, his fingers fumbling with some papers. The fat man went around the empty desk and pulled up a chair. The bony man did not look up.

Will stood in front of the empty desk and watched the fat man sit down behind it. The fat man swung his chair around until he faced the little man.

"Charlie," he said.

"Yeah, Sam," Charlie said, not looking up from his work.

"Charlie. This boy here says he come to register."

"You sure? You sure that's what he said, Sam?" Still not looking up. "You sure? You better ask him again, Sam."

"I'm sure, Charlie."

"You better be sure, Sam."

"All right, Charlie. All right. I'll ask him again," the fat man said. He looked up at Will. "Boy. What you come here for?"

"I came to register."

The fat man stared up at him. He didn't say anything. He just stared, his lips a thin line, his eyes wide open. His left hand searched behind him and came up with a handkerchief. He raised his left arm and mopped his face with the handkerchief, his eyes still on Will.

The odor from under his sweat-soaked arm made Will step back. Will held his breath until the fat man finished mopping his face. The fat man put his handkerchief away. He pulled a desk drawer open, and then he took his eyes off Will. He reached in the desk drawer and took out a bar of candy. He took the wrapper off the candy and threw the wrapper on the floor at Will's feet. He looked at Will and ate the candy.

Will stood there and tried to keep his face straight. He kept telling himself: I'll take anything. I'll take anything to get it done.

The fat man kept his eyes on Will and finished the candy.

He took out his handkerchief and wiped his mouth. He grinned, then he put his handkerchief away.

"Charlie." The fat man turned to the little man.

"Yeah, Sam."

"He says he come to register."

"Sam, are you sure?"

"Pretty sure, Charlie."

"Well, explain to him what it's about." The bony man still had not looked up.

"All right, Charlie," Sam said, and looked up at Will.

"Boy, when folks come here, they intend to vote, so they register first."

"That's what I want to do," Will said.

"What's that? Say that again."

"That's what I want to do. Register and vote."

The fat man turned his head to the bony man.

"Charlie."

"Yeah, Sam."

"He says . . . Charlie, this boy says that he wants to register and vote."

The bony man looked up from his desk for the first time. He looked at Sam, then both of them looked at Will.

Will looked from one of them to the other, one to the other. It was hot, and he wanted to sit down. *Anything. I'll take anything.*

The man called Charlie turned back to his work, and Sam swung his chair around until he faced Will.

"You got a job?" he asked.

"Yes, sir."

"Boy, you know what you're doing?"

"Yes, sir."

"All right," Sam said. "All right."

Just then, Will heard the door open behind him, and someone came in. It was a man.

"How you all'! How about registering?"

Sam smiled. Charlie looked up and smiled.

"Take care of you right away," Sam said, and then to Will. "Boy. Wait outside."

As Will went out, he heard Sam's voice: "Take a seat, please. Take a seat. Have you fixed up in a little bit. Now, what's your name?"

"Thanks," the man said, and Will heard the scrape of a chair.

Will closed the door and went back to his bench.

Anything. Anything. Anything. I'll take it all.

Pretty soon the man came out smiling. Sam came out behind him, and he called Will and told him to come in. Will went in and stood before the desk. Sam told him he wanted to see his papers: Discharge, High School Diploma, Birth Certificate, Social Security Card, and some other papers. Will had them all. He felt good when he handed them to Sam.

"You belong to any organization?"

"No, sir."

"Pretty sure about that?"

"Yes, sir."

"You ever heard of the 15th Amendment?"

"Yes, sir."

"What does that one say?"

"It's the one that says all citizens can vote."

"You like that, don't you, boy? Don't you?"

"Yes, sir. I like them all."

Sam's eyes got big. He slammed his right fist down on his desk top. "I didn't ask you that. I asked you if you liked the 15th Amendment. Now, if you can't answer my questions . . ."

"I like it," Will put in, and watched Sam catch his breath.

Sam sat there looking up at Will. He opened and closed his desk-pounding fist. His mouth hung open.

"Charlie."

"Yeah, Sam." Not looking up.

"You hear that?" looking wide-eyed at Will. "You hear that?"

"I heard it, Sam."

Will had to work to keep his face straight.

"Boy," Sam said. "You born in this town?"

"You got my birth certificate right there in front of you. Yes, sir."

"You happy here?"

"Yes, sir."

"You got nothing against the way things go around here?"

"No, sir."

"Can you read?"

"Yes, sir."

"Are you smart?"

"No, sir."

"Where did you get that suit?"

"New York."

"New York?" Sam asked, and looked over at Charlie. Charlie's head was still down. Sam looked back to Will.

"Yes, sir," said Will.

"Boy, what you doing there?"

"I got out of the Army there."[27]

"You believe in what them folks do in New York?"

"I don't know what you mean."

"You know what I mean. Boy, you know good and well what I mean. You know how folks carry on in New York. You believe in that?"

"No, sir," Will said, slowly.

"You pretty sure about that?"

"Yes, sir."

"What year did they make the 15th Amendment?"

" . . . 18 . . . 70," said Will.

"Name a signer of the Declaration of Independence who became President."

" . . . John Adams."

"Boy, what did you say?" Sam's eyes were wide again.

Will thought for a second. Then he said, "John Adams."

Sam's eyes got wider. He looked to Charlie and spoke to a bowed head, "Now, too much is too much." Then he turned back to Will.

He didn't say anything to Will. He narrowed his eyes first, then spoke. "Did you say *just* John Adams?"

"*Mister* John Adams," Will said, realizing his mistake.

"That's more like it," Sam smiled. "Now, why do you want to vote?"

"I want to vote because it is my duty as an American citizen to vote,"

"Hah," Sam said, real loud. "Hah," again, and pushed back from his desk and turned to the bony man.

"Charlie."

"Yeah, Sam."

"Hear that?"

"I heard, Sam."

Sam leaned back in his chair, keeping his eyes on Charlie. He locked his hands across his round stomach and sat there.

"Charlie."

"Yeah, Sam."

"Think you and Elnora be coming over tonight?"

"Don't know, Sam," said the bony man, not looking up. "You know Elnora."

"Well, you welcome if you can."

"Don't know, Sam."

"You ought to, if you can. Drop in, if you can. Come on over and we'll split a corn whisky."

The bony man looked up.

"Now, that's different, Sam."

"Thought it would be."

"Can't turn down corn if it's good."

"You know my corn."

"Sure do. I'll drag Elnora. I'll drag her by the hair if I have to."

The bony man went back to work.

Sam turned his chair around to his desk. He opened a desk drawer and took out a package of cigarettes. He tore it open and put a cigarette in his mouth. He looked up at Will, then he lit the cigarette and took a long drag, and then he blew the smoke, very slowly, up toward Will's face.

The smoke floated up toward Will's face. It came up in front of his eyes and nose and hung there, then it danced and played around his face and disappeared.

Will didn't move, but he was glad he hadn't been asked to sit down.

"You have a car?"

"No, sir."

"Don't you have a job?"

"Yes, sir."

"You like that job?"

"Yes, sir,"

"You like it, but you don't want it."

"What do you mean?" Will asked.

"Don't get smart, boy," Sam said, wide-eyed. "I'm asking the questions here. You understand that?"

"Yes, sir."

"All right. All right. Be sure you do."

"I understand it."

"You a Communist?"

"No, sir."

"What party do you want to vote for?"

"I wouldn't go by parties. I'd read about the men and vote for a man, not a party."

"Hah," Sam said, and looked over at Charlie's bowed head. "Hah," he said again, and turned back to Will.

"Boy, you pretty sure you can read?"

"Yes, sir."

"All right. All right. We'll see about that." Sam took a book out of his desk and flipped some pages. He gave the book to Will.

"Read that loud," he said.

"Yes, sir," Will said, and began: "'When in the course of human events, it becomes necessary for one people to dissolve the political bands which have connected them with another, and to assume among the powers of the earth the separate and equal station to which the Laws of Nature and of Nature's God entitle them, a decent respect to the opinions of mankind requires that they should declare the causes which impel them to the separation.'"

Will cleared his throat and read on. He tried to be distinct with each syllable. He didn't need the book. He could have recited the whole thing without the book.

"'We hold these truths to be self-evident, that all men are created equal, that they . . . '"

"Wait a minute, boy," Sam said. "Wait a minute. You believe that? You believe that about 'created equal'?"

"Yes, sir," Will said, knowing that was the wrong answer.

"You really believe that?"

"Yes, sir." Will couldn't make himself say the answer Sam wanted to hear.

Sam stuck out his right hand, and Will put the book in it. Then Sam turned to the other man.

"Charlie."

"Yeah, Sam."

"Charlie, did you hear that?"

"What was it, Sam?"

"This boy, here, Charlie. He says he really believes it."

"Believes what, Sam? What you talking about?"

"This boy, here . . . believes that all men are equal, like it says in The Declaration."

"Now, Sam. Now you know that's not right. You know good and well that's not right. You heard him wrong. Ask him again, Sam. Ask him again, will you?"

"I didn't hear him wrong, Charlie," said Sam, and turned to Will. "Did I, boy? Did I hear you wrong?"

"No, sir."

"I didn't hear you wrong?"

"No, sir."

Sam turned to Charlie.

"Charlie."

"Yeah, Sam."

"Charlie. You think this boy trying to be smart?"

"Sam. I think he might be. Just might be. He looks like one of them that don't know his place."

Sam narrowed his eyes.

"Boy," he said. "You know your place?"

"I don't know what you mean."

"Boy, you know good and well what I mean."

"What do you mean?"

"Boy, who's . . ." Sam leaned forward, on his desk. "Just who's asking questions, here?"

"You are, sir."

"Charlie. You think he really is trying to be smart?"

"Sam, I think you better ask him."

"Boy."

"Yes, sir."

"Boy. You trying to be smart with me?"

"No, sir."

"Sam."

"Yeah, Charlie."

"Sam. Ask him if he thinks he's good as you and me."

"Now, Charlie. Now, you heard what he said about The Declaration."

"Ask, anyway, Sam."

All right," Sam said. "Boy. You think you good as me and Mister Charlie?"

"No, sir," Will said.

They smiled, and Charlie turned away.

Will wanted to take off his jacket. It was hot, and he felt a drop of sweat roll down his right side. He pressed his right arm against his side to wipe out the sweat. He thought he had it, but it rolled again, and he felt another drop come behind that one. He pressed his arm in again. It was no use. He gave it up.

"How many stars did the first flag have?"

"... Thirteen."

"What's the name of the mayor of this town?"

"... Mister Roger Phillip Thornedyke Jones."

"Spell Thornedyke."

"... Capital T-h-o-r-n-e-d-y-k-e, Thornedyke."

"How long has he been mayor?"

"... Seventeen years."

"Who was the biggest hero in the War Between the States?"

"... General Robert E. Lee."

"What does that 'E' stand for?"

"... Edward."

"Think you pretty smart, don't you?"

"No, sir."

"Well, boy, you have been giving these answers too slow. I want them fast. Understand? Fast."

"Yes, sir."

"What's your favorite song?"

"*Dixie*," Will said, and prayed Sam would not ask him to sing it.

"Do you like your job?"

"Yes, sir."

"What year did Arizona come into the States?"

"1912."

"There was another state in 1912."

"New Mexico, it came in January and Arizona in February."

"You think you smart, don't you?"

"No, sir."

"Don't you think you smart? Don't you?"

"No, sir."

"Oh, yes, you do, boy."

Will said nothing.

"Boy, you make good money on your job?"

"I make enough."

"Oh. Oh, you not satisfied with it?"

"Yes, sir. I am."

"You don't act like it, boy. You know that? You don't act like it."

"What do you mean?"

"You getting smart again, boy. Just who's asking questions here?"

"You are, sir."

"That's right. That's right."

The bony man made a noise with his lips and slammed his pencil down on his desk. He looked at Will, then at Sam.

"Sam," he said. "Sam, you having trouble with that boy? Don't you let that boy give you no trouble, now, Sam. Don't you do it."

"Charlie," Sam said. "Now, Charlie, you know better than that. You know better. This boy here knows better than that, too."

"You sure about that, Sam? You sure?"

"I better be sure if this boy here knows what's good for him."

"Does he know, Sam?"

"Do you know, boy?" Sam asked Will.

"Yes, sir."

Charlie turned back to his work.

"Boy," Sam said. "You sure you're not a member of any organization?"

"Yes, sir. I'm sure."

Sam gathered up all Will's papers, and he stacked them very neatly and placed them in the center of his desk. He took the cigarette out of his mouth and put it out in the full ash tray. He picked up Will's papers and gave them to him.

"You've been in the Army. That right?"

"Yes, sir."

"You served two years. That right?"

"Yes, sir."

"You have to do six years in the Reserve. That right?"

"Yes, sir."

"You're in the Reserve now. That right?"

"Yes, sir."

"You lied to me here, today. That right?"

"No, sir."

"Boy, I said you lied to me here today. That right?"

"No, sir."

"Oh, yes, you did, boy. Oh, yes, you did. You told me you wasn't in any organization. That right?"

"Yes, sir."

"Then you lied, boy, You lied to me because you're in the Army Reserve. That right?"

"Yes, sir. I'm in the Reserve, but I didn't think you meant that. I'm just in it, and don't have to go to meetings or anything like that. I thought you meant some kind of civilian organization."

"When you said you wasn't in an organization, that was a lie. Now, wasn't it, boy?"

He had Will there. When Sam had asked him about organizations, the first thing to pop in Will's mind had been the communists, or something like them.

"Now, wasn't it a lie?"

"No, sir."

Sam narrowed his eyes.

Will went on.

"No, sir, it wasn't a lie. There's nothing wrong with the Army Reserve. Everybody has to be in it. I'm not in it because I want to be in it."

"I know there's nothing wrong with it," Sam said. "Point is, you lied to me here, today."

"I didn't lie. I just didn't understand the question," Will said.

"You understood the question, boy. You understood good and well, and you lied to me. Now, wasn't it a lie?"

"No, sir."

"Boy. You going to stand right there in front of me big as anything and tell me it wasn't a lie?" Sam almost shouted. "Now, wasn't it a lie?"

"Yes, sir," Will said, and put his papers in his jacket pocket.

"You right, it was," Sam said.

Sam pushed back from his desk.

"That's it, boy. You can't register. You don't qualify. Liars don't qualify."

"But . . ."

"That's it." Sam spat the words out and looked at Will hard for a sound, and then he swung his chair around until he faced Charlie.

"Charlie."

"Yeah, Sam."

"Charlie. You want to go out to eat first today?"

Will opened the door and went out. As he walked down the stairs he took off his jacket and his tie and opened his collar and rolled up his shirt sleeves. He stood on the courthouse steps and took a deep breath and heard a noise come from his throat as he breathed out and looked at the flag in the court yard. The flag hung from its staff, still and quiet, the way he hated to see it; but it was there, waiting, and he hoped that a little push from the right breeze would lift it and send it flying and waving and whipping from its staff, proud, the way he liked to see it.

He took out a cigarette and lit it and took a slow deep drag. He blew the smoke out. He saw the cigarette burning in his right hand, turned it between his thumb and forefinger, made a face, and let the cigarette drop to the court-house steps.

He threw his jacket over his left shoulder and walked on down to the bus stop, swinging his arms.

"Liars Don't Qualify," *Urbanite: Images of the American Negro* 1, no. 4 (June 1961): 18–19, 32–33.

Related writing by Junius Edwards: *If We Must Die* (1963).

MICHAEL S. HARPER

Michael S. Harper was born in Brooklyn, New York, in 1938. He was a prolific poet and the recipient of a Guggenheim fellowship and other awards. Harper taught at Brown University from 1970 to 2013. He published a number of poetry collections including *Dear John, Dear Coltrane* (1970), *History Is Your Heartbeat* (1971), which won the poetry award from Black Academy of Arts and Letters, and *Songlines in Michaeltree: New and Collected Poems* (2000). He edited *The Collected Poems of Sterling Brown* (1980) and co-edited *Chant of Saints: A Gathering of Afro-American Literature, Art, and Scholarship*. From 1988–1993, Michael Harper was the first poet laureate of Rhode Island. He died 7 May 2016 in Rhinebeck, New York.

American History

Those four black girls blown up
in that Alabama church[28]
remind me of five hundred
middle passage[29] blacks,
in a net, under water
in Charleston harbor
so redcoats[30] wouldn't find them.
Can't find what you can't see
can you?

"American History," in *Dear John, Dear Coltrane* (Pittsburgh: University of Pittsburgh Press, 1970), 62.

ROBERT E. HOLCOMB

Army Specialist 4 Robert E. Holcomb served in the army after he was arrested for refusing to report for the draft during the War in Vietnam. He held antiwar views, shaped by the Black Liberation/Black Power movement and the burgeoning antiwar sentiments in the nation. Holcomb participated in Wallace Terry's oral history project on African Americans in the war. His account appears in Terry's *Bloods* (1984).

"I was sworn into the Army in manacles"[31]

The FBI was on a rampage looking for me. Around the Fourth of July 1969. So I called the FBI and I told them I was out on the Long Island Expressway. And they came and picked me up and put me in manacles again. Then they took me to Whitehall Street, where everybody in New York City gets inducted.

One of the agents said, "Holcomb, this time we're gonna make sure you take the oath so in case this time you leave, you'll be a problem for the Army and not us. We don't wanna be bothered with you anymore."

They took me inside to say the oath, and I refused. So they took me outside.

The other agent said, "Listen, Bob, if you don't say the oath, we're gonna lock you up forever. You just won't be seen around anymore."

So I said, "All right." And we went back inside.

I raised my hands and said the oath.

I was sworn into the Army in manacles.

Then the agents took the manacles off, and they left. It was really a strange scene. Because there were a lot of very young Spanish guys who were very proud to be getting inducted into the Marine Corps while this was going on with me. They were excited about becoming Marines and getting to wear that uniform. They couldn't understand me. They thought I was a degenerate or something. But they didn't say anything. They just stayed as far away from me as they could.

I had evaded the draft for more than a year, but my antiwar views were shaped long before, while I was a student at Tennessee State University.

After two semesters at Indiana University, I transferred to Tennessee State in Nashville to get farther away from home. I was rebelling from the middle-class values and way of life my parents, both schoolteachers, were grooming me in. I think my first protest came in a march for civil rights that Martin Luther King had organized back home in Gary when I was a junior in high school. I had printed a huge sign to carry in the march. From the time I could hold a pencil, I was always drawing something. The sign said, "*Nunc Es Tempos*." "Now is the time."

Tennessee State was a hotbed of social and political unrest in the mid-sixties. Black awareness was on the rise. People like Nikki Giovanni, Kathleen Cleaver, and Rap Brown[32] would be on campus and join our marches. We staged sit-ins at the governor's office and mansion, protesting poor living conditions for black people in the state, some of whom lacked food, decent shelter, and even real toilet facilities. We got into Che Guevara's theories on guerilla warfare, read Mao's little red book, and the revolutionary writings of Camus and Jean-Paul Sartre.

We thought the government was gonna begin to be more and more oppressive, especially to black and other minority people. So some of us even took our philosophy to the point that we felt we should arm ourselves and develop skills so that we could survive in the hillsides. We were essentially carrying the student movement into a revolutionary mold.

We wanted the war in Vietnam to cease and desist. We felt that it was an attack on minority people, minority people were being used to fight each other. Some of us would give safe haven to soldiers who went AWOL from Fort Campbell, Kentucky, because they did not want to go to Vietnam. They would hope to stay around the college campus scene until things just blew away. But they wouldn't blow away. You had to do something about it; otherwise, they'd be following you for the rest of your life.

I was arrested for violations of curfew after a riot. And for that and other infractions of school policies aimed at stopping protests, I was expelled. As tensions between the police and the black community continued to rise, I decided to leave Nashville. I just had the feeling that I was under surveillance and one day I'd be walking down the street and someone would roll down his window and I would be shot. The revolution I left behind petered out like it did everywhere else. [...]

I decided to move to New York to continue my art study. Soon afterwards, I got a draft letter. At that point, I decided that I was gonna resist, because I didn't believe in the war. I had read tons of books about the war, including literature from Cuba and from China and from Hanoi itself, material that had filtered here through Canada and other sources. Wars are only fought over property, really. And the war in Vietnam was basically about economics. As I saw it, we were after a foothold in a small country in the Orient with rubber plantations, rice, timber, and possibly oil. And the people. A cheap source of labor, like you have in Hong Kong and Taiwan, making designer jeans and the insides of TV sets. That's what I understood the war to be about—a war that was not really for the many but for the few. I didn't have any problems fighting for capitalism, but I was not interested in fighting for a war in which I would not enjoy the rewards.

I considered the conscientious objector status, but I couldn't do that because I was not a religious fanatic. I decided that the best thing for me to do would be to leave the country. I was not interested in being locked into Canada. I was not interested in Cuba, because it had a very pure form of socialism and didn't permit the kinds of freedoms that I was accustomed to here. I did not consider myself an African. I was concerned with the better distribution of wealth and authority at home. I never really left the idea of capitalism and the idea of democratic government. I would have gone to a European or African country. [. . .]

My family did not support my ideas, so I really didn't have any support from them. They wanted me to straighten up, perform as I was trained to, forget my ideas about changing the government, and go into the Army. After a while, I was at the point I was no longer in a viable position to do anything constructive with my life, so I decided to turn myself in.

I was charged with draft evasion. The FBI offered me an option. I could work for them as a plant, an informant, or I could go to the service. For two weeks they kept me locked up in the Federal House of Detention hoping to sweat me into working for them. They wanted to plant me within various black or radical groups, like the Black Panthers, the Student Nonviolent Coordinating Committee, and the Symbionese Liberation Army.[33] They said we could start off in New York, but there might be other cities involved. They would provide me with an apartment and with a subsistence allowance. For each person that I helped them capture on an outstanding warrant, they would pay me from $1,000 to $3,000. My questions to them were, Would I get concessions against the charge against me, how long would I have to do it, and would I be permitted to carry an arm to protect myself? They offered no promises of leniency or a time when I could get out. And no, I wouldn't be permitted to carry any kind of weapon. I said no deal. I did not want to fulfill that kind of role, especially unarmed.

Then I went before a federal district court judge and told him I'd prefer to go to war than go to jail or be an informant. He stamped my papers approved to go into the Army.

When they took me to the induction center on Whitehall the first time, the agent said, "You're not gonna go anywhere, are you?"

I said, "No."

He took the manacles off me and left me in the hands of the Army. The Army treated me just as they did any other recruit. They didn't know what my history was. I was free to roam around, so what I did was to roam around and roamed right out of the building. [. . .] After two weeks to rest and recuperate with a friend, I told the FBI to pick me up.

After I finished basic training, they made me a security holdover for two months because they weren't sure whether I'd be subversive to the government in a war situation. I had [. . .] to prove to them that I'd be a loyal trooper and fight for the red, white, and blue. [. . .]

But an odd thing happened before I left Fort Gordon, Georgia. I was training some troops on how to fight with a bayonet. One of them came running down a path to stick the dummy with his bayonet. It was a guy I was in college with who had his ear severely damaged when he was beaten by the Nashville police. I thought to myself they must be taking all of us who were involved in any sort of black political struggle and putting us into the Army as soon as they could so we wouldn't be a problem anymore.

I landed in Cam Ranh Bay[34] in January 1970. It was just a big sand bowl. There was nothing there. It could have been Long Island beach with some nondescript buildings. It could have been the beach in Mexico with some nondescript buildings. It could have been anywhere. The headquarters of the 4th Division in Pleiku[35] seemed the same way. Little Army buildings. A desolate-looking area. Nothing that reflected the difference in the culture of Vietnam. After two days, I told my commanding officer to send me to the field immediately. I was bored. And I wanted to be somewhere where I could get involved more with the Vietnamese people, but not necessarily fighting against them. [. . .]

There were signs the Communists put up in the Ashau Valley which told the black soldier this was not his war. Finally, in the 3rd [regiment] of the 506th [infantry], about 20 black guys refused to go to the field for a good week. They thought more blacks were going to the field, because blacks were less likely to get shot at. They were confined to quarters and threatened with Articles 15[36] until they ended their protest.

A few of us black soldiers were able to get into positions where we could have some freedom, make our lives a little better, even though we were in a war that we didn't really believe in. But most blacks couldn't, because they didn't have the skills. So they were put in the jobs that were the most dangerous, the hardest, or just the most undesirable. A white soldier would probably get a better position. And Hispanic soldiers and Jewish soldiers and Polish soldiers would catch some flak, too. But not as much as a Blood. [. . .] Our unit was called the Black Panthers.

I came home the day after Christmas. When I changed planes in Seattle, I put on some civilian clothes. But I felt so uncomfortable that I put the Army clothes back on. Before I returned to New York, I went to see my parents in Gary. It really made Christmas for 'em. They told me that I was right in protesting the war and that they felt bad telling me to go. Then they made a bed for me upstairs in my old room. But I didn't really feel comfortable sleeping above ground in a bed. So I moved down into a corner of the basement and put everything around my bed. Gun here. Stereo here. All your pot right here. Just like in the war. Then I could go to sleep. [. . .]

I don't think we failed to win the war, because we didn't fight a war. When Ho Chi Minh[37] asked us for help against the French, we should have told him we can't help him militarily against the French but we can use pressure to get the French out. Once the French were gone, we should have dealt with Ho Chi Minh, instead of letting the country get divided and backing puppet government after puppet government which did not work. We would have saved a lot of money, a lot of lives. [. . .]

Excerpted from "Specialist 4: Robert E. Holcomb, New York City," in *Bloods: An Oral History of the Vietnam War by Black Veterans*, edited by Wallace Terry (New York: Random House, 1984), 200–218.

STEPHEN HOPKINS

Stephen Hopkins enlisted in the army, serving in the 1st Battalion, 9th Infantry Regiment in Korea. He was a prisoner of war for three and a half years. His highest rank was army corporal.

"Uncle Sam didn't do much for me. I am proud of my service."[38]

I went into the Army when I was only eighteen. My father died when I was four and my mother raised us during the Depression. I thought it would be a way to bring more money into the house. I joined up a month before the Korean War started and fought for five months before I was caught.

We were on patrol for a couple of days and we had this new captain. He was a gung ho captain who, instead of standing behind us, would lead, so the fellows liked him. This one morning he took the whole company and set us up on a hill and then took a squad of about ten of us to shake up the enemy. [. . .] The ten of us took off across the rice paddy field. When we entered the village we saw what looked like the whole Chinese army. There were about six or seven hundred of them coming out of the village like rodents. We were trapped.

When the company saw the Chinese, they started firing at them, and we were right in the middle. The battle went on for three or four hours. When it was over, we were still stuck in the rice paddy and the Chinese were still there. One by one, a soldier from the Chinese army would walk up to one of us, point a gun to our head, and say something that sounded like "Move," but all the guys hesitated and were shot in the head. When it was my turn, I just got up and did what he said. [. . .]

We marched from winter to spring, and it was so cold. I always thought they were going to get tired of carrying us around and shoot us. By the time we made it to the prison camp, we were burying two to three guys a day. Out of three hundred guys, only about a hundred were left. The guys were dying from just about everything. I was always scared. You never knew if you were going to be taken somewhere and be shot. A couple of guys tried to escape, and you saw the Chinese bash their heads in or shoot them.

Our first job at the camp was to catch fifty flies a day. It seemed silly, but it was for your own good. There were all these flies around, attracted to the open sores. The place was infested. We also had to clear roads and set up makeshift playgrounds where we would go for these lectures, which were propaganda speeches. They would have pictures and films of how the black man was treated in the United States. They would have pictures of lynchings and houses burning and things like that. Then they'd ask you why you wanted to fight for these imperialists. [...]

I had seen hard days, and I think it helped me to survive. When I was growing up, there was never enough to eat. [...] Some of the guys who'd had easier lives would break down. They would do anything to get a cigarette or an extra bit of sugar.

We would cook in a hibachi pit in the barracks and it was always the same thing—cracked corn and sorghum. If a boll weevil fell in the food, at least you got a meat ration. Otherwise we never got any meat. We slept on the floor. [...]

It was joyful when we heard the war was over. They gave us better food so we wouldn't look so bad—we got rice. Fifteen days after the war was over, they let me go. [...]

I've [...] got real bad arthritis. My feet swell up really bad in the summer. When I went to get benefits and things, Uncle Sam didn't do much for me.

I'm proud of my service. It means a lot to me. Every Memorial Day and Veterans Day I march in the parades, and I'm active with the local chapter of the Korean War Veterans Association. You hear a lot of people saying you don't owe this country anything because of your color and what's going on. But I look at it this way: If you live over there and see how people live, it's a blessing to be here.

Excerpted from "Stephen Hopkins, Army Corporal, 1950–1953," in *We Were There: Voices of African American Veterans from World War II to the War in Iraq*, edited by Yvonne Latty (New York: Amistad, 2004), 63–66.

JOHN OLIVER KILLENS

Writer, activist, and educator John Oliver Killens was born in Macon, Georgia in 1916. During World War II, he served in the South Pacific. Killens was among the founders of the Harlem Writers' Guild in 1950 and also founded the National Black Writers Conference in 1986. He was twice nominated for a Pulitzer Prize, first for his World War II era novel *And Then We Heard the Thunder* (1962) and then for his satirical novel of the Black Liberation/Black Power era, *The Cotillion, or One Good Bull Is Half the Herd* (1971). His novel *'Sippi* (1967) focuses on the lack of full citizenship and voting rights for African Americans during the 1950s and 1960s. At the time of his death in 1987, Killens lived in Brooklyn, New York.

God Bless America[39]

Joe's dark eyes searched frantically for Cleo as he marched with the other Negro soldiers up the long thoroughfare towards the boat. Women were running out to the line of march, crying and laughing and kissing the men good-bye. But where the hell was Cleo?

Beside him Luke Robinson, big and fat, nibbled from a carton of Baby Ruth candy as he walked. But Joe's eyes kept traveling up and down the line of civilians on either side of the street. She would be along here somewhere; any second now she would come calmly out of the throng and walk alongside him till they reached the boat. Joe's mind made a picture of her, and she looked the same as last night when he left her. As he had walked away, with the brisk California night air biting into his warm body, he had turned for one last glimpse of her in the doorway, tiny and smiling and waving good-bye.

They had spent last night sitting in the little two-by-four room where they had lived for three months with hardly enough space to move around. He had rented it and sent for her when he came to California and learned that his outfit was training for immediate shipment to Korea, and they had lived there fiercely and desperately, like they were trying to live a whole lifetime. But last night they had sat on the side of the big iron bed, making conversation, half-listening to a portable radio, acting like it was just any night. Play-acting like in the movies.

It was late in the evening when he asked her, "How's little Joey acting lately?"

She looked down at herself. "Oh, pal Joey is having himself a ball." She smiled, took Joe's hand, and placed it on her belly; and he felt movement and life. His and her life, and he was going away from it and from her, maybe forever.

Cleo said, "He's trying to tell you good-bye, darling." And she sat very still and seemed to ponder over her own words. And then all of a sudden she burst into tears.

She was in his arms, and her shoulders shook. "It isn't fair! Why can't they take the ones that aren't married?"

He hugged her tight, feeling a great fullness in his throat. "Come on now, stop crying, hon. Cut it out, will you? I'll be back home before little Joey sees daylight."

"You may never come back. They're killing a lot of our boys over there. Oh, Joe, Joe, why did they have to go and start another war?"

In a gruff voice he said, "Don't you go worrying about Big Joey. He'll take care of himself. You just take care of little Joey and Cleo. That's what you do."

"Don't take any chances, Joe. Don't be a hero!"

He forced himself to laugh and hugged her tighter. "Don't you worry about the mule going blind."

She made herself stop crying and wiped her face. "But I don't understand, Joe. I don't understand what colored soldiers have to fight for—especially against other colored people."

"Honey," said Joe gently, "we got to fight like anybody else. We can't just sit on the sidelines."

But she just looked at him and shook her head.

"Look," he said, "when I get back, I'm going to finish college. I'm going to be a lawyer. That's what I'm fighting for."

She kept shaking her head as if she didn't hear him. "I don't know, Joe. Maybe it's because we were brought up kind of different, you and I. My father died when I was four. My mother worked all her life in white folks' kitchens. I just did make it through high school. You had it a whole lot better than most Negro boys." She went over to the box of Kleenex and blew her nose.

"I don't see where that has a thing to do with it."

He stared at her, angry with her for being so obstinate. Couldn't she see any progress at all? Look at Jackie Robinson. Look at Ralph Bunche.[40] Damn it! they'd been over it all before. What did she want him to do about it anyway? Become a deserter?

She stood up over him. "Can't see it, Joe—just can't see it! I want you here, Joe. Here with me where you belong. Don't leave me, Joe! Please—" She was crying now. "Joe, Joe, what're we going to do? Maybe it would be better to get rid of little Joey—" Her brown eyes were wide with terror. "No, Joe, no! I didn't mean that! I didn't mean it, darling! Don't know what I'm saying . . ."

She sat down beside him, bent over, her face in her hands. It was terrible for him, seeing her this way. He got up and walked from one side of the little room to the other. He thought about what the white captain from Hattiesburg, Mississippi, had said. "Men, we have a job to do. Our outfit is just as damn important as any outfit in the United States Army, white or colored. And we're working towards complete integration. It's a long, hard pull, but I guarantee you every soldier will be treated equally and without discrimination. Remember, we're fighting for the dignity of the individual." Luke Robinson had looked at the tall, lanky captain with an arrogant smile.

Joe stopped in front of Cleo and made himself speak calmly. "Look, hon, it isn't like it used to be at all. Why can't you take my word for it? They're integrating colored soldiers now. And anyhow, what the hell's the use of getting all heated up about it? I got to go. That's all there is to it."

He sat down beside her again. He wanted fiercely to believe that things were really changing for his kind of people. Make it easier for him—make it much easier for him and Cleo, if they both believed that colored soldiers had a stake in fighting the war in Korea. Cleo wiped her eyes and blew her nose, and they changed the subject, talked about the baby; suppose it turned out to be a girl, what would her name be? A little after midnight he kissed her good night and walked back to the barracks.

The soldiers were marching in full field dress, with packs on their backs, duffle bags on their shoulders, and carbines and rifles. As they approached the big white ship, there was talking and joke-cracking and nervous laughter. They were the leading Negro outfit, immediately following the last of the white troops. Even at route step there was a certain uniform cadence in the sound of their feet striking the asphalt road as they moved forward under the midday sun, through a long funnel of people and palm trees and shrubbery. But Joe hadn't spotted Cleo yet, and he was getting sick from worry. Had anything happened?

Luke Robinson, beside him, was talking and laughing and grumbling. "Boy, I'm telling you, these peoples is a bitch on wheels. Say, Office Willie, what you reckon I read in your Harlem paper last night?" Office Willie was his nickname for Joe because Joe was the company clerk—a high school graduate, two years in college, something special. "I read where some of your folks' leaders called on the President and demanded that colored soldiers be allowed to fight at the front instead of in quartermaster.[41] Ain't that a damn shame?"

Joe's eyes shifted distractedly from the line of people to Luke, and back to the people again.

"Percy Johnson can have my uniform any day in the week," said Luke. "He want to fight so bad. Them Goddamn Koreans ain't done me nothing. I ain't mad with a living ass."

Joe liked Luke Robinson, only he was so damn sensitive on the color question. Many times Joe had told him to take the chip off his shoulder and be somebody. But he had no time for Luke now. Seeing the ship plainly, and the white troops getting aboard, he felt a growing fear. Fear that maybe he had passed Cleo and they hadn't seen each other for looking so damn hard. Fear that he wouldn't get to see her at all—never-ever again. Maybe she was ill, with no way to let him know, too sick to move. He thought of what she had said last night, about little Joey. Maybe. . . .

And then he saw her, up ahead, waving at him, with the widest and prettiest and most confident smile anybody ever smiled. He was so damn glad he could hardly move his lips to smile or laugh or anything else.

She ran right up to him. "Hello, soldier boy, where you think you're going?"

"Damn," he said finally in as calm a voice as he could manage. "I thought for a while you had forgotten what day it was. Thought you had forgotten to come to my going-away party."

"Now, how do you sound?" She laughed at the funny look on his face and told him he looked cute with dark glasses on, needing a shave and with the pack on his back. She seemed so cheerful, he couldn't believe she was the same person who had completely broken down last night. He felt the tears rush out of his eyes and spill down his face.

She pretended not to notice and walked with him till they reached the last block. The women were not allowed to go any further. Looking at her, he wished somehow that she would cry, just a little bit anyhow. But she didn't cry at all. She reached up and kissed him quickly. "Good-bye, darling; take care of yourself. Little Joey and I will write every day, beginning this afternoon." And then she was gone.

The last of the white soldiers were boarding the beautiful white ship, and a band on board was playing "God Bless America." He felt a chill, like an electric current, pass across his slight shoulders, and he wasn't sure whether it was from "God Bless America" or from leaving Cleo behind. He hoped she could hear the music; maybe it would make her understand why Americans, no matter what their color, had to go and fight so many thousands of miles away from home.

They stopped in the middle of the block and stood waiting till the white regiment was all aboard. He wanted to look back for one last glimpse of Cleo, but he wouldn't let himself. Then they started again, marching toward the ship. And suddenly the band stopped playing "God Bless America" and jumped into another tune—"The Darktown Strutters' Ball. . . ."[42]

He didn't want to believe his ears. He looked up at the ship and saw some of the white soldiers on deck waving and smiling at the Negro soldiers, yelling "Yeah, man!" and popping their fingers. A taste of gall crept up from his stomach into his mouth.

"Damn," he heard Luke say, "that's the kind of music I like." The husky soldier cut a little step. "I guess Mr. Charlie want us to jitterbug onto his pretty white boat. Equal treatment. . . . We ain't no soldiers; we're a bunch of damn clowns."

Joe felt an awful heat growing inside his collar. He hoped fiercely that Cleo was too far away to hear.

Luke grinned at him. "What's the matter, good kid? Mad about something? Damn—that's what I hate about you colored folks. Take that damn chip off your shoulder. They just trying to make you people feel at home. Don't you recognize the Negro national anthem[43] when you hear it?"

Joe didn't answer. He just felt his anger mounting, and he wished he could walk right out of line and to hell with everything. But with "The Darktown Strutters' Ball" ringing in his ears, he put his head up, threw his shoulders back, and kept on marching towards the big white boat.

"God Bless America," *California Quarterly* 1, no. 3 (1952): 37–40.

Related writings by John Oliver Killens: *And Then We Heard the Thunder* (1962); *'Sippi* (1967).

MARTIN LUTHER KING JR.

Martin Luther King Jr. served as the leader of the Southern Christian Leader-ship Conference (SCLC) from its inception in 1957. The SCLC is a civil rights organization founded after the Montgomery bus boycott, which launched the Rev. Dr. Martin Luther King Jr. into the national spotlight. Born in 1929 in Atlanta, Georgia, he later would become a prominent spokesperson for the nonviolent Civil Right Movement in the United States until he was slain on 4 April 1968. This speech, delivered at Riverside Baptist Church in New York City, exactly one year before his death, marks King's public criticism of the War in Vietnam and its costs in the light of dwindling governmental support for anti-poverty funding and anti-discrimination legislation in the United States.

Strange Liberators: A Speech at Riverside Church, 4 April 1967[44]

[. . .] I come to this magnificent house of worship tonight because my conscience leaves me no other choice. I join you in this meeting because I am in deepest agreement with the aims and work of the organization which has brought us together: Clergy and Laymen Concerned about Vietnam.[45] The recent statements of your executive committee are the sentiments of my own heart, and I found myself in full accord when I read its opening lines: "A time comes when silence is betrayal." And that time has come for us in relation to Vietnam. [. . .]

The truth of these words is beyond doubt, but the mission to which they call us is a most difficult one. Even when pressed by the demands of inner truth, men do not easily assume the task of opposing their government's policy, especially in time of war. Nor does the human spirit move without great difficulty against all the apathy of conformist thought within one's own bosom and in the surrounding world. Moreover, when the issues at hand seem as perplexed as they often do in the case of this dreadful con-flict, we are always on the verge of being mesmerized by uncertainty. But we must move on.

And some of us who have already begun to break the silence of the night have found that the calling to speak is often a vocation of agony, but we must speak. We must speak with all the humility that is appropriate to our limited vision, but we must speak. And we must rejoice as well, for surely this is the first time in our nation's history that a significant number of its religious leaders have chosen to move beyond the prophesying of smooth patriotism to the high grounds of a firm dissent based upon the mandates of conscience and the reading of history. Perhaps a new spirit is rising among us. If it is, let us trace its movements and pray that our own inner being may be sensitive to its guidance, for we are deeply in need of a new way beyond the darkness that seems so close around us.

Over the past two years, as I have moved to break the betrayal of my own silences and to speak from the burnings of my own heart, as I have called for radical departures from the destruction of Vietnam, many persons have questioned me about the wisdom of my path. At the heart of their concerns this query has often loomed large and loud: "Why are you speaking about the war, Dr. King?" "Why are you joining the voices of dissent?" "Peace and civil rights don't mix," they say. "Aren't you hurting the cause of your people," they ask? And when I hear them, though I often understand the source of their concern, I am nevertheless greatly saddened, for such questions mean that the inquirers have not really known me, my commitment or my calling. Indeed, their questions suggest that they do not know the world in which they live. [. . .]

I come to this platform tonight to make a passionate plea to my beloved nation. This speech is not addressed to Hanoi or to the National Liberation Front.[46] It is not addressed to China or to Russia. Nor is it an attempt to overlook the ambiguity of the total situation and the need for a collective solution to the tragedy of Vietnam. Neither is it an attempt to make North Vietnam or the National Liberation Front paragons of virtue, nor to overlook the role they must play in the successful resolution of the problem. While they both may have justifiable reasons to be suspicious of the good faith of the United States, life and history give eloquent testimony to the fact that conflicts are never resolved without trustful give and take on both sides. [. . .]

There is at the outset a very obvious and almost facile connection between the war in Vietnam and the struggle I, and others, have been waging in America. A few years ago there was a shining moment in that struggle. It seemed as if there was a real promise of hope for the poor—both black and white—through the poverty program. There were experiments, hopes, new beginnings. Then came the buildup in Vietnam, and I watched this program broken and eviscerated, as if it were some idle political plaything of a society gone mad on war, and I knew that America would never invest the necessary funds or energies in rehabilitation of its poor so long as adventures like Vietnam continued to draw men and skills and money like some demonic destructive suction tube. So I was increasingly compelled to see the war as an enemy of the poor and to attack it as such.

Perhaps the more tragic recognition of reality took place when it became clear to me that the war was doing far more than devastating the hopes of the poor at home. It was sending their sons and their brothers and their husbands to fight and to die in extraordinarily high proportions relative to the rest of the population. We were taking the black young men who had been crippled by our society and sending them eight thousand miles away to guarantee liberties in Southeast Asia which they had not found in south-west Georgia and East Harlem. And so we have been repeatedly faced with the cruel irony of watching Negro and white boys on TV screens as they kill and die together for a nation that has been unable to seat them together in the same schools. And so we watch them in brutal solidarity burning the huts of a poor village, but we realize that they would hardly live on the same block in Chicago. I could not be silent in the face of such cruel manipulation of the poor. [. . .]

As I have walked among the desperate, rejected, and angry young men, I have told them that Molotov cocktails and rifles would not solve their problems. I have tried to offer them my deepest compassion while maintaining my conviction that social change comes most meaningfully through non-violent action. But they ask—and rightly—so what about Vietnam? They ask if our own nation wasn't using massive doses of violence to solve its problems, to bring about the changes it wanted. Their questions hit home, and I knew that I could never again raise my voice against the violence of the oppressed in the ghettos without having first spoken clearly to the greatest purveyor of violence in the world today—my own government. For the sake of those boys, for the sake of this government, for the sake of the hundreds of thousands trembling under our violence, I cannot be silent.

For those who ask the question, "Aren't you a civil rights leader?" and thereby mean to exclude me from the movement for peace, I have this further answer. In 1957 when a group of us formed the Southern Christian Leadership Conference, we chose as our motto: "To save the soul of America." We were convinced that we could not limit our vision to certain rights for black people, but instead affirmed the conviction that America would never be free or saved from itself until the descendants of its slaves were loosed completely from the shackles they still wear. In a way we were agreeing with Langston Hughes, that black bard of Harlem, who had written earlier:

O, yes,
I say it plain,
America never was America to me,
And yet I swear this oath—
America will be!

[...] Beyond the calling of race or nation or creed is this vocation of son-ship and brotherhood, and because I believe that the Father [God] is deeply concerned especially for his suffering and helpless and outcast children, I come tonight to speak for them.

This I believe to be the privilege and the burden of all of us who deem ourselves bound by allegiances and loyalties which are broader and deeper than nationalism and which go beyond our nation's self-defined goals and positions. We are called to speak for the weak, for the voiceless, for the victims of our nation and for those it calls "enemy," for no document from human hands can make these humans any less our brothers. [...]

[The Vietnamese] must see Americans as strange liberators. The Viet-namese people proclaimed their own independence [...] in 1945 [...] after a combined French and Japanese occupation and before the commu-nist revolution in China. They were led by Ho Chi Minh.[47] Even though they quoted the American Declaration of Independence in their own docu-ment of freedom, we refused to recognize them. Instead, we decided to support France in its reconquest of her former colony. Our government felt then that the Vietnamese people were not ready for independence, and we again fell victim to the deadly Western arrogance that has poisoned the international atmosphere for so long. With that tragic decision we rejected a revolutionary government seeking self-determination and a government that had been established not by China—for whom the Vietnamese have no great love—but by clearly indigenous forces that included some com-munists. For the peasants this new government meant real land reform, one of the most important needs in their lives.

For nine years following 1945 we denied the people of Vietnam the right of independence. For nine years we vigorously supported the French in their abortive effort to recolonize Vietnam. Before the end of the war we were meeting eighty percent of the French war costs. Even before the French were defeated at Dien Bien Phu, they began to despair of their reck-less action, but we did not. We encouraged them with our huge financial and military supplies to continue the war even after they had lost the will.

Soon we would be paying almost the full costs of this tragic attempt at recolonization.

After the French were defeated, it looked as if independence and land reform would come again through the Geneva Agreement.[48] But instead there came the United States, determined that Ho should not unify the temporarily divided nation, and the peasants watched again as we supported one of the most vicious modern dictators, our chosen man, Premier Diem.[49] The peasants watched and cringed as Diem ruthlessly rooted out all opposition, supported their extortionist landlords, and refused even to discuss reunification with the North. The peasants watched as all this was presided over by United States' influence and then by increasing numbers of United States' troops who came to help quell the insurgency that Diem's methods had aroused. When Diem was overthrown they may have been happy, but the long line of military dictators seemed to offer no real change, especially in terms of their need for land and peace.

The only change came from America, as we increased our troop commitments in support of governments which were singularly corrupt, inept, and without popular support. All the while the people read our leaflets and received the regular promises of peace and democracy and land reform. Now they languish under our bombs and consider us, not their fellow Vietnamese, the real enemy. They move sadly and apathetically as we herd them off the land of their fathers into concentration camps where minimal social needs are rarely met. They know they must move on or be destroyed by our bombs. [...]

What do they think as we test out our latest weapons on them, just as the Germans tested out new medicine and new tortures in the concentration camps of Europe? Where are the roots of the independent Vietnam we claim to be building? Is it among these voiceless ones? [...]

Perhaps a more difficult but no less necessary task is to speak for those who have been designated as our enemies. What of the National Liberation Front, that strangely anonymous group we call "VC" or "communists"?[50] What must they think of the United States of America when they realize that we permitted the repression and cruelty of Diem, which helped to bring them into being as a resistance group in the South? What do they think of our condoning the violence which led to their own taking up of arms? How can they believe in our integrity when now we speak of "aggression from the North" as if there were nothing more essential to the war? How can they trust us when now we charge them with violence after the murderous reign of Diem and charge them with violence while we pour every new weapon of death into their land? Surely we must understand their feelings, even if we do not condone their actions. Surely we must see that the men we supported pressed them to their violence. Surely we must see that our own computerized plans of destruction simply dwarf their greatest acts. [. . .]

Here is the true meaning and value of compassion and nonviolence, when it helps us to see the enemy's point of view, to hear his questions, to know his assessment of ourselves. For from his view we may indeed see the basic weaknesses of our own condition, and if we are mature, we may learn and grow and profit from the wisdom of the brothers who are called the opposition. [. . .]

As we counsel young men concerning military service, we must clarify for them our nation's role in Vietnam and challenge them with the alternative of conscientious objection. I am pleased to say that this is a path now chosen by more than seventy students at my own alma mater, Morehouse College, and I recommend it to all who find the American course in Vietnam a dishonorable and unjust one. Moreover, I would encourage all ministers of draft age to give up their ministerial exemptions and seek status as conscientious objectors. These are the times for real choices and not false ones. We are at the moment when our lives must be placed on the line if our nation is to survive its own folly. Every man of humane convictions must decide on the protest that best suits his convictions, but we must all protest. [. . .]

A true revolution of values will lay hand on the world order and say of war, "This way of settling differences is not just." This business of burning human beings with napalm, of filling our nation's homes with orphans and widows, of injecting poisonous drugs of hate into the veins of peoples normally humane, of sending men home from dark and bloody battlefields physically handicapped and psychologically deranged, cannot be reconciled with wisdom, justice, and love. A nation that continues year after year to spend more money on military defense than on programs of social uplift is approaching spiritual death. [. . .]

These are revolutionary times. All over the globe men are revolting against old systems of exploitation and oppression, and out of the wounds of a frail world, new systems of justice and equality are being born. The shirtless and barefoot people of the land are rising up as never before. The people who sat in darkness have seen a great light. We in the West must support these revolutions. [. . .]

Communism is a judgment against our failure to make democracy real

470 · These Truly Are the Brave

and follow through on the revolutions that we initiated. Our only hope to-day lies in our ability to recapture the revolutionary spirit and go out into a sometimes hostile world declaring eternal hostility to poverty, racism, and militarism. With this powerful commitment we shall boldly challenge the status quo and unjust mores, and thereby speed the day when "every valley shall be exalted, and every mountain and hill shall be made low, and the crooked shall be made straight, and the rough places plain." [...]

We must find new ways to speak for peace in Vietnam and justice throughout the developing world, a world that borders on our doors. If we do not act, we shall surely be dragged down the long, dark, and shameful corridors of time reserved for those who possess power without compassion, might without morality, and strength without sight. [...]

If we will make the right choice, we will be able to transform the jangling discords of our world into a beautiful symphony of brotherhood.

Excerpted from "Beyond Vietnam," address delivered to the clergy and laymen concerned about Vietnam at Riverside Church, New York City, 4 April 1967, available at "Martin Luther King, Jr. and the Global Freedom Struggle," Martin Luther King, Jr. Research and Education Institute, http://mlk-kpp01.stanford.edu/index.php/encyclopedia/document-sentry/doc_beyond_vietnam/, accessed 10 October 2014.

Related writings by Martin Luther King Jr.: "Give Us the Ballot" (1957); "The Time for Freedom Has Come" (1961); "The American Dream" (1961); "Equality Now: The President Has the Power" (1961); "Sign Your Own Emancipation Proclamation" (1962); "I Have a Dream" (1963); "Civil Right No. 1: The Right to Vote" (1965); "Conscience and the Vietnam War" (1967); "A Christmas Sermon on Peace" (1967); "Black Power Defined" (1967); "Remaining Awake through a Great Revolution" (1968).

YUSEF KOMUNYAKAA

Yusef Komunyakaa was born in 1947 in Bogalusa, Louisiana, and is a veteran of the War in Vietnam. He won a Bronze Star for his journalism during the war. Komunyakaa later published *Dien Cai Dau* (1988), a poetry collection that focuses on his war experiences and that won the Dark Room Poetry Prize. He has won numerous national and international awards for his poetry, including a Pulitzer Prize and the Kingsley Tufts Poetry Award for *Neon Vernacular: New and Selected Poems 1977–1989* (1994). In 1999, Komunyakaa was elected to the Board of Chancellors of the Academy of American Poets. He currently teaches creative writing at New York University.

Re-Creating the Scene[51]

The metal door groans
& folds shut like an ancient turtle
that won't let go
of a finger till it thunders.
The Confederate flag
flaps from a radio antenna,
& the woman's clothes
come apart in their hands.
Their mouths find hers
in the titanic darkness
of the steel grotto,
as she counts the names of dead
ancestors, shielding a baby in
her arms. The three men
ride her breath, grunting
over lovers back in Mississippi.
She floats on their rage
like a torn water flower,
defining night inside a machine
where men are gods.
The season quietly sweats.
They hold her down
with their eyes,
taking turns, piling stones
on her father's grave.

The APC[52] rolls with curves of the land,
up hills & down into gullies,
crushing trees & grass,
droning like a constellation
of locusts eating through bamboo,
creating the motion for their bodies. [. . .]

"Re-creating the Scene," in *Dien Cai Dau* (Middletown, Conn.: Wesleyan University Press, 1988), 19–20.

The One-legged Stool[53]

Semidarkness. A black POW[54] is seated on a one-legged stool. He looks all round, slowly stands, then lets the stool hit the dirt floor. He's in a state of delirium, partly hallucinating. Periodically a shadow of a face appears at the peephole in the door.

You didn't see that. My stool never touched the floor, guard. I'm still sitting on my stool. It's all in your head. Would you just drag me out into the compound, then put a bullet through my brains for nothing? Do you call that honor? I never left my stool! It never touched the fucking floor! Look, I've been sitting here hypnotized by dawn crawling under the door like a bamboo viper. (*Pause.*) Sometimes there's a distant bird singing just for me. That's right. Just for me. I sit here on this one-legged stool, watching your eyes pressed against the face-window. Don't you know I'll never cooperate? No, don't care what you whisper into the darkness of this cage like it came out of my own head, I won't believe a word. Lies, lies, lies. You're lying. Those white prisoners didn't say what you say they said. They ain't laughing. Ain't cooperating. They ain't putting me down, calling me names like you say. Lies. Lies. It ain't the way you say it is. I'm American. (*Pause.*) Doctor King,[55] he ain't dead like you say. Lies. How many times are you trying to kill me? Twice, three times, four, how many? You can't break me. Drops of water beating on my head for weeks, that didn't work. Bamboo under my fingernails, that didn't work either. The month I laid cramped in that body-cave of yours, with a pain running through me like a live wire, that didn't make me talk into your microphone. (*Pause.*) What you say? You gook, dink, slant-eyed sloe! That's right. I can get nasty too, just as cruel, you bastard. Standing there with your face in the window like a yellow moon that never goes down. I can give the devil hell. I can be Don Quixote[56] fighting fields of windmills. You should've seen me at Khe Sanh![57] You think you're bad? Shit. Our machine gunner, Johnson, a kid we called Chi, he got hit. I took his M-60, walked that burning hill for a solid straight hour with the Pig. Charlies[58] didn't know what to do. I was dancing, swaying with that machine gun. (*Pause.*) You didn't see that. The hand's quicker than the eye. You didn't see that. I'm still sitting on my stool. I sleep, I live here on my damn stool. (*Pause.*) You've pitted me against them. Against those white troops over there behind those trees. I only half hear their voices through these bamboo walls. For my good, huh? You really think I believe that shit? I know how to protect myself, you can bet your life on that. I also know your games, VC.[59] Anything to break a man, right? Anything to grind his mind to dust. But I know how to walk out of a nightmare backwards. I can survive. When you kicked me awake, then back into a stupor, did I break? Maybe I slipped back a few feet deeper into the darkness, but I didn't break. Maybe I pulled back into myself. Pulled back till there's nowhere to go. Sometimes it's like holding back a flood, but I'm still standing here. Crouched in this place, just listening to my stupid heart. With you always two steps away, always so goddamn close, listening to my thoughts. Sometimes I can hear empty locust shells crack under my feet when I was a boy, but I'm not broken yet. (*Pause.*) I wasn't scratching for earthworms. I was sitting here, not batting an eyelid. I wasn't sniffing the ground like a dog on all fours. That wasn't me. Your eyes must be tricking you or something. Watch this. Do you see that dung beetle? Look! You see, the hands are quicker than the eyes. You didn't see me eat that bug, did you? No, don't think about how the dampness in here hurts. Just concentrate. (*Roars with laughter.*) You know what I was thinking? I was thinking a hundred ways I could bury you. Charlie, you can kill me, you can turn me into an animal, you can make me wish I was never born, but you can't break me. I won't cooperate. (*Pause.*) You didn't see that. I'm still sitting here on my stool. Name, rank—Sergeant First Class Thomas J. Washington. Serial number—321-45-9876. Mission—try to keep alive. (*Pause.*) Yeah, VC. I've been through Georgia. Yeah, been through 'Bama too. Mississippi, yeah. You know what? You eye me worse than those rednecks. They used to look at me in my uniform like I didn't belong in it. (*Struts around in a circle.*) I'd be sharper than sharp. My jump boots spit-shined till my face was lost in them. You could cut your fingers on the creases in my khakis. My brass, my ribbons, they would make their blood boil. They'd turn away, cursing through their teeth. With your eyes pressed against the face-window, you're like a white moon over Stone Mountain.[60] You're everywhere. All I have to go back to are faces just like yours at the door.

"The One-legged Stool," in *Dien Cai Dau* (Middletown, Conn.: Wesleyan University Press, 1988), 40–42.

Related writing by Yusef Komunyakaa: *Dien Cai Dau* (1988).

ALLIA ABDULLAH MATTA

An educator and writer, Allia Abdullah Matta was born in 1962. She currently teaches at the City University of New York La Guardia Community College.

From Mymerica

Sunshine in red, black, black, black
Revolution in red, black, & green
Revolution
Revolution
Revolution

   If I hear one more poem about the revolution
   I'm gonna make sure them darkies can't read and write
   no more

   send them back to multicolored loin cloths
   outlined in feathers

   back to their $7.00 slave wardrobe [. . .]

If I hear one more rapper talk about
getting paid and slaying cops,
I'm gonna retire my hood from the closet
and string up a darkie rapper till his lips can't move.

Problem is
too many darkies ain't swinging
from strong-ass country oaks
and them sandniggers
done rode into Mymerica too.

Mymerica was NOT made for all these peoples peeping
into my shit trying to make it theirs
Mymerica is for pure breed white skin like snow.

My country tis of thee
didn't include darkies and the like
and we didn't thump, thump, thump enough
for all of these tan and brown skins to be here.

And I don't care how many flags you post
And you can also sing God bless America
Till your ass is red, white, & blue
This here America is Mymerica!
And that's the way it's gonna stay too!

Sushine in red, black, black, black,
Revolution in red, black & green
Revolution
Revolution
Revolution.

Excerpted from "Mymerica," TRGGR Media Collective: The Aesthetics of Justice, 21 August 2006, http://trggradio.wordpress.com/2006/08/21/mymerica-by-allia-matta/.

Eric Mitchell

U.S. Air Force Captain Eric Mitchell grew up in a military family; both parents had served. He attended the Air Force Academy in Colorado Springs and graduated top in his flight school class in 1997. He served in Operation Iraqi Freedom and was cited for outstanding achievement. An e-mail that Captain Mitchell wrote to his family and friends from Baghdad follows the interview excerpt.

"Pray 4 a quick ending to this"[61]

My parents were in the military. They met in the military. My father was a loadmaster on C-141 cargo planes. While I was growing up, he was always going on trips around the world, and bringing stuff back. I was born on a base in Delaware, and then we moved to South Carolina, then Alabama, and then I moved to Buffalo, New York, and lived with my grandmother. Ever since I can remember, I always wanted to fly—at whatever cost, I always wanted to fly. I would ride my bike out and just sit at the end of the runway and watch the planes and think, Wow. It was always a dream, a goal that I worked toward, and I was blessed to have it happen for me.

I graduated from high school and got an appointment to the Air Force Academy in Colorado Springs. First, in 1991, I had to go to the Air Force Academy Prep School for a year because my SAT scores weren't high enough to get into the Academy. I started the Air Force Academy the next year and struggled there academically. I went to high school in the inner city of Buffalo, and there was no way that I was prepared for the type of academics I encountered at the Academy, even though I went to prep school. I would be up until two, three in the morning studying. I graduated in 1996 and got a slot for flight school, which I finished in 1997, and was number one in my class.

When most people think of Air Force pilots they think of fighter pilots, but I didn't want to drop bombs and blow up stuff. I was an anomaly in that sense. I had no desire to fly fighter planes. I wanted to fly medevac. I wanted to save people, not kill them. I had to get "counseled" for not wanting to fly fighters. My first assignment was in Germany, flying medevac. I would fly patients in Europe to the military hospital in Germany. That was the most incredible three years of my life. The impact I had on people, directly contributing to their health and well-being, was the most incredible feeling. But then it was over and I was sent to McGuire Air Force Base[62] and started flying KC-10 Extenders, which is basically a flying gas station. Now I'm working as part of an air refueling squadron, doing things that directly support dropping bombs. It has been a big adjustment for me. [. . .]

My first mission as a commander was over Afghanistan. I left in November, and twelve hours later we landed at the base we were stationed at in the Middle East. The reason the KC-10 Extenders are such a valuable asset is because we can take gas and we can stay in the air forever, because we can give away all our gas and then another tanker can give us some more. [. . .]

Our missions were long; the average mission was ten to twelve hours. There was a lot of concern, because it was the first time we were dealing with a country where our enemy was landlocked. In previous conflicts, in Vietnam and the Gulf War, the tankers weren't in harm's way—they were over the water. This was the first time in history we had to put the tankers right over the country we were dealing with. We had no defenses at all, so we were basically up there like sitting ducks. We knew exactly what was happening on the ground; we heard the explosions when the bombs dropped.

I was in charge of a crew of four. [. . .] The first time I saw explosions, people in my crew cheered. I thought that I would feel proud of that, but I wasn't. I was happy to be doing my part, but I thought with those explosions, people were dying, people probably my equal, a person just like me or not like me who is just trying to feed his family. Perhaps he's been taught to hate Americans. He doesn't, but has to say he does to feed his family. What choice does he have? I had thoughts like that at times.

I never think of what I achieved. I'm thankful for the Tuskegee Airmen and Gen. Benjamin O. Davis.[63] Their stories were motivating for me. If it weren't for them, I wouldn't be sitting here now. I had the opportunities to pursue a dream, a goal. I was blessed with determination. I don't think I'm that smart at all—like I said, I struggled through the Academy. I was surrounded by a whole lot of people who were smarter than me, but none worked harder than me.

Two weeks after this interview, Mitchell was sent to the Persian Gulf to prepare for the upcoming Operation Iraqi Freedom. [. . .] But Mitchell had a tough time emotionally during the war. During the bombing of Baghdad, he wrote, "I appreciate all the prayers and support, but I think we all need to focus on the Iraqi people and the immense terror they are experiencing. [. . .] We need to focus on that eighteen-year-old Marine who is on his way to downtown Baghdad, who only a year ago was enjoying his high school prom. We need to focus on that unborn child who will never get the opportunity to meet his father because he gave his life in a land so far away. We need to focus on the newlyweds who will never get the chance to enjoy their first wedding anniversary. We need to focus on the Iraqi soldier who will die because he was trying to find a way to feed his family. Pray 4 a quick ending to this."

He came home on April 27, 2003.

Excerpted from "Eric Mitchell, Air Force Captain, 1996–[2004]," in *We Were There: Voices of African American Veterans from World War II to the War in Iraq*, edited by Yvonne Latty (New York: Amistad, 2004), 171–75.

JANET PENNICK

Janet Pennick served as a first sergeant in Saudi Arabia during the War in Iraq. In the selection below, she provides an honest assessment of her experiences at war.

"Everything about war was horrible"[64]

When the problems in the Gulf[65] started, I had just been promoted to first sergeant in the 304th Civil Affairs Unit, an Army Reserve unit that oversees everything. We control the comings and goings of the troops; we give them their assignments, take care of paperwork and all the little details that make things go smoothly. I wasn't very confident that I could do the job. My first sergeant had volunteered to go to the Persian Gulf and I was asked to take his place. At first, I told them no—I didn't have the experience or knowledge to do the job—but another officer pulled me aside and said he would help me. He was a really nice man who knew a lot and I thought, Well, this could be my chance to move up and learn. So I took the job. Next thing you know he gets sent to the Gulf. Shortly after that they decide to call us up.

When I first heard I was getting called up, I was in shock. I had been watching the war on TV. I knew they were calling up troops, but I didn't really believe they would call my unit up. When I heard they were sending us, I was so scared and nervous. I didn't think I knew enough to do the job right. But I spent so much time calming down other people, it kept me focused. So many wives came to me crying because they didn't want us to take their husbands. I spent more time counseling than anything else. My own daughter was away at her first year of college, so I didn't have to worry about her.

After three weeks of training at Fort Bragg, North Carolina, we were sent to Saudi Arabia. We were attacked as soon as we landed on the airstrip in Saudi Arabia. As we got off the plane, there were Scuds[66] overhead. I had heard of Scuds. We had been trained to deal with them, but it was nothing like the real thing. [...] When I looked up I saw like sparks and flashes of light and debris falling down. Our missiles were hitting the Scuds. But it dawned on me as I was running toward the building that I'm the first sergeant and I better make sure my troops all get to safety. So I went back to make sure everyone had come to the building. [...]

They told us when we first got there not to worry, that they don't normally fire Scuds during the day, only at night. Well, we believed them. That first night nothing happened, so our hearts stopped racing. But after that night it started again. The Scud missile attacks never stopped; they were fired day and night. They would last all night, or just a couple of hours. [. . .] We never knew if there were chemicals in the Scuds. I was scared, [but] I had to keep my fears inside. I couldn't let the troops know. I had to perform. After a while I adjusted to it. Just as if you live in a neighborhood where there's drugs all around you—you adjust. After six months it was time to leave. I was ready. I was anxious. [. . .] I couldn't wait to get out of there. All of us in my unit got back in one piece, but I know of other civil affairs units that had casualties.

I'm proud of what I did there—I just wouldn't want to do it again. When I got back, troops were being diverted to Somalia and other places. I didn't want to go. Everything about war was horrible. I couldn't wait to get out of there. For twenty-one years I served in the Army, and I had a lot of good years. It's just war that I don't like.

Excerpted from "Janet Pennick, Army, 1974–1977; Army Reserves, 1977–1998," in *We Were There: Voices of African American Veterans from World War II to the War in Iraq*, edited by Yvonne Latty (New York: Amistad, 2004), 147–51.

Marie Rodgers

Marie Rodgers, who was born in Alabama, enlisted in the U.S. Army Nurse Corps in 1952. She worked at the U.S. Army hospital in Puerto Rico during the Korean War and then served in Vietnam. Rodgers retired in 1977 at the rank of colonel and was awarded the Bronze Star for her service. In the excerpt below, she discusses her work leading nurses at the 24th Evacuation Hospital at Long Binh.

"I asked to go to Vietnam"[67]

I asked to go to Vietnam because I had never been in combat. I had been an operating room nurse, since I served in Puerto Rico during the Korean War. I was fast on my feet; I had friends who were nurses in World War II and they were always talking about it. I wanted to know how I would perform. I wanted to know how I would do if I had to make do and be innovative.

In Vietnam we were right there. We did cranium, neurological, and facial injuries. We had specialists there. We had eight or nine head wounds a day. Every day we had lots of cases, lots of wounded. What we would do is irrigate and clean the wound, make sure the wounds would not get gangrene. Three days later, if there was no infection, we'd close them up, and then they were on their way home. [...]

Most of them were conscious when we were in the operating room. Some were scared but most of them thought they were in good hands. Some of them were surprised that the Army had a hospital, but this is what the Army promises the soldier: Wherever the soldier goes, there will be a hospital to take care of them. I was glad we were there to help them. I have had people ask me why we [the United States] were in Vietnam. I never wondered why I was there: I was there to take care of the soldiers. As an Army nurse, there was never any doubt. To see the look on their faces, they were happy we were there. [...]

I got a Bronze Star for what I did in Vietnam. President Lyndon Johnson pinned it on me. I got it because of how smooth my unit ran. In all these missions, the operating room supervisor, the nurses, we set everything up. All the doctors had to do was operate. I was surprised I got the Bronze Star. I had no idea. My supervisor called me up and asked me to make sure my uniform was all right, but she didn't tell me why. She told me to go to the surgeon general's office at nine A.M. When I got there she and my chief nurse in Vietnam were there, and they told me. [. . .]

The Army system of promotion really helped. In other situations, as a black nurse, I wouldn't have gotten the kind of jobs I had. In the Army they always had to give you the job you were trained for, and with that, the rank. No matter what they thought of me, they had to put me in the operating room. My sister was in telephone repair; they would hire a white man and she'd teach him everything she knew and next thing you know, he would be her boss.

I can't say I experienced any racism. I was pretty fortunate, but there were not a lot of black nurses. Most times I was the only black nurse. Sometimes when there's a crowd of blacks, they are more apt to be prejudiced than when there is just one or two of us. I never worked with a black doctor. I never had a black surgeon work with me. I never even had a black nurse on my staff. I think I was blessed; I guess competent, too. I was always able to get the job done.

Excerpted from "Marie Rodgers, Colonel, Army Nurse Corps, 1952–1978, Korea and Vietnam," in *We Were There: Voices of African American Veterans from World War II to the War in Iraq*, edited by Yvonne Latty (New York: Amistad, 2004), 127–31.

SONIA SANCHEZ

Sonia Sanchez was born in Birmingham, Alabama, in 1934. She is an educator, a poet, a playwright, and a peace activist. Sanchez participated in the 1960s and 1970s Black Arts Aesthetics Movement and is a prolific and widely fêted writer. Her numerous books include *Homecoming* (1969), *We a Baddddd People* (1970), *A Blues Book for Blue Black Magical Women* (1974), and her collection of plays *I'm Black When I'm Singing, I'm Blue when I Ain't, and Other Plays* (2010). Sanchez has received the American Book Award, a Pew Fellowship in the Arts, the Robert Frost Medal, and the Peace and Freedom Award from the Women's International League for Peace and Freedom. She remains active in peace and justice activities and continues to publish and perform her poetry.

From Reflections after the June 12th March for Disarmament[68]

I have come to you tonite out of the depths
   of slavery
   from white hands peeling black skins over
   america;
I have come out to you from reconstruction eyes
   that closed on black humanity
   that reduced black hope to the dark
   huts of america;
I have come to you from the lynching years,
   the exploitation of black men and women by
   a country that allowed the swinging of
   strange fruits from southern trees;[69]
I have come to you tonite thru the
   delany[70] years, the du bois years, the
   b.t. washington years, the robeson[71]
   years, the garvey[72] years, the
   depression years, the you can't eat
   or sit or live just die here years,
   the civil rights years, the black power
   years, the black nationalist years, the
   affirmative action years, the liberal
   years, the neoconservative years;

I have come to say that those years
    were not in vain, the ghosts of our
    ancestors searching this american dust for
    rest were not in vain, black women
    walking their lives in clots were not
    in vain, the years walked
    sideways in a forsaken land were not
    in vain;
I have come to you tonite as an equal,
    as a comrade, as a black woman
    walking down a corridor of tears,
    looking neither to the left or the right,
    pulling my history with bruised
    heels,
    beckoning to the illusion of America
    daring you to look me in the eyes to
    see these faces, the exploitation of a
    people because of skin pigmentation; [...]
I have come to you tonite not just for the stoppage
    of nuclear proliferation, nuclear
    plants, nuclear bombs, nuclear
    waste, but to stop the proliferation
    of nuclear minds, of nuclear generals
    of nuclear presidents, of nuclear scientists,
    who spread human and nuclear waste
    over the world;
I come to you because the world needs to be
    saved for the future generations who must
    return the earth to peace, who will not
    be startled by a man's/woman's skin color; [...]
I am here between the voices of our ancestors
    and the noise of the planet,
    between the surprise of death and life;
I am here because I shall not give the
    earth up to non-dreamers and earth molesters;
I am here to say to you:
    my body is full of veins
    like the bombs waiting to burst
    with blood.

we must learn to suckle life not
bombs and rhetoric
rising up in redwhiteandblue patriotism;
I am here. and my breath/our breaths
must thunder across this land
arousing new breaths. new life.
new people, who will live in peace
and honor.

Excerpted from "Reflections after the June 12th March for Disarmament," in *Homegirls and Handgrenades* (New York: Thunder's Mouth Press, 1984), 65–68.

Related writing by Sonia Sanchez: "A Letter to Dr. Martin Luther King" (1984).

JOHN A. WILLIAMS

The following is an excerpt from *Captain Blackman*. See part 1, p. 181 for biographical note.

'Nam[73]

[Abraham Blackman is a hero of the War in Vietnam who, while recuperating from war injuries, dreams that he has traveled through time and has relived events from a black military history course that he teaches. While time traveling, he takes part in almost all of the wars the United States has participated in, beginning with the Revolutionary War for Independence. Blackman actually has suffered life-changing injuries in Vietnam, resulting in the loss of one lung and amputation of his right leg. He is a reluctant recipient of the Medal of Honor for heroism and an unenthusiastic participant in a photo session with military brass. He also receives a promotion to the rank of major. While medicated in the military hospital, Blackman hallucinates about a future war involving black soldiers.]

The AK-47s[74] were chewing up everything. Not supposed to be any tough stuff out here. Looks like the Major [Whittman] snapped the string in on me.

Abraham Blackman tried to force himself down into the wet ground. Buttoned down and they're looking for me, especially that one, he thought, as a patch of grass was chopped up close to his face. Blackman pressed down again, and with that extra movement, thought he saw a cobra slither away. Once any kind of snake might have made him recoil for a few seconds; not now. It was the cobra or that 47; he'd take his chances with the cobra, or two or three of them.

There, finally, he thought, hearing a couple of bursts of M-16 fire.[75] But that hungry 47 was still hunting him; its rounds chewed another trail past him, not four inches away; he heard the rounds thud-thudding into the marsh, a sound like ripping out a wet stitch.

"Captain!"

"Captain-Brother. You in there? You all right?"

Blackman was both relieved and annoyed. They were out there, Harrison, Griot, Woodcock, and the others. He'd have to let them know he was okay, but once he opened his mouth . . .

"Okay!" he shouted. "But I'm pinned." Once more he tried to disappear into the ground as the 47 opened up again, spattering water into his eyes from its bullets. Blackman began to shake. He heard his men firing at will. They were splashing toward him. Blackman hunched and another 47, a forty-five degree angle away, sent him burrowing into the ground again.

The guys'll come splashing down here, Blackman thought, thinking there's only one or two of 'em out there, and they'll drop the hammer on them. What to do?

"Captain?"

Why didn't they keep quiet? Why didn't they figure it out?

"Okay," he called. In the momentary stillness he tried to imagine what it felt like being hit with about twenty rounds of 47 ammo. That many rounds, he told himself, you don't feel anything, because you're dead. Five, then, or maybe three. He could not imagine it.

Blackman pushed a blade of marsh grass out of his eye. He heard the 16s again, and Griot's M-60,[76] which he liked to hold the way they did in the movies. He heard them closer now, splashing, and he was relieved, because he didn't want to die. But he was angry, too. Only yesterday he'd told them again at the end of his black military history seminar that he didn't want any heroes in his company. Things were close to the end, and even if they weren't, they had nothing to prove. He'd told them time and again, these legs with their mushrooming Afros and off duty dashikis, that they were not the first black soldiers to do what they were doing. He'd gone back to the American Revolution to Prince Estabrook, Peter Salem, Crispus Attucks,[77] and all of the unnamed rest; from there to the War of 1812, the Civil War, the Plains Wars, the Spanish-American War—all the wars. He'd conducted the seminar during their off-duty time, without the blessing of the brass, with the obvious, smoldering resentment of the Major, who, for some reason, had let him carry on.

"We don't have anything to prove to anybody," he said. "We've done it over and over and over again. No heroes. Just do your jobs."

Blackman's body was tense with momentary indecision. They were walking into what looked like a trap. He recalled in a flash that when the seminar ended, they stood and gave him the salute, the fist, the arm. The same one being used all over the Army these days, wherever there were Brothers. He'd saluted back. He hoped they'd remember the lessons he tried to teach. He hoped they now had that sense of continuity that everyone tried to keep from them, from kindergarten up.

They were closer. He knew the little brown men holding the 47s were waiting. He'd have to do it now; five seconds more would be too late. His mouth was dry, his legs trembling. He thought of Mimosa.

And he sprang up, not wanting them to die for him, thrust his six-four frame skyward, swinging around his 16, screaming, "Get down! Get back!" and felt his weapon kicking against him, felt, rather than saw its bullets attracting the rounds of the 47s, then took the first ones in the thigh, spun around as they clawed for his torso, and he splashed down, sliding in his own blood. He came to rest against a stump that forced his face skyward toward the bright blue Vietnam sky. [. . .]

*   *   *

Major Whittman had been absently listening to the radio. He was sucking on his ragged, wet-ended Roi Tan,[78] his mind back in Saigon[79] on the talk of promotions. He hoped he'd made the lists this time; time to trade in the gold leaf for a silver one and then, chicken colonel, goddamn. But the crackle of the radio and the operator's monotonous southern voice irritated him. Out of space-blue eyes he stared at the kid. Faulkner, a redneck from Georgia. The Army was knee deep in rednecks, mountaineers, spics, and niggers. Handle 'em all but the niggers, and the spics were getting out of hand, and shit, some of the peacenik white kids—

"What's that about Charlie Company?" he asked the operator. He leaned close to the crackling set over which a flood of monotonous voices, very much like Faulkner's, were crowding in.

"Captain Blackman's been hit, Major. They're tryin to reach him." Major Whittman straightened up slowly. He ran a hand through his close-cropped flaxen hair. Good, he thought. *Good*! I hope that fucker got it real *good*. "Is he dead?" he asked aloud.

"They doan know, sir. They ain't been able to reach him yet."

Whittman spun around on his heel, biting hard into his cigar.

"Black military history," he muttered. "Teach that black cocksucker. Sonofabitch. I hope they cream his ass good."

"Sir?" the operator called, leaning away from the set.

"Nothing!" Whittman snapped. He stood. "I'm going to my quarters, Faulkner. Let me know as soon as word comes in on Blackman. Got that?"

"Sure, Major." [. . .]

*   *   *

Robert Doctorow, clumsy in his wheelchair, nevertheless rolled himself fearlessly through the halls, seeking out the officer's wing of the hospital. He had to see about the Captain while he could to settle the phrases and ideas flitting through his head. Now he'd have time, lots of it, to think about the book he was going to write about this lousy war and what happened to the men in it.

As Doctorow was rolling up this hall and down that one, Abraham Blackman peered up into the black face of a man he knew to be a doctor by the insignia on his collar. A major. The doctor smiled. "So you're Captain Blackman. You're going to be all right, Captain. Just fine. Some damage here and there. We're going to have to take your right leg, Captain, your right leg. Do you understand?"

Blackman shifted his eyes from those of the doctor to the man's hairline.

"And I'm afraid you've lost one lung."

Blackman said, "What's the pain around my balls?"

"You took a slug through the bag. Not a testicle, through the bag. That's the least of your worries. That's already fixed up."

"Umm," Blackman said. How did you screw with one leg? He turned now to study his room for the first time, or to give the doctor that impression. He heard the doctor say something about prosthetic devices, and he thought, fuck prosthetic devices. He thought about Mims. Get word to her? What for? Forget it, man. You're going to wind up like some of those black amputees you've seen skidding along the subway platforms, intimidating people into giving them handouts. The only pussy you'll get will be from broads who get kicks out of balling one-legged dudes. You can take your wooden leg and shove it up. How about that?

"When?" he finally asked.

"Tomorrow. Have to do it tomorrow, Captain."

"Yeah, I suppose so. Do you know anything about my men?"

"Sorry, I don't know. On the basis that you're getting a medal, I'd suppose they were all right." The major waited for a response. He leaned close to Blackman again and said, "A medal. You're a hero. I think it's the Medal—"

"Hey, man, can you give me something to put me back out? I don't want to have to lay here all night hurting and thinking about the leg. Okay?"

"Certainly, Captain. We were going to give you something to make you sleep, anyway. By the way, you're not on anything? I mean, there's so much of—"

"No. I'm clean. Shoot me up." Blackman didn't feel like talking anymore. He wanted to be out of it. Forget the whole mess. It's over. Just get me on out of it, man. Zap me. He closed his eyes. [. . .]

* * *

Luther Woodcock rounded the corner and came through the opened door of the room, slowing to a stop in his wheelchair. For before him, bent over the bed in which Captain Blackman lay, he saw a woman. He savored the instant in which he had the complete advantage, the view of extraordinarily good legs, a fine behind with full-curved, strong buttocks. He knew when she turned around, as she was now doing, she would be just as fine in front.

The Captain's eyes were still closed, he saw, and the drainage tubes curved out of his thorax into bottles, now filling slowly. The Captain was in a sitting position. Hastily, almost angrily, Woodcock looked for the stump on the right leg; he wanted to see it before starting a conversation with the woman. You didn't see too many black women out here. But he also wanted to assess the Captain's wounds, see if he was going to make it, shot up, stumped, but make it, anyway.

"Hello," the woman said.

"Hi."

"I'm a friend of Captain Blackman. You?"

Oh. This was the babe from down at the Embassy. "My name's Woodcock. I'm a medic in the Captain's company."

"Are you hurt bad?"

"No. I'll be outa this thing in a few days. How's the Captain?"

"He'll live."

Woodcock peered at the bed again, not able to clearly see where the leg had been amputated. "They took his leg?"

"Yes. Look, let's talk outside, all right? You wouldn't mind?"

Woodcock shook his head and she took the back of his chair, turned him around, and rolled him out of the room. Did she know he'd probably wind up being a pulmonary invalid, with the pleura thickening every day? Maybe she was going to get her hat, now, anyway.

Behind him, Mimosa Rogers was studying his shaggy Afro. Certainly one of the most impressive she'd seen; it was meant to tell the world that, although almost fair enough to pass, its owner was black from his chitlins out. What wise eyes these kids had, she thought, stopping and turning him around. She took a cushioned seat beside him.

Some sadness about her impelled him to gentleness. He took out his cigarettes and offered her one and lit it for her. She was in her late twenties, he guessed. Kind of Amazonian, and it was probably that that brought them together; a big man, a big woman.

"A buddy of mine," Woodcock began, wondering at the shyness he now felt under her cool gaze, "name of Doctorow—he's in here, too—says the Captain's gonna get the Medal of Honor . . ."

"Yes. That's how I found out what'd happened. The Medal of Honor; I'm sure he's wanted that all his life." She flicked her cigarette ash viciously.

"Yeah," Woodcock said. "It's not much of an exchange."

"No." She shouldn't be giving in to her bitterness, she thought, so she asked, "Were you in his black military history seminar?"

"Yes. Really great stuff. I mean, the Captain-Brother told us a whole lot that we didn't know, you know. A lot of the Brothers, they come over here and think they're the first Brothers to ever get into the sh-stuff"

"Into the shit. Yes, I know."

"But the Captain, like, he brought everything down in front for us and—I still can't get over it. Like, you know, Chuck's[80] been f—"

"Fucking over you—"

Woodcock smiled. "Yeah. For so long, and not letting us know, and tellin' us how great it is to die for him . . ." Woodcock's voice trailed away when he saw a set, weary, bitter expression creep back across her face. "Well, the Captain really turned our company around, man."

She ground her cigarette and stared at the floor. Woodcock sat silently, letting his own cigarette go dead at the filter. Once or twice he cleared his throat and thought about his thigh wound. He played with the spokes in his chair. He dropped the butt and rolled over it. "Miss," he said. She looked up, a polite smile on her face.

"I guess I'd better be getting back to the ward. Would you tell the Captain Woodcock came over to see him, please?"

"I'd be happy to. Come back. I know he'd like to see you."

Woodcock, already rolling, nodded. "Miss, I'm sorry. We didn't want nothin' to happen to the Captain, really. We all dug him and—well, we just didn't want to see nothin' happen to him." Woodcock gave a mighty push and rolled out of the room before the tears brimming up in the woman's eyes splashed out on her face.

She rose and walked quietly back into the room and stood staring at the drainage bottles, the shockingly empty place under the sheet, emphasized all the more by the fullness just beside it; no leg and much leg.

She'd been staring for a long time and trying to analyze her feelings, which lay behind the great wall of sadness, when he said, weakly:

"Hello."

How long had he been watching? What had he read in her face? She smiled. "Hello, Abraham."

A thin smile faded up and then down on his face, now stubbled with beard. Perhaps she should try to shave him.

"I've been dreaming about you."

"Don't jive me, man. You sure it wasn't about one of those rice paddy whores?"

He liked the response, she saw; his face curled for a laugh, but nothing came out. He gave a caricature of a laugh. "I read somewhere, a guy had his leg taken off. He wakes, dig, and his toe's itching, only he doesn't have a toe, let alone a foot, ankle, or leg, to itch." He gave his soundless laugh again, then said, in mock puzzlement, "No itch, baby."

She touched his shoulder, kissed him, and went out to find Dr. Jackson, suddenly anxious to get away from the smell of the fluids in the bottles, the lingering odor of feces and urine, the mixed sweat and rubbing alcohol scents. [. . .]

*   *   *

Back through the corridors filled with nurses, GIs, orderlies, Vietnamese help; back through the broken and punctured bodies, their smells; back through the desperately perfumed nurses, the doctors with their heavy, tired attitudes.

Dr. Jackson's eyes swept the bottles and the tubes, took in the stumped leg, gone to just above the knee. "Captain?"

Blackman worked up a weak smile, his eyes watchful, even as the doctor unpocketed his stethoscope and listened to his chest and then took his pulse. Then he said, "I'm afraid you're going to have to sit up like this for a while to help the drainage. And as soon as this"—here he touched the thigh—"toughens up, we'll start with the weights. The rest is mostly in the hands of time."

As though he hadn't been listening, Blackman said, "Where you from, Doctor?" Once Blackman knew what city a black person was from, he could almost decipher his makeup. America was peculiar that way, in the manner in which it inadvertently, or perhaps not, formulated its racial codes.

"Berkeley. You know it?"

Blackman nodded. He'd been at Ord[81] for a short time before going to Korea. Berkeley then was the university and that ever-growing black community of former shipyard workers and Navy people; of southern blacks seeking new lives on the Coast. Berkeley, Oakland, and San Francisco. Wasn't there an A-train that you took from San Francisco to Oakland? He couldn't remember, but now Ellington's song, complete with the full-bodied riffs of the sax front line, jumped into his consciousness. Wrong A-train. The one that hurtled Brooklynites to Harlem and Harlemites to Brooklyn for weekends of partying, that was the Duke's A-train.

"Captain. You know Berkeley?" Dr. Jackson was conscious of Miss Rogers moving closer to the bed.

"Yeah. I used to know it. Nice place." "How about you, where you from?"

"Binghamton."

"Birmingham?"

"Binghamton. New York," Mimosa whispered.

"Oh, Binghamton. Yes. New York State. Young fellow from there, a football player, died of something like leukemia—"

"Ernie Davis, that's right."

Major Jackson slowly stuffed his stethoscope back in his pocket. "I'd like you to get some rest now, Captain. Press your light if you want anything. I'll take Miss Rogers with me, but she'll be in my office or her quarters."

"Quarters?"

"I'm with the nurses for a few days, Abraham." She patted his hand and was surprised at how thin and unalive it was. "I'll be back later." She kissed him again.

"Can we talk, Miss Rogers?" Dr. Jackson asked.

"Sure."

In his office, [. . .] Mimosa now had only to fight down the age-old doubts of the ability a black doctor might or might not have.

For Dr. Jackson this was old stuff; you always sense it, even if you didn't know it. Once, this doubt that managed to reveal itself, even from behind elaborate disguises, had made him doubt himself. But he had got hold of his reality. Meharry, Provident, and the rare black presence at Alta Bates.[82] He knew his business, and people like Miss Rogers could be as uncertain about him as they wished.

"Miss Rogers," he began, once she'd lit a cigarette, crossed her legs, and settled back, waiting in that black niche where Negroes waited for the bad things to happen to them, "I have to take it that you and Captain Blackman are into a special thing. Your being down here proves that, the *conditions* under which you're here. Unusual, you know?"

She waited, her eyes twin probes sinking into his face.

"He's got a bad hurt."

"I can see that, Dr. Jackson."

Okay, baby, he thought, then said, "What I wanted to know was about your future with the Captain. I mean, there is a future?"

She caught the snideness, the suggestion that now that Abraham was broken, she'd catch the first thing smoking, and it took her by surprise. She lurched forward, uncrossing her legs, her cigarette jabbing dangerously close to his face. Boiling within her was the unjustness of it all. In Saigon she'd been waiting, ready. No Abraham. No Abraham the next morning. Worrying, but rejecting the possibility of this. Always in the back of the mind, but always rejecting it. Then, days later, Peggy, in the Ambassador's office, surprised at the quickness with which this particular award was being processed, and remembering the name, came rushing in with the news. Then pressure on Bunk to get her up here. A rough flight. Nurses not really sympathetic because she had too much pull, and finally, Abraham, broken, thin, just this side of dying. Now this jive-ass nigger doctor.

"Now, you listen to me, you—"

But suddenly he changed before her eyes, became hard and in command; it had nothing to do with the Army; it went deeper and farther back than all that. He said, "No, you listen, Sister. You listen!" and his finger was more formidable than her cigarette, his eyes more piercing than she could've imagined. He took her off balance and she paused, wondering. "There is a black man in there who's hurt bad. Bad. Now you come out of the Embassy to see him. I make something of that. I'm not prying. I'm concerned about Captain Abraham Blackman. Ever since you've been here, you've been carrying your ass on your shoulders with me. Well, all right. Get down. Let's talk about that man. If you're not in his future, then, dammit, say so, so I can make other plans. There's nothing wrong with you. You're not my concern. He is." Suddenly and with more gentleness he said, "I know it's tough. Most women from the moment of the hurt are determined to play Hollywood, and stick to the guy through thick and thin. Right from jump. I can see, Miss Rogers, that you're thinking about whether you want to go or stay."

"Yes, you bastard," she said without anger as she started to cry. She talked through the tears. "I don't have any choice to make, Major. Yes, I'm his future, I'm his future, but I know we're both going to spend so much time thinking about the past when he was—you know, and he's not going to want me now. He's too proud a black man to want to have me around doing things for him that he can no longer do for himself, and you know, these are things I have to *deal* with, *me*, and I need just a little more time, just a very little."

"Sister, I don't mean to be rough on you, but you know as well as I do that none of us have that much time, black people especially. I'm glad you came up. I hope you can arrange to stay awhile. He's through with the Army. He'll go to a hospital back home. And even when he's out, Miss Rogers, he's going to have trouble with that lung—"

"But, Doctor, he won't want to get married."

"I didn't say one thing about marriage." He looked levelly at Mimosa. "What's marriage got to do with it? You're either with him or not, and in fact, you know, that may be just the way to make it work."

"So that he doesn't feel that we got married because I felt sorry for him."

"That's right."

"And children?"

"If that happens, then I'm sure he'd want the papers and you're home without sweat."

They sat without speaking for a few moments, she wiping her eyes, grinding out her last cigarette and lighting another, until he said, "All right now?"

"As good as I'll ever be."

"Why don't you get some rest and come back later. You'll feel better. And he'll feel better, not having you there at times, wondering what you're thinking and how you feel about him now."

"Yeah," she said, standing. "He'd better get used to my being around, because I'm going to start getting ready to resign; I'm going back on the same boat or plane or helicopter that he's going back on. I mean, that's all there is to it."

Grinning, Dr. Jackson said, "Sister, that's all I was trying to find out. From what I know, you've got yourself a special kind of man." [. . .]

BLACKMAN'S CADENCE

It was a mistake. I mean to expect my enemy, which he was, always has been, to reward my service with equality. A serious misjudgment. Worse, tragic. The tactics—well, they were dangerous. I mean there were things I was catching from him, just being in his company. I could feel it deep in my soul, I could see it happening, if not to me completely, to others. Soldiering to him was just like any other gig black folks stumble into with white folks. A soldier should get the credit due him for being responsible for the most abrupt and drastic changes that can be effected on any society. Man, they sing about soldiers. Give them land. Salt. Women. Money. Pensions. Medals (!). Allowances. They do the cats up in bronze. They look so noble, even the pigeon shit doesn't matter. But when they don't give you no credit, they're not obligated to honor you one bit, or to give you one mothafucking thing, baby.

Oh, maybe I wasn't too bright like some of the legs they got running around over here now, but things came after a while. Life begins at dit-dat,[83] yeah? A strategic withdrawal, a real one, not that line that comes out of the four-star's office every time the Viet Cong goes upside his head. (Some shit does come outa his office. Like they always find in some Viet Cong colonel's body with maps and plans on his dead ass. A massive attack planned. Yeah.) But I'm talking about a real withdrawal and a reappraisal of the best way to break Chuck's fuckin head wide open, break his will, overrun him militarily, since that's his stick, but not with that jive morality we both been dealing like a Pitty-Pat hand.[84]

We insisted that we belonged, that we were Americans. Oh, yeah, we ran that down for a long time, without once realizing what the enemy always knew: the most basic instrument of warfare was possession of terrain from which to either launch an attack or fight a defensive action. We don't have any. American terrain wasn't ours; it was in our possession only as a figment of the imagination. We didn't even share it with him. Almost four million square miles and what'd we have? Less than one-half of one percent of it. Man, we were as free to use most of that land as animals are free to walk in a goddamn zoo.

What then? Guerrilla warfare; cadres would strike at the cities and vanish into the black communities; acts of critical sabotage would bring Chuck to his knees. Oh, that rappin; oh, them empty phrases; oh, them sacrificial lambs. Let's go to P'eng:[85] "The people are the water and the guerrillas the fish, and without water the fish will die."

A great concept simply put. A concept based on like peoples. Or like colors. A German couldn't tell a partisan from a farmer just from the color of his skin; nor could he tell a maquis from a clochard[86] simply by looking at his skin. A black guerrilla in the United States would be just about as inconspicuous as a white guerrilla in Nam. Inasmuch as the black communities are already captive cities, ghettos, inner cities, etc., the black guerrilla, once he steps outside those areas, is no longer a guerrilla passing unseen through the enemy territory. Now, listen to what I'm saying. He might just as well be followed by King Kong and Mighty Joe Young and the Cardiff Giant.[87] Inconspicuous! But you know, ole P'eng's shit could work—you know where, maybe.

Where, where in the United States could large groups of black people as-

semble to learn the art of war? Where could they escape the agents and electronic devices on the ground and in the air? Which blacks among us could we truly trust? Nowhere. None.

Africa, yes, where sky surveillance was almost nonexistent. But Chuck saw to it that African and Afro-American relationships were chomped and stomped, but there was Africa. This wouldn't be swift, man. Everybody's in a hurry. Brother Hannibal[88] took his time and was hurting the Romans anytime he wanted to. Like, we haven't any odds working for us. No equipment, no diplomats, only cadres of bitter civilians and Armed Forces vets. And they wouldn't be the strike force, except as individuals and under special circumstances. Our war would be quiet. And it would take time.

Those twenty-five cities in Africa. Not fifty. We wouldn't need fifty. Now, suppose we just moved our people over there, not as soldiers in the strict sense, and became twenty-five interlocking colonies, learning languages and dialects and truly becoming one with the people, Brothers and Sisters without the bullshit phrases. We'd have to fend for ourselves, I guess. I don't think the premiers or presidents have ever wished to throw their people into direct competition with Afro-Americans. I hope that's changed a little since World War II.

We'd have our own communications systems; we'd have the know-how, and we'd have the pilots, if we could hustle up small craft for them, to fly back and forth. Lotsa Brothers out here pushing three-million-dollar planes around. We could get things. Arms manufacturers are businessmen. We'd go through fronts, like the Israelis, if we had to, we'd get the shit. And we'd get the people. America is scared. I keep hearing and reading about white folks leaving for New Zealand and Australia and Canada. Well, white folks got the bread. Black folks gonna start taking the hint; they gonna get over that African romanticism and face the fact that it's going to be hard and not always fair, and they'll go, man. Even the white man's money is fallin apart, from Washington to Zurich, from Chase Manhattan to Biddly-bop Savings. Depression coming on; like the 1930s is gonna look like groovy times, compared to this one.

What else? Oh, yeah. They fuckin with the Constitution. Not that it was ever such a hot piece of paper for the Folks, but looks like right now they're ready to riddle it. We'll get the People. Hell, they might even begin a program to depart blacks to Africa. That'd be a help, but of course, you'd have more faith in the cats who'd come voluntarily.

The strike force, heh, heh. Oh, man, the strike force. In the States and in Africa we'd train these people. Tear out their minds and replace them. These *could stay in America safely; they'd be invisible; they'd be as much like fish in the water as those of us in Africa would be. Work this out.*

In war, like in individual combat, a cat more powerful than you can defeat himself by having too much momentum, which doesn't allow him to stop to protect himself when he chooses to. Brother Hannibal at Cannae[89] knew this; did up the Romans real good. How do you level Troy except by deception, a device used in love and war?

In America today, right now, there are at least thirty million Trojan Horses, or, if you will, fishes. Some know who they are, some do not. We can make it if we can win several hundred thousand to our side.

An American Trojan Horse or Pisces americanus—either one, baby, we know what we're talking about, right? Anyway, this is a person who causes absolutely no reaction when he is in places like a governor's mansion or Burning Tree Country Club. No stillness greets him when he walks through doors of places where a person pronouncedly black would set the glasses on the bar to trembling.

People like this would be seen every day, but not perceived. How do you tear them away from the enticements of Elysium?[90] War begins with pride in self, kind, and country. The cultural revolution they talk about back home, that was going to be a big help. It could bring us a lot of fish. Oh, I know that historically mulattoes, quadroons, and octoroons seem to have dealt treacherously, on the whole, with their darker Brothers, because the enemy was willing to share somewhat with them what he withheld completely from us.

You gotta count on some of them falling by the wayside. So be it; we'd have to help them fall a long way. How long would it take to train them? Thirty years or so. (Damn! I'll be seventy!) We would put them back in the pit out of which they climbed; make them relive the shame and bitterness of blackness, touch upon and understand why they went Down the River to Chuckville. Then we'd bring them back up, hone them, train them, pick through the past with a microscope, goad them. Step by step, we'd show the making of a military state, the interlocking connections, the cartels. We'd show the illogicality of the Soviets and Chinese wishing to conquer the U.S. What nation today could afford to take on the problems of a vassal state won by conquest, when it's so goddamn clear that no state that now exists is even close to solving its own internal problems? And we'd have to teach this: If America could make military power relevant to political bargaining with other superpowers, couldn't we, once that military power was in our hands, or short-circuited by us, bargain politically for all we never got? Wasn't America more vulnerable now than at any other time in history, man, since all aspects of its society were gathered at the toe-jam-smelling feet of its military monuments? Neutralize that power and what have you? The world's strong boy unmasked as an impotent masturbator. Most important around the world, a collective sigh that at least one superpower, the one most likely to, would no longer be able to end the world in fifteen minutes.

Sshhhhh. Careful. America has dependents. No talk of bringing America to its knees alone. Fish at U.S. installations in other countries would have to function in concert with those at home, neutralize the West European systems. Systems, yeah; the jugular! For in these, America had concentrated its greatest strength, most of its wealth, its most cunning and clever men and machines.

Okay, so we got our force. We've penetrated the center of gravity of enemy power by the simple expedient of utilizing the enemy's weakness, his momentum, his inability to perceive anything beyond color. How large a force? Well, man, just picture any large Western city at that time of day when the offices close and everyone starts legging for home; picture all those whites crowding the buses and trams, the subways and undergrounds; picture the white floods gushing along the sidewalks of London, Paris, New York, Berlin, Amsterdam, and then tell yourself, them folks ain't white. Say it again. Again. And again, until the concept of all that means begins to take hold, maybe in the root hairs at the back of your neck. Dig their eyes, blue, green, hazel, brown, black; see the pink cheeks, the "un-Negroid" features; picture, man, picture it! White hands brushing through blond, brown, red, raven hair, and now—quickly!—superimpose upon those faces the Sphinx, Benin heads, Olmec heads, 28th Dynasty[91] (that's all they want to give us, baby) pharaohs; see now the flash-images of movie stars, women with full pouty lips and "un Anglo" cheekbones; see presidents and governors and businessmen and others. See them all pass with strange little not-unpleasant smiles on their faces.

Now, fast! Transpose the faces. Set them at the controls of Advanced Massed Strategic Aircraft, in the stomachs of Polaris submarines, in subsea floor missile stations, at the controls of the Safeguard ABM[92] systems, in the missile silos; set them there and know they are only white-looking.

Oh, yes. Take thirty years, about. Set them in NORAD,[93] the Skylab probes, SAC,[94] the Pentagon; to the tracking stations at Kano, Tananarive, Santa Cruz, Canton Island, Kauai, Woomera, Houston, Kennedy; to Grand Forks, Denver, Cheyenne, Omaha; to the ice stations.[95] And sit there lookin white, but be as black as a mothafucker. Get to Plattsburg, Johnston Island. Gon, Blackman! Dig it, Jesus! A fish in the crew of every AMSA—over six hundred men; at key controlling positions in eighteen hundred ICBM silos;[96] *in the crews of fifty four Polaris subs; in the three thousand nuclear-armed tactical aircraft making it back and forth over Europe; in the crews of ground tactical nuclear weapons systems in Europe and other nations bordering Russia and China. Ah, yes. Glory, glory!* [. . .]

Excerpted from John A. Williams, *Captain Blackman* (New York: Doubleday, 1972).

SELECTED ADDITIONAL LITERATURE ON CITIZENSHIP AND WAR

Davis, Frank Marshall. "Give Us Our Freedom Now! (100 Years after the Signing of the Emancipation Proclamation)." [1963.] In *Black Moods: Collected Poems*, edited by John Edgar Tidwell, 175–78. Urbana: University of Illinois Press, 2002.

Davis, George. *Coming Home*. Washington, D.C.: Howard University Press, 1984.

Everett, Percival. "The Appropriation of Cultures." In *damned if i do*. Minneapolis: Graywolf Press, 2004.

Flowers, A. R. *De Mojo Blues*. New York: Ballantine, 1986.

Gaines, Ernest. "The Sky Is Gray." *Bloodline: Five Stories*. New York: Vintage, 1968.

Grooms, Anthony. *Bombingham*. New York: Ballantine, 2001.

Harper, Michael. *Songlines in Michaeltree: New and Collected Poems*. Urbana: University of Illinois Press, 2000.

Heyen, William, ed. *September 11, 2001: American Writers Respond*. Silver Springs, Md.: Etruscan Press, 2002.

Jones, Edward P. "The Store." In *Lost in the City*. New York: Amistad/HarperCollins, 1992.

Lattany, Kristin Hunter. *The Lakestown Rebellion*. St. Paul: Coffee House Press, 2003.

Madhubuti, Haki (Don L. Lee). "The Long Reality." In *think black*. Detroit: Broadside Press, 1967.

———. "Message to a Black Soldier." In *Black Pride*. Detroit: Broadside Press, 1968.

———. "The Third World Bond." In *Don't Cry, Scream*. Detroit: Broadside Press, 1969.

Morrison, Toni. *Home*. New York: Knopf, 2012.

Parks, David. *GI Diary*. Washington, D.C.: Howard University Press, 1984.

Shange, Ntozake. "a nite with beau willie brown." In *for colored girls who have considered suicide/when the rainbow is enuf*. New York: Bantam, 1977.

Thomas, Lorenzo. "Last Call." In *Dancing on Main Street: Poems by Lorenzo Thomas*. Minneapolis: Coffee House Press, 2004.

Walker, Alice. "Petunias." In *You Can't Keep a Good Woman Down*. New York: Harcourt, 1981.

Williams, John A. *Captain Blackman*. Garden City, New York: Doubleday, 1972.

ENDNOTES

1. E. Franklin Frazier: Prominent African American sociologist. His influential studies of black people in the United States include *Black Bourgeoisie* (1957) and *The Negro Church in America* (1963).

2. This line, which has been transmitted through African American oral culture and appears in a variety of versions, is from the spiritual "Free at Last, Free at Last."

3. The *Progressive* magazine received its name in 1929. *La Follette's Weekly*, the predecessor of *The Progressive*, was founded in 1909 by Robert "Fighting Bob" La Follette Sr., a Wisconsin politician and founder in 1924 of the United States Progressive Party.

4. War in Vietnam.

5. The Royal Lao Army of the Kingdom of Laos was established after Laos gained autonomy from France in 1953. It trained rural hill people such as the Hmong, Khmu, and Dao peoples to fight secretly with the United States against the Vietnamese National Liberation Front. Laos officially remained a neutral nation during the War in Vietnam.

6. A mild stimulant obtained from leaves of the betel vine found in parts of Asia.

7. The United States Agency for International Development is a federal agency that supports the foreign policies of the United States by distributing material assistance and financial support.

8. May 1968 (mai 68) marked a period of political and social upheaval in Paris that included student demonstrations and labor strikes.

9. The Pine Ridge Indian Reservation in South Dakota is the home of the Oglala Sioux (Lakota), and the nearby town of Wounded Knee is the location of the 1973 conflict, lasting over two months, between members of the American Indian Movement and the FBI.

10. The Mekong Delta and waterways are in South Vietnam.

11. The Vietnamese People's Army is the military arm of the Socialist Republic of Vietnam. During the Vietnam War, the People's Army, located in North Vietnam, became the People's Army of Vietnam/North Vietnamese Army; in South Vietnam the People's Army was referred to as the National Liberation Front.

12. Ho Chi Minh was the Communist leader of the Democratic Republic of Vietnam (North Vietnam) during the Viet Minh independence movement, which began in 1941. He also had supported the U.S. against the Japanese during World War II. Ho Chi Minh sandals were made from discarded auto and truck tires and inner tubes.

13. The National Liberation Front was the organized militia as well as the regular army that fought against the United States in South Vietnam.

14. War against Terrorism.

15. Trent Lott was a Mississippi senator from 1989 to 2007; David Duke is a white supremacist and former member of the Ku Klux Klan who was a member of the Louisiana House of Representatives from 1990 to 1992; Rudolph "Rudy" Giuliani was the mayor of New York City from 1994 to 2001; Brett Schundler was mayor of Jersey City from late 1991 to mid-2001; Jesse Helms was a U.S. Senator from North Carolina from 1973 to January 3, 2003.

16. The forced removal and relocation (1831–1839) of Native American Indians from their ancestral lands in the South to the Indian Territory (Oklahoma) established by the United States following the 1830 Indian Removal Act.

17. Fulgencio Batista was a U.S.-backed Cuban dictator who was overthrown during the Cuban Revolution in 1959; Theodore Bilbo, a white supremacist, was governor of Mississippi from 1935 to 1947; Chiang Kai-shek was the premier of China (1928–1931, 1943–1948), chairman of the National Military Council of China (1931–1946), and the first president of the Republic of China (1948–1985).

18. The precise location of blackdotpress is unclear.

19. Title supplied by volume editors.

20. This order specifically disallowed discrimination in the armed services and officially ended legal segregation in the U. S. military. Truman's Executive Order extended FDR's Order #8802, which had allowed segregation in the armed services while banning discrimination in defense industries.

21. An army base near Harrisburg, Pennsylvania.

22. The National War College, part of the National Defense University in Washington, D.C., prepares military personnel for high-level positions.

23. *The Student Voice* was a newsletter published by SNCC, a group developed following a conference organized in 1960 by Ella Baker at Shaw University. At that time, she was director of the Southern Christian Leadership Conference. SNCC was involved in sit-ins, freedom rides, community organizing, and protests during the Civil Rights Movement of the 1960s.

24. War against Terrorism.

25. A version of the first poem in Lucille Clifton's "september suite" was published with the title "tuesday 9/11/01" in *September 11, 2001: American Writers Respond*, edited by William Heyen (Silver Springs, Md.: Etruscan Press, 2002), 80–84.

26. Korean War.

27. Will is a Korean War veteran.

28. White supremacists bombed the 16th Street Baptist Church in Birmingham on 15 September 1963, killing four girls aged 11–14, Addie Mae Collins, Carole Robertson, Cynthia Wesley, and Denise McNair.

29. The journey from Africa to the New World during chattel slavery.

30. British soldiers during the Revolutionary War for Independence.

31. War in Vietnam. Title supplied by volume editors.

32. Nikki Giovanni is a poet and was a prominent participant in the Black Arts Aesthetics Movement of the 1960s and 1970s; Kathleen Cleaver held leadership positions in the Black Panther Party and was the wife of Black Panther Party minister of information Eldridge Cleaver; H. Rap Brown was a member of the Student Nonviolent Coordinating Committee and later became the minister of justice in the Black Panther Party.

33. The Black Panthers (Black Panther Party for Self-Defense), founded on 15 October 1966 in Oakland, California, by Huey P. Newton and Bobby Seale, were part of the 1960s Black Liberation/Power Movement; the Student Nonviolent Coordinating Committee developed during the Civil Rights Movement and was founded in April 1960 following a meeting at Shaw University organized by Ella Baker, an activist since the 1930s and a leader in the Southern Christian Leadership Conference; the Symbionese Liberation Army was a fringe, mostly white, organization started in 1973 by Soledad prison escapee Donald DeFreeze and his partner Patricia Soltysik; they committed murders, kidnapped Patty Hearst, and robbed banks.

34. Cam Ranh Bay was the site of a U.S. military base in South Vietnam.

35. Pleiku is a town in Vietnam and the site of Camp Holloway, a U.S. military base. In 1965, the Vietnamese army attacked Camp Holloway in Pleiku and U.S. barracks at Qui Nhon within days of each other. President Lyndon Johnson used these attacks as the rationale for sending troops to Vietnam.

36. Article 15 of the Uniform Code of Military Justice authorizes noncriminal military punishment.

37. Ho Chi Minh was the Communist leader of the Democratic Republic of Vietnam (North Vietnam) during the Viet Minh independence movement, which began in 1941.

38. Title supplied by volume editors.

39. Korean War.

40. Jackie Robinson was a World War II veteran who also was the first African American baseball athlete to play Major League Baseball in the twentieth century when he signed with the Brooklyn Dodgers in 1947. Ralph Bunche was a civil rights activist who in 1950 became the first African American recipient of the Nobel Peace Prize for his role as a mediator for the United Nations during the Arab-Israeli conflict. He also worked for the Office of Strategic Services (renamed the CIA) and was an educator, having chaired the political science department at Howard University.

41. Quartermaster units are responsible for provisions and supplies other than ammunition and medicine.

42. A popular song by Stephen Brooks performed by Ella Fitzgerald, Fats Waller, and many other well-known jazz singers.

43. James Weldon Johnson's song "Lift Every Voice and Sing" (1899), written in honor of Booker T. Washington, is traditionally regarded as the "Negro National Anthem" or "Black National Anthem," not "Darktown Strutters' Ball."

44. War in Vietnam. Title supplied by volume editors.

45. Clergy and Laymen Concerned about Vietnam organized in 1965, aiming to influence thought on the war.

46. Hanoi, the capital of Vietnam prior to the war, became the capital of North Vietnam during the war. In the United States, the National Liberation Front was popularly and disparagingly referred to as the Viet Cong; they were the local militia as well as the regular army that fought against the United States in South Vietnam.

47. Ho Chi Minh was the Communist leader of the Democratic Republic of Vietnam (North Vietnam) during the Viet Minh independence movement, which began in 1941. He also had supported the U.S. against the Japanese during World War II.

48. The Geneva Agreements of 1954 divided French Indochina into Laos, Cambodia, and Vietnam.

49. John-Baptiste Ngo Dinh Diem became the first leader of South Vietnam in 1955.

50. Viet Cong, a derogatory phrase.

51. War in Vietnam.

52. Armored personnel carriers are tanks designed to transport personnel rather than weapons.

53. War in Vietnam.

54. Prisoner of war.

55. Martin Luther King Jr.

56. Don Quixote, the title character in Miguel de Cervantes' novel, has read too many books and has gone mad. He lives in a chivalric fantasy world in which he engages in strange behavior such as bowing to and attacking windmills, which he believes to be giants.

57. The location of a U.S. Marine Corps post in South Vietnam and the site of the battle of Khe Sanh.

58. A slang term for soldiers in the National Liberation Front. The term is derived from the derogatory phrase Viet Cong, which sometimes was altered to Victor Charlie (V.C.).

59. In the United States, the National Liberation Front was popularly and disparagingly referred to as the Viet Cong.

60. Stone Mountain in Georgia is the site of a massive carving of Jefferson Davis, Stonewall Jackson, and Robert E. Lee, the leaders of the Confederate States of America, by Gutzon Borglum. He also carved the presidents at Mount Rushmore in South Dakota.

61. Title supplied by volume editors; War against Terrorism.

62. In New Jersey.

63. Tuskegee Airmen, members of the 332nd Fighter Group and the 447th Bombardment Group of the United States Army Air Forces, were trained as pilots. They saw combat in World War II in Morocco. Benjamin O. Davis Sr. and Benjamin O. Davis Jr. were military pioneers: Davis Sr. became a brigadier general in the U.S. Army and Davis Jr. became a general.

64. Title supplied by volume editors.

65. Gulf War (Iraq).

66. Tactical ballistic missiles.

67. Title supplied by volume editors.

68. In New York City on 12 June 1982, throngs of people gathered at the United Nations to protest for peace and to call for an end to the arms race, especially nuclear weapons. They moved to Central Park to continue the rally, which lasted all day.

69. strange fruits: An allusion to the song and poem "Strange Fruit" (1937), initially titled "Bitter Fruit," by the Jewish political activist and school teacher Abel Meeropol writing under the name Lewis Allan. Billie Holiday popularized the song in 1939 after her stirring performance at Café Society in New York City and subsequent recording that same year.

70. Martin R. Delany was born to a free mother in Virginia. Before the Civil War he advocated for emigration to Africa. During the war he became a field major in the Union Army. He also wrote the serialized novel *Blake, or, The Huts of America*, which appeared in the *Weekly Anglo-African* in 1861 and 1862. The novel envisioned a Pan-African New World extricated from slavery. Delany's narrative was published in book form in 1970 (Boston: Beacon Press). W.E.B. Du Bois was a leading twentieth-century intellectual and advocate for political and social justice.

71. Booker T. Washington founded Tuskegee Institute and advocated industrial education and gradual equality for African Americans. Paul Robeson was an athlete, singer, actor, attorney, and civil rights activist during the 1940s and 1950s.

72. Marcus Garvey founded the Universal Negro Improvement Association and African Communities League (UNIA-ACL) in Jamaica in 1914, and he established the UNIA-ACL in the United States in 1917. He also advocated establishing a Pan-African settlement on the African continent.

73. Title supplied by volume editors.

74. An assault rifle designed in the Soviet Union during World War II. It was the primary weapon of the North Vietnamese People's Army.

75. An automatic assault rifle designed in the United States and introduced into the military during the War in Vietnam.

76. A machine gun manufactured in the United States and introduced into the military during the War in Vietnam.

77. Black participants in the U.S. Revolutionary War for Independence. Prince Estabrook, formerly enslaved, was wounded at the battle of Lexington; Peter Salem, a freedman, fought in the Battle at Bunker Hill and is believed to have killed British major John Pitcairn in battle; Crispus Attucks, likely escaped from slavery, was the first person shot during the Boston Massacre on 5 March 1770.

78. A brand of cigars.

79. Saigon was the capital of the former Cochinchina region (*la colonie de Cochinchine*) of the southern part of Vietnam, which was colonized by the French. From 1954 to 1975, Saigon was the name of the capital of the independent state of South Vietnam. In 1975, the city's name was changed to Ho Chi Minh City.

80. In African American vernacular speech the name is usually "Charlie or Mr. Charlie"; this term typically refers to white persons with power in the United States, yet it can refer more generally to persons who operate within systems of power and carry out their oppressive policies and actions. During the war, Charlie or Chuck was another derogatory slang term for the equally disparaging term Viet Cong. Black soldiers sometimes used it to signify or hide their actual reference.

81. Fort Ord is an army base in the Monterey Bay area in California.

82. These are references to medical facilities associated with the training of black doctors. Meharry Medical College, founded in 1876 in Nashville, Tennessee was the first historically black medical school in the South. Renowned African American cardiac surgeon Dr. Daniel Hale Williams founded Provident Hospital in 1893 in Chicago. Alta Bates is a hospital in Berkeley, California.

83. Slang for when the signal occurs. The word is onomatopoeia for the sound of Morse code. Here it also is used as a nonsense phrase to add a flourish or to code meaning.

84. A card game.

85. Probably the Chinese politician and military leader Peng Te-huai, who was imprisoned during the Cultural Revolution in China.

86. Maquis are guerilla fighters; clochards are destitute or homeless people.

87. Characters with no basis in reality. King Kong and Mighty Joe Young are oversized gorillas in eponymous movies made in 1933 and 1949, respectively. The Cardiff Giant was a hoax perpetrated in 1869 involving the supposed mummified remains of a giant human.

88. Hannibal is seen as a brilliant military strategist whose most famous action involved his army's incursions into northern Italy on the backs of elephants and then his occupation of the region.

89. An Italian town.

90. In Greek mythology, a place for the dead.

91. Bronze and stone sculptures with African features: the Sphinx in Egypt; bronze heads from the Benin Empire of West Africa; colossal pre-Columbian Olmec heads lo-

cated in Mexico. The Twenty-Eighth Dynasty of Egypt is considered to have been an African dynasty.

92. Anti-ballistic missile.

93. NORAD is an acronym for North American Aerospace Defense Command, a joint airspace defense organization of the United States and Canada.

94. Strategic Air Command.

95. Kano is the capital city of Kano State, Nigeria; Tananarive is the capital of Madagascar; Canton Island is located in the South Pacific; Kauai is one of the Hawaiian Islands; Woomera is a village in Australia; Houston is probably a reference to NASA; Kennedy is probably a reference to the Kennedy Space Center in Cape Canaveral, Florida.

96. AMSA is the acronym for Advanced Manned Strategic Aircraft; ICBM is the acronym for Intercontinental Ballistic Missile.

Appendix

List of Titles by Themes and Wars

Citizenship, Civil Rights, and Peace

Baker, Ella, "The Black Woman in the Civil Rights Struggle" (1969)

Baldwin, James, "My Dungeon Shook: Letter to My Nephew on the One Hundredth Anniversary of the Emancipation" (1962)

Bond, Julian, "I Too, Hear America Singing" (1960)

Domingo, W. A., "If We Must Die" (1919)

Douglass, Frederick, "Fellow Citizens: On Slavery and the Fourth of July" (1852)

———, "What country have I?" (1847)

Du Bois, W.E.B., "My Country 'Tis of Thee" (1907)

Forten, James, *Letters from a Man of Colour on a Late Bill before the Senate of Pennsylvania* (1813)

Forten Purvis, Sarah Louisa, "My Country" (1834)

Freedom Petition, Black Abolitionists Declare Rights to Revolutionary Freedom (1777)

Garnet, Henry Highland, "An Address to the Slaves of the United States of America" (1843)

Harper, Frances Ellen Watkins, "An Appeal to My Countrywomen" (1871)

Harper, Michael S., "American History" (1970)

Johnson, James Weldon, "To America" (1917)

Matta, Allia Abdullah, "Mymerica" (2006)

Niagara Movement, "Address to the Country" (1906)

Owen, Chandler, "The Failure of Negro Leadership" (1918)

Sanchez, Sonia, "Reflections after the June 12th March for Disarmament" (1984)

Simpson, Joshua McCarter, "Song of the 'Aliened' American" (1852)

Walker, David, *Walker's Appeal, in Four Articles: Together with a Preamble to the Coloured Citizens of the World, but in Particular, and Very Expressly, to Those of the United States of America* (1829)

Wheatley, Phillis, "Liberty and Peace, a Poem" (1784)

Whitfield, James Monroe, "America" (1853)

Whitman, Albery Allson, "The End of the Whole Matter" (1877)

French and Indian Wars/Seven Years' War (1754–1763)

Equiano, Olaudah, "Life at Sea during the French and Indian War (Seven Years' War)" (1789)

Terry, Lucy, "Bars Fight" (1855)

Revolutionary War for Independence (1775–1783)

Bush-Banks, Olivia, "Crispus Attucks" (1899)

Chesnutt, Charles Waddell, "Acquit Yourselves Like Men: An Address to Colored Soldiers at Grays Armory, Cleveland, Ohio" (1917)

Dunbar, Paul Laurence, "Black Samson of Brandywine" (1903)

Freedom Petition, Black Abolitionists Declare Rights to Revolutionary Freedom (1777)

King, Boston, "Freedom and fear fighting for the Loyalists" (1798)

Wheatley, Phillis, "His Excellency Gen. Washington" (1776)

———, Letter Accompanying a Poem to General George Washington (1775)

———, "Liberty and Peace, a Poem" (1784)

———, "On the Death of General Wooster" (1980)

Whitfield, James Monroe, "America" (1853)

Whitman, Albery Allson, "Hymn to the Nation" (1877)

War of 1812 (1812–1815)

Williams, John A., "1812" (1972)

Indian Wars (1816–1858)

Whitman, Albery Allson, *Twasinta's Seminoles; or, Rape of Florida* (1884)

U.S.-Mexico War (1846–1848)

Douglass, Frederick, "Peace! Peace! Peace!" (1848)

———, "The War with Mexico" (1848)

Francis, Vievee, "Frederick Douglass Speaks before the Anti-Mexican War Abolitionists" (2006)

———, "South of Houston" (2006)

Civil War (1861–1865)

Augusta, Alexander T., "Colored men have their rights that white men are bound to respect" (1863)

Bell, James Madison, *A Poem Entitled, the Day and the War* (1864)

Brawley, Benjamin Griffith, "My Hero (To Robert Gould Shaw)" (1915)

Brown, William Wells, *Clotelle; or the Colored Heroine* (1867)

Cabble, Samuel, "I look forward to a brighter day" (1863)

Chesnutt, Charles Waddell, "Acquit Yourselves Like Men: An Address to Colored Soldiers at Grays Armory, Cleveland, Ohio" (1917)

Douglass, Frederick, "How to End the War" (1861)

Douglass, Lewis Henry, "If I die tonight I will not die a coward" (1863)

Dunbar, Paul Laurence, "The Colored Soldiers" (1895)

———, "Lincoln" (1903)

———, "Robert Gould Shaw" (1900)

Forten Grimké, Charlotte, "True manhood has no limitations of color" (1864)
Graham Du Bois, Shirley, *It's Morning* (1940)
Horton, George Moses, "Jefferson in a Tight Place" (1865)
Johnson, Fenton, "De Ol' Sojer" (1916)
Randall, Dudley, "Memorial Wreath" (1962)
Ray, Henrietta Cordelia, "Robert G. Shaw" (1910)
Rowe, George Clinton, "The Reason Why (1887)
Shuften, Sarah E., "Ethiopia's Dead" (1865)
Smalls, Robert, "Commandeering Freedom: Robert Smalls Pilots the Confederate Ship *Planter*" (1864)
Stephens, George E., "How dare I be offered half the pay of any man, be he white or red?" (1864)
Taylor, Susie Baker King, "A Nurse for the 33rd USCT" (1902)
Trethewey, Natasha, "Elegy for the Native Guards" (2006)
Trotter, James Monroe, "The Fifty-Fourth at Wagner" (1883)
Truth, Sojourner, "The Valiant Soldiers" (1878)
Whitman, Albery Allson, "The End of the Whole Matter" (1877)
——, "Hymn to the Nation" (1877)
——, *Twasinta's Seminoles; Or, Rape of Florida* (1884)

Spanish-Cuban-U.S. War (1898)

A.M.E. Church: *Voice of Missions*, "The Negro Should Not Enter the Army" (1899)
Beadle, Samuel Alfred, "Lines" (1899)
Bush-Banks, Olivia, "A Hero of San Juan" (1899)
Dunbar, Paul Laurence, "The Conquerors: The Black Troops in Cuba" (1898)
Holliday, Presley, "The colored soldier . . . properly belongs among the bravest and most trustworthy in the land" (1899)
Johnson, Fenton, "De Ol' Sojer" (1916)

U.S.-Philippines War (1899–1902)

A.M.E. Church: *Voice of Missions*, "The Negro Should Not Enter the Army" (1899)
A Black Soldier in the Philippine Islands, "We don't want these islands" (1900)
Gilmore, F. Grant, "A Battle in the Philippines" (1915)

World War I (1914–1918)

Burrill, Mary, *Aftermath: A One-Act Play of Negro Life* (1919)
Chesnutt, Charles Waddell, "Acquit Yourselves Like Men: An Address to Colored Soldiers at Grays Armory, Cleveland, Ohio" (1917)
Cotter, Joseph Seamon, Jr., "Moloch" (1921)
Du Bois, W.E.B., "Close Ranks" (1918)
——, "A Philosophy in Time of War" (1918)
——, "Our Special Grievances" (1918)
——, "Returning Soldiers" (1919)

Dunbar-Nelson, Alice, *Mine Eyes Have Seen* (1918)
——, "I Sit and Sew" (1920)
Jamison, Roscoe Conkling, "The Negro Soldiers" (1917)
Johnson, Fenton, "The New Day" (1919)
Matheus, John F., *'Cruiter* (1927)
McKay, Claude, "If We Must Die" (1919)
Owen, Chandler, "The Failure of Negro Leadership" (1918)
Spencer, Anne Bethel, "The Wife-Woman" (1922)
Tolson, Melvin Beaunorus, Sr., "A Legend of Versailles" (1944)
Watkins, Lucian Bottow, "The Negro Soldiers of America: What We Are Fighting For" (1918)

World War II (1939–1945)

Bells, Aeron D., "Local prejudice, or an official order from Washington" (1982)
Brooks, Gwendolyn, "Negro Hero" (1945)
——, "the white troops had their orders but the Negroes looked like men" (1945)
Goodwin, Ruby Berkley, "Guilty" (1948)
Graham Du Bois, Shirley, "Tar" (1945)
Hughes, Langston, "Beaumont to Detroit: 1943" (1943)
Johnson, Georgia Douglas, "Black Recruit" (1948)
Kaufman, Bob, "War Memoir: Jazz, Don't Listen to It at Your Own Risk" (1981)
Moten, Cora Ball, "Negro Mother to Her Soldier Son" (1943)
Petry, Ann Lane, "In Darkness and Confusion" (1947)
Soldiers at Ft. Logan, Colorado, "We'd rather die on our knees as a man, than to live in this world as a slave" (1943)
Thomas-Anderson, Gladys O., "An honor to be in the Army and be black, too. We were the beginning." (2004)
Wideman, John Edgar, "Valaida" (1989)
Williams, Gwendolyn, "Heart against the Wind" (1944)

Korean War (1950–1953)

Becton, Julius W., Jr., "We were pioneers" (2004)
Edwards, Junius, "Liars Don't Qualify" (1961)
Hopkins, Stephen, "Uncle Sam didn't do much for me. I am proud of my service." (2004)
Killens, John Oliver, "God Bless America" (1952)
Rodgers, Marie, "I asked to go to Vietnam" (2004)

War in Vietnam (1955–1973)

Bambara, Toni Cade, "The Sea Birds Are Still Alive" (1977)
Becton, Julius W., Jr., "We were pioneers" (2004)
Holcomb, Robert, "I was sworn into the Army in manacles" (1984)

King, Martin Luther Jr., "Strange Liberators: A Speech at Riverside Church, 4 April 1967" (1967)

Komunhakaa, Yusef, "Re-Creating the Scene" (1988)

———, "The One-legged Stool" (1988)

Rodgers, Marie, "I asked to go to Vietnam" (2004)

Williams, John A., " 'Nam" (1972)

Gulf War (1990–1991) and War on Terrorism (2001–present)

Baraka, Amiri, *Somebody Blew Up America* (2001)

Clifton, Lucille, "september song: a poem in 7 days" (2002)

Mitchell, Eric, "Pray 4 a quick ending to this" (2004)

Pennick, Janet, "Everything about war was horrible" (2004)

BIBLIOGRAPHY

Adams, Virginia M., ed. *On The Altar of Freedom*. Amherst: University of Massachusetts Press, 1991.

Adams-Earley, Charity. *One Woman's Army: A Black Officer Remembers the WAC*. College Station: Texas A&M University Press, 1989.

Allen, Ernest. "Waiting for Tojo: The Pro-Japan Vigil of Black Missourians, 1932–1943." *Gateway Heritage* 16 (Fall 1995): 38–55.

———. "When Japan Was 'Champion of the Darker Races': Satokata Takahashi and the Flowering of Black Messianic Nationalism." *Black Scholar* 24 (Winter 1994): 23–46.

Amar, Akhil Reed. *America's Constitution: A Biography*. New York: Random, 2005.

———. *The Bill of Rights*. New Haven, Conn.: Yale University Press, 1998.

Anderson, Benedict. *Imagined Communities: Reflections on the Origins and Spread of Nationalism*. New York: Verso, 1990.

Aptheker, Herbert. *American Negro Slave Revolts*. New York: International Publishers, 1974.

———. *The Negro in the American Revolution*. New York: International Publishers, 1940.

Ash, Stephen V. *Firebrand of Liberty: The Story of Two Black Regiments that Changed the Course of the Civil War*. New York: W. W. Norton, 2008.

Astor, Gerald. *The Right to Fight: A History of African Americans in the Military*. Cambridge, Mass.: Da Capo Press, 1998.

Bailey, Beth, and David Farber. "The Double-V Campaign in World War II Hawaii: African Americans, Racial Ideology, and Federal Power." *Journal of Social History* 26, no. 4 (1993): 817–43.

Baldwin, James. "The American Dream and the American Negro." *New York Times Magazine*, 7 March 1965, SM32.

———. *The Price of the Ticket: Collected Nonfiction, 1948–1985*. New York: St. Martins, 1985.

Barbeau, Arthur E., and Florette Henri. *The Unknown Soldiers: African-American Troops in World War I*. 1974. Reprint, Cambridge, Mass.: Da Capo, 1996.

Barrow, Charles Kelly, J. H. Segars, and R. B. Rosenburg, eds. *Black Confederates*. Gretna, La.: Pelican Publishing, 1995.

Berlin, Ira, ed. *Freedom: A Documentary History of Emancipation. 1861–1867: The Black Military Experience*. Series 2. New York: Cambridge University Press, 1982.

Berlin, Ira, Joseph Patrick Reidy, and Leslie S. Rowland. *Freedom's Soldiers: The Black Military Experience in the Civil War*. Cambridge, UK: Cambridge University Press, 1998.

Black, Samuel W., ed. *Soul Soldiers: African Americans and the Vietnam Era*. Pittsburgh: Heinz Pittsburgh Regional History Center and the Historical Society of Western Pennsylvania, 2006.

Blassingame, John, Richard G. Carlson, Clarence L. Mohr, Julie S. Jones, John R. McKivigan, David R. Roediger, and Jason H. Silverman, eds. *The Frederick Douglass Papers*.

Series 1, *Speeches, Debates, and Interviews*, vol. 2, *1847–1854*. New Haven, Conn.: Yale University Press, 1979.

Blight, David W. *Beyond the Battlefield: Race, Memory and the American Civil War*. Amherst: University of Massachusetts Press, 2002.

Bogin, Ruth. "'Liberty Further Extended': A 1776 Antislavery Manuscript by Lemuel Haynes." *William and Mary Quarterly* 40, no. 1 (1983): 85–105.

Bolster, W. Jeffrey. *Black Jacks: African American Seamen in the Age of the Sail*. Cambridge, Mass.: Harvard University Press, 1997.

Bond, Horace Mann. "The Negro in the Armed Forces of the United States Prior to World War I." *Journal of Negro Education* 12, no. 3 (1943): 268–87.

Bonsal, Stephen, "The Negro Soldier in War and Peace." *North American Review* 185, no. 616 (1907): 321–27.

Bowers, William T, William M. Hammond, and George MacGarrigle. *Black Soldiers, White Army: The 24th Infantry Regiment in Korea*. Berlin: University Press of the Pacific, 2005.

Bracker, Milton. "Negro Unit Proud of Gains in Italy." *New York Times*, 1 November 1944, 10.

Brandt, Nat. *Harlem at War: The Black Experience in WWII*. Syracuse: Syracuse University Press, 1996.

Branham, Robert James. "'Of Thee I Sing': Contesting 'America.'" *American Quarterly* 48, no. 4 (1996): 632–52.

Brasher, Glenn D. *The Peninsula Campaign and the Necessity of Emancipation: African Americans and the Fight for Freedom*. Chapel Hill: University of North Carolina Press, 2014.

Brawley, Benjamin. *A Social History of the American Negro: Being a History of the Negro Problem in the United States, Including a History and Study of the Republic of Liberia*. 1921. Reprint, Charleston, S.C.: Bibliobazaar, 2007.

Brooks, Jennifer. *Defining the Peace: World War II Veterans, Race, and the Remaking of Southern Political Tradition*. Chapel Hill: University of North Carolina Press, 2004.

Brown, Earl, and George Leighton. *The Negro and the War*. New York: Public Affairs Committee, 1942.

Brown, William Wells, *The Negro in the American Rebellion: His Heroism and His Fidelity*. Athens: Ohio University Press, 2003.

Buckley, Gail. *American Patriots: The Story of Blacks in the Military from the Revolution to Desert Storm*. New York: Random House, 2001.

Bussey, Charles M. *Firefight at Yechon: Courage and Racism in the Korean War*. Lincoln, Neb.: Bison Books, 2002.

Butler, John Sibley. "Affirmative Action in the Military." *Annals of the American Academy of Political and Social Science* 523 (September 1992): 196–206.

Campbell, J. P. "Give Us Equal Pay and We Will Go to War." [1864.] In *Lift Every Voice: African American Oratory, 1787–1900*, edited by Philip S. Foner and Robert James Branham, 426–28. Tuscaloosa: University of Alabama Press, 1998.

Carroll, Joseph. *Slave Insurrections in the United States, 1800–1865*. New York: Dover Publications, 2004.

Cecelski, David, and Timothy Tyson, eds., *Democracy Betrayed: The Wilmington Race Riot of 1898 and Its Legacy*. Chapel Hill: University of North Carolina Press, 1998.

Chambers, John Whiteclay, ed. *The Oxford Companion to American Military History*. New York: Oxford University Press, 1999.

Charles, Patrick. *Washington's Decision: The Story of George Washington's Decision to Reaccept Black Enlistments in the Continental Army, December 31, 1775*. Charleston: Booksurge.com, 2006.

Childers, Thomas. *Soldier from the War Returning: The Greatest Generation's Troubled Homecoming from World War II*. Boston: Houghton Mifflin Harcourt, 2009.

Cimprich, John. *Fort Pillow, a Civil War Massacre, and Public Memory*. Baton Rouge: Louisiana State University Press, 2011.

Clark, Kathleen Ann. *Defining Moments: African American Commemoration and Political Culture in the South, 1863–1913*. Chapel Hill: University of North Carolina Press, 2005.

Clavin, Matthew J. *Toussaint Louverture and the American Civil War: The Promise and Peril of a Second American Revolution*. Philadelphia: University of Pennsylvania Press, 2009.

Clifford, Mary Louise. *From Slavery to Freetown: Black Loyalists after the American Revolution*. Jefferson: McFarland, 2006.

Clinton, Catherine, and Nina Silber, eds. *Divided Houses: Gender and the Civil War*. New York: Oxford University Press, 1992.

Coddington, Ronald S. *African American Faces of the Civil War: An Album*. Baltimore, Md.: Johns Hopkins University Press, 2012.

Colaiaco, James A. *Frederick Douglass and the Fourth of July Oration*. New York: Palgrave, 2006.

Cornish, Dudley Taylor. *The Sable Arm: Black Troops in the Union Army, 1861–1865*. Lawrence: University Press of Kansas, 1987.

Countryman, Edward. *Enjoy the Same Liberty: Black Americans and the Revolutionary Era*. Lanham, Md.: Rowman & Littlefield Publishers, 2011.

Cox, Clinton. *The Forgotten Heroes: The Story of the Buffalo Soldiers*. New York: Scholastic, 1993.

Creighton, Margaret S. *The Colors of Courage: Gettysburg's Forgotten History: Immigrants, Women, and African Americans in the Civil War's Defining Battle*. New York: Basic Books, 2005.

Dailey, Jane, Glenda Elizabeth Gilmore, and Bryant Simon, eds. *Jumpin' Jim Crow: Southern Politics from Civil War to Civil Rights*. Princeton, N.J.: Princeton University Press, 2000.

Dalfiume, Richard M. *Desegregation of the U.S. Armed Forces: Fighting on Two Fronts, 1939–1953*. Columbia: University of Missouri Press, 1969.

Davis, David Brion. *The Problem of Slavery in the Age of Revolution, 1770–1823*. 1975. Reprint, New York: Oxford University Press, 1999.

Davis, Frank Marshall. "To Those Who Sing America." In *Frank Marshall Davis: Black Moods, Collected Poems*, edited by John Edgar Tidwell, 129–30. Urbana: University of Illinois Press, 2002.

Delany, Martin R. *The Condition, Elevation, Emigration and Destiny of the Colored People of the United States*. In *Martin R. Delany: A Documentary Reader*, edited by Robert S. Levine, 189–216. Chapel Hill: University of North Carolina Press, 2003.

Desnoyers-Colas, Elizabeth. *Marching as to War: Narratives of African American Women's Experiences in the Gulf Wars*. New York: University Press of America, 2014.

Douglas, H. Ford. "I Do Not Believe in the Antislavery of Abraham Lincoln." [1860.] In *Lift Every Voice: African American Oratory, 1787–1900*, edited by Philip S. Foner and Robert James Branham, 340–54. Tuscaloosa: University of Alabama Press, 1998.

Douglass, Frederick. "Country, Conscience, and the Anti-Slavery Cause: An Address Delivered in New York, New York, on 11 May 1847." In *The Frederick Douglass Papers: Speeches, Debates, and Interviews*. Series 1, vol. 2, edited by John Blassingame et al., 57–68. New Haven, Conn.: Yale University Press, 1979.

———. "The Present Condition and Future Prospects of the Negro People (Speech at Annual Meeting of the American Foreign Anti-Slavery Society, New York City, May 1853)." In *The Life and Writings of Frederick Douglass: Pre-Civil War Decade, 1850–1860*. Vol. 2, edited by Philip S. Foner, 243–54. 1950. Reprint, New York: International Publishers, 1975.

———. "What the Black Man Wants." In *The Life and Writings of Frederick Douglass*. Vol. 4, edited by Philip S. Foner, 157. New York: International Publishers, 1950.

Du Bois, W.E.B. *Autobiography of W.E.B. Du Bois*. New York: International Publishers, 1980.

———. *Black Reconstruction, 1860–1880*. 1935. Reprint, New York: Free Press, 1998.

———. *Dusk of Dawn*. In *Du Bois: Writings: The Suppression of the Slave Trade; The Souls of Black Folk; Dusk of Dawn; Essays*, 549–802. New York: Library of America, 1986.

———. "The Negro Soldier in Service Abroad during the First World War." *Journal of Negro Education* 12, no. 3 (1943): 324–34.

———. *The Souls of Black Folk*. 1903. New York: Vintage/LOA, 1990.

———. *The Suppression of the Slave Trade*. In *Du Bois: Writings: The Suppression of the Slave Trade; The Souls of Black Folk; Dusk of Dawn; Essays*, 1–356. New York: Library of America, 1986.

Dudziak, Mary L. *Cold War and Civil Rights: Race and the Image of Democracy*. Princeton, N.J.: Princeton University Press, 2000.

Early, Gerald., ed. *The Muhammad Ali Reader*. New Jersey: Ecco Press, 1998.

Early, Gerald, and Alan Lightman. "Race, Art, and Integration: The Image of the African American Soldier in Popular Culture during the Korean War." *Bulletin of the American Academy of Arts and Sciences* 57, no. 1 (2003): 32–38.

Edgerton, Robert B. *Hidden Heroism: Black Soldiers in America's Wars*. New York: Basic Books, 2002.

Egerton, Douglas R. *Death or Liberty: African Americans and Revolutionary America*. New York: Oxford University Press, 2009.

Eggleston, Larry G. *Women in the Civil War: Extraordinary Stories of Soldiers, Spies, Nurses, Doctors, Crusaders and Others*. Jefferson: McFarland, 2003.

Ellis, Richard J. *To the Flag: The Unlikely History of the Pledge of Allegiance.* Lawrence: University of Kansas Press, 2005.

Ellison, Ralph. *Invisible Man.* New York: Random House, 1952.

——. "What America Would Be Like without Blacks." *Time*, April 6, 1970, 54–55.

Emanuel, James. "Renaissance Sonneteers." *Black World* (September 1975), 32–45, 92–97.

Emanuel, James A., and Theodore L. Gross, eds. *Dark Symphony: Negro Literature in America.* New York: Free Press, 1968.

Emilio, Luis F. *A Brave Black Regiment: The History of the 54th Massachusetts, 1863–1865.* 2nd ed. 1894. Reprint, New York: Da Capo Press, 1995.

Farrar, Hayward "Woody." "The Black Soldier in Two World Wars." In *A Companion to African American History*, edited by Alton Hornsby Jr., 349–63. Oxford: Blackwell, 2005.

Faust, Drew Gilpin. *The Creation of Confederate Nationalism: Ideology and Identity in the Civil War South.* Baton Rouge: Louisiana State University Press, 1990.

——. *This Republic of Suffering: Death and the American Civil War.* New York: Vintage, 2008.

Fendrich, James M. "The Returning Black Vietnam-Era Veteran." *Social Service Review* 46, no. 1 (1972): 60–75.

Finkle, Lee. *Forum for Protest: The Black Press during World War II.* Madison, N.J.: Fairleigh Dickinson University Press, 1975.

Foner, Eric. *Reconstruction: America's Unfinished Revolution, 1863–1877.* 1988. Reprint, New York: HarperCollins, 2002.

Foner, Philip S. *Blacks in the American Revolution.* Westport, Conn.: Greenwood, 1975.

——, ed. *The Life and Writings of Frederick Douglass: Pre–Civil War Decade, 1850–1860.* Vol. 2. 1950. Reprint, New York: International Publishers, 1975.

——, ed. *The Life and Writings of Frederick Douglass: The Civil War.* Vol. 3. 1952. Reprint, New York: International Publishers, 1975.

Foner, Philip, and Robert Branham, eds. *Lift Every Voice: African American Oratory 1787–1900.* Tuscaloosa: University of Alabama Press, 1998.

Forbes, Ella. *African American Women during the Civil War.* New York: Routledge, 1998.

Forman, James. *The Making of Black Revolutionaries.* New York: Macmillan, 1972.

Franklin, John Hope, and Genna Rae McNeil, eds. *African Americans and the Living Constitution.* Washington: Smithsonian, 1995.

Franklin, John Hope, and Loren Schweninger. *Runaway Slaves: Rebels on the Plantation.* New York: Oxford University Press, 2000.

Frey, Sylvia. *Water from the Rock: Black Resistance in a Revolutionary Age.* Princeton, N.J.: Princeton University Press, 1991.

Gaines, Kevin. *Uplifting the Race: Black Leadership, Politics, and Culture in the Twentieth Century.* Chapel Hill: University of North Carolina Press, 1996.

Gartner, Scott Sigmund, and Gary M. Segura. "Race, Casualties, and Opinion in the Vietnam War." *Journal of Politics* 62, no. 1 (2000): 115–46.

Garvin, Charles Herbert. "The Negro in the Special Services of the U.S. Army: Medical Corps, Dental Corps and Nurse Corps." *Journal of Negro Education* 12, no. 3 (1943): 335–44.

Gates, Henry Louis, Jr., and Gene Andrew Jarrett, eds. *The New Negro: Readings on Race, Representation, and African American Culture, 1892–1938*. Princeton, N.J.: Princeton University Press, 2007.

Gatewood, Willard B., Jr. "Black Americans and the Quest for Empire, 1898–1903." *Journal of Southern History* 38, no. 4 (1972): 545–66.

———. "Negro Troops in Florida, 1898." *Florida Historical Quarterly* 49, no. 1 (1970): 1–15.

———. *"Smoked Yankees" and the Struggle for Empire: Letters from Negro Soldiers, 1898–1902*. Urbana: University of Illinois Press, 1971.

Gerstle, Gary. *American Crucible: Race and the Nation in the Twentieth Century*. Princeton, N.J.: Princeton University Press, 2002.

Gerzina, Gretchen Holbrook. *Mr. and Mrs. Prince: How an Extraordinary Eighteenth-Century Family Moved out of Slavery and into Legend*. New York: Harper, 2008.

Gilbert, Alan. *Black Patriots and Loyalists: Fighting for Emancipation in the War for Independence*. Chicago: University of Chicago Press, 2012.

Gilmore, Glenda E. *Defying Dixie: The Radical Roots of Civil Rights, 1919–1950*. New York: W. W. Norton, 2008.

Gore, Dayo. *Radicalism at the Crossroads: African American Women Activists in the Cold War*. New York: New York University Press, 2011.

Gorn, Elliott J., ed. *Muhammad Ali: The People's Champ*. Urbana: University of Illinois Press, 1995.

Gould, William B. IV. *Diary of a Contraband: The Civil War Passage of a Black Sailor*. Stanford, Calif.: Stanford University Press, 2002.

Grant, Joanne. *Ella Baker: Freedom Bound*. New York: John Wiley & Sons, 1998.

Greenberg, Amy S. *Manifest Manhood and the Antebellum American Empire*. New York: Cambridge University Press, 2005.

Greene, Lorenzo. "Some Observations on the Black Regiment of Rhode Island in the American Revolution." *Journal of Negro History* 37, no. 2 (1952): 142–72.

Grimké, Angelina Weld. *Rachel: A Play in Three Acts*. Boston: Cornhill Company, 1920.

Guglielmo, Thomas A. "'Red Cross, Double Cross': Race and America's World War II-Era Blood Donor Service." *Journal of American History* 91, no. 1 (2010): 63–90.

Guy, Rosa. *Bird at My Window*. Philadelphia: Lippincott, 1966.

Hachey, Thomas. "Walter White and the American Negro Soldier in World War II: A Diplomatic Dilemma for Britain." *Phylon* 39, no. 3 (1978): 241–49.

Halberstam, David. *The Best and the Brightest*. 1972. Reprint, New York: Ballantine, 1993.

———. *The Coldest Winter: America and the Korean War*. New York: Hyperion, 2007.

Halbert, H. S., and T. H. Hall. *The Creek War of 1813 and 1814*. Tuscaloosa: University of Alabama Press, 1969.

Hall, Richard H. *Women on the Civil War Battlefront*. Lawrence: University Press of Kansas, 2006.

Hall, Simon. "The Response of the Moderate Wing of the Civil Rights Movement to the War in Vietnam." *Historical Journal* 46, no. 3 (2003): 669–701.

Hamlin, Françoise Nicole. *Crossroads at Clarksdale: The Black Freedom Struggle in the Mississippi Delta after World War II*. Chapel Hill: University of North Carolina Press, 2012.

Hammon, Jupiter. "A Dialogue Entitled the Kind Master and Dutiful Servant: A Line on the Present War." In *Jupiter Hammon and the Biblical Beginnings of African-American Literature*, ed. Sondra A. O'Neale. Metuchen, N.J.: American Theological Library Association and Scarecrow Press, 1993.

———. "An Evening's Improvement." In *Jupiter Hammon and the Biblical Beginnings of African-American Literature*, edited by Sondra A. O'Neale, 160–74. Metuchen, N.J.: The American Theological Library Association and Scarecrow Press, 1993.

Hardwick, Kevin R. "'Your Old Father Abe Lincoln Is Dead and Damned': Black Soldiers and the Memphis Race Riot of 1866." *Journal of Social History* 27, no. 1 (1993): 109–28.

Harris, Stephen L. *Harlem's Hell Fighters: The African-American 369th Infantry in World War I*. Washington, D.C.: Brassey's, 2003.

Harris-Perry, Melissa V. *Sister Citizen: Shame, Stereotypes, and Black Women in America*. New Haven, Conn.: Yale University Press, 2011.

Hastie, William H. "Negro Officers in Two World Wars." *Journal of Negro Education* 12, no. 3 (1943): 316–23.

Hellwig, David. "Strangers in Their Own Land: Patterns of Black Nativism, 1830–1930." *American Studies Today* 23, no. 1 (1982): 85–98.

Henderson, George W. "History of Negro Citizenship." *A.M.E. Church Review* 15, no. 3 (January 1899): 689–708.

Henry, Aaron. *Fire Ever Burning*. Jackson: University Press of Mississippi, 2000.

Higginbotham, A. Leon. *Shades of Freedom: Racial Politics and the Presumptions of the American Legal Process*. New York: Oxford University Press, 1996.

Hill, Errol G., and James V. Hatch. *A History of African American Theater*. Cambridge, UK: Cambridge University Press, 2005.

Hill, Patricia Liggins, Bernard W. Bell, Trudier Harris, William J. Harris, R. Baxter Miller, and Sondra A. O'Neale. "'No Other Music'll Ease My Misery': African American History and Culture, 1960 to the Present: Social Revolution, New Renaissance, and Social Reconstruction." In *Call and Response: The Riverside Anthology of the African American Literary Tradition*, edited by Patricia Liggins Hill et al., 1343–385. Boston: Houghton Mifflin, 1998.

Hill, Patricia Liggins, Bernard W. Bell, Trudier Harris, William J. Harris, R. Baxter Miller, and Sondra A. O'Neale, eds. *Call and Response: The Riverside Anthology of the African American Literary Tradition*. Boston: Houghton Mifflin, 1998.

Hine, Darlene Clark. "Black Professionals and Race Consciousness: Origins of the Civil Rights Movement, 1890–1950." *Journal of American History* 89 (March 2003): 1279–294.

Hine, Darlene Clark, Elsa Barkley Brown, and Rosalyn Terborg-Penn, eds. *Black Women in America: An Historical Encyclopedia*. Bloomington: Indiana University Press, 1993.

Hollandsworth, James G. *The Louisiana Native Guard: The Black Military Experience during the Civil War*. Baton Rouge: Louisiana State University Press, 1995.

Hollern, Susan, ed. *Women and Motorcycling: The Early Years*. Summer Hill Lake, N.Y.: Pink Rose Publications, 1999.

Holton, Woody. *Black Americans in the Revolutionary Era: A Brief History with Documents*. New York: St. Martin's, 2009.

Homen, Lynn M., and Thomas Reilly. *Black Knights: The Story of the Tuskegee Airmen*. Gretna, La.: Pelican Publishing, 2001.

Honey, Maureen, ed. *Bitter Fruit: African American Women in World War II*. Columbia: University of Missouri Press, 1999.

Horne, Gerald. *The Counter-Revolution of 1776: Slave Resistance and the Origins of the United States of America*. New York: New York University Press, 2014.

————. *The White Pacific: U.S. Imperialism and Black Slavery in the South Seas after the Civil War*. Honolulu: University of Hawai'i Press, 2007.

Hughes, Langston. "I, Too, Sing America." In *Collected Poems of Langston Hughes*, edited by Arnold Rampersad and David Roessel, 46. New York: Knopf, 1994.

————. "The Red Cross Nurses," *Monthly* 19 (February 1918): 13.

Hunton, Addie W., and Kathryn M. Johnson. *Two Colored Women with the American Expeditionary Forces*. 1920. Reprint, New York: G. K. Hall, 1997.

Hurston, Zora Neale. "Crazy for this Democracy." In *I Love Myself When I Am Laughing . . . and Then Again When I Am Looking Mean and Impressive*, edited by Alice Walker, 165–68. New York: Feminist Press, 1979.

Jackson, Maurice, and Jacqueline Bacon, eds. *African Americans and the Haitian Revolution: Selected Essays and Historical Documents*. New York: Routledge, 2009.

James, Jennifer. *A Freedom Bought with Blood*. Chapel Hill: University of North Carolina Press, 2007.

Johnson, Charles. *Middle Passage*. New York: Scribner's, 1990.

Johnson, James Weldon. "Fifty Years." *New York Times*, 1 January 1913, 16.

Kachun, Mitch. *Festivals of Freedom: Memory and Meaning in African American Emancipation Celebrations, 1808–1915*. Amherst: University of Massachusetts Press, 2003.

Kantrowitz, Stephen. *More Than Freedom: Fighting for Black Citizenship in a White Republic, 1829–1889*. New York: Penguin Books, 2012.

Kaplan, Sidney, and Emma Kaplan. *The Black Presence in the Era of the American Revolution, 1770–1800*. 1973. Reprint, Amherst: University of Massachusetts Press, 1988.

Keene, Jennifer D. "Americans as Warriors: 'Doughboys' in Battle during the First World War." *Magazine of History* 17, no. 1 (2002): 15–18.

Keith, Jeanette. *Rich Man's War, Poor Man's Fight: Race, Class, and Power in the Rural South during the First World War*. Chapel Hill: University of North Carolina Press, 2004.

Kelley, Robin D. G. "'We Are Not What We Seem': Rethinking Black Working-Class Opposition in the Jim Crow South." *Journal of American History* 80, no. 1 (1993): 75–112.

Kelley, William Melvin. *dem*. New York: Doubleday, 1967.

Killens, John Oliver. *And Then We Heard the Thunder*. New York: Knopf, 1963.

Kimbrough, Natalie. *Equality or Discrimination? African Americans in the U.S. Military during the Vietnam War*. New York: University Press of America, 2006.

Kletzing, Henry F., and William Henry Crogman. *Progress of a Race: Or the Remarkable Advancement of the Afro-American from the Bondage of Slavery, Ignorance, and Poverty* to the Freedom of Citizenship, Intelligence, Affluence, Honor and Trust. 1902. Reprint, Atlanta: J. L. Nichols & Co., 1903.

Knoblock, Glen A. *African American World War II Casualties and Decorations in the Navy, Coast Guard and Merchant Marine: A Comprehensive Record*. Jefferson: McFarland, 2009.

Komunyakaa, Yusef. *Dien Cai Dau*. Middletown, Conn.: Wesleyan University Press, 1988.

Krenn, Michael L., ed. *Race and U.S. Foreign Policy from the Colonial Period to the Present*. New York: Garland, 1998.

Kryder, Daniel. "The American State and the Management of Race Conflict in the Workplace and in the Army, 1941–1945." *Polity* 26, no. 4 (1994): 601–34.

Kuncio, Robert C. "Some Unpublished Poems of Phillis Wheatley." *New England Quarterly: A Historical Review of New England Life and Letters* 43, no. 2 (1970): 287–97.

Lanning, Michael. *Defenders of Liberty: African Americans in the Revolutionary War*. New York: Citadel Press, 2000.

Larson, Kate Clifford. *Bound for the Promised Land: Harriet Tubman, Portrait of an American Hero*. New York: Ballantine Books, 2004.

Latty, Yvonne, ed. *We Were There: Voices of African American Veterans from World War II to the War in Iraq*. New York: Amistad, 2004.

Leckie, William H. *The Buffalo Soldiers: A Narrative of the Negro Cavalry in the West*. Norman: University of Oklahoma Press, 1967.

Lederer, Richard. "The Didactic and the Literary in Four Harlem Renaissance Sonnets." *English Journal* 62, no. 2 (1973): 219–23.

Lee, Don L. *Think Black*. Detroit: Broadside Press, 1967.

Lee, Ulysses. "The Draft and the Negro." In *Cavalcade: Negro American Writing from 1760 to the Present*, edited by Arthur P. Davis and Saunders Redding, 587–97. Boston: Houghton Mifflin, 1971.

———. *The Employment of Negro Troops*. 1966. Reprint, Honolulu: University Press of the Pacific, 2004.

Leepson, Marc. *Flag: An American Biography*. New York: St. Martins, 2005.

Lehman, Christopher. *American Animated Cartoons of the Vietnam Era*. Jefferson: McFarland, 2007.

Lemmon, Sarah McCulloh. *Frustrated Patriots: North Carolina and the War of 1812*. Chapel Hill: University of North Carolina Press, 1973.

Lentz-Smith, Adriane. *Freedom Struggles: African Americans and World War I*. Cambridge, Mass.: Harvard University Press, 2009.

Levin, Robert S., ed. *Martin Delany, Frederick Douglass, and the Politics of Representative Identity*. Chapel Hill: University of North Carolina Press, 1997.

Lewis, David Levering. *W.E.B. Du Bois: Biography of a Race, 1868–1919*. New York: Henry Holt, 1993.

Liliuokalani. *Hawaii's Story by Hawaii's Queen*. Boston: Lee and Shepard, 1898. https://archive.org/details/hawaiisstorybyh00goog.

Linebaugh, Peter, and Marcus Rediker. *The Many-Headed Hydra: Sailors, Slaves, Commoners, and the Hidden History of the Revolutionary Atlantic*. Boston: Beacon Press, 2000.

Lipsyte, Robert. "'I Don't Have to Be What You Want Me to Be,' Says Muhammad Ali." In *The Muhammad Ali Reader*, edited by Gerald Early, 90–100. New Jersey: Ecco Press, 1998.

Little, Arthur W. *From Harlem to the Rhine: The Story of New York's Colored Volunteers*. New York: Covici-Friede Publishers, 1936.

Little, Lawrence S. *Disciples of Liberty: The African Methodist Episcopal Church in the Age of Imperialism, 1884–1916*. Knoxville: University of Tennessee Press, 2000.

Litwack, Leon. *Trouble in Mind: Black Southerners in the Age of Jim Crow*. New York: Vintage Books, 1998.

Loeb, Jeff. "MIA: African American Autobiography of the Vietnam War." *African American Review* 31, no. 1 (1997): 105–23.

Lowry, Beverly. *Harriet Tubman: Imagining a Life*. New York: Anchor, 2008.

Lusane, Clarence. *Hitler's Black Victims: The Historical Experiences of Afro-Germans, European Blacks, Africans, and African Americans in the Nazi Era*. New York: Routledge, 2003.

Lutz, Tom, and Susanna Ashton, eds. *These "Colored" United States: African American Essays from the 1920s*. New Brunswick, N.J.: Rutgers University Press, 1996.

Maier, Pauline. *American Scripture: Making the Declaration of Independence*. New York: Vintage, 1997.

Malcolm, Joyce. *Peter's War: A New England Slave Boy and the American Revolution*. New Haven, Conn.: Yale University Press, 2009.

McBride, James. *Miracle at St. Anna*. New York: Riverhead Books, 2002.

McGuire, Phillip, ed. *Taps for a Jim Crow Army: Letters from Black Soldiers in World War II*. Lexington: University of Kentucky Press, 1983.

McMillen, Neil R., ed. *Remaking Dixie: The Impact of World War II on the American South*. Jackson: University Press of Mississippi, 1997.

McPherson, James M. *The Negro's Civil War: How American Blacks Felt and Acted during the War for the Union*. 1965. Reprint, New York: Vintage, 2003.

McWhirter, Cameron. *Red Summer: The Summer of 1919 and the Awakening of Black America*. New York: Henry Holt, 2011.

Mennell, James. "African-Americans and the Selective Service Act of 1917." *Journal of Negro History* 84, no. 3 (1999): 275–87.

Miller, Kelly. *The History of the World War for Human Rights*. 1919. Reprint, Whitefish, Mont.: Kessinger, 2005.

Miller, Randall M., and Jon W. Zophy. "Unwelcome Allies: Billy Yank and the Black Soldier." *Phylon* 39, no. 3 (1978): 234–40.

Mitchell, Koritha. *Living with Lynching: African American Lynching Plays, Performance, and Citizenship, 1890–1930*. Urbana: University of Illinois Press, 2011.

Moore, Brenda L. *To Serve My Country, To Serve My Race: The Story of the Only African American WACs Stationed Overseas during World War II*. New York: New York University Press, 1996.

Moore, Christopher Paul. *Fighting for America: Black Soldiers—The Unsung Heroes of World War II*. New York: Ballantine Books, 2005.

Moore, George. "The Name 'Columbia.'" *Proceedings of the Massachusetts Historical Society* 2 (1885–1886): 159–65.

Morehouse, Maggi M. *Fighting in the Jim Crow Army: Black Men and Women Remember World War II*. Lanham, Md.: Rowman & Littlefield, 2000.

Morgan, Philip D., and Andrew Jackson O'Shaughnessy. "Arming Slaves in the American Revolution." In *Arming Slaves from Classical Times to the Modern Age*, edited by Christopher Leslie Brown and Philip D. Morgan, 180–208. New Haven, Conn.: Yale University Press, 2006.

Morrison, Toni. *A Mercy*. New York: Knopf, 2008.

———. *Beloved*. New York: Knopf, 1987.

———. *The Bluest Eye*. New York: Holt, Rinehart & Winston, 1970.

———. *Home*. New York: Knopf, 2012.

———. *Jazz*. New York: Knopf, 1992.

———. *Love*. New York: Knopf, 2003.

———. *Paradise*. New York: Knopf, 1997.

———. *Song of Solomon*. New York: Knopf, 1977.

———. *Sula*. New York: Knopf, 1973.

———. *Tar Baby*. New York: Knopf, 1981.

Moses, Wilson Julius. "The Poetics of Ethiopianism: W. E. B. Du Bois and Black Nationalism." *American Literature* 47, no. 3 (1975): 411–26.

Motley, Mary Penick, ed. *The Invisible Soldier: The Experience of the Black Soldier in World War II*. Detroit, Mich.: Wayne State University Press, 1975.

Moye, J. Todd. *Freedom Flyers: The Tuskegee Airmen of World War II*. New York: Oxford University Press, 2010.

Nalty, Bernard C. *Strength for the Fight: A History of Black Americans in the Military*. 1986. Reprint, Florence, Mass.: Free Press, 1989.

Nalty, Bernard C., and Morris J. MacGregor, eds. *Blacks in the Military: Essential Documents*. Wilmington, Del.: Scholarly Resource, 1981.

Nash, Gary B. *The Forgotten Fifth: African Americans in the Age of Revolution*. Cambridge, Mass.: Harvard University Press, 2006.

———. *Race and Revolution*. Lanham, Md.: Madison House, 1990.

———. "Thomas Peters: Millwright and Deliverer." The American Revolution: National Discussions of Our Revolutionary Origins Web site. http://revolution.h-net.msu.edu/essays/nash.html.

Neal, Larry. "Some Reflections on the Black Aesthetic." [1971.] In *The Black Aesthetic*, edited by Addison Gayle Jr., 12–15. New York: Doubleday, 1971.

Nell, William Cooper. *Colored Patriots of the American Revolution, with Sketches of Several Distinguished Colored Persons: To Which Is Added a Brief Survey of the Condition and Prospects of Colored Americans*. 1855. Reprint, New York: Beaufort Books, 1968.

Newman, Richard, Patrick Rael, and Phillip Lapsansky, eds. *Pamphlets of Protest: An Anthology of Early African American Protest Literature, 1790–1860*. New York: Routledge, 2001.

Niagara Movement. "Negroes Want Equal Rights: The Niagara Movement Issues an Address to the Country," *New York Times*, 20 August 1906, 4.

"No Closed Ranks Now, Says *Crisis*." *Pittsburgh Courier*, 17 January 1942, 2.

Ochs, Stephen J. *A Black Patriot and a White Priest: André Cailloux and Claude Paschal Maistre in Civil War New Orleans*. Baton Rouge: Louisiana State University Press, 2000.

Ogletree, Charles J., Jr., and Austin Sarat. *From Lynch Mobs to the Killing State: Race and the Death Penalty in America*. New York: New York University Press, 2006.

O'Leary, Cecilia Elizabeth. *To Die For: The Paradox of American Patriotism*. Princeton, N.J.: Princeton University Press, 1999.

O'Shaughnessy, Andrew Jackson. "Arming Slaves in the American Revolution." In *Arming Slaves from Classical Times to the Modern Age*, edited by Christopher Leslie Brown and Philip D. Morgan, 180–208. New Haven, Conn.: Yale University Press, 2006.

Outlaw, Lucius T. "Philosophy, African-Americans, and the Unfinished American Revolution." In *On Race and Philosophy*, 33–50. New York: Routledge, 1996.

Painter, Nell Irvin. *The History of White People*. New York: W. W. Norton, 2010.

———. *Standing at Armageddon: A Grassroots History*. New York: W. W. Norton, 1989.

Parker, Christopher S. "When Politics Becomes Protest: Black Veterans and Political Activism in the Postwar South." *Journal of Politics* 71, no. 1 (2009): 113–31.

Patton, Venetria, and Maureen Honey. "Contested Periodization." In *Double Take: A Revisionist Harlem Renaissance Anthology*, xxv–xxvii. New Brunswick, N.J.: Rutgers University Press, 2001.

Petry, Ann. *The Street*. Boston: Houghton Mifflin, 1946.

Phillips, Kimberley L. *War! What Is It Good For? Black Freedom Struggles and the U.S. Military from World War II to Iraq*. Chapel Hill: University of North Carolina Press, 2012.

Piep, Karsten H. *Embattled Home Fronts: Domestic Politics and the American Novel of World War I*. New York: Rodopi, 2009.

Plummer, Brenda Gayle. *Rising Wind: Black Americans and U.S. Foreign Affairs, 1935–1960*. Chapel Hill: University of North Carolina Press, 1996.

Pollard, Kisha (Miss Flame). "Girls at War." *Voices from the Frontline*. CD. Released 2006. Crosscheck Records 8962.

Porter, Dorothy B. "Selected References on the American Negro in World War I and World War II." *Journal of Negro Education* 12, no. 3 (1943): 579–84.

Powell, Colin. *My American Journey*. New York: Ballantine Books, 1995.

Purvis, Robert. *An Appeal to Forty Thousand Citizens, Threatened with Disenfranchisement, to the People of Pennsylvania*. In *Pamphlets of Protest: An Anthology of Early African American Protest Literature, 1790–1860*, edited by Richard Newman, Patrick Rael, and Phillip Lapsansky, 133–42. New York: Routledge, 2001.

Pybus, Cassandra. *Epic Journeys of Freedom: Runaway Slaves of the American Revolution and Their Global Quest for Liberty*. Boston: Beacon Press, 2006.

Quarles, Benjamin. *Black Abolitionists*. 1969. Reprint, Cambridge, Mass.: Da Capo Press, 1991.

———. *Black Mosaic: Essays in Afro-American History and Historiography*. Amherst: University of Massachusetts Press, 1988.

———. *The Negro in the American Revolution*. 1961. Reprint, Chapel Hill: University of North Carolina Press, 1996.

———. *The Negro in the Civil War*. 1953. Reprint, New York: Da Capo, 1989.

Rael, Patrick, ed. *African American Activism before the Civil War*. New York: Routledge, 2008.

Raines, Howell. *My Soul Is Rested: Movement Days in the Deep South Remembered*. New York: G. P. Putnam's Sons, 1977.

Ramold, Steven J. *Slaves, Sailors, Citizens: African Americans in the Union Navy*. DeKalb: Northern Illinois University Press, 2002.

Rampersad, Arnold. *The Life of Langston Hughes: I, Too, Sing America*. Vol. 1. New York: Oxford University Press, 1986.

Randolph, A. Philip. "Call to Negro America 'To March on Washington for Jobs and Equal Participation in National Defense' on July 1, 1941." [1970.] In *Afro-American History: Primary Sources*, edited by Thomas R. Frazier, 291–94. Belmont, Calif.: Wadsworth Publishing Company, 1988.

Redkey, Edwin S. *A Grand Army of Black Men: Letters from African American Men in the Union Army*. New York: Cambridge University Press, 1992.

Reidy, Joseph P. "Armed Slaves and the Struggles for Republican Liberty in the U.S. Civil War." In *Arming Slaves from Classical Times to the Modern Age*, edited by Christopher Leslie Brown and Philip D. Morgan, 274–303. New Haven, Conn.: Yale University Press, 2006.

Remnick, David. *King of the World: Muhammad Ali and the Rise of an American Hero*. New York: Random House, 1998.

Report of the Adjutant General of the State of Kansas, 1861–'65. Topeka, Kansas: J. K. Hudson, State Printer, 1896. https://archive.org/stream/reportofadjutant12kans#page/n5/mode/2up.

Richardson, Henry J., III. "The Gulf Crisis and African-American Interests under International Law." *American Journal of International Law* 87, no. 1 (1993): 42–82.

Ripley, C. Peter. *The Black Abolitionist Papers*. Vol. 5, *The United States, 1859–1865*. Chapel Hill: University of North Carolina Press, 1992.

Rishell, Lyle. *With a Black Platoon in Combat: A Year in Korea*. College Station: Texas A&M University Press, 1993.

Roberts, Frank E. *The American Foreign Legion: Black Soldiers of the 93rd in World War I*. Annapolis, Md.: U.S. Naval Institute Press, 2004.

Robinson, Charles M., III. *The Fall of a Black Army Officer: Racism and the Myth of Henry O. Flipper*. Norman: University of Oklahoma Press, 2008.

Rock, John S. "I Will Sink or Swim with My Race." In *Lift Every Voice: African American Oratory, 1787–1900*, edited by Philip S. Foner and Robert James Branham, 313–18. Tuscaloosa: University of Alabama Press, 1998.

Roosevelt, Theodore. "The Rough Riders." *Scribner's Magazine* 25 (1899).

Ross, Marlon. *Reforming Black Men in the Jim Crow Era*. New York: New York University Press, 2004.

Russ, William Adam, Jr. *The Hawaiian Revolution (1893–94)*. Selinsgrove, Pa.: Susquehanna University Press, 1992.

Sammons, Jeffrey T., and John H. Morrow Jr. *Harlem's Rattlers and the Great War: The Undaunted 369th Regiment and the African American Quest for Equality*. Lawrence: University Press of Kansas, 2014.

Sasser, Charles W. *Patton's Panthers: The African-American 761st Tank Battalion in World War II*. New York: Pocket Books, 2004.

Schubert, Frank N. *Voices of the Buffalo Soldier: Records, Reports, and Recollections of the Military Life and Service in the West*. Albuquerque: University of New Mexico Press, 2003.

Scott, Edward Van Zile. *The Unwept: Black American Soldiers and the Spanish-American War*. Montgomery: Black Belt Press, 1996.

Scott, Emmett J. "The Participation of Negroes in World War I: An Introductory Statement." *Journal of Negro Education* 12, no. 3 (1943): 288–97.

———. *Scott's Official History of the American Negro in the World War*. 1919. Self-published.

Scott, Lawrence P. *Double V: The Civil Rights Struggle of the Tuskegee Airmen*. East Lansing: Michigan State University Press, 1994.

Scott, William R. "Black Nationalism and the Italo-Ethiopian Conflict, 1934–1936." In *Race and U.S. Foreign Policy from the Colonial Period to the Present*, edited by Michael L. Krenn, 134–50. New York: Garland, 1998.

Segars, J. H., and Charles Kelly Barrow, eds. *Black Southerners in Confederate Armies: A Collection of Historical Accounts*. Gretna, La.: Pelican Publishing, 2007.

Shenk, Gerald. *"Work or Fight": Race, Gender, and the Draft in World War One*. New York: Palgrave, 2005.

Sinha, Manisha. "To 'Cast Just Obloquy' on Oppressors: Black Radicalization in the Age of Revolution." *William and Mary Quarterly* 64, no. 1 (2007): 149–60.

Slotkin, Richard. *Lost Battalions: The Great War and the Crisis of American Nationality*. New York: Holt, 2006.

Smith, Gary. "The Black Protest Sonnet." *American Poetry* 2 (1984): 2–12.

Smith, Graham. *When Jim Crow Met John Bull: Black Soldiers in World War II Britain*. New York: Palgrave Macmillan, 1988.

Smith, John David, ed. *Black Soldiers in Blue: African American Troops in the Civil War Era*. Chapel Hill: University of North Carolina Press, 2002.

Spencer, Tracey Lovette, James E. Spencer Jr., and Bruce G. Wright. "World War I as I Saw It: The Memoir of an African American Soldier." *Massachusetts Historical Review* 9 (2007): 134–65.

Spurgeon, Ian. *Soldiers in the Army of Freedom: the 1st Kansas Colored, the Civil War's First African American Combat Unit*. Norman: University of Oklahoma Press, 2014.

Stanford, Karin L. *If We Must Die: African American Voices on War and Peace*. Lanham, Md.: Rowman & Littlefield, 2008.

Stepto, Robert. "'Intimate Things in Place': A Conversation with Toni Morrison." *Massachusetts Review* 18, no. 3 (1977): 473–89.

Sterling, Dorothy, ed. *Speak Out in Thunder Tones: Letters and Other Writings by Black Northerners, 1787–1865*. New York: Da Capo, 1998.

Steward, T. G. *Buffalo Soldiers: The Colored Regulars in the United States Army*. Philadelphia: AME Book Concern, 1904. http://www.gutenberg.org/ebooks/16750.

Stewart, Maria W. "Sufferings during the War." In *Maria W. Stewart, America's First Black Woman Political Writer: Essays and Speeches*, edited by Marilyn Richardson, 98–109. Bloomington: Indiana University Press, 1987.

———. "Why Sit Ye Here and Die?" In *Lift Every Voice: African American Oratory, 1787–1900*, edited by Philip S. Foner and Robert James Branham, 125–289. Tuscaloosa: University of Alabama Press, 1998.

Stillman, Richard, II. "Negroes in the Armed Forces." *Phylon* 30, no. 2 (1969): 139–59.

Stillwell, Paul, ed. *The Golden Thirteen: Recollections of the First Black Naval Officers*. New York: Berkley Books, 1994.

Stouffer, Samuel A., Edward A. Suchman, Leland C. DeVinney, Shirley A. Star, and Robin M. Williams. *The American Soldier: Adjustment during Army Life*. Princeton, N.J.: Princeton University Press, 1949.

Sullivan, Patricia. *Lift Every Voice: The NAACP and the Making of the Civil Rights Movement*. New York: New Press, 2009.

Takaki, Ronald. *Democracy and Race: Asian Americans and World War II*. New York: Chelsea, 1995.

———. *Double Victory: A Multicultural History of America in World War II*. New York: Little, Brown, 2000.

Taylor, Quintard. "African American Men in the American West, 1528–1990." *Annals of the American Academy of Political and Social Science* 569 (May 2000): 102–19.

Taylor, Ula. *The Veiled Garvey: The Life and Times of Amy Jacques Garvey*. Chapel Hill: University of North Carolina Press, 2002.

Terry, Wallace. *Bloods: An Oral History of the Vietnam War by Black Veterans*. New York: Ballantine, 1985.

Thompson, James G. "Should I Sacrifice to Live Half-American?" *Pittsburgh Courier*, 31 January 1942, 3.

Thompson, Shirley E. "The Black Press." In *A Companion to African American History*, edited by Alton Hornsby Jr., 332–45. Oxford: Blackwell, 2005.

Thorne, Christopher. "Britain and the Black G.I.s: Racial Issues and Anglo-American Relations in 1942." In *Race and U.S. Foreign Policy from the Colonial Period to the Present*, edited by Michael L. Krenn, 342–51. New York: Garland, 1998.

Torres, Rodolfo D., Louis F. Mirón, and Jonathan Xavier Inda, eds. *Race, Identity, and Citizenship: A Reader*. Malden, Mass.: Blackwell, 1999.

Treadwell, Mattie E. *United States in World War II, Special Studies: The Women's Army Corps*. Washington, D.C.: Office of the Chief of Military History, Department of the Army, 1954.

Trethewey, Natasha. *Native Guard*. New York: Marina Books, 2007.

Trudeau, Noah Andre. *Like Men of War: Black Troops in the Civil War, 1862–1865*. Boston: Little, Brown, 1999.

Tucker, Phillip Thomas. *Cathy Williams: From Slave to Buffalo Soldier*. Mechanicsburg: Stackpole Books, 2002.

Tuttle, William N. *Race Riot: Chicago in the Red Summer of 1919*. Urbana: University of Illinois Press, 1970.

Tylee, Claire M., Elaine Turner, and Agnes Cardinal, eds. *War Plays by Women: An International Anthology*. New York: Routledge, 1999.

Urwin, George J. W. *Black Flag over Dixie: Racial Atrocities and Reprisals in the Civil War*. Carbondale: Southern Illinois University Press, 2005.

VanderVelde, Lea. *Redemption Songs: Suing For Freedom before Dred Scott*. New York: Oxford University Press, 2014.

Varon, Elizabeth R. *Southern Lady, Yankee Spy: The True Story of Elizabeth Van Lew, a Union Agent in the Heart of the Confederacy*. New York: Oxford University Press, 2003.

Vollers, Maryanne. *Ghosts of Mississippi: The Murder of Medgar Evers, the Trials of Byron De La Beckwith, and the Haunting of the New South*. London: Little, Brown, 1995.

Waldstreicher, David. *In the Midst of Perpetual Fetes: The Making of American Nationalism, 1776–1820*. Chapel Hill: University of North Carolina Press, 1997.

Walker, Alice. *You Can't Keep a Good Woman Down: Stories*. New York: Harcourt, 1981.

Ware, Gilbert. *William Hastie: Grace Under Pressure*. New York: Oxford University Press, 1985.

Watkins [Harper], Frances Ellen. *Poems on Miscellaneous Subjects*. Boston: J. B. Yerrinton & Son, 1854.

Weigert, Kathleen Mass. "Stratification, Ideology, and Opportunity Beliefs among Black Soldiers." *Public Opinion Quarterly* 38, no. 1 (1974): 57–68.

Westheider, James. *The African American Experience in Vietnam: Brothers in Arms*. Lanham, Md.: Rowman & Littlefield Publishers, 2007.

———. *Fighting on Two Fronts: African Americans and the Vietnam War*. New York: New York University Press, 1999.

Whalan, Mark. *The Great War and the Culture of the New Negro*. Gainesville: University Press of Florida, 2008.

Wheatley, Phillis. *Phillis Wheatley: Complete Writings*. Edited by Vincent Carretta. New York: Penguin, 2001.

———. *Poems on Various Subjects, Religious and Moral*. London: A. Bell, 1773.

Whitaker, Robert. *On the Laps of Gods: The Red Summer of 1919 and the Struggle for Justice that Remade a Nation*. New York: Crown, 2008.

White, Walter. *A Man Called White*. New York: Arno Press, 1969.

Whitehead, Ruth Holmes. *Black Loyalists: Southern Settlers of Nova Scotia's First Free Black Community*. Halifax, Nova Scotia: Nimbus Publishing, 2013.

Whitman, T. Stephen. *Challenging Slavery in the Chesapeake: Black and White Resistance to Human Bondage, 1775–1865*. Baltimore: Maryland Historical Society, 2006.

Williams, Chad L. *Torchbearers of Democracy: African American Soldiers in the World War I Era*. Chapel Hill: University of North Carolina Press, 2010.

Williams, David. *I Freed Myself: African American Self-Emancipation in the Civil War Era*. Cambridge, UK: Cambridge University Press, 2014.

Williams, Eric. *Capitalism and Slavery*. 1944. Reprint, Chapel Hill: University of North Carolina Press, 1994.

Williams, George Washington. *A History of the Negro Troops in the War of the Rebellion, 1861–65*. 1888. Reprint, New York: Bergman Publishers, 1968.

Williams, John A. *Clifford's Blues*. Minneapolis: Coffee House Press, 1998.

Wilson, Joseph. *The Black Phalanx: African American Soldiers in the War of Independence, the War of 1812, and the Civil War*. 1890. Reprint, New York: Da Capo Press, 1994.

Wilson, Keith P. *Campfires of Freedom: The Camp Life of Black Soldiers during the Civil War*. Ohio: Kent State University Press, 2002.

Winch, Julie. "The Making and Meaning of James Forten's *Letters from a Man of Colour*." *The William and Mary Quarterly*, 3rd series. 64, no. 1 (January 2007): 129–38.

Wong, Edlie L. *Neither Fugitive nor Free: Atlantic Slavery, Freedom Suits, and the Legal Culture of Travel*. New York: New York University Press, 2009.

Woodruff, Nan Elizabeth. *American Congo: The African American Freedom Struggle in the Delta*. Cambridge, Mass.: Harvard University Press, 2003.

Woodward, Colin E. *Marching Masters: Slavery, Race, and the Confederate Army during the Civil War*. Charlottesville: University of Virginia Press, 2014.

Wright, Kai. *Soldiers of Freedom: An Illustrated History of African Americans in the Armed Forces*. New York: Black Dog and Leventhal, 2002.

Wynn, Neil. *The Afro-American and the Second World War*. 1977. Reprint, Teaneck, N.J.: Holmes and Meier, 1993.

Yacovone, Donald, ed. *Freedom's Journey: African American Voices of the Civil War*. Chicago: Lawrence Hill Books, 2004.

Zinn, Howard, and Anthony Arnove. *Voices of a People's History of the United States*. New York: Seven Stories Press, 2004.

Zobel, Hiller. *The Boston Massacre*. 1970. Reprint, New York: W. W. Norton, 1996.

PERMISSIONS

Author Index

Title Index

A Yẹmisi Jimoh is professor of African American studies at the University of Massachusetts Amherst. She has published scholarly articles and coedited scholarly collections on African American literature and culture and is the author of *Spiritual, Blues, and Jazz People in African American Fiction: Living In Paradox.*

* * *

Françoise N. Hamlin is associate professor in the Departments of Africana studies and history at Brown University. Her book *Crossroads at Clarksdale: The Black Freedom Struggle in the Mississippi Delta after World War II* (2012) won the 2013 Lillian Smith Book Award and Best First Book Prize for 2012 at the Berkshire Conference on the History of Women. She has written articles about black activist mothering during the Civil Rights Movement, the role of oral history in recovering historical narratives, grassroots organizing in Mississippi, rethinking notions of success in the mass movement, and the pedagogy of experiential learning. Her current research focuses on children and youth in the black freedom struggle.

www.ingramcontent.com/pod-product-compliance
Lightning Source LLC
LaVergne TN
LVHW051940060925
820435LV00015B/104